Why Do You Need This New Edition?

If you're wondering why you should buy this new edition of *Along These Lines: Writing Paragraphs and Essays, Sixth Edition,* here are ten good reasons:

1. **All of the exercises in the writing chapters are new** and will help you appreciate the importance of the **prewriting, planning, drafting, and revising stages** of the writing process.

2. **New revision and editing exercises in the grammar chapters** will help you appreciate the grammatical principles so crucial for success in your future composition classes and in real-world settings.

3. **New, expanded essay coverage,** including instruction on writing the **multipattern essay,** will enable you to select the best format for expressing your ideas.

4. **New writing and discussion topics,** many designed to promote **critical thinking,** will motivate you to analyze and address the enormous challenges facing today's students on campus, in the workplace, and in their community.

5. **New collaborative and Web-based activities** will provide you with ample opportunities for group work and positive interaction with your classmates.

6. **Updated coverage of slang, clichés, and wordiness (and better alternatives)** will help you **become a more effective communicator,** a valuable asset in today's competitive job market.

7. **New MLA guidelines for documenting sources** are included in Chapter 14, "Using Research to Strengthen Essays," a section that shows you, step-by-step, how to incorporate expert opinion and professional sources smoothly and properly in your papers.

8. **A new, streamlined appendix** contains the comprehension strategies of prereading and summarizing and includes a new sample of a marked reading.

9. **New, engaging, and well-structured readings** cover timely topics ranging from the dangers of intervening on a stranger's behalf to the humor of student excuses for missed assignments. Related writing topics encourage you to think critically and write analytically, two skills vital for success in college and careers.

10. **Chapter Objectives & MyWritingLab:** Each chapter in *Along These Lines: Writing Paragraphs and Essays* now opens with a listing of chapter objectives and ties them into Pearson's **MyWritingLab** (www.mywritinglab.com). Now you can truly master chapter content and test your understanding of that content with MyWritingLab in a more meaningful way!

PEARSON

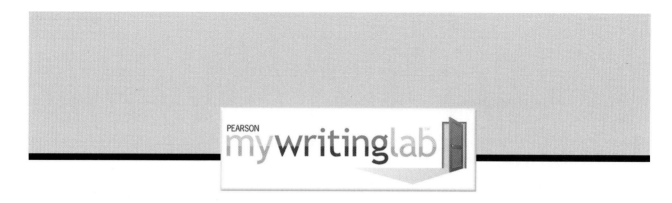

MyWritingLab™ has helped students like you from all over the country.

MyWritingLab™ can help you become a better writer and help you get a better grade.

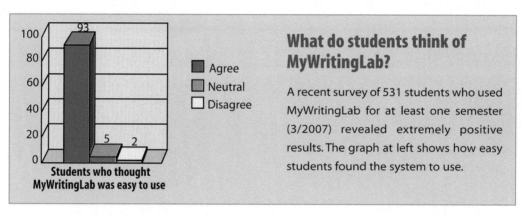

Students who thought MyWritingLab was easy to use

What do students think of MyWritingLab?

A recent survey of 531 students who used MyWritingLab for at least one semester (3/2007) revealed extremely positive results. The graph at left shows how easy students found the system to use.

MyWritingLab helped me achieve a higher grade.

Bottom Line: Do students feel the program helped them achieve a higher grade?

85% of the students believe MyWritingLab helped them achieve higher grades.

Better practice really does make better writers!

www.mywritinglab.com

Helping Students Succeed . . .

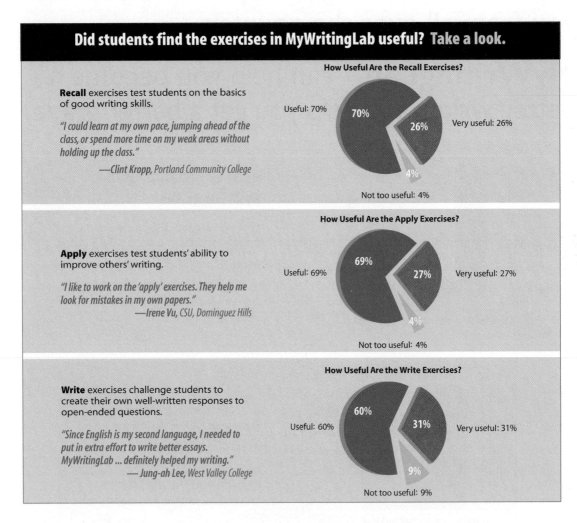

Did students find the exercises in MyWritingLab useful? Take a look.

Recall exercises test students on the basics of good writing skills.

"I could learn at my own pace, jumping ahead of the class, or spend more time on my weak areas without holding up the class."

　　　　　—*Clint Kropp, Portland Community College*

How Useful Are the Recall Exercises?

Useful: 70%　70%　26%　Very useful: 26%

4%

Not too useful: 4%

Apply exercises test students' ability to improve others' writing.

"I like to work on the 'apply' exercises. They help me look for mistakes in my own papers."
　　　　—*Irene Vu, CSU, Dominguez Hills*

How Useful Are the Apply Exercises?

Useful: 69%　69%　27%　Very useful: 27%

4%

Not too useful: 4%

Write exercises challenge students to create their own well-written responses to open-ended questions.

"Since English is my second language, I needed to put in extra effort to write better essays. MyWritingLab ... definitely helped my writing."
　　　　— *Jung-ah Lee, West Valley College*

How Useful Are the Write Exercises?

Useful: 60%　60%　31%　Very useful: 31%

9%

Not too useful: 9%

Students just like you are finding MyWritingLab's Recall, Apply, and Write exercises useful in their learning.

www.mywritinglab.com

Along These Lines

Writing Paragraphs and Essays

Sixth Edition

John Sheridan Biays, professor emeritus of English
Broward College

Carol Wershoven, professor emerita of English
Palm Beach State College

PEARSON

Boston   Columbus   Indianapolis   New York   San Francisco   Upper Saddle River
Amsterdam   Cape Town   Dubai   London   Madrid   Milan   Munich   Paris   Montreal   Toronto
Delhi   Mexico City   Sao Paulo   Sydney   Hong Kong   Seoul   Singapore   Taipei   Tokyo

Senior Acquisitions Editor: Matthew Wright
Assistant Editor: Amanda Dykstra
Senior Development Editor: Katharine Glynn
Marketing Manager: Kurt Massey
Supplements Editor: Cyndy Taylor
Senior Media Producer: Stefanie Liebman
Digital Project Manager: Janell Lantana
Project Coordination, Text Design,
and Electronic Page Makeup: Laserwords / Rebecca Lazure
Cover Design Manager: John Callahan
Cover Designer: Laura Shaw
Cover Art: Natthawat Wongrat / Shutterstock
Text Permissions: Glenview / Lisa Yakmalian
Photo Research: PreMediaGlobal / Marta Johnson
Procurement Specialist: Mary Ann Gloriande
Printer/Binder: Courier / Kendallville
Cover Printer: Lehigh-Phoenix / Hagerstown

Credits and acknowledgments borrowed from other sources and reproduced, with permission, in this textbook appear on page 663.

This title is restricted to sales and distribution in North America only.

Library of Congress Cataloging-in-Publication Data
Biays, John Sheridan.
    Along these lines: writing paragraphs and essays / John Sheridan Biays;
        Carol Wershoven.—6th ed.
        p. cm.
    ISBN-13: 978-0-205-11013-1
    ISBN-10: 0-205-11013-4
        1. English language—Rhetoric—Problems, exercises, etc.   2. English
        language—Grammar—Problems, exercises, etc.   3. Report writing—Problems,
        exercises, etc.   I. Wershoven, Carol.   II. Title.
    PE1408.B4933 2011
    808'.042—dc23   2011022137

10 9 8 7 6 5 4 3 2—CKV—15 14 13 12

Student edition:
ISBN 10:   0-205-11013-4
ISBN 13: 978-0-205-11013-1

Annotated Instructor's Edition:
ISBN 10:   0-205-11018-5
ISBN 13: 978-0-205-11018-6

www.pearsonhighered.com

Contents

Photo Assignments to Accompany the Writing Chapters

Preface for Instructors

As a developmental writing instructor, you know all too well that striking a balance between teaching creatively and meeting statewide or departmental "exit test" objectives can be a monumental feat. We applaud your commitment to quality instruction in this era of pervasive budget cuts, ever-increasing class sizes, and more state mandates than ever. Despite such challenges, we firmly believe that beginning writers who engage in a variety of instructional activities (e.g., individual, collaborative, creative, computer-based) can master core competencies and even gain an appreciation for the writing process.

Along These Lines: Writing Paragraphs and Essays, 6/e, recognizes the myriad learning styles and backgrounds your students bring to the classroom; it also respects their innate desire to learn and succeed. Based on the advice and support of fellow developmental educators, we have incorporated several new features and refinements aimed at motivating students to think critically, write coherently, and revise carefully. We have been gratified and encouraged by the positive reception of the *Along These Lines* series over the years, and we trust that you will find this new edition visually appealing and pedagogically sound.

NEW FEATURES AND ENHANCEMENTS IN THE SIXTH EDITION

- **New and expanded writing-process exercises** help students recognize the importance of the prewriting, planning, drafting, revising, and proofreading stages of their work.

- **New editing exercises in the grammar chapters** enable students to apply the relevant grammar principles to real-world writing.

- **New revision exercises and updated coverage of slang, clichés, and wordiness** help students improve their style.

- **New and expanded essay instruction includes 48 new exercises and a new section on writing the multipattern essay;** annotated samples enable students to devise topics adaptable to a variety of formats.

- **New, timely, professional readings** cover such wide-ranging subjects as the importance of online etiquette in job searches, the meaning of a rich life, and the perceived dangers of intervening in a stranger's plight; related assignments challenge students to think critically and write analytically.

- **Increased emphasis on critical-thinking strategies** prepares students to address pressing issues on their campus, in the workplace, and in their community.

- **Updated MLA rules for documenting sources** guide students as they employ basic research to strengthen their essays.

A SAMPLING OF PRAISE FROM *ALONG THESE LINES* ADOPTERS

"I love the Info Boxes and checklists! I draw my students' attention to them in every chapter. The boxes summarize the information so neatly, and the checklists remind them not to leave anything out. These attractive features make **Along These Lines** *stand out from competing texts!"*

Lisa Jackson, Black River Technical College

"I look for a textbook that is well organized with a clear table of contents, index, and a common-sense organization of material within the chapters. Grade for **Along These Lines***: A."*

Marta Anderton, Jackson State Community College

"Along These Lines *[presents material] clearly, and the sequence of skills makes sense. It can be used as a primary tool for teaching or to supplement lessons. There are plenty of exercises for the teacher to use for student practice. Overall, using this book has been a good experience."*

Lisa Tittle, Harford Community College

POPULAR FEATURES RETAINED

Based on suggestions from current users and new reviewers, we have retained these popular, distinctive features:

The Writing Chapters

- Visually appealing checklists, charts, and "Info Boxes" for quick reference and reminders
- Boxed examples of an outline, draft, and final version of a writing assignment in each chapter to reinforce the crucial role of revision
- A "Walk-Through" writing assignment in each chapter that guides students, step-by-step, through the stages of the writing process
- More Web-based activities, ideal for group work and peer interaction

The Grammar Chapters

- Three types of grammar exercises: **Practice** (simple reinforcement), **Collaborate** (partner or group work), and **Connect** (application of the grammar principles to editing paragraphs)
- Grammar concepts taught step-by-step, as in "Two Steps to Check for Fragments"
- A Chapter Test at the end of each grammar chapter, ideal for class review or quick quizzes

The Reading Section

- Professional reading selections grouped and categorized in an attractive appendix, "Readings for Writers," for easy reference
- Comprehension strategies including prereading and summarizing techniques

- Vocabulary definitions based on the specific context of the author's intent
- Writing options sparked by a selection's content and designed to promote critical thinking, not merely rote replication of a model

WRITING RESOURCES AND SUPPLEMENTS

Book-Specific Ancillary Material

Annotated Instructor's Edition for Along These Lines: Writing Paragraphs and Essays 6/e ISBN 0205110185
The Annotated Instructor's Edition contains all the answers to all the exercises throughout the book and includes general teaching tips and general guidance on tailoring instruction.

Instructor's Resource Manual for Along These Lines: Writing Paragraphs and Essays 6/e ISBN 0205110193
A detailed instructor's manual, written by Lavonne McIver of Essex County College, provides teaching suggestions, more activities, additional exercises, handouts, and MyWritingLab www.mywritinglab.com information that instructors can use with each chapter of the text. In addition, the IM also provides a detailed outline of all student and instructor supplements for the developmental writing classroom.

PowerPoint Slide Set for Along These Lines: Writing Paragraphs and Essays 6/e ISBN 0205217354
A comprehensive PowerPoint slide set contains multiple slides for each chapter of the book.

ADDITIONAL RESOURCES FOR INSTRUCTORS AND STUDENTS

The Pearson Writing Package: Pearson is pleased to offer a variety of support materials to help make teaching writing easier for teachers and to help students excel in their coursework. Many of our student supplements are available free or at a greatly reduced price when packaged with *Along These Lines*. Visit www.pearsonhighereducation.com, contact your local Pearson sales representative, or review a detailed listing of the full supplements package in the *Instructor's Resource Manual* for more information.

Media Resources

mywritinglab **Where better practice makes better writers!**
www.mywritinglab.com

MyWritingLab, a complete online learning program, provides additional resources and better practice exercises for developing writers.

What Makes the Practice in MyWritingLab Better?

- **Diagnostic Testing:** MyWritingLab's diagnostic test comprehensively assesses students' skills in grammar. Students are given an individualized learning path based on the diagnostic's results, identifying the areas where they most need help.

- **Progressive Learning:** The heart of MyWritingLab is the progressive learning that takes place as students complete the exercises within each topic. Students move from literal comprehension to critical understanding to the ability to demonstrate a skill in their own writing. This progression of critical thinking, not available in any other online resource, enables students to truly master the skills and concepts they need to become successful writers.
- **Online Gradebook:** All student work in MyWritingLab is captured in the Online Gradebook. Students can monitor their own progress through reports explaining their scores on the exercises in the course. Instructors can see which topics their students have mastered and access other detailed reports, such as class summaries, that track the development of their entire class and display useful details on each student's progress.
- **eText:** The *Along These Lines* eText is accessed through MyWritingLab. Students now have the eText at their fingertips while completing the various exercises and activities within MyWritingLab. Students can highlight important material in the eText, tab areas they add notes to any section for reflection and/or study throughout the semester.

ACKNOWLEDGMENTS

We are immensely grateful to the many individuals who helped us shape and refine the *Along These Lines* series. We thank the following new reviewers and survey respondents for their insight and practical advice:

Marta Anderton	Jackson State Community College
Anna Harrington	Edison State College
Deedra Herington	Pensacola State College
Deanna Highe	Central Piedmont Community College
Lisa Jackson	Black River Technical College
Jonathan Lowndes	Broward College–South Campus
Linda Mobley	Bishop State Community College
Gretchen Polnac	University of Texas at Austin
Christine Prendergast	Pensacola State College
Sharon Rinkiewicz	Broward College
Carol Sinclair	Bainbridge College
Elizabeth Teagarden	Central Piedmont Community College
Melanie Thomas	Three Rivers Community College
Lisa Tittle	Harford Community College
Carmen Wong	John Tyler Community College

We are also indebted to Matt Wright, senior acquisitions editor for developmental English, for keeping us updated and on task throughout the revision process. He remained consistently upbeat about our revisions, and his faith in our work never waivered. We also want to thank Katharine Glynn, our senior development editor, for her judicious suggestions and her skill at juggling various conference calls and numerous editorial responsibilities.

We are very fortunate to have worked with Rebecca Lazure, our full-service production manager at Laserwords Maine. Rebecca somehow managed to resolve scheduling snags, tackle design challenges, meet page-count mandates, and handle our venting sessions with grace and good humor. Rebecca gently reassured us that all would be fine, and we couldn't have been in kinder or more caring hands. Joan Foley, our project manager at Pearson headquarters, oversaw the entire enterprise, and we can't thank her enough for her calm but confident demeanor on several *ATL* editions over the years.

Any new edition relies on a wealth of expertise from talented individuals, and kudos are extended to Laura Patchkofsky, copy editor; Laura Shaw, cover designer; Lisa Yakmalian, permissions specialist; Kelly Carroll, editorial assistant; and Megan Zuccarini, marketing assistant. We are also grateful to Kurt Massey, marketing manager, and Tom DeMarco, former marketing manager, for his enthusiastic support of the *Along These Lines* series and for serving as our liaison to the excellent sales team at Pearson.

Not only were we guided by Pearson's finest, we were also blessed to have the support of friends and family who tolerated our manic behavior as deadlines loomed with increasing frequency. We extend heartfelt thanks to Huck and Sophie Biays; Bill and Chris Childers; B.G., Nancy, and Pixie Thompson; Ted and Carol Cushmore; and Kathleen and Willow Bell for their patience and camaraderie along *all* lines.

Finally, and most importantly, we thank the countless developmental writing students who exemplify perseverance in the face of adversity. We sincerely hope the *Along These Lines* series will continue to help developmental writers find their voice, accept new challenges, and reach their potential.

John Sheridan Biays
Carol Wershoven

Writing in Stages: The Process Approach

INTRODUCTION

Learning By Doing

Writing is a skill, and like any skill, writing improves with practice. This book provides you with ample practice to improve your writing through a variety of individual and group activities. Whether you complete assignments at home or in the classroom, just remember that *good writing takes practice:* you can learn to write well by writing.

Steps Make Writing Easier

Writing is easier if you *do not try to do too much at once.* To make the task of writing easier, *Along These Lines* breaks the process into stages:

PREWRITING

In this stage, you think about your topic, and you *gather ideas*. You *react* to your own ideas and add even more thoughts. You can also react to other people's ideas as a way of expanding your own.

PLANNING

In this stage, you *examine your ideas* and begin to *focus* them around one main idea. Planning involves combining, dividing, and even eliminating some ideas. Placing your specific details in a logical order often involves *outlining*.

DRAFTING AND REVISING

In this stage, the thinking and planning begin to take shape as a piece of writing. You complete a draft of your work, a *rough version* of the finished product. Then you examine the draft and consider ways to *revise* it, a process that may require extensive *editing* and several versions of your original draft.

PROOFREADING

In this stage, the final version of your writing gets one last, careful *review* when you are rested and alert. You concentrate on identifying and correcting any mistakes in spelling, mechanics, or punctuation you may have overlooked. This stage is the *final check* of your work to make your writing the best it can be.

These four stages in the writing process—*prewriting, planning, drafting and revising*, and *proofreading*—may overlap. You may be changing your plan even as you work on the draft of your paper. Throughout this book, you will have many opportunities to become familiar with the stages of effective writing. Working individually and with your classmates, you can become a better writer along *all* lines.

Writing a Paragraph

Jumping In

Where do you get your ideas for writing? Do they seem to come at you all at once? Working with a jumble of ideas is often part of the writing process, and a key step is sorting through these ideas. By sorting, you will be working toward one **paragraph** that focuses on one idea or point.

Chapter Objectives

Students will be able to (1) recognize and write clear topic sentences, (2) engage in planning and revision strategies, and (3) write a paragraph reflecting effective unity, support, and coherence.

WHAT IS THE ROLE OF A PARAGRAPH?

Usually, students write because they have a writing assignment requiring them to write on some topic or choice of topics, and the writing is due by a certain day. So assume that you get such an assignment and it calls for one paragraph. You might wonder, "Why a paragraph? Why not something large, like a two- or three-page paper? After all, many classes will ask for papers, not just paragraphs."

For one thing, all essays are a series of paragraphs. If you can write one good paragraph, you can write more than one. The **paragraph** is the basic building block of any essay. It is a group of sentences focusing on *one idea* or one point. Keep this concept in mind: *one idea to a paragraph*. Focusing on one idea or one point gives a paragraph **unity**. If you have a new point, start a new paragraph.

You may ask, "Doesn't this mean a paragraph will be short? How long should a paragraph be, anyway?" To convince a reader of one main point, you need to make it, support it, develop it, explain it, and describe it. There will be shorter and longer paragraphs, but for now, you can assume your paragraph will be somewhere between seven and twelve sentences long.

This chapter guides you through each stage of the writing process:

- **Prewriting**—how to generate and develop ideas for your paragraph
- **Planning**—how to organize your ideas
- **Drafting and Revising**—how to create, revise, and edit rough drafts
- **Proofreading**—how to proofread and make one final check

We give extra emphasis to the prewriting stage in this chapter to give you some extra help in getting started.

PREWRITING A PARAGRAPH

Suppose your instructor asks you to write a paragraph about your favorite city or town. Writing about your favorite city or town is your general **topic**, but you must choose one city or town to make the topic more specific. With this topic, you already know your **purpose**—to write a paragraph that makes some point about the city or town. You have an **audience** since you are writing this paragraph for your instructor and classmates. Often, your purpose is to write a specific kind of paper for a class. Occasionally, you may have to write with a different purpose or audience, such as writing instructions for a new employee at your workplace, or a letter of complaint to a manufacturer, or a short biographical essay for a scholarship application. Knowing your audience and purpose is important in writing effectively.

Freewriting, Brainstorming, and Keeping a Journal

Once you have identified your purpose and audience, you can begin by finding some way to *think on paper*. You can use the techniques of freewriting, brainstorming, or keeping a journal to gather ideas and potential details.

Freewriting Give yourself fifteen minutes to write whatever comes into your mind on your subject. If your mind is a blank, write, "My mind's a blank. My mind's a blank," over and over until you think of something else. The main goal here is to *write without stopping*. Do not stop to tell yourself, "This is stupid," or "I can't use any of this in a paper." Do not stop to correct your spelling or punctuation. Just write. Let your ideas flow. Write *freely*. Here is an example:

Freewriting About a Favorite City or Town

Favorite city or town. City? I like New York. It's so big and exciting. Haven't been there much, though. Only once. My hometown. I like it. It's just another town but comfortable and friendly. Maybe St. Augustine. Lots of fun visits there. Grandparents there. Hard to pick a favorite. Different places are good for different reasons.

Brainstorming This technique is like freewriting because you write whatever comes into your head, but it is a little different because you can pause *to ask yourself questions* that will lead to new ideas. When you brainstorm alone, you "interview" yourself about a subject. You can also brainstorm and ask questions within a group.

Brainstorming About a Favorite City or Town

Favorite place

City or town

What's the difference between a city and a town?

Doesn't matter. Just pick one. Cities are bigger.

How is city life different from town life?

Cities are bigger. More crowded, like Atlanta.

Which do you like better, a city or a town?

Sometimes I like cities.

Why?

There is more to do.

So, what city do you like?

I like New York and St. Augustine.

Is St. Augustine a city?

Yes. A small one.

Do you like towns?

I loved this little town in Mexico.

If you feel like you are running out of ideas in brainstorming, try to form a question out of what you've just written. *Go where your questions and answers lead you.* For example, if you write, "There is more to do in cities," you could form these questions:

What is there to do? Sports? Entertainment? Outdoor exercise? Meeting people?

You could also make a list of your brainstorming ideas, but remember to *do only one step at a time.*

Keeping a Journal A **journal** is a notebook of your personal writing, a notebook in which you write *regularly and often. It is not a diary, but it is a place to record your experiences, reactions, and observations.* In it, you can write about what you have done, heard, seen, read, or remembered. You can include sayings that you would like to remember, news clippings, snapshots—anything that you would like to recall or consider. A journal provides an enjoyable way to practice your writing, and it is a great source of ideas for writing.

Journal Entry About a Favorite City or Town

I'm not going south to see my grandparents this winter. They're coming here instead of me going to St. Augustine. I'd really like to go there. I like the warm weather. It's better than months of snow, ice, and rain here in Easthampton. I'll miss going there. I've been so many times that it's like a second home. St. Augustine is great around Christmastime.

Finding Specific Ideas

Whether you freewrite, brainstorm, or consult your journal, you end up with something on paper. Follow those first ideas; see where they can take you. You are looking for specific ideas, each of which can focus on the general topic you started with. At this point, you do not have to decide which specific idea you want to write about. You just want to *narrow your range* of ideas.

You might think, "Why should I narrow my ideas? Won't I have more to say if I keep my topic big?" But remember that a paragraph has one idea; you want to state it clearly and with convincing details for support. If you try to write one paragraph on city life versus town life, for example, you will probably make so many general statements that you will say very little, or you will bore your reader with big, sweeping statements. General ideas are big, broad ones. Specific ideas are smaller, narrower ones. If you scanned the freewriting example on a favorite city or town, you might underline many specific ideas as possible topics:

> Favorite city or town. City? I like <u>New York</u>. It's so big and exciting. Haven't been there much, though. Only once. <u>My hometown</u>. I like it. It's just another town but comfortable and friendly. Maybe <u>St. Augustine</u>. Lots of fun visits there. Grandparents there. Hard to pick a favorite. Different places are good for different reasons.

Consider the underlined terms. They are specific places. You could write a paragraph about any one of these places. Or you could underline specific places in your brainstorming questions and answers:

> Favorite place
> City or town
>
> **What's the difference between a city and a town?**
> Doesn't matter. Just pick one. Cities are bigger.
>
> **How is city life different from town life?**
> Cities are bigger. More crowded, like <u>Atlanta</u>.
>
> **Which do you like better, a city or a town?**
> Sometimes I like cities.
>
> **Why?**
> There is more to do.
>
> **So, what city do you like?**
> I like <u>New York</u> and <u>St. Augustine</u>.
>
> **Is St. Augustine a city?**
> Yes. A small one.
>
> **Do you like towns?**
> I loved this <u>little town in Mexico</u>.

Each of these specific places could be a topic for your paragraph.

If you reviewed the journal entry on a favorite city or town, you would also be able to underline specific places:

> I'm not going south to see my grandparents this winter. They're coming here instead of me going to <u>St. Augustine</u>. I'd really like to go there. I like the warm

weather. It's better than months of snow, ice, and rain here in <u>Easthampton</u>. I'll miss going there. I've been so many times that it's like a second home. St. Augustine is great around Christmastime.

Remember if you follow the steps, they can lead you to specific ideas.

Selecting One Topic

Once you have a list of specific ideas that can lead you to a specific topic, you can pick one topic. Let's say you decided to work with the list of places you gathered through brainstorming:

Atlanta
New York
St. Augustine
a little town in Mexico

Looking at this list, you decide you want to write about St. Augustine as your favorite city.

Exercise 1   **Practice: Creating Questions for Brainstorming**

Following are several topics. For each one, brainstorm by writing at least six questions related to the topic that could lead you to further ideas. The first topic is done for you.

1. topic: dogs

Question 1. Why are dogs such popular pets?

Question 2. What kind of dog is a favorite pet in America?

Question 3. Are dogs hard to train?

Question 4. What dog, in your life, do you remember best?

Question 5. What's the most famous dog on television?

Question 6. Are there dogs as cartoon characters?

2. topic: driving

Question 1. _____

Question 2. _____

Question 3. _____

Question 4. _____

Question 5. _____

Question 6. _____

3. topic: phones

Question 1. _____

Question 2. _____

Question 3. _____

Question 4. _____

Question 5. _____

Question 6. _____

Exercise 2 **Practice: Finding Specific Details in Freewriting**

Below are two samples of freewriting. Each is a written response to a different topic. Read each sample, and then underline any words and phrases that could become the focus of a paragraph.

Freewriting Reaction to the Topic of Summer

Summer used to be summer vacation. Now I have to work in the summer, just like I work the rest of the year. At least the days are longer in summer. Can get outdoors after work. Can go for a walk. Jog. Do yard work or sit on the porch. Summer holidays, too. July 4th. Labor Day. Warm weather means summer food and barbecues.

Freewriting Reaction to the Topic of Gossip

I hate gossip. Mean and nasty words. Often lies. People who gossip want to hurt others. Every day unhappy people spread rumors. It can be hard not to listen. Gossip can be exciting. Cruel , too. Powerful and dangerous. I've been a victim of gossip. Mean and hurtful. Jealousy can lead to gossip. Who gossips more, men or women?

Exercise 3 **Practice: Finding Specific Details in a List**

Below are several lists of words or phrases. In each list, one item is a general term; the others are more specific. Underline the words or phrases that are more specific. The first list is done for you.

1. <u>apple pie</u>
   <u>ice cream</u>
   desserts
   <u>butterscotch pudding</u>
   <u>jello</u>
   <u>chocolate brownies</u>

2. garment bag
   duffle bag
   suitcase
   knapsack
   luggage

3. parka
   winter clothing
   wool scarf
   overcoat
   lined gloves
   ski cap

4. ring
   necklace
   bracelet
   jewelry
   earring
   watch

5. rock 'n roll
   rap
   music
   jazz
   country and western

6. health care
   prescription medicine
   health insurance
   emergency room
   surgery
   checkups

Collaborate

Exercise 4 **Collaborate: Finding Topics Through Freewriting**

The following exercise must be completed with a partner or a group. Below are several topics. Pick one and freewrite on it for ten minutes. Then read your freewriting to your partner or group. Ask your listener(s) to jot down any words or phrases from your writing that could lead to a specific topic for a paragraph.

Your listener(s) should read the jotted-down words or phrases to you. You will be hearing a collection of specific ideas that came from *your* writing. As you listen, underline the words in your freewriting.

Freewriting topics (pick one):

1. A dream
2. A disappointment
3. A childhood memory

Freewriting on (name of topic chosen): _____

_____

_____

_____

_____

_____

Adding Details to a Specific Topic

You can develop the specific topic you picked in a number of ways:

1. *Check your list* for other ideas that seem to fit with the specific topic you've picked.
2. *Brainstorm*—ask yourself more questions about your topic, and use the answers as details.
3. *List* any new ideas you have that may be connected to your topic.

One way to add details is to go back and check your brainstorming for other ideas about St. Augustine:

I like St. Augustine.
a small city

Now you can **brainstorm** some questions that will lead you to more details. The questions do not have to be connected to each other; they are just questions that could lead you to ideas and details:

What's a small city?

It doesn't have skyscrapers or freeways or millions of people.

So, what makes it a city?

Thousands of visitors come there every day.

What's so great about St. Augustine?

You can go to the beach nearby.

Is it a clean, big beach?

Sure. And the water is a clear blue.

What else can you do in St. Augustine?

There's lots of history.

Like what?

A fort. The oldest schoolhouse. Old houses.

Another way to add details is to list any ideas that may be connected to your topic. The list might give you more specific details:

grandparents live there
warm in winter
grandparents feed me
I use their car

If you had tried all three ways of adding detail, you would end up with this list of details connected to the topic of a favorite city or town:

a small city	clear blue water
no freeways	lots of history
no skyscrapers	a fort
not millions of people	oldest schoolhouse
thousands of visitors every day	grandparents live there
can always visit family for free	warm in winter
beach nearby	grandparents feed me
clean, big beach	I use their car

INFO BOX: Beginning the Prewriting: A Summary

The prewriting stage of writing a paragraph enables you to gather ideas. This process begins with several steps:

1. **Think on paper and write down any ideas that you have about a topic.** You can do this by freewriting, by brainstorming, or by keeping a journal.

2. **Scan your writing for specific ideas that have come from your first efforts.** List these specific ideas.

3. **Pick one specific idea.** Then, by reviewing your early writing, by questioning, and by thinking further, you can add details to the one specific idea.

This process may seem long, but once you have worked through it several times, it will become nearly automatic. When you think about ideas before you try to shape them into a paragraph, you are off to a good start. Confidence comes from having something to say, and once you have a specific idea, you will be ready to begin shaping and developing details that support your idea.

Exercise 5   Practice: Adding Details to a Topic by Brainstorming

Below are two topics. Each is followed by two or three details. Brainstorm more questions, based on the existing details, that can lead to more details.

1. **topic:**   advantages of bringing your lunch to work or school
   details: saves money
                  healthier

Question 1. _____

Question 2. _____

Question 3. _____

Question 4. _____

Question 5. _____

Question 6. _____

2. **topic:**   getting a flat tire
   details: causes stress
                  forces a change of plans
                  can be frightening

Question 1. _____

Question 2. _____

Question 3. _____

Question 4. _____

Question 5. _____

Question 6. _____

Exercise 6   **Practice: Adding Details By Listing**

Following are three topics for paragraphs. For each topic, list details that seem to fit the topic.

1. **topic:**   inexpensive gifts

   details: a. _____   c. _____

                  b. _____   d. _____

2. **topic:**   an ideal Saturday

   details: a. _____   c. _____

                  b. _____   d. _____

3. **topic:**   nosy neighbors

   details: a. _____   c. _____

                  b. _____   d. _____

Focusing the Prewriting

The next step of writing is to *focus your ideas around some point.* Your ideas will begin to take a focus if you reexamine them, looking for *related ideas.* Two techniques that you can use are

- marking a list of related ideas
- mapping related ideas

Listing Related Ideas

To develop a marked list, take another look at the list we developed under the topic of a favorite city or town. The same list is shown below, but you will notice some of the items have been marked with symbols that show related ideas:

N marks ideas about St. Augustine's natural good points
H marks ideas about St. Augustine's history
F marks ideas about family in St. Augustine

Here is the marked list of ideas related to the topic of a favorite city or town:

a small city	**N** clear blue water
no freeways	**H** lots of history
no skyscrapers	**H** a fort
not millions of people	**H** oldest schoolhouse
thousands of visitors every day	**F** grandparents live there
F can always visit family for free	**N** warm in winter
N beach nearby	**F** grandparents feed me
N clean, big beach	**F** I use their car

You have probably noticed that some items are not marked: a small city, no freeways, no skyscrapers, not millions of people, thousands of visitors every day. Perhaps you can come back to them later, or you may decide you do not need them in your paragraph.

To make it easier to see what ideas you have, and how they are related, try *grouping related ideas,* giving each list a title, like this:

Natural Good Points of St. Augustine

beach nearby	clear blue water
clean, big beach	warm in winter

History in St. Augustine

lots of history	oldest schoolhouse
a fort	

Family in St. Augustine

can always visit family for free	grandparents live there
grandparents feed me	I use their car

Mapping

Another way to focus your ideas is to mark your first list of ideas, and then cluster the related ideas into separate lists. You can **map** your ideas, like this:

Whatever way you choose to examine and group your details, you are working toward *a focus, a point.* You are asking and beginning to answer the question, "Where do the details lead?" The answer will be the **topic sentence** of your paragraph. It will be the *main idea* of your paragraph.

Forming a Topic Sentence

To form a topic sentence, you can do the following:

1. Review your details and see if you can form some general idea that can summarize the details.
2. Write that general idea as one sentence.

Your sentence that summarizes the details is the **topic sentence**. It makes a general point, and the more specific details you have gathered will support this point.

To form a topic sentence about your favorite city, St. Augustine, review the many details you have listed about the city. It is time to ask questions about those details. You could ask yourself, "What kind of details do I have? Can I summarize them?" You might then write the summary as the topic sentence:

I love St. Augustine because it has sun and sea, history, and family.

Check the sentence against your details. Does it cover the natural good points of St. Augustine? Yes. The topic sentence sums them up as *sun and sea.* Does it cover history and family? Yes. The topic sentence says the place has *history and family.*

Writing Good Topic Sentences

Be careful. *Topics are not the same as topic sentences. Topics are the subjects you will write about.* A topic sentence states the *main idea* you have developed on a topic. Consider the differences between the topics and the topic sentences below:

topic: Why courtesy is important
topic sentence: Courtesy takes the conflict out of unpleasant
    encounters.

topic: Dogs and their owners
topic sentence: Many dog owners begin to look like their pets.

Topic sentences *do not announce; they make a point*. Look at the sentences below, and notice the differences between the sentences that announce and the topic sentences.

announcement: I will discuss the process of changing a tire.
topic sentence: Changing a tire is easy if you have the right tools and follow a simple process.

announcement: An analysis of why recycling paper is important will be the subject of this paper.
topic sentence: Recycling paper is important because it saves trees, money, and even certain animals.

Topic sentences can be too big to develop in one paragraph. A topic sentence that is *too broad* may take many paragraphs, even pages of writing, to develop. Look at the very broad sentences below, and then notice how they can be narrowed.

too broad: Athletes get paid too much money. (This sentence is too broad because the term "athletes" could mean anything from professional boxers to college football players to neighborhood softball teams; "too much money" could mean any fee that basketball players receive for endorsing products to bonuses that professional football players get if they make the Super Bowl. The sentence could also refer to all athletes in the world at any time in history.)
a narrower, better topic sentence: Last year, several professional baseball players negotiated high but fair salaries.

too broad: I changed a great deal in my last year of high school. (The phrase "changed a great deal" could refer to physical changes, intellectual changes, emotional changes, changes in attitude, changes in goals, or just about any other change you can think of.)
a narrower, better topic sentence: In my last year of high school, I overcame my shyness.

Topic sentences can be too small to develop in one paragraph. A topic sentence that is *too narrow* cannot be supported by detail. It may be a fact, which cannot be developed. A topic sentence that is too narrow leaves you with nothing more to say.

too narrow: I hate broccoli.
an expanded topic sentence: I hate broccoli for two reasons.

too narrow: It takes twenty minutes to get out of the airport parking lot.
an expanded topic sentence: Congestion at the airport parking lot is causing problems for travelers.

The prewriting stage begins with free, unstructured thinking and writing. As you work through the prewriting process, your thinking and writing will become more focused.

Focusing the Prewriting: A Summary

The prewriting stage of writing a paragraph enables you to develop an idea into a topic sentence and related details. You can focus your thinking by working in steps.

1. Try marking a list of related detail, or try mapping to group your ideas.

2. Write a topic sentence that summarizes your details.

3. Check that your topic sentence is a sentence, not a topic. Make sure that it is not too broad or too narrow, and that it is not an announcement. Check that it makes a point and focuses the details you have developed.

Exercise 7   **Practice: Grouping Related Items in Lists of Details**

Below are lists of details. In each list, circle the items that seem to fit into one group; then underline the items that seem to belong to a second group. Some items may not belong in either group. The first list is done for you.

1. **topic:** blizzards
   <u>power outages</u>   (freedom from school)
   (sit by a warm fire)   snows most in February
   (drink hot chocolate)   <u>travel is hazardous</u>
   (snuggle up with loved ones) (build a snowman)
   weather reports   <u>damage to trees</u>

2. **topic:** clothes
   jeans   shirts
   evening gown   silk tie
   high heels   sneakers
   underwear   tuxedo
   sweatpants   flip-flops

3. **topic:** fame
   public admiration   media interviews
   sudden riches   loss of privacy
   false friends   photographers
   nasty Internet rumors personal power
   famous athletes   stalkers

Exercise 8   **Practice: Writing Topic Sentences for Lists of Details**

Below are lists of details that have no topic sentence. Write an appropriate topic sentence for each one.

1. **topic sentence:** _____

   _____

   Latino families celebrate *quinceanera*, the fifteenth birthday of their daughters.

   Jewish families celebrate the *bar mitzvah,* or coming of age of thirteen-year-old Jewish boys.

Jewish girls have their own similar ceremony, the *bat mitzvah*.

For many young American women, a Sweet Sixteen party is a tradition to mark a teen's growth into adulthood.

Every year, thousands of twenty-year-old Japanese men and women come together on one day.

They participate in a traditional ceremony, similar to a graduation ceremony, with speeches and celebrations.

Wealthy parents in England and America celebrate the "coming out" into society of their teenage daughters by holding elaborate debutante balls.

2. topic sentence: _____

_____

Emily Dominguez was the prettiest girl in my first grade class.

She had long hair and wide eyes.

I used to watch her in class, admiring the way she held her pencil or raised her hand.

One day she caught me looking at her.

Emily smiled and turned her head.

Now I was truly in love because I believed Emily liked me.

For a few days, I lived in a dream in which Emily, the princess, chose me as her hero.

Then I saw her at recess, giggling with Tommy Malone on the playground.

I knew my dream would not come true.

3. topic sentence: _____

_____

My roommate Etienne is Haitian, so at first I had a hard time understanding his English.

He also seemed very shy.

I didn't see him much, so I figured he was socializing with his own friends and didn't like me.

Then one night I had an important algebra test to study for. I went to the Tutoring Center to get some help with my math.

Etienne was there, wrapped up in books.

Later, I learned he was there every night, studying English, but also tutoring other people in math.

Etienne and I are good friends now; I help him with English, and he teaches me algebra.

Exercise 9   **Practice: Turning Topics into Topic Sentences**

Below is a list. Some of the items in the list are topic sentences, but some are topics. Put an *X* by the items that are topics. In the lines below the list, rewrite the topics into topic sentences.

1. _____ Two simple ways to lose weight without following a strict diet or taking diet pills.

2. _____ The happiest day in my life started out as a bad day.

3. _____ Choosing the wrong friends and facing the consequences.

4. _____ Worrying about the future can become an obsession.

5. _____ How I met the man I married.

6. _____ Why procrastinating is a destructive habit.

7. _____ One strong family can survive many tragedies.

8. _____ College classes are not what I expected.

9. _____ Volunteering at a nature preserve gives me a break from my worries.

10. _____ My ten-year-old niece is obsessed with makeup.

Rewrite the topics. Make each one into a topic sentence.

_____

_____

_____

_____

_____

_____

_____

_____

Exercise 10   **Practice: Revising Topic Sentences That Are Too Broad**

Below is a list of topic sentences. Some of them are too broad to support in one paragraph. Put an *X* by the ones that are too broad. Then, on the lines below the list, rewrite those sentences, focusing on a limited idea, a topic sentence that could be supported in one paragraph.

1. _____ Childhood is a time of innocence.

2. _____ The worst part of working at the supermarket's fish department was the fish smell.

3. _____ Trust is the most important factor in negotiations.

4. _____ Omar needs to be more realistic about his goals.

5. _____ Colin has two jobs so that he can afford to go to college next year.

6. _____ American teenagers are deeply troubled.

7. _____ Two of my cousins were victims of the epidemic of teen depression.

8. _____ When I finish my education, I want to do some meaningful work.

9. _____ My mother would have liked to be a stay-at-home mother.

10. _____ My life as a thirty-year-old student is nothing like the lives of college students in most movies.

Rewrite the broad sentences. Make each one more limited.

_____

_____

_____

_____

_____

_____

_____

_____

_____

_____

Exercise 11 **Practice: Making Announcements into Topic Sentences**

Below is a list of sentences. Some are topic sentences. Some are announcements. Put an *X* by the announcements. Then, on the lines below the list, rewrite the announcements, making them into topic sentences.

1. _____ Sticking to a budget can be difficult for a college student.

2. _____ This paper will be about the loss of green space in our town.

3. _____ I became a vegetarian for several reasons.

4. _____ Flowers are a great, all-purpose gift, but they can be expensive.

5. _____ Why my brother is in prison is the subject of this essay.

6. _____ The need for more and better campus lighting is the area to be discussed.

7. _____ The smartest change I made all year was to give up soft drinks and switch to water.

8. _____ The topic of this paper will be the recent carjacking on Patriot Road.

9. _____ I will discuss the reasons for taking the bus to work.

10. _____ Arthur O'Malley deserves a reward for heroism.

Rewrite the announcements. Make each one a topic sentence.

_____

_____

_____

_____

_____

_____

_____

_____

_____

_____

_____

| Exercise 12 | **Practice: Revising Topic Sentences That Are Too Narrow** |

Below is a list of topic sentences. Some of them are topics that are too narrow; they cannot be developed with details. Put an *X* by the ones that are too narrow. Then, on the lines below, rewrite those sentences as broader topic sentences that could be developed in one paragraph.

1. _____ My father has to sell my grandmother's house.

2. _____ Every night, I cook dinner for my children.

3. _____ Adrian Levine's people skills made him a good psychologist.

4. _____ Armando has a commercial pilot's license.

5. _____ The movie theater is across the street from the mall.

6. _____ Once the supermarket closed, the small stores around it struggled to survive.

7. _____ Heavy flooding drove hundreds of people from their Kansas homes.

8. _____ There was a fire at the abandoned bowling alley on Dowling Road.

9. _____ Our first night of camping was full of surprises.

10. _____ Ted and I played basketball all Saturday afternoon and most of Sunday morning.

Rewrite the narrow sentences. Make each one broader.

_____

_____

_____

_____

_____

_____

_____

_____

_____

_____

_____

PLANNING A PARAGRAPH

Checking Your Details

Once you have a topic sentence, you can begin working on an **outline** for your paragraph. The outline is a plan that helps you stay focused in your writing. The outline begins to form when you write your topic sentence and write your list of details beneath the topic sentence. You can now look at your list and ask yourself an important question: "Do I have **enough details** to **support** my topic sentence?" Remember, your goal is to write a paragraph of seven to twelve sentences.

Consider this topic sentence and list of details:

topic sentence: People can be very rude when they shop in supermarkets.

details: push in line
express lane
too many items

Does the list contain enough details for a paragraph of seven to twelve sentences? Probably not.

Adding Details When There Are Not Enough

To add details, try brainstorming. Ask yourself some questions like these:

Where else in supermarkets are people rude?
Are they rude in other lanes besides the express lane?
Are they rude in the aisles? How?
Is there crowding anywhere? Where?

By brainstorming, you might come up with this detail:

topic sentence: People can be very rude when they shop in supermarkets.

details: push in line
express lane
too many items
hit my cart with theirs in aisles
block aisles while they decide
push ahead in deli area
will not take a number
argue with cashier over prices
yell at the bagger

Keep brainstorming until you feel you have enough details for a seven- to twelve-sentence paragraph. Remember that it is better to have too many details than too few, for you can always edit the extra details later.

If you try brainstorming and still do not have many details, you can refer to your original ideas—your freewriting or journal—for other details.

Eliminating Details That Do Not Relate to the Topic Sentence

Sometimes, what you thought were good details do not relate to the topic sentence because they do not fit or support your point. Eliminate details that do not relate to the topic sentence. For example, the following list contains details that really do not relate to the topic sentence. Those details are crossed out.

topic sentence:	Waiters have to be very patient in dealing with their customers.
details:	customers take a long time ordering
	~~waiter's salary is low~~
	waiters have to explain specials twice
	customers send orders back
	customers blame waiters for any delays
	customers want food instantly
	waiters can't react to sarcasm of customers
	waiters can't get angry if customer gets angry
	~~waiters work long shifts~~
	customers change their mind after ordering

From List to Outline

Take another look at the topic sentence and list of details on a favorite city or town:

topic sentence: I love St. Augustine because it has sun and sea, history, and family

details:

a small city	clear blue water
no freeways	lots of history
no skyscrapers	a fort
not millions of people	oldest schoolhouse
thousands of visitors every day	grandparents live there
can always visit family for free	warm in winter
beach nearby	grandparents feed me
clean, big beach	I use their car

After you scan that list, you are ready to develop the outline of the paragraph.

An outline is a plan for writing, and it can be a type of draft in list form. It sketches what you want to write and the order in which you want to present it. *An organized, logical list will make your writing unified since each item on the list will relate to your topic sentence.*

When you plan, keep your topic sentence in mind:

I love St. Augustine because it has <u>sun</u> and <u>sea</u>, <u>history</u>, and <u>family</u>.

Notice the underlined key words, which lead to three key parts of your outline:

sun and sea
history
family

You can put the details on your list together so that they connect to one of these parts:

sun and sea

>   beach nearby, clean, big beach, clear blue water, warm in winter

history

>   lots of history, a fort, oldest schoolhouse

family

>   can always visit family for free, grandparents live there, grandparents
>   feed me, I drive their car

With this kind of grouping, you have a clearer idea of how to organize a paragraph.

Now that you have grouped your ideas with key words and details, you can write an outline.

An Outline for a Paragraph

topic sentence:	I love St. Augustine because it has sun and sea, history, and family.
details: **sun and sea**	It is warm in the winter. There is a beach nearby. It is big and clean. The water is clear blue.
history	It has lots of history. There is a fort. The oldest schoolhouse is there.
family	My grandparents live in St. Augustine. I stay at their house. They feed me. I use their car.

As you can see, the outline combined some of the details from the list. Even with these combinations, the details are very rough in style. As you reread the list of details, you will notice places that need more combination, places where ideas need more explaining, and places that are repetitive. Keep in mind that an outline is merely a very rough organization of your paragraph. As you work through the steps of devising an outline, you can check for the following.

Checklist for an Outline

✔ **Unity:** Do all the details relate to the topic sentence? If they do, the paragraph will be unified.

✔ **Support:** Do you have enough supporting ideas? Can you add to these ideas with even more specific details?

✔ **Coherence:** Are the details listed in the right order? If the order of points is logical, the paragraph will be coherent.

Coherence: Putting Your Details in Proper Order

Check the sample outline again, and you will notice that the details are grouped in the same order as the topic sentence: first, details about sun and sea; next, details about history; last, details about family in St. Augustine. Putting the details in an order that matches the topic sentence is a logical order for this paragraph.

Putting the details in logical order makes the ideas in your paragraph easy to follow. The most logical order for a paragraph depends on the subject of the paragraph. If you are writing about an event, you might use **time order** (such as telling what happened first, second, and so forth); if you are arguing some point, you might use **emphatic order** (such as saving your most convincing idea for last); if you are describing a room, you might use **space order** (such as from left to right, or from top to bottom).

The format of the outline helps to organize your ideas. The topic sentence is written above the list of details. This position helps you to remember that the topic sentence is the *main idea*, and the details that support it are written under it. The topic sentence is the most important sentence of the paragraph. You can easily check the items on your list, one by one, against your main idea. You can also develop the *unity* (relevance) and *coherence* (logical order) of your details.

When you actually write a paragraph, the topic sentence does not necessarily have to be the first sentence in the paragraph. Read the paragraphs below, and notice where each topic sentence is placed.

Topic Sentence at the Beginning of the Paragraph

<u>Watching a horror movie on the late show can keep me up all night</u>. The movie itself scares me to death, especially if it involves a creepy character sneaking up on someone in the dark. After the movie, I'm afraid to turn out all the lights and be alone in the dark. Then every little noise seems like the sound of a sinister intruder. Strange shapes seem to appear in the shadows. My closet becomes a place where someone could be hiding. There might even be a creature under the bed! And if I go to sleep, these strange invaders might appear from under the bed or in the closet.

Topic Sentence in the Middle of the Paragraph

The kitchen counters gleamed. In the spice rack, every jar was organized neatly. The sink was polished, and not one spot marred its surface. The stove burners were surrounded by dazzling stainless steel rings. <u>The chef kept an immaculate kitchen.</u> There were no finger marks on the refrigerator door. No sticky spots dirtied the floor. No crumbs hid behind the toaster.

Topic Sentence at the End of the Paragraph

On long summer evenings, we would play softball in the street. Sometimes we'd play until it was so dark we could barely see the ball. Then our mothers would come to the front steps of the row houses and call us in, telling us to stop our play. But we'd pretend we couldn't hear them. If they insisted, we'd beg for a few minutes more or for just one more game. It was so good to be outdoors with our friends. It was warm, and we knew we had weeks of summer vacation ahead. There was no school in the morning; there would be more games to play. <u>We loved those street games on summer nights.</u>

Note: Many of your paragraph assignments will require a clear topic sentence, so be sure you follow your own instructor's directions about placement of the topic sentence.

Exercise 13 **Practice: Adding Details to Support a Topic Sentence**

The topic sentences below have some—but not enough—details. Write sentences to add details to the list below each topic sentence.

1. **topic sentence:** A bad cold can be a miserable experience.

   a. No one wants to be around a person with a cold.

   b. My head hurts because of congestion.

   c. A constantly dripping nose makes it hard to do any work.

   d. _____

   e. _____

   f. _____

   g. _____

2. **topic sentence:** Unexpected time off can be a great gift.

   a. I used to love snow days when I was in elementary school.

   b. I could stay home, play in the snow, or watch television.

   c. _____

   d. _____

   e. _____

   f. _____

   g. _____

3. **topic sentence:** Anyone who has moved to a new place knows what loneliness means.

   a. There is no old friend to visit nearby.

   b. At work, everyone seems to have a closed group of friends.

   c. Those groups don't need a new person at the workplace.

   d. _____

   e. _____

f. _____

g. _____

Practice: Eliminating Details That Do Not Fit

Below are topic sentences and lists of supporting details. Cross out the details that do not fit the topic sentence.

1. **topic sentence:**   A gray and rainy day has a special kind of appeal for me.

   details: When I wake up on a dark, rainy morning, I appreciate my bed.

It is warm and comfortable.

I like to stay in bed for a few minutes and savor the sound of the rain.

Unfortunately, I can't stay in bed forever.

Drinking a hot cup of coffee and seeing the dripping trees outside, I feel safe and protected.

Even when I have to drive to work in the rain, I enjoy the glistening streets and misty air.

Everywhere I look, I see drivers racing through puddles and splashing the poor pedestrians on the sidewalks.

2. **topic sentence:**   A new seatbelt law has made me angry and upset.

   details: The old law allowed the police to check for a seatbelt violation only if they spotted another violation first.

The new law says police can now randomly check for seatbelt violations.

Last week, police offers stopped me and about forty other students just as we pulled out of the parking lot at our college.

I was so busy trying to pull out of my parking space and slip into the long line of cars that I forgot to buckle up.

Between classes, the parking lot is jammed with people coming and going.

Instead of giving me a warning, an officer issued a ticket that costs more than a hundred dollars.

I am furious about this unfair treatment.

My mother says that the officer was trying to protect me, but she's just being silly.

Practice: Coherence: Putting Details in the Right Order

These outlines have details that are in the wrong order. In the space provided, number the sentences in the right order: 1 would be the number for the first sentence, and so on.

1. **topic sentence:** Finding emergency day care for my son was difficult.

_____ My four-year-old son was a little grumpy at breakfast on Friday morning.

_____ Michelle said my son had a slight fever and a runny nose.

_____ By 8:00 A.M., when I dropped him off at his regular day care facility, he seemed better.

_____ My second was to call my sister, but I reached her at my aunt's house, two hours away.

_____ Michelle wanted me to pick up my son immediately so that the other children would not be infected.

_____ My first option was to leave work and risk being fired.

_____ At noon, while I was at work, I got a call from Michelle, the owner of the day care facility.

_____ As I listened to Michelle, I examined my options.

_____ Finally, my brother, who works at night, brought Ryan home and stayed with him until I finished work.

2. **topic sentence:** My argument with Patrick was a silly quarrel between two stubborn people.

_____ Our quarrel ended when the theater ran out of tickets before we reached the ticket window.

_____ It started over a movie that we both wanted to see.

_____ We arranged to go to a nine o'clock showing.

_____ When we got to the theater, a huge line snaked around the building.

_____ At 9:20, we were still in line, and I wanted to leave.

_____ "You won't miss any of the movie," Patrick answered, "just the advertisements and the coming attractions."

_____ "I hate to miss any of the movie," I said," so let's go and come back another time."

_____ Patrick's words irritated me, so I replied, "You go to the movie if you want to. I'll just wait in the car."

_____ "Fine," Patrick snarled, "you sit in the car for two hours."

DRAFTING AND REVISING A PARAGRAPH

Drafting a Paragraph

The outline is a draft in list form. You are now ready to write the list in paragraph form, to "rough out" a draft of your assignment. This stage of writing is the time to draft, revise, edit, and draft again. You may write several drafts in this stage, but don't think of this as an unnecessary chore or a punishment.

It is a way of taking the pressure off yourself. By revising in steps, you are reminding yourself that the first try does not have to be perfect.

Review the outline on a favorite city or town on page 21. You can create a first draft of this outline in the form of a paragraph. (Remember that the first line of each paragraph is indented.) In the draft of the paragraph below, the first sentence of the paragraph is the topic sentence.

A First Draft of a Paragraph

I love St. Augustine because it has sun and sea, history, and family. St. Augustine is warm in the winter. There is a beach nearby. It is clean and big. The water is clear blue. St. Augustine has lots of history. There is an old stone fort. The oldest schoolhouse is there. I can always visit my family for free. My grandparents live in St. Augustine. They feed me. I use their car.

Revising

Once you have a first draft, you can begin to think about revising and editing it. **Revising** means rewriting the draft by making changes in the structure, in the order of the sentences, and in the content. **Editing** includes making changes in the choice of words, in the selection of details, in punctuation, and in the pattern and kinds of sentences. It may also include **adding transitions**, which are words, phrases, or sentences that link ideas.

One way to begin revising and editing is to read your work aloud to yourself. Listen to your words, and consider the following questions in the checklist below.

Checklist for Revising the Draft of a Paragraph (with key terms)

✔ Am I staying on my point? (unity)

✔ Should I take out any ideas that do not relate? (unity)

✔ Do I have enough to say about my point? (support)

✔ Should I add any details? (support)

✔ Should I change the order of my sentences? (coherence)

✔ Is my choice of words appropriate? (style)

✔ Is my choice of words repetitive? (style)

✔ Are my sentences too long? Too short? (style)

✔ Should I combine any sentences? (style)

✔ Am I running sentences together? (grammar)

✔ Am I writing complete sentences? (grammar)

✔ Can I link my ideas more smoothly? (transitions)

If you apply the checklist to the draft of the paragraph on a favorite city or town, you will probably find these rough spots:

- The sentences are very short and choppy.
- Some sentences could be combined.
- Some words are repeated often.
- Some ideas would be more effective if they were supported by more details.
- The paragraph could use a few transitions.

Consider the following revised draft of the paragraph, and notice the changes, underlined, that have been made in the draft:

A Revised Draft of a Paragraph

topic sentence	I love St. Augustine, <u>Florida</u>, because it has sun and sea,
sentences combined	history, and family. <u>St. Augustine is warm in the winter,</u>
transition added	<u>and a big, clean beach with clear blue water is nearby.</u> <u>In</u>
sentences combined,	<u>addition,</u> St. Augustine has lots of history, including an
transition added	<u>old stone fort that looks out on the water.</u> It <u>also</u> has the old-
details added,	est schoolhouse <u>in America, a tiny wooden building.</u> <u>Best</u>
transition added,	<u>of all,</u> my grandparents live in St. Augustine. They are <u>my</u>
details added	<u>favorite</u> relatives, <u>and</u> <u>they make me feel very welcome.</u>
sentences combined	<u>When I am in St. Augustine, I stay with them, enjoy their</u>
	<u>food, and use their car.</u>

When you are revising your own paragraph, you can use the checklist to help you. Read the checklist several times; then reread your draft, looking for answers to the questions on the list. If your instructor agrees, you can work with your classmates. You can read your draft to a partner or a group. Your listener(s) can react to your draft by applying the questions on the checklist and by making notes about your draft as you read. When you are finished reading aloud, your partner(s) can discuss the notes about your work. **Remember that writing and revising several drafts may be necessary before you are satisfied with your paragraph.**

Exercise 16   **Practice: Revising a Draft by Combining Sentences**

The paragraph below has many short, choppy sentences. The short, choppy sentences are underlined. Wherever you see two or more underlined sentences clustered next to each other, combine the clustered sentences into one clear, smooth sentence. Write your revised version of the paragraph in the spaces above the lines.

Paragraph to be revised:

I have often claimed that I would love a rainy holiday. <u>I swore that it would</u>

<u>be a perfect time for me. It would be a time for me to relax. It would be a time for</u>

<u>me to enjoy my solitude.</u> I was wrong. Last week, because of the Memorial Day

holiday, I had a free three-day weekend. The rain began on Saturday morning. <u>I watched the water splatter the windows. It gushed from the gutters.</u> "Fine," I thought. I planned to enjoy every minute of my freedom. <u>I started with a leisurely cup of coffee. I spent some time calling all my friends.</u> How wonderful it is to have all this time, I thought. By late afternoon, it was raining hard. <u>I was bored. I did a few chores. I took a nap.</u> I woke up to darkness and pouring rain. The rain continued on Sunday. Now I was feeling cheated of my great weekend. <u>I could not play softball. I could not sunbathe in the park. I could not have a picnic or go for a walk.</u> My friends did not want to get together in the nasty weather. By Monday, as the rain continued, I had to admit that rainy holidays do not put me in a holiday mood.

Collaborate

Exercise 17   Collaborate: Adding Details to a Draft

Complete this exercise with a partner or a group. The paragraph below lacks the kind of details that would make it more interesting. Working with a partner or a group, add the details to the blank spaces provided. When you are finished with the additions, read the revised paragraph to the class.

Paragraph to be revised:

     Students are busy and often broke. As a result, their meals are not always healthy and often eaten on the run. Instead of eating a nutritional breakfast, many students grab _____, _____, or _____ and eat or drink it on their way to class. Lunch is likely to come from a vending machine and be filled with sugar or fat. Every day, students drink soft drinks such as _____ or _____ when they have a break between classes; they munch on bags of _____ or little plastic packets of _____. Of course, every student appreciates the student activities that include free food; these include fairs sponsored by various clubs, multicultural celebrations, and _____. Some students who sign up for an evening class fortify themselves by grabbing fast food from popular restaurants like _____, _____, and _____ so that they will have the energy for a two- or three-hour class.

PROOFREADING A PARAGRAPH

The final version of your paragraph is the result of careful thinking, planning, and revising. After as many drafts as necessary for you to be satisfied, you then *proofread*. You can avoid too many last-minute corrections if you check your last draft carefully. Check the draft for the following:

> spelling errors
> punctuation errors
> word choice
> a final statement

Take a look at the last draft of the paragraph on a favorite city or town. Wherever something is crossed out, the draft has been corrected directly above the crossed-out material. At the end of the paragraph, you will notice a concluding sentence has been added to unify the paragraph.

Correcting the Last Rough Draft of a Paragraph

                                      Florida

I love St. Augustine, ~~Fla.~~, because it has sun and sea, history, and fam-

                                       winter

ily. St. Augustine is warm in the ~~Winter~~, and a large, clean beach with clear

blue   lots

~~blew~~ water is nearby. In addition, St. Augustine has ~~lot's~~ of history, includ-

                                          has

ing an old stone fort that looks out on the water. It also ~~have~~ the oldest

schoolhouse in America, a tiny wooden building. Best of all, my grandpar-

ents live in St. Augustine. They are my favorite relatives, and they make me

feel

~~fell~~ very welcome. When I am in St. Augustine, I stay with them, enjoy their

                     their

food, and use ~~there~~ car. St. Augustine has the perfect natural advantages,

                           connections

history, and family ~~connection~~ to make it my favorite city.

Giving Your Paragraph a Title

When you prepare the final version of your paragraph, you may be asked to give it a title. The title should be short and should fit the subject of the paragraph. For example, an appropriate title for the paragraph on a favorite city or town could be "My Favorite City" or "The City I Love." Check with your instructor to see if your paragraph needs a title. In this book, the paragraphs do not have titles.

The Final Version of a Paragraph

Following is the final version of the paragraph on a favorite city or town. As you read it, you will notice a few more changes. Even though the paragraph went through several drafts and many revisions, the final copy still reflects some changes even as the final version was prepared. Some details have been added, some have been made more specific, and some words have been changed. (These changes are underlined for your reference.)

Final Version of a Paragraph

(Changes from the previous draft are underlined.)

I love St. Augustine, Florida, because it has sun and sea, history, and family. St. Augustine is warm in the winter, and a <u>wide</u>, clean beach with clear blue water is <u>ten minutes away</u>. In addition, St. Augustine is <u>filled with</u> history, including an old stone fort that looks out on the water. It also has the oldest schoolhouse in America, a tiny wooden building <u>smaller than a two-car garage</u>. Best of all, my grandparents live in St. Augustine. They are my favorite relatives, and they make me feel very welcome. When I am in St. Augustine, I stay with them, enjoy their <u>delicious Spanish</u> food, and use their car. St. Augustine has the natural advantages, history, and family connections to make it my favorite city.

Reviewing the Writing Process

This chapter has taken you through four important stages in writing. As you become more comfortable with them, you will be able to work through them more quickly. For now, try to remember the four stages.

INFO BOX: **The Stages of the Writing Process**

Prewriting: gathering and developing ideas, thinking on paper through freewriting, brainstorming, mapping, or keeping a journal

Planning: planning the paragraph by combining and dividing details, focusing the details with a topic sentence, listing the supporting details in proper order, and devising an outline

Drafting and Revising: writing and revising several drafts of the paragraph and editing them extensively

Proofreading: reviewing the final version of the paragraph to check for careless errors in preparation, punctuation, and spelling

---

Exercise 18 **Practice: Proofreading to Prepare the Final Version**

Following are two paragraphs with the kind of errors it is easy to overlook when you prepare the final version of an assignment. Correct the errors by writing above the lines. There are eleven errors in the first paragraph and nine errors in the second paragraph.

1. Andrew is working hard, but is having a hard time coping with the pressures of his first semester in college. Andrew was not a very good student in High School because he had other intrests. He was friends with some ruff people and even got arrested 2 times. Andrew managed to get a high school diploma but really didn't know what to do next? After two years of working at jobs such as delivering pizza and washing cars, Andrew faced the reality. He knew he needed a

better education so he could find more satisfying work. The decision was a huge

first step in Andrew's journey to a better life. How ever, Andrew is not use to tak-

ing the small and difficult steps toward success in college. Concentrating in class

is difficult for a man who never paid much attention in his high school classes.

Homework seems to pile up and threatens to overwhelm him. Fortunately, he has

an advisor who encourages him to be patience and take one small step, at a time.

2. Because I dont have a car, I depend on half a dozen people to get me to

my job, my classes, the supermarket, and my mother's house. My cousin and I

work in the same mall so I ride with him. Since our schedules are nearly identicle,

this plan works fairly well, especially because, I split the cost of gas with my

cousin. Of course, if he misses a day of work, I have to find someone to get me to

my job. Then I beg one of my coworkers to take me home. Fortunately, I have a

room mate who attends college, owns a car, and has several classes at times

when I am also in class. My roommate also drive me to visit my mother because

my mother cooks us fabulous dinners. Grocery shopping, visiting a pharmacy, or

taking advantage of bargains at a big discount store, present problems. sometimes my

sister takes me to a supermarket. I wish that I could afford a car or lived near a bus

line, but I'm lucky to have a kind and generous support system of friends and families.

Critical Thinking and the Writing Process

As you know by now, one of the popular methods of prewriting is called
brainstorming, the practice of asking yourself key questions that can lead
you to new ideas and directions related to your writing topic. During your
college career, you will find that such questioning can enable you to engage in
critical thinking, a type of reasoning that has several meanings and practical uses. For now, just remember that any time you evaluate the relevance
of supporting details, determine their order of importance, and attempt to
justify their inclusion, you are making judgments that are considered *critical*. Making such judgments will become more common for you as you tackle
college writing assignments.

You will soon appreciate the crucial role critical thinking plays in effective writing, whether you are comparing and contrasting ideas, identifying
a trend's causes and effects, arguing rationally for or against a proposal, or
questioning what you read. Additionally, whenever you evaluate a piece of
writing based on such criteria as unity, support, coherence, and intended
audience, you will be sharpening your critical thinking skills.

Critical thinking and writing options can be found at the end of each writing chapter and at the end of each reading selection in this book. These topics may require you to take a stand, defend a choice, imagine a certain scenario, or examine a trend. Whether you discuss these topics with peers or decide to write about them, keeping an open mind will help you become a better writer and a stronger critical thinker.

Lines of Detail: A Walk-Through Assignment

This assignment involves working within a group to write a paragraph.

Step 1: Read the three sentences below. Pick the one sentence you prefer as a possible topic sentence for a paragraph. Fill in the blank for the sentence you chose.

Pick one sentence and fill in the blank:

a. The most frightening movie I've ever seen was

_____ (fill in the title).

b. If money were no problem, the car I'd buy is

_____ (fill in the name of the car).

c. The one food I refuse to eat is _____

(fill in the name of the food).

Collaborate

Step 2: Join a group composed of other students who picked the same topic sentence you picked. In your class, you'll have "movie" people, "car" people, and "food" people. Brainstorm in a group. Discuss questions that could be used to get ideas for your paragraph.

For the movie topic, sample questions could include, "What was the most frightening part of the movie?" or "What kind of movie was it—a ghost story, a horror movie, etc.?" For the car topic, sample questions could include, "Have you ever driven this kind of car?" or "Do you know anyone who has one?" For the food topic, sample questions could include, "Did you hate this food when you were a child?" or "Where has this food been served to you?"

As you discuss, write the questions, not the answers, below. Keep the questions flowing. Do not stop to say, "That's silly," or "I can't answer that." Try to devise **at least ten questions.**

Ten Brainstorming Questions:

1. _____

2. _____

3. _____

4. _____

5. _____

6. _____

7. _____

8. _____

9. _____

10. _____

Step 3: Split up. Alone, begin to think on paper. Answer as many questions as you can, or add more questions and answers, or freewrite.

Step 4: Draft an outline of the paragraph. You will probably have to change the topic sentence to fit the details you have gathered. For example, your new topic sentence might be something like:

_____ was the most frightening movie

I have ever seen; it creates fear by using _____

_____, _____, and

_____.

or

If money were no problem, I would buy a _____

for its performance, _____, and

_____.

or

I refuse to eat _____ because _____

_____.

     Remember to look at your details to see where they lead you. The details will help you to refine your topic sentence.

Step 5: Prepare the first draft of the paragraph.

Step 6: Read the draft aloud to your writing group, the same people who met to brainstorm. Ask each member of your group to make at least one positive comment and one suggestion for revision.

Step 7: Revise and edit your draft, considering the group's ideas and your own ideas for improvement.

Step 8: Prepare a final version of the paragraph.

Topics for Writing a Paragraph

When you write on any of these topics, follow the four basic stages of the writing process in preparing your paragraph.

Collaborate

1. Begin this assignment with a partner. The assignment requires an interview. Your final goal is to write a paragraph that will introduce a class member, your partner, to the rest of the class. In the final paragraph, you may design your own topic sentence or use one of the topic sentences below, filling in the blanks with the material you have discovered:

   There are several details you should know about

   _____ (fill in your partner's name).

   or

   Three unusual events have happened to _____

   (fill in your partner's name).

   Before you write the paragraph, follow these steps:

Step 1: Prepare to interview a classmate. Make a list of six questions you might want to ask. They can be questions like, "Where are you from?" or "Have you ever done anything unusual?" Write *at least six questions* before you start the interview. List the questions on the following interview form, leaving room to fill in short answers later.

Interview Form

Question 1: _____

Answer: _____

Question 2: _____

Answer: _____

Question 3: _____

Answer: _____

Question 4: _____

Answer: _____

Question 5: _____

Answer: _____

Question 6: _____

Answer: _____

Additional questions and answers: _____

_____

_____

_____

Step 2: Meet and interview your partner. Ask the questions on your list. Jot down brief answers. Ask *any other questions* you think of as you are talking; write down the answers on the additional lines at the end of the interview form.

Step 3: Change places. Let your partner interview you.

Step 4: Split up. Use the list of questions and answers about your partner as the prewriting part of your assignment. Work on the planning and drafting stages.

Step 5: Ask your partner to read the draft version of your paragraph, to write any comments or suggestions for improvement below the paragraph, and to mark any spelling or grammar errors in the paragraph itself.

Step 6: When you have completed a final version of the paragraph, read the paragraph to the class.

2. Below are some topic sentences. Select one and use it to write a paragraph.

I am easily irritated by _____.

My first experience with college registration was

_____.

My secret dream is to become a _____.

Most of my friends tend to be _____.

3. Write a paragraph on one of the topics below. Create your own topic sentence; explain and support it with specific details.

a favorite activity   a dreaded chore   a challenging class
a special song   a patriotic moment   a model athlete

4. Examine the two photographs of families. After you have looked at them carefully, write a paragraph with this topic sentence:

Families can be as varied as their members.

You can write about several kinds of families, not just the ones shown in the photographs.

5. Examine the photograph of the dog. After you have looked at it carefully, write a paragraph with this topic sentence:

Some owners treat their pets like people

The details of the photograph can provide you with some details, but come up with other details on your own.

Topics for Critical Thinking and Writing

Note: College writing assignments will often require you to engage in *critical thinking*. Evaluating and questioning your own views and assumptions is a natural part of critical thinking and the writing process. The following topics will involve a careful analysis of some of your basic attitudes and opinions.

1. Do you make major decisions quickly, or do you take considerable time evaluating your options? Write about a major decision, perhaps a life-changing one, you have made. Include the factors that led to this decision and how pleased or dissatisfied you are with yourself for having made it.

2. Imagine that someone has given you an acre of land in your town to use any way you desire. What, if anything, would you do with this land? Include the specific reasons for your choice.

Note: Additional writing options can be found after the professional reading, "Getting Carded," in the "Readings for Writers" appendix of this book.

Name _____ Section _____

Peer Review Form for a Paragraph

After you have written a draft of your paragraph, let a writing partner read it. When your partner has completed the form below, discuss the comments. Then repeat the same process for your partner's paragraph.

The topic sentence of this paragraph is _____

_____

_____

_____

_____

The detail that I liked best begins with the words _____

_____

The paragraph has _____ (enough, too many, too few) details to support

the topic sentence.

A particularly good part of the paragraph begins with the words _____

_____

I have questions about or would like to know more about _____

_____

Other comments on the paragraph _____

_____

_____

_____

_____

_____

_____

_____

_____

_____

_____

Reviewer's name _____

Illustration

CHAPTER 2

Jumping In

*People who must stand in long lines react in a variety of ways. Do some become visibly or verbally impatient? Do some try to cut in line? Do some begin conversations with strangers who are also in line? By answering such questions, you will be **illustrating** ways people cope with standing in long lines.*

Chapter Objectives

Students will be able to (1) distinguish between general statements and specific details, and (2) write an illustration paragraph containing a clear topic sentence and sufficient supporting details.

WHAT IS ILLUSTRATION?

Illustration uses specific examples to support a general point. In your writing, you often use illustration because you frequently want to support a point by providing a specific example.

Hints for Writing an Illustration Paragraph

Knowing what is specific and what is general.

A *general* statement is a broad point. The following statements are general:

Traffic can be bad on Hamilton Boulevard.
Car insurance costs more today than it did last year.
It is difficult to meet people at my college.

You can support a general statement with specific examples:

general statement: Traffic can be bad on Hamilton Boulevard.

specific examples:	During the morning rush hour, the exit to First Avenue is jammed.
	If there is an accident, cars can be backed up for a mile.
general statement:	Car insurance costs more today than it did last year.
specific examples:	Last year I paid $150 a month; this year I pay $200 a month.
	My mother, who has never had a traffic ticket, has seen her insurance premium rise fifty percent.
general statement:	It is difficult to meet people at my college.
specific examples:	After class, most students rush to their jobs.
	There are very few places to sit and talk between classes.

When you write an illustration paragraph, be careful to support a general statement with specific examples, not with more general statements.

not this—general statement:	College is harder than I thought it would be.
~~**more general statements:**~~	~~It is tough to be a college student.~~
	~~Studying takes a lot of my time.~~
but this—general statement:	College is harder than I thought it would be.
specific examples:	I cannot afford to miss any classes.
	I have to study at least two hours a day.

If you remember to illustrate a broad statement with specific examples, you will have the key to this kind of paragraph.

Exercise 1   **Practice: Recognizing Broad Statements**

Each list below contains one broad statement and three specific examples. Underline the broad statement.

1. Students who come to class early often start conversations.

    Some students get to know each other in study groups formed in class.

    As a class ends, students tend to share their reactions to the latest quiz or assignment.

    Classes are a good place to start new friendships.

2. One of my roommates always borrows my shampoo even if there is very little left.

    Borrowing even small items can become a nasty habit.

    A man in my business class relies on me for a pencil and never returns one.

    I used to infuriate my father by scooping all his spare change off the hall table each day.

3. Photographs of adorable babies are nearly impossible to resist.

    My refrigerator is covered with photos of my sister's two-year-old twins.

    A photo of a smiling or sleeping baby sells fabric softener or toilet tissue.

    When a celebrity gives birth, the first published baby pictures are worth millions.

4. People fill the movie theaters when rain spoils their plans for a holiday outdoors.

Malls are popular places on a wet, hot, or snowy holiday.

Bad weather on a holiday can mean big profits for certain businesses.

When the weather gets too nasty, many people call a pizza delivery service.

Exercise 2   **Practice: Distinguishing the General Statement From the Specific Example**

Each general statement below is supported by three items of support. Two of these items are specific examples; one is too general to be effective. Underline the one that is too general.

1. general statement: Adolescent boys are very choosy about their footwear.

support: They know that some shoes will make them outcasts at school.

Shoes chosen by their parents make teenage boys cringe.

They select their sneakers and other footwear according to strict standards.

2. general statement: Vegetarian food choices are more popular than ever.

support: More and more people are turning to vegetarian dishes.

Today, veggie burgers are sold in almost every supermarket.

Major restaurant chains have vegetarian meals on their menus.

3. general statement: Preteen girls adore the color pink.

support: Many young girls dream of an all-pink bedroom.

Pink handbags, shoes, and clothing dominate the aisles in the preteen sections of department stores.

Every girl between the ages of two and twelve loves pink.

4. general statement: A person who coughs in public can make others nervous.

support: People sitting near someone who coughs fear catching a cold.

Everyone is uneasy when a cougher enters public space.

Some are afraid the cougher is a carrier of some new form of flu.

Exercise 3   **Collaborate: Adding Specific Examples to a General Statement**   Collaborate

With a partner or group, add four specific examples to each general statement below.

1. general statement: Mother's Day is associated with several popular gifts.

examples: _____

_____

_____

_____

2. **general statement:**   A crowded store, mall, or restaurant can bring out the worst in people.

examples: _____

_____

_____

_____

3. **general statement:**   The sense of being ignored is a painful feeling.

examples: _____

_____

_____

_____

4. **general statement:**   People caught in a sudden rainstorm have creative ways to stay dry.

examples: _____

_____

_____

_____

WRITING THE ILLUSTRATION PARAGRAPH IN STEPS

PREWRITING   ILLUSTRATION

Suppose your instructor asks you to write a paragraph about some aspect of **serving the community.** You can begin by thinking about your subject to gather ideas and to find a focus for your paragraph. Looking through entries in your journal might lead you to the following underlined entry:

Journal Entry About Serving the Community

Tomorrow I'm going to <u>help my father.</u> He's <u>giving out Thanksgiving baskets.</u> We'll go to the <u>Harvest Center Food Bank.</u> It <u>sounds sad.</u> I did it last year. It was <u>a happy experience</u> for me. The <u>families</u> who got baskets <u>were pleased.</u> Everybody waited in line. They were <u>patient.</u> <u>Volunteering put me in a good mood.</u> Now <u>I volunteer at</u> <u>the food bank on weekends.</u> We are a <u>father-and-son team.</u>

The underlined terms can lead you to a list:

help my father	families were pleased
giving out Thanksgiving baskets	patient
Harvest Center Food Bank	Volunteering put me in a good mood
sounds sad	I volunteer at the food bank on weekends
a happy experience	father-and-son team

Consider the underlined terms. Many of them are specific ideas about serving the community. You could write a paragraph about one item or about several related items on the list.

Adding Details to an Idea

Looking at the list of ideas on page 42, you might decide you want to write something about this topic: family volunteering. To add details, you decide to brainstorm:

Who else in your family volunteers?

My mother does. So does my sister.

What do they do?

My mother helps visitors. My sister walks dogs.

Where do they volunteer?

My mother goes to the hospital. My sister goes to the animal shelter.

Who benefits from the volunteering?

Hungry people, worried people, animals.

Why do your family members volunteer?

To help people or pets in trouble. To give to the community. To feel good.

How stressful is volunteering?

Seeing suffering is tough.

You now have this list of ideas connected to the topic of family volunteering:

help my father	mother and sister volunteer
giving out Thanksgiving baskets	mother helps visitors at the hospital
Harvest Center Food Bank	sister walks dogs at the animal shelter
sounds sad	people and animals benefit
I did it last year	family wants to help people or pets in trouble
a happy experience	
families pleased	family wants to give to the community
put me in a good mood	family wants to feel good seeing suffering is tough
father-and-son team	

Creating a Topic Sentence

If you examine this list, looking for *related ideas*, you can create a topic sentence. The ideas on the list include (1) details on who volunteers, (2) details about why they volunteer, and (3) details about who benefits from the volunteering. Not all the details fit into these three categories, but many do.

Grouping the related ideas into the three categories can help you focus your ideas into a topic sentence.

Who Volunteers

Father and son volunteer at Harvest Center Food Bank
Mother helps visitors at the hospital
Sister volunteers at the animal shelter

Why They Volunteer

Help people or pets in trouble
Family wants to give to the community
Family wants to feel good

Who Benefits

Hungry adults and children
Animals at the shelter
The volunteers

You can summarize these related ideas in a topic sentence:

In my family, volunteering is a way to give to the community and to share our good fortune.

Check the topic sentence against your details. Does it explain who volunteers? Yes. It says that the writer's family volunteers. Does it explain why they volunteer? Yes. It says that the family members want "to give to the community and to share our good fortune." Does it cover the people who get rewarded? Yes. It talks about the community that receives the benefits of others' volunteering, and it mentions that the volunteers themselves are rewarded.

The topic sentence has given you a focus for your illustration paragraph.

Exercise 4   Practice: Finding Specific Ideas in Freewriting

Following are two samples of freewriting. Each is a response to a broad topic. Read each sample, and then underline any words that could become a more specific topic for a paragraph.

Freewriting Reaction to the Topic of Gambling

I never gamble. Well, I have bought a lottery ticket or two. Of course, I've never won anything. Lottery tickets are just a form of wishful thinking. Would I like to go to Las Vegas? Just to see it once. Afraid to lose a lot of money there. Maybe I'd play the slot machines just once. I guess I do have a gambling streak in me.

Freewriting Reaction to the Topic of Physical Exercise

I don't get enough exercise. Running. Basketball. Going to a gym regularly. Regular exercise takes time out of a person's schedule. Only a super-organized person schedules exercise. Or a fanatic like my brother. He works out every morning at 6:00 A.M. I can't imagine sweating in a gym at dawn. So, how can I get easy exercise? Walk. Jog. Take the stairs. Just burn a few calories when I can. Exercise videos. Why are they popular?

Exercise 5   Practice: Finding Specific Ideas in Lists

Following are two lists. Each is a response to a broad topic. Read each list, and then underline any words that could become a more specific topic for a paragraph.

1. **topic:** the environment

environmental issues	a community garden
water pollution	dangers of greenhouse gases
recycling at my workplace	saving rainwater in your yard
cloth shopping bags	endangered species
Environmental Protection Agency	wasting paper at home

2. **topic:** crime

international drug laws	crime-proofing my car
college students and crime	maximum-security prisons
dangerous criminals	service dogs in police work
the best film about crime	security on my campus
shoplifters' tricks	fighting a speeding ticket

Exercise 6   **Practice: Grouping Related Ideas in Lists of Details**

Following are lists of details. In each list, circle the items that seem to fit into one group; then underline the items that seem to fit into a second group. Some items may not fit into either group.

1. **topic:** courage

seeking treatment for depression	attending patriotic events
volunteering for military service	bullying a child
recovering from addiction	reading books about heroes
accepting one's mistakes	confronting a gang member
rescuing a drowning person	admitting an addiction

2. **topic:** snacks

barbecue potato chips	ice cream cone
apple sauce	jello
low-fat yogurt	doughnut
midnight snack	chocolate brownie
ready-made snacks	banana

3. **topic:** living with a roommate

less loneliness	too little privacy
male or female	different concepts of neatness
risk of clashing personalities	international students
can share a social life	split the cost of rent
possible lifelong friendship	unauthorized borrowing

Exercise 7   **Practice: Writing Topic Sentences for Lists of Details**

Following are lists of details that have no topic sentences. Write an appropriate topic sentence for each one.

1. **topic sentence:** _____

_____

A salesperson who made a big sale may rush home to share the news with a loved one.

A worker who gets a promotion could celebrate with friends at a local restaurant.

Someone who gets an "A" on a test may rush out after class to call a parent.

A mother watching her child perform in a school play is likely to take her child to McDonald's afterwards.

A man who just became a father could react by telling everyone he knows.

A child who got a new toy will squeal as he or she rips open the box.

A lottery winner may keep staring at the winning ticket, safely stashed away.

2. topic sentence: _____

_____

A small child needs a tolerant, playful, and protective dog.

Apartment dwellers do best with a small dog that doesn't need much exercise.

A farmer who raises sheep could use a herding dog.

Police officers train intelligent, strong dogs such as German shepherds to become crime-fighting comrades.

Therapy dogs must love people and be trained to sit quietly with nursing home residents and children in hospitals.

Firehouse dogs are active dogs, often Dalmatians, who can learn when to be calm.

Teams of large, furry dogs who thrive in cold weather can pull sleds in Alaska.

3. topic sentence: _____

_____

Alexander Depree was born in Haiti in the same month that his father died.

Alexander and his mother struggled against the constant threat of starvation in their village.

When Alexander was ten, he and his mother were admitted to the United States as refugees.

Alexander and his mother knew only a few words of English.

To support herself and her son, Alexander's mother worked at two jobs.

Alexander struggled to survive in a school where almost all the students spoke English or Spanish.

Lonely, afraid, but determined, he graduated from high school with the rest of the senior class.

After high school, he found a night job as a janitor in a large business complex; in the daytime, he attended the police academy.

Now a police officer, Alexander is respected by his fellow officers and a mentor to boys in the growing Haitian community.

Exercise 8 **Practice: Choosing the Better Topic Sentence**

Following are lists of details. Each list has two possible topic sentences. Underline the better topic sentence for each list.

1. possible topic sentence:

a. High school can be a source of exciting memories.

b. Reunions can be disappointing when one friend has grown up but the other hasn't.

Michael had the same best friend for all four years of high school.

He and Brian, his friend, were known for their carefree attitudes and crazy pranks.

After they finished high school, Michael joined the U.S. Navy.

Brian left their hometown in Virginia to look for work in California.

Michael lost touch with Brian but liked to remember their wild times.

Five years after their high school graduation, the two friends reunited.

Michael was home on leave from his Army base in Germany.

Brian was visiting his family and having another wild time.

Although Michael had looked forward to the reunion, he was saddened by the meeting.

Michael shared the adventures and struggles he had experienced in the military.

Brian had worked at a series of jobs, but none of the jobs had worked out, he said.

All Brian wanted to do was to relive their glory days in high school.

2. possible topic sentence:

a. Being popular sometimes means not being yourself.

b. Friendship can be strange and confusing.

My sister Tanya feels sorry for me because I'm not as popular as she is.

Her phone is always ringing, and she has hundreds of friends online and locally.

On the other hand, I have just a few friends.

Many of Tanya's friends are interested in parties and drinking.

I like sports, hiking, and nature.

I have tried to fit in with Tanya's friends.

However, I realized that, in order to fit in, I would have to pretend I liked socializing all night and getting drunk.

My group of friends doesn't go to huge parties or drink much.

They understand me.

I decided to be myself and enjoy my small circle of friends.

3. possible topic sentence:

a. Snack bars are not good for students.

b. Bringing lunch to school can be practical and healthy.

If students take a bagged lunch to school, they can save time.

Students don't have to walk to the student center to buy food.

Instead of standing in line at the student center waiting to be served, they have their food with them.

It can be eaten outside a classroom, on a patio, or even under a shady tree.

A homemade lunch can be cheaper than a snack for lunch.

Leftovers from home don't cost anything.

A bottle of water or soda brought from a pack at home costs less than one bought in a vending machine or at a snack bar.

Finally, lunches from home can be more nutritious than most campus food.

School cafeterias and fast-food chains on campus focus on sugary, high-fat selections.

Such food offers a quick jolt of pleasure followed by a sudden drop in energy.

Students who pack a bagged lunch can bring whole-grain bread and leftovers such as cheese, chicken, and fresh fruit or vegetables to sustain their energy.

PLANNING **ILLUSTRATION**

When you plan your outline, keep your topic sentence in mind:

In <u>my family,</u> volunteering is a way to <u>give to the community</u> and to <u>share our good fortune.</u>

Notice the three key phrases:

my family
give to the community
share our good fortune

Assign each detail to **one** of the key phrases:

my family

my father and I volunteer at the food bank
my mother helps visitors at the local hospital
my sister volunteers at the animal shelter

give to the community

help hungry people
help other people or pets in trouble

share our good fortune

a happy experience
needy families pleased
animals at the shelter
family members feel good

With this kind of grouping, you have a clearer idea of how to organize a paragraph.

Outline for an Illustration Paragraph

topic sentence: In my family, volunteering is a way to give to the community and to share our good fortune.

details:

who volunteers
{ My father and I volunteer every weekend at a local food bank.
My mother helps visitors at the hospital.
My sister volunteers at the animal shelter.

why they volunteer
{ My father and I want to help hungry people.
Some family members want to help other people or pets in trouble.
Family members want to feel good.

who shares our good fortune
{ Hungry adults and children are fed.
Visitors to the hospital are comforted.
Homeless pets receive love.
Family members get to give back to the community.
Family members get to feel good.

As you can see, the outline combined some of the details from the list. You can combine other details, avoid repetition, and add more details as you draft your essay.

Collaborate

Exercise 9   **Collaborate: Adding Details to an Outline**

Below are three partial outlines. Each has a topic sentence and some details. Working with a partner or group, add more details that support the topic sentence.

1. topic sentence: Sleeping habits vary a great deal.

   a. Some people like to sleep without a pillow.

   b. Others like to sleep with a pillow covering their face.

   c. Some people like to sleep with a window open, even in winter.

   d. _____

   e. _____

   f. _____

   g. _____

2. topic sentence: There is no safe, quick, and easy way to lose weight.

   a. Stomach stapling is expensive and can be risky.

   b. Diet pills can be dangerous.

   c. Eating only protein and no carbohydrates is no long-term solution.

   d. _____

   e. _____

   f. _____

   g. _____

3. topic sentence: License plates give car owners a chance to be creative.

   a. For a fee, car owners can request a series of numbers or letters on their state license plates.

   b. The letters may spell out a name or represent a driver's initials.

   c. The numbers could refer to a date such as a birthday.

   d. _____

   e. _____

   f. _____

   g. _____

Exercise 10   **Eliminating Details That Are Repetitive**

In the following outlines, some details use different words to repeat an example given earlier in the list. Cross out the repetitive details.

1. topic sentence: Lying may help a person in the short term, but it can be self-destructive in the long term.

Lying as an excuse for lateness or for broken promises can work for a while.

Eventually the excuses aren't believable and make a bad habit more obvious.

People who lie about their money or background to impress others may gain admiration at first.

Sooner or later, people will spot the lying braggart and become resentful or contemptuous.

Telling too many elaborate stories about car problems, family emergencies, or illness does not work forever.

Lies of infidelity may get a husband or wife out of a difficult situation.

However, a cheating spouse can become entangled in too many lies.

Someone who creates a phony image of wealth is bound to be exposed and mocked.

2. **topic sentence:** Nosy neighbors can be helpful people, even lifesavers.

They may appear to be gossipy, nasty people.

However, they may be lonely and just want something to fill their time.

They will collect your mail when you are away.

If you are away for a few days, you can ask them to keep an eye on your house.

The neighbors who are not minding their own business could spot a crime such as a burglary in progress.

You can ask them to check your mailbox if you are going to be out of town.

People who observe the comings and goings of their neighbors can spot a change in someone's routine.

That change could involve someone who hasn't left the house for days.

A person who slipped or fell at home, can't walk, and can't crawl to a phone would welcome a rescue by a nosy neighbor.

A nosy neighbor acts like your own Neighborhood Crime Watcher.

He or she can be almost as good as a paramedic.

3. **topic sentence:** Talking all day is a tough way to make a living.

People who work in phone sales have to be upbeat and polite.

Telemarketers must present themselves as cheerful, courteous callers.

People who respond to complaints about a product or service struggle to show patience and understanding to angry customers.

Teachers spend hours talking, trying to be clear and to motivate students.

Those who work at information booths at the airport say the same phrases all day.

It takes a huge amount of self-control to work with unhappy customers losing their temper at the complaint department.

People who offer samples of new products at the supermarket are on their feet, smiling and positive, while many shoppers ignore them.

DRAFTING AND REVISING   **ILLUSTRATION**

Review the outline on family volunteering on page 48. You can create a first draft of this outline in the form of a paragraph. Then as you begin to revise your drafts, you can combine some of the short, choppy sentences of the outline, add details, and add transitions to link your ideas. You can use the following checklist.

> ### Checklist for Revising an Illustration Paragraph
> ✔ Should some of the sentences be combined?
> ✔ Do I need more or better transitions?
> ✔ Should I add more details to support my points?
> ✔ Should some of the details be more specific?

Transitions

As you revise your illustration paragraph, you may find places where one idea ends and another begins abruptly. This problem occurs when you forget to add **transitions,** which are words, phrases, or sentences that connect one idea to another. Using transitions effectively will make your writing clear and smooth. When you write an illustration paragraph, you will need some transitions that link one example to another and other transitions to link one section of your paragraph to another section. Here are some transitions you may want to use in writing an illustration paragraph.

> **INFO BOX:** **Transitions for an Illustration Paragraph**
>
> | | | |
> |---|---|---|
> | another example | in the case of | other kinds |
> | a second example | like | such as |
> | for example | one example | the first instance |
> | for instance | one instance | another instance |
> | in addition | other examples | to illustrate |

Look carefully at the following draft of the paragraph on family volunteering, and note how it combines sentences, adds details, and uses transitions to transform the outline into a clear and developed paragraph.

Revised Draft of an Illustration Paragraph

topic sentence	In my family, volunteering is a way to give to
transition	the community and to share our good fortune. <u>One</u>
	<u>example</u> of this volunteering is the weekend work
detail added	my father and I do at the <u>Harvest Center Food Bank.</u>
transition added	<u>A second example</u> is the work of my mother, who
detail added	<u>spends her Thursdays</u> helping visitors at the local
transition added	hospital. <u>Another example of a</u> <u>volunteer</u> is my sis-
detail added	ter, who <u>devotes a part of each weekend</u> to working
transition sentence added	at the animal shelter. <u>The family members have sev-</u>
	<u>eral reasons for volunteering.</u> My father, mother, and
detail added	I like to help people in trouble. My sister <u>comforts</u>
	<u>homeless pets by walking and</u> <u>playing with them.</u>
	Every member of the family wants to give something
detail added	to the community. <u>The community has been good to</u>
	<u>us.</u> Most of all, we enjoy the good feeling that comes
	with sharing time, food, or love. In our volunteering,
transition, sentences combined	everyone benefits. <u>For instance, hungry adults and</u>
	<u>children receive food; friends and family of the sick</u>
	<u>receive comfort; and homeless animals receive love.</u>
transition, sentences combined	<u>In addition, everyone in my family gets the great</u>
	<u>reward that comes from sharing.</u>

Exercise 11	**Revising a Draft by Combining Sentences**

The paragraph below has many short, choppy sentences, which are underlined. Wherever you see two or more underlined sentences clustered next
to each other, combine them into one clear, smooth sentence. Write your
revised version of the paragraph in the spaces above the lines.

My sister Patrice loves the color red. <u>She has red shoes. She has six pairs of</u>

<u>them.</u> <u>They include bright red sneakers, tomato-colored platform heels, and scar-</u>

<u>let boots.</u> Her love of red does not end with clothing. <u>Her hair is dyed crimson. It</u>

<u>is not a natural shade.</u>

Of course, her nails are always painted bright red, and she never appears in public

without a shiny red coating of lipstick. Patrice collects red purses and bags, too.

<u>She haunts thrift shops in search of vintage bags in red. She hits the sales at the</u>

<u>mall. She looks for designer handbags in red.</u> All this searching makes Patrice

happy because she can survey her collection and know that she will never run out of red accessories. The greatest and most beloved item in her collection is not an

item at all. <u>It is her dog Pepper. He is a red Irish setter.</u>

Practice: Revising a Draft by Adding Transitions

The paragraph below needs some transitions. Add appropriate transitions
(words or phrases) to the blanks.

Meeting people is difficult for me. I never know what to say after shaking hands

or mumbling "Hi." Should I say "Nice to meet you"? Should I ask "How are you

doing?"? Then there is the problem of eye contact. This problem has many

facets. <u>For instance</u> , making eye contact is supposed to indicate openness

and good character. <u>In addition</u> , eye contact shows that a person is con-

fident. However, I am afraid to hold the eye contact for too long or too short a

time. <u>To illustrate</u>, I can remember a time when I felt myself looking down

at the floor too soon. I must have looked as if I were ashamed of something. Other

examples involve holding eye contact for too long. _____ I felt as

if I were invading the other person's space. _____ I felt uncom-

fortable because my lengthy eye contact made me look too needy. To cope with

my fears about meeting people, I pay close attention to television and movie

scenes where people meet. The actors always seem confident and suave. Actors

_____Will Smith and Denzel Washington never seem nervous or

tongue-tied. Maybe I can learn to act confident even when I feel nervous.

Adding Details to a Draft

Collaborate

The paragraph below lacks the kind of details that would make it more interesting. Working with a partner or group, add details to the blank spaces
provided. When you are finished, read the revised paragraph to the class.

People who need to cut back on their spending handle the challenge in different

ways. One of the first cuts involves nonessential clothing purchases. Teens may buy

fewer _____, _____, and _____. Their parents

may decide not to buy any more of the _____, _____, and

_____ they regularly wear to work. Some people decide to cut their

spending on fuel. To save money on gasoline, they may limit their driving and

avoid trips to _____ and _____. To save on gas or electric

heating and cooling at home, residents will turn up the thermostat on their air

conditioning, and _____.

    Finally, food shopping changes when people are short of money. In good times,

a food budget may leave room for a few luxuries such as _____,

_____, and _____. In more challenging times,

shoppers are likely to replace pricey goodies with cheaper treats such as

_____, _____, and _____.

PROOFREADING **ILLUSTRATION**

As you prepare the final version of your illustration paragraph, look for any errors in spelling, punctuation, typing, and formatting. You may also want to make a few changes in word choice or transitions that can refine your writing.

    Following is the final version of the paragraph on family volunteering. As you read it, you will notice a few more changes: unnecessary words have been eliminated, better word choice has solved a problem with repetition, "homeless pets" has been changed to the more specific "homeless dogs," more details about the family's gratitude to the community have been added, and the phrase "enjoy the great reward" has been changed to a more specific phrase, "know the joy." These changes were made as the final version was prepared. (They are underlined for your reference.)

Final Version of an Illustration Paragraph

(Changes from the last draft are underlined.)

    In my family, volunteering is a way to give to the community and to share our good fortune. One example of this volunteering is the weekend work my father and I do at the Harvest Center Food Bank. A second example is the work of my mother, who spends her Thursdays helping visitors at the local hospital. Another <u>volunteer</u> is my sister, who spends many hours at the animal shelter. The family members have several reasons for <u>giving their time and effort.</u> My father, mother, and I like to help people in trouble. My sister comforts homeless <u>dogs</u> by walking and playing with them. Every member of the family wants to give something to the community <u>that was very generous to us when a fire damaged our house.</u> Most of all, we <u>know the joy</u> that comes with sharing time, food, or love. In our volunteering, everyone benefits. For instance, hungry adults and children receive food; friends and family of the sick receive comfort; and homeless animals receive love. In addition, everyone in my family receives the great reward that comes from sharing.

For your information: A sample illustration essay based on the same topic and following the same writing steps can be found in Chapter 12.

Exercise 14 **Practice: Proofreading to Prepare the Final Version**

Following are two illustration paragraphs with the kinds of errors that are easy to overlook when you prepare the final version of an assignment. Correct the errors by writing above the lines. There are twelve errors in the first paragraph and ten errors in the second paragraph.

1. When I was 16, I learned the right way to dress for success. During my first two weeks of summer vactation, I tried to find work but no one would hire me. I filled out several applications, but no one called me back. I complained to my Aunt Denise, who works at a bank, and she looked at me critically. Then she quizzed me about the clothes I had worn When I applied for work. I told her I dressed the way I always did. "Be specific," she demanded. I were becoming a little defensive, but I said that I had worn a clean, long, lose tee-shirt, shorts, and my best flip-flops. "Where did you look for work?" she demanded. I tell her I had applied at several stores in the Mall, a movie theater, and a motel. My aunt was horrified. "Did you look around you"? she asked. "Were any of the employees dressed the way you were?" When I said no, she added, "What were you thinking?" Even tho she humiliated me. she gave me some good advice. In the following week, I continued my job search. This time I wore a shirt with a collar, khaki trousers, and real shoes. Two weeks later, I had a job at large discount store.

2. Sleep is a precious gift, but not all sleep are equal. People with deep anxieties or sorrows can suffer thru a broken sleep that leaves them exhausted and trouble. Passengers in a car, bus, train, or plane often fall into a long doze interrupted by periods of semi-consciousness. They incorporate the sound of engines, the talk of other passenger, and the jolts of travel into their sleep. They wake up feeling, grimy, disoriented, and cramped. A person who has worked for too many hours without sleeping may finally fall into a exhausted sleep. However, that sleep is'nt alway's refreshing. The best sleep is a soft, gentle fall into peace and silence. Its' rare and valuable, and the people who enjoy it regularly should be greatful.

Lines of Detail: A Walk-Through Assignment

Your assignment is to write an illustration paragraph about music.

Step 1: Freewrite or brainstorm on this broad topic for ten minutes.

Step 2: Review your freewriting or brainstorming. Underline any parts that are a specific idea related to the broad topic of music.

Step 3: List all the specific ideas. Choose one as the narrowed topic for your paragraph.

Step 4: Add related ideas to your chosen, narrowed topic. Do this by reviewing your list for related ideas and by brainstorming for more related ideas.

Step 5: List all your related ideas and review their connection to your narrowed topic. Then write a topic sentence for your paragraph.

Step 6: Write a first draft of your paragraph.

Step 7: Revise your first draft. Be sure it has enough details and clear transitions. Combine any choppy sentences.

Step 8: After a final check for any errors in punctuation, spelling, and word choice, prepare the final version of the paragraph.

Topics for Writing an Illustration Paragraph

When you write on any of these topics, follow the four basic stages of the writing process in preparing your illustration paragraph.

Collaborate

Computer

1. Begin this assignment with a partner or group. Together, write down as many old sayings as you can. (Old sayings include statements like, "It's not whether you win or lose; it's how you play the game that's important," or "Money can't buy happiness.") If anyone in your group speaks a second language, ask him or her to translate and explain any old sayings from that language. To review quotations categorized by topics, visit **www.quoteland.com**.

   Once you have a long list of sayings, split up. Pick one saying; then write a paragraph on that saying. Your paragraph should give several examples that illustrate the truth of the saying.

2. Below are some topic sentences. Select one and use it to write a paragraph in which you use examples to support (illustrate) the topic sentence.

   _____ makes me nervous.

   _____ takes great courage.

A rainy day is a good day to _____.

The friendliest person in my neighborhood is _____.

3. Select one of the topics listed below. Write an illustration paragraph on some narrowed part of the topic. If you choose the topic of jobs, for example, you might narrow the topic to illustrate the benefits or drawbacks of your job.

jobs	fears	dreams	mistakes
stress	money	food	mysteries
computers	children	sleep	surprises
fashion	challenges	anger	kindness

4. Examine the photograph of fast-food outlets. After you have looked at it carefully, write a paragraph using the following topic sentence:

   Fast-food restaurants appeal to a variety of ages and tastes.

   (The photograph may help you think of examples to support the topic sentence.)

5. Examine the image of the angry driver. After you have looked at it carefully, write a paragraph with this topic sentence:

   Whenever I am delayed by a traffic jam on a major highway, I can react in several ways.

Topics for Critical Thinking and Writing

1. Everyone has made general statements such as "This town has nothing to make young people want to stay here" or "People who don't have children have no idea how stressful life can be." Think of a similar generalization and use specific examples to illustrate the degree of truth in that statement. Be careful to avoid further generalizations in your supporting details.

2. Assume that you are a member of a student advisory board at your college, and you have been charged with identifying several potential safety hazards. After reviewing your list of potential dangers, choose the most severe hazard and illustrate why it poses such a serious threat to students and/or campus life in general. (You may want to share your initial list with your peers to elicit their feedback.)

> **Note:** Additional writing options suitable for illustration-related assignments can be found after the professional reading, "A Life Full of Riches," in the "Readings for Writers" appendix at the end of this book.

Name _____   Section _____

Peer Review Form for an Illustration Paragraph

After you have written a draft of your illustration paragraph, let a writing partner read it. When your partner has completed the form below, discuss the comments. Then repeat the same process for your partner's paragraph.

The examples in this paragraph relate to this topic sentence _____

_____

_____

_____

_____

The paragraph has _____ (enough, too few) details to support the topic sentence.

The most effective example was the one about _____

_____

Three words or phrases of specific detail in the paragraph are _____

Two transitions (words or phrases) in the paragraph are _____

_____

I have questions about or would like to know more about _____

_____

Other comments _____

_____

_____

_____

_____

_____

_____

_____

_____

_____

Reviewer's name _____

CHAPTER **3**	# Description

Jumping In

What is your strongest impression of this scene? Does the scene evoke feelings of power? Excitement? Anxiety? Examining the scene carefully, along with your reactions, will help you **describe** it effectively.

Chapter Objectives

Students will be able to write a descriptive paragraph that (1) supports a dominant impression, and (2) contains effective sense details.

WHAT IS DESCRIPTION?

Description shows a reader what a person, place, thing, or situation is like. When you write description, you try to *show, not tell about*, something. You want to make the reader see that person, place, or situation, and then, perhaps, to make the reader think about or act on what you have shown.

HINTS FOR WRITING A DESCRIPTIVE PARAGRAPH

Using Specific Words and Phrases

Using specific words and phrases will help the reader "see" what you are describing. If a word or phrase is *specific*, it is *exact and precise*. The opposite of specific language is language that is vague, general, or fuzzy. Think of the difference between specific and general in this way:

Imagine that you are browsing through a used car lot. A salesman approaches you.

"Can I help you?" the salesman asks.
"I'm looking for a good, reliable car," you say.
"Well, what kind of car did you have in mind?" asks the salesman.
"Not too old," you say.
"A sports car?" asks the salesman.
"Maybe," you say.

The conversation could go on and on. You are being very general in saying that you want a "good, reliable" car. The salesman is looking for specific details: How old a car do you want? What model of car?

In writing, if you use words like *good* or *nice* or *bad* or *interesting*, you will not have a specific description or a very effective piece of writing. Whenever you can, try to use a more precise word instead of a general term. To find a more explicit term, ask yourself such questions as, "What type?" or "How?" The examples below show how a general term can be replaced by a more specific one.

general word: hat (Ask "What type?")
more specific words: beret, fishing hat, baseball cap

general word: lettuce (Ask "What type?")
more specific words: iceberg lettuce, Romaine, arugula

general word: ran (Ask "How?")
more specific words: raced, sprinted, loped

general word: nice (Ask "How?")
more specific words: friendly, outgoing, courteous

Exercise 1   Practice: Identifying General and Specific Words

Below are lists of words. Put an *X* by the one term in each list that is a more general term than the others. The first one is done for you.

List 1

____X____ science

_____ botany

_____ biology

_____ astronomy

_____ geology

List 2

_____ physical exercise

_____ lifting weights

_____ running

_____ swimming

_____ rock climbing

List 3

_____ squash

_____ vegetable

_____ cucumber

_____ carrot

_____ peas

List 4

_____ neurologist

_____ pediatrician

_____ obstetrician

_____ physician

_____ endocrinologist

Exercise 2   **Practice: Ranking General and Specific Items**

Below are lists of items. In each list, rank the items, from the most general (1) to the most specific (4).

List 1

_____ car interiors

_____ seats in cars

_____ cars

_____ leather seats in cars

List 2

_____ chicken

_____ fried chicken

_____ southern fried chicken

_____ cooked chicken

List 3

_____ money

_____ coins

_____ silver-colored coins

_____ quarters

List 4

_____ makeup for the face

_____ makeup

_____ eye makeup

_____ mascara

Collaborate

Exercise 3   **Collaborate: Interviewing for Specific Answers**

To practice being specific, interview a partner. Ask your partner to answer the questions below. Write his or her answers in the spaces provided. When you have finished, change places. In both interviews, your goal is to find specific answers, so you should both be as explicit as you can in your answers.

Interview Questions

1. What is your favorite flavor of ice cream?

_____

_____

2. What did you eat and drink for breakfast this morning?

_____

_____

3. What is your favorite professional sports team?

_____

_____

4. What performer would you most like to see (in a live performance)?

_____

_____

5. If you could buy any car in the world, what car would you choose?

_____

_____

6. What kind of pillow do you like to sleep on (soft, firm, no pillow, several pillows, etc.)?

_____

_____

7. When you think of a brave person, who comes to mind?

_____

_____

8. What smell reminds you of a family holiday?

_____

_____

9. What specific piece of your clothing is the most itchy?

_____

_____

10. What is the most enjoyable city or town you have visited?

_____

_____

Exercise 4   Practice: Finding Specific Words or Phrases

List four specific words or phrases beneath the (underlined) general one in each list. The first word on List 1 is done for you.

List 1

general word: After dinner, we ate some <u>dessert</u>.

specific word or phrase: _coconut cake_

banana pudding

chocolate chip cookies

brownies

List 2

general word: Kenny was my <u>buddy</u>.

specific word or phrase: _____

_____

_____

_____

List 3

general word: I need some <u>rest</u>.

specific word or phrase: _____

_____

_____

_____

List 4

general word: Carl looked <u>funny</u>.

specific word or phrase: _____

_____

_____

_____

Exercise 5 **Practice: Identifying Sentences That Are Too General**

Below are lists of sentences. Put an *X* by one sentence in each group that is general and vague.

1. a. _____ I thrive on excitement.

b. _____ I like violent movies.

c. _____ I can't stay home alone on the weekends.

2. a. _____ She won't make eye contact with me.

b. _____ She never talks to her classmates.

c. _____ She is a real snob.

3. a. _____ My history class is long and boring.

b. _____ My history class consists of 75 minutes of lecturing.

c. _____ My history class does not include any discussion.

4. a. _____ At the free concert, the crowd cried for an encore.

b. _____ Everyone had a nice time at the free concert.

c. _____ Everyone clapped their hands and danced at the free concert.

Using Sense Words in Your Descriptions

One way to make your description specific and vivid is to *use sense words*. As you plan a description, ask yourself,

What does it **look** like?
What does it **sound** like?
What does it **smell** like?
What does it **taste** like?
What does it **feel** like?

The sense details can make the description vivid. Try to include details about the five senses in your descriptions. Often you can brainstorm sense details more easily if you focus on specific details that relate to each sense.

Collaborate

Exercise 6 **Collaborate: Brainstorming Sense Details for a Descriptive Paragraph**

Review the Info Box on the next page. Then, with a partner or a group, brainstorm the topics ideas for a paragraph by listing at least six questions and answers that could help you find sense details. Be prepared to read your completed exercise to another group or to the class.

INFO BOX: **Devising Sense Details**

For the sense of	think about
sight	colors, light and dark, shadows, or brightness
hearing	noise, silence, or the kinds of sounds you hear
smell	fragrance, odors, scents, aromas, or perfume
taste	bitter, sour, sweet, or compare the taste of one thing to another
touch	the feel of things: texture, hardness, softness, roughness, smoothness

1. topic: The bouquet of flowers was beautiful.
Brainstorm questions and answers:

Q: _____

Q: _____

Q: _____

Q: _____

Q: _____

Q: _____

2. topic: The closet was a mess.
Brainstorm questions and answers:

Q: _____

Q: _____

Q: _____

Q: _____

Q: _____

Q: _____

3. topic: The stew was disgusting.
Brainstorm questions and answers:

Q: _____

Q: _____

Q: _____

Q: _____

Q: _____

Q: _____

| Exercise 7 | **Practice: Writing Sense Words**

Write sense descriptions for the items below.

1. Write four words or phrases to describe the texture of sand on a beach:

   _____

   _____

2. Write four words or phrases to describe what a kitten looks like:

   _____

   _____

3. Write four words or phrases to describe the sounds of a garbage truck collecting your garbage:

   _____

   _____

WRITING THE DESCRIPTIVE PARAGRAPH IN STEPS

| PREWRITING | **DESCRIPTION**

Writing a descriptive paragraph begins with thinking on paper, looking for specific details and sense descriptions. You can think by brainstorming, free-writing, or writing in a journal. For example, you might decide to write about the contents of your garage. Brainstorming might lead you to something like the following list of ideas.

Brainstorming a List for a Descriptive Paragraph

- my husband
- Bradley's motorcycle in the garage
- cycle always in pieces
- his tools for the cycle, yard work, home repairs
- paint cans
- bulletin board with photos
- his little plastic containers of nails, screws
- dusty shelves on walls
- oil stains and smells on the floor
- Bradley's work bench
- musty smell of Bradley's boxes of junk on the floor
- noise of engine running
- bags of fertilizer
- garbage can smells
- gasoline smells
- Bradley's camping gear, a tent
- my collection of hand-painted ceramic bowls doesn't fit

The Dominant Impression

When you think you have enough details, you can begin to think about focusing them. Look over these details and consider where they are taking you. If you were to look at the list above, you might identify ideas that keep appearing in the details:

- my husband
- Bradley's motorcycle in the garage
- cycle always in pieces
- his tools for the cycle, yard work, and home repairs
- bulletin board with photos
- little plastic containers of nails, screws
- dusty shelves on walls
- oil stains and smells on the floor
- Bradley's work bench
- musty smell of Bradley's boxes of junk on the floor
- noise of engine running
- bags of fertilizer
- garbage can smells
- gasoline smells
- Bradley's camping gear, a tent

Reading over this list, you realize that all the items and details connect to Bradley. The cycle, work bench, tools, and camping gear reflect his hobbies and interests. The garbage can and tools may relate to his chores. Therefore, the garage seems to be Bradley's territory. This idea is the **dominant impression,** or the main point of the description. In a descriptive paragraph, the dominant impression is the topic sentence. For example, the topic sentence could be:

The garage is my husband's territory.

Once you have a dominant impression, you are ready to add more ideas to explain and support it. You should try to make the added details specific by using sense description where appropriate.

Exercise 8 **Practice: Adding Details to a Dominant Impression**

Following are sentences that could be used as a dominant impression in a descriptive paragraph. Some details to explain and support the dominant impression are already given. Add more details.

1. **dominant impression:**   The bodyguard looked intimidating.

   details: a. He was over six feet tall.

   b. He weighed about 250 pounds.

   c. _____

   d. _____

   e. _____

2. **dominant impression:**   My toddler enjoyed the wrapping paper more than the gift inside it.

   details: a. _____

   b. _____

   c. He concentrated on the bright paper.

d. _____

e. _____

3. **dominant impression:** The sound of screeching brakes in the road ahead made me cringe.

details: a. _____

b. _____

c. Then I heard the sound of metal scraping metal. _____

d. _____

e. _____

Exercise 9   **Practice: Creating a Dominant Impression from a List of Details**

Following are lists of details. For each list, write one sentence that could be used as the dominant impression created by the details.

1. **dominant impression:** _____

_____

details: Clarice's hair was tangled. The hair on the back of her head was flat.

She was wearing rumpled pajamas.

Her eyes were dull.

She was barefoot.

She walked hesitantly.

2. **dominant impression:** _____

_____

details: The salespeople stared from behind the counters.

They did not make eye contact with each other.

They avoided looking at the shoppers browsing through the departments.

When they made a sale, the clerks spoke without any emotion.

"Thank you for shopping at Pleasant Mart," they said softly.

After they completed the transition, they stared into space again.

3. **dominant impression:** _____

_____

details: My five-year-old son David begins to jump when he sees an ice cream cone in my hand.

He grabs it from me, crying, "Yum!"

Of course he licks it from the top, pushing the soft ice cream out of the sides of the cone.

Soon he is covered in dripping ice cream, but he doesn't care.

He concentrates on enjoying the soft, sweet, gooey mess.

To get the last drops of ice cream out of the cone, he turns the cone upside down.

He licks the inside of the cone with gusto.

Finally, he crushes the cone, eats it, and grins.

PLANNING DESCRIPTION

The sentence you created as the dominant impression can be the topic sentence for your outline. Beneath the topic sentence, list the details you have collected. Once you have this rough list, check the details by asking:

> Do all the details relate to the topic sentence?
> Are the details in logical order?

Following are the topic sentence and list of details for the paragraph describing the contents of the garage. The details that are crossed out don't "fit" the topic sentence.

topic sentence: The garage is my husband's territory.

- my husband
- Bradley's motorcycle in the garage
- cycle always in pieces
- his tools for the cycle, yard work, home repairs
- paint cans
- bulletin board with photos
- his little plastic containers of nails, screws
- dusty shelves on walls
- oil stains and smells on the floor
- Bradley's work bench
- musty smell of Bradley's boxes of junk on the floor
- ~~noise of engine running~~
- bags of fertilizer
- garbage can smells
- gasoline smells
- Bradley's camping gear, a tent
- ~~my collection of hand-painted ceramic bowls doesn't fit~~

Notice what is crossed out. The detail about the noise of the engine running doesn't fit because the paragraph is about the contents of the garage, not what happens in the garage. In addition, the detail about the wife's collection of ceramic bowls is not related to the topic sentence because the topic sentence focuses on the garage as Bradley's place. It is about his interests and responsibilities.

Remember that as you write and revise, you may decide to eliminate other ideas, to reinsert ideas you once rejected, or even to add new ideas. Changing your mind is a natural part of revising.

Once you have decided upon your best list of details, check their order. Remember, when you write a description, you are trying to make the reader *see*. It will be easier for the reader to imagine what you see if you put your description in a simple, logical order. You might want to put descriptions in order by **time sequence** (first to last), by **spatial position** (top to bottom, or right to left), or by **similar types** (for example, all about the flowers, then all about the trees in a park).

If you are describing a house, for instance, you may want to start with the outside of the house and then describe the inside. You do not want the details to shift back and forth, from outside to inside and back to outside. If you are describing a person, you might want to group all the details about his face before you describe his body. You might describe a meal from first course to dessert.

Look again at the details describing the garage. It is logical to use these categories: from the bare floor, to the covered floor, and to the walls. Now look at the following outline and notice how this order works.

Outline for a Descriptive Paragraph

topic sentence:	The garage is my husband's territory.
details: **bare floor**	The area of bare floor is covered in oil stains. It smells like gasoline. This area is very small.
covered floor	Most of the garage floor is filled. Boxes of Bradley's junk give off a musty odor. Bradley's work bench is pushed into one corner. Bradley's camping gear and a tent fill another corner. His motorcycle, usually in pieces, fills one third of the space. The garbage can smells of rotting food.
walls	The back and side walls are covered with dusty metal shelves. They contain tools for cycle repair, yard work, and home repair. Old, crusty paint cans are on the shelves. Bags of fertilizer are on the shelves. Dozens of small plastic containers of nails and screws are there. One wall has a bulletin board with photos.

You probably noticed that the outline has more details than the original list. These details help to make the descriptions more specific. You can add them to the outline and to the drafts of your paragraph.

Once you have a list of details focused on a topic sentence and arranged in some logical order, you can begin writing a draft of your description paragraph.

Exercise 10   **Practice: Finding Details That Do Not Relate**

Survey the following lists. Each includes a topic sentence and several details.
In each list, cross out the details that do not relate to the topic sentence.

1. **topic sentence:**   At my apartment building, the laundry facilities are
   inadequate and unreliable.

   details: Twenty apartments share one washer and one dryer.

   Whenever I try to do laundry, the machines are full
   of someone else's clothes.

   The washer is medium-sized, so I have to pay for
   two loads instead of one.

   The washer breaks down at least once a week.

   The dryer is inefficient.

   The dryer tends to spin my sheets of clothes into a
   long, rope-like tangle.

   I never remember to bring enough money to the
   laundry room.

   The laundry room shares a little hut with the mail
   boxes.

2. **topic sentence:**   Bernard is a good listener.

   details: He is genuinely interested in what I have to say.
   He likes to sit in a quiet place.

   Bernard never interrupts me with his opinions or
   criticism.

   He maintains eye contact.

   After I finish talking, he asks questions that show he
   has been listening carefully.

   He can keep a secret.

3. **topic sentence:**   The Bread Basket is a great restaurant for college
   students.

   details: It has a wide choice of soups, salads, sandwiches,
   fresh bread, and bagels.

   A big menu is posted on one wall.

   It also offers the cookies, muffins, and brownies
   that students love.

   For those who need to wake up or stay awake, the
   coffee is excellent.

   The prices are reasonable.

   The parking lot is usually overcrowded.

   Many students come to eat and socialize indoors or
   on the patio.

   Others place their laptops on the wide tables and
   booths indoors, do their homework, and study in
   peace.

   No one pushes out the students who linger over
   their homework or conversation.

Exercise 11   **Practice: Putting Details in Order**

Following are lists that start with a topic sentence. The details under each topic sentence are not in the right order. Put the details in logical order by labeling them, with 1 being the first detail, 2 the second, and so forth.

1. topic sentence: My job interview at a local restaurant confused me. (Arrange the details in time order.)

details: _____ After fifteen minutes of waiting, the manager led me to a small table near the kitchen.

_____ When I came in, a hostess told me to wait because the manager was busy.

_____ Waiting, I felt lost in a crowd of customers in line for tables.

_____ At the table, I struggled to hear the manager's words over the noise from the kitchen.

_____ I did my best to answer the manager's questions, but I couldn't hear half of what she was saying.

2. topic sentence: The exterior of the candy store was designed to bring out the love of candy in all children and adults. (Arrange the details from the top of the store to the bottom.)

details: _____ Hanging from the bottom of the sign, a line of brightly lighted gingerbread men danced.

_____ On either side of the store's entrance, huge windows displayed enormous piles of dark chocolate, milk chocolate, and white chocolate bonbons.

_____ The strangest part of the store was the roof, topped by a giant candy cane.

_____ Directly below the roof, huge pink gumdrops spelled out the words "Candy Haven" on a brightly colored sign.

_____ Even the welcome mat at the store's entrance looked like a line of red and black licorice sticks.

3. topic sentence: As soon as Michelle and Liam saw the house, they dreamed of owning it.
(Arrange the details from outside to inside.)

details: _____ A stone walkway began at the front gate.

_____ The walkway, bordered by brightly colored flowers, led to the front door.

_____ The small brick home was set back from the street.

_____ Inside the front door, a small tiled hall contained a framed mirror, an antique wooden table, and a dark green coat rack.

_____ The living room, which followed the hall, had a brick fireplace, soft carpet, and large windows facing the sun.

Exercise 12   **Practice: Creating Details Using a Logical Order**

The following lists include a topic sentence and indicate a required order for the details. Write five sentences of details in the required order.

1. topic sentence: The first class meeting with my math instructor was a little frightening.
(Describe the meeting from beginning to end.)

a. _____

b. _____

c. _____

d. _____

e. _____

2. topic sentence: The noise and lighting at the amusement park contributed to the carnival atmosphere.
(Describe the noise; then describe the lighting.)

a. _____

b. _____

c. _____

_____

d. _____

e. _____

3. topic sentence: As my sister ran her first marathon, her expression changed.
(Describe the changes from beginning to end.)

a. _____

b. _____

c. _____

d. _____

e. _____

DRAFTING AND REVISING   **DESCRIPTION**

After you have an outline, the next step is creating a first rough draft of the paragraph. At this point, you can begin combining some of the ideas in your outline, making two or more short sentences into one longer one. You can also write your first draft in short sentences and combine the sentences later. Your goal is simply to put your ideas in paragraph form so that you can see how they look and you can check them to see what needs to be improved.

The first draft of a paragraph will not be perfect. If it were perfect, it wouldn't be a first draft. Once you have the first draft, check it using the following list.

Checklist for Revising a Descriptive Paragraph

✔ Are there enough details?

✔ Are the details specific?

✔ Do the details use sense words?

✔ Are the details in order?

✔ Is there a dominant impression?

✔ Do the details connect to the dominant impression?

✔ Have I made my point?

A common problem in writing description is creating a fuzzy, vague description. Take a look at the following fuzzy description:

> The football fans were rowdy and excited. They shouted when their team scored. Some people jumped up. The fans showed their support by cheering and stomping. They were enjoying every minute of the game.

The description could be revised so that it is more specific and vivid:

> The football fans were rowdy and excited. When their team scored, they yelled, "Way to go!" or "Stomp 'em! Crush 'em!" until they were hoarse. Three fans, wearing the team colors of blue and white on their shirts, shorts, and socks, jumped up, spilling their drinks on the teenagers seated below them. During timeouts, the fans chanted rhythmically, and throughout the game they stomped their feet in a steady beat against the wooden bleachers. As people chanted, whooped, and woofed, they turned to grin at each other and thrust their clenched fists into the air.

The vivid description meets the requirements of the checklist. It has sufficient specific details. The details use sense words to describe what the fans looked and sounded like. The details also support a dominant impression of rowdy, excited fans. The vivid, specific details make the point.

As you revise the drafts of your essay, you will notice how the right details, sense words, and a focus on the dominant impression (the topic sentence) improve your description.

Exercise 13 **Practice: Revising a Paragraph, Finding Irrelevant Sentences**

Following are two descriptive paragraphs. In each, there are sentences that are irrelevant, meaning they do not have anything to do with the first sentence, the topic sentence. Cross out the irrelevant sentences in the paragraphs below.

1. The heavy rain made driving difficult. The downpour was so strong that drivers could barely see. It was a typical autumn storm. The huge drops, falling fast and hard, covered the cars' windshields. Drivers could barely make out the shapes of the cars and trucks around them. Surrounded by a curtain of water, the drivers inched their way down the road. A few impatient drivers created a hazard by racing past the cautious ones, causing dangerous waves of water. Anyone trying to get out of a parked car would be soaked in seconds. Within minutes, the pounding rain had left four or five inches of water on the road. Now the sound of drivers testing their brakes joined the noise of the downpour.

2. My six-month-old nephew has the face of an angel. His soft, fuzzy hair barely covers his scalp, but it looks like a halo. I like to touch the strands of his hair because it is so different from mine. Benjamin's eyes are large and round; they radiate innocence and joy. They always seem to show his surprise at the wonderful world he has entered. He has a perfect little snub nose. Finally, his small mouth is exactly like the mouths of the angels shown on valentines and Christmas cards. When he smiles, Benjamin looks a little more mischievous than an angel.

Exercise 14   Practice: Revising a Paragraph for More Specific Details

In the following paragraphs, the details that are underlined are not specific. Change the underlined sentences to more specific descriptions. Write the changes in the lines below each paragraph.

1. The eccentric millionaire dressed in an odd combination of clothing. On his head was a weird hat. He wore an expensive silk tie around his neck, but his shirt was made of faded cotton with a flower print. The sleeves were rolled up, and the ragged shirttails hung over a pair of expensive, neatly pressed khakis. He wore white socks with a dark blue band around the top. His shoes, however, did not match the socks.

revisions: _____

_____

2. The plane taking us to Hayden Springs represented air travel at its worst. The roof of the aircraft was low, threatening each entering passenger with decapitation. After one step inside, passengers wanted to leave. The interior of the plane smelled

<u>awful.</u> The storage bins held only tiny bags or boxes, and the doors on the bins would not close. The hard, narrow seats imprisoned the passengers. <u>There was hardly any leg room.</u> In addition, those with window seats could barely see through the filthy window.

revisions: _____

_____

Transitions

As you revise your descriptive paragraph, you may notice places in the paragraph that seem choppy or abrupt. That is, one sentence may end, and another may start, but the two sentences don't seem to be connected. Reading your paragraph aloud, you may sense that it is not very smooth.

You can make the writing smoother and make the content clearer by using **transitions,** which are words or phrases that link one idea to another idea. They tell the reader what he or she has just read and what is coming next. Below are some transitions you may want to use in writing a description.

INFO BOX: **Transitions for a Descriptive Paragraph**

To show ideas brought together:

and also		in addition	next

To show a contrast:

although	however	on the contrary	unlike
but	in contrast	on the other hand	yet

To show a similarity:

all	each	like	similarly
both			

To show a time sequence:

after	first	next	then
always	second (etc.)	often	when
before	meanwhile	soon	while

To show a position in space:

above	between	in front of	over
ahead of	beneath	inside	there
alongside	beyond	near	toward
among	by	nearby	under
around	close	next to	up
away	down	on	underneath
below	far	on top of	where
beside	here	outside	

There are many other transitions you can use, depending on what you need to link your ideas. Take a look at a draft of the description paragraph of a garage. Compare it to the outline on page 70. A sentence of details has been added to the end of the paragraph; it gives specific details about another of Bradley's interests. You will also notice that more sense details have been added. Transitions have been added, too. Pay particular attention to the transitions in this draft.

Revised Draft of a Descriptive Paragraph

transition added	The garage is my husband's territory. <u>Near</u> the entrance
added details	to the garage is a small <u>area of bare floor</u>. This area is covered in
transition added	oil stains and smells like gasoline. <u>Next to</u> this patch of open floor
details, transition added	is the <u>long, cluttered part of the floor</u>. <u>On one side</u>, boxes of Bradley's junk give off a musty odor. Bradley's work bench is pushed into one
transition added	corner. <u>In front of</u> it is Bradley's motorcycle, which is usually in pieces. The cycle fills one third of the space in the garage. Pushed
transition added	<u>close to</u> the bench and the cycle, the garbage can smells of rotting food. Dusty metal shelves cover the back and side walls. The shelves
transition added	<u>next to</u> the motorcycle contain tools for motorcycle repair and <u>a few</u>
details, transition added, details added,	<u>items</u> for home repair and yard work. <u>On the opposite wall</u>, old, crusty paint cans <u>share space with</u> dozens of small plastic containers of nails and screws. <u>Heavy</u> bags of <u>lawn</u> fertilizer <u>cause the shelves of</u>
details, transition added, sentence of detail added	<u>of the back wall</u> to sag. Sitting <u>on</u> the <u>top shelf</u> of this wall, a <u>cork</u> board is covered with photographs. <u>Bradley's camping gear and a small tent are stuffed into the lower shelves of the back wall.</u>

<u>Exercise 15</u> **Practice: Recognizing Transitions**

Underline the transitions in the paragraph below.

My college roommate and I found an apartment in a perfect location. Nearby was a bus stop where we could catch the regularly scheduled buses to campus. A huge supermarket a block away from our apartment met our needs for groceries and snacks; next to it were a pizza shop, a drug store, and an Asian restaurant. About a mile beyond our apartment, a huge public park attracted us. It offered jogging trails, a bike path, a small lake, and acres of huge green trees. Here we could exercise, study, and relax. In addition, we could meet new people who might soon become friends.

Exercise 16 **Practice: Combining Sentences and Using Transitions**

The following description has some choppy sentences that could be combined to create a smoother paragraph. Combine each pair of underlined sentences by revising them in the space above each pair and using appropriate transitions.

At Thanksgiving, my Aunt Christine, the worst cook in the world, insists on cooking dinner for victims who cannot say "no." Her entire family gathers for a meal that always begins with a fruit cocktail. She serves tiny glass bowls with tiny chunks of pears and peaches, red grapes, and one or two red cherries. All the fruit has come straight out of a can. It is swimming in the sugary sweet liquid that also came from the can. Next is the main course. The side dishes are always the same. We guests have a choice of vegetables. We can eat tough green beans. They come from a can. Corn is another choice. It is not on the cob. It is corn kernels from a freezer bag. Aunt Christine also serves sweet potatoes. These potatoes have been baked. They have not been baked long enough. Nothing is worse than trying to put a fork into a potato that is hard in the middle. The turkey arrives last. Unfortunately, Aunt Christine tends to burn the bird. The turkey may not be perfect. It is edible. All that is left is dessert, and even Aunt Christine can't spoil an apple pie from the local bakery. My aunt is pleased that the pie is a hit. Yet she can't understand why, after a large holiday meal, all her guests have such a huge appetite for dessert.

PROOFREADING **DESCRIPTION**

In preparing the final version of a descriptive paragraph, you make a final check for errors in spelling, punctuation, typing, and copying. You might also add a few finishing touches to your paragraph, making changes in words, changing or adding transitions, and sharpening details. In the final version of the description paragraph, you will notice these changes:

- To identify him sooner, the name of the husband, Bradley, has been added to the topic sentence.
- Instead of describing Bradley's boxes as containers of "junk," the contents are now more specific: "old sweatshirts, rags, books, and motorcycle manuals."
- Finally, the paragraph ends with a concluding sentence. This sentence reinforces the topic sentence, which describes the garage

as "Bradley's territory." It also summarizes Bradley's duties (yard work, home repair, taking out the garbage) and describes his pleasures (maintaining his motorcycle and camping).

Final Version of a Descriptive Paragraph

(Changes from the draft are underlined.)

The garage is my husband <u>Bradley's</u> territory. Near the entrance to the garage is a small area of bare floor. This area is covered in oil stains and smells like gasoline. Next to this patch of open floor is the large, cluttered part of the floor. On one side, boxes of Bradley's <u>old sweatshirts, rags, books, and motorcycle manuals</u> give off a musty odor. Bradley's work bench is pushed into one corner. In front of it is Bradley's motorcycle, which is usually in pieces. The cycle fills one third of the space in the garage. Pushed close to the bench and the cycle, the garbage can smells of rotting food. Dusty metal shelves cover the back and side walls. The shelves next to the motorcycle contain tools for motorcycle repair and a few items for home repair and yard work. On the opposite wall, old, crusty paint cans share space with dozens of small plastic containers of nails and screws. Sitting on the top shelf of this wall, a cork board is covered with photographs of classic motorcycles. Bradley's camping gear and a small tent are stuffed into the lower shelves of the back wall. <u>This garage gives a portrait of my husband, a man who maintains the house and the yard and who loves outdoor adventures.</u>

For your information: A sample descriptive essay based on the same topic and following the same writing steps can be found in Chapter 12.

Exercise 17   **Proofreading to Prepare the Final Version**

Following are two descriptive paragraphs with the kinds of errors it is easy to overlook when you write the final version of an assignment. Correct the errors, writing above the lines. There are nine errors in the first paragraph and twelve errors in the second.

1. My boyfriend has an old, cap that belongs in the trash bin. It's a battered gray baseball cap. The name of the team on the cap is ragged because the stitching is falling out. Sweat stains have left their marks around the bottom of the cap. Tim, my boy friend, constantly pushes the cap in to a shape that suits his head. Unfortunately. The constant shaping have left the cap looking shapeless. At the back of the cap, the band that tightens or loosens the cap is useless, for it has lost it's grip. Inside the cap, the lining is discolored by sweat, hair gel, and suntan lotion It's a hideous piece of headware; however, my boyfriend loves it. To him, the cap offers comfort and brings back memories of adventure and fun.

2. At one shop in the mall, I feel like an intruder. The store is a clothing store, and it offers clothes for people in my age group. However, I do not feel comftable in the store. The windows draw me in with glimpses of attractive jeans, shirts, sweater, and jackets. Unfortunately, when I take a few steps inside the store, I sense that I do not belong. The store is unnaturaly quiet; no one seems to be shopping. In addition, The racks of clothing are in perfect order. Not a hanger is out of place. The color-coded shirts and sweaters on the shelves are stacked in immaculate piles. On look at the price of a sweater tells me I cant afford the style, and fashion in this place. I leave before 1 of the salespeople approach me and reconizes me as to broke, two sloppy, or too unfashionable for this establishment.

Lines of Detail: A Walk-Through Assignment

Your assignment is to write a paragraph describing a popular place for socializing. Follow these steps:

Step 1: To begin, freewrite about a place where people socialize. For example, you could write about a place where people go to eat, or dance, or swim, or just "hang out."

Step 2: Read your freewriting. Underline all the words, phrases, and sentences of description.

Step 3: List everything you underlined, grouping the ideas in some order. Maybe the details can be listed from inside to outside, or maybe they can be put into categories, like walls, floor and furniture, or scenery and people.

Step 4: After you've surveyed the list, write a sentence about the dominant impression of the details.

Step 5: Using the dominant impression as your topic sentence, write an outline. Add specific details where you need them. Concentrate on details that appeal to the senses.

Step 6: Write a first draft of your paragraph. Be sure to check the order of your details. Combine short sentences and add transitions.

Step 7: Revise your first draft version, paying particular attention to order, specific details, and transitions.

Step 8: After a final check for punctuation, spelling, and word choice, prepare the final version of the paragraph.

Topics for Writing a Descriptive Paragraph

When you write on any of the following topics, work through the stages of the writing process in preparing your descriptive paragraph. Be sure that your paragraph is based on a dominant impression, and put the dominant impression into your topic sentence.

1. Write a paragraph that describes one of the items below:

a favorite pair of shoes	a hospital waiting room
your favorite meal	an eccentric friend
a tranquil retreat	a messy car
a very young baby	an irritating relative
a vacation spot	a person who changed your life
an ugly hairdo	an activity that energizes you

2. Describe a place that creates one of these impressions:

peace	tension	warmth
cheerfulness	danger	safety

3. Describe a person who conveys one of these impressions:

confidence	friendliness	pride
fear	style	shyness
intelligence	nervousness	strength

4. Visit the Web site of your local newspaper and find a photograph of a local event involving two or more individuals. Describe where the people are, what the event is, what the people are doing, what their facial expressions suggest, and anything you find unique about the setting. You may have to look through the archives of the Web site until you find a photograph that prompts such details. Be sure your details relate to a dominant impression of the scene, and be sure to select a photograph that you find interesting or unique. Attach the photograph to the completed paragraph.

Computer

5. Interview a partner so that you and your partner can gather details and then write a description paragraph with the title, "My Ideal Room."

Collaborate

   First, prepare a list of at least six questions to ask your partner. Write down the answers your partner gives and use those answers to form more questions. For example, if your partner says her ideal room would be a game room, ask her what games she'd like to have in it. If your partner says his ideal room would be a workshop, ask him what kind of workshop.

   When you've finished the interview, switch roles. Let your partner interview you. Feel free to add more questions or to follow up on previous ones.

   Give your partner his or her interview responses. Take your own responses and use them as the basis for gathering as many details as you can on your perfect room. Then go on to the outline, draft, and final version of your paragraph. Be prepared to read your completed paragraph to your partner.

6. Study the photograph below. Then write a paragraph that describes and explains the dominant impression of this scene.

7. Look carefully at the face in the photograph. Write a description that focuses on the aura of the face. Does the face give an impression of wisdom? Pain? Sorrow? Peace? Strength? You decide, and support your decision by describing the details of the photograph.

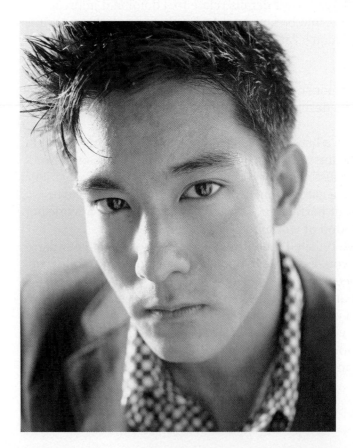

Topics for Critical Thinking and Writing

1. Have you ever heard the old saying, "First impressions are lasting ones"? Do you agree with that statement? If so, describe a person or place that, on further acquaintance, proved to be very similar to your first impressions. If you do not accept the truth of the saying, describe a person or place that proved to be very different from your first assessment.

2. Imagine that one of your relatives from another state or country planned to visit you for the first time and wanted to see a little bit of your town. Make a list of some of your town's more memorable natural attractions, buildings, or landmarks. If your visitor had time to see only one place, which one would you choose? Describe your choice by using as many sense details as possible.

Note: Additional writing options suitable for illustration-related assignments can be found after the professional reading, "A Life Full of Riches," in the "Readings for Writers" appendix of this book.

Name _____   Section _____

Peer Review Form for a Descriptive Paragraph

After you've written a draft of your descriptive paragraph, let a writing partner read it. When your partner has completed the form below, discuss the comments. Then repeat the same process for your partner's paragraph.

The dominant impression of the paragraph is this sentence _____

_____

_____

_____

_____

The details of the description are in a specific order. That order is (for example, top to bottom, time order, etc.) _____

The part of the description I liked best begins with the words _____

_____

The part that could use more or better details begins with the words _____

_____

I have questions about or would like to know more about _____

_____

I noticed these transitions _____

_____

_____

_____

_____

A place where transitions could be added or improved is right before the words _____

_____

Other comments _____

_____

_____

_____

Reviewer's name _____

Narration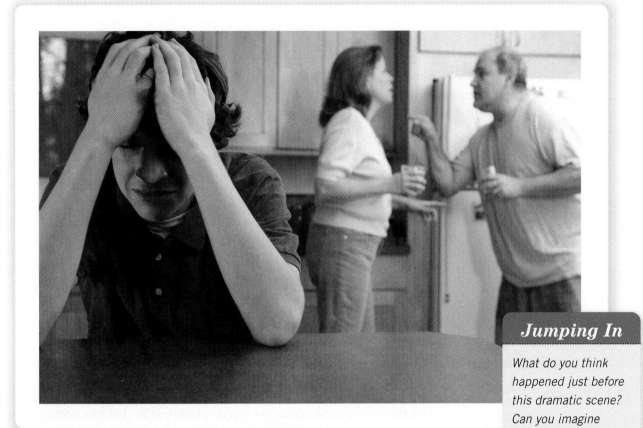

*What do you think happened just before this dramatic scene? Can you imagine what led to the tense atmosphere? There must be a story behind this picture, and if you write the story, you will be writing a **narrative** paragraph.*

Chapter Objectives

Students will be able to write a narrative paragraph that (1) has a narrow focus, (2) presents details in a clear order, and (3) uses effective transitional words and phrases.

WHAT IS NARRATION?

Narration means telling a story. Everybody tells stories; some people are better storytellers than others. When you write a **narrative** paragraph, you can tell a story about something that happened to you or to someone else, or about something that you saw or read.

A narrative, like a description, relies on specific details, but it is also different from a description because it covers events in a time sequence. While a description can be about a person, a place, or an object, a narrative is always about happenings: events, actions, incidents.

Interesting narratives do more than just tell what happened. They help the reader become involved in the story by providing vivid details. These details come from your memory, your observation, or your reading. Using good details, you don't just tell the story; you *show* it.

Give the Narrative a Point

We all know people who tell long stories that seem to lead nowhere. These people talk on and on; they recite an endless list of activities and soon become boring. Their narratives have no point.

The difficult part of writing a narrative is making sure that it has a point. That point will be included in the topic sentence. The point of a narrative is the meaning of the incident or incidents you are writing about. To get to the point of your narrative, ask yourself questions like these:

What did I learn?
What is the meaning of this story?
What is my attitude toward what happened?
Did it change me?
What emotion did it make me feel?
Was the experience a good example of something (such as unfairness, kindness, generosity, or some other quality)?

The answers to such questions can lead you to a point. An effective topic sentence for a narrative is

not this: I'm going to tell you about the time I flunked my driving test. (This is an announcement; it does not make a point.)
but this: When I failed my driving test, I learned not to be overconfident.

not this: Yesterday my car stalled in rush-hour traffic. (This identifies the incident but does not make a point. It is also too narrow to be a good topic sentence.)
but this: When my car stalled in rush-hour traffic, I was annoyed and embarrassed.

The topic sentence, stating the point of your narrative paragraph, can be placed in the beginning, middle, or end of the paragraph. You may want to start your story with the point so that the reader knows exactly where your story is headed, or you may want to conclude your story by leaving the point until last. Sometimes the point can even fit smoothly into the middle of your paragraph.

Consider the narrative paragraphs below. The topic sentences are in various places.

Topic Sentence at the Beginning

<u>When I was five, I learned how serious it is to tell a lie.</u> One afternoon, my seven-year-old friend Tina asked me if I wanted to walk down the block to play ball in an empty lot. When I asked my mother, she said I couldn't go because it was too near dinner time. I don't know why I lied, but when Tina asked me if my mother had said yes, I nodded my head in a lie. I wanted to go play, and I did. Yet as I played in the dusty lot, a dull buzz of guilt or fear distracted me. As soon as I got home, my mother confronted me. She asked me whether I had gone to the sandlot and whether I had lied to Tina about getting permission. This time, I told the truth. Something about my mother's tone of voice made me feel very dirty and ashamed. I had let her down.

Topic Sentence in the Middle

When I was little, I was afraid of diving into water. I thought I would go down and never come back up. Then one day, my father took me to a pool where we swam and fooled around, but he never forced me to try a dive. After about an hour of playing, I walked round and round the edge of the pool, trying to get the courage to dive in. Finally, I did it. <u>When I made that first dive, I felt blissful because I had done something I had been afraid to do.</u> As I came to the surface, I wiped the water from my eyes and looked around. The sun seemed more dazzling, and the water sparkled. Best of all, I saw my father looking at me with a smile. "You did it," he said. "Good for you! I'm proud of you."

Topic Sentence at the End

It seemed like I'd been in love with Reeza for years. Unfortunately, Reeza was always in love with someone else. Finally, she broke up with her boyfriend Nelson. I saw my chance. I asked Reeza out. After dinner, we talked and talked. Reeza told me all about her hopes and dreams. She told me about her family and her job, and I felt very close to her. We talked late into the night. When she left, Reeza kissed me. "Thanks for listening," she said. "You're like a brother to me." <u>Reeza meant to be kind, but she shattered my hopes and dreams.</u>

Exercise 1   Practice: Finding the Topic Sentence in a Narrative Paragraph

Underline the topic sentence in each narrative paragraph below.

Paragraph 1

I love to take my dog with me wherever I go, so I was happy to take her to my friends' house. My friends have a dog of their own, and they don't mind my pet visiting. When I arrived at their house, Ben and Denise welcomed me, and their dog Callie and my dog River sniffed each other happily. Soon the dogs were chasing each other through the house, and the adults were socializing over a pizza. After about forty minutes, I saw Callie under the kitchen table. "Where's River?" I asked. "He must be up to some mischief," I joked. I checked the living room, the hall, the two bedrooms, and the garage. Meanwhile, Ben and Denise looked under tables and beds, behind the couch, and in the closets. Next I thought that River must have found some way to the outside. I walked the neighborhood, crying, "River! River!" I imagined the night coming and my dog lost in a strange neighborhood. Finally, I returned indoors. Then something made me open the bathroom door. Inside was River, waiting quietly to be freed from the small place. At that moment, when I saw my beautiful dog, I knew how much he meant to me.

Paragraph 2

After I finished high school, I wanted to have some fun. I was sick of studying and worrying about test scores. I spent the summer going to the beach, surfing, and socializing with my friends. I kept my part-time job at a discount store and lived at my parents' house so that I could afford to live a carefree life. Summer was great, and the days went by quickly. Soon it was fall, and my friends became too busy for fun. They found full-time work, started college, or combined work and school. On a rainy day in October, I sat alone on a sand dune. I realized that it was time for me to grow up.

My friends had moved on, and here I was, feeling anxious about my future. I did not want to become known as the oldest surfer in town. Soon after, I started looking for a full-time job. Then I spoke with a counselor at a local community college. She told me about early registration for the next term. We also discussed careers.

Paragraph 3

Hurting my knees gave me a small hint of what it means to be disabled or elderly. In a silly accident, I slipped on the wet pavement near my house. I went flying onto my hands and knees. My knees were bloody, but I picked myself up and kept walking. At first, all that concerned me was the blood on my knees. People might see me and wonder if I had been mugged, I thought. Later, I felt an ache in my shoulders. Then my knees began to hurt whenever I sat or bent down. When I got out of bed the next morning, the pain was worse. I avoided bending over or picking up heavy bags. Walking was unpleasant. The discomfort was not great, but it was there. I had never had to think about whether a simple physical movement like kneeling or bending over was worth the effort or pain it might bring. I felt overcautious, constricted, and conscious of my weakness.

Exercise 2   **Practice: Writing the Missing Topic Sentences in Narrative Paragraphs**

Following are three paragraphs. If the paragraph already has a topic sentence, write it in the lines provided. If it does not have a topic sentence, create one. (Two of the paragraphs have no topic sentence.)

Paragraph 1

In high school, I avoided eye contact and kept my head down. There were many cliques, but I felt sure that no group would want me. I was not fit, not smart, not very attractive, not outgoing, and not wealthy. I expected college to be another place where I would be a loner. I thought that it might be even more lonely because it was so much larger. However, on my first day of college, during an orientation for new students, I saw hundreds of people. Almost all of them seemed lost. Only a few were with a friend. The rest had a slightly worried expression. They looked the way I must have looked in high school. Maybe the college students would be more open to my friendship.

If the paragraph already has a topic sentence, write it here. If it does not

have a topic sentence, create one. _____

_____

_____

Paragraph 2

I have never felt as much shame as the shame I felt after my one involvement in shoplifting. At fourteen, I had my first boyfriend, and I was infatuated. Part of my attraction to Jimmie was his daring and rebellious nature. Unfortunately, Jimmie had friends who liked to test the boundaries of the law. One day, Jimmie and two friends decided to steal some steaks from a supermarket. They planned to slip the packages of steak into the front of their jeans. I was supposed to be the lookout. I entered the store with my heart thumping against my chest. I was sure everyone was looking at me and the three thugs with me. I thought of the security mirrors, the security cameras, and the vigilant managers at the store. As Jimmie and his friends approached the refrigerator cases of meat, I stayed behind. I didn't see them slip the steaks into their pants, but I saw them turn and walk confidently through the store. I rushed to join them. We made our escape without any trouble. All I felt was a sickening mix of anxiety and self-hatred.

If the paragraph already has a topic sentence, write it here. If it does not

have a topic sentence, create one. _____

_____

_____

Paragraph 3

My seventh birthday was here, and I was sure that I wouldn't celebrate it much. My father was living in a distant state, and he had stopped sending child support checks for me and my sisters several months earlier. At school, I thought of better birthdays when my folks had been together and money had not been such a problem. As I walked slowly home from school, I told myself, "A cake will be fine." However, I kept hoping that at least one small gift would be waiting for me. My little sisters, smiling, opened the door. My mother, trying to smile, stood by the kitchen table. On it were six chocolate cupcakes, each with a blue candle in the chocolate icing. "So this is it," I thought. I loved my mother and sisters, and they loved me. However, this wasn't much of a birthday celebration for a seven-year-old. Suddenly my four-year-old sister Rosalee began to jump up. "Look under the table!" she cried. There was a big box beneath the table. I picked it up, and it felt heavy, with the weight in it shifting from side to side. Inside the box was the most beautiful orange and white kitten I had ever seen.

If the paragraph already has a topic sentence, write it here. if it does not

have a topic sentence, create one. _____

_____

_____

Hints for Writing a Narrative Paragraph

Everyone tells stories, but some people tell stories better than others. When you write a story, be sure to

- Be clear.
- Be interesting.
- Stay in order.
- Pick a topic that is not too big.

1. Be clear. Put in all the information the reader needs in order to follow your story. Sometimes you need to explain the time or place or the relationships of the people in your story in order to make the story clear.

Sometimes you need to explain how much time has elapsed between one action and another. This paragraph is not clear:

> I've never felt so stupid as I did on my first day of work. I was stocking the shelves when Mr. Cimino came up to me and said, "You're doing it wrong." Then he showed me how to do it. An hour later, he told me to call the produce supplier and check on the order for grapefruit. Well, I didn't know how to tell Mr. Cimino that I didn't know what phone to use or how to get an outside line. I also didn't know how to get the phone number of the produce supplier, or what the order for the grapefruit was supposed to be and when it was supposed to arrive. I felt really stupid asking these questions.

What is wrong with the paragraph? It lacks all kinds of information. Who is Mr. Cimino? Is he the boss? Is he a produce supervisor? And, more importantly, what kind of place is the writer's workplace? The reader knows the place has something to do with food, but is it a supermarket, a fruit market, or a warehouse?

2. Be interesting. A boring narrative can make the greatest adventure sound dull. Here is a dull narrative:

> I had a wonderful time on prom night. First, we went out to dinner. The meal was excellent. Then we went to the dance and saw all our friends. Everyone was dressed up great. We stayed until late. Then we went out to breakfast. After breakfast we watched the sun come up.

Good specific details are the difference between an interesting story and a dull one.

3. Stay in order. Put the details in a clear order so that the reader can follow your story. Usually, time order is the order you follow in narration. This narrative has a confusing order:

> My impatience cost me twenty dollars last week. There was an expensive pair of shoes I really wanted. I had wanted them for weeks. So, when payday came around, I went to the mall and checked the price on the shoes. I had been checking the price for weeks before. The shoes were expensive, but I really wanted them. On payday, a friend who works at the shoe store told me the shoes were about to go on sale. But I was impatient. I bought them at full price, and three days later, the shoes were marked down twenty dollars.

There's something wrong with the order of events here. Tell the story in the order it happened: first, I saw the expensive shoes and wanted them; second, I checked the price for several weeks; third, I got paid; fourth, on the same day, I checked the price again; fifth, my friend at the store told me the shoes were about to go on sale; sixth, I paid full price right away; seventh, three days later the shoes went on sale. A clear time sequence helps the reader follow your narrative.

4. Pick a topic that is not too big. If you try to write about too many events in a short space, you run the risk of being superficial. You cannot describe anything well if you cover too much. This paragraph covers too much:

> Starting my sophomore year at a new high school was a difficult experience. Because my family had just moved to town, I didn't know anybody at school. On the first day of school, I sat by myself at lunch. Finally, two students at another table started a conversation with me. I thought they were just feeling sorry for me. At the end of the first week, it seemed like the whole school was talking about exciting plans for the weekend. I spent Friday and Saturday night at home, doing all kinds of things to keep my mind off my loneliness. On Monday, people casually asked, "Have a good weekend?" I lied and said, "Of course."

This paragraph would be better if it discussed one shorter time period in greater depth and detail. It could cover the first day at school, or the first lunch at school, or the first Saturday night at home alone, when the writer was doing "all kinds of things" to keep from feeling lonely.

Using a Speaker's Exact Words in Narrative

Some of the examples of narrative that you have already seen have included the exact words someone said. You may want to include part of a conversation in your narrative. To do so, you need to know how to punctuate speech.

A person's exact words get quotation marks around them. If you change the words, you do not use quotation marks.

exact words: "You're being silly," he told me.
not exact words: He told me that I was being silly.

exact words: My sister said, "I'd love to go to the party."
not exact words: My sister said she would love to go to the party.

There are a few other points to remember about punctuating a person's exact words. Once you've started quoting a person's exact words, periods and commas generally go inside the quotation marks. Here are two examples:

Richard said, "Nothing can be done."
"Be careful," my mother warned us.

When you introduce a person's exact words with phrases like *She said* or *The teacher told us*, put a comma before the quotation marks. Here are two examples:

She said, "You'd better watch out."
The teacher told us, "This will be a challenging class."

> If you are using a person's exact words and have other questions about punctuation, read about the use of quotation marks in Chapter 27 of the grammar section of this book.

WRITING THE NARRATIVE PARAGRAPH IN STEPS
PREWRITING   NARRATION

Finding something to write about can be the hardest part of writing a narrative paragraph because it is usually difficult to think of anything interesting or significant that you have experienced. By answering the following questions you can gather topics for your paragraph.

Collaborate

Exercise 3   **Collaborate: Questionnaire for Gathering Narrative Topics**

Answer the questions below and list details in the spaces provided. Then read your answers to a group. The members of the group should then ask you follow-up questions. Write your answers on the lines provided; the answers will add details to your list.

Finally, ask each member of your group to circle one topic or detail on your questionnaire that could be developed into a narrative paragraph. Discuss the suggestions. Repeat this process for each member of the group.

Narrative Questionnaire

1. Have you ever gotten lost (in a new town, on strange streets, in a mall, at a college, or elsewhere)? When? Write four details you remember about the occasion:

   a. _____

   b. _____

   c. _____

   d. _____

   Additional details, to be added after working with the group:

   _____

   _____

2. Have you ever had a pleasant surprise? Write four details about what happened before, during, and after:

   a. _____

   b. _____

   c. _____

   d. _____

   Additional details, to be added after working with the group:

   _____

   _____

3. Have you ever won anything (a game, a contest, a raffle, some other prize or competition?) Write four details about the experience:

   a. _____

   b. _____

   c. _____

   d. _____

Additional details, to be added after working with the group:

_____

_____

Freewriting for a Narrative Topic

One good way to discover something to write about is to freewrite. For example, if your instructor asks you to write a narrative paragraph about something that changed you, you might begin by freewriting.

Freewriting for a Narrative Paragraph

Topic: Something That Changed Me

Something that changed me. I don't know. What changed me? Lots of things happened to me, but I can't find one that changed me. Graduating from high school? Everybody will write about that, how boring, and anyway, what was the big deal? I haven't gotten married. No big change there. Divorce. My parents' divorce really changed the whole family. A big shock to me. I couldn't believe it was happening. I was really scared. Who would I live with? They were really calm when they told me. I've never been so scared. I was too young to understand. Kept thinking they'd just get back together. They didn't. Then I got a stepmother. The year of the divorce was a hard time for me. Kids suffer in divorce.

Narrowing and Selecting a Suitable Narrative Topic

After you freewrite, you can assess your writing, looking for words, phrases, or sentences that you could expand into a paragraph. The sample writing has several ideas for a narrative:

> high school graduation
> learning about my parents' divorce
> adjusting to a stepmother
> the year of my parents' divorce

Looking for a topic that is not too big, you could use:

> high school graduation
> learning about my parents' divorce

Since the freewriting has already called graduation a boring topic, the divorce seems to be a more attractive subject. In the freewriting, you already have some details related to the divorce; add to these details by brainstorming. Follow-up questions and answers might include the following:

How old were you when your parents got divorced?

I was seven years old when my mom and dad divorced.

Are you an only child?

My sister was ten.

Where did your parents tell you? Did they both tell you at the same time?

They told us at breakfast, in the kitchen. Both my folks were there. I was eating toast. I remember I couldn't eat it when they both started talking. I remember a piece of toast with one bite out of it.

What reasons did they give?

They said they loved us, but they couldn't get along. They said they would always love us kids.

If you didn't understand, what did you <u>think</u> was happening?

At first I just thought they were having another fight.

Did you cry? Did they cry?

I didn't cry. My sister cried. Then I knew it was serious. I kept thinking I would have to choose which parent to live with. Then I knew I'd really hurt the one I didn't choose. I felt so much guilt about hurting one of them.

What were you feeling?

I felt ripped apart.

Questions can help you form the point of your narrative. After brainstorming, you can go back and survey all the details. Do they lead you to a point? Try asking yourself the questions listed earlier in this chapter: What did I learn? What is the meaning of this story? What is my attitude toward what happened? Did it change me? What emotion did it make me feel? Was the experience a good example of something (like unfairness, or kindness, or generosity)?

For the topic of the divorce, the details mention a number of emotions: confusion, pain, shock, disbelief, fear, guilt. The *point* of the paragraph cannot list all these emotions, but it could be started this way:

When my parents announced they were divorcing, I felt confused by all my emotions.

Now that you have a point and several details, you can move on to the planning stage of writing a narrative paragraph.

Exercise 4 **Practice: Distinguishing Good Topic Sentences from Bad Ones in Narration**

Below are sentences. Some would make good topic sentences for a narrative paragraph. Others would not: they are too big to develop in a single paragraph, or they are so narrow they can't be developed, or they make no point about an incident or incidents. Put an *X* by the sentences that would not make good topic sentences.

1. _____ At a ceremony at the courthouse, I became a U.S. citizen

2. _____ Nothing has pleased me more than my mother's words to me at my high school graduation.

3. _____ My sister's drug abuse is causing problems for our entire family.

4. _____ When I passed my driving test, I felt an enormous sense of freedom.

5. _____ Last Tuesday night, I spend five hours waiting in a local hospital's emergency room.

6. _____ One day of volunteering at a homeless center taught me about respecting other people's dignity.

7. _____ I come from a small Midwestern town where everybody knows everyone else.

8. _____ Years of working at a bakery made me hate the smell of baking bread.

9. _____ I blamed myself when I saw what vandals had done to my car.

10. _____ After my last experience at Crescent Beach, I will never again swim in rough seas.

Exercise 5   **Practice: Developing a Topic Sentence from a List of Details**

Following are two lists of details. Each has an incomplete topic sentence. Read the details carefully; then complete each topic sentence.

1. **topic sentence:** One hour alone with _____ gave me a

better understanding of _____

    details: My neighbor Sonya had an emergency yesterday.

               Her mother had a flat tire on the turnpike.

               Sonya's twin boys, five years old, could not be left home alone.

               She asked if I, single and childless, could watch them for an hour.

               I agreed, and Sonya brought Andrew and Anthony to my apartment.

               They looked like angels, and I felt confident that we would have a happy time together.

               I turned on the Cartoon Network and, transfixed, they sat in front of the television.

               Unfortunately, their interest in cartoons lasted about ten minutes.

               Then Anthony hit Andrew.

               Andrew hit back, and the boys began running around my small apartment.

               Eager to stop them, I offered milk and cookies.

               Soon cookie crumbs and spilled milk were all over the floor and the furniture.

               Then the boys began to wrestle.

               For the next forty minutes, I tried threats, bribes, and begging to get the boys to behave.

               When Sonya returned, I was overjoyed.

2. **topic sentence:** Losing my driver's license caused me to feel

_____

_____

    details: I had just written a check at a local bookstore.

               To provide some identification, I reached for my driver's license, which I carry in my wallet.

It wasn't in its usual slot.

While the cashier waited, I searched every part of my wallet.

I couldn't find my license.

I felt shamed in front of the cashier and the customers waiting behind me.

I paid for my purchases with a credit card and left the store.

In the store's parking lot, I checked my car.

No license appeared in the glove compartment, on the seats, under the seats, or on the floor.

At home, I desperately retraced my steps, trying to remember when I had last seen my license.

I was angry at myself for being careless.

I also worried about the consequences of the loss.

Without a license, I was afraid to drive anywhere.

I knew I needed to get a replacement license as soon as possible.

To me, the license bureau meant waiting in endless lines and dealing with overworked clerks.

I knew I could not relax until I had a replacement license in my hand.

PLANNING NARRATION

The topic of how an experience changed you has led you to a point and a list of details. You can now write a rough outline, with the point as the topic sentence. Once you have the rough outline, check it for these qualities:

Relevance: Do all the details connect to the topic sentence?
Order: Are the details in a clear order?
Development: Does the outline need more details? Are the details specific enough?

Your revised outline might look like the following:

Outline for a Narrative Paragraph

topic sentence: When my parents announced that they were divorcing, I felt confused by all my emotions.

details: I was seven when my mom and dad divorced.
My sister was ten.
background of the narrative   Both my folks were there.
They told us at breakfast, in the kitchen.
I was eating toast.
I remember I couldn't eat anything when they started talking.
I remember a piece of toast with one bite out of it.

story of the divorce announcement	My parents were very calm when they told us. They said they loved us but couldn't get along. They said they would always love us kids. It was a big shock to me.
my reactions at each stage	I couldn't believe it was happening. At first I just thought they were having another fight. I was too young to understand. I didn't cry. My sister cried. Then I knew it was serious. I kept thinking I would have to choose which parent to live with. I knew I'd really hurt the one I didn't choose. I felt so much guilt about hurting one of them. I felt ripped apart.

Once you have a revised outline, you're ready to write a draft of the narrative paragraph.

Exercise 6   Practice: Finding Details That Are Out of Order in a Narrative Outline

The outlines below have details that are out of order. Put the details in correct time order by numbering them 1, 2, and so forth.

1. **topic sentence:** An argument with my sister led to hurt feelings for both of us.

    details: _____ A week ago, I was foolish enough to tell my older sister Kelly about the speeding ticket I had just received.

    _____ Yesterday, she told our mother about the ticket.

    _____ Today, I cornered Kelly in her room and accused her of being a blabbermouth and a spy.

    _____ An hour after Kelly had spoken to our mother, I faced a grilling and a warning from both my parents.

    _____ Kelly's first reaction to my accusations was to shout at me.

    _____ Then she told me it was her duty to warn my parents about my bad behavior.

    _____ Hearing the words "bad behavior," I told her *she* had behaved badly and had betrayed my trust.

    _____ Before she threw me out of her room, she said, "Trust? All you wanted was my money to pay for your ticket!"

    _____ When I left her room, she was in tears, and I felt there was some truth in her words.

2. topic sentence: A small surprise changed my attitude on Sunday.

details: _____ Sunday started as a rainy day.

_____ The rain matched my mood.

_____ Even if it had been sunny, I couldn't have gone outdoors because I had responsibilities.

_____ After two hours with my chemistry text-book, my head was exploding.

_____ I began by dealing with the worst part of the day: studying for a chemistry test.

_____ Working through the chapters I had never read, I felt doomed to fail.

_____ I decided to give my head a break, but it was not an enjoyable break.

_____ During this break, I began to sort the dirty laundry piled in my closet.

_____ Frustrated and irritated, I tossed the dirty clothes back into the closet.

_____ As I sorted, I realized that I was too broke to do my laundry.

_____ As a pair of jeans hit the closet floor, I heard a clink.

_____ I looked in the direction of the clink and saw a quarter.

_____ After retrieving the coin, I checked the pockets of the jeans.

_____ I didn't find any more coins, but I did find a ten-dollar bill.

_____ Life no longer seemed so bleak, for I could skip the laundry and get a pizza.

Exercise 7   **Practice: Recognizing Irrelevant Details in a Narrative Outline**

Below are two outlines. One of them has details that are not relevant to the topic sentence. Cross out the details that do not fit.

1. topic sentence: Meeting my uncle led me to an important decision.

details: My Uncle Benjamin lives far away from us, so I first met him when I was twelve years old.

He is a cook in a famous restaurant in California, and he visited us to cook for my sister's engagement party.

My sister is the kind of person who enjoys elaborate parties.

Bored by the fancy celebration, I watched my uncle in the kitchen.

He prepared the kitchen efficiently, assembling bowls, utensils, pots, pans, and spices.

Working quickly, he chopped vegetables, sautéed garlic, onions, and capers, and sliced meat into thin strips.

It's not a big kitchen, but Uncle Benjamin was able to work efficiently in a small space.

When he began to cook, he expertly managed all four burners on the stove at once.

My uncle concentrated intently on managing complicated tasks.

The guests in the living room were drinking toasts to my sister and her fiancé.

My uncle sautéed, he blended, he mixed sauces, and he added spices with precision.

His work was like an art.

Uncle Benjamin's talent and skill made me want to learn what he knew: the culinary art.

2. topic sentence: Lola got caught in a moment of hypocrisy yesterday.

details: My friend Lola and I were taking a break between classes, sitting on a bench near the building where our next class would start.

It was a sunny day, so we didn't have to wear coats.

As we sat, enjoying the good weather, we saw Ryan, one of our classmates, approach.

Ryan, who is shy but friendly, smiled when he recognized us.

Ryan gets better grades than Lola and I do.

"How are you doing?" Lola asked.

"Pretty good," Ryan said.

"I like your tee-shirt," Lola added. "Is it new?"

Ryan, pleased, smiled.

"No," Ryan said, "but thanks for the compliment."

A few students were walking slowly toward the classrooms.

Lola turned to me and muttered, "Did you see his disgusting shirt? What a loser."

I waited for a few seconds, then I whispered, "Lola, he heard you. You should have seen his face."

DRAFTING AND REVISING   **NARRATION**

After you have a revised outline for your narration paragraph, you can begin working on a rough draft of the paragraph. As you write your first draft, you can combine some of the short sentences of the outline. Once you have a draft, you can check it for places you would like to improve. The list below may help you to check your draft.

Checklist for Revising the Draft of a Narrative Paragraph

✔   Is my narrative vivid?

✔   Are the details clear and specific?

✔   Does the topic sentence fit all the details?

✔   Are the details written in a clear order?

✔   Do the transitions make the narrative easy to follow?

✔   Have I made my point?

Revising for Sharper Details

A good idea for a narrative can be made better if you revise for sharper details. In the paragraph below, the underlined words and phrases could be revised to create better details. In the following example, see how the second draft has more vivid details than the first draft.

First Draft: Details Are Dull

A woman at the movies showed me just how rude and selfish people can be. It all started when I was in line with <u>a lot</u> of other people. We had been waiting <u>a long time</u> to buy our tickets. We were outside, and it <u>wasn't pleasant.</u> We were impatient because time was running out and the movie was about to start. Some people were <u>making remarks,</u> and <u>others were pushing.</u> Then <u>a woman cut to</u> the front of the line. The cashier at the ticket window <u>told</u> the woman there was a line and she would have to go to the end of it. The woman <u>said she didn't want to wait because her son didn't want to miss the beginning of the movie.</u>

Second Draft: Better Details

A woman at the movies showed me just how rude and selfish people can be. It all started when I was in line with <u>forty or fifty other people.</u> We had been waiting to buy our tickets for <u>twenty minutes.</u> We were outside, <u>where the temperature was about 90 degrees and it looked like rain.</u> We were all getting impatient because time was running out and the movie was about to start. <u>I heard two people mutter about how ridiculous the wait was, and someone else kept saying, "Let's go!" The man directly behind me kept pushing me, and each new person at the end of the line pushed the whole line forward against the ticket window.</u> Then a woman <u>with a loud voice and a large purse thrust her purse and her body in front of the ticket window.</u> The cashier <u>politely</u> told the woman there was a line and she had to go to the end of it. But the woman answered <u>indignantly. "Oh no," she said. "I'm with my son Mickey. And Mickey really wants to see this martial arts movie. And he hates to miss the first part of any movie. So I can't wait. I've got to have those tickets now."</u>

Checking the Topic Sentence

Sometimes you think you have a good idea, a good topic sentence, and specific details, but when you write the draft of the paragraph, you realize the topic sentence does not quite fit all the details. When that happens, you can either revise the details or *rewrite the topic sentence.*

In the paragraph below, the topic sentence (underlined) does not quite fit all the details, so the topic sentence should be rewritten.

> <u>I didn't know what to do when a crime occurred in front of my house.</u> At 9:00 P.M., I was sitting in my living room, watching television, when I heard what sounded like a crash outside. At first I thought it was a garbage can that had fallen over. Then I heard another crash and a shout. I ran to the window and I looked out into the dark. I couldn't see anything because the street light in front of my house was broken. I heard at least two voices, and they sounded angry and threatening. I heard another voice, and it sounded like someone moaning. I was afraid. I ran to the telephone. I was going to call 911, but then I froze in fear. What if the police came, and people got arrested? Would the suspects find out I was the one who had called the police? Would they come after *me?* Would I be a witness at a trial? I didn't want to get involved. So I just stood behind the curtain, peeking out and listening. Pretty soon the shouting stopped, but I still heard sounds like hitting. I couldn't stand it anymore. I called the police. When they came, they found a young teenager, badly beaten, in the street. They said my call may have saved his life.

The paragraph above has good details, but the story has more of a point than "I didn't know what to do." The person telling the story did, finally, do something. Following is a better topic sentence that covers the whole story.

topic sentence rewritten: I finally found the courage to take the proper action when a crime occurred in front of my house.

Exercise 8 **Practice: Combining Sentences in a Draft of a Narrative**

The following paragraph contains some short, choppy sentences, which are underlined. Wherever you see two or more underlined sentences clustered next to each other, combine them into one clear, smooth sentence. Write your revised version of the paragraph in the spaces above the lines.

Mother Nature pulled me out of a dark mood this morning. Caught in a rainstorm, I was driving to work in rush hour traffic and checking my watch every two minutes. I began making a mental list of all my worries. In addition to being afraid of getting to work late, I was worried about being broke. My last credit card bill had been astronomical. <u>I couldn't afford to get caught in a cycle. The cycle would be dangerous. The cycle would involve high interest rates and increasing debt.</u> School was another worry. <u>I had a quiz coming up in my accounting class. I was nervous about it. I was afraid that I wouldn't pass the quiz.</u> All these fears and the frustration of a slow ride in heavy traffic made me feel that I was drowning in misery. Then I looked up. <u>Beyond the rain was a beautiful sight. I saw a bright, clear</u>

rainbow. It curved across the horizon like an arch of glowing colors. <u>I felt that</u>

<u>the rainbow was a sign. The sign told me to be cheerful.</u> Almost against my will, I

began to feel better.

Exercise 9   **Practice: Adding Better Details to a Draft of a Narrative**

The following paragraph has some details that could be more vivid. Rewrite
the paragraph in the lines below, replacing the underlined details with more
vivid words, phrases, or sentences.

Even the most stubborn people have to admit they are sometimes
wrong. My father is extremely <u>bad</u> when he drives to a new destination. He
insists that he knows how to get to the place. He refuses to look at a map
or at a tracking system before we all pile into the car. Then we watch him
drive happily in the wrong direction, but we hesitate to correct him. If we try
to steer my father to the right route, he reacts <u>badly</u>. He says that he knows
exactly where he is going. <u>Things</u> deteriorate when we passengers begin to
notice certain landmarks appearing three or four times as my father blindly
circles and recircles the wrong streets. Meanwhile, my father is getting <u>mad,</u>
and we are getting <u>madder</u>. Eventually, my father does acknowledge that he
is lost. We feel <u>good</u> now that my father is ready to take directions.

Rewrite: _____

_____

_____

_____

_____

_____

_____

_____

_____

_____

_____

_____

_____

Exercise 10   Practice: Writing a Better Topic Sentence for a Narrative

The paragraphs below could use better topic sentences. (In each paragraph, the current topic sentence is underlined.) Read each paragraph carefully, then write a new topic sentence for it in the lines below.

1. Last week my brother told me a terrible story. It started when he left his workplace. His boss had just promised to give him some extra hours of work, and my brother was happy to hear of the opportunity. As my brother drove out of the parking lot, he wanted to share the good news with Nicole, his girlfriend. Merging slowly into traffic, my brother began texting Nicole. Soon after, he was absorbed in writing her his news. Suddenly, he heard horns honking and metal crunching. My brother, intent on text-messaging, had run a red light. A woman had been injured when my brother, preoccupied, had driven into the driver's side of her car. If only he had waited to contact his girlfriend and had concentrated on driving, an innocent woman would not be suffering from bruises and broken bones. In addition, my brother would still be celebrating his good news.

New topic sentence: _____

_____

2. Janelle and I saw a beautiful red fox recently. We live in a typical suburban neighborhood, and the most exotic animals we see are the squirrels and mice that appear near the dumpsters at our apartment. However, we do have a few wooded areas between the houses and apartment buildings that make up our town. One day, Janelle and I were walking through our neighborhood when she grabbed my arm. "Look," she said, nodding her head toward an undeveloped area of trees and bushes. I saw a blur of fur, about the size of a large cat. It was standing at the edge of the property as if it were waiting to cross the street. "It's a fox," Janelle whispered. When we stood still, we were able to focus on its long legs, its red and white body, and its black nose. Then the animal seemed to sense our presence and loped gracefully back into the bush. Janelle and I looked at each other, stunned by the sight of a wild animal hiding and surviving in the middle of our civilized, regulated environment.

New topic sentence: _____

_____

Using Transitions Effectively in Narration

When you tell a story, you have to be sure that your reader can follow you as you move through the steps of your story. One way to make your story easier to follow is to use transitions. Most of the transitions in narration have to do with time. Below is a list of transitions writers often use in writing narration.

A Revised Draft

Below is a revised draft of the paragraph on divorce. As you read it, you will notice some changes that are typical of narrative writing. Because telling a

---

INFO BOX: Transitions for a Narrative Paragraph

after	before	in the meantime	soon after
again	during	later	still
always	finally	later on	suddenly
at first	first	meanwhile	then
at last	second (etc.)	next	until
at once	frequently	now	when
at the same time	immediately	soon	while

---

story (narrative) involves events in time order, a first draft tends to focus on simply putting those events in the correct sequence. However, once the time order is correct, a writer has to focus on two important issues: (1) making sure that the narrative is more than a list of the details, in time sequence, and (2) avoiding short, choppy writing. When you study this revised draft, you will notice the many **transitions** that help create a smooth movement from one stage of the divorce announcement to another. You will also notice several places where **sentences** from the outline have been **combined** for smoother, more logical connections. Finally, using the exact words of **dialogue** in part of the story adds realistic detail.

Revised Draft of a Narrative Paragraph

(Changes from the outline are underlined.)

	When my parents announced that they were
transition	divorcing, I felt confused by all my emotions. <u>At the</u>
sentences combined	<u>time</u> of their announcement, <u>I was seven and my sister</u> <u>was ten.</u> Both my folks were there to tell us. They told
sentences combined	us at breakfast, in the kitchen. <u>I was eating toast, but</u> <u>I remember I couldn't eat anything when they started</u>
transition	<u>talking. In fact,</u> I remember a piece of toast with one bite taken out of it. My parents were very calm when
dialogue added	they told us. <u>"We love both you kids very much,"</u>

sentences combined	<u>my dad said, "but your mother and I aren't get-</u> <u>ting along."</u> They said they would always love us. <u>The announcement was such a shock to me that</u> <u>I couldn't believe it was happening.</u> At first, I just
sentences combined transition	thought they were having another fight. <u>Because I</u> <u>was too young to understand, I didn't cry.</u> <u>Suddenly,</u>
sentences combined, and transition added	<u>my sister started to cry, and then I knew it was seri-</u> <u>ous.</u> I kept thinking I would have to choose which
sentence combined, and transition added	parent to live with. <u>I knew I'd really hurt the one I</u> <u>didn't choose, so I felt so much guilt about hurting one</u> <u>of them.</u> I felt ripped apart.

Practice: Recognizing Transitions in a Narrative Paragraph

Underline the transitions in the following paragraph.

A little work in my mother's garden provided a tough lesson for me. My

mother has always loved her plants and flowers, and I had always thought of her

yard work as a sweet little hobby. Frequently, she would ask me to come outside,

enjoy the fresh air, and join her in a little pruning, trimming, and weeding. Finally, I

agreed. At once she handed me a pair of heavy gardening gloves and a bucket. Then

she led to a patch of lawn covered in feathery green stalks. "Pull out the weeds,"

she said, pointing to the feathery stalks, "and put them in the bucket." It couldn't

be much work to pull out a clump of these little green things, I told myself. When I

began my work, I discovered that the weeds could not be pulled in clumps, and even

a single feathery weed did not come out without a fight. Soon I realized that squat-

ting on the ground is hard on the knees. After what seemed like hours, I had to get

up and stretch. Looking at my watch, I saw that I had been working for fifteen min-

utes. Meanwhile, my mother had filled a huge bucket with the ornery weeds.

Practice: Adding the Right Transitions to a Narrative Paragraph

In the following paragraph, circle the correct transition in each of the pairs.

When/After I was ten, I had my first infatuation, which was a blend of ela-

tion and pain. My beloved was a singer on the Disney Channel, and I watched

his performances faithfully. Now/Soon I could repeat every word of his dialogue

on his show and every lyric in his songs. Until/Then I discovered his Web site, and my heart beat faster. Frequently/During I created elaborate fantasies in which my loved one met me and was immediately/still stricken with a burning love. These dreams sustained me through months of the ordinary days of a ten-year-old at school and home. Suddenly/Before my fantasies became nightmares. Pictures of my hero with a beautiful teenage girl began to appear on the Web. The two seemed to be in love. At first/Always I was overcome by a sense of loss. Immediately/Later my grief began to subside. However, I can finally/still remember the strong and often terrible emotions of my fantasy romance.

PROOFREADING NARRATION

As you prepare the final version of the narration paragraph, check your work for any errors in punctuation, spelling, or preparation of the paragraph. You may also want to make any minor changes in word choice or transitions that can refine your writing. Below is the final copy of the narrative paragraph on divorce. Notice these changes in the final version:

- The draft version used both formal and informal words like "folks" and "parents" and "dad." The final version uses only "parents" and "father."
- A few details have been added.
- A few details have been changed.

Final Version of a Narrative Paragraph

(Changes from the draft are underlined.)

When my parents announced that they were divorcing, I felt confused by all my emotions. At the time of the announcement, I was seven and my sister was ten. Both <u>my parents</u> were there to tell us. They told us at breakfast, in the kitchen. I was eating toast, but I remember I couldn't eat anything when they started talking. In fact, I remember <u>staring at</u> a piece of toast with one bite taken out of it. My parents were very calm when they told us. <u>"We both love you very much,"</u> my <u>father</u> said. "But your mother and I aren't getting along." They said they would always love us. The announcement was such a shock to me that I couldn't believe it was happening. At first, I just thought they were having another fight. Because I was too young to understand, I didn't cry. Suddenly, my sister started to cry, and then I knew it was serious. I kept thinking I would have to choose which parent to live with. I knew I'd really hurt the one I didn't choose, so I felt <u>terrible</u> guilt about hurting one of them. I felt ripped apart.

For your information: A sample narrative essay based on this topic and following the same writing steps can be found in Chapter 12, "Different Essay Patterns: Part One."

Exercise 13   Proofreading to Prepare the Final Version

Following are two narrative paragraphs with the kinds of errors that are easy
to overlook when you prepare the final version of an assignment. Correct the
errors, writing above the lines. There are twelve errors in the first paragraph
and eleven in the second.

Paragraph 1

I discovered a new world when a friend dragged me, to a lecture on the

star's. I had no thing to do last Tuesday nite and my best friend encouraged me

to accompany him to a lecture at the college planetarium. He had to go so that

he could earn some extra credit in his astronomy class. I had never cared much

about the stars or the planets; but I didn't want to spend the evening sitting in my

room. Consequently, I followed my freind into the planetarium. First, I noticed

that the building was impressive. We passed a giant telescope as we made our way

to a Theater with stadium seating. When the lecture began, the lights dimmed, the

speaker pressed a button, an the ceiling disappeared. A glass dome took it's place.

Beyond it, we could see the stars. Soon, the lecture became a sound and light

show with thrilling music spectacular close-ups, and dramatic language. After the

presentation, my friend and me left the building and immediately looked up at the

night sky.

Paragraph 2

Standing up to my roommate forced me to show some courage. I am a shy

person, and I am usally afraid of conflict. How ever, last weekend I was pushed to

the brink of rage. For weeks, I had accepted the filthy condition of our apartment.

I had done my best to clean the slimy bathroom and the filthy kitchen. Then, last

Saturday night, I wake up at 5:00 A.M., and had a horrible surprise. Looking for a

glass of water, I turned on the kitchen lite and saw a dozen cockroaches scurrying

on the floor, racing under the refrigerator, and crawling into the sink. My roomate

had left dishes caked with food on the counters and chicken bones on the table.

Spilled Pepsi stuck to my feet as I left the room. Next, I woke up my roommate.

"You've got to clean up after yourself," I said. I'm not going to live in a pigpen any longer." I think my roommate was astonished at my words. My heart beet hard as

I waited for his reaction. He glared at me and stormed out from the apartment.

I soon left, too, so that I could avoid a argument. When I returned several hours

later, my roommate was not there, and I soon noticed a small victory. The kitchen,

had been cleaned.

Lines of Detail: A Walk-Through Assignment

Write a paragraph about an incident in your life that embarrassed, amused, frightened, saddened, or angered you. In writing the paragraph, follow these steps:

Step 1: Begin by freewriting. Then read your freewriting, looking for both the details and focus of your paragraph.

Step 2: Brainstorm for more details. Then write all the freewriting and brainstorming as a list.

Step 3: Survey your list. Write a topic sentence that makes a point about the details.

Step 4: Write an outline. As you write the outline, check that your details fit the topic sentence and are in clear order. As you revise your outline, add details where they are needed.

Step 5: Write and revise a draft of your paragraph. Revise until your details are specific and in a clear order and your transitions are smooth. Combine any sentences that are short and choppy. Add a speaker's exact words if they will make the details more specific.

Step 6: In preparing the final version, check for punctuation, spelling, and word choice.

Topics for Writing a Narrative Paragraph

When you write on any of the following topics, be sure to work through the stages of the writing process in preparing your narrative paragraph.

Collaborate

1. Write about some surprising event you saw that you will never forget. Begin by freewriting. Then read your freewriting, looking for both the details and the focus of your paragraph.

   If your instructor agrees, ask a writing partner or group to (a) listen to you read your freewriting, (b) help you focus it, and (c) help you add details by asking questions.

2. Write a narrative paragraph about a mistake you made at your first job. Include how that mistake proved to be a valuable lesson.

3. Have you ever had a wonderful surprise? It might be an unannounced visit from a loved one, a piece of good luck in a competition, a good grade on an exam, or any other unexpected moment of happiness. Write about it.

4. Interview an older family member or friend. Ask him or her to tell you an interesting story about his or her past. Ask questions as the person speaks. Take notes. If you have a recorder, you can record the interview, but take notes as well.

 When you've finished the interview, review the information with the person you've interviewed. Ask the person if he or she would like to add anything. If you wish, ask follow-up questions.

 Next, on your own, find a point to the story. Work through the stages of the writing process to turn the interview into a narrative paragraph.

5. Visit the Web site of your local newspaper and find a news article about a crime that involved a sequence of events leading to a confrontation, arrest, or escape. Write the details of the story in time order, and be sure to use effective transitions. Your topic sentence should state what type of crime occurred as well as the outcome of it. (As you take notes from the article, be aware that newspaper accounts are not written in time order, so you will have to do some reordering of events.) Include a copy of the article with your paragraph.

Computer

6. Write a narrative paragraph about the couple in the photograph. Look carefully at their expressions and body language and write about events you imagine happened before, during, and after this scene. You may want to include some dialogue in your paragraph.

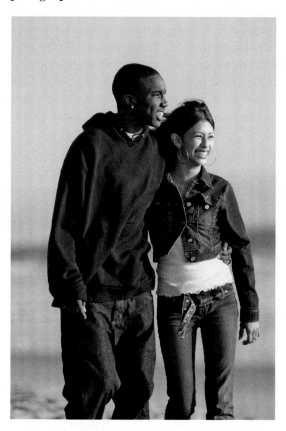

7. Write a narrative about the disaster in the photograph on the next page. You can include events you imagine happened before, during, and after the dramatic scene in the photograph.

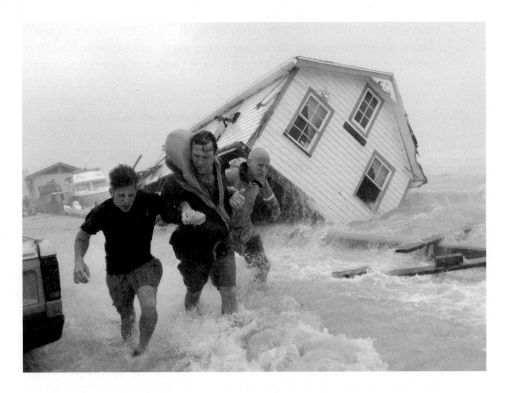

Topics for Critical Thinking and Writing

1. Have you ever been involved in a car accident, a serious dispute with a friend or family member, a sudden ending to a relationship, or some other emotionally difficult event? Write a narrative paragraph about this moment, but write it from the perspective of another person involved in the event. For example, how would the other driver involved in an accident tell his story? How would a friend tell the story of his or her unpleasant encounter with you?

2. If your job involves dealing with the public, write a narrative about one of your best or worst experiences with a customer or client. Afterwards, imagine that you are the customer, and write a narrative from his or her perspective. Use the same verb tense and sequence of events for both versions. Share your narratives with your classmates to see which version they prefer.

Note: Additional writing options suitable for narrative-related assignments can be found after the professional reading "The Good Father," in the "Readings for Writers" appendix at the end of this book.

mywritinglab   For support in meeting this chapter's objectives, log in to www.mywritinglab.com and select **Paragraph Development–Narrating**.

Name _____   Section _____

Peer Review Form for a Narrative Paragraph

After you have written a draft of your narrative paragraph, let a writing partner read it. When your partner has completed the form below, discuss the responses. Repeat the same process for your partner's paragraph.

I think the topic sentence of this paragraph is _____

_____

_____

_____

_____

I think the topic sentence (a) states the point well or (b) could be revised. (Choose one.)

The part of the narrative I liked best begins with the words _____

_____

The part that could use more or better details begins with the words _____

An effective transition was _____

_____

I have questions about or would like to know more about _____

I would like to take out the part about_____

I think the narrative is (a) easy to follow or (b) a little confusing. (Choose one.)

Other comments _____

_____

_____

_____

_____

_____

_____

Reviewer's name _____

CHAPTER 5

Process

Could you teach a
person who has never
used a digital camera
or camera phone how
to take photos with it?
How would you start
your explanation? How
many steps would your
instructions take?
Teaching in steps
involves one kind of
process.

Chapter Objectives

Students will be able to (1) recognize the difference between directional and informational process papers, and (2) write a process paragraph that contains a logical sequence, consistency in person and verb tense, and effective transitional devices.

WHAT IS PROCESS?

Process writing explains how to do something or describes how something happens or is done. When you tell the reader how to do something (a **directional process**), you speak directly to the reader, giving clear, specific instructions about performing some activity. Your purpose is to explain an activity so that a reader can do it. For example, you may have to leave instructions telling a new employee how to close the cash register or use the copier. A directional process uses "you," or in the way it gives directions, the word "you" is understood.

When you describe how something happens or is done (an **informational process**), your purpose is to explain an activity without telling a reader how to do it. For example, you can explain how a boxer trains for a fight or how a special effect for a movie was created. Instead of speaking directly to the reader, an informational process speaks about "I," "he," "she," "we," "they," or about a person by his or her name.

A Process Involves Steps in Time Order

Whether a process is directional or informational, it describes something that is done in steps, and these steps are in a specific order: a **time order.** The process can involve steps that are followed in minutes, hours, days, weeks, months, or even years. For example, the steps in changing a tire may take minutes, whereas the steps taken to lose ten pounds may take months.

You should keep in mind that a process involves steps that *must follow a certain order*, not just a range of activities that can be placed in any order.

This sentence *signals a process:*

> Learning to search the Internet is easy if you follow a few simple directions. (Using the Internet involves following steps in order; that is, you cannot search before you turn on the computer.)

This sentence *does not signal a process:*

> There are several ways to get a person to like you. (Each way is separate; there is no time sequence here.)

Telling a person, in a conversation, how to do something or how something is done gives you the opportunity to add important points you may have overlooked or to throw in details you may have skipped at first. Your listener can ask questions if he or she does not understand you. Writing a process, however, is more difficult. Your reader is not there to stop you, to ask you to explain further, or to question you. In writing a process, you must be organized and clear.

Hints for Writing a Process Paragraph

1. In choosing a topic, find an activity you know well. If you write about something familiar to you, you will have a clearer paragraph.

2. Choose a topic that includes steps that must be done in a specific time sequence.

> **not this:** I find lots of things to do on a rainy day.
> **but this:** I have a plan for cleaning the garage.

3. Choose a topic that is fairly small. A complicated process cannot be covered well in one paragraph. If your topic is too big, the paragraph can become vague, incomplete, or boring.

> **too big:** There are many stages in the process of a bill becoming a law.
> **smaller and manageable:** Will power and support were the most important elements in my struggle to quit smoking.

4. Write a topic sentence that makes a point. Your topic sentence should do more than announce. Like the topic sentence for any paragraph, it should have a point. As you plan the steps of your process and gather details, ask yourself some questions: What point do I want to make about this process? Is the process hard? Is it easy? Does the process require certain tools? Does the process require certain skills, like organization, patience, endurance?

> **an announcement:** This paragraph is about how to change the oil in your car.
> **a topic sentence:** You do not have to be a mechanic to change the oil in your car, but you do have to take a few simple precautions.

5. Include all of the steps. If you are explaining a process, you are writing for someone who does not know the process as well as you do. Keep in mind that what seems clear or simple to you may not be clear or simple to the reader, and be sure to tell what is needed before the process starts. For instance, what ingredients are needed to cook the dish? Or what tools are needed to assemble the toy?

6. Put the steps in the right order. Nothing is more irritating to a reader than trying to follow directions that skip back and forth. Careful planning, drafting, and revision can help you get the time sequence right.

7. Be specific in the details and steps. To be sure you have sufficient details and clear steps, keep your reader in mind. Put yourself in the reader's place. Could you follow your own directions or understand your steps?

If you remember that a process explains how to do something or how something is done, you will focus on being clear. Now that you know the purpose and strategies of writing a process, you can begin the prewriting stage.

Exercise 1   Practice: Recognizing Good Topic Sentences for Process Paragraphs

If a sentence is a good topic sentence for a process paragraph, put *OK* on the line provided. If a sentence has a problem, label that sentence with one of these letters:

A This is an announcement; it makes no point.

B This sentence covers a topic that is too big for one paragraph.

S This sentence describes a topic that does not require steps.

1. _____ You can use a simple procedure to remove stains from a carpet.

2. _____ When I became a babysitter, I discovered a simple way of getting and holding a child's attention.

3. _____ This essay is about the way to wash a car so that it gleams in the sunshine.

4. _____ Many things contribute to giving a dynamic speech in front of a business organization.

5. _____ Selling items on e-Bay is a business that grew over several years.

6. _____ Finding the right Valentine's Day gift for a loved one demands some creative thinking and strategic shopping.

7. _____ Several tips can help you to get a good deal on a laptop.

8. _____ The process of training for a career in nursing is not for those without a true commitment to quality, compassionate care.

9. _____ How a security system in a twenty-four-hour food mart works is the subject of this paper.

10. _____ If you know how to bargain, you can get a good deal on used furniture at a garage sale.

Exercise 2   Collaborate: Including Necessary Materials in a Process

Collaborate

Below are three possible topics for a process paragraph. For each topic, work with a partner or a group and list the items (materials, ingredients, tools, utensils, supplies) the reader would have to gather before he or she began the process. When you've finished the exercise, compare your lists with another group's list to see if you've missed any items.

1. topic: cutting a person's hair

needed items: _____

_____

_____

2. topic: gift wrapping a fragile object

needed items: _____

_____

_____

3. topic: cleaning out a crowded, dirty garage

needed items: _____

_____

_____

WRITING THE PROCESS PARAGRAPH IN STEPS

PREWRITING **PROCESS**

The easiest way to start writing a process paragraph is to pick a small topic, one that you can cover well in one paragraph. Then you can gather ideas by listing or freewriting or both.

If you decide to write about how to find the right apartment, you might begin by freewriting.

Then you might check your freewriting, looking for details that have to do with the process of finding an apartment. You can underline those details, as in the example that follows.

Freewriting for a Process Paragraph

Topic: Finding the right apartment

You have to look around. Don't pick the first apartment you see. Sean did that, and he ended up with a dump. Look at a bunch. But not too many, or you'll get confused. The lease, too. Check it carefully. How much is the security deposit? Do you want a one-bedroom? Friends can help if they know of any nice apartments. I found my place that way. Maybe somebody you know lives in a good neighborhood. A convenient location can be more expensive. But can save you money on transportation.

Next, you can put what you've underlined into a list, in correct time sequence:

before the search

Do you want a one-bedroom?
Friends can help.
a good neighborhood
a convenient location can be more expensive
can save you money on transportation

during the search

look around
Don't pick the first apartment you see.
Look at a bunch.
not too many

after the search

Check the lease carefully.
How much is the security deposit?

Check the list. Are some details missing? Yes. A reader might ask, "What other ways (besides asking friends) can help you find apartments? What else should you do before you search? When you're looking at apartments, what should you be looking for? What questions should you ask? After the search, how do you decide which apartment is best? And what, besides the security deposit, should you check on the lease?" Answers to questions like these can give you the details needed to write a clear and interesting directional process.

Writing a Topic Sentence for a Process Paragraph

Freewriting and a list can now help you focus your paragraph by identifying the point of your process. You already know what the subject of your paragraph is: finding the right apartment. But what's the point? Is it easy to find the right apartment? Is it difficult? What does it take to find the right apartment?

Maybe a topic sentence could be

Finding the right apartment takes planning and careful investigation.

Once you have a topic sentence, you can think about adding details that explain your topic sentence and you can begin the planning stage of writing.

Exercise 3   **Practice: Finding the Steps of a Process in Freewriting**

Read the following freewriting, then reread it, looking for all the words, phrases, or sentences that relate to steps. Underline all those items. Then once you've underlined the freewriting, put what you've underlined into a list in a correct time sequence.

How To Cut Back on Complaining: Freewriting

Cut back? Wouldn't it be better just to stop complaining? Everybody complains. Maybe it's impossible to stop complaining. After you've started counting complaints, notice what you complain about. Decide that you will make a conscious effort to reduce the number of times you complain. Start by noticing how often you complain. Next, focus on changing your conversations. As soon as you hear yourself starting to complain, change the subject or cut off your whining. Try to shift your dark mood to a lighter one. It's tough to shift from a negative attitude to a positive one; you may feel a little bit phony. However, if you focus on the positive, you'll eventually feel better and make others feel better, too.

Your List of Steps in Time Sequence

1. _____
   _____
2. _____
   _____
3. _____
   _____
4. _____
   _____
5. _____
   _____
6. _____
   _____
7. _____
   _____

PLANNING   **PROCESS**

Using the freewriting and topic sentence on finding an apartment, you can make an outline. Then you can revise it, checking the topic sentence and the list of details, improving them where you think they could be better. A revised outline on finding the right apartment is shown below.

Outline for a Process Paragraph

topic sentence:	Finding the apartment you want takes planning and careful investigation.
details:	Decide what you want.
	Ask yourself, "Do I want a one-bedroom?" "What can I afford?"
	A convenient location can be expensive.
before the search	It can also save you money on transportation.
	Friends can help you with names of nice apartments.
	Maybe somebody you know lives in a good neighborhood.
	Check the advertisements in the newspapers and online.
	Look around.
	Don't pick the first apartment you see.
	Look at several.
	But don't look at too many.
during the search	Check the cleanness, safety, plumbing, and appliances of each one.
	Ask the manager about the laundry room, additional storage, parking facilities, and maintenance policies.
	Compare the two best places you saw.
after the search	Consider the price, location, and condition of the apartments.
	Check the leases carefully.
	Check the requirements for first and last month's rent deposits.

The following checklist may help you revise an outline for your own process paragraph.

Checklist for Revising a Process Outline

✔ Is my topic sentence focused on some point about the process?

✔ Does it cover the whole process?

✔ Do I have all the steps?

✔ Are they in the right order?

✔ Have I explained the steps clearly?

✔ Do I need better details?

Exercise 4 **Practice: Revising the Topic Sentence in a Process Outline**

The topic sentence below doesn't cover all the steps of the process. Read the outline several times; then write a topic sentence that covers all the steps of the process and has a point.

topic sentence: You can make a bathroom sink shine if you take your time.

details: First, assemble a few tools and products.

You need a small bucket of warm, soapy water.

You need an old washcloth or other clean, absorbent cloth.

You need a cleaning product that will remove soap scum and grit but is not too abrasive.

You need an old toothbrush.

Begin the cleaning by using the old toothbrush.

Use it to scrub the grimy dirt that collects around the bottom of the faucets and the opening of the drain.

This part of the cleaning takes time and determination because the dirt is hard to reach.

Once this dirt has fallen into the sink, rinse the dirt down the drain.

Rinse the old toothbrush clean.

Now, use a little bit of the cleaner and a wet cloth to scrub away the soap scum in the sink.

Scrub all over the sink, not just at the bottom of it.

Finally, rinse off the scum, rinse out the cloth, and enjoy the sight of a shiny sink.

revised topic sentence: _____

_____

_____

Exercise 5   Practice: Revising the Order of Steps in a Process Outline

The steps in each of these outlines are out of order. Put numbers in the spaces provided, indicating what step should be first, second, and so on.

1. **topic sentence:** Whenever my brother sits down to study, he gets sidetracked in a process that defeats him.

   details: _____ As he places his books, a notebook, pencils, and his laptop on the table, he seems focused and serious.

   _____ Mike starts the process with good intentions.

   _____ His first mistake is to turn on his computer before he looks at his textbooks or checks his assignments.

   _____ Once his laptop is on, Mike does a quick check of his e-mail.

   _____ The quick check of the e-mail takes time because Mike is popular.

   _____ Checking the e-mail leads Mike to deleting some of the e-mail and replying to most of it.

   _____ Once Mike has finished dealing with his e-mail, he makes his second big mistake.

   _____ By the time he has checked his favorite blogs and sites, an hour has passed.

   _____ The second mistake is his decision to check a few sites and blogs, just to see what is new.

   _____ After an hour of focusing on his laptop, Mike feels a slight headache coming on.

   _____ He decides to treat his headache by taking a break before he deals with his homework.

   _____ Most of the time, Mike's break lasts until the next day, and he never gets around to studying.

2. **topic sentence:** Sal's Sports Center has survived for twenty years because Sal, the owner, has a perfect system for making his customers feel free to roam but never ignored.

   details: _____ A bell rings as soon as a customer enters Sal's Sports Center.

   _____ Most customers say, "No thanks; I'm just looking around."

   _____ Once he hears the bell, Sal approaches and says, "Can I help you with anything?"

   _____ Sal knows how to respond to "No thanks"; he just goes back to the counter and leaves the customer to roam the aisles.

   _____ Usually, Sal's customers, grateful for his relaxed attitude, leave with a purchase.

   _____ Every ten or fifteen minutes, Sal walks through the store, stocking or straightening the shelves.

_____ "Have a great day!" Sal says, as another satisfied customer leaves with a purchase.

_____ On these periodic trips, Sal is available to answer questions or give help, but he never pushes himself on a shopper.

3. topic sentence: My brother Eddie and his wife Leona have come up with a bedtime routine that allows their daughter to sleep comfortably in her own bed.

details: _____ Five-year-old Sonya used to be terrified of the dark and would not sleep alone.

_____ Eager to help Sonya with her fears, Eddie and Leona developed a process that moved Sonya out of their bed and into her own.

_____ After the story is over, both parents check Sonya's room for the "ghosts" she fears, and Sonya watches.

_____ Every night, fifteen minutes before Sonya's bedtime, Eddie or Leona sits on Sonya's bed and reads her a story.

_____ First, they check the closet.

_____ Then they check the windows.

_____ After they check the windows, they check under the bed and behind the dresser.

_____ Finally, just before they leave, they kiss Sonya and tell her they will be in the room next to hers so that she will be safe.

_____ When they have completed the "security" check of the room, the parents turn on soft, relaxing music.

_____ They leave, and Sonya falls asleep to soft music in a ghost-free room.

Exercise 6   **Practice: Listing All of the Steps in an Outline**

Following are three topic sentences for process paragraphs. Write all the steps needed to complete an outline for each sentence. After you've listed all the steps, number them in the correct time order.

1. topic sentence: You can make restaurant-quality garlic bread at home with a few simple ingredients, some basic kitchen supplies, and very little skill.

steps: _____

_____

_____

_____

_____

_____

_____

_____

_____

_____

_____

_____

_____

_____

_____

_____

_____

_____

_____

2. topic sentence: A simple system for taking care of your dirty clothes
can make your clothes last longer and look better.

steps: _____

_____

_____

_____

_____

_____

_____

_____

_____

_____

_____

_____

_____

_____

_____

3. topic sentence: A few simple steps will help you to make the most
of a free outdoor concert.

steps: _____

_____

_____

_____

_____

_____

_____

_____

_____

_____

_____

_____

_____

PROCESS

You can take the outline and write it in paragraph form, and you'll have a first draft of the process paragraph. As you write the first draft, you can combine some of the short sentences from the outline. Then you can review your draft and revise it for organization, details, clarity, grammar, style, and word choice.

Using the Same Grammatical Person

Remember that the _directional_ process speaks directly to the reader, calling him or her "you." Sentences in a directional process use the word "you," or they imply "you."

> **directional:**　_You_ need a good paintbrush to get started.
> Begin by making a list. ("You" is implied.)

Remember that the _informational_ process involves somebody doing the process. Sentences in an informational process use words like "I," "we," "he," "she," or "they" or a person's name.

> **informational:**　_Chip_ needed a good paintbrush to get started.
> First, _I_ can make a list.

One problem in writing a process is shifting from describing how somebody did something to telling the reader how to do an activity. When that shift happens, the two kinds of processes get mixed. That shift is called a **shift in person.** In grammar, the words "I" and "we" are considered to be in the first person, "you" is the second person, and "he," "she," "it," and "they" are in the third person.

If these words refer to one, they are _singular;_ if they refer to more than one, they are _plural._ The following list may help.

INFO BOX:　A List of Persons

First person singular:	I
Second person singular:	you
Third person singular:	he, she, it, or a person's name
First person plural:	we
Second person plural:	you
Third person plural:	they, or the names of more than one person

In writing your process paragraph, decide whether your process will be directional or informational, and stay with one kind.

Below are two examples of a shift in person. Look at them carefully and study how the shift is corrected.

shift in person:	After *I* preheat the oven to 350 degrees, *I* mix the egg whites and sugar with an electric mixer set at high speed. *Mix* until stiff peaks form. Then *I* put the mixture in small mounds on an ungreased cookie sheet. ("Mix until stiff peaks form" is a shift to the "you" person.)
shift corrected:	After *I* preheat the oven to 350 degrees, *I* mix the egg whites and sugar with an electric mixer set at high speed. *I* mix until stiff peaks form. Then *I* put the mixture in small mounds on an ungreased cookie sheet.
shift in person:	*A salesperson* has to be very careful when a customer tries on clothes. *The clerk* can't hint that a suit may be a size too small. *You* can insult a customer with a hint like that. (The sentences shifted from "salesperson" and "clerk" to "you.")
shift corrected:	*A salesperson* has to be very careful when customers try on clothes. *The clerk* can't hint that a suit may be a size too small. *He or she* can insult a customer with a hint like that.

Using Transitions Effectively

As you revise your draft, you can add transitions. Transitions are particularly important in a process paragraph because you are trying to show the steps in a *specific sequence*, and you are trying to show the *connections* between steps. Effective transitions will also keep your paragraph from sounding like a choppy, boring list.

Following is a list of some of the time transitions you can use in writing a process paragraph. Be sure that you use transitional words and phrases only when it is logical to do so, and try not to overuse the same transitions in a paragraph.

INFO BOX: **Transitions for a Process Paragraph**

after	during	last	the second step, etc.
afterward	eventually	later	then
as	finally	meanwhile	to begin
as he/she is	first	next	to start
as soon as	second, etc.	now	until
as you are	first of all	quickly	when
at last	gradually	sometimes	whenever
at the same time	in the beginning	soon	while
before	immediately	suddenly	while I am . . .
begin by	initially	the first step	

When you write a process paragraph, you must pay particular attention to clarity. As you revise, keep thinking about your audience to be sure your steps are easy to follow. The following can help you revise your draft.

Checklist for Revising a Process Paragraph

✔ Does the topic sentence cover the whole paragraph?

✔ Does the topic sentence make a point about the process?

✔ Is any important step left out?

✔ Should any step be explained further?

✔ Are the steps in the right order?

✔ Should any sentences be combined?

✔ Have I used the same person throughout the paragraph to describe the process?

✔ Have I used transitions effectively?

Exercise 7   **Practice: Correcting Shifts in Person in a Process Paragraph**

Below is a paragraph that shifts from being an informational to a directional process in several places. Those places are underlined. Rewrite the underlined parts directly above the original ones so that the whole paragraph is an informational process.

My sister Colleen has a system for getting the most out of a bottle of shampoo. As soon as she stands in the shower and opens a new bottle of shampoo, she is careful to pour only a tiny portion of the liquid into the palm of her hand. She knows the temptation to slap a huge glop of shampoo right onto <u>your</u> head. Pouring on the shampoo is wasteful, and it also saturates her hair with too many soapy suds. Colleen carefully takes the liquid from the palm of her hand and smears it onto the top of her head. Then she carefully adds a little water to the shampoo on her head. Now <u>you</u> can massage the mixture into her hair and scalp. She doesn't waste shampoo or water on a rinse followed by a second shampooing. Instead, she simply rinses her hair thoroughly once. Then <u>you cap</u> the shampoo so that it will not drip or collect dripping water. Next, <u>you</u> must place the shampoo bottle in a safe part of the shower so that the bottle will not fall, pop open, and leak. When she is near the end of her bottle of shampoo, <u>add</u> a little water to the bottle and <u>you</u> can get enough shampoo to last a week or more.

Exercise 8   **Revising Transitions in a Process Paragraph**

The transitions in this paragraph could be better. Rewrite the underlined transitions directly above each one so that the transitions are smoother.

Walking on wet or muddy pavement can be treacherous if you're not prepared and vigilant. <u>First,</u> wear sensible footwear. "Sensible" means shoes or boots with some traction on the soles, not flip-flops or high heels. <u>Second,</u> as you walk, concentrate on walking. That is, don't think about your plans, your worries, or your fantasies. Focus on the process of walking on slippery terrain. <u>Third,</u> be careful about hazards such as steps, curbs, or cracks in the pavement. <u>Fourth,</u> look ahead for deep puddles or oily pavement that can lead you into a sudden slide onto your knees or back. <u>Fifth,</u> do not let down your guard until you are safely indoors in a dry, not slippery, hallway or room. <u>Six,</u> you can relax and take off your muddy shoes.

Exercise 9   **Practice: Combining Sentences in a Process Paragraph**

The paragraph following has many short, choppy sentences, which are underlined. Wherever you see two or more underlined sentences clustered next to each other, combine them into one clear, smooth sentence. Write your revised versions of those sentences in the space above the original.

My dog has a clever way of telling me that she needs a bedtime visit outdoors. First, her bedtime is not my bedtime. If it were, my dog's system for getting outside would not be necessary. However, my dog gets restless about half an hour before I want to turn off the television and go to bed. <u>Her routine always begins at the same time. I am watching a contest or a drama. It is about to reach its peak.</u> Just as the winner is about to be announced or the criminal exposed, my dog begins to stir. <u>She wakes up from her nap. She has been dozing on the couch. She begins to look around.</u> This is my first clue that my dog is nearly ready to travel outdoors. <u>Soon, she begins licking my hand. She also licks my face.</u> When these forms of persuasion do not work, she resorts to her final tactic. <u>She jumps onto the floor. Then she starts to moan.</u> Now I begin to think that she needs to go outside immediately. When I open the door to the backyard, my dog runs out happily. <u>She sniffs the bushes. She explores the area beneath the trees. She checks for any animal intruders.</u> Finally, she relieves herself and runs inside for her nighttime dog biscuit. While I have been waiting at the open door and have missed

the climax of the television show, my dog has gotten just what she wanted.

The Draft

Below is a revised draft of the process paragraph on finding an apartment. This draft has more details than the outline on page 117. Some short sentences have been combined, and transitions, many of them time transitions, have been added. Added details make the directional process seem more authoritative and complete.

Revised Draft of a Process Paragraph

transition added	Finding the apartment you want takes planning and investigation. <u>First of all,</u> you must decide what you want. Ask yourself, "Do I want a one-bedroom
added detail and transition	apartment?" or "<u>Do I want a studio apartment?</u>" <u>Most</u> <u>important,</u> ask yourself, "What can I afford?" <u>A con-</u>
sentences combined, and transition	<u>venient location can be expensive; on the other hand,</u> <u>that location can save you money on transportation.</u>
transition added	<u>Before</u> you start looking for a place, do some research. Friends can help you with the names of nice apart-ments. Be sure to check the advertisements in the
transition added	newspaper and online. <u>Once</u> you begin your search,
sentences combined	don't pick the first place you see. <u>You should look at</u> <u>several places, but looking at too many can make your</u> <u>search confusing.</u> Just remember to check each apart-ment's cleanness, safety, plumbing, and appliances.
transition added	<u>Then</u> ask the manager about the laundry room, addi-tional storage, parking facilities, and maintenance
transition added	policies. <u>After</u> you've completed your search, compare the two best places you saw. Consider each one's price, location, and condition. Carefully check each
detail added	lease, <u>studying the amount of the security</u> deposit, the
detail added	deposit for first and last month's rent, <u>and the rules for</u> <u>tenants.</u>

PROOFREADING PROCESS

Before you prepare the final copy of your process paragraph, you can check your latest draft for grammar, word choice, and style that need revising. You may also decide to make a few final changes to polish your writing. Following is the final version of the process paragraph on finding the apartment you want. You'll notice that it contains several changes from the previous draft.

- The word "nice" has been changed to "suitable" to make the description more specific.
- The sentence that began, "You should look" has been rewritten so that it follows the pattern of the preceding sentences. Three sentences in a row now include the parallel pattern of "Be sure," "don't pick," and "Look at."

- A final sentence that relates to the topic of the paragraph has been added.

Final Version of a Process Paragraph

(Changes from the draft are underlined.)

Finding the apartment you want takes planning and investigation. First of all, you must decide what you want. Ask yourself, "Do I want a one-bedroom apartment?" or "Do I want a studio apartment?" Most important, ask yourself, "What can I afford?" A convenient location can be expensive; on the other hand, that location can save you money on transportation. Before you start looking for a place, do some research. Friends can help you with the names of <u>suitable</u> apartments. Be sure to check the advertisements in the newspaper and online. Once you begin your search, don't pick the first place you see. <u>Look at</u> several places, but looking at too many can make your search confusing. Just remember to check each apartment's cleanness, safety, plumbing, and appliances. Then ask the manager about the laundry room, additional storage, parking facilities, and maintenance policies. After you've completed your search, compare the two best places you saw. Consider each one's price, location, and condition. Carefully check each lease, studying the amount of the security deposit, the deposit for first and last month's rent, and the rules for tenants. <u>When you've completed your comparison, you're ready to choose the apartment you want.</u>

> **For your information:** A sample process essay based on this topic and following the same writing steps can be found in Chapter 12, "Different Essay Patterns: Part One."

Exercise 10   **Practice: Proofreading to Prepare the Final Paragraph**

Following are two process paragraphs with the kind of errors it is easy to overlook when you prepare the final version of an assignment. Correct the errors, writing above the lines. There are ten errors in the first paragraph and twelve in the second paragraph.

1. Sooner or later, every one gets a cold, so I dealing with a cold by preparing

for it, and accepting it. To prepare for a cold, I stock up on supplies. I make sure

that I have tea, honey, and chicken noodle soup in my kitchen When I feel a cold

begining, I decide to give in to it. Instead of trying to endure my stuffy head, sneez-

ing, and general misery at work and school; I stay home. I can sleep as long as

I need to, and I can sneeze without spreading my germs at work or in class. Once

I get out of bed, I do not force myself to eat when I feel sick. Instead, I do what

I can to make myself feel comftable. I lay on the couch, and cover my self with a

blanket. I watch videos or television Until I fall asleep again. If I am feeling ener-

getic, I get up to make myself some soothing tea with honey or a bowl of soup.

2. I have learned the hard way that you have to start off rite on the 1st day of class if you want to succeed. You can do two things before the first day. One is to by yourself something to write with and something to write on School supplies matter. Teachers do not appreciate a student who has to borrow basic supplies like a pencil or paper while they are trying to introduce the course and motivate the class. The other thing you can do is to make an early visit to the building and room where your class will be held. Knowing where to go helps you to arrive on time for the first class. Teachers can become frazzled when some one arrives late, even on the first day. They feel that each late arrival disrupts a day when important class busness is being conducted. On that day, dress reasonably well. That means, avoiding the appearance of someone who have just climbed out of bed. Bring your supplies. When you get to the classroom, sit in the front. Sitting in the front allows you to make eye contact with your Instructor and encourages you to pay more attention than you might if you sat at the back of the classroom. During my first term at college, I never followed any of these guidelines. It took me awhile and a few disappointing grades to realize that feeling or looking foolish on the first day of class is not a effective way to begin. On the other hand, you can use your first day of class to sit a pattern for success.

Lines of Detail: A Walk-Through Assignment

Your assignment is to write a paragraph on how to plan a special day. Follow these steps:

Step 1: Focus on one special day. If you want to, you can begin by using your own experience. Ask yourself such questions as, Have I ever planned a birthday party? A baby or wedding shower? A surprise party? A picnic? A reunion? A barbecue? A celebration of a religious holiday? Have I ever seen anyone else plan such a day? If so, how would you teach a reader about planning for such a day?

Step 2: Once you have picked the day, freewrite. Write anything you can remember about the day and how you or someone else planned it.

Step 3: When you've completed the freewriting, read it. Underline all the details that refer to steps in planning that event. List the underlined details in time order.

Step 4: Add to the list by brainstorming. Ask yourself questions that can lead to more details. For example, if an item on your list is "Send out invitations early," ask questions like "How early?" and "How do you decide whom to invite?"

Step 5: Survey your expanded list. Then write a topic sentence that makes some point about your planning for this special day. To reach a point, think of questions like these: "What makes a plan successful?" or "If you are planning for a special day (birthday, barbecue, surprise party, and so forth), what must you remember?"

Step 6: Use the topic sentence to prepare an outline. Be sure that the steps in the outline are in the correct time order.

Step 7: Write a first draft of the paragraph, adding details and combining short sentences.

Step 8: Revise your draft. Be careful to use smooth transitions, and check that you have included all the necessary steps.

Step 9: Prepare and proofread the final version of your paragraph.

Topics for Writing a Process Paragraph

When you write on one of these topics, be sure to work through the stages of the writing process in preparing your process paragraph. Also, be sure to write from your own experience.

1. Write a **directional** or **informational process** about one of these topics:

cleaning out a closet	fixing a clogged drain
preparing for a garage sale	changing the oil in a car
painting a room	waxing a car
taking a test	breaking a specific habit
losing weight	gaining weight
training a roommate	giving a pet a bath
coping with rejection	walking for better health
getting to work on time	preparing for a marathon
getting good tips as a server	preparing for a job interview
performing a family ritual	asking for a raise

2. Write about the wrong way to do something, or the wrong way you (or someone else) did it. You can use any of the topics in the list above, or you can choose your own topic.

3. Imagine that a relative who has never been to your state is coming to visit. This relative will arrive at the nearest airport, rent a car, and drive to your house. Write a paragraph giving your relative clear directions for getting from the airport to your house. Be sure to have an appropriate topic sentence.

4. Interview one of the counselors at your college. Ask the counselor to tell you the steps for applying for financial aid. Take notes or record the interview, get copies of any forms that are included in the application process, and ask questions about these forms.

After the interview, write a paragraph explaining the process of applying for financial aid. Your explanation is directed at a high school senior who has never applied for aid.

Collaborate

5. Interview someone whose cooking you admire. Ask that person to tell you the steps involved in making a certain dish. Take notes or tape the interview. After the interview, write a paragraph, *not* a recipe, explaining how to prepare the dish. Your paragraph will explain the process to someone who is a beginner at cooking.

Computer

6. Brainstorm about a particular task or function of a word-processing program that took considerable practice for you to master. (For example, you could write about moving text, highlighting, finding or creating a file, and so forth.) Write a paragraph that explains how to master this specific skill. Conclude your paragraph by stressing the benefits and/or practical uses of this skill.

Computer

7. Visit your college's Web site and follow any links that are associated with your campus bookstore. After reviewing the information about shopping for books and supplies, and based on your own experience, write a paragraph that explains the most efficient way to avoid long lines and waiting periods. If your college bookstore offers online purchasing, be sure to include the steps involved in this option.

8. Study the photograph of the dog and the man, and notice the connection between them. Then write a process paragraph on how to train a dog to catch a ball or a Frisbee in midair.

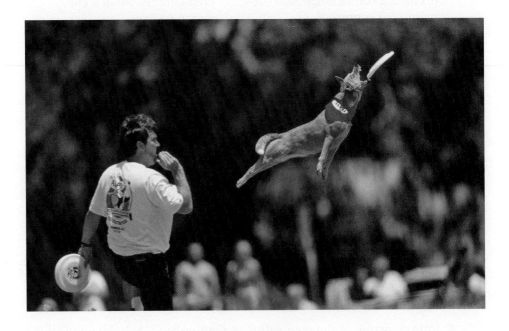

9. Examine the photograph of the basketball player, and then write a paragraph on how an athlete can focus his or her concentration for maximum benefit.

Topics for Critical Thinking and Writing

1. What steps do you follow when you are faced with a major decision? Do you consult others to help you make a choice? Do you seek information that will clarify your choices and help you weigh the pros and cons of your options? If you can identify the steps involved in your decision making, write a process paragraph about a major decision you have made as an adult. Be sure to provide specific details for each of the steps you cover, including why or how you undertook each step.

2. Many students have to work either part time or full time to afford college tuition and fees. Learning to manage time efficiently can be a difficult process. In a process paragraph, describe the steps you undertook to manage work and school responsibilities. You can consider how you worked out a schedule that recognizes the commitment of time and effort involved in meeting school and work demands.

Note: Additional writing options suitable for process-related assignments can be found after the professional reading "Breath of Life," in the "Readings for Writers" appendix at the end of this book.

Name _____   Section _____

Peer Review Form for a Process Paragraph

After you've written a draft of your process paragraph, let a writing partner read it. When your partner has completed the form below, discuss. Repeat the same process for your partner's paragraph.

The steps that are most clearly described are _____

_____

_____

_____

_____

I'd like more explanation about this step _____

_____

Some details could be added to the part that begins with the words _____

_____

I noticed these transitions _____

_____

_____

_____

_____

A transition could be added to the part that begins with the words _____

_____

I have questions about _____

_____

The best part of this paragraph is _____

_____

Other comments _____

_____

_____

_____

Reviewer's name _____

Comparison and Contrast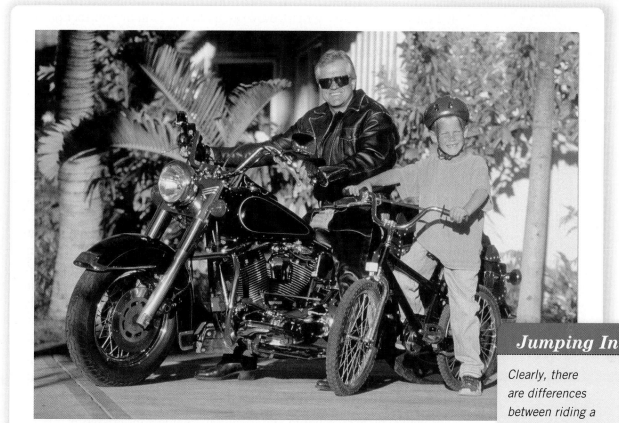

CHAPTER 6

Jumping In

*Clearly, there are differences between riding a bike and riding a motorcycle. Can you think of several differences? Are there any similarities? Examining similarities and differences is a way of **comparing** and **contrasting**.*

Chapter Objectives

Students will be able to (1) compare or contrast two entities, (2) demonstrate knowledge of the subject-by-subject and point-by-point patterns of exposition, and (3) write a process paragraph that incorporates appropriate transitions for a specific pattern.

WHAT IS COMPARISON? WHAT IS CONTRAST?

To **compare** means to point out *similarities*. To **contrast** means to point out *differences*. **When you compare or contrast, you need to come to some conclusion.** It's not enough to say, "These two things are similar" or "They are different." Your reader will be asking, "So what? What's your point?" You may be showing the differences between two restaurants to explain which is the better buy:

> If you like Mexican food, you can go to either Café Mexicana or Juanita's, but Juanita's has lower prices.

Or you may be explaining the similarities between two family members to explain how people with similar personalities can clash.

> My cousin Bill and my brother Karram are both so stubborn they can't get along.

Hints for Writing a Comparison or Contrast Paragraph

1. Limit your topic. When you write a comparison or contrast paragraph, you might think that the easiest topics to write about are broad ones with many similarities or differences. However, if you make your topic too large, you will not be able to cover it well, and your paragraph will be full of very large, boring statements.

Here are some topics that are too large for a comparison or contrast paragraph: two countries, two periods in history, two kinds of addiction, two wars, two economic or political systems, two presidents.

2. Avoid the obvious topic. Some people think it is easier to write about two items if the similarities or differences between them are obvious, but with an obvious topic, you will have nothing new to say, and you will risk writing a boring paragraph.

Here are some obvious topics: the differences between high school and college, the similarities between *Saw* and *Saw II*. If you are drawn to an obvious topic, *try a new angle* on the topic. Write about the unexpected, using the same topic. Write about the similarities between high school and college, or the differences between *Saw* and *Saw II*. You may have to do more thinking before you come up with ideas, but your ideas may be more interesting to write about and to read.

3. Make your point in the topic sentence of your comparison or contrast paragraph. Indicate whether the paragraph is about similarities or differences in a topic sentence like this:

> Because he is so reliable and loyal, Michael is a much better friend to me than Stefan. (The phrase "much better" indicates differences.)

> My two botany teachers share a love of the environment and a passion for protecting it. (The word "share" indicates similarities.)

4. Do not announce in the topic sentence. The sentences below are announcements, not topic sentences:

> This paper will explain the similarities between my two botany teachers.

> Let me tell you how Michael is a different kind of friend than Stefan.

5. Make sure your topic sentence has a focus. It should indicate similarities or differences; it should focus on the specific kind of comparison or contrast you will make.

> **not focused:** My old house and my new one are different.
> **focused:** My new home is bigger, brighter, and more comfortable than my old one.

6. In the topic sentence, cover both subjects to be compared or contrasted.

> **covers only one subject:** The beach at Santa Lucia was dirty and crowded.
> **covers both subjects:** The beach at Santa Lucia was dirty and crowded, but the beach at Fisher Bay was clean and private.

Be careful. It is easy to get so carried away by the details of your paragraph that you forget to put both subjects into one sentence.

Exercise 1 **Practice: Identifying Suitable Topic Sentences for a Comparison or Contrast Paragraph**

Following is a list of possible topic sentences for a comparison or contrast paragraph. Some would make good topic sentences. The ones that wouldn't make good topic sentences have one or more of these problems: they are announcements, they don't indicate whether the paragraph will be about similarities or differences, they don't focus on the specific kind of comparison or contrast to be made, they cover subjects that are too big to write about in one paragraph, or they don't cover both subjects.

Mark the problem sentences with an *X*. If a sentence would make a good topic sentence for a comparison or contrast paragraph, mark it *OK*.

1. _____ Both expensive jeans and bargain-priced jeans appeal to a wide range of ages, offer a variety of styles, and can be worn almost anywhere.

2. _____ Driving in heavy rain and driving in heavy snow require similar precautions.

3. _____ On the one hand, there are Siamese cats; on the other, there are Persian cats.

4. _____ Child actors and child singers can become rich, famous, and loved by audiences.

5. _____ Ricci's Restaurant has a more extensive menu, a better location, and friendlier service.

6. _____ Forest Park High School and Richmond Academy have demanding academic programs, caring teachers, and various extracurricular activities.

7. _____ This essay will discuss the similarities between my first summer job and my first summer at band camp.

8. _____ Siamese cats and Persian cats are regal, beautiful, and smart.

9. _____ On the one hand, there are expensive jeans; on the other hand, there are bargain-priced jeans.

10. _____ Texting is more convenient, saves more time, and is less of an interruption than phoning.

Organizing Your Comparison or Contrast Paragraph

Whether you decide to write about similarities (to compare) or differences (to contrast), you will have to decide how to organize your paragraph. You can choose between two patterns of organization: subject-by-subject or point-by-point.

Subject-by-Subject Organization In the subject-by-subject pattern, you support and explain your topic sentence by first writing all your details on one subject and then writing all your details on the other subject. If you choose a subject-by-subject pattern, be sure to discuss the points for your second subject *in the same order* as you did for the first subject. For example, if your first subject is an amusement park, and you cover (1) the price of admission, (2) the long lines at rides, and (3) the quality of the rides, when you discuss the second subject, another amusement park, you should write about its prices, lines, and quality of rides *in the same order.*

Look carefully at the outline and comparison paragraph below for a subject-by-subject pattern.

Comparison Outline: Subject-by Subject Pattern

topic sentence:	Once I realized that my brother and my mother are very much alike in temperament, I realized why they don't get along.
details:	
subject 1,	My brother James is a hot-tempered person.
James—temper	It is easy for him to lose control of his temper.
unkind words	When he does, he often says things he later regrets.
stubbornness	James is also very stubborn.
	In an argument, he will never admit he is wrong.
	Once we were arguing about baseball scores.
	Even when I showed him the right score printed in the paper, he wouldn't admit he was wrong.
	He said the newspaper had made a mistake.
	James' stubbornness overtakes his common sense.
subject 2,	James has inherited many of his character traits from our mother.
mother—temper	She has a quick temper, and anything can provoke it.
	Once, she got angry because she had to wait too long at a traffic light.
unkind words	She also has a tendency to use unkind words when she's mad.
stubbornness	She never backs down from a disagreement or concedes she was wrong.
	My mother even quit a job because she refused to admit she'd made a mistake in taking inventory.
	Her pride can lead her into foolish acts.
	After I realized how similar my brother and mother are, I understood how such inflexible people are likely to clash.

A Comparison Paragraph: Subject-by-Subject Pattern

subject 1,	Once I realized that my brother and my mother are very much alike in temperament, I realized why they don't
James—temper	get along. My brother James is a hot-tempered person.
unkind words,	It is easy for him to lose control of his temper, and when
stubbornness	he does, he often says things he regrets. James is also very stubborn. In an argument, he will never admit he is wrong. I remember one time when we were arguing about baseball scores. Even when I showed him the right scores printed in the newspaper, he wouldn't admit he was wrong. James insisted that the newspaper must have made a mistake in printing the score. As this example shows, sometimes James' stubbornness overtakes his

subject 2,
mother—temper

unkind words,

stubbornness

common sense. It took me a while to realize that my stubborn brother James has inherited many of his traits from our mother. Like James, she has a quick temper, and almost anything can provoke it. She once got angry because she had to wait too long at a traffic light. She also shares James' habit of saying unkind things when she's angry. And just as James refuses to back down when he's wrong, my mother will never back down from a disagreement or concede she's wrong. In fact, my mother once quit a job because she refused to admit she'd made a mistake in taking inventory. Her pride is as powerful as James' pride, and it can be just as foolish. After I realized how similar my mother and brother are, I understood how such inflexible people are likely to clash.

Look carefully at the paragraph in the subject-by-subject pattern, and you'll note that it

- begins with a topic sentence about both subjects—James and his mother,

- gives all the details about one subject—James,

- then gives all the details about the second subject—his mother, in the same order.

Point-by-Point Organization In the point-by-point pattern, you support and explain your topic sentence by discussing each point of comparison or contrast, switching back and forth between your subjects. You explain one point for each subject, then explain another point for each subject, and so on.

Look carefully at the outline and the comparison paragraph below for the point-by-point pattern.

Comparison Outline: Point-by-Point Pattern

topic sentence:	Once I realized that my brother and my mother are very much alike in temperament, I realized why they don't get along.
details:	
point 1,	My brother James is a hot-tempered person.
temper	It is easy for him to lose control of his temper.
James and mother	My mother has a quick temper, and anything can provoke it. Once she got angry because she had to wait too long at a traffic light.
point 2,	When my brother gets mad, he often says things he regrets.
unkind words	My mother has a tendency to use unkind words when she's
James and mother	mad.

continued

point 3, **stubbornness** **James and mother**	James is very stubborn. In an argument, he will never admit he is wrong. Once we were arguing about baseball scores. Even when I showed him the right score printed in the news-paper, he wouldn't admit he was wrong. He said the newspaper had made a mistake. James' stubbornness overtakes his common sense. My mother will never back down from a disagreement or admit she is wrong. She even quit a job because she refused to admit she'd made a mistake in taking inventory. She was foolish in her stubbornness. After I realized how similar my mother and brother are, I understood how such inflexible people are likely to clash.

Comparison Paragraph: Point-by-Point Pattern

point 1, temper **James and mother** **point 2,** **unkind words** **James and mother** **point 3, stubbornness** **James and mother**	Once I realized that my brother and my mother are very much alike in temperament, I realized why they don't get along. My brother is a hot-tempered person, and it is easy for him to lose control of his temper. My mother shares James' quick temper, and anything can provoke her anger. Once, she got angry because she had to wait too long at a traffic light. When my brother gets mad, he often says things he regrets. Similarly, my mother is known for the unkind things she's said in anger. James is a very stubborn person. In an argument, he will never admit he's wrong. I can remember one argument we were having over baseball scores. Even when I showed him the right score printed in the news-paper, he wouldn't admit he had been wrong. He simply insisted the paper had made a mistake. At times like that, James' stubbornness overtakes his common sense. Like her son, my mother will never back down from an argument or admit she was wrong. She even quit a job because she refused to admit she'd made a mistake in taking inventory. In that case, her stubbornness was as foolish as James'. It took me a while to see the similari-ties between my brother and mother. Yet after I realized how similar these two people are, I understood how two inflexible people are likely to clash.

Look carefully at the paragraph in the point-by-point pattern, and you'll note that it

- begins with a topic sentence about both subjects—James and his mother;

- discusses how both James and his mother are alike in these points: their quick tempers, the unkind remarks they make when they are angry, and their often foolish stubbornness;

- switches back and forth between the two subjects.

The subject-by-subject and point-by-point patterns can be used for either a comparison or contrast paragraph. But whatever pattern you choose, remember these hints:

1. Be sure to use the same points to compare or contrast two subjects. If you are contrasting two cars, you can't discuss the price and safety features of one, then the styling and speed of the other. You must discuss the price of both, or the safety features, styling, or speed of both.

You don't have to list the points in your topic sentence, but you can include them, like this: "My old Ford turned out to be a cheaper, safer, and faster car than my boyfriend's new Mazda."

2. Be sure to give roughly equal space to both subjects. This rule doesn't mean you must write the same number of words—or even sentences—on both subjects. It does mean you should be giving fairly equal attention to the details of both subjects.

Since you will be writing about two subjects, this type of paragraph can involve more details than other paragraph formats. Thus, a comparison or contrast paragraph may be longer than twelve sentences.

Using Transitions Effectively for Comparison or Contrast

How and when you use transitions in a comparison or contrast paragraph depend on the answers to two questions:

1. Are you writing a comparison or contrast paragraph?

   - When you choose to write a *comparison* paragraph, you use transitional words, phrases, or sentences that point out *similarities*.

   - When you choose to write a *contrast* paragraph, you use transitional words, phrases, or sentences that point out *differences*.

2. Are you organizing your paragraph in the point-by-point or subject-by-subject pattern?

   - When you choose to organize your paragraph in the *point-by-point* pattern, you need transitions *within* each point *and between points*.

   - When you choose to organize in the *subject-by-subject pattern*, you need *most of your transitions* in the *second half* of the paragraph, to remind the reader of the points you made in the first half.

Here are some transitions you can use in writing comparison or contrast. Many others you may think of will also be appropriate for your ideas.

INFO BOX: **Transitions for a Comparison or Contrast Paragraph**

To show similarities:

additionally	both	in the same way	similar to
again	each of	just like	similarly
also	equally	like	so
and	furthermore	likewise	too
as well as	in addition		

To show differences:

although	even though	instead of	though
but	except	nevertheless	unlike
conversely	however	on the other hand	whereas
despite	in contrast to	otherwise	while
different from	in spite of	still	yet

Writing a comparison or contrast paragraph challenges you to make decisions: Will I compare or contrast? Will I use a point-by-point or a subject-by-subject pattern? Those decisions will determine what kind of transitions you will use and where you will use them.

Exercise 2   **Practice: Writing Appropriate Transitions for a Comparison or Contrast Paragraph**

Below are pairs of sentences. First, decide whether each pair shows a comparison or contrast. Then combine the two sentences into one, using an appropriate transition (either a word or a phrase). You may have to rewrite parts of the original sentences to create one smooth sentence. The first pair is done for you.

1. My mother loves to go out dancing.
   My father has danced only once: at his wedding.

   combined: My mother loves to go out dancing, yet my father has

   danced only once: at his wedding.

2. Red hair may be considered a sign of a fiery temper.
   Blond hair is sometimes associated with a lack of intelligence.

   combined: _____

   _____

3. Young children should go to bed at the same time each night.
   Young children should have regularly scheduled meal times.

   combined: _____

   _____

4. A steady job can be tiring and stressful.
   Unemployment can be painful and terrifying.

   combined: _____

   _____

5. Playing chess with my uncle taught me to think deeply and plan my next move.
   When I was a member of a high school football team, I learned about the importance of strategy.

   combined: _____

   _____

6. Taking a long walk in a quiet place can be a way of clearing the mind of negative thoughts.
   Sitting alone in nature helps a person escape his or her worries.

combined: _____

_____

WRITING THE COMPARISON OR CONTRAST PARAGRAPH IN STEPS

PREWRITING   COMPARISON OR CONTRAST

One way to get started on a comparison or contrast paragraph is to list as many differences or similarities as you can on one topic. Then you can see whether you have more similarities (comparisons) or differences (contrasts), and decide which approach to use. For example, if you are asked to compare or contrast two restaurants, you could begin with a list like the one that follows.

List for Two Restaurants: Victor's and The Garden

similarities

both offer lunch and dinner

very popular

nearby

differences

Victor's	The Garden
formal dress	informal dress
tablecloths	placemats
food is bland	spicy food
expensive	moderate
statues, fountains, fresh flowers	dark wood, hanging plants

Getting Points of Comparison or Contrast

Whether you compare or contrast, you are looking for points of comparison or contrast, items you can discuss about both subjects.

    If you surveyed the list on the two restaurants and decided you wanted to contrast the two restaurants, you'd see that you already have these points of contrast:

      dress   food
      decor prices

To write your paragraph, start with several points of comparison or contrast. As you work through the stages of writing, you may decide you don't need all the points you've jotted down, but it is better to start with too many points than with too few.

Exercise 3   **Collaborate: Developing Points of Comparison or Contrast**

Do this exercise with a partner or a group. Below are some topics that could be used for a comparison or contrast paragraph. Underneath each topic, write three points of comparison or contrast. Be ready to share your answers with another group or with the class. The first topic is done for you.

1. **topic:** Compare or contrast two rooms.
   points of comparison or contrast:

   a. their size

   b. their furniture

   c. their color scheme

2. **topic:** Compare or contrast two breakfast cereals.
   points of comparison or contrast:

   a. _____

   b. _____

   c. _____

3. **topic:** Compare or contrast two popular actors or actresses.
   points of comparison or contrast:

   a. _____

   b. _____

   c. _____

4. **topic:** Compare or contrast two annual holidays.
   points of comparison or contrast:

   a. _____

   b. _____

   c. _____

Exercise 4   **Practice: Finding Differences in Subjects That Look Similar**

Following are pairs of subjects that seem very similar but that do have differences. List three differences for each pair.

1. **subjects:**   fried chicken and grilled chicken

   differences: a. _____

   b. _____

   c. _____

2. **subjects:**   pens and pencils

   differences: a. _____

   b. _____

   c. _____

3. **subjects:** regular coffee and decaffeinated coffee

   differences: a. _____

                        b. _____

                        c. _____

4. **subjects:** dumpster and garbage can

   differences: a. _____

                        b. _____

                        c. _____

Exercise 5 **Practice: Finding Similarities in Subjects That Look Different**

Following are pairs of subjects that are different but have some similarities. List three similarities for each pair.

1. **subjects:** getting fired and getting hired

   similarities: a. _____

                        b. _____

                        c. _____

2. **subjects:** becoming a senior citizen and becoming a teenager

   similarities: a. _____

                        b. _____

                        c. _____

3. **subjects:** spending money and saving money

   similarities: a. _____

                        b. _____

                        c. _____

4. **subjects:** loving and hating

   similarities: a. _____

                        b. _____

                        c. _____

Adding Details to Your Points

Once you have some points, you can begin adding details to them. The details may lead you to more points. If they do not, they will still help you develop the ideas of your paragraph. If you were to write about the differences in restaurants, for example, your new list with added details might look like this:

List for a Contrast of Restaurants

Victor's	The Garden
dress—formal	informal dress
men in jackets, women in dresses	all in jeans
decor—pretty, elegant	placemats, on table is a card
statues, fountains	listing specials, lots of dark wood,
fresh flowers on tables	and brass, green hanging plants
tablecloths	
food—bland tasting	spicy and adventurous
traditional, broiled fish or	pasta in tomato sauces, garlic
chicken, traditional steaks,	in everything, curry,
appetizers like shrimp cocktail,	appetizers like tiny tortillas,
onion soup	ribs in honey-mustard sauce
price—expensive	moderate
everything costs extra,	price of dinner includes
like appetizer, salad	appetizer and salad

Reading the list about restaurants, you might conclude that some people may prefer The Garden to Victor's. Why? There are several hints in your list. The Garden has cheaper food, better food, and a more casual atmosphere. Now that you have a point, you can put it into a topic sentence. A topic sentence contrasting the restaurants could be

> Some people would rather eat at The Garden than at Victor's because The Garden offers better, cheaper food in a more casual environment.

Once you have a possible topic sentence, you can begin working on the outlines stage of your paragraph.

Exercise 6 Practice: Writing Topic Sentences for Comparison or Contrast

Below are lists of details. Some lists are for comparison paragraphs; some are for contrast paragraphs. Read each list carefully; then write a topic sentence for each list.

1. topic sentence: _____

_____

List of Details

cats	dogs
needs	**needs**
need affection	need outdoor exercise
need play	need companionship
	need comfort
	need approval

temperament	**temperament**
solitary	companionable
quiet	boisterous
independent	loyal and trusting
ideal home	**ideal home**
small or large home	a large home
comfortable furniture	a big yard

2. topic sentence: _____

List of Details

cats	**dogs**
training	**training**
litter box training	toilet training
using a scratching post	walking on a leash
jumping on kitchen counters	behaving around people or pets
	obeying commands
benefits of personality	**benefits of personality**
affectionate	loving
mysterious	unpredictable
amusing	always entertaining
intuitive	sympathetic
great moments	**great moments**
curling up in bed	sneaking into bed
greeting owner	joyfully jumping on owner
playing with a cat toy	playing fetch

3. topic sentence: _____

List of Details

red	**blue**
emotional impact	**emotional impact**
a hot color	a cool color
red face = ashamed or angry	blue mood = sad, depressed
red peppers = hot	blue ocean = cool
red lipstick = passionate	big blue eyes = innocence

messages in public spaces	**messages in public spaces**
red fire engine means danger or an emergency	blue police uniforms mean calm and order
red lines on the pavement or floor signal "do not cross"	blue rooms in hospitals are calm and soothing

messages in clothing	**messages in clothing**
red velvet dress signals luxury and daring	blue jeans are ordinary almost like a uniform
red suspenders are worn by eccentrics	blue suits are worn by traditional business people

4. topic sentence: _____

_____

List of Details

red	**blue**
patriotism	**patriotism**
U.S. flag has red stripes	U.S. flag has white stars on a blue field
red, white, and blue caps worn as a patriotic statement	red, white, and blue tee-shirts worn as a patriotic statement
red, white, and blue decorations on public holidays such as Veterans' Day	red, white, and blue fireworks on Fourth of July

jewelry	**jewelry**
rubies are expensive gems	turquoise jewelry is popular and stylish
garnets are less expensive	a blue topaz is a lower-cost gem for rings
red beads are common in multistrand necklaces	dark blue stones appear on bangle bracelets

transportation	**transportation**
red sports cars are a popular image of money and daring	many airlines paint their planes blue and white (or blue and silver)
a red convertible is another image of adventure	police cars are often blue and white

PLANNING   **COMPARISON OR CONTRAST**

With a topic sentence, you can begin to draft an outline. Before you can write an outline, however, you have to make a decision: What pattern do you want to use in organizing your paragraph? Do you want to use the subject-by-subject or the point-by-point pattern?

The following is an outline of a contrast paragraph in point-by-point form.

Outline of a Contrast Paragraph: Point-by-Point Pattern

topic sentence:	Some people would rather eat at The Garden than at Victor's because The Garden offers better, cheaper food in a more casual environment.
details:	Food at Victor's is bland-tasting and traditional.
	The menu has broiled fish, chicken, traditional steaks.
	The spices used are mostly parsley and salt.
	The food is the usual American food with a little French food on the list.
point 1, food	Appetizers are the usual things like shrimp cocktail or onion soup.
	Food at The Garden is more spicy and adventurous.
	There are many pasta dishes in tomato sauce.
	There is garlic in just about everything.
	The Garden serves four different curry dishes.
	It has all kinds of ethnic food.
	Appetizers include items like tiny tortillas and hot, honey-mustard ribs.
	The prices of the two restaurants differ.
	Victor's is expensive.
point 2, prices	Everything you order costs extra.
	An appetizer and a salad costs extra.
	Food at The Garden is more moderately priced.
	The price of a dinner includes an appetizer and a salad.
	Certain diners may feel uncomfortable in Victor's, which has a formal environment.
point 3, environment	Everyone is dressed up, the men in jackets and ties and the women in dresses.
	Less formal diners would rather eat in a more casual place.
	People don't dress up to go to The Garden; they wear jeans.
conclusion	Many people prefer a place where they can relax, with reasonable prices and unusual food, to a place that's a little stuffy, with a traditional and expensive menu.

Once you've drafted an outline, check it. Use the following checklist to help you review and revise your outline.

Checklist for an Outline of a Comparison or Contrast Paragraph

✔ Do I have enough details?

✔ Are all my details relevant?

✔ Have I covered all the points on both sides?

✔ If I'm using a subject-by-subject pattern, have I covered the points in the same order on both sides?

✔ Have I tried to cover too many points?

✔ Have I made my main idea clear?

Using this checklist as your guide, compare the outline with the prewriting list on page 141. You may notice several changes:

- Some details on decor in the list have been omitted because there were too many points.

- A concluding sentence has been added to reinforce the main idea.

Exercise 7 **Practice: Adding a Point and Details to a Comparison or Contrast Outline**

The following outline is too short. Develop it by adding a point of comparison and details to both subjects to develop the comparison.

topic sentence: People who wear caps and those who wear hats often choose them for similar reasons.

details: Caps and hats both make a statement.

Caps are often marked with the name of a tractor company, a football team, or a college, so they indicate an affiliation or interest.

Hats often indicate a person's interests, hobbies, or employment.

Fishing hats are worn by people who fish for fun or profit.

Cowboy hats appear on the heads of working ranchers and people on vacation.

Caps and hats can be a way for people to fit in.

Most people at a football or basketball game want to be seen with their team's insignia on their caps.

New students at a college like to wear the college's name on a cap.

In some places of worship, women like to wear elaborate hats on special occasions.

People who attend country music concerts like to come in cowboy hats.

Add a new point of comparison, and details, about caps and hats:

_____

_____

_____

_____

_____

_____

_____

Exercise 8 **Practice: Finding Irrelevant Details in a Comparison or Contrast Outline**

The following outline contains some irrelevant details. Cross out the details that don't fit.

topic sentence: Fibs and lies are quite different in intention, consequences, and in the nature of fibbers and liars.

details: Fibs tend to be small distortions of the truth.

When people have to choose between hurting another person's feelings by telling the truth and sparing that person
some pain, they tell a fib.

"Your haircut looks great," a fibber will say.

Hair is a very sensitive subject with some people.

Lies are larger falsehoods.

Some people lie about being faithful to a partner.

So that they will not get caught cheating, they may say they
were working late.

Many people are unemployed these days.

The consequences of telling a fib are not likely to be as serious
as the consequences of lying.

Because a fib is about a small matter, it has a fairly small impact.

A fib told to avoid hurting another person may not be kind in the
long run, but it isn't cruel.

It would be difficult for an average person to count all the fibs
he or she has told.

Lies, on the other hand, can create great harm.

Lies about infidelity can poison a marriage.

The unsuspecting partner can sense a painful distance growing
between the spouses.

The cheater is caught in a web of guilt.

Cheating is often portrayed on television as funny, but it is not.

Essentially, fibbers and liars are different types of people.

Young children may sense that fibbing is wrong, but their fibs
are meant to save themselves, not to hurt others.

In the same way, adults who fib usually mean to avoid an awkward situation, but the fibs are not intentionally cruel.

Liars are most often adults, and their lies can be toxic.

Although unfaithful partners tell themselves they are not hurting
anyone, they know better.

Their lies are both selfish and dangerous.

Everyone is human and therefore flawed, but fibbers are far less
dangerous than liars.

Exercise 9   Practice: Revising the Order in a Comparison or Contrast Outline

Below is an outline written in the subject-by-subject pattern. Rewrite the part of
the outline that is in italics so that the points in the second half follow the order
of the first half. You do not have to change any sentences; just rearrange them.

topic sentence: Carl and Sean could not have been more different, yet
they were college roommates who became best friends.

details: Carl was a country boy.

Carl's family lived on a ten-acre property fifteen miles from the nearest mall.

Carl had two horses, which he cared for himself.

He was used to seeing foxes, snakes, and possum in his back yard.

Carl loved football.

He had been a star player at his high school.

He drove two hours to attend every football game at the nearest university.

On his satellite television, he watched every professional game he could find.

Carl also loved country music.

When he wasn't watching football on television, he turned to country music channels.

The only concerts he attended featured country music superstars.

Sean loved hip-hop.

Hip-hop blasted from his MP-3 player.

Clubs that offered hip-hop entertainment were Sean's favorite hangouts.

Sean was a typical suburban teen.

He and his family lived in a three-bedroom house with a two-car garage and a small back yard.

Sean had never had a pet, but his mother had a Yorkshire terrier.

The creatures that lived in his yard were likely to be crows, squirrels, and worms.

He lived within a ten-minute drive to two huge malls, ten restaurants, and a multiplex movie theater.

A major part of Sean's life was basketball.

He had played basketball in high school.

He attended all the games at the nearby college.

He regularly drove half an hour to a nearby sports center where he watched nationally known teams play.

Rewritten order: _____

_____

_____

_____

_____

_____

_____

_____

_____

_____

_____

_____

_____

_____

_____

DRAFTING AND REVISING **COMPARISON OR CONTRAST**

When you've revised your outline, you can write the first draft of the restaurant paragraph. As you work through several drafts, you may decide to rearrange your points or refine your topic sentence. Adding vivid details can make the paragraph more than just a list of comparisons or contrasts. You may also need to add transitions, and the transitions may include transitional devices such as words, phrases, and even sentences.

The Draft

Here is a final draft version of the paragraph on contrasting two restaurants. As you read it, notice the changes from the outline on page 147: the order of some details in the outline has been changed, sentences have been combined, and transitional devices have been added.

Draft of a Contrast Paragraph, Point-by-Point Pattern

        Some people would rather eat at The Garden than at Victor's because The Garden offers better, cheaper food in a more casual environment. The food at Victor's is bland-tasting and traditional. The menu has broiled fish, chicken, and traditional steaks. The food is the usual American food with a little French food on the list. Appetizers are the usual things like shrimp cocktail and onion soup. The spices used are mainly parsley and salt. Food at

transition
sentence order changed

The Garden, <u>however,</u> is more spicy and adventurous. <u>The restaurant has all kinds of ethnic food.</u> There are many pasta dishes with tomato sauce. The menu has five kinds of curry on it. The appetizers include items like tiny tortillas and hot, honey-mustard ribs.

transition

<u>And if parsley is the spice of choice at Victor's,</u> garlic is the favorite spice at The Garden. The prices at the restaurants differ, <u>too.</u> Victor's is expensive because everything you order costs extra.

continued

sentences combined transition	An appetizer or a salad costs extra. Food at The Garden, <u>in contrast, is more moderately priced because the price of a dinner includes an appetizer and a salad. Price and menu are important, but the most important difference between the restaurants has to do with environment.</u> Certain diners may feel uncomfortable at Victor's, which has a formal kind of atmosphere. Everyone is dressed up, the men in jackets and ties and the women in dresses.
sentences combined	<u>Less formal diners would rather eat in a more casual place like The Garden, where everyone wears jeans.</u> Many people prefer a place where they can relax, with reasonable prices and unusual food, to a place that is a little stuffy, with a traditional and expensive menu.

The following checklist may help you to revise your own draft.

Checklist for Revising the Draft of a Comparison or Contrast Paragraph

✔ Did I include a topic sentence that covers both subjects?

✔ Is the paragraph in a clear order?

✔ Does it stick to one pattern, either subject by subject or point by point?

✔ Are both subjects given roughly the same amount of space?

✔ Do all the details fit?

✔ Are the details specific and vivid?

✔ Do I need to combine any sentences?

✔ Are transitions used effectively?

✔ Have I made my point?

Exercise 10   Practice: Revising the Draft of a Comparison or Contrast Paragraph by Adding Vivid Details

You can do this exercise alone, with a writing partner, or with a group. The following contrast paragraph lacks the vivid details that could make it interesting. Read it; then rewrite the underlined parts in the space above them. Replace the original words with more vivid details.

I had always planned on getting a dog, but when I finally got one, the experience was not at all what I had expected. First of all, I had always imagined myself visiting the local animal shelter where I would find the largest dog in the place. He would be a great watchdog and know how to <u>do a lot of things</u>. After I selected him, I would take him back to <u>my place</u>, and he would <u>fit right in</u>. I felt sure that the dog would soon <u>learn the rules and be cool.</u> Finally, I dreamed of a dog that

would love to <u>have all kinds of fun.</u> However, the reality of getting a dog was

nothing like my fantasy. First, I didn't find my dog; she found me. I saw her on

campus, and her tongue was hanging out. After I gave her some water, she fol-

lowed me all day. She even tried to follow me into <u>some places at college.</u> When I

had to leave at the end of the day, I picked her up and put her in my car. She was

easy to pick up because, unlike the dog of my dreams, she <u>was not big</u>. When I

took her to my apartment, she didn't exactly conform to my fantasies of a pet.

Instead of fitting in, she took over my territory. Within the first ten minutes of her

arrival, she had jumped on the sofa, chewed one of my old sneakers, and eaten

part of a roll of toilet paper. Finally, I discovered that my idea of fun is not hers.

She does not want to catch a ball, and she does not want to learn any tricks. How-

ever, she is fearless and loves to <u>do some wild stuff</u>. My dog is not the fantasy pet

I expected to own, but she is a real dog with a courage and a joy for living that is

all her own.

Exercise 11   Practice: Revising a Draft by Combining Sentences

The paragraph below has many short, choppy sentences, which are underlined. Whenever you see two or more underlined sentences clustered next
to each other, combine them into one smooth, clear sentence.

Whenever I visit a doctor, I feel as if I were going to prison. First, there is the

weird atmosphere of the doctor's waiting room. The room is unusually quiet. It is

full of people. <u>They are sitting. They are staring ahead. They are awaiting their</u>

<u>doom.</u> The staff behind the glass partition reminds me of a group of prison guards

who keep the latest prisoners in order until the big door opens and incarceration

begins. At long intervals, each patient's name is called. Each time, I look up. I hope

the name is mine so that, like a prisoner, I can begin my ordeal and soon end it. On

the other hand, I dread entering the space behind the big door. <u>That space con-</u>

<u>tains another kind of waiting room. This is the solitary waiting area. Here I gener-</u>

<u>ally sit on a chair or on the edge of an examination table. Here I can dwell on what</u>

is wrong with me. In a similar way, prisoners are supposed to use their incarceration to think about what they have done wrong. <u>I sit alone in the small, cell-like room. I fear the arrival of the doctor.</u> I have gone to the doctor to find out what is wrong. <u>However, I feel that I have committed some crime. Maybe I have eaten too much fatty food. Maybe I have skimped on exercise.</u> As I wait for the doctor to examine me, I feel as if a warden were about to enter, study me critically, and frown. Like a prisoner, I am unable to escape.

PROOFREADING   **COMPARISON OR CONTRAST**

Contrast Paragraph: Point-by-Point Pattern

When you prepare the final version of your comparison or contrast paragraph, you can check for errors in spelling, grammar, or preparation. You may also notice that some choice of words needs improvement. In the final version of the contrast essay, which used a point-by-point pattern, several changes from the draft on page 151 were made:

- "Usual" or "usually" was used too often, so synonyms were substituted.

- "<u>Onion soup</u>" became "<u>French</u> onion soup" to improve this detail.

- "Everything <u>you</u> order" was changed to "everything <u>a person</u> orders" for better grammar.

- "A formal <u>kind of atmosphere</u>" became "<u>a formal environment</u>" to eliminate extra words.

Final Version of a Contrast Paragraph: Point-by-Point Pattern

(Changes from the draft are underlined.)

    Some people would rather eat at The Garden than at Victor's because The Garden offers better and cheaper food in a more casual environment. The food at Victor's is bland-tasting and traditional. The menu has broiled fish, chicken, and traditional steaks. The food is <u>typical</u> American food with a little French food on the list. Appetizers are <u>standard</u> things like shrimp cocktail and <u>French</u> onion soup. The spices are mostly parsley and salt. Food at The Garden, however, is more spicy and adventurous. The restaurant has all kinds of ethnic food. There are many pasta dishes with tomato sauce. The menu has four kinds of curry on it. The appetizers include items like tiny tortillas and hot, honey-mustard ribs. And if parsley is the spice of choice at Victor's, garlic is the favorite spice at The Garden. The prices at the restaurants differ, too. Victor's is expensive because everything <u>a person</u> orders costs extra. An appetizer or a salad costs extra. Food at The Garden, in contrast, is more moderately priced because the price of a dinner includes an appetizer and a salad. Price and menu are important, but the most important difference between the two restaurants has to do with environment. Certain diners may feel uncomfortable at Victor's, which has a formal <u>environment</u>. Everyone is dressed up, the men in jackets and ties and the women in dresses. Less formal diners would rather eat in a more casual place like The Garden, where everyone wears jeans. Many people prefer a place where they can relax, with reasonable prices and unusual food, to a place that is a little stuffy, with a traditional and expensive menu.

Before you prepare the final copy of your comparison or contrast paragraph, check your latest draft for errors in spelling, punctuation, typing, and copying.

> **For your information:** A sample point-by-point contrast essay based on this topic and following the same writing steps can be found in Chapter 12, "Different Essay Patterns: Part One."

The Same Contrast Paragraph: Subject-by-Subject Pattern

To show you what the same paragraph contrasting restaurants would look like in a subject-by-subject pattern, the outline, draft, and final version are shown below.

Outline: Subject-by-Subject Pattern

topic sentence: Some people would rather eat at The Garden than at Victor's because The Garden offers better, cheaper food in a more casual environment.

details:

subject 1, Victor's
Food at Victor's is bland-tasting and traditional.
The menu has broiled fish, chicken, and traditional steaks.
The spices used are mostly parsley and salt.
The food is the usual American food with a little French food on the list.
Appetizers are the usual things like shrimp cocktail and onion soup.
Victor's is expensive.
Everything you order costs extra.
An appetizer or salad costs extra.
Certain diners may feel uncomfortable at Victor's, which has a formal environment.
Everyone is dressed up, the men in jackets and ties and the women in dresses.

subject 2, The Garden
Food at The Garden is more spicy and adventurous.
There are many pasta dishes in tomato sauce.
There is garlic in just about everything.
The Garden serves four different curry dishes.
It has all kinds of ethnic food.
Appetizers include items like tiny tortillas and hot, honey-mustard ribs.
Food at The Garden is moderately priced.
The price of a dinner includes an appetizer and a salad.
The Garden is casual.
People don't dress up to go there; they wear jeans.

conclusion Many people prefer a place where they can relax, with reasonable prices and unusual food, to a place that's a little stuffy, with a traditional and expensive menu.

Draft: Subject-by-Subject Pattern

Some people would rather eat at The Garden than at Victor's because The Garden offers better, cheaper food in a more casual environment. The food at Victor's is bland-tasting and traditional. The menu has broiled fish, chicken, and traditional steaks on it. The food is the usual American food with a little French food on the list. Appetizers are the usual things like shrimp cocktail and onion soup. <u>At Victor's, the spices are</u> <u>mostly parsley and salt.</u> <u>Eating</u> <u>traditional food at Victor's is expensive, since everything</u> <u>you order costs extra.</u> An appetizer or a salad, <u>for instance,</u> costs extra. <u>Victor's prices make some people nervous, and</u> <u>the restaurant's formal environment makes them uncomfort-</u> <u>able.</u> At Victor's, everyone is dressed up, the men in jackets and ties and the women in dresses. <u>The formal atmosphere,</u> <u>the food, and the prices attract some diners, but others</u> <u>would rather go to The Garden for a meal.</u> The food at The Garden is more spicy and adventurous <u>than the offerings</u> <u>at Victor's.</u> The place has all kinds of ethnic food. <u>There are</u> <u>many pasta dishes in tomato sauce, and The Garden serves</u> <u>four different curry dishes.</u> Appetizers include items like tiny tortillas and hot, honey-mustard ribs. <u>If Victor's relies</u> <u>on parsley and salt to flavor its food,</u> The Garden sticks to garlic, which is in just about everything. Prices are lower at The Garden <u>than they are at Victor's.</u> The Garden's meals are more moderately priced because, <u>unlike Victor's,</u> The Garden includes an appetizer and a salad in the price of a dinner. <u>And in contrast to Victor's,</u> The Garden is a casual restaurant. People don't dress up to go to The Garden; everyone wears jeans. Many people prefer a place where they can relax, with unusual food at reasonable prices, to a place that's a little stuffy, with a traditional and expensive menu.

Margin annotations:

sentence order changed,
sentences combined
transition
transition sentence

transition sentence

transition
sentence order changed, sentences combined

transition

transition
transition

transition

Final Version: Subject-by-Subject Pattern

(Changes from the draft are underlined.)

Some people would rather eat at The Garden than at Victor's because The Garden offers better, cheaper food in a more casual environment. The food at Victor's is bland-tasting and traditional. The menu has broiled fish, chicken, and traditional steaks on it. The food is typical American food, with a little French food on the list. Appetizers are the <u>standard</u> things like shrimp cocktail and <u>French</u> onion soup. At Victor's, the spices are mostly parsley and salt. Eating traditional food at Victor's is expensive, since everything <u>a person</u> orders costs extra. An appetizer or a salad, for instance, costs extra. Victor's prices make some people nervous, and the restaurant's formal environment makes them uncomfortable. At Victor's, everyone is dressed up, the men in jackets and ties and the women in dresses. The formal <u>environment</u> and the prices attract some diners, but others would rather go to The Garden for a meal. The food at The Garden is more spicy and adventurous than the offerings at Victor's. The place has all kinds of ethnic food. There are many pasta dishes in tomato sauce, and The Garden serves four different curry dishes. Appetizers include items like tiny tortillas and hot, honey-mustard ribs. If Victor's relies on parsley and salt to flavor its food, The Garden sticks to garlic, which is in just about everything. Prices are lower at The Garden than they are at Victor's. The Garden's meals are moderately priced because, unlike Victor's, The Garden includes an appetizer and a salad in the price of a dinner. And in contrast to Victor's, The Garden is a casual restaurant. People don't dress up to go to The Garden; everyone wears jeans. Many people prefer a place where they can relax, with unusual food at reasonable prices, to a place that's a little stuffy, with a traditional and expensive menu.

For your information: A sample contrast essay based on this topic and following the same writing steps can be found in Chapter 12, "Different Essay Patterns: Part One."

Exercise 12 Proofreading to Prepare the Final Version

Following are two comparison or contrast paragraphs with the kinds of errors it is easy to overlook in a final copy of an assignment. Correct the errors, writing your corrections above the lines. There are twelve errors in the first paragraph and fourteen in the second.

    1. Anyone who love hamburgers knows that a hamburger cooked indoors

and a hamburger cooked outdoors are significantly different. One look at each

kind of Burger reveals the first difference. A burger that has been prepared in a

frying pan on a kitchen stove is gray-brown inn color. It is also the same color

all over it's surface. On the other hand, a burger cooked outdoors on a grill has a

darker color. Sometimes it is nearly black, or has an uneven color because of the

mark's left by the hot grill. Each kind of burger has a different texture, too. the

hamburger cooked in a pan is usually fired with a little oil or butter, so the meat

is likely to be a little greasy. The meat that is grilled is simply placed on a very

hot surface. The grilled burger looks dry on the outside but are filled with natural

juices. Finally, burgers cooked inside and burgers cooked outside taste different.

Burgers cooked indoors taste good. They taste like beef, but the flavor can be a

little bland. Burgers cooked on the grill have a smoky, charcoal flavor. Because

they are cooked in fresh air, they seem to have a more natural taste. A hamburger

is popular food choice, but some burger's are better then others.

2. My car is an old Toyota Camry that used to belong to my Mother, and I was thrilled when I get the chance to drive my uncle's newer BMW for a few weeks while he was out of town. However, I was surprised that my life did not change very much when I get the newer, sportier car. First, I axpected to attract more attention when I drove the BMW. No one looks twice at an old Camry in need of a paint job, so I always felt invisible when I drove it. People did look more closely at the BMW, but they didnt look at me. Another disappointment was related to the excessories and upgrades in my uncles car. At first, the BMW was a like a great toy for me, with every automotive option, every entertainment choice, and every comfort I could imagine. It took me several days to learn what I could do, and how I could do it in this luxury car. It was wonderful to try out the satellite radio, the temperature controls, and all the other options in the car. Unfortunately, learning how to play with these gadgets and remembering how to use the upgrades becomes irritating after a while, especially when I couldn't get them to work. My greatest disappointment related to the car as a driving machine. At first, I enjoy the power of the BMW. I could weave in and out of Traffic, turn corners easily, and feel the car respond instantly when I stepped on the gas. But once I had been driving the car for a week, I felt less of a sense of adventure. After all, driving fast on the highway and burning to much gas is thrilling for only a short time. I loved my uncle's car, and I'm glad I got to drive it. However, I'm quite satisfied to be back in my old Camry. I'v learned that a car with a glamorous image, great accessories, and a terrific engine are fun, but the car doesn't make a new person out of the driver.

Lines of Detail: A Walk-Through Assignment

Write a paragraph that compares or contrasts any experience you've heard about with the same experience as you lived it. For example, you could compare or contrast what you heard about starting college with your actual experience of starting college. You could compare or contrast what you heard about falling in love with your experience of falling in love, or what you heard about playing a sport with your own experience playing that sport. To write your paragraph, follow these steps:

Step 1: Choose the experience you will write about; then list all the similarities and differences between the experience as you heard about it and the experience as you lived it.

Step 2: To decide whether to write a comparison or contrast paragraph, survey your list to see which has more details, the similarities or the differences.

Step 3: Add details to your comparison or contrast list. Survey your list again, and group the details into points of comparison or contrast.

Step 4: Write a topic sentence that includes both subjects, focuses on comparison or contrast, and makes a point.

Step 5: Decide whether your paragraph will be in the subject-by-subject or point-by-point pattern. Write your outline in the pattern you choose.

Step 6: Write a draft of your paragraph. Revise your draft, checking the transitions, the order of the points, the space given to each subject, and the relevance and vividness of details. Combine any short, choppy sentences.

Step 7: Before you prepare the final copy of your paragraph, edit for word choice, spelling, punctuation, and transitions.

Topics for Writing a Comparison or a Contrast Paragraph

When you write on one of these topics, be sure to follow the stages of the writing process in preparing your comparison or contrast paragraph.

1. Compare or contrast what is most important in your life now to what was most important to you as a child. You may want to brainstorm about your values then and now before narrowing your focus to specific similarities or differences.

2. Compare or contrast any of the following:

two neighbors	two relatives	two college classes
two gifts	two jobs	two apartment complexes
two supervisors	two role models	two friends' Facebook pages
two clubs	two athletic teams	two flat-screen televisions

   If your instructor agrees, you may want to brainstorm points of comparison or contrast with a writing partner or a group.

3. Imagine that you are a reporter who specializes in helping consumers get the best for their money. Imagine that you are asked to rate two brands of the same supermarket item. Write a paragraph advising your readers which is the better buy. You can rate two brands of cola, yogurt, potato chips, toothpaste, ice cream, chocolate chip cookies, or paper towels—any item you can get in a supermarket.

   Be sure to devise *enough* points to contrast. You can't, for example, do a well-developed paragraph on just the taste of two cookies. But you can also discuss texture, color, smell, price, fat content, calories, number of chocolate chips, etc. If your instructor agrees, you may want to brainstorm topics or points of contrast with a group as a way of beginning the writing process. Then work on your own on the outline, drafts, and final version.

4. Compare or contrast your taste in music, or dress, or ways of spending leisure time with that of a close friend or family member.

5. If you have ever shopped online for sales or bargains offered by your favorite department store, contrast this experience with shopping inside the store itself. Select one specific store for this assignment, but be sure to contrast the specific differences between the two shopping choices. You should include three points of contrast in your paragraph.

Collaborate

6. Interview a person of your age group who comes from a different part of the country. (Note: There may be quite a few people from different parts of the country in your class.) Ask him or her about similarities or differences between his or her former home and this part of the country. You could ask about similarities or differences in dress, music, dating, nightlife, ways to spend leisure time, favorite entertainers, or anything else that you like.

   After the interview, write a paragraph that either shows how people of the same age group but from different parts of the country have different tastes in something like music or dress or share the same tastes in music, dress, etc. Whichever approach you use, include details you collected in the interview.

7. Examine the photograph of the two buildings. Then write a paragraph contrasting them. You can start by asking such questions as the following: Which is more elegant? Which seems less impressive? Which is more serene? Which is more modern? Use the details of the photograph to support your topic sentence.

8. Look carefully at the photograph of the two boys. Write a paragraph contrasting the mood of the boys with the atmosphere of the background.

Topics for Critical Thinking and Writing

1. When you were five or ten years younger, what did you expect to be doing and how did you expect to be living at the age you are now? Have you reached certain goals? If so, write about how closely your life today reflects those goals. If you haven't reached those goals yet, contrast the ways your present life is better or less satisfying than you once anticipated.

2. As a child, you probably admired several individuals whom you considered heroes or role models. Today, you may have different individuals you admire. Write a paragraph about the ways a hero or role model from your childhood is similar to or different from one you currently admire. To develop your details, you may need to examine the values you held as a child and the ones you deem important today.

> **Note:** Additional writing options suitable for comparison or contrast–related assignments can be found after the professional reading "Honesty and Dishonesty," in the "Readings for Writers" appendix at the end of this book.

Name _____   Section _____

Peer Review Form for a Comparison or Contrast Paragraph

After you've written a draft of your paragraph, let a writing partner read it. When your partner has completed the form below, discuss the comments. Then repeat the same process for your partner's paragraph.

I think the topic sentence of this paragraph is _____

_____

_____

_____

_____

The pattern of this paragraph is (a) subject by subject or (b) point by point. (Choose one.)

The points used to compare or contrast are _____

_____

_____

The part of the paragraph I liked best is about _____

The comparison or contrast is (a) easy to follow or (b) a little confusing. (Choose one.)

I have questions about or would like to know more about _____

I would like to see a few more details about _____

I would like to take out the part about _____

I would like to add or change a transition in front of the words _____

Other comments _____

_____

_____

_____

_____

_____

_____

_____

Reviewer's name _____

Classification

CHAPTER 7

Jumping In

*If you were hungry for a snack, which one of the foods in the photographs would you prefer to eat? Are the foods all equally fattening? If not, which is the most fattening? Which is the least? If you can rank the foods from least to most fattening, you will be using a technique called **classification.***

Chapter Objectives

Students will be able to (1) determine a clear basis for classifying a topic, (2) develop at least three basis-related categories, and (3) write a classification paragraph by devising key supporting details for each category.

WHAT IS CLASSIFICATION?

When you **classify,** you divide something into different categories, and you do it according to some basis. For example, you may classify the people in your neighborhood into three types: those you know well, those you know slightly, and those you don't know at all. Although you may not be aware of it, you have chosen a basis for this classification. You are classifying the people in your neighborhood according to *how well you know them.*

Hints for Writing a Classification Paragraph

1. **Divide your subject into three or more categories or types.** If you are thinking about classifying DVD players, for instance, you might think about dividing them into cheap players and expensive players. Your basis for classification would be the price of DVD players. But you would need at least one more type—moderately priced players. Using at least three types helps you to be reasonably complete in your classification.

2. Pick one basis for classification and stick with it. If you are classifying DVD players by price, you cannot divide them into cheap, expensive, and Chinese. Two of the categories relate to price, but "Chinese" does not.

In the following examples, notice how one item does not fit its classification and has been crossed out.

fishermen
fishermen who fish every day
weekend fishermen
~~fishermen who own their own boat~~

(If you are classifying fishermen on the basis of how often they fish, "fishermen who own their own boat" does not fit.)

tests
essay tests
objective tests
~~math tests~~
combination essay and objective tests

(If you are classifying tests on the basis of the type of questions they ask, "math tests" does not fit, because it describes the subject being tested.)

3. Be creative in your classification. While it is easy to classify drivers according to their age, your paragraph will be more interesting if you choose another basis for comparison, such as how drivers react to a very slow driver in front of them.

4. Have a reason for your classification. You may be classifying to help a reader understand a topic, or to help a reader choose something, or you may be trying to prove a point, to criticize, or to attack.

A classification paragraph must have a unifying reason behind it, and the detail for each type should be as descriptive and specific as possible. Determining your audience and deciding why you are classifying can help you stay focused and make your paragraph more interesting.

Exercise 1 **Practice: Finding a Basis for Classifying**

Write three bases for classifying each of the following topics. The first topic is done for you.

1. **topic to classify:** cats
   You can classify cats on the basis of

   a. _their age_____

   b. _their color_____

   c. _how friendly they are_____

2. **topic to classify:** bicycles
   You can classify bicycles on the basis of

   a. _____

   b. _____

   c. _____

3. **topic to classify:** breakfast cereal
   You can classify breakfast cereal on the basis of

   a. _____

   b. _____

   c. _____

4. **topic to classify:** greeting cards
   You can classify greeting cards on the basis of

   a. _____

   b. _____

   c. _____

Exercise 2   **Practice: Identifying What Does Not Fit the Classification**

In each list below, one item does not fit because it is not classified on the same basis as the others on the list. First, determine the basis for the classification. Then cross out the one item on each list that does not fit.

1. **topic:** pizza

   basis for classification: _____

   list: pepperoni pizza
           medium pizza
           mushroom pizza
           peppers and onions pizza

2. **topic:** scary movies

   basis for classification: _____

   list: special effects movies
           alien invasion movies
           slasher movies
           ghost movies

3. **topic:** candles

   basis for classification: _____

   list: candles on a cake
           candles at a community vigil
           candles in a candle shop
           candles on a dinner table

4. **topic:** teachers

   basis for classification: _____

   list: psychology teachers
           kindergarten teachers
           high school teachers
           college teachers

Exercise 3   **Practice: Finding Categories That Fit One Basis for Classification**

In the lines under each topic, write three categories that fit the basis of classification that is given. The first one is done for you.

1. **topic:** cartoons on television
   basis for classification: when they are shown
   categories:

   a. Saturday morning cartoons

   b. weekly cartoon series shown in the evening

   c. cartoons that are holiday specials

2. **topic:** football players
   basis for classification: at what level they play
   categories:

   a. _____

   b. _____

   c. _____

3. **topic:** sunburn
   basis for classification: how much damage it causes
   categories:

   a. _____

   b. _____

   c. _____

4. **topic:** business people
   basis for classification: how frequently they interact with the public
   categories:

   a. _____

   b. _____

   c. _____

WRITING THE CLASSIFICATION PARAGRAPH IN STEPS

PREWRITING CLASSIFICATION

First, pick a topic for your classification. The next step is to choose some basis for your classification.

Brainstorming a Basis for Classification

Sometimes the easiest way to choose one basis is to brainstorm about different types related to your topic and to see where your brainstorming leads you. For example, if you were to write a paragraph classifying phone calls, you could begin by listing anything about phone calls that occurs to you.

Phone Calls

sales calls at dinner time	people who talk too long
short calls	calls I hate getting
calls in the middle of the night	wrong numbers
calling plans	waiting for a call

The next step is to survey your list. See where it is leading you. The list on phone calls seems to have a few items about *unpleasant phone calls:*

> sales calls at dinner time
> wrong numbers
> calls in middle of night

Maybe you can label these "Calls I Do Not Want," and that will lead you toward a basis for classification. You might think about calls you *do not* want and calls you *do* want. You think further and realize that you want or do not want certain calls because of their effect on you.

You decide to use the effect of the calls on you as the basis for classification. Remember, however, that you need at least three categories. If you stick with this basis for classification, you can come up with three categories:

> calls that please me
> calls that irritate me
> calls that frighten me

By brainstorming, you can then gather details about your three categories.

Added Details for Three Categories

calls that please me

from boyfriend

good friends

catch-up calls—someone I haven't talked to for a while

make me feel close

calls that irritate me

sales calls at dinner time

wrong numbers

calls that interrupt

invade privacy

calls that frighten me

emergency call in middle of night

break-up call from boyfriend

change my life, indicate some bad change

Matching the Points Within the Categories

As you begin thinking about details for each of your categories, try to write about the same points in each type. For instance, in the list on phone calls, each category includes some details about who made the call:

> calls that please me—from good friends, my boyfriend
> calls that irritate me—from salespeople, unknown callers
> calls that frighten me—from the emergency room, my boyfriend

Each category also includes some details about why you react to them in a specific way:

> calls that please me—make me feel close
> calls that irritate me—invade privacy
> calls that frighten me—indicate some bad change

You achieve unity by covering the same points for each category.

Writing a Topic Sentence for a Classification Paragraph

The topic sentence for a classification paragraph should do two things:

1. It should mention what you are classifying,
2. It should indicate the basis for your classification by stating the basis or by listing your categories, or both.

Consider the details on phone calls. To write a topic sentence about the details, you

1. mention what you are classifying: phone calls,
2. indicate the basis for classifying by (a) stating the basis (their effect on me) or (b) listing the categories (calls that please me, calls that irritate me, and calls that frighten me). You may also state both the basis and the categories in the topic sentence.

Following these guidelines, you can write a topic sentence like this:

> I can classify phone calls according to their effect on me.

or

> Phone calls can be grouped into the ones that please me, the ones that irritate me, and the ones that frighten me.

Both of these topic sentences state what you're classifying and give some indication of the basis for the classification. Once you have a topic sentence, you are ready to begin the planning stage of writing the classification paragraph.

Collaborate

Exercise 4 **Collaborate: Creating Questions to Get Details for a Classification Paragraph**

Do this exercise with a partner or group. Each list below includes a topic, the basis for classifying that topic, and three categories. For each list, think of three questions that you could ask to get more details about the types. The first list is done for you.

1. **topic:** sports fans expressing support for a team
   basis for classification: how supportive they are
   categories: loyal fans, extremely loyal fans, fanatic fans
   questions you can ask:

   a. How will team support be expressed on each type's car?

   b. How much team-related clothing will each type wear to a game?

   c. How will each type's support be reflected in body decoration?

2. topic: college students waiting in line to register for classes
   basis for classification: how stressed they are
   categories: the calm, the mildly stressed, and the overstressed
   questions you can ask:

   a. _____

   b. _____

   c. _____

3. topic: dogs riding in cars
   basis for classification: how enthusiastic they are
   categories: the wildly ecstatic, the calm co-pilot, the unhappy traveler
   questions you can ask:

   a. _____

   b. _____

   c. _____

4. topic: peppers
   basis for classification: how hot they are
   categories: hot peppers, very hot peppers, unbearably hot peppers
   questions you can ask:

   a. _____

   b. _____

   c. _____

Exercise 5   **Practice: Writing Topic Sentences for a Classification Paragraph**

Review the topics, bases for classification, and categories in Exercise 4. Then, using that material, write a good topic sentence for each topic.

Topic Sentences

   for topic 1: _____

   _____

   for topic 2: _____

   _____

   for topic 3: _____

   _____

   for topic 4: _____

   _____

PLANNING **CLASSIFICATION**

Effective Order in Classifying

After you have a topic sentence and a list of details, you can create an outline. Think about which category you want to write about first, second, and so on. The order of your categories will depend on what you're writing about. If you're classifying ways to meet people, you can save the best for last. If you're classifying three habits that are bad for your health, you can save the worst one for last.

If you list your categories in the topic sentence, list them in the same order you will use to explain them in the paragraph.

Following is an outline for a paragraph classifying phone calls. The details have been put into categories. The underlined sentences have been added to clearly define each category before the details are given.

Outline for a Classification Paragraph

topic sentence: Phone calls can be grouped into the ones that please me, the ones that irritate me, and the ones that frighten me.

category 1, details

There are some calls that please me.
They make me feel close to someone.
I like calls from my boyfriend, especially when he calls just to say he is thinking of me.
I like to hear from good friends.
I like catch-up calls.
These are calls from people I haven't talked to in a while.

category 2, details

There are some calls that irritate me.
These calls invade my privacy.
Sales calls always come at dinner time.
Most are recorded and offer me help with my credit card bills.
I get at least four wrong-number calls each week.
All these calls irritate me, and I have to interrupt what I'm doing to answer them.

category 3, details

There are some calls that frighten me.
They are the calls that tell me about some bad change in my life.
I once got a call in the middle of the night.
It was from a hospital emergency room.
The nurse said my brother had been in an accident.
I once got a call from a boyfriend.
He said he wanted to break up.

You can use the following checklist to help you revise your own classification outline.

Checklist for Revising the Classification Outline

✔ Do I have a consistent basis for classifying?

✔ Does my topic sentence mention what I am classifying and indicate the basis for classification?

✔ Do I have enough to say about each category in my classification?

✔ Are the categories presented in the most effective order?

✔ Am I using clear and specific details?

With a revised outline, you can begin writing your draft.

Exercise 6   **Practice: Recognizing the Basis for Classification Within the Topic Sentence**

The topic sentences below do not state a basis for classification, but you can recognize the basis nevertheless. After you've read each topic sentence, write the basis for classification on the lines provided. The first one is done for you.

1. **topic sentence:** People at the supermarket can be classified into those who qualify for the express lane, those who push a moderately filled cart, and those who drag overloaded carts.

   basis for classification: how much they have in their carts

2. **topic sentence:** Cakes can be classified into those without icing, those with a glaze of icing, and those with more icing than cake.

   basis for classification: _____

3. **topic sentence:** Male singers fall into three categories: the ones pre-teens adore, the ones college students enjoy, and the ones grandparents remember.

   basis for classification: _____

4. **topic sentence:** There are three types of traffic police: the kind, the reasonable, and the rigid.

   basis for classification: _____

Exercise 7   **Collaborate: Adding Details to a Classification Outline**

Collaborate

Do this exercise with a partner or group. In this outline, add details where the blank lines indicate. Match the points covered in the other categories.

topic sentence: Talkers in my family can be classified into the non-stop conversationalists, the moderately talkative, and the silent minority.

details: My little brother is a nonstop conversationalist.

He has just started kindergarten.

He comes home full of excitement.

He wants to tell me about his day.

He is full of stories about his activities, his class-mates, and even the pet turtles in his classroom.

My mother is less talkative.

She works in a dentist's office.

She is tired when she comes home.

_____

_____

My father, unlike my little brother and my mother, rarely talks unless he must.

_____

He doesn't want to talk about his job, where he is under constant stress.

He will answer "yes" and "no" if I ask him a direct question.

I know the members of my family well, and I understand the reasons behind each one's level of communication.

DRAFTING AND REVISING **CLASSIFICATION**

You can transform your outline into a first draft of a paragraph by writing the topic sentence and the details in paragraph form. As you write, you can begin combining some of the short sentences, adding details, and inserting transitions.

Transitions in Classification

Various transitions can be used in a classification paragraph. The transitions you select will depend on what you are classifying and the basis you choose for classifying. For example, if you are classifying roses according to how pretty they are, you can use transitions like, "*one lovely kind* of rose," and "*another, more beautiful kind,*" and "*the most beautiful kind.*" In other classifications you can use transitions like, "the first type," "another type," or "the final type." In revising your classification paragraph, use the transitions that most clearly connect your ideas.

As you write your own paragraph, you may want to refer to a "kind" or a "type." For variety, try such other words as "class," "group," "species," "form," or "version" if it is logical to do so.

After you have a draft of your paragraph, you can revise and review it. The checklist below may help you with your revisions.

Checklist for Revising the Draft of a Classification Paragraph
✔ Does my topic sentence state what I am classifying?
✔ Does it indicate the basis of my classification?
✔ Should any of my sentences be combined?
✔ Do my transitions clearly connect my ideas?
✔ Should I add more details to any of the categories?
✔ Are the categories presented in the most effective order?

Following is a draft of the classification paragraph on phone calls. Compare these changes to the outline on page 170:

- An introduction has been added, in front of the topic sentence, to make the paragraph smoother.

- Some sentences have been combined.

- Some details have been added.

- Transitions have been added.

- A final sentence has been added, so that the paragraph makes a stronger point.

Draft of a Classification Paragraph

introduction added	I get many phone calls, but most of them fit into three types. Phone calls can be grouped into the ones that please me, the ones that irritate me, and the ones that
sentences combined	frighten me. There are some calls that please me because they make me feel close to someone. I like calls from my boyfriend, especially when he calls just to say he is thinking of me. I like to hear from my good friends. I
sentences combined and added detail	like catch-up calls, the calls from people I haven't talked to in a while that fill me in on
transition, sentences combined	what they have been doing. There are also calls that irritate me because they invade my privacy. Sales calls that feature recorded
transition	voices offering me help with my credit card bills always come at dinner time. In addition, I get at least four wrong-number calls each
transition	week. All these calls irritate me, and I have to interrupt what I'm doing to answer them. The more serious calls are the ones that frighten
sentences combined	me. They are the calls that tell me about some bad change in my life. I once got a midnight
transition, sentences combined	call from a hospital emergency room, informing me my brother had been in an accident.
final sentence added	Another time, a boyfriend called to tell me he wanted to break up. When I get bad news by phone, I realize that the telephone can bring frightening calls as well as friendly or irritating ones.

Exercise 8   **Practice: Combining Sentences for a Better Classification Paragraph**

The paragraph below has some short sentences that would be more effective if they were combined. Combine each pair of underlined sentences into one sentence. Write the new sentence in the space above the old ones.

The three types of worries in my life are brief worries, nagging little worries, and deep, serious worries. <u>Brief worries are frequent. They don't bother me for long.</u> A brief worry may occur when I notice that I need air in my left front tire. <u>For a moment, I have a vision. I see myself stranded on the highway. I am stranded because my left front tire is completely flat.</u> As soon as I make a mental note to put air in the tire the next time I use the car, the worry goes away. Nagging little worries are different. <u>They are minor concerns. They keep returning.</u> For instance, I know that I need to lose some weight. <u>I can push this concern to the back of my mind. I can even keep this worry out of my awareness for days. It still comes back.</u> Until I make a real effort to get more exercise, I will continue to worry about my weight. The worst kind of worry is the dark and serious kind. <u>For example, I lost a cousin last year. He was an innocent bystander. He happened to be near a drive-by shooting.</u> Now I fear for the safety of all the people I love. <u>However, I am working hard. I want to accept the loss of my cousin. I would also like to live my life as fully as I can in spite of my fear.</u>

Exercise 9 Practice: Identifying Transitions in a Classification Paragraph

Underline all the transitions in the paragraph below. The transitions may be words or groups of words.

Insects that sneak into my house can be classified into the ones I expect to find, the ones that startle me, and the ones that horrify me. The first type, the ones I expect to find, are mainly ants. I am used to seeing trails of ants in my kitchen. These ants make their way across the floor when I have spilled a few drops of a sugary drink or a few crumbs of a cookie. It is easy to get rid of these insects. I simply spray a bit of insect spray or wipe up the ants with a wet paper towel. There is another kind of insect that appears in my house frequently but still makes me cringe. This group of bugs includes all species of roaches, especially the ones that fly. Roaches are sly, and they can be large. When they fly, I feel as if they are trying to bomb me. I hate to kill a roach by stepping on it or swatting it with a newspaper because the roach may not die, or worse, it may die and leave a gooey mess. As a result, I waste about half of a can of insecticide on one roach. The final

kind of intruder insect is rare. However, I am now on the lookout for it. This spe-

cies showed up just outside my back door recently. It was a three-inch, fat, brown,

and shiny centipede. The idea that this form of garden pest was waiting to enter

my house sent me into shock. In this case, I called on my friend to deal with the

scary creature. However, I continue to think about the possibility that, barefoot,

I could have stepped out the back door and onto this latest version of an insect

intruder.

PROOFREADING CLASSIFICATION

As you prepare the final copy of your paragraph, you need to look carefully for easily overlooked errors in spelling, grammar, and punctuation. However, you can also use this stage to make a few changes such as adding a transition or two or improving your choice of words. These are the kinds of changes you will notice in the final version of the classification paragraph on phone calls. Compare the draft of the paragraph on page 173 to the final version and you'll notice several improvements:

- A transition, "My," links the second sentence to the first.

- The word choice has been refined: "someone" has been changed to "a person I care about" to make the detail more precise, and a reference to "irritate" has been changed to "annoy" to avoid repetition. The phrase "bad change in my life" has been replaced by "some crisis in my life," a more precise description.

Final Version of a Classification Paragraph

(Changes from the draft are underlined.)

    I get many phone calls, but most of them fall into one of three types. <u>My</u> phone calls can be grouped into the ones that please me, the ones that irritate me, and the ones that frighten me. There are some calls I want to receive because they make me feel close to <u>a person I care about.</u> I like calls from my boyfriend, especially when he calls just to say he is thinking of me. I like to hear from my good friends. I like catch-up calls, the calls from people I haven't talked to in a while that fill me in on what friends are doing. There are also calls I don't want because they invade my privacy. Sales calls that feature recorded voices offering me help with my credit card bills always come at dinner time. In addition, I get at least four wrong-number calls each week. All these calls <u>annoy</u> me, and I have to interrupt what I'm doing to answer them. The more serious calls are the ones I really don't want to receive. They are the calls that tell me about <u>some crisis in my life.</u> I once got a midnight call from a hospital emergency room, informing me my brother had been in an accident. Another time, a boyfriend called to tell me he wanted to break up. When I get bad news by phone, I realize that the telephone can bring frightening calls as well as friendly or irritating ones.

> **For your information:** A sample classification essay based on this topic and following the same writing steps can be found in Chapter 13, "Different Essay Patterns: Part Two."

Exercise 10 **Practice: Proofreading to Prepare the Final Version**

Following are two classification paragraphs with the kind of errors it is easy to overlook when you prepare the final version of an assignment. Correct the errors, writing above the lines. The first paragraph has eleven errors; the second has twelve errors.

Paragraph 1

When I helped my father cleanout the garage, I realized the mess fill into three categories: useful tools, useless gadgets, and objects with possibilities. The best part of this chore was finding a few forgotten tools. These ranged from a snow shovel that would work just fine after I had chipped away the crusted dirt, to a set of small screwdrivers, to a tire gauge. Someone in my family are always looking for a tire gauge, and now Id located one. Another small but useful item was, a clear plastic bottle with a spray cap. My mother is always combining powdery plant fertilizer with water so that she can apply the mixture to her flowers. A spray bottle will help her do her gardening. Useless gadgets outnumbered useful tools. One useless item was a hand-held portable plastic fan. Of course, it had no batteries inside, and the fan was worth less than the batteries would cost. at one time, I had probably given this fan, to my father, and it had found it's way to the dark corners of the garage. Another bad idea disguised as a cute gift was an inflatable shark. My father had bought the huge plastic shark for my little sister to float on when she was at a nearby lake, but everyone, including my sister, had fallen off the shark and in to the lake within minutes. Finally, I found a few objects with possibilities. A small whisk broom was dusty, but if I wash and rinse it, I can use the brush to clean the tires and trunk of my car. In addition, a stack of old, cracked flower pots are just right for holding the assortment of nails, screws, scissors, and electric

Tape my father has scattered around the garage. I knew that cleaning the garage would not be fun, but the sorting and saving was satisfying.

Paragraph 2

People who do not own a car have several options for getting from one place to another; and these options include taking a bus, riding a bicycle, and walking. Each of the options have its advantages. For example riding a bus keeps a person out of rain, snow, and other, bad weather. In addition, riding a bus is generally a safe and reliable way to get around. Another advantage is that passengers on a bus have time to read, study, call their friends, or make new friends with other passengers. For other reasons, ridding a bike is attractive. One great reason is the healthy exercise that bike riding provides. Also, a person who owns a bike owns transportation that is always available as long as they takes minimal care of the bike. Best of all, bikeriders can weave their way around traffic jams and often reach their destination faster than car's and buses can. Walkers enjoy unique benefits, to. They don't have to pay bus fair, so they can save money. They don't have to maintain a bicycle find a place to put it, or worry about someone stealing it. Walkers rely souly on their bodies to get them where they want to go. Walking is an uncomplicated way to travel.

Lines of Detail: A Walk-Through Assignment

Write a paragraph that classifies bosses on the basis of how they treat their employees. To write the paragraph, follow these steps:

Step 1: List all the details you can remember about bosses you have worked for or known.

Step 2: Survey your list. Then list three categories of bosses, based on how they treat their employees.

Step 3: Now that you have three categories, study your list again, looking for matching points for all three categories. For example, all three categories could be described by this matching point: where the boss works.

Step 4: Write a topic sentence that (a) names what you are classifying and (b) states the basis for classification or names all three categories.

Step 5: Write an outline. Check that your outline defines each category, uses matching points for each category, and puts the categories in an effective order.

Step 6: Write a draft of the classification paragraph. Check the draft, revising it until it has specific details, smooth transitions, and effective word choice.

Step 7: Before you prepare the final copy of your paragraph, check your last draft for any errors in punctuation, spelling, word choice, or mechanics.

Topics for Writing a Classification Paragraph

When you write on any of these topics, be sure to work through the stages of the writing process in preparing your classification paragraph.

Collaborate

1. Write a classification paragraph on any of the topics listed below. As a first step, you will need to narrow the topic. For example, instead of classifying all cars, you can narrow the topic to *sports* cars, or food to *food at a barbecue.* If your instructor agrees, brainstorm with a partner or a group to come up with (1) a basis for your classification, (2) categories related to the basis, and (3) points you can make to give details about each of the categories.

cartoon heroes	food	haircuts
horror movies	drivers	restaurants
romantic movies	birthdays	dreams
children	cars	scams
parents	cell phone options	salespeople
students	e-mail	dancers
professors	sportscasters	weddings
coaches	rumors	apologies
cameras	shoes	hobbies

Collaborate

2. Below are some topics. Each one already has a basis for classification. Write a classification paragraph on one of these choices. If your instructor agrees, work with a partner or group to brainstorm categories, matching points and details for the categories.

Classify the Following:
a. Exams on the basis of how *difficult they are*
b. Weekends on the basis of how *busy they are*
c. Valentines on the basis of how *romantic they are*
d. Breakfasts on the basis of how *healthy they are*
e. Holidays on the basis of *how pleasant they are for you*
f. Singers on the basis of *how popular they are with your friends*
g. Relatives on the basis of *how close they are to you*
h. Radio stations on the basis of *what kind of music they play*
i. Urban legends on the basis of *how illogical they are*

3. Look carefully at the photograph on next page. Then use its details to write a classification paragraph with this topic sentence:

College students can be classified according to the way they react to a professor's explanation of a concept.

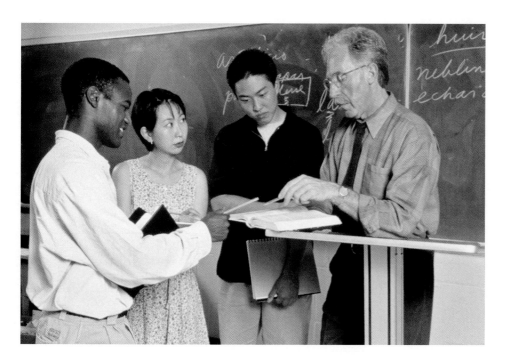

Topics for Critical Thinking and Writing

1. Make a list or freewrite about your major goals and then see if you can classify them according to a single basis. For example, you might group them according to how long it will take to fulfill them (immediate, mid-range, and long-term), or you might group them according to quality-of-life goals (such as career, relationship, and humanitarian goals). You may even have several secret goals that you do not share with many people. After you have determined the basis for classifying these goals, be sure your details about each goal relate to your basis of classification.

2. Music is an integral part of many people's lives, and some individuals believe that it plays a crucial role in coping with or celebrating life itself. Consider how important music is to people you know and classify them on the basis of how much they depend on music in their lives.

> **Note:** Additional writing options suitable for classification-related assignments can be found after the professional reading "The Dog Ate My Disk," which can be found in the "Readings for Writers" appendix at the end of this book.

PEARSON
mywritinglab   For support in meeting this chapter's objectives, log in to
www.mywritinglab.com and select **Paragraph Development—**
Division/Classification.

Name _____ Section _____

Peer Review Form for Classification Paragraph

After you've written a draft of your classification paragraph, let a writing partner read it. When your partner has completed the form below, discuss his or her comments. Then repeat the same process for your partner's paragraph.

This paragraph classifies _____ (write the topic).

The basis for the classification is _____
_____

The matching points are _____
_____

The part that could use more or better details is _____
_____

I have questions about or would like to know more about _____
_____

I would like to see more specifics about _____
_____

I would like to take out the part about _____
_____

The part of this paragraph I like best is _____
_____

Other comments _____
_____
_____
_____
_____
_____
_____
_____

Reviewer's name _____

Definition

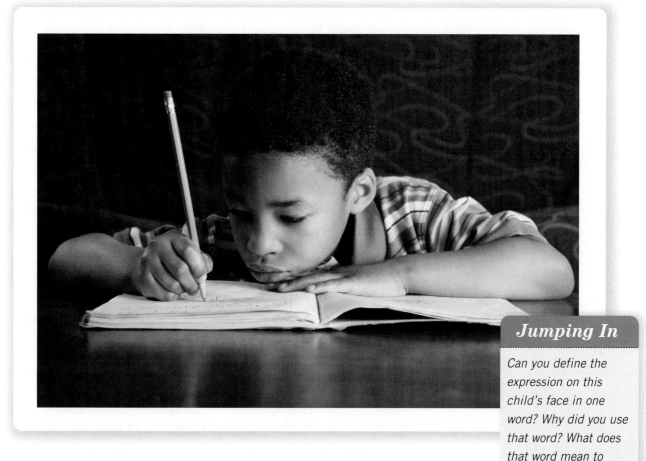

CHAPTER 8

Jumping In

*Can you define the expression on this child's face in one word? Why did you use that word? What does that word mean to you? By exploring such questions, you are now working toward a personal **definition**.*

Chapter Objectives

Students will be able to (1) identify formal and personal definitions, (2) recognize abstract and concrete terms, and (3) write a definition paragraph by defining a term according to its distinguishing characteristics.

WHAT IS DEFINITION?

A **definition** paragraph is one that explains *what a term means to you*. You can begin thinking about what a term means by consulting the dictionary, but your paragraph will include much more than a dictionary definition. It will include a personal definition.

You can select several ways to explain the meaning of a term. You can give examples, you can tell a story, or you can contrast your term with another term. If you were writing a definition of perseverance, for example, you could do one or more of the following: You could give examples of people you know who have persevered, you could tell a story about someone who persevered, or you could contrast perseverance with another quality, like impatience. You could also write about times when perseverance is most needed or about the rewards of perseverance.

Hints for Writing a Definition Paragraph

1. Pick a word or phrase that has a personal meaning for you and that allows you room to develop your idea. Remember that you will be writing a full paragraph on this term. Therefore, a term that can be defined quickly, in only one way, is not a good choice. For example, you would not have much to say about terms like "cauliflower" or "dental floss" unless you have strong personal feelings about cauliflower or dental floss. If you don't have such feelings, your paragraph will be very short.

When you think about a term to define, you might think about some personal quality you admire or dislike. If some quality provokes a strong reaction in you, you will probably have something to write about that term.

2. The topic sentence should have three parts. Include these items:

- the *term* you are defining
- the broad *class* or *category* into which your term fits
- the specific *distinguishing characteristics* that make the term different from all the others in the class or category

Each of the following topic sentences could be a topic sentence for a definition paragraph because it has the three parts.

              term   **category**   **distinguishing characteristics**
Resentment is the *feeling* that *life has been unfair.*

              term   **category**   **distinguishing characteristics**
A *clock watcher* is a *worker* who *is just putting in time, not effort.*

3. Select an appropriate class or category when you write your topic sentence.

    not this: Resentment is a thing that makes you feel life has been unfair. (Resentment is a feeling or an attitude. Say so.)

    not this: Resentment is when you feel life has been unfair. ("When" is a word that refers to a time, like noon or 7:00 P.M. Resentment is a feeling, not a time.)

    not this: Resentment is where a person feels life has been unfair. ("Where" is a word that refers to a place, like a kitchen or a beach. Resentment is not a place; it is a feeling.)

    but this: Resentment is the feeling that life has been unfair.

4. Express your attitude toward the term you are defining in the "distinguishing characteristics" part of the topic sentence. Make that attitude clear and specific.

    not this: Resentment is the feeling that can be bad for a person. (Many feelings can be bad for a person. Hate, envy, anger, and impatience, for instance, can all be bad. What is special about resentment?)

    not this: Resentment is an attitude of resenting another person or a circumstance. (Do not define a word with another form of the word.)

    but this: Resentment is the feeling that life has been unfair.

5. Use specific and concrete examples to explain your definition.
Concrete terms refer to things you can see, touch, taste, smell, or hear. Using concrete terms and specific examples will make your definition interesting and clear.

You may be asked to define an *abstract* idea like happiness. Even though an abstract idea cannot be seen, touched, tasted, smelled, or heard directly, you can give a personal definition of it by using concrete terms and specific examples.

> **not this:** Happiness takes place when you feel the joy of reaching a special goal. ("Joy" and "special goal" are abstract terms. Avoid defining one abstract term by using other abstract terms.)

> **but this:** I felt happiness when I saw my name at the top of the list of athletes picked for the team. Three months of daily, six-hour practices had paid off, and I had achieved more than I had set out to do. (The abstract idea of happiness is linked to a specific, concrete example of feeling happiness.)

If you remember to show, not tell, your reader what your term means, you'll have a better definition. Be especially careful not to define a term with another form of that term.

Exercise 1 | Practice: Recognizing Abstract and Concrete Words

In the list below, put an *A* by the abstract words and a *C* by the concrete words.

1. ____ elegance | 11. ____ courtesy
2. ____ respect | 12. ____ surgeon
3. ____ aspirin | 13. ____ patriotism
4. ____ trust | 14. ____ donor
5. ____ propeller | 15. ____ beauty
6. ____ traitor | 16. ____ song
7. ____ fear | 17. ____ suspicion
8. ____ sorrow | 18. ____ bracelet
9. ____ island | 19. ____ rainbow
10. ____ automobile | 20. ____ dignity

Exercise 2 | Practice: Completing a Topic Sentence for a Definition Paragraph

Following are unfinished topic sentences for definition paragraphs. Finish each sentence, so that the sentence expresses a personal definition of the term and has the three requirements for a definition's topic sentence.

1. A penny pincher is a person who _____

_____

2. A game plan is a strategy for _____

_____

3. A blabbermouth is a person who _____

_____

4. Tailgating is the traffic offense of _____

_____

5. A garage sale is an event in which _____

_____

6. A sore loser is a competitor who _____

_____

7. An angel of mercy is a person who _____

_____

8. Nitpicking is the habit of _____

_____

9. A lemon is a car that _____

_____

10. Cyber crime is a term for illegal activity that _____

_____

Exercise 3 **Practice: Recognizing Problems in Topic Sentences for Definition Paragraphs**

Review the three components that should be included in the topic sentence for a definition paragraph. Then read the topic sentences below, put an *X* next to each sentence that has a problem, and underline the part of the sentence that is faulty.

1. _____ A sense of fun is a gift for enjoying the humor in everyday situations.

2. _____ An amusement park is a place where people go to amuse themselves.

3. _____ Rage is when a person feels uncontrollable anger at another person or about a situation.

4. _____ Emotional stability is where someone feels in control of his or her emotions.

5. _____ Doubt is the inability to trust another person or oneself.

6. _____ Adolescence is the thing that all teenagers struggle to endure.

7. _____ A crisis is a sudden situation that creates fear and extreme stress.

8. _____ A temper tantrum is a loud and juvenile expression of anger.

9. ____ An old wives' tale is a story that is passed on from generation to generation and is most likely unreliable.

10. ____ A sweet tooth is a tendency to eat anything that contains a large quantity of sugar.

Exercise 4   **Collaborate: Writing Examples for Definition Paragraphs**

Below are incomplete statements from definition paragraphs. Complete them in the spaces below by writing specific examples. When you have completed the statements, share your work with a group. After each group member has read his or her examples aloud, discuss the examples. Which examples did you like best? Which are the clearest and most specific? Do some examples lead to a different definition of a term than other examples do?

Collaborate

The first part of each sentence has been started for you.

1. I first experienced bullying when _____

_____

_____

Another example of bullying took place at _____ and the

victim was _____

_____

_____

2. One person who was extremely generous to me was my older

brother. He gave me _____

when _____

_____

Some people are generous to family members; others perform acts

of generosity to total strangers. For example, _____

_____

_____

3. A person who represents courage to me is _____

because this person _____

_____

I showed some courage when _____

_____

_____

4. A time when a person must learn to forgive is when _____

_____

_____

I saw forgiveness in action when _____

_____

_____

WRITING THE DEFINITION PARAGRAPH IN STEPS

PREWRITING DEFINITION

To pick a topic for your definition paragraph, begin with some personality trait or type of person. For instance, you might define "the insecure person." If you listed your first thoughts, your list might look like this:

> the insecure person
> someone who is not emotionally secure
> wants (needs?) other people to make him or her feel good
> no self-respect

Using Questions to Get Details

Often, when you look for ideas to define a term, you get stuck with big, general statements or abstract words, or you simply cannot come up with enough to say. If you are having trouble getting ideas, think of questions about your term. Jot these questions down without stopping to answer them. One question can lead you to another question. Once you have five or more questions, you can answer them, and the answers will provide details for your definition paragraph.

If you were writing about the insecure person, for example, you could begin with questions like these:

> What are insecure people like?
> What behavior shows a person is insecure?
> How do insecure people dress or talk?
> What makes a person insecure?
> Why is insecurity a bad trait?
> How do insecure people relate to others?
> Does insecurity hurt the insecure person? If so, how?
> Does the insecure person hurt others? If so, how?

By scanning the questions and answering as many as you can, you can add details to your list. Once you have a longer list, you can review it and begin to group the items on the list. Following is a list of grouped details on the insecure person.

Grouped Details on the Insecure Person

wants (needs?) other people to make him or her feel important

no self-respect

insecure people have to brag about everything

a friend who brags about his car

they tell you the price of everything

they put others down

saying bad things about other people makes insecure people feel better

insecure people can never relax inside

can never enjoy being with other people

other people are always their competitors

must always worry about what others think of them

The Topic Sentence

Grouping the details can help you arrive at several main ideas. Can they be combined and revised to create a topic sentence? Following is a topic sentence on the insecure person that meets the requirements of naming the term, placing it in a category, and distinguishing the term from others in the category:

term   **category**   **distinguishing characteristics**

The *insecure person* is *someone* who *needs other people to make him or her feel respected and important.*

Once you have a topic sentence, you can begin working on the planning stage of the paragraph.

Exercise 5   **Practice: Designing Questions to Gather Details**

Following are terms that could be defined in a paragraph. For each term, write five questions that could lead you to details for the definition. The first one has been done for you as an example.

1. **term:** arrogance

   questions: a. Do I know anyone who displays arrogance?

   b. Is there any celebrity I think is arrogant?

   c. What is an arrogant action?

   d. What kind of remark is an example of arrogance?

   e. Why are people arrogant?

2. **term:** a nagger

   questions: a. _____

   b. _____

   c. _____

   d. _____

   e. _____

3. **term:** competence

   questions: a. _____

   b. _____

   c. _____

   d. _____

   _____

   e. _____

4. **term:** flexibility

   questions: a. _____

   b. _____

   c. _____

d. _____

e. _____

| Exercise 6 | **Practice: Grouping Related Ideas for a Definition Paragraph** |

Following is a list of ideas for a definition paragraph. Read the list several times; then group all the ideas on the list into one of the three categories below. Put the letter of the category next to each idea.

Categories:

G = how secrecy can be **good**

B = how secrecy can be **bad**

D = **dealing** with secrecy

List

1. _____ Too much secrecy can poison a marriage or other close relationship.

2. _____ A surprise birthday party can be a wonderful secret.

3. _____ To protect national security, some countries have to keep certain weapons programs a secret.

4. _____ A shameful family secret can poison generations who try to hide the truth.

5. _____ Trusting a friend or sibling can mean allowing that person the privacy of small secrets such as the content of his or her e-mail.

6. _____ Spying to discover a secret is rarely a good idea unless life-or-death matters are involved.

7. _____ Secret codes or ID numbers protect consumers' credit.

8. _____ Children should be allowed the privacy of having a secret, imaginary friend.

9. _____ In most cases, if a friend confides a secret pain or sorrow to another friend, the listener should keep the secret.

10. _____ A bank that hides the reality of its failing investments puts the well-being of thousands in jeopardy.

PLANNING   **DEFINITION**

To make an outline for a definition paragraph, start with the topic sentence and list the grouped details. Often, a first outline does not have many examples or concrete, specific details. A good way to be sure you put specific details and concrete examples into your paragraph is to include shortened versions of them in your revised outline. If you compare the following outline to the grouped list of details on page 186, you will see how specific details and concrete examples have been added.

Outline for a Definition Paragraph

topic sentence:	The insecure person is someone who needs other people to make him or her feel respected and important.
details:	Insecure people have to brag about everything.
	An insecure friend may brag about his car.
added detail	Insecure people wear expensive jewelry and tell you what it costs.
added detail	They brag about their expensive clothes.
added detail	They make sure they wear clothes with trendy labels, another kind of bragging.
	Insecure people put others down.
	Saying bad things about others makes insecure people feel better.
added example	When some friends were talking about Susan's great new job, Jill had to make mean remarks about Susan.
	Jill hated having Susan look like a winner.
	Insecure people can never relax inside.
	They can never enjoy being with other people.
	Other people are always their competitors.
added example	Luke can't enjoy any game of basketball unless he is the star.
	Insecure people must always worry about what others think of them.

When you prepare your own definition outline, use the following checklist to help you revise.

Checklist for Revising a Definition Outline

✔ Does my topic sentence include a category and the characteristics that show how my term is different from others in the category?

✔ Have I defined my term so that it is different from any other term?

✔ Am I being concrete and specific in the details?

✔ Do I have enough examples?

✔ Do my examples relate to the topic sentence?

✔ Are my details in the most effective order?

With a revised outline, you are ready to begin writing a rough draft of your definition paragraph.

Exercise 7 **Practice: Rewriting a Topic Sentence for a Definition Paragraph**

Below is an outline in which the topic sentence does not make the same point as the rest of the outline. Rewrite the topic sentence so that it relates to the details.

topic sentence:	A sixth sense is a strange sense.
details:	My grandmother believes that her sixth sense changed the course of her life.

At seventeen, my grandmother was engaged to be married to a man she had known all her life.

He was kind, handsome, and hardworking.

A month before the wedding, she met a new man, Daniel, at a cousin's party.

Daniel was a tall, skinny man with few social skills.

Although my grandmother thought Daniel was quite unattractive and irritating, she could not stop thinking about him.

A week later, she cancelled her wedding to her fiancé.

Daniel and my grandmother soon married and have been happy together for forty-five years.

I never believed in a sixth sense until recently.

I have taken the same route to work for years.

It involves crossing an old bridge.

One day last month, I was approaching the bridge when I had a sick feeling.

I decided to turn around and take a different way to work.

Later that day, a portion of the old bridge collapsed into the water.

Two drivers were seriously hurt.

Even animals seem to have a sixth sense.

I recently read the story of a mutt and his family.

At 4:00 A.M., the dog began whining, trying to wake up the mother and father.

Then the dog began running to the baby in her crib.

The father got up to push the dog outside.

Outside, the dog began to cry.

At last, the father opened the door and the dog ran inside, still crying.

Finally, both parents looked inside the crib.

The baby was unconscious and had a dangerously high fever.

In the emergency room, a doctor said the dog had saved the baby's life.

Rewrite the topic sentence: _____

_____

Exercise 8   **Practice: Revising an Example to Make It More Concrete and Specific**

The following outline contains one example that is too abstract. In the lines provided, rewrite the example that is too abstract, using more specific, concrete details.

topic sentence:	Culture shock is an extreme reaction to a new way of living.
details: **example 1**	I first experienced culture shock when I was sent away to summer camp.
	At first I was horrified by the living conditions at the camp.
	I and five other boys had to sleep in a rustic cabin with rickety bunk beds.
	The bathrooms were primitive.
	We went to bed early and were awakened even earlier.
	I hated the food, but there was no place to buy snacks.
	It took me a week of misery before I adjusted to the campers' lifestyle.
example 2	A weekend visit to New York City was my next experience of culture shock.
	I could not believe the thousands of people cramming the sidewalks.
	I tried hard to keep up with the pace of the New Yorkers as they confidently and aggressively made their way.
	The crush of travelers on the subway made me nervous.
	In my grandfather's New York apartment, I couldn't see how the man could live in such a small, dark, dirty place surrounded by constant noise.
example 3	Culture shock also struck on my first days on a college campus.
	Students looked different than they did in high school.
	Classes were different, too.
	My schedule seemed so easy.
	I felt a little confused because the rules seemed looser than those in high school.
	On the other hand, I was nervous about messing up.

The revised example: _____

_____

_____

_____

_____

_____

_____

_____

_____

_____

_____

_____

_____

_____

DRAFTING AND REVISING　**DEFINITION**

To write the first draft of your definition paragraph, you can rewrite the outline in paragraph form, combining some of the short sentences and adding more details. Remember that your purpose in this definition paragraph is to explain your personal understanding of a term. Therefore, you want to be sure that your topic sentence is clear and that your explanation connects your details to the topic sentence. Careful use of transitions will link your details to your topic sentence.

Transitions

Since you can define a term in many ways, you can also use many transitions. If you are listing several examples in your paragraph, you can use transitions like "first," "second," and "finally." If you are contrasting your term with another, you can use transitions like "on the other hand" or "in contrast." You may want to alert or remind the reader that you are writing a definition paragraph by using phrases like "can be defined as," "can be considered as," "means that," or "implies that."

Because many definitions rely on examples, the transitions below are ones you may want to use.

INFO BOX: **Transitions for a Definition Paragraph**

a classic case of ____ is ____	in fact	another time
another case	in one case	sometimes
for example	in one instance	specifically
for instance	one time	

Sample Draft

Following is a draft of the definition paragraph on the insecure person. When you read it, you'll notice several changes from the outline on page 189.

- Transitions have been added in several places. Some transitions let the reader know an example is coming, some transitions link one point about the topic to another point, other transitions connect an example to the topic sentence.

- Examples have been made concrete and specific.

- The word choice has been improved.

Draft of a Definition Paragraph

	The insecure person is someone who needs other people to make him or her feel respected and important. The insecure
transition	person loves to brag about everything. <u>For instance,</u> a friend
specific details	may brag about his car. <u>He tells everyone he meets that he</u> <u>drives a Hyundai Genesis Coupe.</u> An insecure person tells you the price of everything. He wears expensive jewelry and tells
transition	you what it costs, <u>like</u> the person who always flashes his
added detail,	<u>Rolex</u> watch. <u>Another</u> insecure person will brag about her expen-
transition	sive clothes or make sure she always wears clothes with trendy
transition	labels, <u>another kind</u> of bragging. <u>Bragging is not the only way</u>
transition	<u>an insecure person tries to look good;</u> he or she may put other people down. Saying bad things about other people can put the
transition	insecure person on top. <u>For instance,</u> some friends were recently talking about another friend, Susan, who had just started a great
added details	new job. Jill had to add some mean remarks <u>about how lucky</u> <u>Susan had been to get the job since Susan really wasn't quali-</u> <u>fied for it.</u> Jill hated having Susan look like a winner. The inse-
transitions	cure person can hurt others <u>but also</u> suffers inside. <u>Such a person</u> can never relax because he or she always sees other people as
transition	competitors. <u>An example of this attitude is</u> seen in Luke, <u>a col-</u>
added details	<u>lege acquaintance who always plays pickup basketball games.</u>
added details	<u>Even though the games are just for fun,</u> Luke can't enjoy any game unless he is the star. Luke is a typically insecure person,
transition	<u>for</u> he must always worry about what others think of him.

The following checklist may help you to revise the draft of your own definition paragraph.

Checklist for Revising the Draft of a Definition Paragraph

✔ Is my topic sentence clear?

✔ Have I written enough to define my term clearly?

✔ Is my definition interesting?

✔ Could it use another example?

✔ Could it use more details?

✔ Do I need to combine any sentences?

✔ Do I need any words, phrases, or sentences to link the examples or details to the topic sentence?

✔ Do I need any words, phrases, or sentences to reinforce the topic sentence?

Exercise 9   **Practice: Adding Examples to a Draft of a Definition Paragraph**

Two of the following paragraphs need examples with concrete, specific details to explain their points. Where the lines indicate, write an example with concrete, specific details. Each example should be at least two sentences long. The first paragraph is done for you.

1. Listlessness is the feeling that nothing is worth starting. After a hectic week, I often wake up on Saturday morning feeling listless. I just do not have the energy to do the things I intended to do. I may have planned to wash my car, for example, but I cannot bring myself to get going. I cannot put together the bucket, detergent, brushes, and window cleaner I need to start the process. I tell myself, "Why wash the car? It will probably rain anyway." Another time I feel listless is when I am faced with a big assignment. For instance, I hate to start a term paper because there is so much to do. I have to think of a topic, do research, read, take notes, plan, write, and revise. When I am faced with so many things to do, I don't do anything. I tell myself it is not worth starting because I will probably get a bad grade on the paper anyway. I put off getting started. I let listlessness get the better of me.

2. Tact is the ability to express oneself without needlessly hurting another person's feelings. My boss at the clothing store where I work is a very tactful person. Customers often ask my boss how they look in an item they are trying on. My boss must be tactful in her answer. _____

_____

_____

_____ I have tried to be tactful in declining an invitation.

_____

_____

_____

_____

Of course, there are times when there is no way to be both tactful and honest.

_____

_____

_____

Although tact cannot always prevent others from feeling embarrassment or pain, tact is a great tool in many situations.

3. A clock watcher is a person who always wants to leave a place early. Clock watchers are commonly seen in the workplace. _____

_____

_____

_____

_____ Clock

watchers have a hard time sitting still in a classroom. _____

_____

_____

_____

Clock watchers sometimes obsess about leaving a large sports or social event

early. _____

_____

_____

_____ Clock watchers cannot really experience

the present moment because they are preoccupied with getting away from it.

Exercise 10 **Practice: Identifying the Words That Need Revision in a Definition Paragraph**

The following paragraph has too many vague, abstract words. Underline the words that you think should be replaced with more specific or concrete words or examples.

Chronic complainers are people who rarely appreciate what they have or

where they are and who like to share their dissatisfaction. A chronic complainer

might have a nice car, but he will always note its flaws. For example, he will

remind others that his car doesn't get the best gas mileage or doesn't have other

stuff. Chronic complainers are also likely to be unhappy with their jobs or financial

situation. A chronic complainer who works in a bank, for example, may whine that

she is only a teller when she should be higher up by now. Another chronic com-

plainer will spend hours moaning that he cannot afford anything because his boss

is unfair. Eventually, friends and relatives tend to spend less time with a chronic

complainer. It is not fun to be around someone who can poison any social event,

even a conversation over a cup of coffee, with bitterness, anger, and whatnot.

Sooner or later, a chronic complainer will be unhappy about losing friends.

| Exercise 11 | **Practice: Combining Sentences in a Definition Paragraph** |

The following definition paragraph has some short, choppy sentences that could be combined. These pairs or clusters of sentences are underlined. Combine each pair or cluster into one smooth sentence, and write the new sentence in the space above the original ones.

A peacemaker is a socially gifted person who knows how to resolve con-flicts. My mother is a peacemaker. <u>She has a natural skill. Her skill enables her to detect a family conflict. It is a family conflict that is about to begin. She can resolve it. She can resolve it quickly.</u> She coaxes the unhappy family members into conversing honestly and calmly. Soon, what could have been a hot argument has cooled down. My high school hockey coach was a peacemaker, too. <u>However, he was different from my mother. He was a tough, often physically involved settler of arguments.</u> Hockey can be a brutal game. My coach could sense anger brewing between players. <u>Before it started and spread, he did something. He grabbed the unhappy players. He scolded, shouted, and threatened them.</u> His talent was his ability to push the players face to face before they created a chaotic situation. In a less physical way, some diplomats can bring nations together. <u>A diplomat can do this by convincing hostile countries to send their representatives. Each country's representatives meet at a neutral location.</u> There the representatives and the dip-lomats talk calmly. <u>In the neutral atmosphere, things can happen. Treaties can be written. Trade agreements can be reached.</u> Peacemaking can be global, or it can be personal. Either way, a special person has to initiate it.

| Exercise 12 | **Practice: Adding the Right Transitions to a Definition Paragraph** |

In the following paragraph, circle the correct transition in each of the pairs.

Calm is a state of mind in which a person can think clearly. Words such as "agitated," "upset," "elated," or "thrilled" describe the opposite of calm. Neither emotional lows nor highs are a good background for making a major decision. For instance /In one case, people making choices about getting a job, leaving col-lege, or starting a relationship must be able to weigh the positive and negative aspects of their choice. In one instance/ Specifically, when they reach a decision, people need to rely on their ability to reason rather than on a momentary high or low mood. That is, they must reach a level of calm. One way that people can recognize a calm state of mind is to be sure that they do not feel rushed into making a decision. Sometimes /In another case, people refer to "calm seas," and the term refers to a good time to sail. In calm seas, ships may not sail as fast, but they are not tossed about by rough waves. In the same way, calm people are not tossing up and down emotionally. One time/ In fact, calm people are slowly but confidently moving to a choice.

PROOFREADING   **DEFINITION**

As you prepare the final version of your definition paragraph, check your latest draft to see if it needs a few improvements in grammar, spelling, and word choice. You may also want to check for good transitions and effective details. If you compare the draft on page 193 to the following final version of the paragraph on the insecure person, you will see a few more revisions:

- To keep the paragraph consistent in person, the word "you" has been taken out.
- The wording has been improved so that it is more precise.
- Transitions have been added to reinforce the topic sentence.

Final Version of a Definition Paragraph

(Changes from the draft are underlined.)

    The insecure person is someone who needs other people to make him or her feel respected and important. <u>To get respect,</u> the insecure person loves to brag about everything. For instance, a friend may brag about his car. He tells everyone he meets that he drives a Hyundai Genesis Coupe. An insecure person tells <u>people</u> the price of everything. He wears expensive jewelry and tells <u>people</u> what it costs, like the man who always flashes his Rolex watch. Another insecure person will brag about her expensive clothes or make sure she wears clothes with trendy labels, another kind of bragging. Bragging isn't the only way an insecure person tries to look good; he or she may also <u>criticize</u> other people. <u>Criticizing</u> others can put the insecure person on top. For instance, some friends were recently talking about another friend, Susan, who had just started a great new job. Jill had to add some mean remarks about how lucky Susan had been to get the job since Susan really wasn't qualified for it. Jill couldn't stand to have Susan look like a winner. The insecure person <u>like Jill</u> can hurt others but also suffers inside. Such a person can never relax because he or she always sees other people as competitors. An example of this attitude can be seen in Luke, a college acquaintance who always plays pick-up basketball games. Even though the games are just for fun, Luke can't enjoy any game unless he is the star. Luke is a typically insecure person, for he must always worry about what others think of him.

> **For your information:** A sample definition essay based on this topic and following the same writing steps can be found in Chapter 13, "Different Essay Patterns: Part Two."

| Exercise 13 | **Practice: Correcting Errors in the Final Version of a Definition Paragraph** |

Below are two definition paragraphs with the kinds of errors that are easy to overlook in a final version. Correct the errors by writing above the lines. There are eleven errors in the first paragraph and thirteen in the second paragraph.

1. A luxury is a pleasant experience that a person does not usally have a chance to enjoy. For example, to a person who works 8 or ten hours a day at a demanding job, getting out of work two hrs. early is a luxury. It gives that person time to do anything he or she choses, from catching up on chores to spending time with a friend. A millionaire whose schedule allows his more freedom may think a luxury is a trip to the Seychelles Islands for sun and scuba diving. On the other hand, a child who doesn't spend much time with his busy parents' will feel that a whole day spent with his mother or father is a luxury. One Strange aspect of luxury is that something that was once a luxury may lose it's appeal if it is experience regularly. For example, the worker who becomes accustomed to leaving work early may gradually take the new schedule for granted. Similarly, a rich woman who can travel anywhere may become bored by cruises and sightseeing. However, lonely children who gets to spend more time with a parent may no longer consider that time a luxury, but they will never become sick of the attention.

2. A brat is a child, or immature adult who craves control. A child brat can be recognize by their frequent tantrums. The child brat screams shakes, runs, kicks, and generally makes a scene when he or she demand something. For example, the child brat may see a toy in a store and scream when a parent refuses to by the toy. Another situation in which a child brat misbehaves occurrs at bedtime. The brat may have to be carried, kicking and screaming, to bed. Adult brats are somewhat different from child brats. Adult brats can be recognized by two kinds of behavior: explosive or silent. They may not want toys, but they do want control.

An adult brat wants to see the movie of his choice and can sulk silently for days

if his friends choose a different film. One the other hand, adult brats can act like

children and resort to more dramatic misbehavior. A male adult brat has been

known to threw a flashlight to the floor when he canot get the flashlight to work.

A female adult brat quietly may toss a pear of earrings into the trash if she is angry

at the person who gave her the jewlry. Brats of all ages are proof that some people

who crave control have not learned to control themself.

Lines of Detail: A Walk-Through Assignment

Write a paragraph that gives a personal definition of the secure person. To
write the paragraph, follow these steps:

Step 1: List all your ideas about a secure person.

Step 2: Write at least five questions that can add details about a
secure person. Answer the questions as a way of adding
details to your list.

Step 3: Group your details; then survey your groups.

Step 4: Write a topic sentence that includes the term you are defining,
puts the term into a category, and distinguishes the term from
others in the category.

Step 5: Write an outline. Begin by writing the topic sentence and
the groups of details. Then add more details and specific
examples.

Step 6: Write a draft of your paragraph. To revise, check that you
have enough examples, that your examples fit your definition,
and that the examples are in an effective order. Combine any
choppy sentences, and add transitions. Remember that careful
revision may involve writing several rough drafts before you
are satisfied.

Step 7: Before you prepare the final version of your definition paragraph, check the punctuation, word choice, transitions, and
grammar of your latest draft.

Topics for Writing a Definition Paragraph

When you write on any of these topics, be sure to work through the stages
of the writing process in preparing your definition paragraph.

1. Define an abstract term using concrete, specific details. Choose
from the following list. You can begin by looking up the term in a
dictionary to be sure you understand the dictionary meaning. Then
write a personal definition.

   You can begin by freewriting. If your instructor agrees, you can
read your freewriting to a group for reactions and suggestions. If
you prefer, you can begin by brainstorming a list of questions to

Collaborate

help you define the term. Again, if your instructor agrees, you can work with a group to develop brainstorming questions. Here is the list of abstract terms:

loyalty	generosity	bliss
superstition	style	betrayal
boredom	charisma	persistence
initiative	charity	prejudice
ambition	selfishness	envy
suspicion	success	independence
loneliness	shame	endurance
rage	self-deception	self-discipline

Collaborate

2. Write a definition of a type of person. Develop your personal definition with specific, concrete details. You can choose one of the following types or choose your own type.

Freewriting on the topic is one way to begin. If your instructor agrees, you can read your freewriting to a group for reactions and suggestions. You can also begin by brainstorming a list of questions to help you define your term. If your instructor agrees, you can work with a group to develop brainstorming questions. Following is the list of types.

the procrastinator	the bully	the daredevil
the braggart	the bodybuilder	the jock
the chocaholic	the neatness fanatic	the apologizer
the organizer	the dieter	the joker
the optimist	the manipulator	the dreamer
the two-timer	the whiner	the buddy
the workaholic	the old reliable friend	the fan
the compulsive liar	the Mr./Ms. Fixit	the achiever

3. Think of one word that best defines you. In a paragraph, define that word, using yourself as a source of examples and details. To begin, you may want to freewrite about several words that define you; then you can select the most appropriate one.

Computer

4. Using Google or a similar search engine, type in the words "Web log" and "blog." Investigate as many definitions as you can of the term "blog." Based on this information, write a definition of this term and assume your audience is a group of adults who have never read or written a blog. Your definition may include examples of blogs from the fields of politics, entertainment, news, business, and education.

5. Study the photograph of the soldiers in battle. Then write a paragraph that defines (1) combat stress or (2) courage under fire.

Topics for Critical Thinking and Writing

1. Think of a word or phrase that has different meanings to different groups (age groups, political groups, people in a variety of socioeconomic levels, and so on). For example, "freedom" means something different to a person in prison than it means to a teen who has a curfew. Choose an abstract word and write at least three meanings of it. Be sure to assign each meaning to a specific group or type of individual.

2. Too often, people resort to using stereotypes when they describe a group or even a type of person. For example, the word "politician" is a derogatory term when it is spoken with a condescending tone of voice in certain circumstances, but not all those who choose a career in public service are the same. As another example, "a free spirit" can be described as someone who is either highly creative and independent or unpredictable and erratic. Consider three terms that are commonly used today as quick, stereotypical definitions for complicated issues. In addition, explain how each term has alternate meanings.

> **Note:** Additional writing options suitable for definition-related assignments can be found after the professional reading "Terrorism," which can be found in the "Readings for Writers" appendix at the end of this book.

Name _____   Section _____

Peer Review Form for a Definition Paragraph

After you've written a draft of your definition paragraph, let a writing partner read it. When your partner has completed the form below, discuss the comments. Then repeat the same process for your partner's paragraph.

In the topic sentence, the term being defined is placed in this category or class _____

_____

In the topic sentence, the characteristic(s) that make(s) the term different from others in its class or category is/are _____

_____

The most enjoyable or interesting part of this definition starts with the words _____

_____

The part that could use a clear example or more details starts with the words _____

_____

I have questions about or would like to know more about _____

_____

I would like to take out the part about _____

_____

Other comments _____

_____

_____

_____

_____

_____

_____

_____

_____

_____

Reviewer's name _____

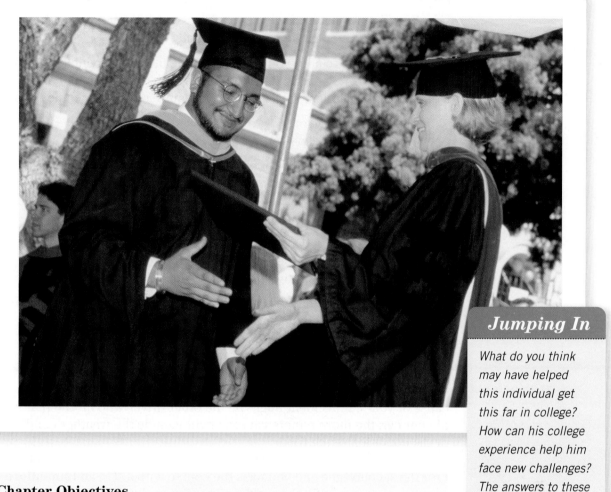

Chapter Objectives

Students will be able to (1) identify immediate and long-range causes and effects, (2) devise suitable topics, and (3) write a cause or effect paragraph that incorporates appropriate transitions and details.

WHAT IS CAUSE AND EFFECT?

Almost every day, you consider the causes or effects of events so that you can make choices and take action. In writing a paragraph, when you explain the **reasons** for something, you are writing about **causes.** When you write about the **results** of something, you are writing about **effects.** Often in writing, you consider both the causes and effects of a decision, an event, a change in your life, or a change in society, but in this chapter, you will be asked to *concentrate on either causes (reasons) or effects (results).*

Hints for Writing a Cause or Effect Paragraph

    1. Pick a topic you can handle in one paragraph. A topic you can handle in one paragraph is one that (a) is not too big and (b) doesn't require research.

Some topics are so large that you probably can't cover them in one paragraph. Topics that are too big include ones like:

Why People Get Angry
Effects of Unemployment on My Family

Other topics require you to research the facts and to include the opinions of experts. They would be good topics for a research paper, but not for a one-paragraph assignment. Topics that require research include ones like:

The Causes of Divorce
The Effects of Television Viewing on Children

When you write a cause or effect paragraph, choose a topic you can write about by using what you already know. That is, make your topic smaller and more personal. Topics that use what you already know are ones like:

Why Children Love Animal Cartoon Characters
The Causes of My Divorce
What Enlistment in the Navy Did for My Brother
How Alcoholics Anonymous Changed My Life

2. Try to have at least three causes or effects in your paragraph. Be sure you consider immediate and remote causes or immediate and remote effects. Think about your topic and gather as many causes or effects as you can *before* you start drafting your paragraph.

An event usually has more than one cause. Think beyond the obvious, the **immediate cause,** to more **remote causes.** Although the immediate cause of your car accident might be the other driver who hit the rear end of your car, the more remote causes might include the weather conditions or the condition of the road.

Situations can have more than one result, too. If you take Algebra I for the second time and you pass the course with a "C," an **immediate result** is that you fulfill the requirements for graduation. But there may be other, **more remote results.** Your success in Algebra I may help to change your attitude toward mathematics courses, may build your confidence in your ability to handle college work, or may lead you to sign up for another course taught by the same teacher.

3. Make your causes and effects clear and specific. If you are writing about why short haircuts are popular, don't write, "Short haircuts are popular because everybody is getting one," or "Short haircuts are popular because they are a trend." If you write either of those statements, you have really said, "Short haircuts are popular because they are popular."

Think further. Have any celebrities been seen with this haircut? Write the names of actors, athletes, or musicians who have the haircut, or the name of the movie and the actor that started the trend. By giving specific details that explain, illustrate, or describe a cause or effect, you help the reader understand your point.

4. Write a topic sentence that indicates whether your paragraph is about causes or effects. You should not announce, but you can *indicate*.

not this: The effects of my winning the scholarship are going to be
    discussed. (an announcement)
but this: Winning the scholarship changed my plans for college.
    (indicates effects will be discussed)

You can *list* a short version of all your causes or effects in your topic sentence, like this:

> The high price of concert tickets has enriched a few performers and promoters, excluded many fans, and threatened the future of live entertainment.

You can just *hint* at your points by summarizing them, like this:

> The high price of concert tickets has brought riches to a few but hurt many others.

Or you can use words that *signal* causes or effects.

words that signal causes: reasons, why, because, motives, intentions
words that signal effects: results, impact, consequences, changed, threatened, improved

Exercise 1   Practice: Selecting a Suitable Topic for a Cause or Effect Paragraph

Below is a list of topics. Some are suitable for a cause or effect paragraph. Some are too large to handle in one paragraph, some would require research, and some are both too large and would require research. Put an *X* next to any topic that is not suitable.

1. _____ Why I Am Afraid of Heights

2. _____ The Effects of Alcoholism on the Children of Alcoholics

3. _____ The Impact of Unemployment on College Students

4. _____ The Reasons I Was Accused of Burglary

5. _____ My Father's Motives for Leaving His Family

6. _____ How a Stranger's Kindness Changed One Baby's Fate

7. _____ The Worldwide Consequences of Texting While Driving

8. _____ The Causes of Drug Addiction

9. _____ How Gambling Changes Personalities

10. _____ What Causes War between Nations

Exercise 2   Practice: Recognizing Cause and Effect in Topic Sentences

In the list below, if the topic sentence is for a cause paragraph, put *C* next to it. If the sentence is for an effect paragraph, put *E* next to it.

1. _____ Once my brother left home, he developed more mature attitudes toward earning, spending, and saving money.

2. _____ Chloe's trip to Brazil had a surprising impact on her career plans.

3. _____ I broke up with my boyfriend to escape his constant criticism, make my own friends, and reconnect with my family.

4. _____ Dr. Menendez has three reasons for opening a free clinic near the farm workers' camp.

5. _____ One successful semester at college changed my mother's hopes, ambitions, and self-esteem.

6. _____ College students need access to caring adults because the students face an overwhelming number of choices and challenges.

7. _____ When adult children leave home, their parents may feel lonely, unfocused, and even unloved.

8. _____ Failing an advanced biology class had an impact on my choice of career.

9. _____ One way to explain Enrique's fear of commitment is to examine his childhood.

10. _____ Working from home is transforming me into a more responsible person.

WRITING THE CAUSE OR EFFECT PARAGRAPH IN STEPS

PREWRITING   CAUSE OR EFFECT

Once you've picked a topic, the next—and very important—step is getting ideas. Because this paragraph will contain only causes *or* effects and details about them, you must be sure you have enough causes or effects to write a developed paragraph.

Freewriting on a Topic

One way to get ideas is to freewrite on your topic. Since causes and effects are so clearly connected, you can begin by freewriting about both and then choose one, causes or effects, later.

If you were thinking about writing a cause or effect paragraph on owning a car, you could begin by freewriting something like this:

Freewriting on Owning a Car

A car of my own. Why? I needed it. Couldn't get a part-time job without one. Because I couldn't get to work. Needed it to get to school. Of course I could have taken the bus to school. But I didn't want to. Feel like a grown-up when you have a car of your own. Freedom to come and go. I was the last of my friends to have a car. Couldn't wait. An old Ford. But I fixed it up nicely. Costs a lot to maintain. Car payments, car loan. Car insurance.

Now you can review the freewriting and make separate lists of the causes and effects you wrote down:

causes (reasons)

needed to get a part-time job
needed to get to school
my friends had cars

effects (results)

feel like a grown-up
freedom to come and go

costs a lot to maintain
car payments
car loan
car insurance

Because you have more details on the effects of owning a car, you decide to write an effects paragraph.

Your list of effects can be used several ways. You can add to it if you think of ideas as you are reviewing your list. You can begin to group ideas in your list and then add to it. Following is a grouping of the list of effects; grouping helps you see how many effects and details you have.

effects of getting my own car

effect 1: I had to pay for the car and related expenses.
details: costs a lot to maintain
                car payments
                car loan
                car insurance

effect 2: I had the freedom to come and go.
details: none

effect 3: I felt like a grown-up.
details: none

Will these effects work in a paragraph? One way to decide is to try to add details to the ones that have no details. Ask questions to get those details.

effect 2: I had the freedom to come and go.

What do you mean?
Well, I didn't have to beg my father for his truck anymore. I didn't have to get rides from friends. I could go to the city when I wanted. I could ride around just for fun.

effect 3: I felt like a grown-up.

What do you mean, "like a grown-up"?
Adults can go where they want, when they want. They drive themselves.

If you look carefully at the answers to the questions above, you'll find that the two effects are really *the same*. By adding details to both effects, you'll find that both are saying that owning a car gives you the adult freedom to come and go.

So the list needs another effect of owning a car. What else happened, how else did things change when you got your car? You might answer:

I worried about someone hitting my car.
I worried about bad drivers.
I wanted to avoid the scratches you get in parking lots.

With answers like these, your third effect could be:

I became a more careful driver.

Now that you have three effects and some details, you can rewrite your list. You can add details as you rewrite.

List of Effects of Getting My Own Car

effect 1:   I had to pay for the car and related expenses.
details: costs a lot to maintain
             car loans
             car insurance

effect 2:   I had the adult freedom to come and go.
details: didn't have to beg my father for his truck
             didn't have to get rides from friends
             could go to the city when I wanted
             could ride around for fun

effect 3:   I became a more careful driver.
details: worried about someone hitting the car
             worried about bad drivers
             wanted to avoid the scratches cars get in parking lots

Devising a Topic Sentence

With at least three effects and some details for each effect, you can create a topic sentence. The topic sentence for this paragraph should indicate that the subject is the *effects* of getting a car. You can summarize all three effects in your topic sentence, or you can just hint at them. A possible topic sentence for the paragraph can be:

Owning my own car cost me money, gave me freedom, and made me more careful about how I drive.

or

Once I got a car of my own, I realized the good and bad sides of ownership.

With a topic sentence and a fairly extensive list of details, you are ready to begin the planning stage in preparing your paragraph.

Collaborate

Exercise 3   **Collaborate: Devising Questions for a Cause or Effect Paragraph**

Below are four topics for cause or effect paragraphs. For each topic below, write five questions that could lead you to ideas on the topic. (The first one is completed for you.) After you've written five questions for each topic, give your list to a member of your writing group. Ask him or her to add one question to each topic and then to pass the exercise on to the next member of the group. Repeat the process so that each group member adds to the lists of all the other members.

Later, if your instructor agrees, you can answer the questions (and add more questions and answers) as a way to begin writing a cause or effect paragraph.

1. **topic:** the effects of cell-phone cameras on crime
   questions that can lead to ideas and details:

   a. _Are unsuspecting people photographed and blackmailed?_

b. <u>Can the cameras be used to photograph confidential documents?</u>

c. <u>Are the cameras being used by Peeping Toms?</u>

d. <u>Can criminals use the camera-phones to photograph banks?</u>

e. <u>Can citizens photograph a crime in progress?</u>

additional questions: <u>Can citizens photograph a suspect or perpetrator?</u>
<u>Can police use the cameras in surveillance?</u>

2. **topic:** the effects of a regularly scheduled, widely available bus service to campus
   questions that can lead to ideas and details:

   a. _____

   b. _____

   c. _____

   d. _____

   e. _____

   additional questions: _____

   _____

3. **topic:** why most students tend to wear a similar college wardrobe
   questions that can lead to ideas and details:

   a. _____

   b. _____

   c. _____

   d. _____

   e. _____

   additional questions: _____

   _____

4. **topic:** why many adults drink beverages full of sugar
   questions that could lead to ideas and details:

   a. _____

   b. _____

   c. _____

   d. _____

   _____

   e. _____

   _____

   additional questions: _____

   _____

Exercise 4 **Practice: Creating Causes or Effects for Topic Sentences**

For each of the following topic sentences, create three causes or effects, depending on what the topic sentence requires. The first one is completed for you.

1. **topic sentence:** Sticking to an exercise routine has both improved and complicated my life.

   a. I am in better physical shape than I have been in years

   b. The physical exercise also gives me a mental boost.

   c. I now have to find time to fit my routine into my busy schedule.

2. **topic sentence:** Studying with a friend can be a useful way to prepare for a test.

   a. _____

   b. _____

   c. _____

3. **topic sentence:** There are several reasons why children love plush toys.

   a. _____

   b. _____

   c. _____

4. **topic sentence:** As more people choose vegetarian meals, the items sold in the supermarket have become more diverse.

   a. _____

   b. _____

   c. _____

PLANNING **CAUSE OR EFFECT**

With a topic sentence and a list of causes (or effects) and details, you can draft an outline of your paragraph. Once you have a rough outline, you can work on revising it. You may want to add to it, to take out certain ideas, to rewrite the topic sentence, or to change the order of the ideas. The following checklist may help you to revise your outline.

Checklist for Revising the Outline of a Cause or Effect Paragraph
✔ Does my topic sentence make my point?
✔ Does it indicate whether my paragraph is about causes or effects?
✔ Does the topic sentence fit the rest of the outline?
✔ Have I included enough causes or effects to make my point?
✔ Have I included enough details?
✔ Should I eliminate any ideas?
✔ Is the order of my causes or effects clear and logical?

The Order of Causes or Effects

Looking at a draft outline can help you decide on the best order for your causes or effects. There is no single rule for organizing causes or effects. Instead, you should think about the ideas you are presenting and decide on the most logical and effective order.

For example, if you are writing about some immediate and some long-range effects, you might want to discuss the effects in a **time order.** You might begin with the immediate effect, then discuss what happens later, and end with what happens last of all. If you are discussing three or four effects that are not in any particular time order, you might save the most important effect for last, for an **emphatic order.** If one cause leads to another, then use the **logical order** of discussing the causes.

Compare the following outline on owning a car to the list of effects on page 208. Notice that, in the outline, the carefree side of owning a car comes first, and the cares of owning a car, the expense and the worry, come later. The topic sentence follows the same order.

Outline for an Effects Paragraph

revised topic sentence:	Owning my own car gave me freedom, cost me money, and made me careful about how I drive.
effect 1 **details**	I had the adult freedom to come and go. I didn't have to beg my father for his truck. I didn't have to get rides from my friends. I could go to the city when I wanted. I could ride around for fun.
effect 2 **details**	I had to pay for the car and related expenses. A car costs a lot to maintain. I had a car loan to pay. I had car insurance.
effect 3 **details**	I became a more careful driver. I worried about someone hitting the car. I worried about bad drivers. I wanted to avoid the scratches cars can get in a parking lot.

Once you have a revised outline of your cause or effect paragraph, you are ready to begin writing your draft.

Exercise 5 **Practice: Writing Topic Sentences for Cause or Effect Outlines**

Following are two outlines. They have no topic sentences. Read the outlines carefully several times. Then write a topic sentence for each.

1. topic sentence: _____

_____

details: I was writing a check at a local store when I was asked to show my driver's license.

I opened my wallet to the place where I keep my driver's license.

My license was not there.

At first, I felt irritated and annoyed.

I felt that I was wasting time looking for the license that I had obviously slipped into the wrong slot in my wallet.

My irritation built as I felt the customers behind me waiting impatiently.

Irritation turned to shame after I had checked every part of my wallet, my pockets, and the floor.

I sensed that the checkout clerk was beginning to mistrust me.

At home, I frantically searched the entire apartment.

The shame began to explode, and I was furious at myself for being so careless.

In my panic, I trapped myself into a circle of questions.

"How would I drive without a license?" I asked myself.

"What would I do if a police officer pulled me over?"

After a sleepless night, I asked my roommate to drive me to the license bureau.

Once I had my new license, the panic and misery subsided.

2. topic sentence: _____

_____

details: Many of my high school friends were planning to attend Coolidge Technical College.

As a result, I would have people to socialize with at the college.

I wouldn't feel as lonely as I would at a college full of strangers.

Coolidge Technical College offered two-year degrees in Culinary Science, and I was thinking of becoming a chef.

I like the idea of learning a marketable skill in two years.

Location was my main reason for choosing to attend Coolidge Technical College.

The college was only fifteen minutes away from my parents' house.

I could save money on rent and food by continuing to live at home.

I could save on transportation costs, too.

Exercise 6   **Practice: Revising the Order of Causes or Effects**

Below are topic sentences and lists of causes or effects. Reorder each list according the directions given at the end of the list. Put "1" by the item that would come first, and so forth.

1. topic sentence: Going on a diet changed my father's life.

_____ He learned the difference between healthy and unhealthy food.

_____ After eating right for a year, my father was better able to control his diabetes.

_____ Once my father began to choose more healthy foods such as fruits, vegetables, and fish, he began to have more energy.

Use this order: Time order

2. topic sentence: My grandparents lost money on the sale of their house for three reasons.

_____ The real estate market was in a steep decline.

_____ The paint colors in the kitchen and dining room seemed outdated.

_____ The garage was small.

Use this order: From least important to most important

3. topic sentence: Reducing my work hours so that I could attend college has had negative and positive effects on me.

_____ I am constantly short of money.

_____ I can see the career possibilities that education can offer.

_____ I enjoy the challenge of college.

Use this order: The order indicated by the topic sentence, from bad to good.

Exercise 7   **Practice: Developing an Outline**

The outlines below need one more cause or effect and details for that cause or effect. Fill in the missing parts.

1. topic sentence: People give many reasons for ending a relationship.

cause 1:   Some say they are not ready for a commitment.

details: They say they need time to find themselves.
They swear that they value their freedom.
They feel that the relationship has developed too quickly.

cause 2:   Others tend to blame the partner in the relationship.

details: Some say the partner is too possessive.
Others claim the partner is too demanding.
Others complain that they do not want to argue anymore.

cause 3: _____

_____

details (at least two sentences): _____

_____

_____

_____

_____

2. **topic sentence:** Telling someone else's secret can make a person feel both powerful and miserable.

    effect 1:   Revealing a friend's secret made me the center of attention.

    details: People love gossip, so they were ready to listen.
They wanted all the details.
They seemed flattered that I had confided in them.

    effect 2:   For a while, I felt superior to my listeners.

    details: I felt that I was above the crowd because I knew a story that others did not know.
I felt needed.
I also felt powerful.

    effect 3:   _____

    details (at least two sentences): _____

_____

_____

_____

_____

DRAFTING AND REVISING   **CAUSE OR EFFECT**

Once you have an outline in good order, with a sufficient number of causes or effects and a fair amount of detail, you can write a first draft of the paragraph. When the first draft is complete, you can read and reread it, deciding how you'd like to improve it. The checklist below may help you revise.

Checklist for Revising the Draft of a Cause or Effect Paragraph

✔ Does my topic sentence indicate cause or effect?

✔ Does it fit the rest of the paragraph?

✔ Do I have enough causes or effects to make my point?

✔ Do I have enough details for each cause or effect?

✔ Are my causes or effects explained clearly?

✔ Is there a clear connection between my ideas?

✔   Have I shown the links between my ideas?

✔   Do I need to combine sentences?

✔   Do I need an opening or closing sentence?

Linking Ideas in Cause or Effect

When you write about how one event or situation causes another, or about how one result leads to another, you have to be very clear in showing the connections between events, situations, or effects.

One way to be clear is to rely on transitions. Some transitions are particularly helpful in writing cause and effect paragraphs.

INFO BOX: **Transitions for a Cause or Effect Paragraph**

For cause paragraphs:

because	for	for this reason	since
due to			

For effect paragraphs:

as a result	hence	so	therefore
consequently	in consequence	then	thus

Making the Links Clear

Using the right transition is not always enough to make your point. Sometimes you have to write the missing link in your line of thinking so that the reader can understand your point. To write the missing link means writing phrases, clauses, or sentences that help the reader follow your point.

not this: Many mothers are working outside the home. Consequently, microwave ovens are popular.

but this: Many mothers are working outside the home and have less time to cook. Consequently, microwave ovens, which can cook food in minutes, are popular.

The hard part of making clear links between ideas is that you have to put yourself in your reader's place. Remember that your reader cannot read your mind, only your paper. Connections between ideas may be very clear in your mind, but you must spell them out on paper.

Revising the Draft

Below is a revised draft of the paragraph on owning a car. When you read it, you'll notice many changes from the outline on page 211.

- The details on "car payments" and "a car loan" said the same thing, so the repetition has been cut.
- Some details about the costs of maintaining a car and about parking have been added.
- The order of the details about the costs of a car has been changed. Now, paying for a car comes first; maintaining it comes after.
- Sentences have been combined.
- Transitions have been added.

Draft of an Effects Paragraph

transition
sentences combined

sentences combined
transition
sentences combined,
order of details
changed, added
details, transition

transition

Owning my own car gave me freedom, cost me money, and made me more careful about how I drive. <u>First of all,</u> my car gave me the adult freedom to come and go. <u>I didn't have to beg my father for his truck or get rides from my friends anymore.</u> <u>I could go to the city or even ride around for fun when I wanted.</u> <u>On the negative side,</u> I had to pay for the car and related expenses. <u>I had to pay for both the car loan and car insurance.</u> <u>A car costs a lot to maintain, too.</u> <u>I paid for oil changes, tune-ups, tires, belts, and filters.</u> <u>With so much of my money put into my car,</u> I became a more careful driver. I worried about someone hitting the car and watched out for bad drivers. <u>In addition,</u> I wanted to avoid the scratches a car can get in a parking lot, so I always parked far away from other cars.

Exercise 8   **Practice: Making the Links Clear**

Following are ideas that are linked, but their connection is not clearly explained. Rewrite each pair of ideas, making the connection clear.

1. It's been raining all week. As a result, I've been taking an allergy pill every day.

   Rewritten: _____

   _____

   _____

   _____

   (**Hint:** What is the connection between your allergies and rain?)

2. Alex wanted a real Cuban dish of beans and rice. Therefore, he went home for the weekend.

   Rewritten: _____

   _____

   _____

   _____

   (**Hint:** Can someone at home make Alex a real Cuban dish of beans and rice?)

3. The first dog I saw at the animal shelter had a long, thick coat of red hair. Consequently, I chose a brown dog with shorter hair.

   Rewritten: _____

   _____

   _____

   _____

   (**Hint:** Were you worried about the amount of hair the first dog would shed?)

4. Craig was able to see the humor in any situation. Therefore I tended to avoid him.

Rewritten: _____

_____

_____

_____

(**Hint:** Was Craig's gift for seeing the funny side of situations sometimes inappropriate?)

Exercise 9   **Practice: Revising a Paragraph by Adding Details**

Each of the paragraphs below is missing details. Add at least two details as you extend each paragraph by two additional sentences.

Paragraph 1

Being diagnosed with diabetes had a tremendous impact on me. When the doctor told me the news, I was horrified. My first thoughts focused on losing a limb or dying young. In addition, the misery of constantly monitoring my blood sugar levels, giving myself frequent injections, and rigidly following a limited diet scared me. Once I became more informed and rational about the challenges I faced, I was angry. I could not understand why I had the bad luck of developing diabetes. I cursed my situation and wallowed in self-pity. Learning to eat healthy foods, to control my blood sugar, and to avoid infections seemed like punishments I did not deserve. When I finally accepted my situation, I understood that the doctor's diagnosis had been a gift of life. _____

_____

_____

_____

_____

_____

Once I let go of misery, fear, and anger, I found a new gratitude for being alive.

Paragraph 2

My sister Lorrie had three foolish reasons for marrying young. First, she was infatuated. Barely out of high school, she met Calvin in August and thought he was her Prince Charming. He was good-looking, funny, and high-spirited. Lorrie never thought about his recklessness and troubles with the law. She saw Calvin only as her one chance for true romance. In addition, Lorrie was bored and restless. She hated the idea of working for hours in a dreary job, but she had no desire to be in a classroom again. To Lorrie, marriage to Calvin was an exciting alternative to years of struggling to earn a little money or of worrying about exams, quizzes, and other academic demands. Most important, Lorrie married so that she could get out of our parents' house. _____

_____

_____

_____

_____

Unfortunately, Lorrie married for all the wrong reasons.

Exercise 10   **Practice: Revising a Draft by Combining Sentences**

Combine the underlined sentences in the following paragraph. Write your combinations in the space above the original sentences.

Quitting smoking changed me in some unexpected ways. First, it gave me a real sense of power. I had been sure that quitting would be impossible for me. I was smoking a pack a day. At that time, I decided to try cutting back. My initial goal was to cut my smoking in half. I was able to do this. It did not take much effort. It took me about three months. When I had achieved this goal, I aimed to push ahead. I tried hard to cut my cigarette habit to five cigarettes per day. Eventually I succeeded in limiting myself to five a day. Then I tried four a day. Next I cut my limit to three. The hardest part was giving them up entirely, but I did it. Once I quit, I changed in another way. I developed a new understanding of the reasons that nonsmokers avoid smokers. I realized that rooms do absorb the smell of cigarettes. The clothes that smokers wear smell, too. Smokers also have bad breath. Suddenly I became someone who avoided smoke-filled people and rooms. Finally, breaking the smoking habit led me to make another big change. I stopped drinking. During the time when I was cutting back on cigarettes, I became aware that nothing made me crave a cigarette more than drinking a beer or mixed drink.

In my final days as a smoker, I avoided any temptation to smoke. As a result, I

stopped drinking. Now I am determined to stay nicotine-free. <u>I am alcohol-free as</u>

<u>well. I have broken two habits. I am twice as healthy as I expected to be.</u>

PROOFREADING   **CAUSE OR EFFECT**

Following is the final version of the paragraph on owning a car. As you check
your final rough draft for errors in grammar, spelling, or preparation, you
can also look out for small improvements in the smoothness and language
of the paragraph. When you contrast the final version with the draft on page
216, you'll notice several changes:

- An introductory sentence has been added.
- Transitions have been revised.
- Some words have been changed so that the language is more
  precise.

Changes in style, word choice, and transitions can all be made before you
decide on the final version of your paragraph. You may also want to add an
opening or closing sentence to your paragraph.

Final Version of an Effects Paragraph

(Changes from the draft are underlined.)

> <u>When I bought my first car, I wasn't prepared for all the changes it made in my</u>
> <u>life.</u> Owning my own car gave me freedom, cost me money, and made me careful
> about how I drive. First of all, my car gave me the adult freedom to come and go.
> I didn't have to beg my father for his truck or get rides from my friends anymore. I
> could go to the city or even ride around for fun when I wanted. On the negative side,
> I had to pay for the car and related expenses. I had to pay for both the car loan and
> car insurance. A car costs <u>money</u> to maintain, too. I paid for oil changes, tune-ups,
> tires, belts, and filters. With so much of my money put into my car, I became a more
> careful driver. I worried about someone hitting the car and watched out for bad
> drivers. <u>To avoid dangers in the parking lot as well as on the road,</u> I always parked
> <u>my car</u> far away from other cars, <u>keeping my car safe from scratches.</u>

For your information: A sample effects essay based on this topic and following
the same writing steps can be found in Chapter 13, "Different Essay Patterns:
Part Two."

Exercise 11   **Practice: Correcting a Final Copy of a Cause or Effect
Paragraph**

Following are one cause and one effects paragraph with the kind of errors
it is easy to overlook when you prepare the final version of an assignment.
Correct the errors, writing above the lines. There are thirteen errors in the
first (cause) paragraph, and twelve errors in the second (effects) paragraph.

Paragraph 1

I got my job at a Discount Appliance store for three reason's. First, I used my imagination and asked myself, "Who would want to hire me"? I didn't have much experience because I had spent the last three years at one job. That job was unpacking merchandise at my uncle's dollar store. When he had to close his store, I started thinking about my skills. I was able to carry heavy loads, I was careful not to break the merchandise, and I knowed how to make the best use of storage space. When, I realized that I did have some skills, I kept looking for a place that needed them. After any employer turned me down, I checked with him or her several more times. Soon I became a familiar, face. I smiled, and learned the names of the boss and the staff at each place of work. However, I also learned not to a nuisance. The last reason that I eventually found work was the more important. I swore that I was willing to work for a low wage. I was not to proud to accept any offer. I now have a job at the delivery entrance to a large household appliance store. I unload and fit large boxes of Refrigerators, stoves, washers, and dryers into tight storeage areas. By selling my skills, persevering, and accepting a minimum wage, I found employment.

Paragraph 2

When I was younger, I had a mania for clothes shopping and the crazyness hurt me in several way. First, I shopped in a state of elation, and I lost my common sense. The first item that caught my eye became irresistible. I felt that bying it would, change my life. I knew that I had to have it. After I bought it, some shoes or jeans or a jacket seemed to be calling me. I craved them, too. In such an irrational state, I bought some hideous clothes. Second, I never truely enjoyed the experience of buying the items because the endless shopping was a compulsion. In every store, I acted like a robot. Hours after I returned home, I look at my purchases and felt disappointed. The new clothes hadn't changed much about my life. In fact; all the new purchases have done was to change my bank balance. The worse affect of my mania was the constant worry about paying for my shopping spree's. This fear became overwhelming as the bills kepped coming. My mania brought me three emotions: a rush of elation, inevitable disappointment, and endless fear.

Lines of Detail: A Walk-Through Assignment

Write a paragraph on this topic: Why Most College Students Tend to Wear a Similar College Wardrobe. To write your paragraph, follow these steps:

Step 1: Go back to Exercise 3 starting on page 208. Topic 3 is the same topic as this assignment. If you have already done that exercise, you have 5 or more questions that can lead you to ideas and details. If you haven't completed the exercise, try topic 3 on page 209.

Step 2: Use the answers to your questions to prepare a list of ideas and details. Put the items on your list into groups of causes and related details. Add to the groups until you have at least three causes (and related details) for the similarity in many college students' wardrobes.

Step 3: Write a topic sentence that fits your causes.

Step 4: Write an outline. Check that your outline has sufficient details and that you have put the causes in the best order.

Step 5: Write a rough draft of your paragraph. Revise it until you have enough specific details to explain each cause and the links between your ideas are smooth and clear. Check whether any sentences should be combined and whether your paragraph could use an opening sentence or a concluding one.

Step 6: Before you prepare the final copy of your paragraph, check your latest draft for word choice, punctuation, transitions, and spelling.

Topics for Writing a Cause or Effect Paragraph

When you write on any of the following topics, be sure to work through the stages of the writing process in preparing your cause or effect paragraph.

1. Write a cause paragraph on one of the following topics. You create the topic by filling in the blanks.

   Why I Chose _____

   Why I Stopped _____

   Why I Enjoy _____

   Why I Started _____

   Why I Lost Interest in _____

2. Write a one-paragraph letter of complaint to the manufacturers of a product you bought or to the company that owns a hotel, a restaurant, an airline, or some other service you used. In your letter, write at least three reasons why you (1) want your money refunded or (2) want the product replaced. Be clear and specific about your reasons. Be sure your letter has a topic sentence.

   If your instructor agrees, read a draft of your letter to a writing partner while your partner pretends to be the manufacturer or the head of the company. Afterwards, ask your partner to point out where your ideas are not clear or convincing and where you make your point effectively.

Collaborate

3. Think of a current fad or trend. The fad can be a popular style of clothing, type of movie, style of music, a sport, a pastime, a kind of food or drink, an athlete, a gadget, an invention, an appliance, and so on. Write a paragraph on the causes of this fad or trend or the effects of it.

Collaborate

If your instructor agrees, begin by brainstorming with a group. Create a list of three or four fads or trends. Then create a list of questions to ask (and answer) about each fad or trend. If you are going to write about **causes,** for example, you might ask questions like these:

What changes in society have encouraged this trend?
Have changes in the economy helped to make it popular?
Does it appeal to a specific age group? Why?
Does it meet any hidden emotional needs? For instance, is it a way to gain status, to feel safe, or to feel powerful?

If you are going to write about **effects,** you might ask questions like these:

Will this trend last?
Has it affected competitors?
Is it spreading?
Is the fad changing business, education, or the family?
Has it improved daily life?

4. If you have a vivid memory of one of the following experiences, write a paragraph about the experience's effects on you.

moving to a new place	losing a job	speaking in public
making a new friend	breaking a promise	camping in the wild
being a victim of a crime	entering a relationship	traveling alone
winning a contest	ending a relationship	defending your
undergoing surgery	getting your first	beliefs
losing a friend	paycheck	

Computer

5. If you currently use a computer for drafting your writing assignments, write a paragraph that summarizes the effects of relying on the computer for composing most, if not all, of your writing assignments. Remember that the effects may be both positive and negative, so you will need to brainstorm or freewrite first. Be sure your final version of the paragraph reflects logical organization of details and appropriate transitions.

6. After looking at the photograph, write a paragraph on why joining an exercise group can have social benefits.

7. After looking at the photograph, write a paragraph on the positive effects of a young and an old person creating a bond.

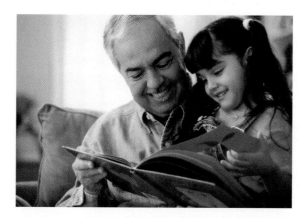

Topics for Critical Thinking and Writing

1. Why do you think so many Americans do not register or even bother to vote? Pose this question to some of your peers and friends to gather as many reasons as you can for so much voter apathy. Determine three main causes and use emphatic order (least to most significant) as you explain each cause.

2. Applying the same techniques suggested in topic 1, ask friends, peers, and family members who are registered voters why they feel voting is so important. Determine three main causes and use emphatic order as you explain each cause.

3. Police often have difficulty finding witnesses to a crime such as a violent street assault or a neighborhood robbery. Why are some eyewitnesses reluctant or afraid to cooperate with authorities? As you brainstorm or freewrite about this topic, consider both rational and irrational reasons people give for not helping with an investigation. Discuss the three most common reasons and include the degree of rationality in each reason.

Note: Additional writing options suitable for cause- or effect-related assignments can be found after the professional reading "Say Something," which can be found in the "Readings for Writers" appendix at the end of this book.

PEARSON
mywritinglab   For support in meeting this chapter's objectives, log in to
www.mywritinglab.com and select **Paragraph Development—**
Cause and Effect.

Name _____   Section _____

Peer Review Form for a Cause or Effect Paragraph

After you've written a draft of your cause or effect paragraph, let a writing partner read it. When your partner has completed the form below, discuss the comments. Then repeat the same process for your partner's paragraph.

This is a cause paragraph/an effect paragraph. (Circle one.)

In this paragraph, the causes or effects are (briefly list all of them) _____

_____

_____

_____

The topic sentence uses these words to indicate cause or effect _____

_____ (Write the exact words.)

The cause or effect that is most clearly explained is _____

_____

I would like to see more details added to _____

_____

I have questions about _____

I would like to take out the part about _____

Other comments _____

_____

_____

_____

_____

_____

_____

_____

_____

_____

_____

Reviewer's name _____

Argument

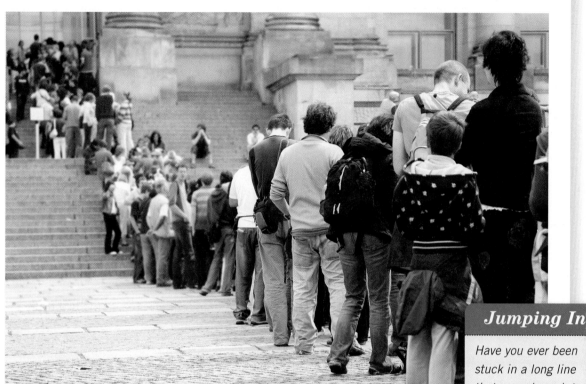

Jumping In

*Have you ever been stuck in a long line that moved much too slowly? How did you feel? Can you think of a way the line could have moved more quickly? If you can propose an effective way to shorten the waiting time, you will be presenting an **argument**.*

Chapter Objectives

Students will be able to write an effective argument paragraph that (1) respects its targeted audience and (2) acknowledges opposing viewpoints.

WHAT IS ARGUMENT?

A written **argument** is an attempt to *persuade* a reader to think or act in a certain way. When you write an argument paragraph, your goal is to get people to see your point so that they are persuaded to accept it and perhaps to act on it.

In an argument paragraph, you take a stand. Then you support your stand with reasons. In addition, you give details for each reason. Your goal is to persuade your reader by making a point that has convincing reasons and details.

Hints for Writing an Argument Paragraph

1. Pick a topic you can handle. Your topic should be small enough to be covered in one paragraph. For instance, you can't argue effectively for world peace in just one paragraph.

2. Pick a topic you can handle based on your own experience and observation. Topics like legalizing drugs, gun control, capital punishment, or air pollution require research into facts, figures, and expert opinions to make a complete argument. They are topics you can write about convincingly in a longer research paper, but for a one-paragraph argument, pick a topic based on what you've experienced yourself.

> **not this topic:** Organized Crime
> **but this topic:** Starting a Crime Watch Program in My Neighborhood

3. Do two things in your topic sentence: name the subject of your argument and take a stand. The following topic sentences do both.

> subject   takes a stand
> The college cafeteria should serve more healthy snacks.

> subject   takes a stand
> High school athletes who fail a course should not be allowed to play on a school team.

You should take a stand, but *don't* announce it:

> **not this:** This paragraph will explain why Springfield needs a teen center.
> **but this:** Springfield should open a teen center. (This is a topic sentence with a subject and a stand.)

4. Consider your audience. Consider why these people should support your points. How will they be likely to object? How will you get around these objections? For instance, you might want to argue to the residents of your community that the intersection of Hawthorne Road and Sheridan Street needs a traffic light. Would anyone object?

At first, you might think, "No. Why would anyone object? The intersection is dangerous. There's too much traffic there. People risk major accidents getting across the intersection." However, if you think further about your audience, which is the people in your community, you might identify these objections: (1) Some town residents may not want to pay for a traffic signal, and (2) some drivers may not want to spend extra time waiting for a light to change.

There are several ways to handle objections:

> You can *refute* an objection. To refute it means to prove that it isn't valid, that it isn't true. For instance, if someone says that a light wouldn't do any good, you might say that a new light has already worked in a nearby neighborhood.

> Sometimes it's best to admit the other side has a point. You have to *concede* that point. For instance, traffic lights do cost money, and waiting for a light to change does take time.

> Sometimes you can *turn an objection into an advantage.* When you acknowledge the objection and yet use it to make your own point, you show that you've considered both sides of the argument. For instance, you might say that the price of a traffic signal at the intersection is well worth the expense because that light will buy safety for all the drivers who try to cross Hawthorne Road and Sheridan Street. As an alternative, you might say that waiting a few moments for the light to change is better than waiting many minutes for an opening in the heavy traffic of the intersection.

5. Be specific, clear, and logical in your reasons. As always, think before you write. Think about your point and your audience. Try to come up with at least three reasons for your position.

Be careful that your reasons do not overlap. For instance, you might write the following:

topic sentence: College students should get discounts on movie tickets.
audience: Owners of movie theaters
reasons: 1. Many college students can't afford current ticket prices.
                  2. The cost of tickets is high for most students.
                  3. More people in the theater means more popcorn and
                     candy sold at the concession stand.

But reasons 1 and 2 overlap; they are really part of the same reason.

Be careful not to argue in a circle. For instance, if you say, "One reason for having an after-school program at Riverside Elementary School is that we need one there," you've just said, "We need an after-school program because we need an after-school program."

Finally, be specific in stating your reasons.

> **not this:** One reason to start a bus service to and from the college is to help people.
>
> **but this:** A bus service to and from the college would encourage students to leave their cars at home and use travel time to study.

Exercise 1   **Practice: Recognizing Good Topic Sentences for an Argument Paragraph**

Some of the topic sentences below are appropriate for an argument paragraph. Some are for topics that are too large for one paragraph, and some are for topics that would require research. Some are announcements. Some do not take a stand. Put *OK* next to the sentences that would work well in an argument paragraph.

1. _____ Residents of the Whispering Pines neighborhood must not let their dogs run loose.

2. _____ Slippery sidewalks at Jackson Elementary School are a danger to adults and children.

3. _____ We must learn to conserve water if we wish to save our planet.

4. _____ Our community needs a local noise ordinance forbidding excessively loud sound systems in cars and trucks.

5. _____ Something must be done about the growing problem of identity theft.

6. _____ Why flu shots should be free to children is the topic to be discussed.

7. _____ More online courses should be available to juniors and seniors at Emerson High School.

8. _____ Fraternities and sororities promote social exclusion and a false sense of superiority.

9. _____ The mini-mart outside of our town should provide better security for its night clerks.

10. _____ Quality First, the largest employer in the county, needs an on-site child care center for the children of its employees.

Collaborate

Exercise 2   **Collaborate: Recognizing and Handling Objections**

Below are the topic sentences of arguments. Working with a group, list two possible objections to each argument that might come from the specific audience identified. Then think of ways to handle each objection, by refuting it, conceding it, or trying to turn it to your advantage. On the lines provided, write the actual sentence(s) you would use in a paragraph.

1. **topic sentence:** The downtown area of Carsonville needs a network of bike paths.

   audience: The residents of Carsonville

   possible objections from this audience:

   a. _____

   _____

   b. _____

   _____

   answering objections:

   a. _____

   _____

   b. _____

   _____

2. **topic sentence:** Large commercial moving vans should not be allowed to park on the streets of Bayside overnight.

   audience: residents of Bayside who are planning to move and need to use a van

   possible objections from this audience:

   a. _____

   _____

   b. _____

   _____

   answering objections:

   a. _____

   _____

   b. _____

   _____

3. topic sentence: The entrance to Laurel Park must be locked
                   at sunset.

audience: Teens who hang out at the park after dark

possible objections from this audience:

a. _____

   _____

b. _____

   _____

answering objections:

a. _____

   _____

b. _____

   _____

WRITING THE ARGUMENT PARAGRAPH IN STEPS

PREWRITING   ARGUMENT

Imagine that your instructor has given you this assignment:

> Write a one-paragraph letter to the editor of your local
> newspaper. Argue for something in your town that needs to
> be changed.

One way to begin is to **brainstorm** for some specific thing that you can
write about.

Is there a part of town that needs to be cleaned up?
Should something be changed at a school?
What do I notice on my way to work or school that needs improvement?
What could be improved in my neighborhood?

By answering these questions, you may come up with one topic, and then
you can list ideas on it.

topic
Cleaning Up Roberts Park

ideas
dirty and overgrown
benches are all cracked and broken
full of trash
could be fixed up
people work nearby
they would use it

You can consider your audience and possible objections:

audience
people of all ages who read the local paper

possible objections from this audience
would cost money
more important things to spend money on

answering objections
Money would be well spent to beautify the downtown.
City children could play there in the fresh air and in nature; workers could
eat lunch there.

Grouping Your Ideas

Once you have a list, you can start grouping the ideas on your list. Some of
the objections you wrote down may actually lead you to reasons that support your argument. That is, by answering objections, you may come up with
reasons that support your point. Following is a list with a point to argue,
three supporting reasons, and some details about cleaning up Roberts Park.

List for an Argument Paragraph

point: We should fix up Roberts Park.

reason: Improving the park would make the downtown area more attractive to shoppers.

details: Shoppers could stroll in the park or rest from their shopping.

           Friends could meet in the park for a day of shopping and lunch.

reason: City children could play in the park.

details: They could get fresh air.

           They could play in a natural setting.

reason: Workers could eat lunch outdoors.

details: Several office complexes are nearby.

           Workers would take a break outdoors.

With three reasons and some details for each, you can draft a topic sentence.
Remember that your topic sentence for an argument should (1) name your
subject and (2) take a stand. Below is a topic sentence about Roberts Park
that does both.

      subject   takes a stand
Roberts Park should be cleaned up and improved.

With a topic sentence, you are ready to move on to the planning stage
of preparing an argument paragraph.

> **Exercise 3** **Practice: Distinguishing Between Reasons and Details**

Each list below has three reasons and details for each reason. Put *reason 1*,
reason 2, and *reason 3* next to the reasons on each list. Then put *detail for 1*,
detail for 2, or *detail for 3* by the items that give details about each reason.
There may be more than one sentence of detail connected to one reason.

1. **topic sentence:** Crystal Lake needs a weekly farmers' market.

_____ Many people want fresh, locally grown produce,
plants, crafts, and baked goods.

_____ Small, local farmers need local outlets for their
produce.

_____ Seasonal vegetables and fruits straight from
the fields taste better than supermarket
produce.

_____ Small family farms can bring their products
to a nearby market and save money on
shipping costs.

_____ Neighbors meet at the market, talk, and share coffee
and homemade muffins.

_____ Fresh produce is healthier than food treated with
preservatives and other chemicals.

_____ Farmers' markets bring a community together.

_____ Those who regularly shop at the market become
friends with the merchants.

_____ Many supermarket chains deal only with
agricultural conglomerates and don't sell
local produce.

_____ When a farmer can tell a customer how to prepare a
vegetable or how to use a fruit in a salad, the farmer
is likely to make a sale.

2. topic sentence: The residents at Midtown Manors Apartments need
more dumpsters.

_____ The trash is an eyesore for residents.

_____ A toddler might pick up a filthy tuna can and taste
the tainted fish.

_____ The trash smells.

_____ One day after the trash is collected, the dumpsters
begin to fill again.

_____ Rotting fruit and vegetables spill onto the pavement,
releasing garbage smells.

_____ The trash is a health hazard.

_____ Roaches crawl among the spilled garbage.

_____ From their apartment windows, residents see the
mounds of trash.

_____ The odor of rotting food carries to the parking lots
and to open apartment windows.

_____ Rats scurry in and out of the piles of garbage.

Exercise 4   Practice: Finding Reasons to Support an Argument

Give three reasons that support each point. In each case, the readers of your
local newspaper will be the audience for an argument paragraph.

1. point: Ridgeview needs regular bus service on the weekends, not
just on the weekdays.

reasons: a. _____

_____

b. _____

_____

c. _____

_____

2. **point:** Backpacks should be banned at elementary schools.

reasons: a. _____

_____

b. _____

_____

c. _____

_____

3. **point:** A softer, light plastic covering must replace the ultra-hard plastic packaging wrapped around tools, flashlights, and small gadgets.

reasons: a. _____

_____

b. _____

_____

c. _____

_____

PLANNING   **ARGUMENT**

With a topic sentence and a list of reasons and details, you can draft an outline. Then you can review it, making whatever changes you think it needs. The checklist below may help you to review and revise your outline.

Checklist for Revising an Argument Outline

✔ Does my topic sentence make my point? Does it state a subject and take a stand?

✔ Have I considered the objections to my argument so that I am arguing intelligently?

✔ Do I have all the reasons I need to make my point?

✔ Do any reasons overlap?

✔ Are my reasons specific?

✔ Do I have enough details for each reason?

✔ Are my reasons in the best order?

The Order of Reasons in an Argument

When you are giving several reasons, it is a good idea to keep the most convincing or most important reason for last. Saving the best for last is called using **emphatic order.** For example, you might have these three reasons to tear down an abandoned building in your neighborhood: (1) The building is ugly. (2) Drug dealers are using the building. (3) The building is infested with rats. The most important reason, the drug dealing, should be used last, for emphatic order.

Following is an outline on improving Roberts Park. When you look at the outline, you'll notice several changes from the list on page 230:

- Since the safety of children at play is important, it is put as the last reason.
- Some details have been added.
- A sentence has been added to the end of the outline. It explains why improving the park is a good idea even to people who will never use the park themselves. It is a way of answering these people's objections.

Outline for an Argument Paragraph

topic sentence:	Roberts Park should be cleaned up and improved.
reason	Improving the park would make the downtown area more attractive to shoppers.
details	Shoppers could stroll through the park or rest there after shopping.
	Friends could meet at the park for a day of shopping and lunch.
reason	Workers from nearby offices and stores could eat lunch outdoors.
details	Several office complexes are nearby.
	An hour outdoors is a pleasant break from work.
reason	City children could play there.
details	They would get fresh air.
	They would play on grass, not on asphalt.
	They would not have to play near traffic.
final idea	An attractive park improves the city, and all residents benefit when the community is beautified.

Exercise 5   **Practice: Working with the Order of Reasons in an Argument Outline**

Below are topic sentences and lists of reasons. For each list, put an *X* by the reason that is the most significant, the reason you would save for last in an argument paragraph.

1. **topic sentence:** Door-to-door sales of candy, raffle tickets, or other fundraising items should be outlawed.

   reason 1: _____ The solicitations are annoying.

   reason 2: _____ Opening a door to a stranger can lead to a crime.

   reason 3: _____ People feel pressured to buy overpriced items.

2. topic sentence: Students at the local college need an emergency health center near the campus.

reason 1: _____ A nearby health center would make a campus epidemic less likely.

reason 2: _____ Many college students think they are invincible and ignore the symptoms of an illness.

reason 3: _____ Flu and other highly contagious illnesses spread quickly on college campuses.

3. topic sentence: Hamilton Apartments need regular exterior maintenance.

reason 1: _____ Broken screens and windows invite strangers to break into residences.

reason 2: _____ Dry grass and dying trees create a landscape of ants' nests and fallen branches.

reason 3: _____ Cracks in the sidewalks make walking a challenge.

Exercise 6   **Practice: Recognizing Reasons That Overlap**

Below are topic sentences and lists of reasons. In each list, two reasons overlap. Put an *X* by the two reasons that overlap.

1. topic sentence: The salad bar at Kiki's Pizza needs improvement.

a. _____ There is little variety in the offerings.

b. _____ The lettuce is limp, and the leaves often have a brown edge.

c. _____ There are mushy chunks of cucumbers.

d. _____ The salad always contains the same items: lettuce from a bag, soft pieces of tomatoes, and shredded carrots.

2. topic sentence: Students who lounge on the steps of campus buildings should find another place to relax.

a. _____ Clogging up the steps is rude.

b. _____ Trying to weave through the stair-sitters, I am afraid of tripping and falling.

c. _____ Someone is going to have an accident because inconsiderate students make the steps into an obstacle course.

d. _____ I'm afraid of being late for class because I have to wait for access to the stairs occupied by sitting students.

3. topic sentence: The Student Action Club should hold a coat give-away each fall.

a. _____ Cold weather hits hard at the homeless and others who are struggling.

b. _____ Children are especially vulnerable to illnesses caused by the cold.

c. _____ Many people have old coats and jackets they would be
willing to give away.

d. _____ Boys and girls need the protection of warm clothing.

Exercise 7   **Practice: Identifying a Reason That Is Not Specific**

For each of the following lists, put an *X* by the reason that is not specific.

1. **topic sentence:** All cell phones should be turned off in movie
theaters.

   a. _____ Movies theaters are filled with strangers who must be con-
siderate of other audience members if they are all to enjoy
the film.

   b. _____ Ringing phones or phone conversations distract and annoy
many people in the audience.

   c. _____ Being aware of the feelings and rights of others is always a
good policy.

   d. _____ When strangers in a theater become irritated by
phone conversations, complaints, insults, and even
violence result.

2. **topic sentence:** The office where I work needs a water cooler.

   a. _____ The office is small, crowded with desks, boxes, and file
cabinets, and very hot.

   b. _____ The office has a bathroom but no refrigerator, so the staff
cannot keep bottled water cool.

   c. _____ The office is a ten-minute drive from a fast-food restaurant
or food mart where bottled water is available.

   d. _____ Having a water cooler in the office would be better for all
the people who work there.

3. **topic sentence:** Crystal River Mall needs more than two maps of the
mall inside the complex.

   a. _____ Shoppers want to have a pleasant experience as they walk
through the mall.

   b. _____ Every shop in the mall wants potential customers to be
able to locate its store quickly.

   c. _____ With four main entrances to the mall, but only two maps,
many shoppers wander around until they become frustrated and leave.

   d. _____ The design of the mall is complicated, with twists, turns,
and dead ends.

Exercise 8   **Practice: Adding Details to an Outline**

Following is part of an outline. It includes a topic sentence and three reasons. Add at least two sentences of details to each reason. Your details may
be examples or descriptions.

topic sentence: Students in evening classes at Crescent Community College deserve the same services that students in day classes enjoy.

reason: Students in evening classes may have jobs or other responsibilities during the day, but, like all students, they need to see counselors.

details: _____

_____

details: _____

_____

reason: Students in evening classes may be on a tight schedule and may need to grab a quick snack on campus.

details: _____

_____

details: _____

_____

reason: Darkness makes it important for every night student to be as safe as a day student.

details: _____

_____

details: _____

_____

DRAFTING AND REVISING   ARGUMENT

Once you are satisfied with your outline, you can write the first draft of your paragraph. When you have completed it, you can begin revising the draft so that your argument is as clear, smooth, and convincing as it can be. The checklist below may help you with your revisions.

Checklist for Revising a Draft of an Argument Paragraph

✔ Do any of my sentences need combining?

✔ Have I left out a serious or obvious reason?

✔ Should I change the order of my reasons?

✔ Do I have enough details?

✔ Are my details specific?

✔ Do I need to explain the problem or issue I am writing about?

✔ Do I need to link my ideas more clearly?

✔ Do I need a final sentence to stress my point?

Checking Your Reasons

Be sure that your argument has covered all the serious or obvious reasons. Sometimes writers get so caught up in drafting their ideas that they forget to mention something very basic to the argument. For instance, if you were arguing for a leash law for your community, you might state that dogs who run free can hurt people and damage property. But don't forget to mention another serious reason to keep dogs on leashes: Dogs who are not restrained can get hurt or killed by cars.

One way to see if you have left out a serious or obvious reason is to ask a friend or classmate to read your draft and to react to your argument. Another technique is to put your draft aside for an hour or two and then read it as if you were a reader, not the writer.

Explaining the Problem or the Issue

Sometimes your argument discusses a problem so obvious to your audience that you do not need to explain it. On the other hand, sometimes you need to explain a problem or issue so that your audience can understand your point. If you tell readers of your local paper about teenage vandalism at Central High School, you probably need to explain what kind of vandalism has occurred and how often. Sometimes it is smart to convince readers of the seriousness of a situation by explaining it a little so that they will be more interested in your argument.

Transitions That Emphasize Your Reasons

In writing an argument paragraph, you can use any transition, depending on how you arrange your reasons and details. However, no matter how you present your reasons, you will probably want to *emphasize* one of them. Below are some transitions that can be used for emphasis.

INFO BOX: **Transitions to Use for Emphasis**

above all	finally	most important	most significant
especially	mainly	most of all	primarily

For example, by saying, "*Most important*, broken windows at Central High School are a safety problem," you put the emphasis for your audience on this one idea.

Revising a Draft

Following is a draft of the argument paragraph on Roberts Park. When you read it, you'll notice these changes from the outline on page 233:

- A description of the problem has been added.
- Details have been added.
- Short sentences have been combined.
- Transitions, including two sentences of transition, have been added. "Most important" and "Best of all"—transitions that show emphasis—have been included.

Draft of an Argument Paragraph

description of the problem	<u>Roberts Park was once a pretty little park, but today it is overgrown with weeds, cluttered with trash and rusty benches.</u> Roberts Park should be cleaned up and improved. Improving the park would make the downtown area more attractive to shoppers. Shoppers
added detail	could stroll through <u>a renovated</u> park or rest there after
transition	shopping. Friends could <u>also</u> meet there for a day of
transition sentence	shopping and lunch. <u>Shoppers are not the only ones who could enjoy the park.</u> Workers from nearby offices and stores could eat lunch outdoors. Several office com-
added details	plexes are near the park, <u>and workers from these offices could bring their lunch to work and eat outside in good weather.</u> I think many people would agree that an hour spent outdoors is a pleasant break from work. <u>Most</u>
transition	
added detail, sentences combined	<u>important,</u> city children could play in <u>an improved</u> Roberts Park. <u>They would get fresh air while they played on grass, not asphalt. Best of all,</u> they would not have
transition	
transition sentence	to play near traffic. <u>Children, shoppers, and workers would benefit from a clean-up of Roberts Park, but so would others.</u> An attractive park improves the city, and all residents benefit when a community is beautified.

Exercise 9   **Practice: Adding an Explanation of the Problem to an Argument Paragraph**

This paragraph could use an explanation of the problem before the thesis. Write a short explanation of the problem in the lines provided.

_____

_____

_____

_____

_____

_____

The local drivers' license bureau needs a larger, better furnished, and elec-

tronically updated waiting area. For the applicants who have come to renew,

reinstate, or be tested for a license, a large room would help them to feel less

stressed. The increased size would reduce the anxiety of being crushed in

a crowd of people, all waiting for an item as important as a driver's license.

Finally, better furniture in the new area would encourage the applicants to feel welcome and respected rather than unwelcome and annoying. Adequate seating would allow people to wait in some comfort and a calmer atmosphere. Finally, waiting would be more bearable if a clock or electric sign posted the estimated wait time. Applicants who arrived on a break from work would know whether to wait or return later. Posting the wait time would also eliminate the many questions about time that the staff must handle. These changes to the waiting room could reduce the irritation, misery, and even resentment of a necessary but unpleasant chore.

Exercise 10 **Practice: Recognizing Transitions in an Argument Paragraph**

Underline all the transitions—words, phrases, or sentences—in the paragraph below. Put a double line under any transitions that emphasize reasons.

On Saturdays, the entrance to many local supermarkets shelters boys or girls accompanied by several caring adults who are the parent sponsors of the children's group. The group can be an athletic team, a school club, or a chapter of a national boys' or girls' club. The children are selling something—cookies, popcorn, chocolate bars—to raise money for their school, team, or charitable organization. Although it is easy to walk past the children, we should support their efforts. First of all, the children are nervous, and they need encouragement. If a child can make a sale while other children and the adults are watching, that child feels proud and empowered. More important, all the children are learning about working hard for a cause. They may be raising money for a club, a school team, or a national organization that helps children. However, each child is collecting money for something bigger than him- or herself. The process brings them pleasure and pride in working for others. Most important, if we buy the item, we become part of something larger than ourselves. By spending a few dollars on chocolate or cookies, we join a circle of giving. The children's parents give their time, support, and protection, the children give their efforts and courage, and the buyers give their money to a needy organization. As a result, each small purchase does a small world of good.

Exercise 11   **Practice: Revising a Draft by Combining Sentences**

In the following paragraph, combine each cluster of underlined sentences into one clear, smooth sentence. Write your combinations in the space above the original sentences.

Nicholson College has an impressive campus of nine large buildings set in green grass, large trees, and open spaces. It is beautiful. It presents a challenge for most people. These people include current students, new students, and applicants. Nicholson College needs more signs on every building. Current students are likely to become bad-tempered at the beginning of a new term. On the first day of class, they check their printed copies of their class schedules. At that moment, they realize their next class is scheduled for a building. The building is one that is far away. The building is one they have never entered. They rush to find the building, but they are lost. At Nicholson College, each structure has its name in one place, on one wall. The sign is impressive. However, even longtime students may not find it. They may be approaching the building from the wrong direction. As a result, these students wander on the outskirts of one, two, or three buildings that they don't know well. New students suffer near panic as they struggle to find their classes. New students have many worries. They worry about arriving late to class. They worry about looking ridiculous in front of a room full of seated students. They are afraid of irritating a professor. Roaming the halls and sidewalks is not a good way to begin a term. However, the worst impact of insufficient signs hits applicants to the college. Applicants may be visiting the campus for the first time. They may be unsure whether the place is right for them. They may be considering several colleges. Anyone new to the college is likely to become irritated and frustrated as he or she wanders aimlessly. College maps are no help if the visitor cannot find signs on the buildings. A first-time visitor may decide to look somewhere else to start his or her college career or give up on college altogether. Nicholson College has much to offer, but it needs to offer clear directions to old, new, and aspiring students.

PROOFREADING   ARGUMENT

Following is the final version of the argument paragraph on Roberts Park. It has been improved through careful checking for errors in spelling, punctuation, and preparation. In addition, it includes several improvements made since preparation of the draft on page 238:

- Some words have been changed to improve the details.
- The first sentence has been changed so that it is more descriptive and uses a parallel pattern for emphasis.

Final Version of an Argument Paragraph

(Changes from the draft are underlined.)

Roberts Park was once a pretty little park, but today it is overgrown with weeds, <u>littered with trash, and cluttered with rusty benches.</u> Roberts Park should be cleaned up and improved. Improving the park would make the downtown area more attractive to shoppers. Shoppers could stroll through a <u>restored</u> park or rest there after shopping. Friends could also meet at the park for a day of shopping and lunch. Shoppers are not the only ones who could enjoy the park. Workers from nearby offices and stores could eat lunch outdoors. Several office complexes are near the park, and workers from these offices could bring <u>a bag</u> lunch to work and eat outside in good weather. I think many people would agree that an hour spent outdoors is a pleasant break from work. Most important, city children could play in an improved Roberts Park. They would get fresh air while they played on grass, not asphalt. Best of all, they would not have to play near traffic. Children, shoppers, and workers would benefit from a clean-up of Roberts Park, but so would others. An attractive park improves the city, and all residents benefit when a community is beautified.

For your information: A sample argument essay based on this topic and following the same writing steps can be found in Chapter 13, "Different Essay Patterns: Part Two."

Exercise 12   Proofreading to Prepare the Final Version

Following are two paragraphs with the kinds of errors that are easy to overlook when you prepare the final version of an assignment. Correct the errors, writing above the lines. There are fifteen errors in the first paragraph and eleven in the second paragraph.

1. Not all college students have access to computers at the homes. Most

colleges have technology labs where students can use the computers to work

on writing assignments or research projects. Unfortunately, the branch campuss

where I attend college does not offer much access to technology. Eastside business

College need to offer more computers and more hours for students to use

them. Today, the college has only 1 computer lab for students' use. Unfortunately, the lab fills up at 7:30 A.M., and most students have to stand in line for access. It is also difficult to concentrate in a glass-walled room while inpatient students line up outside the windows. Meanwhile, the students outside are wasting their time. Another reason that access is poor involves the computer lab's hours. The lab closes at 9:00 P.M. on weekdays, 5:00 P.M. on Saturdays, and is not open on Sundays. The students who takes evening classes and has a full-time day job rarely gets access to the lab unless they come to the College on Saturday mornings. Saturday afternoons at the lab are especially crowded. Finally, many of the student's who rely on the college's one lab are already struggling to stay focused on college. Most likely, they, cannot afford there own computers. Many of them have very little free time to commute to campus on Saturdays. Eastside Business College must consider it's students' needs, and goals. It must offer wider and better access to basic technology.

2. The residents in the Southern part of Millbrook need a small children's library staffed by children's libarians. Southern Millbrook is not, a fancy part of town. The residents are mostly working people who do not have excess to the variety of activities that wealthier communities offer to children. There is no private dance studio, soccer clinic, craft center, or indoor sports center for children. After school, children in southern Millbrook dont do much except play video games indoors or look for some distraction outdoors. The library would offer them an alternative place to be after school. In addition, it would offer excitement. Children's librarians know how to plan activities for every child from a toddler who likes story time, to a preteen who wants computer time, to an six-year-old who wants to join an early evening pajama party that features ghost stories. A children's library is a place for the whole family, too. Retired grandparents can enjoy guiding the first-time visitors through the facilities or listening to a beginning reader decipher the words of a book. Teens could volunteers to read a story to a group of children or to dress up as a character in a children's book and act in a short drama Parents who reglarly accompany their children to the library would bond over their children pleasure. For every age group, the library would offer a place of safety, excitement, and learning.

Lines of Detail: A Walk-Through Assignment

Write a one-paragraph letter to the editor of your local newspaper. Argue for some change you want for your community. You could argue for a traffic light, turn signal, or stop sign at a specific intersection. Or you could argue for bike paths in certain places, a recycling program, more bus service, or for any other specific change you feel is needed. To write your paragraph, follow these steps:

Step 1: Begin by listing all the reasons and details you can about your topic. Survey your list and consider any possible objections. Answer the objections as well as you can, and see if the objections can lead you to more reasons.

Step 2: Group your reasons, listing the details that fit under each reason. Add details where they are needed and check to see if any reasons overlap.

Step 3: Survey the reasons and details and draft a topic sentence. Make sure that your topic sentence states the subject and takes a stand.

Step 4: Write an outline; then revise it, checking that you have enough reasons to make your point. Also check that your reasons are specific and in an effective order. Make sure that you have sufficient details for each reason. Check that your outline includes answers to any significant objections.

Step 5: Write a draft of your argument. Revise the draft until it includes any necessary explanations of the problem being argued, all serious or obvious reasons, and sufficient specific details. Also check that the most important reason is stated last. Add all the transitions that are needed to link your reasons and details.

Step 6: Before you prepare the final copy of your paragraph, decide whether you need a final sentence to stress your point and whether your transitions are smooth and logical. Refine your word choice. Then check for errors in spelling, punctuation, and grammar.

Topics for Writing an Argument Paragraph

When you write on any of the topics below, be sure to work through the stages of the writing process in preparing your argument paragraph.

1. Write a paragraph for readers of your local newspaper, arguing for one of the following:
   a. A local ban on all advertising of alcohol
   b. Mandatory jail terms for those convicted of drunk driving

c. Mandatory school uniforms for all public elementary and middle schools

d. A fine for all dog or cat owners who have not had their animals neutered, to be used to support animal shelters

Collaborate

2. In a paragraph, argue one of the following topics to the audience specified. If your instructor agrees, brainstorm your topic with a group before you start writing. Ask the group to "play audience" by reacting to your reasons, raising objections, and asking questions.

topic a: Early-morning classes should be abolished at your college.
audience: The dean of academic affairs

topic b: College students should get discounts at movie theaters.
audience: The owner of your local movie theater

topic c: Your college should provide a day-care facility for students with children.
audience: The president of your college

topic d: Businesses should hire more student interns.
audience: The president of a company (name it) you'd like to work for

3. Write a paragraph for or against any of the following topics. The audience for this argument is your classmates and your instructor.

For or Against

a. Allowing police to stop drivers solely for a seat-belt check
b. A city's hidden cameras to catch drivers who run red lights
c. Cheaper tuition for Saturday and evening classes
d. The elimination of preferred parking (except for the handicapped) on campus
e. Mandatory student activities fees for commuter students at colleges and universities
f. A law requiring a month waiting period between buying a marriage license and getting married
g. A higher tax on cigarettes to be used to pay the health costs of smokers with smoking-related illnesses
h. More minimum-wage student jobs on campus

Computer

4. Visit your state's Department of Motor Vehicles Web site. Review the penalties for DUI (driving under the influence of alcohol) or DWI (driving while intoxicated). Argue for or against one of these penalties, and be sure to be as logical as possible. As an alternative, argue in favor of stricter penalties for either DUI or DWI in your city or state.

Computer

5. Some educators and parents are very concerned about the potentially harmful effects of violent video games on children. Using a search engine such as Google™, type in the words "video games" and "action." See if you can find the manufacturer's description of a video game you have played, and find the targeted age range. Using this information, argue for or against this point: (*Name of the video game*) is suitable for children ages _____ to _____.

6. Study the photograph of the traffic jam. One way to relieve such congestion is for more commuters to use carpooling. Write an argument for starting a carpooling program at your school or workplace, and be sure to include specific benefits to your fellow students or colleagues.

7. Study the photograph of the dumpster, garbage bags, and graffiti in a back alley. Imagine that this alley is near your home, and propose a practical method to keep it clean. As you make your case, include the immediate and long-range benefits of your proposal.

Topics for Critical Thinking and Writing

1. Many drivers often complain about dangerous street conditions and the high rate of accidents and fatalities near their neighborhood. Commonly proposed solutions involve traffic calming, a way of slowing down impatient drivers and reducing the number of deadly collisions. Traffic-calming methods include traffic circles ("roundabouts") and narrower lanes to discourage drivers from passing in a turn lane. Argue for or against a particular traffic-calming method and consider how it would or would not be practical for alleviating dangerous driving conditions on your commute to work or school. You may need to research the principles and practices of traffic calming and imagine how various methods apply to your local roadways.

2. Assume that a university wants to build a research center in your area of the state. You live in a region that is home for some major corporations but also has thousands of acres of farmland. Argue in favor of establishing either an agricultural-related research center or a business-related research center based on the most pressing needs of your region.

Note: Additional writing options suitable for argument-related assignments can be found in the professional reading "The Case for a Tax on Sodas," which can be found in the "Readings for Writers" appendix at the end of this book.

Name _____   Section _____

Peer Review Form for an Argument Paragraph

After you've written a draft of your argument paragraph, let a writing partner read it. When your partner has completed the form below, discuss the comments. Then repeat the same process for your partner's paragraph.

The topic sentence has this subject _____

_____

It takes this stand _____

_____

The most convincing part of the paragraph started with the words _____

_____ and ended with the words _____

_____

After reading this paragraph, I can think of an objection to this argument. The objection is _____

_____

The paragraph has/has not handled this objection. (Choose one.)

The part of the argument with the best details is the part about _____

_____

The part that could use more or better details is the part about _____

_____

The order of the reasons (a) is effective or (b) could be better. (Choose one.)

I have questions about _____

_____

Other comments _____

_____

_____

_____

_____

_____

_____

Reviewer's name _____

CHAPTER 11

Writing an Essay

Jumping In

*A quality home often reflects logical design, solid foundation and support, and careful attention to finishing touches. Similarly, an effective **essay** stems from careful preliminary work (prewriting and outlining techniques), well-constructed body paragraphs for thesis support (through drafting and revising), and meticulous attention to final details (editing and proofreading).*

Chapter Objectives

Students will be able to (1) identify the basic components of an essay, (2) recognize the differences between a topic sentence and a thesis statement, and (3) write a multi-paragraph essay containing sufficient supporting details and effective transitions.

WHAT IS AN ESSAY?

You write an essay when you have more to say than can be covered in one paragraph. An **essay** can consist of one paragraph, but in this book, we take it to mean a writing of more than one paragraph. An essay has a main point, called a *thesis*, supported by subpoints. The subpoints are the *topic sentences*. Each paragraph in the *body*, or main part, of the essay has a topic sentence. In fact, each paragraph in the body of the essay is like the paragraphs you've already written because each one makes a point and then supports it.

Comparing the Single Paragraph and the Essay

Read the paragraph and the essay that follow, both about Bob, the writer's brother. You will notice many similarities.

A Single Paragraph

I think I'm lucky to have a brother who is two years older than I am. For one thing, my brother Bob fought all the typical child–parent battles, and I was the real winner. Bob was the one who made my parents understand that sixteen-year-olds shouldn't have an 11:00 P.M. curfew on weekends. He fought for his rights. By the time I turned sixteen, my parents had accepted the later curfew, and I didn't have to fight for it. Bob also paved the way for me at school. He was such a great athlete that I benefited from his reputation. When I tried out for the basketball team, I had an advantage before I hit the court. I was Bob Cruz's younger brother, so the coach thought I had to be pretty good. At home and at school, my big brother was a big help to me.

An Essay

Some people complain about being the youngest child or the middle child in the family. These people believe older children get all the attention and grab all the power. I'm the younger brother in my family, and I disagree with the complainers. I think I'm lucky to have a brother who is two years older than I am.

For one thing, my brother Bob fought all the typical child–parent battles, and I was the real winner. Bob was the one who made my parents understand that sixteen-year-olds shouldn't have an 11:00 P.M. curfew on weekends. He fought for his rights, and the fighting wasn't easy. I remember months of arguments between Bob and my parents as Bob tried to explain that not all teens on the street at 11:30 are punks or criminals. Bob was the one who suffered from being grounded or who lost the use of my father's car. By the time I turned sixteen, my parents had accepted the later curfew, and I didn't have to fight for it.

Bob also paved the way for me at school. Because he was so popular with the other students and the teachers, he created a positive image of what the boys in our family were like. When I started school, I walked into a place where people were ready to like me, just as they liked Bob. I remember the first day of class when the teachers read the new class rolls. When they got to my name, they asked, "Are you Bob Cruz's brother?" When I said yes, they smiled. Bob's success opened doors for me in school sports, too. He was such a great athlete that I benefited from his reputation. When I tried out for the basketball team, I had an advantage before I hit the court. I was Bob Cruz's younger brother, so the coach thought I had to be pretty good.

I had many battles to fight as I grew up. Like all children, I had to struggle to gain independence and respect. In my struggles at home and at school, my big brother was a big help to me.

If you read the two selections carefully, you noticed that they make the same main point, and they support that point with two subpoints.

main point: I think I'm lucky to have a brother who is two years older than I am.

subpoints: 1. My brother Bob fought all the typical child–parent battles, and I was the real winner.

2. Bob also paved the way at school.

You also noticed that the essay is longer because it has more details and examples to support the points.

ORGANIZING AN ESSAY

When you write an essay of more than one paragraph, the **thesis** is the focus of your entire essay; it is the major point of your essay. The other important points that relate to the thesis are in topic sentences.

> **thesis:** Working as a salesperson has changed my character.
> **topic sentence:** I have learned patience.
> **topic sentence:** I have developed the ability to listen.
> **topic sentence:** I have become more tactful.

Notice that the thesis expresses a bigger idea than the topic sentences below it, and it is supported by the topic sentences. The essay has an introduction, a body, and a conclusion.

1. **Introduction:** The first paragraph is usually the introduction. The thesis is included in this paragraph.
2. **Body:** This central part of the essay is the part where you support your main point (the thesis). Each paragraph in the body of the essay has its own topic sentence.
3. **Conclusion:** Usually one paragraph long, the conclusion reminds the reader of the thesis.

Writing the Thesis

There are several characteristics of a thesis:

1. It is expressed in a sentence. A thesis is *not* the same as the topic of the essay or the title of the essay.

> **topic:** quitting smoking
> **title:** Why I Quit Smoking
> **thesis:** I quit smoking because I was concerned for my health, and I wanted to prove to myself that I could break the habit.

2. A thesis *does not announce;* it makes a point about the subject.

> **announcement:** This essay will explain the reasons why young adults should watch what they eat.
> **thesis:** Young adults should watch what they eat so they can live healthy lives today and prevent future health problems.

3. A thesis *is not too broad.* Some ideas are just too big to cover well in an essay. A thesis that tries to cover too much can lead to a superficial or boring essay.

> **too broad:** People all over the world should work on solving their interpersonal communication problems.
> **acceptable thesis:** As a Southerner, I had a hard time understanding that some New Yorkers think slow speech is ignorant speech.

4. A thesis *is not too narrow.* Sometimes, writers start with a thesis that looks good because it seems specific and precise. Later, when they try to support such a thesis, they can't find anything to say.

> **too narrow:** My sister pays forty dollars a week for a special formula for her baby.
> **acceptable thesis:** My sister had no idea what it would cost to care for a baby.

Hints for Writing a Thesis

1. Your thesis can **mention the specific subpoints** of your essay. For example, your thesis might be as follows:

> I hated *The Revenge of the Shark People* because the film's plot was disorganized, its conflict was unrealistic, and its scenes were overly violent.

With this thesis, you have indicated the three subpoints of your essay: *The Revenge of the Shark People* had a disorganized plot, it had an unrealistic conflict, and it had overly violent scenes.

2. You can **make a point** without listing your subpoints. For example, you can write a thesis like this:

> I hated *The Revenge of the Shark People* because it was a bloody mess.

With this thesis, you can still use the subpoints stating that the movie had a disorganized plot, an unrealistic conflict, and overly violent scenes. You just don't have to mention all your subpoints in the thesis.

Exercise 1   Practice: Recognizing Good Thesis Sentences

Following is a list of thesis statements. Some are acceptable, but others are too broad or too narrow. Some are announcements; others are topics, not sentences. Put a *G* next to the good thesis sentences.

1. _____ Fighting a speeding ticket involved me in plenty of frustration and drama.

2. _____ My landlord is evicting the family in the apartment next to mine.

3. _____ Ultraviolent movies are desensitizing viewers to the realities of suffering around the world.

4. _____ Why too much sugar is unhealthy for adults and children.

5. _____ Learning a second language was more difficult than I had expected.

6. _____ Rising unemployment rates affect every age group and social class.

7. _____ By the time I got married, I had learned three important rules about apologizing.

8. _____ Addiction is a terrible thing in any kind of family.

9. _____ Habits that can keep a person from financial success.

10. _____ How the cost of electricity is causing local residents to change their ways.

Exercise 2   Practice: Selecting a Good Thesis Sentence

In each pair of thesis statements below, put a *G* next to the good one.

1. a. _____ After losing a wallet, a person suffers from fear, frustration, and guilt.

   b. _____ Losing a wallet and the fear, frustration, and guilt that follow.

2. a. _____ Global water shortages threaten to change the face of the earth in our lifetime.

   b. _____ Residents in Santa Elisa can adopt three simple ways to save water.

3. a. _____ Excessive sunbathing leads to leathery skin, wrinkles, and skin cancer.

   b. _____ The dangers of excessive sunbathing are the subject to be discussed in this essay.

4. a. _____ Arturo was involved in a bad accident recently.

   b. _____ Because he had been driving for eighteen hours and fell asleep at the wheel of his truck, Arturo was involved in a bad accident.

5. a. _____ I found the perfect roommate through sheer luck.

   b. _____ How I found the perfect roommate is the topic of this essay.

Exercise 3 Practice: Writing a Thesis That Relates to the Subpoints

Following are lists of subpoints that could be discussed in an essay. Write a thesis for each list. Remember that there are two ways to write a thesis: you can write a thesis that includes the specific subpoints, or you can write one that makes a point without listing the subpoints. As an example, the first one is done for you, using both kinds of topic sentences.

1. **one kind of thesis:** If you want a pet, a cat is easier to care for than a dog.

   _____

   another kind of thesis: Cats make better pets than dogs because cats don't need to be walked, don't mind being alone, and don't make any noise.

   subpoints: a. Cats don't have to be walked and exercised like dogs do.
   b. Cats are independent and don't mind being home alone, but a dog gets lonely.
   c. Cats are quieter than dogs.

2. **thesis:** _____

   _____

   subpoints: a. A star college athlete can win fame and opportunity.
   b. A star college athlete's reputation can be destroyed before graduation arrives.

3. **thesis:** _____

   _____

   subpoints: a. A professional athlete risks permanent damage from injuries such as concussions or broken bones.
   b. The use of steroids is a constant temptation in many professional sports.

    c. A professional athlete who must travel constantly and perform flawlessly endures high stress levels.

    d. Media attention can create a superstar but deprive a professional athlete of a private life.

4. thesis: _____

_____

subpoints: **a.** Many high school graduates will long remember the most popular song of their senior year.

    b. Married couples reminisce about the song played for the first dance of their wedding celebration.

    c. Parents remember the song they sang to help their baby fall asleep.

WRITING THE ESSAY IN STEPS

In an essay, you follow the same steps you learned in writing a paragraph—prewriting, planning, drafting and revising, and proofreading—but you adapt them to the longer essay form.

PREWRITING   AN ESSAY

Often you begin by *narrowing a topic.* Your instructor may give you a large topic so that you can find something smaller, within the broad one, that you would like to write about.

Some students think that because they have several paragraphs to write, they should pick a big topic, one that will give them enough to say. But big topics can lead to boring, superficial, general essays. A smaller topic can challenge you to find the specific, concrete examples and details that make an essay effective.

If your instructor asked you to write about college, for instance, you might *freewrite* some ideas as you narrow the topic:

narrowing the topic of college

what college means to me—too big, and it could be boring
college versus high school—everyone might choose this topic
college students—too big
college students who have jobs—better!
problems of working and going to college—OK!

In your freewriting, you can consider your *purpose*—to write an essay about some aspect of college—and *audience*—your instructor and classmates. Your narrowed topic will appeal to this audience because many students hold jobs and instructors are familiar with the problems of working students.

Listing Ideas

Once you have a narrow topic, you can use whatever process works for you. You can brainstorm by writing a series of questions and answers about your topic, you can freewrite on the topic, you can list ideas on the topic, or you can do any combination of these processes.

Following is a sample listing of ideas on the topic of the problems of working and going to college.

problems of working and going to college

early classes
too tired to pay attention
tried to study at work
got caught
got reprimanded
slept in class
constantly racing around
no sleep
little time to do homework

weekends only time to study
no social life
apartment a mess
missed work for makeup test
get behind in school
need salary for tuition
rude to customers
girlfriend ready to kill me

Clustering the Ideas

By clustering related items on the list, you'll find it easier to see the connections between ideas. The following items have been clustered (grouped), and they have been listed under a subtitle.

Problems of Working and Going to College: Ideas in Clusters

problems at school

early classes
too tired to pay attention
slept in class
little time to do homework
get behind in school

problems at work

tried to study at work
got caught
got reprimanded
missed work for makeup test
rude to customers

problems outside of work and school

weekends only time to study
no social life
apartment a mess
girlfriend ready to kill me

When you surveyed the clusters, you probably noticed that some of the ideas from the original list were left out. These ideas—constantly racing around, not getting enough sleep, and needing tuition money—could fit into more than one place and might not fit anywhere. You might come back to them later.

When you name each cluster by giving it a subtitle, you move toward a focus for each body paragraph of your essay. And by beginning to focus the body paragraphs, you start thinking about the main point, the thesis of the essay. Concentrating on the thesis and on focused paragraphs helps you to *unify* your essay.

Reread the clustered ideas. When you do so, you'll notice that each cluster is about problems at a different place. You can incorporate that concept into a thesis with a sentence like this:

> Students who work while they attend college face problems at school, at work, and at home.

Once you have a thesis and a list of details, you can begin working on the planning part of your essay.

Exercise 4 **Collaborate: Narrowing Topics**

Working with a partner or a group, narrow these topics so that the new topics are related, but smaller and suitable for short essays between four and six paragraphs long. The first topic is narrowed for you.

1. **topic:** summer vacation
   smaller, related topics:

   a. _a car trip with children_____

   b. _finding the cheapest flight to Mexico_____

   c. _my vacation job_____

2. **topic:** luck
   smaller, related topics:

   a. _____

   b. _____

   c. _____

3. **topic:** music
   smaller, related topics:

   a. _____

   b. _____

   c. _____

4. **topic:** anger
   smaller, related topics:

   a. _____

   b. _____

   c. _____

Exercise 5 **Practice: Clustering Related Ideas**

Below are two topics, each with a list of ideas. Mark all the related items on the list with the same number (1, 2, or 3). Not all items will get a number. When you've finished marking the list, write a title for each number that explains the cluster of ideas.

1. **topic:** my worst birthday celebration

   _____ my girlfriend gave me some smelly cologne

   _____ the birthday cake collapsed into a mess of melted icing and crumbling yellow layers

   _____ celebrated my twenty-second birthday in May

   _____ my best friend showed up an hour late

   _____ the burgers were char-burnt, not char-grilled

   _____ my nosy neighbor crashed the birthday party

   _____ my cousin ate all the chips and salsa

   _____ one friend gave me a set of wooden bowls I had seen in the dollar store

_____ I hate surprise parties

_____ I also got a gift certificate for a store that had gone out of business

The ideas marked *1* can be titled _____

The ideas marked *2* can be titled _____

The ideas marked *3* can be titled _____

2. topic: when tears are a universal reaction

_____ a loved one dies

_____ the birth of a baby

_____ at a wedding

_____ a comedian tells a string of hilarious jokes

_____ watching a long, funny scene in a movie

_____ your employment is terminated

_____ attending a child's graduation

_____ carrying tissues to wipe away tears

_____ parents announce they are divorcing

_____ children who are called crybabies

The items marked *1* can be titled _____

The items marked *2* can be titled _____

The items marked *3* can be titled _____

PLANNING AN ESSAY

In the next stage of writing your essay, draft an outline. Use the thesis to focus your ideas. There are many kinds of outlines, but all are used to help a writer organize ideas. When you use a **formal outline,** you show the difference between a main idea and its supporting detail by *indenting* the supporting detail. In a formal outline, Roman numerals (numbers I, II, III, and so on) and capital letters are used. Each Roman numeral represents a paragraph, and the letters beneath the numeral represent supporting details.

The Structure of a Formal Outline

first paragraph	I. Thesis
second paragraph	II. Topic sentence
details	A. B. C. D. E.
third paragraph	III. Topic sentence
details	A. B. C. D. E.

fourth paragraph	IV. Topic sentence
	A.
	B.
details	C.
	D.
	E.
fifth paragraph	V. Conclusion

Hints for Outlining

Developing a good, clear outline now can save you hours of confused, disorganized writing later. The extra time you spend to make sure your outline has sufficient details and that *each paragraph stays on one point* will pay off in the long run.

1. Check the topic sentences. Keep in mind that each topic sentence in each body paragraph should support the thesis sentence. If a topic sentence is not carefully connected to the thesis, the structure of the essay will be confusing. Here are a thesis and a list of topic sentences; the topic sentence that does not fit is crossed out:

thesis:	I.	A home-cooked dinner can be a rewarding experience for the cook and the guests.
topic sentences:	II.	Preparing a meal is a satisfying activity.
	III.	It is a pleasure for the cook to see guests enjoy the meal.
	IV.	~~Many recipes are handed down through generations.~~
	V.	Dinner guests are flattered that someone cooked for them.
	VI.	Dining at home is a treat for everyone at the table or in the kitchen.

Since the thesis of this outline is about the pleasure of dining at home for the cook and the guests, topic sentence IV doesn't fit: it isn't about the joy of cooking *or* of being a dinner guest. It takes the essay off track. A careful check of the links between the thesis and the topic sentences will help keep your essay focused.

2. Include enough details. Some writers believe that they don't need many details in the outline. They feel they can fill in the details later, when they actually write the essay. Even though some writers do manage to add details later, others who are in a hurry or who run out of ideas will have problems.

For example, imagine that a writer has included very few details in an outline, like this outline for a paragraph:

II. A burglary makes the victim feel unsafe.
    A. The person has lost property.
    B. The person's home territory has been invaded.

The paragraph created from that outline might be too short, lack specific details, and look like this:

    A burglary makes the victim feel unsafe. First of all, the victim has lost property. Second, a person's home territory has been invaded.

If you have difficulty thinking of ideas when you write, try to tackle the problem in the outline. The more details you put into your outline, the more detailed and effective your draft essay will be. For example, suppose the same outline on the burglary topic had more details, like this:

II. A burglary makes the victim feel unsafe.

more details about burglary	A. The person has lost property.
	B. The property could be worth hundreds of dollars.
	C. The victim can lose a television or camera or DVD player.
	D. The burglars may take cash.
	E. Worse, items with personal value, like family jewelry or heirlooms, can be stolen.
more details about safety concerns	F. Even worse, a person's territory has been invaded.
	G. People who thought they were safe know they are not safe.
	H. The fear is that the invasion can happen again.

You will probably agree that the paragraph will be more detailed, too.

3. Stay on one point. It is a good idea to check the outline of each body paragraph to see whether the paragraph stays on one point. Compare each topic sentence, which is at the top of the list for the paragraph, against the details indented under it. Staying on one point gives each paragraph unity.

Below is the outline for a paragraph that has problems staying on one point. See if you can spot the problem areas.

III. Sonya is a generous person.

   A. I remember how freely she gave her time when our club had a car wash.
   B. She is always willing to share her lecture notes with me.
   C. Sonya gives ten percent of her salary to her church.
   D. She is a member of Big Sisters and spends every Saturday with a disadvantaged child.
   E. She can read people's minds when they are in trouble.
   F. She knows what they are feeling.

The topic sentence of the paragraph is about generosity. However, sentences E and F talk about Sonya's insight, not her generosity.

When you have a problem staying on one point, you can solve the problem two ways:

1. Eliminate details that do not fit your main point.
2. Change the topic sentence to cover all the ideas in the paragraph.

For example, you could cut sentences E and F about Sonya's insight, getting rid of the details that do not fit. As an alternative, you could change the topic sentence in the paragraph so that it relates to all the ideas in the paragraph. A better topic sentence would be "Sonya is a generous and insightful person."

Revisiting the Prewriting Stage

Writing an outline can help you identify undeveloped places in your plan, places where your paragraphs will need more details. You can get these details in two ways:

1. Go back to the writing you did in the prewriting stage. Check whether items on a list or ideas from prewriting can lead you to more details for your outline.

2. Brainstorm for more details by a question-and-answer approach. For example, if the outline includes "My apartment is a mess," you might ask, "Why? How messy?" Or if the outline includes "I have no social life," you might ask, "What do you mean? No friends? No activities? Or what about school organizations?"

The time you spend writing and revising your outline will make it easier for you to write an essay that is well developed, unified, and coherently structured. The checklist below may help you to revise.

Checklist for Revising the Outline of an Essay

✔ **Unity:** Do the thesis and topic sentences all lead to the same point? Does each paragraph make one, and only one, point? Do the details in each paragraph support the topic sentence? Does the conclusion unify the essay?

✔ **Support:** Do the body paragraphs have enough supporting details?

✔ **Coherence:** Are the paragraphs in the most effective order? Are the details in each paragraph arranged in the most effective order?

A sentence outline on the problems of working and going to college follows. It includes the thesis in the first paragraph. The topic sentences have been created from the titles of the ideas clustered earlier. The details have been drawn from ideas in the clusters and from further brainstorming. The conclusion has just one sentence that unifies the essay.

Outline for an Essay

paragraph 1	I. Thesis: Students who work while going to college face problems at school, at work, and at home.
paragraph 2 **topic sentence**	II. Trying to juggle job and school responsibilities creates problems at school.
	A. Early classes are difficult.
details	B. I am too tired to pay attention.
problems at school	C. Once I slept in class.
	D. I have little time to do homework.
paragraph 3	E. I get behind in school assignments.
topic sentence	III. Work can suffer when workers attend college.
details	A. I tried to study at work.
problems at work	B. I got caught by my boss.
	C. I was reprimanded.
	D. Sometimes I come to work very tired.
	E. When I don't have enough sleep, I can be rude to customers.
	F. Rudeness gets me in trouble.
	G. Another time, I had to cut work to take a makeup test.

continued

paragraph 4
topic sentence

IV. Working students suffer outside of classes and the workplace.
   A. I work nights during the week.

details
problems at home

   B. The weekends are the only time I can study.
   C. My apartment is a mess since I have no time to clean it.
   D. Worse, my girlfriend is ready to kill me because I have no social life.
   E. We never even go to the movies anymore.
   F. When she comes over, I am busy studying.

paragraph 5
conclusion

V. I have learned that working students have to be very organized to cope with their responsibilities at college, work, and home.

Exercise 6 Practice: Completing an Outline for an Essay

Following is part of an outline that has a thesis and topic sentences, but no details. Add the details and write in complete sentences. Write one sentence for each capital letter. Be sure that the details are connected to the topic sentence.

I. Thesis: Many college students who live on their own do very little cooking.

II. For many students, fast-food restaurants are more popular than supermarkets.

   A. _____

   _____

   B. _____

   _____

   C. _____

   _____

   D. _____

   _____

   E. _____

   _____

III. A microwave or toaster is the only cooking device that students need.

   A. _____

   _____

   B. _____

   _____

   C. _____

   _____

   D. _____

   _____

   E. _____

   _____

IV. When hunger strikes college students, they can resort to delivery services.

A. _____

_____

B. _____

_____

C. _____

_____

D. _____

_____

E. _____

_____

V. College students may no longer enjoy home cooking or a healthy diet, but they have plenty of choices.

Exercise 7   **Practice: Focusing an Outline for an Essay**

The outline below has a thesis and details, but it has no topic sentences for the body paragraphs. Write the topic sentences.

I. Thesis: Just once in my life, I would love the luxury of a new car.

II. _____

_____

A. No dirt would soil the floor.

B. There would be no scratches or tears on the upholstery.

C. I would own an elaborate car sound system that worked perfectly.

D. The only smell in the automobile would be the distinctive smell of a new car.

E. The interior of the car would be filled with gadgets I had never dreamed of.

III. _____

_____

A. The hubcaps and rims would shine.

B. There would be no scratches on the paint.

C. The paint would not be faded.

D. No dents would appear in the fenders or bumpers.

E. As for the tires, not a bit of wear would be evident.

IV. I have always dreamed of the day when I would drive a brand new car out of the car dealer's lot.

DRAFTING AND REVISING **AN ESSAY**

When you are satisfied with your outline, you can begin drafting and revising the essay. Start by writing a first draft of the essay, which includes these parts: introduction, body paragraphs, and conclusion.

WRITING THE INTRODUCTION

Where Does the Thesis Go?

The **thesis** should appear in the introduction of the essay, in the first paragraph. But most of the time, it should not be the first sentence. In front of the thesis, write a few (three or more) sentences of introduction. Generally, the thesis is the *last sentence* in the introductory paragraph.

Why put the thesis at the end of the first paragraph? First of all, writing several sentences in front of your main idea gives you a chance to lead into it, gradually and smoothly. This will help you build interest and gain the reader's attention. Also, by placing the thesis after a few sentences of introduction, you will not startle the reader with your main point.

Finally, if your thesis is at the end of the introduction, it states the main point of the essay just before that point is supported in the body paragraphs. Putting the thesis at the end of the introduction is like putting an arrow pointing to the supporting ideas in the essay.

Hints for Writing the Introduction

There are a number of ways to write an introduction.

   1. **You can begin with some general statements** that gradually lead to your thesis:

general statements	Students face all kinds of problems when they start college. Some students struggle with a lack of basic math skills; others have never learned to write a term paper. Students who were stars in high school have to cope with being just another Social Security number at a large institution. Students with small children have to find a way to be good parents and good students, too. Although all these problems are common, I found
thesis at end	an even more typical conflict. My biggest problem in college was learning to organize my time.

   2. **You can begin with a quotation** that smoothly leads to your thesis. The quotation can be from someone famous, or it can be an old saying. It can be something your mother always told you, or it can be a slogan from an advertisement or the words of a song.

quotation	Everybody has heard the old saying, "Time flies," but I never really thought about that statement until I started college. I expected college to challenge me with demanding coursework. I expected it to excite me with the range of people I would meet. I even thought it might amuse me with the fun and intrigue of dating and romance. But I never expected college to exhaust
thesis at end	me. I was surprised to discover that my biggest problem in college was learning to organize my time.

> **Note:** Remember that you can add transitional words or phrases to your thesis, as in the preceding example.

3. You can tell a story as a way of leading into your thesis. You can open with the story of something that happened to you or to someone you know, a story you read about or heard on the news.

story	My friend Phyllis is two years older than I am, and so she started college before I did. When Phyllis came home from college for the Thanksgiving weekend, I called her with plans for fun, but Phyllis told me she planned to spend most of the weekend sleeping. I didn't understand her when she told me she was worn out. When I started college myself, I understood her perfectly. Phyllis was a victim of that old college ailment: not knowing how to handle time. I developed
thesis at end	the same disease. <u>My biggest problem in college was learning to organize my time.</u>

4. You can explain why this topic is worth writing about. Explaining could mean giving some background on the topic, or it could mean discussing why the topic is an important one.

explain	I do not remember a word of what was said during my freshman orientation, and I wish I did. I am sure somebody somewhere warned me about the problems I would face in college. I am sure somebody talked about getting organized. Unfortunately, I didn't listen, and I had to learn the hard way. I hope other students will listen and learn and be spared my hard lesson and
thesis at end	my big problem. <u>My biggest problem in college was learning to organize my time.</u>

5. Use one or more questions to lead into your thesis. You can open with a question or questions that will be answered by your thesis. Or you can open with a question or questions that catch the reader's attention and move toward your thesis.

question	Have you ever stayed up all night to study for an exam, then fallen asleep at dawn and slept right through the time of the exam? If you have, then you were probably the same kind of college student I was. I was the student who always ran into class three minutes late, the one who begged for an extension on the term paper, the one who pleaded with the teacher to postpone the test. I just could not get things done on
thesis at end	schedule. <u>My biggest problem in college was learning to organize my time.</u>

6. You can open with a contradiction of your main point as a way of attracting the reader's interest and leading to your thesis. You can begin with an idea that is the opposite of what you will say in your thesis. The opposition of your opening and your thesis creates interest.

contradiction   People who knew me in my freshman year probably felt really sorry for me. They saw a girl with dark circles under her bloodshot eyes, a girl who was always racing from one place to another. Those people probably thought I was exhausted from overwork. But they were wrong. My problem in college was definitely not too much work; it was the way I handled my

thesis at end   work. <u>My biggest problem in college was learning to organize my time.</u>

Exercise 8   **Practice: Writing an Introduction**

Below are five thesis sentences. Pick one. Then write an introductory paragraph on the lines provided. Your last sentence should be the thesis sentence. If your instructor agrees, read your introduction to others in the class who wrote an introduction to the same thesis, or read your introduction to the entire class.

Thesis Sentences:

1. Being alone makes some people uncomfortable.

2. Three people have supported me in times when I was under stress.

3. Fame does not always bring happiness.

4. Texting can be a means for connecting or a tool for avoiding close contact.

5. People have a number of reasons for paying attention to weather reports.

6. (Write an introduction) _____

_____

_____

_____

_____

_____

_____

_____

WRITING THE BODY OF THE ESSAY

In the body of the essay, the paragraphs *explain, support, and develop* your thesis. In this part of the essay, each paragraph has its own topic sentence. The topic sentence in each paragraph does two things:

1. It focuses the sentences in the paragraph.
2. It makes a point connected to the thesis.

The thesis and the topic sentences are ideas that need to be supported by details, explanations, and examples. You can visualize the connections among the parts of an essay like this:

Introduction with Thesis

Body {
Topic Sentence
Details
Topic Sentence
Details
Topic Sentence
Details
}

Conclusion

When you write topic sentences, refer to the checklist below to help you organize your essay.

Checklist for Topic Sentences of an Essay

✔ Does the topic sentence give the point of the paragraph?

✔ Does the topic sentence connect to the thesis of the essay?

How Long Are the Body Paragraphs?

Remember that the body paragraphs of an essay are the place where you explain and develop your thesis. Those paragraphs should be long enough to explain your points, not just list them. To do this well, try to make your body paragraphs *at least seven sentences* long. As you develop your writing skills, you may find that you can support your ideas in fewer than seven sentences.

Developing the Body Paragraphs

You can write well-developed body paragraphs by following the same steps you used in writing single paragraphs for the earlier assignments in this course. By working through the stages of gathering ideas, outlining, drafting, revising, editing, and proofreading, you can create clear, effective paragraphs.

To focus and develop the body paragraphs, ask the questions below as you revise:

Checklist for Developing Body Paragraphs for an Essay

✔ Does the topic sentence cover everything in the paragraph?

✔ Do I have enough details to support the topic sentence?

✔ Do all the details in the paragraph explain, develop, or illustrate the topic sentence?

Exercise 9 **Practice: Creating Topic Sentences**

Following are thesis sentences. For each thesis, write topic sentences (as many as indicated by the numbered blanks). The first one is done for you.

1. thesis: Cats make good pets.

topic sentence 1: Cats are independent and don't mind being home alone.

topic sentence 2: Cats are easy to litter-train. _____

_____

topic sentence 3: Cats are fun to play with. _____

_____

2. **thesis:** Most college students live on a tight budget.

   topic sentence 1: _____

_____

   topic sentence 2: _____

_____

   topic sentence 3: _____

_____

3. **thesis:** When a crowd camps out overnight to be the first customers at a special sale, chaos can break out.

   topic sentence 1: _____

_____

   topic sentence 2: _____

_____

4. **thesis:** The loss of a job can signal a time of crisis, but it can also be a time of opportunity.

   topic sentence 1: _____

_____

   topic sentence 2: _____

_____

   topic sentence 3: _____

_____

   topic sentence 4: _____

_____

WRITING THE CONCLUSION

The last paragraph in the essay is the **conclusion.** It does not have to be as long as a body paragraph, but it should be long enough to unify the essay and remind the reader of the thesis. You can use any of these strategies in writing the conclusion.

   1. **You can restate the thesis in new words.** Go back to the first paragraph of your essay and reread it. For example, this could be the first paragraph of an essay:

introduction

Even when I was a child, I did not like being told what to do. I wanted to be my own boss. When I grew up, I figured that the best way to be my own boss was to own my own business. I thought that being in charge would be easy. I now know how difficult being an independent business person can

thesis at end

be. <u>Independent business owners have to be smart, highly motivated, and hard-working.</u>

The thesis, underlined above, is the sentence that you can restate in your conclusion. Your task is to *keep the point but put it in different words.* Then work that restatement into a short paragraph, like this:

restating the thesis

People who own their own business have to be harder on themselves than any employer would ever be. Their success is their own responsibility; they cannot blame company policy or rules because they set the policy and make the rules. <u>If the business is to succeed, their intelligence, drive, and effort are essential.</u>

2. You can make a judgment, valuation, or recommendation.
Instead of simply restating your point, you can end by making some comment on the issue you've described or the problem you've illustrated. If you were looking for another way to end the essay on owning one's own business, for example, you could end with a recommendation.

ending with a recommendation

People often dream of owning their own business. Dreaming is easy, but the reality is tough. <u>Those who want to succeed in their own venture should find a role model.</u> Studying a role model would teach them how ambition, know-how, and constant effort lead to success.

3. You can conclude by framing your essay. You can tie your essay together neatly by *using something from your introduction* as a way of concluding. When you take an example, a question, or even a quotation from your first paragraph and refer to it in your last paragraph, you are "framing" the essay. Take another look at the introduction to the essay on owning your own business. The writer talks about not liking to be told what to do, being one's own boss, and believing that being in charge would be easy. The writer also mentions the need to be smart, highly motivated, and hard-working. Now consider how the ideas of the introduction are used in this conclusion:

frame
frame

Children <u>who do not like to take directions</u> may think that <u>being their own boss will be easy.</u> Adults who try to start a business soon discover that they must be totally self-directed; that is, they must be strong enough

frame
frame

to <u>keep learning,</u> to <u>keep pushing forward,</u> and to <u>keep working.</u>

Exercise 10   **Practice: Choosing a Better Way to Restate the Thesis**

Following are four clusters. Each cluster consists of a thesis sentence and two sentences that try to restate the thesis. Each restated sentence could be used as part of the conclusion to an essay. Put *B* next to the sentence in each pair that is a better restatement. Remember that the better choice repeats the same idea as the thesis but does not rely on too many of the same words.

1. **thesis:** Drinking water instead of soft drinks can improve a person's health.

   restatement 1: ___ People can improve their health when they drink water instead of soft drinks.

   restatement 2: ___ Water is a healthy substitute for soft drinks.

2. **thesis:** Some people will avoid a large party because they fear making conversation with strangers.

   restatement 1: ___ Because they are afraid of knowing what to say to strangers, some people stay away from large parties.

   restatement 2: ___ There are people who will avoid a large party, for they fear making conversation with strangers.

3. **thesis:** One act of kindness can lead the way to many other good deeds.

   restatement 1: ___ One kind act can be like a seed that grows and spreads.

   restatement 2: ___ Several other good deeds can result from one act of kindness.

4. **thesis:** Regularly playing a sport or getting another form of exercise helps a person stay sane in a crazy world.

   restatement 1: ___ A person can stay sane in a world of craziness if he or she regularly plays a sport or gets another form of exercise.

   restatement 2: ___ When the world has gone mad, a person who exercises regularly can remain sane.

Revising the Draft

Once you have a rough draft of your essay, you can begin revising it. The following checklist may help you to make the necessary changes in your draft.

Checklist for Revising the Draft of an Essay
✔ Does the essay have a clear, unifying thesis?
✔ Does the thesis make a point?
✔ Does each body paragraph have a topic sentence?
✔ Is each body paragraph focused on its topic sentence?
✔ Are the body paragraphs roughly the same size?
✔ Do any of the sentences need combining?

✔ Do any of the words need to be changed?

✔ Do the ideas seem to be smoothly linked?

✔ Does the introduction catch the reader's interest?

✔ Is there a definite conclusion?

✔ Does the conclusion remind the reader of the thesis?

Transitions Within Paragraphs

In an essay, you can use two kinds of transitions: those within a paragraph and those between paragraphs.

Transitions that link ideas *within a paragraph* are the same kinds you used earlier. Your choice of words, phrases, or even sentences depends on the kind of connection you want to make. Here is a list of some common transitions and the kinds of connections they express.

INFO BOX: **Common Transitions Within a Paragraph**

To join two ideas:

again	another	in addition	moreover
also	besides	likewise	similarly
and	furthermore		

To show a contrast or a different opinion:

but	instead	on the other hand	still
however	nevertheless	or	yet
in contrast	on the contrary		

To show a cause-and-effect connection:

accordingly	because	for	therefore
as a result	consequently	so	thus

To give an example:

for example	in the case of	such as	to illustrate
for instance	like		

To show time:

after	first	recently	subsequently
at the same time	meanwhile	shortly	then
before	next	soon	until
finally			

Transitions Between Paragraphs

When you write something that is more than one paragraph long, you need transitions that link each paragraph to the others. There are several effective ways to link paragraphs and remind the reader of your main idea and of how the smaller points connect to it. Restatement and repetition are two of these ways:

1. Restate an idea from the preceding paragraph at the start of a new paragraph. Look closely at the two paragraphs below and notice how the second paragraph repeats an idea from the first paragraph and provides a link.

> If people were more patient, driving would be less of an an ordeal. If, for instance, the driver behind me didn't honk his horn as soon as the traffic light turned green, both he and I would probably have lower blood pressure. He wouldn't be irritating himself by pushing so hard. Also, I wouldn't be reacting by slowing down, trying to irritate him even more, and getting angry at him. When I get impatient in heavy traffic, I just make a bad situation worse. My hurry doesn't get me to my destination any faster; it just stresses me out.

**transition
restating an idea**

> <u>The impatient driver doesn't get anywhere; neither does</u> the impatient customer at a restaurant. Impatience at restaurants doesn't pay. I work as a hostess at a restaurant, and I know that the customer who moans and complains about waiting for a table won't get one any faster than the person who makes the best of the wait. In fact, if a customer is too aggressive or obnoxious, the restaurant staff may actually slow down the process of getting that customer a table.

2. Use synonyms and repetition as a way of reminding the reader of an important point. For example, in the two paragraphs below, notice how certain repeated words, phrases, and synonyms all remind the reader of a point about facing fear. The repeated words and synonyms are underlined.

> Some people just <u>avoid</u> whatever they <u>fear</u>. I have an uncle who is <u>afraid</u> to fly. Whenever he has to go on a trip, he does anything he can to <u>avoid</u> getting on an airplane. He will drive for days, travel by train, take a bus trip. Because he is so <u>terrified</u> of flying, he lives with <u>constant anxiety</u> that some day he may have to fly. He is always thinking of the one emergency that could force him to <u>confront what he most dreads.</u> Instead of <u>dealing directly with his fear,</u> he lets it <u>haunt</u> him.

> Other people are even worse than my uncle. He won't <u>attack his fear</u> of something external. But there are people who won't <u>deal with their fear</u> of themselves. My friend Sam is a good example of this kind of person. Sam has a serious drinking problem. All of Sam's friends know he is an alcoholic. But Sam <u>will not admit</u> his addiction. I think he is <u>afraid to face</u> that part of himself. So he <u>denies</u> his problem, saying he can stop drinking any time he wants to. Of course, until Sam has the courage to <u>admit what he is most afraid of,</u> his alcoholism, he won't be able to change.

A Draft Essay

Below is a draft of the essay on working and going to college. As you read it, you'll notice many changes from the outline on pages 259–260:

- An introduction has been added, written in the first person, "I," to unify the essay.
- Transitions have been added within and between paragraphs; many transitions are complete sentences.
- General statements have been replaced by more specific ones.
- Many new, specific details and examples develop the body paragraphs.
- Word choice has been improved.
- A conclusion has been added. Some of the ideas added to the conclusion came from the original list of ideas about the topic of work and school. They are ideas that do not belong in the body paragraphs but are useful in the conclusion.

Draft of an Essay

introduction added	I work thirty hours a week at the front desk of a motel in Riverside. When I first signed up for college classes, I figured college would be fairly easy
tells a story	to fit into my schedule. After all, college students are not in class all day, as high school students are. So I thought the twelve hours a week I'd spend in class wouldn't be too much of a load. But I was in for a big
thesis sentence at the end of the paragraph	surprise. <u>My first semester at college showed me that students who work while going to school face problems at school, at work, and at home.</u>
transition, topic sentence	<u>First of all, trying to juggle job and school responsibilities creates problems at school.</u> Early-
transition	morning classes, <u>for example</u>, are particularly difficult for me. <u>Because I work every weeknight from</u>
added sentence of detail	<u>six to midnight, I don't get home until 1:00 A.M., and I can't fall asleep until 2:00 A.M. or later.</u> I am too
added detail	tired to pay attention in <u>my 8:00 A.M.</u> class. Once, I
added detail transition	even fell asleep <u>in that class.</u> <u>My work hours cre-</u>
sentence added	<u>ate other conflicts.</u> They <u>cut into my study time</u>, so I
added detail	have little time to do <u>all the assigned reading and</u>
added detail	<u>papers.</u> I get behind in these assignments, and <u>I</u>
added detail	<u>never seem to have enough time to catch up.</u> <u>Conse-</u>
transition	<u>quently, my grades are not as good as they could be.</u>
transition	<u>Because I both work and go to school, I have</u>
topic sentence	<u>problems doing well at school. But work can also</u>
transition sentence	<u>suffer when workers attend college. Students can</u> <u>bring school into the workplace.</u> One night I tried
added detail	to study at work, but my boss caught me <u>reading</u> <u>my biology textbook at the front desk.</u> I was repri-
added detail	manded, and <u>now my boss doesn't trust me.</u> Some- times I come to work very tired. When I don't get

continued

added detail transition added example	enough sleep, I can be rude to motel guests <u>who give me a hard time. Then</u> the rudeness can get me into trouble. <u>I remember one particular guest who reported me because I was sarcastic to her. She had spent a half hour complaining about her bill, and I had been too tired to be patient. Once again, my boss reprimanded me.</u> Another time, school
transition	interfered with my job when I had to cut work to
added detail	take a makeup test at school. <u>I know my boss was unhappy with me then, too.</u>
transition sentence topic sentence, transition sentences combined	<u>As a working student, I run into trouble on the job and at college. Working students also suffer outside of classes and the workplace.</u> Since I work nights during the week, the weekends are the only
transition sentence	time I can study. <u>Because I have to use my weekends to do schoolwork, I can't do other things.</u> My apartment is a mess since I have no time to clean it. Worse, my girlfriend is ready to kill me because I have no social life. We never even go to the movies any more. When she comes over, I am busy studying.
repeats focus of body paragraphs	With responsibilities at <u>home</u>, <u>work</u>, and <u>college</u>, I face a cycle of stress. I am constantly racing around, and I can't break the cycle. I want a college education, and I must have a job to pay my tuition. The only way I can manage is to learn to manage
topic sentence restates thesis in new words	my time. <u>I have learned that working students have to be very organized to cope with their responsibilities at college, work, and home.</u>

Exercise 11 **Practice: Identifying the Main Points in the Draft of an Essay**

Below is the draft of a five-paragraph essay. Read it, then reread it and underline the thesis and the topic sentences in each body paragraph and in the conclusion.

Until this year, I had never considered spending my free time helping others in my community. Volunteer work, I thought, was something retired folks and rich people did to fill their days. Just by chance, I became a volunteer for the public library's Classic Connection, a group that arranges read-a-thons and special programs for elementary school children. Although I don't receive a salary, working with some perceptive and entertaining third graders has been very rewarding in other ways.

Currently, I meet with my small group of four girls and three boys each Saturday morning from ten to eleven o'clock, and they have actually taught me more than I ever thought possible. I usually assign the children various passages in an illustrated children's classic like *The Little Prince*, and I help them with the difficult words as they read aloud. When I occasionally read to them, they follow right along, but when it's their turn, they happily go off track. I've learned that each child has a mind of his or her own, and I now have much more respect for day-care workers and elementary school teachers who must teach, entertain, and discipline thirty rowdy children all day long. I'm tired after one hour with just seven children.

I have also learned the value of careful planning. I arrive at each session with a digital voice recorder and have the children record sound effects related to the story we'll be reading. At certain points during the session, we stop to hear the sound effects. They love to hear themselves and seem more focused on reading when I use this method. I feel more relaxed when I am well prepared and the sessions go smoothly.

I have enjoyed making several new friends and contacts through the Classic Connection. I've become friendly with the parents of the kids in my reading group, and one of the fathers has offered me a good-paying job at his printing business. He even mentioned he could be flexible about my schedule. I asked him if he could help me put a collection together of the group's most outrageous original stories, and he said he'd be glad to do it in *his* free time. I've thus learned that the spirit of volunteerism is indeed contagious.

I plan to keep volunteering for the Classic Connection's programs and look forward to a new group that should be starting soon. I don't know if I'm ready to graduate to an older group. After all, third graders still have much to teach me.

Exercise 12   Practice: Adding Transitions to an Essay

The following essay needs transitions. Add the transitions where indicated, and add the kind of transition—word, phrase, or sentence—indicated.

I am a fairly good student, but I have to work hard to earn decent grades. Most of that work is the long, sometimes boring time spent studying. Since I need to study as much as I can, I have found three places that offer me at least a little study time.

The first place isn't meant for studying. _____ (add a word) I have managed to slip a few minutes of cramming into the hours I spend there. This place is the supermarket where I work. Of course, work at a supermarket is constant, and I am always under supervision. _____ (add a word or phrase) I have found ways to incorporate a little mental work. When I have a test coming up, I write key terms, rules, or definitions on note cards. On my ten-minute breaks at the store, I sit outside and study my cards. When I return to the store, I try to repeat the information I have just learned. Of course, this repetition is silent _____ (add a word) I don't want to alarm the customers by muttering in the aisles.

The second place is more appropriate for studying. It is the college I attend. I try to find a quiet place like an empty bench where I can sit between classes. If I have a free hour or more, I go somewhere more private _____ (add a word or phrase) the library. Sometimes the library has too many students talking in the aisles or at the computers _____ (add a word or phrase), I find a spot under a tree and sit on the lawn.

_____

_____ (add a sentence). That place is my home. I am lucky to have my own bedroom, and when my family has finished dinner, I retreat to my room. First, I close the door. _____ (add a word) I spread out my books and notes on the bed. Sometimes I sit on the bed to study, but when I feel myself getting sleepy, I move to the floor. On the floor, I am less comfortable but more alert. My room is a quiet place. _____ (add a word or phrase) I do suffer one or two interruptions. Before she goes to bed, my little sister comes in to chat or kiss me goodnight. She can break my train of thought _____ (add a word or phrase) she is a sweet and affectionate visitor. Most of the time, my room gives me the peace that I need.

Studying for my college classes takes up more of my time than I had ever expected. _____ (add a word or phrase) it is more difficult than I had expected. _____ (add a word or phrase) my efforts are carrying me through the challenges of college. _____ (add a word or phrase) I am happy to spend the time on the work that will determine my future.

Exercise 13 **Practice: Recognizing Synonyms and Repetition Used to Link Ideas in an Essay**

In the following essay, underline all the synonyms and repetition (of words or phrases) that help remind the reader of the thesis sentence. (To help you, the thesis is underlined.)

We can make many changes in our lives. We can choose to move to a new town, to attend a certain college, or to train for a specific career. However, sometimes the changes in our lives are not our choices. In such cases, the changes can signal trouble. <u>Like everyone, I have felt the pain and the loss of control that can come with change, but I have also learned that loss can lead me to a better life.</u>

The first time that I suffered from a sudden change was when my best friend left the area. At the time, my friend and I were fourteen, and we spent most of our free time together. We confided in each other and created our private world of jokes, adventures, and pranks. When my friend's mother was offered a good job in a distant city, there was nothing I could do to keep my friend near me. At first, I was so upset that I became angry at my friend, and I refused to acknowledge that he was suffering, too. When the day came for him to leave, we were both resigned to the pain of separating.

My second experience of such misery came years later when my girlfriend announced that she was leaving me. One day she decided that she wanted to "move on" in her relationships. I was unprepared for the hurt of her blunt speech. Nothing that I said could change her mind, and I could not escape the suffering that followed. When the shock wore off, I struggled to cope with the inevitable loneliness. The worst part of this conflict was my fear of getting hurt again. This fear kept me locked in misery.

A year later, my life changed again when the terror began to lose its grip on me. Slowly, I began to move closer to people who could be my friends. Each step was risky, but each step helped me to get stronger. When I began to trust again and feel that I had some value, I started to believe that other people might accept me. I admitted that I would never be able to control all my interactions with other people. I might be hurt again, but I might also find friends and even someone to love.

As I began to let go of my fears, I also gave up the past: I let go of the suffering and self-doubt that had come when I could not hold on to my friend or girlfriend. I made these changes by taking a risk. I stepped back into the real world where I could lose control of events again, but where I could also find fulfillment.

PROOFREADING AN ESSAY

Creating a Title

When you are satisfied with the final version of your essay, you can begin preparing a good copy. Your essay will need a title. Try to think of a short title that is connected to your thesis. Since the title is the reader's first contact with your essay, an imaginative title can create a good first impression. If you can't think of anything clever, try using a key phrase from your essay.

The title is placed at the top of your essay, about an inch above the first paragraph. Always capitalize the first word of the title and all major words such as nouns, pronouns, verbs, adjectives, and adverbs. Minor words such as articles (*the, an, a*), prepositions (*of, in, between*), and coordinating conjunctions (*and, but, so*) are not capitalized unless they are the first or last words of the title. *Do not* underline or put quotation marks around your title.

The Final Version of an Essay

As you prepare the final version of your essay, you need to consider many aspects of your work. Aside from checking for errors in spelling, punctuation, and formatting (such as indenting for each new paragraph), you have more writing to examine than you would if you were proofreading a paragraph. For instance, you need to consider your choice of title, the balance (in size) of your body paragraphs, and the word choice of four or more paragraphs.

Following is the final version of the essay on working and going to college. When you compare it to the draft on page 271, you will notice some changes:

- In the first paragraph, the words "I thought" have been added to make it clear that the statement is the writer's opinion.

- One topic sentence, in paragraph two, has been revised so that it includes the word "students" and the meaning is more precise.

- Words have been changed to sharpen the meaning.
- Transitions have been added.
- A title has been added.

Final Version of an Essay

(Changes from the draft are underlined.)

Problems of the Working College Student

I work thirty hours a week at the front desk of a motel in Riverside. When I first <u>registered</u> for college classes, I figured college would be fairly easy to fit into my schedule. After all, <u>I thought,</u> college students are not in class all day, as high school students are. So I <u>assumed</u> the twelve hours a week I'd spend in class wouldn't be too much of a load. But I was in for a big surprise. My first semester at college showed me that students who work while going to college face problems at school, at work, and at home.

First of all, <u>students who try</u> to juggle job and school responsibilities <u>find trouble at school.</u> Early-morning classes, for example, are particularly difficult for me. Because I work every weeknight from six to midnight, I don't get home until 1:00 A.M., and I can't fall asleep until 2:00 A.M. or later. <u>Consequently,</u> I am too tired to pay attention in my <u>eight o'clock class.</u> Once, I even fell asleep in that class. My work hours create other conflicts. They cut into my study time, so I have little time to do all the assigned reading and papers. I get behind in the assignments, and I never seem to have enough time to catch up. <u>As a result,</u> my grades are not as good as they could be.

Because I both work and go to school, I have problems doing well at school. But work can also suffer when workers attend college. Students can bring school into the workplace. <u>I've been guilty of this practice and have paid the price.</u> One night I tried to study at work, but my boss caught me reading my biology textbook at the front desk. I was reprimanded, and now my boss doesn't trust me. Sometimes I come to work very tired, <u>another problem.</u> When I don't get enough sleep, I can be rude to <u>motel</u> guests who give me a hard time. Then the rudeness can get me into trouble. I remember one particular guest who reported me because I was sarcastic to her. She had spent a half hour complaining about her bill, and I had been too tired to be patient. Once again, my boss reprimanded me. Another time, school interfered with my job when I had to cut work to take a makeup test at school. I know my boss was unhappy with me then, too.

As a working student, I run into trouble on the job and at college. Working students also suffer outside of classes and the workplace. <u>My schedule illustrates the conflicts of trying to juggle too many duties.</u> Since I work nights during the week, the weekends are the only time I can study. Because I have to use my weekends to do schoolwork, I can't do other things. My apartment is a mess since I have no time to clean it. Worse, my girlfriend is ready to kill me because I have no social life. We never even go to the movies anymore. When she comes over, I am busy studying.

With responsibilities at home, work, and college, I face a cycle of stress. I am constantly racing around, and I can't break the cycle. I want a college education, and I must have a job to pay my tuition. The only way I can manage is to learn to manage my time. <u>In my first semester at college, I've realized</u> that working students have to be very organized to cope with the responsibilities of college, work, and home.

Exercise 14   **Practice: Proofreading to Prepare the Final Version**

Following are two essays with the kinds of errors that are easy to overlook when you prepare the final version of an assignment. Correct the errors, writing above the lines. There are nineteen errors in the first essay and twenty-two in the second.

A Free Morning

Most mornings begin with responsibilities. A person has to work at a certain ~parallel~ time, follow a specific routine, and rush to work, school, or to other commitments. A morning without duties, chores, or schedules is rare. When someone has the gift of a free morning, they can consider three of the best ways to spend it.

One of the most luxurious ways to enjoy a morning without chores is to turn off the alarm clock and to go back to sleep. The irritating sound of the alarm makes the freedom to stop the noise a pleasure. If someone turns off the clock the night *before* be fore the free morning, he or she will not enjoy the luxury of hearing the noise, at first assuming that the sound signals another hectic morning, and then realizeing that the clock is powerless on this day. Next, the sleeper can enjoy the pleasure of staying in bed, snuggling into the pillows, and *Slipping* slip into a long nap.

A morning without responsibilities can also be a time to wake up at a reasonable hour but to have nothing planned. A person can linger over a cup of coffee. On a free morning, he or she may have time to eat toast or cereal instead of rushing off to begin another round of work and worry. The gift of time *means* mean a chance to check phone messages, sit calmly at a computer, read a book, or listen to music. Without a plan, a person can choose to do nearly anything or nothing at all.

The the best way to enjoy a free morning is to spend it *outdoors* out doors. Since *there* their are many *ways* way to enjoy nature, a person can do as little or as much as he or she desires. An athlete can run, bike, or power-walk in the neighborhood. Someone less active can sit on a porch or patio and enjoy the trees, the birds, or the squirrels. Parks, benches, lakes, and mountains may be nearby, and nature can be as calming or invigorating as someone wants it to be.

Most people are constantly short of time. They are behind in their responsibilities at work and at home. A free morning should be a time without responsibilities. Instead of using it to catch up on endless chores and duties, peo-

ple should think of the morning as a gift with know[*no*] strings attached.

Myths About college[*C*]

Before I started College[*C*], many people told me what to expect in this new

place. Some gave me accurate description[*S*] and good advice. Others did not offer

a real picture of higher education. Their advice and descriptions focused on three

myths about college.

The first myth appeared constantly in comments and pieces of advice. "Your

college years are the best years of your life"[*life,*], many people said, "so make the most

of them." These words usually came from people who had attended college many

years earlier or had never gone to college at all. They had forgotten or had never

know[*known*] the stress of applying for a college loan, or the anxiety of starting classes as

a stranger among strangers. They never told me about the fear, of feeling stupid

among so many smart students.

The second mistaken belief came from fellow high school students. A stu-

dent who hated mathematics would say, "I'm so glad this is my last math class.

When I get to college, I will take only the classes that interest me." I heard ver-

sions of this statement from seniors who sweared[*swore*] never to take English or biol-

ogy, or history in college. My friends and I were convinced that we would take

only the classes connected to our major field of study. One visit to a councilor[*Counselor*]

revealed the truth. Anyone who wants a college degree has to take some core

classes. Weather[*Whether*] I planned to study physical education, psychology, or accounting,

I would have to sign up for a core of classes outside of my field.

When the last myth was revealed to me, I felt relieved. In high school, a

few teachers warned me, "If you don't learn this material now, you'll never get

a chance to learn it." The material could be fractions, writing a book report, or

whatever subject I had trouble learning. Some said, "In college, no body will help[*nobody*]

you learn this material because you will just be a number in a crowd."[*be just*] Fortunately, these gloomy teachers were wrong. In college, my teachers are patient and help-

ful. There are Tutors available, and there is a Student learning Center with a help

desk. I've also joined a study group of other students who are taking my most

challenging subject. We work together to prepare for exams.

I learned the truth about three college myth's only when I entered College.

College is not a fantasy world of total freedom and fulfillment. On the other hand,

it is not a cold world where I am left alone to succeed or fail. In reality, college is

more complicated then I expected, but I can handle the challenges.

Lines of Detail: A Walk-Through Assignment

Think of two careers that you believe would be right for you. They do not
have to be careers for which you are studying or preparing now but can be
the kind of work that you would choose if you had unlimited funds, time to
study, train, or otherwise prepare, and the freedom to change your circumstances so that you could begin focusing on one of these two careers.

Step 1: Begin with some investigation. Even if you are extremely
familiar with these two careers, do as much of the following
as you can: talk to an expert in the college's career center and
begin to investigate each career's required training/educa-
tional requirements as well as the necessary mental, psychological, and physical ability that this career demands. You can
talk to a person who is presently working in this career field
or to a student who is preparing for the field. Online research
and time spent in the college or local public library will help
you to become more informed.

Step 2: As you investigate, take notes. Keep in mind that your purpose
is to discover what to expect if you were to work toward earning the qualifications for employment in this field.

Step 3: After your visit, survey your notes. Try to focus on a point that you
can make about the two possible careers. Do they both require
the same type of personality? What are the rewards of each? What
are the drawbacks? What is the job market for those whose education or training prepares them for either of the two careers?
The answers to such questions can help you focus on a
thesis.

Step 4: Once you have a thesis, you can begin to cluster the details
you gathered in your visits.

Step 5: Once you have a thesis and clustered details, draft an outline.
Revise your draft outline until it is unified, expresses the ideas
in a clear order, and has enough supporting details.

Step 6: Write a draft of your essay. Revise the draft, checking it for
balanced paragraphs, relevant and specific details, a strong
conclusion, and smooth transitions.

Step 7: Before you prepare the final version of your essay, check for spelling, word choice, and punctuation errors. Also, give your essay a title.

Topics for Writing an Essay

When you write on any of these topics, be sure to work through the stages of the writing process in preparing your essay.

Collaborate

1. Take any paragraph you have already written for this class and develop it into an essay of four or five paragraphs. If your instructor agrees, read the paragraph to a partner or group, and ask your listener(s) to suggest points inside the paragraph that could be developed into paragraphs of their own.

2. Write an essay using one of the following thesis statements:

   If I did not have to work for a living, I would spend my time doing _____.

   Most families waste natural resources every day, simply by going through their daily routines.

   I would love to live in _____ because _____.

   I believe that in fifty years, the planet will be in better/worse shape than it is today.

   Three items that every college student needs are _____, _____, and _____.

   City living (or suburban living or country living) has its advantages.

   Pets can bring comfort and joy to any age group.

Collaborate

3. Write an essay on earliest childhood memories. Interview three class-mates to gather detail and to focus your essay. Ask each one to tell you about the earliest memory he or she has of childhood. Before you begin interviewing, make a list of questions like these: What is your earliest memory? How old were you at the time of that recollection? What were you doing? Do you remember other people or events in that scene? If so, what were the others doing? Were you indoors? Out-doors? Is this a pleasant memory? Why do you think this memory has stayed with you? Use the details collected at the interviews to write a five-paragraph essay with a thesis sentence like one of the following:

   Childhood memories vary a great deal from person to person.

   The childhood memories of different people are surprisingly similar.

   Although some people's first memories are painful, others remember a happy time.

   Some people claim to remember events from their infancy, but others can't remember anything before their third (or fourth, fifth, etc.) birthday.

4. Freewrite for ten minutes on the two best days of your life. After you've completed the freewriting, review it. Do the two days have much in common? Or were they very different? Write a four-paragraph essay based on their similarities or differences, with a thesis like one of these:

   The two best days of my life were both _____. (Focus on similarities.)

While one of the best days of my life was _____, the other great day was _____. (Fill in with differences.)

5. Write a five-paragraph essay on one of the following topics:

Three Careers for Me   The Three Worst Jobs
Three Workplace Hazards   Three Workplace Friends
Three Lucky People   Three Wishes
Three Family Traditions   Three Decisions for Me

6. Narrow one of the following topics and then write an essay on it. Remember that brainstorming and freewriting can help you narrow your focus.

nature	dreams	crime	music	celebrities
fears	family	lies	health	romance
habits	books	money	animals	travel
students	teachers	games	secrets	fashion

Computer

7. Many people are turning to online dating services as a way to meet people and potential partners. Find an online dating service and investigate its methods, claims, and fees. Based on your research, write an essay that takes a stand on the following statement: _____, an online dating service, is ethical/unethical (choose one) in its promises.

As an alternative, if you or someone you know has ever used an online dating service, write an essay based on the following statement: Finding a suitable mate through an online dating service can be a(n) _____ experience.

8. Look closely at the photo of the couple seeking a ride to New York. Write a five-paragraph essay in which you describe a situation that the picture may represent. In one body paragraph, you can write about how these two people met and decided to head for New York; in another paragraph, about what they are hoping for as they stand together hitchhiking; and in another paragraph, about what may happen to them next.

9. Look closely at the photo of the couple in the field on the next page. Write a four-paragraph essay in which you describe the relationship between the people in the photograph. You can use your imagination, but try to base your assumptions on the facial expressions and body language of the individuals.

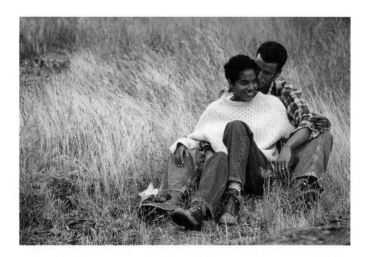

Topics for Critical Thinking and Writing

1. Everyone has to make compromises. The father of a large family, for example, may have dreamed of buying a big house for his family. However, economic realities may have forced him to compromise by renting a smaller duplex. Your brother may have dreamed of becoming a professional athlete but settled for spending weekends playing on a city softball team. Write an essay about three compromises you have made, explaining what you dreamed of, what you settled for, and how you accepted these compromises.

2. Social media networks such as Twitter, Facebook, and LinkedIn are popular among a wide spectrum of users for both personal and professional reasons. Freewrite about the ways in which social media improves the quality of life for its users, and then write an essay about the top three benefits of using social media outlets.

or

If you feel that the drawbacks of social media outweigh the benefits, write about the three most significant negative aspects. Be sure to incorporate specific details and examples for each drawback.

Note: Additional writing options suitable for essay assignments can be found after the professional readings "How to Twitter," "A Brother's Murder," and "Navajo Code Talkers: The Century's Best Kept Secret," all of which can be found in the "Readings for Writers" appendix at the end of this book.

PEARSON **mywritinglab** For support in meeting this chapter's objectives, log in to www.mywritinglab.com and select **Recognizing the Essay, Essay Organization, Essay Introductions, Conclusions, and Titles,** and **Thesis Statements**.

Name _____   Section _____

Peer Review Form for an Essay

After you've written a draft of your essay, let a writing partner read it. When your partner has completed the form below, discuss the comments. Then repeat the same process for your partner's essay.

The thesis of this essay is _____

The topic sentences for the body paragraphs are _____

_____

_____

_____

The topic sentence in the conclusion is _____

_____

The best part of the essay is the _____ (first, second, third, etc.) paragraph.

I would like to see details added to the part about _____ I would take out the part about _____

The introduction is (a) good or (b) could be better. (Choose one.)

The conclusion is (a) good or (b) could be better. (Choose one.)

I have questions about _____

Other comments _____

_____

_____

_____

_____

_____

_____

_____

_____

_____

Reviewer's name _____

Different Essay Patterns: Part One

CHAPTER 12

Jumping In

*Snowflakes come in an infinite variety of shapes and sizes, and while no two flakes are identical, they do share basic elements. Similarly, essays can be structured in **different patterns** and still share basic writing elements. Which pattern of writing covered in previous chapters (illustration, description, narration, etc.) did you find most effective for developing a paragraph? Do you think this pattern could also work well if you expanded your paragraph into an essay?*

Chapter Objective

Students will be able to apply the stages of the writing process and the basic essay format to a variety of rhetorical patterns.

You can write essays in a number of patterns, but any pattern will develop more easily if you follow the writing steps in preparing your essay. The examples in this chapter take you through the steps of preparing an essay in several patterns. Each sample essay expands on its related paragraph pattern in an earlier chapter of this book.

ILLUSTRATION

Hints for Writing an Illustration Essay

1. Use specific examples to support a general point. Remember that a *general* statement is a broad point, and a *specific* example is narrow.

> **general statement:** The weather was terrible yesterday.
> **specific example:** It rained for six hours.

general statement: I am having trouble in my math class.
specific example: I can't understand the problems in Chapter 12.

2. Be sure that you support a general statement by using specific examples instead of merely writing another general statement.

not this: general statement: The weather was terrible yesterday.
more general statements: ~~It was awful outside.~~
~~Yesterday brought nasty weather.~~

but this: general statement: The weather was terrible yesterday.
specific examples: It rained for six hours.
Several highways were flooded.

3. Be sure that you have sufficient examples and that you develop them well. If you use one or two examples and do not development them effectively, you will have a skimpy paragraph. You can use fewer examples and develop each one, or you can use more examples and develop them less extensively.

not this: a skimpy paragraph:

The weather was terrible yesterday. It rained for six hours. Several highways were flooded.

but this: a paragraph with a few examples, each one well developed:

The weather was terrible yesterday. It rained for six hours. The rain was heavy and harsh, accompanied by high winds that lashed the trees and signs on stores and restaurants. The downpour was so heavy that several highways were flooded. Drivers who usually take the Collins Road Expressway were diverted to a narrow city street and crawled home at 30 mph. Additionally, traffic on the interstate highway was at a standstill because drivers slowed to gawk at the numerous accidents caused by the lack of visibility and water-slicked roads.

or this: a paragraph developed with more examples:

The weather was terrible yesterday. It rained for six hours, and several highways were flooded. Cedar Forest Elementary School closed early because of a leak in the auditorium's roof. The standing water also collected in low-lying residential areas where some children put on their swimsuits and splashed in four to six inches of water. Their parents, meanwhile, were trying to sweep the water out of porches and patios and praying that more rain would not seep into their houses. The high winds that accompanied the rain snapped tree branches and littered the area with debris. Two small "For Sale" signs were blown into the drive-through window at Burger King.

WRITING THE ILLUSTRATION ESSAY IN STEPS

PREWRITING   **ILLUSTRATION ESSAY**

If you were asked to write an illustration essay about some aspect of serving the community, you might first freewrite.

Freewriting for an Illustration Essay

Police serve the community. I'd like a job in law enforcement. What other kinds of people serve the community? Firefighters. Do you have a job serving the community? What about volunteers? Even volunteer firefighters. My mother works at the hospital one day a week. She's been doing it for years. Volunteering on her day off from work. Then there's the food bank. That's my father's place. I go there, too. That's serving the community.

Some additional brainstorming might lead you to recognize that everyone in your family, including your sister, volunteers. You might ask yourself some questions about why each family member volunteers and receives the benefits of the volunteering. Next, you are able to write a thesis sentence:

In my family, volunteering is a way for all of us to give to the community and to share our good fortune.

This thesis contains three parts: it explains who volunteers (all the family members), it explains why they volunteer ("to give to the community and to share our good fortune"), and who benefits ("the community").

With a thesis sentence and some of the ideas from your freewriting and brainstorming, you can begin to think about an outline.

PLANNING   ILLUSTRATION ESSAY

Following is an outline for an illustration essay on family volunteering. Study the outline carefully and be prepared to respond to the exercise that follows it.

Outline for an Illustration Essay

paragraph 1	I. Thesis: In my family, volunteering is a way for all of us to give to the community and to share our good fortune.
paragraph 2 **topic sentence and details**	II. Parents and children all volunteer.
	A. My father and I volunteer at a local food bank every weekend.
who volunteers and where	B. We work in the warehouse.
	C. We sort and stack donations of food from several sources.
they volunteer	D. My mother spends every Thursday helping visitors at the local hospital.
	E. She is a greeter at the information desk directly inside the main entrance.
	F. My sister volunteers at an animal shelter.
	G. She spends her time with homeless dogs.
paragraph 3 **topic sentence and details**	III. Each member of the family has several reasons for volunteering.
	A. My father likes the work of organizing the food and stacking each item neatly.
different **reasons**	B. I enjoy surveying the amount and kind of donations and seeing what is new.
	C. We both like knowing that many hungry people will be able to eat.

continued

D. My mother likes comforting the sick or supporting their loved ones.

E. She is the first person that people see when they enter the hospital.

F. My sister finds her own comfort with homeless animals.

G. They spend almost all their time in cages.

paragraph 4
topic sentence
and details
one shared
motive

IV. All of us want to give back to the community.

A. The town helped us when our house caught fire.

B. We have shelter, food, work, and good educations.

C. The best feelings come when we share our time, food, and love with others.

D. My father and I like to think about a hungry child getting dinner.

E. My mother likes to see people in crisis find some relief.

F. My sister loves to see a dog play or pull at a leash in joy.

paragraph 5
conclusion

V. When we volunteer, comfort and happiness spreads.

The outline combined some of the ideas from the freewriting and new details gathered during the outlining process. As you write and revise your draft, you can continue to add details. You can also combine sentences, add transitions, and work on word choice.

Exercise 1 **Practice: Keeping the Examples in Order**

In the outline for the essay on family volunteering, each body paragraph uses the same order in giving the examples of who volunteers, their different reasons for volunteering, and their one shared motive. Survey the three body paragraphs and list that order.

_____

_____

_____

_____

DRAFTING AND REVISING **ILLUSTRATION ESSAY**

Following is a revised draft of the essay on family volunteering. As you read it, you'll notice many changes from the outline on pages 287–288.

- An introduction has been added.
- Transitions have been added within and between paragraphs.
- Details have been added.
- Sentences have been combined.
- A concluding paragraph has been added.

Study the draft carefully and be prepared to respond to the exercises that follow it.

Draft of an Illustration Essay

(Thesis and topic sentences are underlined.)

The members of my family do not spend much free time at home. Our home is often empty because each one of us is busy somewhere else. We rarely go to a mall, a fitness club, or a pub. We do have a social life, but socializing is not the largest part of our free time. <u>In my family, volunteering is a way to give to the community and to share our good fortune.</u>

<u>Parents and children all volunteer.</u> My father and I volunteer at a local food bank every weekend. We work in the warehouse, sorting and stacking different kinds of food donations from several sources. My mother spends every Thursday, her day off from work, helping visitors at the local hospital. She is a greeter at the information desk directly inside the main entrance. On Saturdays, my sister works at a the county animal shelter where she spends her time with homeless dogs.

<u>Each member of the family has several reasons for volunteering.</u> At the food bank, my father likes the work of organizing the food and stacking each item neatly. I like surveying the amount and kind of donations and seeing what is new. We both like knowing that many people will be able to eat. My mother likes comforting the sick or supporting their loved ones. She is the first person that people see when they enter the hospital. My sister finds her own comfort in working with homeless animals. They spend most of their time in cages.

<u>All of us share one motive: we want to give back to the community.</u> We are grateful for the help we received from our town when a fire damaged our home. Today we have a safe place to live, enough food, steady work, and good educations. Most of all, we know that happiness comes to us when we share our time, food, and love with others. My father and I like to think about a hungry child getting dinner. My mother likes to see people in crisis find some relief. My sister often walks or plays with a shelter dog. She loves to see one jump, run, or pull at a leash in joy. Then she finds pleasure herself.

My parents, sister, and I may not spend much of our free time at home. Pubs, malls, and fitness clubs are not part of our social life. In my family, we have other interests. Because we volunteer, hungry people get food, frightened people find comfort, and homeless animals receive love. In addition, everyone in my family enjoys the great rewards of sharing. <u>When we volunteer, comfort and happiness spreads.</u>

Exercise 2   **Practice: Recognizing Combined Sentences**

Paragraph 2 of the draft essay contains two examples of sentences from the outline that were combined in the draft. Compare the outline to the draft paragraph and underline the new, combined sentences.

Exercise 3   **Practice: Using Framing to Conclude an Essay**

Framing, which is discussed in Chapter 11 ("Writing an Essay"), is one way to tie an essay together neatly. It involves using something from the introduction as a way of concluding. You can take an example, a question, or even some general statement from the introduction and use that idea (though not necessarily the same words) in your conclusion. In the essay on volunteering, the conclusion uses the framing device.

Reread the introduction, then reread the conclusion. Notice the repetition of certain ideas. Underline that repetition in the concluding paragraph.

PROOFREADING   **ILLUSTRATION ESSAY**

Following is the final version of the essay on family volunteering. When you compare it to the draft on page 289, you will notice some changes:

- A title has been added.

- Some of the word choices have been polished to make a description more precise or to eliminate an awkward phrase.

- A transition sentence has been added to the first paragraph so that the thesis sentence does not come so abruptly.

- New details have been added to paragraph 2.

- Paragraphs 3 and 4 contain new examples of sentence combining.

Study the final version carefully and be prepared to respond to the exercise that follows it.

Final Version of an Illustration Essay

The Power of Volunteering

The members of my family do not spend much free time at home. Our home is often empty because each one of us is busy somewhere else. We rarely go to a mall, a fitness club, or a pub. We do have a social life, but socializing is not the largest part of our free time. Instead, we spend our time volunteering. In my family, volunteering is a way to give to the community and to share our good fortune.

Parents and children all volunteer. My father and I volunteer at a local food bank every weekend. We work in the warehouse, sorting and stacking different kinds of food donations from several sources such as supermarkets, bakeries, and local farms. My mother spends every Thursday, her day off from work, helping visitors at the local hospital. She is a greeter at the information desk directly inside the main entrance. On Saturdays, my sister works at the county animal shelter where she spends her time with homeless dogs.

Each member of the family has several reasons for volunteering. At the food bank, my father likes the work of organizing the food and stacking each item neatly. I like surveying the amount and kind of donations and seeing what is new. We both like knowing that many people will be able to eat. My mother likes comforting the sick or supporting their loved ones. She is the first person that people see when they enter the hospital. On Saturdays, my sister finds her own comfort in working with homeless animals who spend most of their time in cages.

All of us share one motive: we want to give back to the community. We are grateful for the help we received from our town when a fire damaged our home. Today we have a safe place to live, enough food, steady work, and good educations. Most of all, we know that happiness comes to us when we share our time, food, and love with others. My father and I like to think about a hungry child getting dinner. My mother likes to see people in crisis find some relief. My sister often walks or plays with a shelter dog. When she sees one jump, run, or pull at a leash in joy, she finds pleasure herself.

My parents, sister, and I may not spend much of our free time at home. Pubs, malls, and fitness clubs are not part of our social life. In my family, we have other interests. Because we volunteer, hungry people <u>receive</u> food, frightened people find comfort, and homeless animals receive love. In addition, everyone in my family enjoys the great rewards of sharing. When we volunteer, comfort and happiness spreads.

Exercise 4   **Practice: Identifying the Changes in a Final Version of an Illustration Essay**

To become more aware of the kinds of changes that can improve an essay, underline the following changes: the transition sentence in paragraph 1, the added details in paragraph 2, the sentences combined in paragraph 3, the sentences combined in paragraph 4.

Topics for Writing an Illustration Essay

When you write on any of these topics, work through the stages of the writing process in preparing your essay.

1. Complete one of the following statements and use it as the thesis for an illustration essay.

   Losing a friend can be _____.

   Angry people may sometimes _____.

   Students under financial pressure are likely to _____.

   A sense of humor can _____.

   A close family is _____.

   My greatest strength is my ability to _____.

2. Choose one of the following topics. Narrow it to a more specific topic and then write a thesis statement about it. Use that thesis to write an illustration essay.

employment	driving	loneliness
money	fatigue	sports
style	safety	popularity
science	legends	ambition

3. To begin this assignment, brainstorm with a partner or a group. Together, write down as many overused slang expressions as you can. For example, many people regularly use "awesome" to describe anything from a beautiful beach to a good dinner. After you have a list of tired slang, work independently on an essay. Begin by picking three examples of overused slang from the list. In a five-paragraph essay, discuss one expression in each body paragraph. Include examples of the many meanings assigned to the slang expression and suggest other, more specific words or phrases that can replace it.

   Collaborate

4. To begin this assignment, look around your classroom. Now, write a general statement about some aspect of the classroom: the furniture, the condition of the room, what the students carry to class, the students' footwear, facial expressions, hairstyles, and so forth. For example, if you observed the size of your classroom and the number of students in it, you might conclude that "Cramming too many students into a small space makes learning difficult." You could write a five-paragraph essay using that general statement as your thesis and supporting it with specific examples from your observation.

Topics for Critical Thinking and Writing

1. In conversation, we often use expressions that are meant to hide what we really mean: we may want to conceal our motives, avoid hurting another person's feelings, or avoid taking responsibility. For instance, a statement from a boy- or girlfriend to a significant other may be, "I think it's time we started seeing other people." This may be coded, softer language for such a message as "I've found somebody I like better than you" or "I'm bored and need more excitement in my life." When talking to the parents of a badly behaved child, we may say, "He has a lot of energy" or "She certainly has a mind of her own, doesn't she?"

   Think of three situations in which people are likely to use less than frank expressions for a variety of reasons. For instance, people tend to be tactful at weddings, at dinners where they are guests, when they have to let an employee go, and so forth. Devote one body paragraph to each situation and illustrate your point with specific examples.

2. Various organizations commonly rely on volunteers to improve the quality of life for many individuals. From your observations or knowledge of various volunteer groups in your hometown or school, illustrate the ways volunteers give more than money to the needy in your community. For example, some volunteers staff emergency hotlines for people in distress while others make quilts for the homeless.

DESCRIPTION

Hints for Writing a Descriptive Essay

1. Use many specific details. Because an essay is usually longer than one paragraph, you will need more details to develop an essay. To ensure that your details create an effective description, make them specific.

2. Decide on a clear order. Without a clear order, a descriptive essay will become a jumble of details spread over several paragraphs. Decide on a clear order (from inside to outside, from top to bottom, and so forth) and stick to it. Each body paragraph can focus on one part of that order.

WRITING THE DESCRIPTIVE ESSAY IN STEPS

PREWRITING   DESCRIPTIVE ESSAY

If you were going to write an essay describing the contents of your garage, you might first brainstorm a list.

Brainstorming a List for a Descriptive Essay

Topic: The Contents of Our Garage
- my husband
- Bradley's motorcycle
- his tools for the cycle, yard work, home repairs
- paint cans
- bulletin board with photos

- little plastic containers of nails, screws
- dusty shelves on the walls
- oil stains and smells on the floor
- Bradley's work bench
- musty smell of Bradley's junk on the floor
- noise of engine running
- garbage can smells
- Bradley's camping gear
- my collection of hand-painted pottery doesn't fit

After surveying the list, you want to think about what point it makes. For this list, your thoughts might lead you to the idea that most of the details connect to Bradley. That main point is the *dominant impression.* For this list, the dominant impression could be this sentence:

> The garage is my husband's territory.

This sentence could be the thesis sentence of the descriptive essay.

PLANNING   DESCRIPTIVE ESSAY

Following is an outline for a descriptive essay on Bradley's garage. Study the outline carefully and be prepared to respond to the exercise that follows it.

Outline for a Descriptive Essay

paragraph 1	I. Thesis: The garage is my husband's territory.
paragraph 2 **topic sentence** **and details**	II. The bare floor is a small space. A. It is an area by the garage door. B. It also includes enough space to enter the door to the house. C. The two spaces have oil stains.
the bare floor	D. They are also gritty with dirt. E. The floor smells like gasoline.
paragraph 3 **topic sentence** **and details**	III. Most of the garage floor is filled. A. Boxes of Bradley's junk give off a nasty odor. B. Bradley's work bench is pushed into one corner and covers a large part of the floor.
the covered floor	C. His camping gear stretches into the middle of the floor. D. His motorcycle, usually in pieces, lies on the floor. E. It fills one third of the space. F. Pieces of other cycles mingle with parts of Bradley's cycle.
paragraph 4 **topic sentence** **and details**	IV. The back and side walls seem to stagger because of the densely packed shelves. A. Dusty metal shelves are packed with tools. B. Old, crusty paint cans are on the shelves.

continued

the walls	C. Open bags of lawn fertilizer sit on a high shelf.
	D. Dozens of small plastic containers of nails and screws are there.
	E. One shelf has a bulletin board
	F. It leans against a mess of tools.
paragraph 5 conclusion	V. Bradley loves this part of our house.

The outline combined some of the details from the list with new details gathered during the outlining process. As you write and revise your drafts, you can continue to add details. You can also combine sentences, add transitions, and work on word choice.

> **Exercise 5**   **Practice: Recognizing Sense Descriptions**

A good description relies on many words that relate to the five senses of sight, sound, taste, touch (or texture), and smell. In the outline above, underline one example of a word or phrase that refers to each of the following: (1) sight, (2) smell, and (3) touch. Use 1, 2, or 3 to identify the type of sense description.

> **DRAFTING AND REVISING**   **DESCRIPTIVE ESSAY**

Following is a revised draft of the essay on Bradley's garage. As you read it, you'll notice many changes from the outline on pages 293–294.

- An introduction has been added.
- Transitions have been added within and between paragraphs.
- Details have been added.
- Sentences have been combined.
- A concluding paragraph has been written.

Study the draft carefully and be prepared to respond to the exercises that follow it.

Draft of a Descriptive Essay

(Thesis and topic sentences are underlined.)

Everyone likes one part of his or her living space better than the other parts. Some people find pleasure in their comfortable living rooms. Others love a bedroom that reflects their tastes. My husband Bradley prefers a different part of our house. <u>The garage is my husband's territory.</u>

<u>The bare floor is a small space.</u> It is an area by the garage door and includes a small space near the door to the house. These two spaces are speckled with oil stains. They are also gritty with dirt. One good aspect of the grit is that it protects people from slipping on the oily patches on the floor. The floor smells like gasoline. Bradley doesn't mind the smell at all.

<u>Most of the garage floor is filled.</u> Boxes of Bradley's junk give off a nasty odor. These boxes contain lots of junk, but Bradley wants to save it all. Although the boxes take up space, Bradley's big work bench fills lots more space. It is pushed

into one corner of the garage. In addition, his camping gear stretches into the middle of the floor. Bradley's motorcycle, which is usually in pieces, lies on the floor. Pieces of other cycles also mingle with parts of Bradley's cycle.

<u>The walls of the garage are also heavily loaded.</u> In fact, the back and side walls seem to stagger because of their densely loaded shelves. Some of these dusty metal shelves are packed with tools. Old, crusty paint cans are also on the shelves. Open bags of lawn fertilizer spill their contents on a high shelf. Dozens of small plastic containers of nails and screws are stacked between piles of cleaning rags and towels. One shelf contains a bulletin board that leans against a mess of tools.

The garage is not a showplace in a model home. It doesn't look like the clean, organized garages that appear in commercials for home improvement stores. However, it is a real garage. <u>Although I cannot imagine spending time in it, Bradley loves his garage.</u>

Exercise 6   Practice: Identifying the Type of Lead-In

Circle the type of lead-in used in this essay: (1) beginning with some general statements, (2) telling a story, or (3) explaining why this topic is worth writing about.

Exercise 7   Practice: Noticing How Contrast Is Used in the Conclusion

In the conclusion, several contrasts are used to lead to a rewording of the thesis. One of these contrasts is the transition to the thesis: "Although I cannot imagine spending time in it." The writer, Bradley's wife, contrasts her attitude toward the garage to the place that her husband loves. Underline one other use of contrast in the final paragraph.

PROOFREADING   DESCRIPTIVE ESSAY

Following is a final version of the essay on Bradley's garage. When you compare it to the draft on pages 294–295, you will notice some changes:

- A new transition sentence opens one of the body paragraphs.
- Some repetitive words, such as the word "space," have been replaced.
- Specific details have been added to all the body paragraphs.
- More sense words have been added.
- Two more sentences have been combined.
- Word choice, such as the replacement of the word "mess" in paragraph 4 with a more specific word, has been improved.
- A title has been added.

Study the final version carefully and be prepared to respond to the exercise that follows it.

Final Version of a Descriptive Essay

One Person's Preference

Everyone likes one part of his or her living space better than the other parts. Some people find pleasure in their comfortable living rooms. Others love a bedroom that reflects their tastes. My husband Bradley prefers a different part of our house. The garage is my husband's territory.

continued

The least noticeable part of the garage is the open floor. The bare floor is a small space. It is an area by the garage door and includes a small space near the door to the house. These two places, are speckled with shiny, smelly oil stains. They are also gritty with dirt. One good aspect of the grit is that it protects people from slipping on the oily patches on the floor. The floor smells like gasoline, but Bradley doesn't mind the smell at all.

Most of the garage floor is filled. It is covered in boxes of Bradley's junk that give off a nasty odor. These boxes contain junk such as rags, cracked plastic flower pots, and rusted garden tools, but Bradley wants to save it all. Although the boxes take up space, Bradley's big work bench fills much more space. It is pushed into one corner of the garage. In addition, his camping gear, including a tent and a sleeping bag, stretches into the middle of the floor. In addition, Bradley's motorcycle, which is usually in pieces, lies on the floor. Pieces of other cycles also mingle with parts of Bradley's cycle.

The walls of the garage are also heavily loaded. In fact, the back and side walls seem to stagger because of their densely loaded shelves. Some of these dusty metal shelves are packed with tools such as wrenches, screwdrivers, and pliers. Old, crusty paint cans, some without any paint, are also on the shelves. Open bags of lawn fertilizer spill their contents on a high shelf. Dozens of small plastic containers of nails and screws are stacked between piles of cleaning rags and towels. One shelf contains a bulletin board that leans against a jumble of tools.

The garage is not a showplace in a model home. It doesn't look like the clean, organized garages that appear in commercials for home improvement stores. However, it is a real garage. Although I cannot imagine spending time in it, Bradley loves his garage.

Exercise 8 **Practice: Recognizing the Changes in the Final Version of a Descriptive Essay**

Compare the draft and the final version of the paragraph. Then, in the final version, underline and number these changes from the draft version: (1) an added transition sentence, (2) a change in word choice to avoid too much repetition of the word "space," (3) additional sense words, and (4) two sentences that have been combined. All of these changes are in paragraph 2.

Topics for Writing a Descriptive Essay

When you write on any of these topics, work through the stages of the writing process in preparing your essay.

Collaborate

1. Think about a place on your campus and consider what emotions you associate with that place. For example, does a crowded campus parking lot create feelings of frustration or tension? Do you feel a certain comfort when you meet a classmate in the computer lab? Describe the place, the feelings it evokes, and why you react to it in a particular way.

2. Begin this essay with a partner. Describe the car, truck, or motorcycle you would love to own. Ask your partner to (1) jot down the details of your description and (2) help you come up with specific

details by asking you follow-up questions each time you run out of ideas. Work together for at least ten minutes. Then change roles. Let your partner describe his or her dream car, truck, or cycle and take notes for your partner. Then split up and use the details you collected to write an essay.

3. Describe a place you never want to see again. It can be a room, a building, an outdoor area such as a beach, or the inside of an airport or government building. Be sure to use specific details that explain why this place is terrible, unpleasant, or unattractive and describe the emotions you connect to the place.

4. If you could choose your own workplace, what would it look like? Would it be a private office? An outdoor space such as a mountain park or a playing field? Would it be a home office? What items would be essential? How would you personalize the space? What would your job be?

5. When you think of a frightening place, what comes to mind? Is it an evil house in a horror movie? A hospital operating room? The ledge of a skyscraper? Describe the place and explain why it causes certain emotions in you.

Topics for Critical Thinking and Writing

1. How important to you is open space such as woods, lakes, beaches, hills, and desert? Are you more content in an urban space surrounded by people and a rush of activity? Consider why your choice of space appeals to you, and predict what environment will be the norm in one hundred years. As you revise your drafts, try to use as many vivid images as possible.

2. If you have fond memories of a particular place (e.g., park, playground, nature path, neighborhood street, and so forth) you liked to visit as a child, see if you can remember specific sights, sounds, smells, or emotions associated with it. Freewrite about these memories and then determine the most vivid images you want to include in your essay. For this descriptive essay, your details should focus on more of the atmosphere and/or appearance of the place rather than merely your activities there.

NARRATION

Hints for Writing a Narrative Essay

1. **Give the essay a point and stick to it.** A narrative essay tells a story. A story without a point becomes a list of moments that lead nowhere. Once you have your point, check that your use of details does not lead you away from the point.

2. **Divide your narrative into clear stages.** In an essay, you divide your narrative into several paragraphs. Check that each body paragraph has a clear focus (in the topic sentence) and that you have a clear reason for your division. You may decide to divide your body paragraphs into (a) before, during, and after or (b) the first part of the story, the middle part, and the ending.

WRITING THE NARRATIVE ESSAY IN STEPS

PREWRITING   **NARRATIVE ESSAY**

If you were asked to write a narrative essay about something that changed you, you might begin by freewriting.

Freewriting for a Narrative Essay

Topic: Something That Changed Me

Something that changed me. I don't know. What changed me? Lots of things happened to me, but I can't find one that changed me. Graduating from high school? Everybody will write about that, how boring, and anyway, what was the big deal? I haven't gotten married. No big change there. Divorce. My parents' divorce really changed the whole family. A big shock to me. I couldn't believe it was happening. I was really scared. Who would I live with? They were real calm when they told me. I've never been so scared. I was too young to understand. Kept thinking they'd just get back together. They didn't. Then I got a stepmother. The year of the divorce was a hard time for me. Kids suffer in divorce.

Reviewing your freewriting, you decide to write on the topic of your parent's divorce. Once you have this topic, you begin to brainstorm about your topic, asking yourself questions that can lead to further details about the divorce.

With more details, you can decide that your essay will focus on the announcement of your parents' divorce and the emotions you felt. You devise the following thesis sentence:

> When my parents announced that they were divorcing, I felt confused by all my emotions.

PLANNING   **NARRATIVE ESSAY**

Following is an outline for a narrative essay on the announcement of your parents' divorce and the emotions you felt. As you read it, note how it divides the announcement into three parts: (1) the background of the announcement, (2) the story of the divorce announcement, and (3) the emotions connected to the announcement. Study the outline carefully and be prepared to respond to the exercise that follows it.

Outline for a Narrative Essay

paragraph 1

I. Thesis: When my parents announced that they were divorcing, I felt confused by all my emotions.

paragraph 2
topic sentence
and details

II. I will never forget how one ordinary day suddenly became a terrible one.
   A. I was seven when my mom and dad divorced.

background of
the announcement

   B. My sister was ten.
   C. Both of my parents were there.
   D. They told us at breakfast, in the kitchen.

        E. I was eating toast.

        F. I remember I couldn't eat anything after they started talking.

        G. I remember a piece of toast with one bite out of it.

paragraph 3
topic sentence
and details

III. When my parents first spoke, I was in shock.

        A. They were very calm when they told us.

        B. They said they loved us, but they couldn't get along.

story of the
announcement

        C. They said they would always love us kids.

        D. It was an unreal moment to me.

        E. I couldn't believe it was happening.

        F. At first I just thought they were having another fight.

        G. I was too young to understand.

paragraph 4
topic sentence
and details

        H. I didn't cry.

IV. When the reality hit me, my emotions overwhelmed me.

        A. My sister cried.

        B. Then I knew it was serious.

        C. I kept thinking I would have to choose which parent to live with.

my emotions

        D. I knew I would really hurt the one I didn't choose.

        E. I loved them both.

        F. I felt so much guilt about leaving one of them.

        G. I also needed both of them.

paragraph 5
conclusion

        H. I felt ripped apart.

V. When my parents' marriage fell apart, so did I.

The outline combined some of the details from the freewriting with new details gathered through brainstorming and during the outlining process. As you write and revise your draft, you can continue to add details. You can also combine sentences, add transitions, and work on word choice.

    Exercise 9 **Practice: Recognizing New Details in the Outline**

Look at the writer's freewriting and note its details on the writer's emotions. Then compare those details to the details about emotions in paragraph 4 of the outline. Underline the additional details in paragraph 4.

    DRAFTING AND REVISING **NARRATIVE ESSAY**

Following is a revised draft of the essay on an announcement of divorce. As you read it, you'll notice many changes from the outline on pages 298–299.

- An introduction has been added.
- Transitions within the paragraphs have been added.
- Details have been added.
- Some dialogue has been added.
- A concluding paragraph has been added.
- Sentences have been combined

Study the draft carefully and be prepared to respond to the exercises that follow it.

Draft of a Narrative Essay

(Thesis and topic sentences are underlined.)

Divorce can be really hard on children. <u>When my parents announced that they were divorcing, I felt confused by all my emotions.</u>

<u>I will never forget how one ordinary day suddenly became a terrible one.</u> I was seven, and my sister was ten on that day. Both of my parents told us at breakfast, in the kitchen. I clearly remember that I was eating toast, but once they started talking, I couldn't eat anything. I can still recall holding a piece of toast with one bite out of it. I stared at the toast stupidly as I listened to what they had to say.

<u>When my parents first spoke, I was in shock.</u> They were very calm when they told us. "We love both of you very much," my dad said, "but your mother and I aren't getting along." "But we will always love you," my mother added. The announcement was such an unreal moment that I couldn't believe it was happening. My parents used to fight a lot, so at first I just thought they were having another fight. I was too young to understand. In fact, I didn't even cry.

<u>When the reality hit me, my emotions overwhelmed me.</u> My sister began to cry, and I suddenly knew it was serious. I kept thinking I would have to choose which parent to live with, and I knew I would really hurt the one I didn't choose. I loved them both. I was filled with guilt about hurting one. I also needed both parents so much that I dreaded separating from one of them. I believed that the one I didn't choose would hate me. I felt ripped apart.

In one morning, my world changed. One minute, I was an ordinary seven-year-old having breakfast with his family. The next, I was experiencing powerful emotions no child should feel. <u>When my parents' marriage fell apart, so did I.</u>

| Exercise 10 | Practice: Spotting Differences Between the Outline and the Draft |

Compare paragraph 2 in the outline to the same paragraph in the draft. The draft of the paragraph is better because it (1) combines sentences (twice) and (2) adds a sentence of new details. Underline and number these changes in the draft.

| Exercise 11 | Practice: Evaluating Effectiveness of the Introduction and Conclusion |

Compare the introduction to the concluding paragraph. Which do you think is more effective, and why?_____

PROOFREADING NARRATIVE ESSAY

Following is the final version of the essay on an announcement of divorce. When you compare it to the draft above, you will notice some changes:

- The introduction has been developed and improved.

- More specific details have been added.

- The word choice has been improved in several places to avoid repetition, to remove an overused phrase ("a lot"), or to change from an informal word for a parent to a more formal one.

- To improve the style in paragraph 4, some sentences have been combined.

- A title has been added.

Study the final version carefully and be prepared to respond to the exercise that follows it.

Final Version of a Narrative Essay

An Emotional Morning

No childhood is perfect, and part of growing up is facing disappointment, change, and loss. However, there is one loss that can be overwhelming. Divorce can be really hard on children. When my parents announced that they were divorcing, I felt confused by all my emotions.

I will never forget how one ordinary day suddenly became a terrible one. I was seven, and my sister was ten on that day. Both of my parents told us at breakfast, in the kitchen. I clearly remember that I was eating toast, but once they started talking, I couldn't eat anything. I can still recall holding a piece of whole wheat toast with one bite out of it. I stared at the toast stupidly as I listened to what they had to say.

When my parents first spoke, I was in shock. They were very calm when they told us. "We love both of you very much," my father said, "but your mother and I aren't getting along." "But we will always love you," my mother added. The announcement was such an unreal moment that I couldn't believe it was happening. My parents used to fight often, so at first I just thought they were having another argument. I was too young to understand. In fact, I didn't even cry.

Then the reality hit me, and my emotions overwhelmed me. My sister began to cry, and I suddenly knew the situation was serious. I kept thinking I would have to choose which parent to live with, and I knew I would really hurt the one I didn't choose. Because I loved them both, I was filled with guilt about hurting one. I also needed both parents so much that I dreaded separating from one of them. I believed that the one I didn't choose would hate me. I felt ripped apart.

In one morning, my world changed. One minute, I was an ordinary seven-year-old having breakfast with his family. The next, I was experiencing powerful emotions no child should feel. When my parents' marriage fell apart, so did I.

Exercise 12 **Practice: Recognizing Changes in the Final Version**

Compare the draft version of this essay to the final version. Underline these changes in word choice: the word that replaced "a lot"; the word that replaced "fight," so that "fight" no longer appears twice in one sentence, the word that replaced "it" in the draft phrase "it was serious."

Topics for Writing a Narrative Essay

When you write on any of these topics, work through the stages of the writing process in preparing your essay.

1. This assignment begins with an interview. Ask one (or both) of your parents to tell you about the day you were born. Be prepared to ask questions. (For example, were you expected that day, or did you

surprise your family? Was there a rush to the hospital?) Get as many details as you can. Then write a narrative essay about that day.

2. Write about a time you learned an important lesson. Use the events of the time to explain how you learned the lesson.

3. Write the story of an argument (one you were involved in or one you observed) and its consequences.

4. Write about a crime you witnessed or were a victim of. Be sure to include details about what happened after the crime was committed.

5. Write about an incident in your life that seemed to be fate (that is, meant to happen).

6. Write the story of an accident. The accident can be one you were involved in or one you observed. It can be any kind of accident: a car accident, a sports injury, and so forth.

7. Write on any of the following topics:

your first day at work   your first day at college
the worst day of your life   the last time you studied hard
the day you witnessed a victory   a day you made a friend
a day you lost a friend   a day with a pleasant surprise
the day you decided on a career   a final goodbye

Topics for Critical Thinking and Writing

1. Write an essay about an incident involving you and a friend or family member. It can be a quarrel, a misunderstanding, a promise, a shared secret, or some other interaction between the two of you. In a five-paragraph essay, write one body paragraph on the way you perceived the incident and how you reacted to it. Then write another body paragraph imagining how the other person must have perceived the same incident based on his or her reactions. In the third body paragraph, include some valuable lessons you learned from these two perspectives.

2. If you have recently enjoyed some success in school, at work, or with others, write a narrative about an event or experience that contributed to your understanding of what it means to be successful.

PROCESS

Hints for Writing a Process Essay

1. **Remember that there are two kinds of process essays:** a **directional** process essay tells the reader how to do something; an **informational** process essay explains an activity without telling the reader how to do it. Whether you write a directional or an informational process essay, be sure to make a point. That point is expressed in your thesis.

When you write a process essay, it is easy to confuse a topic with a thesis.

topic: How to change the oil in your car
thesis: You don't have to be an expert to learn how to change the oil in your car.

topic: How gardeners squirrel-proof their backyards
thesis: Gardeners have to think like squirrels to keep the critters away from plants and trees.

2. Find some logical way to divide the steps into paragraphs. If you have seven steps, you probably don't want to put each one into a separate paragraph, especially if they are short steps. You would run the risk of having a list instead of a well-developed essay. To avoid writing a list, try to cluster your steps according to some logical division.

For instance, if you are writing about how to prepare for a yard sale, you could divide your steps into groups such as (1) what to do a week before the sale, (2) what to do the day before the sale, and (3) what to do early on the day of the sale. Or if you are writing about how to cope with a bad cold, you could divide the steps into (1) recognizing the first signs of a cold, (2) assembling cold-fighting foods and vitamins, and (3) struggling through the days of misery.

3. Develop your paragraphs by explaining each step thoroughly and by using details. If you are explaining how to make a cake, you can't simply tell the reader to mix the combined ingredients well. You need to explain how long to mix and whether to mix with a fork, spoon, spatula, or electric mixer. Fortunately, an essay gives you the time and space to be clear. And you will be clear if you put yourself in the reader's place and anticipate his or her questions.

WRITING THE PROCESS ESSAY IN STEPS

PREWRITING **PROCESS ESSAY**

If you were writing a process essay about finding an apartment, you might first freewrite your ideas on the topic. Brainstorming and listing your ideas might lead you to group your ideas into three categories, organized in time order:

Listing and Grouping Ideas for a Process Essay

Topic: Finding an Apartment

before the search

Do you want a one-bedroom?

Friends can help

A good neighborhood

A convenient location can be more expensive

Can save you money on transportation

during the search

Look around

Don't pick the first apartment you see

Look at a bunch

But not too many

after the search

Check the lease carefully

How much is the security deposit?

After some more thinking, you could summarize these ideas in a thesis:

Finding the apartment you want takes planning and careful investigation.

With a thesis sentence and some ideas clustered in categories, you can write an outline for your essay.

PLANNING   **PROCESS ESSAY**

Following is an outline for a process essay on finding an apartment. Study the outline carefully and be prepared to respond to the exercise that follows it.

Outline for a Process Essay

paragraph 1	I. Thesis: Finding the apartment you want takes planning and careful investigation.

paragraph 2
topic sentence
and details
 	
before the
search
	II. You can save yourself stress by doing some preliminary work.
	  A. Decide what you want.
	  B. Ask yourself, "Do I want a one-bedroom?" and "What can I afford?"
	  C. Weigh the pros and cons of your wishes.
	  D. A convenient location can be expensive.
	  E. It can also save you money on transportation.
	  F. Friends can help you with the names of nice apartments.
	  G. Maybe somebody you know lives in a good neighborhood.
	  H. Check the classified advertisements in the newspapers.

paragraph 3
topic sentence
and details
 	
during the
search
	III. On your search, be patient, look carefully, and ask questions.
	  A. Look around.
	  B. Don't pick the first apartment you see.
	  C. Look at several.
	  D. But don't look at too many.
	  E. Check the cleanness, safety, plumbing, and appliances of each one.
	  F. Ask the manager about the laundry room, additional storage, parking facilities, and maintenance policies.

paragraph 4
topic sentence
and details
 	
after the
search
	IV. When you've seen enough apartments, take time to examine your options.
	  A. Compare the two best places you saw.
	  B. Consider the price, locations, and condition of the apartments.
	  C. Check the leases carefully.
	  D. Are pets allowed?
	  E. Are there rules about getting roommates?
	  F. Check the amount of the security deposit.
	  G. Check the requirements for the first and last month's rent deposit.

paragraph 5 conclusion	V.	With the right strategies and a thorough search, you can get the apartment that suits you.

The outline used each cluster of steps as one body paragraph. A topic sentence for each body paragraph made some point about that group of steps. It also added many new details gathered during the outline process. As you write and revise your draft, you can continue to add details. You can also combine sentences, add transitions, and work on word choice.

Exercise 13   Practice: Recognizing Added Details in the Outline Stage

Paragraph 2 of the outline is quite different from the list of ideas grouped for the same category (Before the Search) earlier. In the outline, a topic sentence and a number of new details have been added. Underline the added details in Paragraph 2.

DRAFTING AND REVISING   PROCESS ESSAY

Following is a revised draft of the essay on finding an apartment. As you read it, you'll notice many changes from the outline on pages 304–305.

- An introduction has been added.
- Transitions have been added within and between paragraphs.
- Details have been added.
- Sentences have been combined.
- A concluding paragraph has been added.

Study the revised draft carefully and be prepared to respond to the exercises that follow it.

Draft of a Process Essay

(Thesis and topic sentences are underlined.)

Some people drive around a neighborhood until they see an apartment complex with a "Vacancy" sign. They talk to the building manager, visit the apartment, and sign a lease. Soon they are residents of their new apartment, and often they are unhappy with their home. These people went about their search the wrong way. They did not realize that finding the apartment you want takes planning and careful investigation.

You can save yourself stress by doing some preliminary work. First of all, decide what you want. Ask yourself, "Do I want a one-bedroom apartment" and "What can I afford?" Weigh the pros and cons of your wishes. You may want a convenient location, but that can be expensive. On the other hand, that location can save you money on transportation. When you've decided what you want, rely on friends to help you with your search. They can help you with the names of nice apartments. Maybe somebody you know lives in a good neighborhood and can help you find an apartment. In addition, check the classified advertisements in the newspapers. They are full of possibilities.

continued

<u>In your search, be patient, look carefully, and ask questions.</u> It's important to look around and not to pick the first apartment you see. Look at several so that you can get a sense of your options. However, don't look at so many apartments that they all become a blur in your memory. As you visit each apartment, check its cleanness, safety, plumbing, and appliances. You don't want an apartment that opens onto a bad area or one with a leaky refrigerator. Be sure to ask the apartment manager whether there are a laundry room, a storage area, and sufficient assigned parking and guest parking. Check to see if a maintenance person lives on the premises.

<u>When you've seen enough apartments, take the time to examine your options.</u> First, compare the two best places you saw. Now that you have narrowed your search, consider the price, location, and condition of each apartment. Check the leases carefully. If you have or are thinking of getting a pet, check to see if pets are allowed. Check the rules about roommates, too. Next, check to see how much money you will have to put up initially. Does the lease specify the amount of the security deposit? Does it require a payment of first and last month's rent? The answers to these questions can help you reach a decision.

Once you have followed the steps of the process, you are ready to make your choice. While these steps take more time than simply picking the first place you see on the street, they are worth it. <u>With the right strategies and a thorough search, you can get the apartment that suits your needs.</u> Finally, you are ready to settle into your new home.

Exercise 14 **Practice: Recognizing How an Outline Can Be Developed into a Draft**

Study Paragraph 3 in its outline form. Then examine the same paragraph in draft form. The paragraph includes new details about (1) a reason to look at several apartments, (2) the danger of looking at too many apartments, (3) why it is important to check the safety of the apartment and the condition of the appliances, and (4) what to ask about maintenance. Underline these new details.

Exercise 15 **Practice: Recognizing Effective Transitions**

The concluding paragraph carries the reader into the final step in the process of finding an apartment. Notice how effective time transitions lead the reader from the first part of the paragraph, then past the restatement of the thesis to the final sentence. Underline the time transitions.

PROOFREADING **PROCESS ESSAY**

Following is the final version of the essay on finding an apartment. When you compare it to the draft on pages 305–306, you will notice some changes:

- A transition has been added to the beginning of paragraph 2 so that there is a smoother movement from the thesis at the end of paragraph 1 and the topic sentence of paragraph 2.

- The words "nice," "good," and "bad" have been changed to more specific descriptions.

- More details have been added to the end of paragraph 3.
- A title has been added.

Study the final version carefully and be prepared to respond to the exercise that follows it.

Final Version of a Process Essay

How to Find a Suitable Apartment

Some people drive around a neighborhood until they see an apartment complex with a "Vacancy" sign. They talk to the building manager, visit the apartment, and sign a lease. Soon they are residents of their new apartment, and often they are unhappy with their home. These people went about their search the wrong way. They did not realize that finding the apartment you want takes planning and careful investigation.

When it comes to choosing an apartment, you can save yourself stress by doing some preliminary work. First of all, decide what you want. Ask yourself, "Do I want a one-bedroom apartment" and "What can I afford?" Weigh the pros and cons of your wishes. You may want a convenient location, but that can be expensive. On the other hand, that location can save you money on transportation. When you've decided what you want, rely on friends to help you with your search. They can help you with the names of suitable apartments. Maybe somebody you know lives in an attractive neighborhood and can help you find an apartment. In addition, check the classified advertisements in the newspapers. They are full of possibilities.

In your search, be patient, look carefully, and ask questions. It's important to look around and not to pick the first apartment you see. Look at several so that you can get a sense of your options. However, don't look at so many apartments that they all become a blur in your memory. As you visit each apartment, check its cleanness, safety, plumbing, and appliances. You don't want an apartment that opens onto a dark and deserted area or one with a leaky refrigerator. Be sure to ask the apartment manager whether there are a laundry room, storage area, and sufficient assigned parking and guest parking. Check to see if a maintenance person lives on the premises or if a rental agency handles emergencies and repairs.

When you've seen enough apartments, take the time to examine your options. First, compare the two best places you saw. Now that you have narrowed your search, consider the price, location, and condition of each apartment. Check the leases carefully. If you have or are thinking of getting a pet, check to see if pets are allowed. Check the rules about roommates, too. Next, check to see how much money you will have to put up initially. Does the lease specify the amount of the security deposit? Does it require a payment of first and last month's rent? The answers to these questions can help you reach a decision.

Once you have followed the steps of the process, you are ready to make your choice. While these steps take more time than simply picking the first place you see on the street, they are worth it. With the right strategies and a thorough search, you can get the apartment that suits your needs. Finally, you are ready to settle into your new home.

Exercise 16 **Practice: Recognizing Small Improvements in the Final Version of a Process Essay**

Underline (1) the more specific descriptions that have replaced the words "nice," "good," and "bad" used in the draft and (2) the new details added to the end of paragraph 3.

Topics for Writing a Process Essay

When you write on any of these topics, work through the stages of the writing process in preparing your essay.

1. Write a directional or informational process essay about one of these topics:

   trying out for a team   childproofing a room
   finding the best airfare   painting a room
   finding the best calling plan   teaching someone to drive
   finding a roommate   applying for a loan
   selling a car   proposing marriage
   getting a good night's sleep   saving money at the flea market
   making new friends   getting the class schedule you want

2. You may work through some process at work. For example, you may have to open or close a store, clean a piece of machinery, fill out a report, use a specific computer program, or follow a process in making telemarketing calls. You may have to maintain the appearance of a work area (like aisles in a supermarket), or follow a procedure in dealing with complaints. If you follow a process at work, write an essay that teaches the process to a new employee.

3. Think of a time when you had to make an important decision. Write an essay about how you reached that decision. You can write about the circumstances that led to making a choice and about the steps you followed. For example, what did you consider first? Did you weigh the pros and cons of your options? What was your first choice? Did you stay with that decision or change your mind? Trace the steps of your thought process.

4. Is there someone you know who has an irritating habit or is hard to live with? For instance, you may be living with someone who leaves the kitchen a mess, or working with someone who always loses items (staplers, pens), and borrows yours. Write an essay in which you teach this person the steps to breaking the bad habit or changing the annoying behavior.

5. Writing this essay will take some deliberate and careful observation. The next time you perform a process that is so automatic for you that you never think about, be very aware of the steps you perform. For example, you may have a morning routine for waking up and getting ready for school, work, or other responsibilities. You may have a process for getting your child ready for school. Be very conscious of each step and consider the practicality and result of each step. Now, write an essay describing how you have always performed the process and how you can improve it.

Topics for Critical Thinking and Writing

1. A turning point in one's life can be the result of taking risks, planning carefully, or even both. Write an essay about the series of steps you followed to make a decision that significantly changed your life.

2. Assume that your manager or supervisor has asked you to gather suggestions about ways to improve employee morale, but these suggestions should not involve raises. He or she has said that it would be entirely up to you how you gather as much information and employee feedback as possible. You have agreed to compile suggestions but need to devise a plan to ensure that as many employees as possible are involved. What are the steps you would undertake to ensure optimal employee participation? You may want to consider such steps as forming a committee, recruiting colleagues, devising a survey, and so forth.

COMPARISON AND CONTRAST

Hints for Writing a Comparison or Contrast Essay

1. Use the thesis of your comparison or contrast to make a statement. Your essay must do more than explain the similarities or differences between two people, places, or things. It must make some statement about the two. For instance, if you are writing about the differences between your first and second semester of college, your thesis may be that a person can change radically in a short time.

2. Use your points of comparison or contrast as a way to organize your body paragraphs. A comparison or contrast essay needs points; each point focuses on a specific similarity or difference. For example, you might use three points to compare two dogs: their appearance, their temperament, and their abilities. You can write one body paragraph on each of these points of comparison.

3. Use a point-by-point pattern. That is, each body paragraph can explain one point of comparison or contrast. The topic sentence can summarize the point, and the details about the two subjects (people, places, or things you are comparing) can support the topic sentence. These details can be grouped so that you first discuss one subject, and then the other. You might, for example, compare the appearance of two dogs. An outline for one body paragraph might look like the following:

topic sentence	II. My German shepherd and my border collie are similar in appearance.
point: appearance	A. Max, my shepherd, has long, shiny
subject 1:	black and brown hair.
my German shepherd	B. His ears stand up as if he is always alert.
	C. His eyes are dark and intelligent.
subject 2: my border collie	D. Sheba, my collie, has glossy black and white hair.
	F. Her pointed ears make it seem as if she is always listening to something.
	G. Her black eyes are knowing and wise.

WRITING THE COMPARISON OR CONTRAST ESSAY IN STEPS

PREWRITING COMPARISON OR CONTRAST ESSAY

One way to get started on a comparison or contrast paragraph is to list as many differences or similarities as you can on one topic. Then you can see whether you have more similarities (comparisons) or differences (contrasts), and decide which approach to use. For example, if you decide to compare or contrast two restaurants, you could begin with a list like this:

Listing Ideas for a Comparison or Contrast Essay

Topic: Two Restaurants: Victor's and The Garden

similarities

both offer lunch and dinner

very popular

nearby

differences

Victor's	The Garden
formal dress	informal dress
tablecloths	placemats
food is bland	spicy food
expensive	moderate
statues, fountains, fresh flowers	dark wood, hanging plants

Getting Points of Comparison or Contrast

Whether you compare or contrast, you are looking for points of comparison or contrast, items you can discuss about both subjects.

If you surveyed the list on the two restaurants and decided you wanted to contrast the two restaurants, you'd see that you already have these points of contrast:

dress   food

decor   prices

To write your essay, start with several points of comparison or contrast. As you work through the stages of writing, you may decide you don't need all the points you've jotted down, but it is better to start with too many points than with too few.

Once you have some points, you can begin adding details to them. The details may lead you to more points. If they do not, they will still help you develop the ideas of your paragraph. If you were to write about the differences in restaurants, for example, your new list with added details might look like this:

Listing Ideas for a Contrast Essay

Topic: Two Restaurants

Victor's	The Garden
dress—formal	informal dress
men in jackets, women in dresses	all in jeans

Victor's	The Garden
decor— pretty, elegant	placemats, on table is a card listing specials
statues, fountains fresh flowers on tables tablecloths	lots of dark wood, brass, green hanging plants
food— bland tasting traditional, broiled fish or chicken, traditional steaks, appetizers like shrimp cocktail, onion soup	spicy and adventurous pasta in tomato sauces, garlic in everything, curry appetizers like tiny tortillas, ribs in honey - mustard sauce
price— expensive	moderate
everything costs extra, like appetizer, salad	price of dinner includes appetizer and salad

Reading the list about restaurants, you might conclude that some people may prefer The Garden to Victor's. Why? There are several hints in your list. The Garden has cheaper food, better food, and a more casual atmosphere. Now that you have a point, you can put it into a topic sentence. A topic sentence contrasting the restaurants could be as follows:

> Some people would rather eat at The Garden than at Victor's because The Garden offers better, cheaper food in a more casual environment.

Once you have a possible topic sentence, you can begin working on the planning stage of your paragraph.

PLANNING   **CONTRAST ESSAY**

Following is an outline for a contrast essay on two restaurants. Study the outline carefully and be prepared to respond to the exercise that follows it.

Outline for a Contrast Essay

paragraph 1	I. Thesis: Some people would rather eat at The Garden than at Victor's because The Garden offers better, cheaper food in a more casual environment.
paragraph 2 topic sentence and details	II. The menus at the two restaurants reveal significant differences.
food—Victor's	A. Food at Victor's is bland-tasting and traditional.
	B. The menu has broiled fish, chicken, and traditional steaks.
	C. The spices used are mostly parsley and salt.
	D. The food is the usual American food, with a little French food on the list.
The Garden	E. Food at The Garden is more spicy and adventurous.
	G. There are many pasta dishes in tomato sauce.
	H. There is garlic in just about everything.
	I. The Garden serves five different curry dishes.
	J. It has all kinds of ethnic food.
	K. Appetizers include items like tiny tortillas and hot honey-mustard ribs.

continued

paragraph 3	III. There is a contrast in prices at the two restaurants.
topic sentence	A. Victor's is expensive.
and details	B. Everything you order costs extra.
price	C. An appetizer or a salad costs extra.
Victor's	D. Even a potato costs extra.
The Garden	E. Food at The Garden is more moderately priced.
	G. The price of a dinner includes an appetizer and a salad.
	H. All meals come with a potato, pasta, or rice.
paragraph 4	IV. At Victor's and The Garden, meals are served in opposing environments.
topic sentence	
and details	A. Certain diners may feel uncomfortable in Victor's, which has a formal atmosphere.
environment	
Victor's	B. Everyone is dressed up, the men in jackets and ties and the women in dresses.
	C. Even the children in the restaurant are in their best clothes and sit up straight.
	D. Less formal diners would rather eat in a more casual place.
The Garden	E. People don't dress up to go to The Garden; they wear jeans.
	F. Some come in shorts and sandals.
	G. The children often wear sneakers and caps.
	H. They wriggle in their seats and even crawl under the table.
paragraph 5	V. Many people prefer a place where they can relax, with rea-
conclusion	sonable prices and unusual food, to a place that's a little stuffy, with a traditional and expensive menu.

The outline added some new details gathered during the outlining process. The topic sentences of the body paragraphs are based on the points of contrast on the earlier list. One point of contrast, the decor of the restaurants, has been omitted. The details about decor may be useful in the introduction or conclusion of the essay.

As you write and revise your draft, you can continue to add details. You can also combine sentences, add transitions, and work on word choice.

Exercise 17 **Practice: Recognizing How an Outline Evolves from a List**

Compare the <u>list</u> of ideas on dress in the two restaurants to the <u>outline</u> section on the topic. Underline the ideas that have been added to the outline.

DRAFTING AND REVISING **CONTRAST ESSAY**

Following is a revised draft of the essay on two restaurants. As you read it, you'll notice many changes from the outline on page 311–312.

- An introduction has been added, and it contains some of the details on decor gathered earlier.
- Transitions have been added within and between paragraphs.
- Details have been added.

- Sentences have been combined.
- The word choice has been improved.
- A concluding paragraph has been added.

Study the draft carefully and be prepared to respond to the exercises that follow it.

Draft of a Contrast Essay

(Thesis and topic sentences are underlined.)

There are two well-known restaurants in town. One, Victor's, is an elegant place with white linen tablecloths and fresh flowers on each table. The other, The Garden, has paper placemats on the tables. The only other item on the tables is a small card listing the day's specials. While it might seem that Victor's is a more attractive setting for a meal, The Garden has its advantages. Some people would rather eat at The Garden than at Victor's because The Garden offers better, cheaper food in a more casual environment.

The menus at the two restaurants reveal significant differences. Food at Victor's is bland-tasting and traditional. The menu offers broiled fish, baked chicken, and typical steaks like T-bone and sirloin. The spices used are mostly parsley and salt. Victor's serves standard American food with a little French food on the list; for example, the appetizers include an American favorite, shrimp cocktail, and French onion soup. While food at Victor's relies on old, safe choices, food at The Garden is more spicy and adventurous. There are many pasta dishes in tomato sauce. Garlic appears in just about everything from mashed potatoes to pork roasts. The Garden serves five different curry dishes. In fact, it has all kinds of ethnic food; tiny tortillas and ribs dipped in honey and hot Chinese mustard are the most popular appetizers.

Food choice is not the only difference between Victor's and The Garden; there is also a contrast in prices at the two restaurants. Victor's is expensive. Everything you order, such as an appetizer or a salad, costs extra. Even a baked potato costs extra. An entree like a steak, for example, comes on a platter with a sprig of parsley. If you want a potato or a vegetable, you have to pay extra for it. Food at The Garden is more moderately priced. The price of a dinner includes an appetizer and a salad; in addition, all meals come with a potato, pasta, or rice, so there are few pricey extras to pay for.

The cost of a meal at Victor's is different from one at The Garden, and the atmosphere in which the meal is enjoyed is different, too. At the two places, meals are served in opposing settings. Certain diners may feel uncomfortable in Victor's, which has a formal atmosphere. Everyone is dressed up, the men in jackets and ties, and the women in dresses. Even the children at Victor's are dressed in their best and sit straight up in their chairs. Less formal diners would rather eat in a more casual place, like The Garden. People don't dress up to go to The Garden; they wear jeans or shorts and sandals. The children often wear sneakers and baseball caps. They wriggle in their seats and even explore under the table.

Sometimes adults want to let go, just as children do. They want to sit back, not up, stretch their legs in casual clothes, not jackets and ties or dresses, and explore new food choices, not the same old standards. The Garden appeals to that child-like need for physical comfort and adventurous dining, at a moderate cost. People choose it over Victor's because they prefer a place where they can relax, with reasonable prices and unusual food, to a place that's a little stuffy, with a traditional and expensive menu.

Exercise 18 **Practice: Spotting Synonyms**

In an essay about food, the word "food" can be overused. One way around this repetition is to use synonyms. These synonyms can be general (such as "menu") or specific (such as "potato"). Search the essay and underline as many words or phrases as you can find that refer to specific things to eat or to spices.

Exercise 19 **Practice: Recognizing the Power of Transitions**

An essay that compares or contrasts needs effective transitions to keep the ideas flowing smoothly. Three paragraphs in this essay open with transitions (sentences or parts of sentences that link a new idea to a previous one). Underline these transitions.

PROOFREADING **CONTRAST ESSAY**

Following is a final version of the essay on two restaurants. When you compare it to the draft on page 313, you will notice some changes:

- More specific details have been added.
- Two sentences in paragraph 3 have been revised so that the shift to "you" is eliminated.
- The phrase "explore under the table" in paragraph 4 has been changed to "explore the spaces under the table" for clarity.
- One sentence in the conclusion has been revised so that it has a stronger parallel structure.
- A title has been added.

Study the final version carefully and be prepared to respond to the exercise that follows it.

Final Version of a Contrast Essay

Victor's and The Garden: Two Contrasting Restaurants

There are two well-known restaurants in town. One, Victor's, is an elegant place with white linen tablecloths and fresh flowers on each table. The other, The Garden, has paper placemats on the tables. The only other item on the tables is a small card listing the day's specials. While it might seem that Victor's is a more attractive setting for a meal, The Garden has its advantages. Some people would rather eat at The Garden than at Victor's because The Garden offers better, cheaper food in a more casual environment.

The menus at the two restaurants reveal significant differences. Food at Victor's is bland-tasting and traditional. The menu offers broiled fish, baked chicken, and typical steaks like T-bone and sirloin. The spices used are mostly parsley and salt; pepper, garlic, and curry are nowhere to be found. Victor's serves standard American food with a little French food on the list; for example, the appetizers include an American favorite, shrimp cocktail, and French onion soup. While food at Victor's relies on old, safe choices, food at The Garden is more spicy and adventurous. There are many pasta dishes, from linguini to lasagna, in a rich tomato sauce. Garlic appears in just about everything from mashed potatoes to pork roasts. The Garden serves five different curry dishes. In fact, it has all kinds of ethnic food; tiny tortillas and ribs dipped in honey and hot Chinese mustard are the most popular appetizers.

Food choice is not the only difference between Victor's and The Garden; there is also a contrast in prices at the two restaurants. Victor's is expensive. Everything a person orders, such as an appetizer or a salad, costs extra. Even a baked potato costs extra. An entree like a steak, for example, comes on a platter with a sprig of parsley. Anyone who wants a potato or a vegetable has to pay extra for it. Food at The Garden is more moderately priced. The price of a dinner includes an appetizer and a salad; in addition, all meals come with a potato, pasta, or rice, so there are few pricey extras to pay for.

The cost of a meal at Victor's is different from one at The Garden, and the atmosphere in which the meal is enjoyed is different, too. At the two places, meals are served in opposing settings. Certain diners may feel uncomfortable in Victor's, which has a formal atmosphere. Everyone is dressed up, the men in jackets and ties, and the women in fancy dresses. Even the children at Victor's are dressed in their best and sit straight up in their chairs. Less formal diners would rather eat in a more casual place, like The Garden. People don't dress up to go to The Garden; they wear jeans or shorts and sandals. The children often wear sneakers and baseball caps. They wriggle in their seats and even explore the spaces under the table.

Sometimes adults want to let go, just as children do. They want to sit back, not up, stretch their legs in casual clothes, not hold their breath in tight ties or fancy dresses, and explore new food choices, not settle for the same old standards. The Garden appeals to that childlike need for physical comfort and adventurous dining, at a moderate cost. People choose it over Victor's because they prefer a place where they can relax, with reasonable prices and unusual food, to a place that's a little stuffy, with a traditional and expensive menu.

Exercise 20   **Practice: Correcting a Shift in Persons**

A shift in persons is a grammar error that occurs when, for example, the third person (*he, she, it, they,* or *the name of a person, place, or thing*) suddenly shifts to another person such as the second person (*you*). In the draft version of the essay, there was a shift in persons from the third person (*people, food, it*) to the second person (*you*). The shift occurs <u>twice</u> in paragraph 3. Read the draft version of paragraph 3; note where the shifts occur, and then check the final version. Underline what replaced "you" and what replaced the verbs that followed "you" in the draft version.

Topics for Writing a Comparison or Contrast Essay

When you write on any of these topics, work through the stages of the writing process in preparing your essay.

1. Compare or contrast any of the following:

two holidays	satellite and cable television
two video games	two Internet providers
two personal goals	two clothing styles
two siblings	two surprises
two role models	two employment opportunities
two expensive purchases	two houses you've lived in
two coworkers	two assignments

2. Find a baby picture of yourself. Study it carefully; then write an essay about the similarities between the baby and the adult you are today. You can use physical similarities or similarities in personality or

attitude (as expressed in the photo). If your instructor agrees, you can ask a classmate to help you find physical resemblances between you as you are today and the baby in the picture.

3. Compare or contrast the person you were two years ago to the person you are today. You might consider such points of comparison as your worries, fears, hopes, goals, or relationships.

4. Begin this assignment by working with a partner or group. Brainstorm to make a list of four or five top performers (singers, actors, comedians) popular with one age group (young teens, high school students, college students, people in their twenties, thirties, and so forth.). Once you have the list, write individual essays comparing or contrasting two of the people on the list.

5. Compare or contrast the way you spend a weekday with the way you spend a day off. You can consider what you do in the morning, afternoon, and evening, as points of comparison or contrast.

6. Compare or contrast your expectations of some aspect of college life (such as the instructors, the grading policies, the classroom environment, and so forth) with the reality you are now experiencing.

Topics for Critical Thinking and Writing

1. Today's consumer has more choices than ever regarding cell phones. Write about the similarities or differences between a basic cell phone and one of the "smart" phones available today. Assume your audience for this essay is someone unfamiliar with various new features, and be objective in your style (i.e., do not take a stand). Be as specific as possible with your examples and details so your reader can decide which type of phone would be best suited for his or her needs.

2. If you have experience working at an independent store (only one of its kind) as well as at a chain or franchised store (multiple locations), write an essay about the stores' similarities or differences in three main areas. Brainstorm about hiring practices, working conditions, opportunities for promotion, sales training, and so forth before you determine the best areas to compare or contrast. Try to incorporate as many details as possible that would be important or surprising to the general public.

mywritinglab   For support in meeting this chapter's objectives, log in to www.mywritinglab.com and select **Essay Development—Illustration, Essay Development—Description, Essay Development—Narration, Essay Development—Process, Essay Development—Compare and Contrast**.

Different Essay Patterns: Part Two

Chapter Objectives

Students will be able to (1) gain further practice in applying the stages of the writing process to various rhetorical patterns and (2) recognize the flexibility of the multipattern essay.

CLASSIFICATION

Hints for Writing a Classification Essay

1. Be sure to have a point in your classification. Remember that you need to do more than divide something into three or more types, according to some basis, and explain and describe these types. You must have a reason for your classification. For example, if you write about three types of scooters, you may be writing to evaluate them, and your point may state which type is the best buy. If you are classifying weight-loss programs, you may be studying each type so that you can prove that two types are dangerous.

2. A simple way to structure your classification essay is to explain each type in a separate body paragraph. Then use the same kind of details to describe each type. For instance, if you describe the medical principles, food restrictions, and results of one type of weight-loss program, describe the medical principles, food restrictions, and results of the other types of weight-loss programs.

WRITING THE CLASSIFICATION ESSAY IN STEPS

PREWRITING   CLASSIFICATION ESSAY

First, pick a topic for your classification. The next step is to choose some basis for your classification. For example, if you were to write a paragraph classifying phone calls, you could write about phone calls on the basis of their effect on you. With this basis for classification, you can come up with three categories:

> calls that please me
> calls that irritate me
> calls that frighten me

By brainstorming, you can then gather details about your three categories as follows:

Added Details for Three Categories of a Classification Essay

Topic: Phone Calls

calls that please me

from boyfriend

good friends

catch-up calls—someone I haven't talked to for a while

make me feel close

calls that irritate me

sales calls at dinnertime

wrong numbers

calls that interrupt

invade privacy

calls that frighten me

emergency call in middle of night

break-up call from boyfriend

change my life, indicate some bad change

With these categories and details, you can write a thesis that (1) mentions what you are classifying and (2) indicates the basis for your classifying by listing all three categories or by stating the basis, or both. Here is a thesis that follows the guidelines:

> Phone calls can be grouped into the ones that please me, the ones that irritate me, and the ones that frighten me.

This thesis mentions what you are classifying: *phone calls*. It indicates the basis for classification, the effect of the phone calls, by listing the types: *the ones that please me, the ones that irritate me, and the ones that frighten me*. Here is another thesis that follows the guidelines:

> I can classify phone calls according to their effect on me.

This thesis also mentions what you are classifying, *phone calls*, but it mentions the basis for classification, *their effect on me*, instead of listing the types.

Once you have a thesis sentence and a list of ideas, you are ready to begin the planning stage of writing the classification essay.

PLANNING   CLASSIFICATION ESSAY

Following is an outline for a classification essay on phone calls. Study the outline carefully and be prepared to respond to Exercise 1 that follows on the next page.

Outline for a Classification Essay

paragraph 1	I. Thesis: Phone calls can be grouped into the ones that please me, the ones that irritate me, and the ones that frighten me.

paragraph 2
topic sentence and details
 	
pleasing calls
	II. Calls that please me make me feel close to someone.
	  A. I like calls from my boyfriend, especially when he calls to say he is thinking of me.
	  B. I like to hear from good friends.
	  C. My two best friends call me at least twice a day.
	  D. I like catch-up calls.
	  E. These are calls from people I haven't talked to in a while.
	  F. A friend I hadn't seen in a year called me from Ecuador to say "Happy Birthday."
	  G. We talked for a long time.

paragraph 3
topic sentence and details
 	
irritating calls
	III. Some calls irritate me because they invade my privacy.
	  A. Sales calls always come at dinnertime.
	  B. They are recorded.
	  C. They offer me help with my credit card bills.
	  D. I get at least four wrong-number calls each week.
	  E. Some of the callers don't even apologize.
	  F. These calls annoy me because I have to interrupt what I'm doing to answer them.

continued

paragraph 4 topic sentence and details frightening calls	IV. The calls that tell me about some bad change in my life frighten me. A. I once got a call in the middle of the night. B. It was from a hospital emergency room. C. The nurse said my brother had been in an accident. D. That was the most terrifying call of my life. E. I once got a call from a boyfriend. F. He said he wanted to break up. G. His words hurt me.
paragraph 5 conclusion	V. A phone is just an instrument; its effect on the person who receives a call makes it a good or bad instrument.

The outline combined some of the details from the list with new details gathered during the writing process. It used the three categories as the basis for the topic sentences for the body paragraph. Each topic sentence has two parts: (1) the name of the category, such as pleasing calls, and (2) the effect of calls in this category. For example, here is one topic sentence:

(1) the category   **(2) the effect of calls in this category**
Calls that please me make me feel close to someone.

Since the point of the essay is to show the effect of different kinds of calls, this topic sentence is effective.

As you write and revise your draft, you can continue to add details. You can also combine sentences, add transitions, and work on word choice.

Exercise 1   **Practice: Identifying the Added Details in Paragraph 2 of the Outline**

Compare the list of details (under the heading "Calls That Please Me") in the Prewriting section for the classification essay with the list of details in the outline. Underline the additional details.

DRAFTING AND REVISING   **CLASSIFICATION ESSAY**

Following is a revised draft of the essay on phone calls. As you read it, you'll notice many changes from the outline on pages 319–320.

- An introduction has been added.
- Transitions have been added within and between paragraphs.
- Details have been added.
- Sentences have been combined.
- A concluding paragraph has been added.

Study the draft carefully and be prepared to respond to the exercises that follow it.

Draft of a Classification Essay

(Thesis and topic sentences are underlined.)

I am lost without a phone. My friends swear that I must have been born holding a tiny phone to my ear. Although I am constantly talking on the phone, I am not always enjoying the process. Not all my phone calls are pleasant. In fact, <u>the calls can be grouped into the ones that please me, the ones that irritate me, and the ones that frighten me.</u>

<u>Calls that please me make me feel close to someone.</u> For example, I like calls from my boyfriend, especially when he calls to say that he is thinking of me. I also like to hear from good friends. My two best friends call me at least twice a day, and it is amazing that we can always find something to talk about. Catch-up calls, calls from people I haven't seen in a while, are another kind of call I enjoy. Recently, a friend I hadn't seen in a year called me from Ecuador to say "Happy Birthday." It was so good to hear from her that we talked for a long time.

The ring of a phone can bring me warm feelings, but it can sometimes bring irritation. <u>Calls that irritate me invade my privacy.</u> Sales calls, for instance, always come at dinnertime. They have recorded voices. The voices offer me help with my credit card bills. Also in this category are wrong-number calls. I get at least four of these a week, and some of the callers don't even apologize for bothering me. These calls annoy me because I have to interrupt what I'm doing to answer them.

Finally, there are the worst calls of all. The calls that frighten me tell me about some bad change in my life. I once got a call in the middle of the night. It was from a hospital emergency room; the nurse told me my brother had been in an accident. That was the most terrifying call of my life. Another time, a boyfriend called to say he wanted to break up. His cold words surprised and hurt me.

I rely on the telephone, but it is not always good to me. Ever since I received the call about my brother's accident, I tremble when the phone rings late at night. However, I have come to realize that a phone is just an instrument; its effect on the person who receives a call makes it a good or bad instrument.

Exercise 2   **Practice: Examining the Introduction**

Look carefully at the introduction in the draft above and notice how smoothly it moves from one idea to another. Underline the sentence that introduces the idea that the writer spends a great deal of time on the phone. Then underline the sentence that moves to another idea: that not all calls are pleasant. Finally, underline the transition that introduces the thesis.

Exercise 3   **Practice: Determining an Effective Style Change**

Which two sentences in paragraph 3 could be combined? Underline them.

PROOFREADING   **CLASSIFICATION ESSAY**

Following is the final version of the essay on phone calls. When you compare it to the draft above, you will notice some changes:

- Two sentences have been combined.

- Some of the word choices have been polished to make details more specific, to eliminate repetition, or to eliminate an awkward phrase.

- A final sentence has been added to paragraph 4 to reinforce the point that both examples in the paragraph are about a life-changing phone call.
- The last sentence in the concluding paragraph has been revised to make a more precise statement about the basis for the classification: the effect of each type of phone call.
- A title has been added.

Study the final version carefully and be prepared to respond to Exercise 4 that follows it.

Final Version of a Classification Essay

Phone Calls: Good, Bad, and Ugly

I am lost without a phone. My friends swear that I must have been born holding a tiny phone to my ear. Although I am constantly talking on the phone, I am not always enjoying the process. Not all the conversations are pleasant. In fact, the calls can be grouped into the ones that please me, the ones that irritate me, and the ones that frighten me.

Calls that please me make me feel close to someone. For example, I like calls from my boyfriend, especially when he calls to say that he is thinking of me. I also like to hear from good friends. My two best friends call me at least twice a day, and it is amazing that we can always find something to talk about. Catch-up calls, calls from people I haven't seen in a while, are another kind of call I enjoy. Recently, a friend I hadn't seen in a year called me from Ecuador to say "Happy Birthday." It was so good to hear from her that we talked for an hour.

The ring of a phone can bring me warm feelings, but it can sometimes bring irritation. Calls that irritate me invade my privacy. Sales calls that feature recorded voices always come at dinnertime. They offer help with my credit card bills. Also in this category are wrong-number calls. I get at least four of these a week, and some of the callers don't even apologize for bothering me. These calls annoy me because I have to interrupt what I'm doing to answer them.

Finally, there are the worst calls of all. The calls that frighten me tell me about some crisis in my life. I once got a call in the middle of the night. It was from a hospital emergency room; the nurse told me my brother had been in an accident. That was the most terrifying call of my life. Another time, a boyfriend called to say he wanted to break up. His cold words surprised and hurt me. Both of these calls brought me news that changed my life, and the news was totally unexpected.

I rely on the telephone, but it is not always good to me. Ever since I received the call about my brother's accident, I tremble when the phone rings late at night. However, I have come to realize that a phone is just an instrument; it conveys a message. Its effect on the person who receives that message makes it a welcome, annoying, or dreaded instrument.

Exercise 4 Practice: Evaluating the Concluding Sentence

Compare the last paragraph of the draft essay to the last paragraph of the final version. Why did the final essay end by describing a phone as a "welcome, annoying, or dreaded instrument"? How is this a more appropriate phrase than the "good or bad instrument" description of the draft version?

_____

_____

Topics for Writing a Classification Essay

When you write on any of these topics, work through the stages of the writing process in preparing your essay.

1. Write a classification essay on any of the topics below. If your instructor agrees, brainstorm with a partner or group to come up with a basis for your classification and categories related to the basis.

Collaborate

your clothes	your dreams	your mistakes
your relatives	your job responsibilities	your goals
photographs	discount stores	broken promises
military heroes	Web sites	vampire films
beloved pets	bargain meals	gossip
traffic violations	lost chances	urban legends

2. You may not know it, but you are probably an expert on something. For example, you may work in a jewelry store and know all about diamonds. You may be a paramedic and know about medical emergencies. If you are a veterinarian's assistant, you know about cats and dogs. If you collect Barbie dolls, you are an expert on these toys. Consider what you know best, through your work, hobbies, education, or leisure activities, and write a classification essay about a subject in that area. If you know about diamonds, you can classify engagement rings. If you work at a veterinarian's office, you can classify pet owners or poodles.

3. Below are some topics. Each one already has a basis for classification. Write a classification essay on one of the choices.

   Classify

   a. babysitters on the basis of how competent they are
   b. small children on the basis of their sleeping habits
   c. teenage boys or girls on the basis of their favorite sport
   d. government offices (like the post office, courthouse) on the basis of how efficient they are
   e. roads on the basis of how safe they are
   f. fads on the basis of how long they last
   g. auto repair shops on the basis of their reliability
   h. classrooms on the basis of how comfortable they are
   i. uniforms on the basis of how attractive they are
   j. uniforms on the basis of how comfortable they are

4. This assignment requires a little research. Write an essay that classifies some product according to price. For example, you can classify laptops or electronic reading devices (or hair dryers, backpacks, hiking boots, motorcycles, and so forth) according to their cost. Assume that you are writing to advise readers who may want to buy this product and want the best deal for their money. Research the details of this product in different price ranges; for example, explain what the most expensive laptop includes and how useful these features are, and then explain what mid-priced and low-priced laptops offer for their price. Use your essay to recommend the best deal for the money.

Topics for Critical Thinking and Writing: Classification Essay

1. Think about the ways in which you may be classified. For example, if you are reading this book, you are probably classified as a college student. But are you classified as a part-time or full-time student? Your racial or ethnic background may be difficult to categorize. Today there are so many ways each person can be classified—by income level, marital status, spending habits, and so forth—that most people defy simple classifications. In your body paragraphs, write about three ways in which you might be classified incorrectly. For each classification, include examples of how these terms do not truly describe you.

2. Throughout your formal education thus far, you have probably been exposed to various teaching methods and settings that may be considered nontraditional. Brainstorm about nontraditional types of schools or teaching methods you have encountered, and classify them on the basis of how effective they were in teaching you new concepts or subject matter. As you make these judgments and draft your essay, include details about why certain methods or environments worked well or were largely ineffective for you.

DEFINITION

Hints for Writing a Definition Essay

1. Write a personal definition, not a dictionary definition. To develop a definition essay, you need to define a term that can be explained by more than the words in a dictionary. You can develop your essay with concrete terms and specific examples that help define the term.

> **terms that won't work in a personal definition:** photosynthesis, DNA, the Colt Revolver, the Renaissance

> **terms that will work in a personal definition:** self-pity, patience, the team player, the pessimist

2. Include in your thesis (1) the term you are defining, (2) the broad class or category into which your term fits, and (3) the specific distinguishing characteristics that make the term different from all others in the class or category. Each of the following sentences could be the thesis for a definition essay.

> term   category   distinguishing characteristics
> *Envy* is *the desire for what others have.*

> term   category   distinguishing characteristics
> A *nit-picker* is a *person who worries excessively about minor details.*

3. Form your body paragraphs from different aspects of your term. For example, if you defined *patience*, you might write one paragraph on the times when patience is necessary and another on the times when people need to stop being patient and take action. If you write about *temptation*, you might write one paragraph on how to resist temptation and another on when to give in to temptation.

WRITING THE DEFINITION ESSAY IN STEPS

PREWRITING **DEFINITION ESSAY**

To pick a topic for your definition essay, you can begin with some personality trait or type of person. For instance, you might define "the insecure person." If you listed your first thoughts, your list might look like this:

> the insecure person
> someone who is not emotionally secure
> wants (needs?) other people to make him or her feel good
> no self-respect

Often, when you look for ideas to define a term, you get stuck with big, general statements or abstract words, or you simply cannot come up with enough to say. If you are having trouble getting ideas, think of questions about your term. Jot these questions down without stopping to answer them. One question can lead you to another question. Once you have five or more questions, you can answer them, and the answers will provide details for your definition paragraph.

If you were writing about the insecure person, for example, you could begin with questions like these:

> What are insecure people like?
> What behavior shows a person is insecure?
> How do insecure people dress or talk?
> What makes a person insecure?
> Why is insecurity a bad trait?
> How do insecure people relate to others?
> Does insecurity hurt the insecure person? If so, how?
> Does the insecure person hurt others? If so, how?

By scanning the questions and answering as many as you can, you can add details to your list. Once you have a longer list, you can review it and begin to group its items. Following is a list of grouped details on the insecure person.

Grouped Details for a Definition Essay

Topic: The Insecure Person

wants (needs?) other people to make him or her feel important
no self-respect

insecure people have to brag about everything
a friend who brags about his car
they tell you the price of everything

they put others down
saying bad things about other people makes insecure people feel better

insecure people can never relax inside
can never enjoy being with other people
other people are always their competitors
must always worry about what others think of them

Grouping the details can help you arrive at several main ideas. Can they be combined and revised to create a topic sentence? Following is a thesis on the insecure person that meets the requirements of naming the term, placing it in a category, and distinguishing the term from others in the category:

term   category   distinguishing characteristics

The *insecure person* is *someone* who *needs other people to make him or her feel respected and important.*

Once you have a thesis sentence, you can begin working on the planning stage of the paragraph.

PLANNING   DEFINITION ESSAY

Following is an outline for a definition essay on the insecure person. Study the outline carefully and be prepared to respond to Exercise 5 that follows it.

Outline for a Definition Essay

paragraph 1	I. Thesis: The insecure person is someone who needs other people to make him or her feel respected and important.
paragraph 2 **topic sentence and** **details** **bragging**	II. Insecure people have to brag about everything. A. An insecure friend may have to brag about his car. B. He is sure to tell you if it is a popular car. C. Insecure people wear expensive jewelry and tell what it cost. D. A man will tell you what his ring cost; a woman will tell you what her boyfriend paid for her ring. E. They make sure they wear clothes with trendy labels. F. They have to have shirts with the designer's logo on the pocket and jackets with the designer's name spread across the front. G. This is another kind of bragging.
paragraph 3 **topic sentence and** **details** **putting others down**	III. Insecure people put others down. A. They make mean remarks about other people's looks, clothes, or style. B. Saying bad things about others makes insecure people feel better. C. When some friends were talking about Susan's great new job, Jill had to make mean remarks about Susan. D. Jill hated having Susan look like a winner. E. Jill wanted all the attention and admiration for herself. F. I work with a man who is always spreading cruel gossip. G. His attacks on others are a cowardly way of making himself look good.

paragraph 4	IV. Insecure people can never relax inside.
topic sentence and	A. They can never enjoy being with other people.
details	B. Other people are always their competition.
never relaxing	C. Luke plays pickup basketball games.
	D. He can't enjoy any game of basketball unless he is the star.
	E. When someone on his team scores, he is not pleased.
	F. Instead, he becomes aggressive and selfish.
	G. Another person I know is always loud and crude at parties.
paragraph 5	H. He is so desperate to be liked that he turns himself into an obnoxious character that he thinks is the life of the party.
conclusion	V. Insecure people must always worry about what others think about them.

The outline combined some of the details from the list with new details and examples gathered during the outlining process. As you write and revise your draft, you can continue to add details. You can also combine sentences, add transitions, and work on word choice.

Exercise 5   **Practice: Recognizing Synonyms**

Paragraph 2 of the outline focuses on how a person's speech can reveal his or her insecurity. The topic sentence and the first item of detail use the word "brag" to refer to this type of speech. There are synonyms for another kind of speech which reveals a person's cruelty, in paragraph 3. Underline them.

DRAFTING AND REVISING   **DEFINITION ESSAY**

Following is a revised draft of the essay on the insecure person. As you read it, you'll notice many changes from the outline on pages 326–327.

- An introduction has been added.
- Transitions have been added within and between paragraphs.
- Details have been added.
- Sentences have been combined.
- A concluding paragraph has been added.

Study the draft carefully and be prepared to respond to the exercises that follow it.

Draft of a Definition Essay

(Thesis and topic sentences are underlined.)

Everybody knows at least one person who seems to feel so superior that no one could ever reach his or her status. Sometimes this person annoys others; at other times, this person hurts them. While it seems to be pride that motivates this person to irritate and belittle others, it is really insecurity disguised as ego. The insecure person is someone who needs other people to make him or her feel respected and important.

continued

One sign of the insecure person is bragging. <u>Insecure people have to brag about everything.</u> An insecure friend may have to brag about his car and will be sure to tell everyone that he drives a Hyundai Genesis Coupe. Some insecure people wear expensive jewelry and brag about what it cost. A man may boast about what his ring cost; a woman will mention what her boyfriend paid for her ring. Others filled with insecurity brag about their expensive clothes. They make sure they wear clothes with trendy labels. They have to have shirts with the designer's logo on the pocket or jackets with the designer's name spread across the front. This is another kind of bragging.

<u>Insecure people</u> not only like to build themselves up, but they also <u>have to put others down.</u> They make mean remarks about other people's looks, clothes, and style. Saying bad things about others makes insecure people feel better. Recently, some friends were talking about our classmate Susan's great new job. While most of us were happy for Susan, Jill had to add some comments about how lucky Susan had been to get the job since Susan was not qualified for it. Because she wants all the attention and admiration for herself, Jill hated having Susan looking like a winner. Another insecure person is a man I work with who is always spreading cruel gossip. His attacks on others are his cowardly way of making himself look good.

The constant need to shine in other people's opinion means that <u>insecure people can never relax inside.</u> Other people are always their competition for attention or approval. One such person is Luke, a college acquaintance who always plays on our pickup basketball games. Even though the games are just for fun, Luke can't enjoy any game of basketball unless he is the star. When someone on his team scores, he isn't pleased. Instead, he becomes aggressive and selfish. He wants to win every game singlehandedly. Another person who is eager to shine is always loud and crude at parties. He is so desperate to be liked that he turns himself into an obnoxious character that he thinks is the life of the party.

Insecure people can be mean and obnoxious, but they are mainly sad. <u>Insecure people must always worry about what others think of them</u>. Because they care so much about others' opinions, they cannot be spontaneous or open. They must get very tired of hiding their fears behind their bragging and criticizing. They must also be very lonely.

Exercise 6   **Practice: Recognizing Variations in Wording**

In paragraph 2 of the preceding draft, each example of bragging uses a slightly different word or phrase to describe the insecure bragger. The first example refers to the "insecure person." The next refers to "insecure people." Underline the other synonyms or variations used in the paragraph.

Exercise 7   **Practice: Spotting Added Details**

The story of Susan, whose new job prompted some mean remarks, gets some added details in the draft of the essay. Underline these new details in paragraph 3.

PROOFREADING   **DEFINITION ESSAY**

Following is the final version of the essay on the insecure person. When you compare it to the draft on pages 327–328, you will notice some changes:

- Sentences in paragraph 2 have been combined for a smoother style.

- The word "this" in the last sentence of paragraph 2 has been replaced with a more specific phrase: "This obsession with designer clothes."

- Some of the word choices have been polished to avoid repetition or to be precise.

- A specific example has been added to paragraph 4.

- A title has been added.

Study the final version carefully and be prepared to respond to Exercise 8 that follows it.

Final Version of a Definition Essay

The Insecure Person

Everybody knows at least one person who seems to feel so superior that no one could ever reach his or her status. Sometimes this person annoys others; at other times, this person hurts them. While it seems to be pride that motivates this person to irritate and belittle others, it is really insecurity disguised as ego. The insecure person is someone who needs other people to make him or her feel respected and important.

One sign of the insecure person is bragging, for insecure people have to brag about everything. An insecure friend may have to brag about his car and will be sure to tell everyone that he drives a Hyundai Genesis Coupe sports car. Some insecure people wear expensive jewelry and brag about what it cost. A man may boast about what his ring cost; a woman will mention what her boyfriend paid for her ring. Others filled with insecurity show off their expensive clothes. They make sure they wear clothes with trendy labels. They have to have shirts with the designer's logo on the pocket or jackets with the designer's name spread across the front. This obsession with designer clothes is another kind of bragging.

Insecure people not only like to build themselves up, but they also have to put others down. They make mean remarks about other people's looks, clothes, and style. Making nasty comments about others makes insecure people feel better. Recently, some friends were talking about our classmate Susan's great new job. While most of us were happy for Susan, Jill had to add some comments about how lucky Susan had been to get the job since Susan was not qualified for it. Because she wants all the attention and admiration for herself, Jill hated having Susan looking like a winner. Another insecure person is a man I work with who is always spreading cruel gossip. His attacks on others are his cowardly way of making himself look good.

The constant need to shine in other people's opinion means that insecure people can never relax inside. Other people are always their competition for attention or approval. One such person is Luke, a college acquaintance who always plays on our pickup basketball games. Even though the games are just for fun, Luke can't enjoy any game of basketball unless he is the star. When someone on his team scores, he isn't pleased. Instead, he becomes aggressive and selfish. He wants to win every game singlehandedly. Another person who is eager to shine is my cousin Jamie, a generally good-natured person, who is always loud and crude at parties. He is so desperate to be liked that he turns himself into an obnoxious character that he thinks is the life of the party.

Insecure people can be mean and obnoxious, but they are mainly sad. Insecure people must always worry about what others think of them. Because they care so much about others' opinions, they cannot be spontaneous or open. They must get very tired of hiding their fears behind their bragging and criticizing. They must also be very lonely.

Exercise 8   **Practice: Distinguishing the Changes**

In draft form, paragraph 4 gave one example that names a specific person. In the final version of the essay, another example now includes a named person. Name the person and consider how a little added description makes him more human.

_____

_____

_____

Topics for Writing a Definition Essay

When you write on any of these topics, work through the stages of the writing process in preparing your essay.

1. What is the one quality you most admire in other people? Is it courage, kindness, drive, or another character trait? Choose a quality and write an essay defining it.

2. Define any of the terms below, using specific details and examples. You can begin by looking up the term in a dictionary to make sure you understand the dictionary meaning. Then write a personal definition.

guilt	satisfaction	longing
worry	stress	contentment
paranoia	trust	shyness
boldness	confidence	will power
sympathy	brotherhood	compassion
nerve	perseverance	generosity

3. Write a personal definition of a specific type of person. Develop your definition by using specific details and examples. Following is a list of types, but you may write about another type of your choosing.

the tattletale	the guardian angel	the loner
the natural athlete	the ideal mate	the planner
the big brother/sister	the technology geek	the nagger
the control freak	the hypochondriac	the sneak
the good sport	the lost soul	the patriot
the rebel	the penny pincher	the critic

4. We often use terms that we understand and that we assume everyone knows but that may not have clear definitions. Write your definition of such a term. Examples of these terms are listed below, but you can also choose your own term. Here are some sample terms:

street smarts	a people person	fashion sense
people skills	negativity	personal issues
comfort zone	people pleaser	alpha male
change agent	street life	wishful thinking

Topics for Critical Thinking and Writing: Definition Essay

1. Think of a slang term or phrase that is currently popular and then define it. In your essay, be sure to include several meanings associated with this term or phrase. You may also want to explain its original definition, popularity, the age groups and backgrounds of the people that use the word or phrase, and the duration of its popularity.

2. As you have matured, your views about life and what is important to you have probably changed numerous times. Today, what does the phrase "a satisfying life" mean to you? You may need to examine your aspirations in several areas of your life (family, relationships, career, hobbies, and so forth) in order to write this essay.

CAUSE AND EFFECT

Hints for Writing a Cause or Effect Essay

1. Choose either causes or effects. If you try to do both in a short essay, you will make your task more difficult. In addition, you need a longer and more complex essay to cover both causes and effects adequately.

2. You can use each cause or effect as the focus of one body paragraph. You can develop the paragraph by explaining and describing that cause or effect.

WRITING THE CAUSE OR EFFECT ESSAY IN STEPS

PREWRITING CAUSE OR EFFECT ESSAY

If you were thinking about writing a cause or effect paragraph on owning a car, you could begin by freewriting something like this:

Freewriting for a Cause or Effect Essay

Topic: Owning a Car

A car of my own. Why? I needed it. Couldn't get a part-time job without one. Because I couldn't get to work. Needed it to get to school. Of course I could have taken the bus to school. But I didn't want to. Feel like a grown-up when you have a car of your own. Freedom to come and go. I was the last of my friends to have a car. Couldn't wait. An old Ford. But I fixed it up nicely. Costs a lot to maintain. Car payments, car loan. Car insurance.

Now you can review the freewriting and make separate lists of causes and effects you wrote down:

causes (reasons)

needed to get a part-time job
needed to get to school
my friends had cars

> **effects (results)**
>
> feel like a grown-up
> freedom to come and go
> costs a lot to maintain
> car payments
> car loan
> car insurance

Because you have more details on the effects of owning a car, you decide to write an effects paragraph.

After brainstorming questions to help you gather more effects and details, you are ready to write another list:

List of Effects for an Effect Essay

Topic: Owning a Car

effect 1: I had to pay for the car and related expenses.

    details: costs a lot to maintain

    car payments

    car loans

    car insurance

effect 2: I had the adult freedom to come and go.

    details: didn't have to beg my father for his truck

    didn't have to get rides from friends

    could go to the city when I wanted

    could ride around for fun

effect 3: I became a more careful driver.

    details: worried about someone hitting the car

    worried about bad drivers

    wanted to avoid the scratches cars get in parking lots

With at least three effects and some details for each effect, you can create a thesis. The thesis for this paragraph should indicate that the subject is the *effects* of getting a car. You can summarize all three effects in your thesis, or you can just hint at them. A possible thesis sentence for the paragraph can be:

> Owning my own car cost me money, gave me freedom, and made me more careful about how I drive.

The thesis summarizes all three effects. Another possible thesis hints at the effects:

> Once I got a car, I realized the good and bad sides of ownership.

With a thesis sentence, three effects, and a list of details, you are ready to write an outline for your essay.

PLANNING   **EFFECTS ESSAY**

Following is an outline for an effects essay on owning a car. Study the outline carefully and be prepared to respond to the exercise that follows it.

Outline for an Effects Essay

paragraph 1	I. Thesis: Owning my own car gave me freedom, cost me money, and made me a more careful driver.
paragraph 2 **topic sentence and details** **effect 1 freedom**	II. The wonderful part of owning a car was the adult freedom it gave me. A. I didn't have to beg my father for his truck. B. Every time I asked him, he seemed reluctant to lend it to me. C. He was always worried that I would get the interior dirty. D. I didn't have to get rides from my friends. E. I was really tired of begging rides from my buddies, and I am sure they were sick of driving me around. F. I could go to the city whenever I wanted. G. I could even ride around for fun.
paragraph 3 **topic sentence and details** **effect 2 costs**	III. I had to pay for the car and related expenses. A. A car costs a lot to maintain. B. There are oil changes and tune-ups. C. My car needed new tires. D. I had car payments. E. I had a car loan to pay. F. I had car insurance. G. I had to work overtime to pay the insurance bills.
paragraph 4 **topic sentence and details** **effect 3 cautiousness**	IV. I became a more careful driver. A. I worried about someone hitting the car. B. I could see my beautiful car dented and dinged. C. I began to worry about bad drivers. D. I became more nervous on the road. E. I worried about parking lots. F. I wanted to avoid the scratches cars can get in parking lots. G. I parked at the end of the row, away from other cars.
paragraph 5 **conclusion**	V. Owning a car gave me adult freedom, but it gave me adult responsibilities and worries, too.

The outline put each effect into a separate body paragraph. It combined some of the details from the list with details gathered during the outlining process. As you write and revise your draft, you can continue to add details. You can also combine sentences, add transitions, and work on word choice. Remember that several drafts may be necessary before you feel ready to prepare the final version of your essay.

Exercise 9   **Practice: Changing the Order of Effects**

Review the order of the effects in the list and then look closely at the order of effects in the outline. Why would a writer begin with the positive effect of owning a car (as in the outline) instead of leaving it in the middle of two negative effects? And how did the thesis change?

_____

_____

_____

DRAFTING AND REVISING   **EFFECTS ESSAY**

Following is a revised draft of the essay on owning a car. As you read it, you'll notice many changes from the outline on page 333.

- An introduction has been added.
- Transitions have been added within and between paragraphs.
- Details have been added.
- Sentences have been combined.
- A concluding paragraph has been added.

Study the draft carefully and be prepared to respond to the exercises that follow it.

Draft of an Effects Essay

(Thesis and topic sentences are underlined.)

Ever since I was six years old, I have dreamed of owning my own car. The day I got my driver's license was one of the happiest days of my life. All that was left, I thought, was having a car of my own. That day came, too, and it changed my life. Owning my own car gave me freedom, cost me money, and made me a more careful driver.

The wonderful part of owning a car was the adult freedom it gave me. First of all, I didn't have to beg my father for his truck anymore. Every time I asked him, he seemed reluctant to lend it to me. He was always worried that I would get the interior dirty. Second, I no longer had to get rides from my friends whenever I wanted to go somewhere. I was really tired of begging rides from my buddies, and I am sure they were sick of driving me around. With my own car, I could go to the city whenever I wanted. I could even ride around for fun.

On the more serious side, I had to pay for the car and related expenses. A car costs a lot to maintain. There are oil changes and tune-ups to keep the car in good running condition. Two months after I got my car, I had to buy four new and very expensive tires. Of course, I had monthly payments on my car loan. I also had to pay for car insurance, which, because of my young age, was unbelievably expensive. My insurance cost so much that I had to work overtime to pay it.

Now that I was paying for the car I drove, I became a more careful driver. I became worried about someone hitting the car; I could imagine my beautiful car dented and dinged. These thoughts made me worry about bad drivers and become more nervous on the road. Parking lots made me nervous, too. To avoid the scratches cars can get in parking lots, I parked at the end of the row, away from other cars.

<u>Owning a car gave me adult freedom, but it gave me adult responsibilities</u> <u>and worries, too.</u> Even with the stress of car payments, insurance payments, and car maintenance, I would never give up my car. My fear of dents and scratches can't keep me from the joy of driving whenever and wherever I want. I'm happy to accept the responsibilities that come with being on the road in my own car.

Exercise 10   **Practice: Seeing How the Essay Develops**

The draft of the essay is structured around a childhood wish for a car, the older phase of wanting to be independent, and the final phase of adult responsibility. Study each body paragraph and underline any words, phrases, or sentences (excluding the topic sentences) that show the stages of growth.

Exercise 11   **Practice: Recognizing the Role of Transitions**

1. Which body paragraph opens with a transition that shows a contrast from the subject of the previous paragraph?

   _____

   _____

2. Which body paragraph opens with a reference to the subject of the previous paragraph?

   _____

   _____

PROOFREADING   **EFFECTS ESSAY**

Following is the final version of the essay on owning a car. When you compare it to the draft on pages 334–335, you will notice some changes:

- Some of the word choices have been polished, replacing a vague term like "costs a lot" with the more specific "costs hundreds of dollars," and avoiding repetition of words like "worry" and "expensive."
- Details have been added; for instance, in paragraph 2 there are new details about what makes a car dirty and about how friends feel ("acting like a taxi service") when they are constantly asked for rides.
- A sentence has been added to paragraph 4 to support the topic sentence. The focus of the paragraph is on careful driving, and the body of the paragraph gives many examples of the fears of a new-car owner, but it needed one more detail to show the change in the owner's driving.
- A title has been added.

Study the final version carefully and be prepared to respond to the exercise that follows it.

Final Version of an Effects Essay

Owning a Car: Driving into Adulthood

Ever since I was six years old, I have dreamed of owning my own car. The day I got my driver's license was one of the happiest days of my life. All that was left, I thought, was having a car of my own. That day came, too, and it changed my life. Owning my own car gave me freedom, cost me money, and made me a more careful driver.

The wonderful part of owning a car was the adult freedom it gave me. First of all, I didn't have to beg my father for his truck anymore. Every time I asked him, he seemed reluctant to lend it to me. He was always worried that I would dirty the interior with food wrappers and empty soda cans. Second, I no longer had to get rides from my friends whenever I wanted to go somewhere. I was really tired of begging rides from my buddies, and I am sure they were sick of acting like a taxi service. With my own car, I could go to the city whenever I wanted. I could even ride around for fun.

On the more serious side, I had to pay for the car and related expenses. A car costs hundreds of dollars to maintain. There are oil changes and tune-ups to keep the car in good running condition. Two months after I got my car, I had to buy four new and very expensive tires. Of course, I had monthly payments on my car loan. I also had to pay for car insurance, which, because of my young age, was unbelievably high. My insurance cost so much that I had to work overtime to pay the bill.

Now that I was paying for the car I drove, I became a more careful driver. I became worried about someone hitting the car; I could imagine my beautiful car dented and dinged. These thoughts made me fear bad drivers and become more nervous on the road. I began to drive more defensively, and instead of challenging aggressive drivers, I began to avoid them. Parking lots made me nervous, too. To avoid the scratches cars can get in parking lots, I parked at the end of the row, away from other cars.

Owning a car gave me adult freedom, but it gave me adult responsibilities and worries, too. Yet even with the stress of car payments, insurance payments, and car maintenance, I would never give up my car. My fear of dents and scratches can't keep me from the joy of driving whenever and wherever I want. I'm happy to accept the responsibilities that come with being on the road, in my own car.

Exercise 12   **Practice: Evaluating Changes in the Final Version**

Underline the details added to paragraph 2. Would you have added these specific details? Defend your answer: _____

Underline the sentence added to paragraph 4. Do you think it is necessary? Why or why not?_____

_____

Topics for Writing a Cause or Effect Essay

When you write on any of these topics, work through the stages of the writing process in preparing your essay.

> 1. Think of a time when you had to make an important choice. Then write an essay explaining the reasons for your choice. Your essay can include an explanation of your options as well as the reasons for your choice.

2. Write an essay about the effects one of the following experiences had on you (or someone you know well).

beginning a new job	the first day at college
surviving an accident	the first day in a new country
losing a wallet	winning a prize
a sudden change of plans	witnessing an act of violence
a random act of kindness	receiving good news

3. Write an essay on one of the following topics:

   Why Speaking in Class Can Be Frightening

   Why (you name the career) is the right career for me.

   Why Clothing Styles Change

   Why College Students May Feel Lonely

   Why _____ is a great sport to watch.

   Why _____ is a great sport to play.

   Why people are willing to spend too much on _____.

   Why my neighborhood needs better (law enforcement, fire service, roads, public transportation, schools, stores) (pick one).

4. Think of a performer that is currently very popular and admired. Write an essay explaining the reasons for that person's popularity.

5. Explain why a certain kind of car has become much more popular than it used to be.

6. Think of a decision that changed your life. Write about the effects of that choice.

Topics for Critical Thinking and Writing: Cause or Effect Essay

1. Some college students select a major or field of study based on what they believe is popular at the moment. Think about a popular major or field at your school, and write about three key reasons students are attracted to it. You may want to interview career counselors or academic advisers to compile reasons and details behind its popularity. To help you plan your essay, consider whether these reasons are practical, idealistic, or simply driven by unrealistic media images.

2. City and county commissions routinely pass ordinances that are unpopular with certain segments of the population. If you are aware of a local ordinance or county law (e.g., a curfew, a noise ordinance, a zoning regulation, and so forth) that has been unpopular with your peers, write about three reasons for its unpopularity. As an alternative, you can write about three effects (consequences) of the ordinance that were unintended at the time it became law.

ARGUMENT

Hints for Writing an Argument Essay

1. Pick a topic based on your own experience and observation. Although you may not realize it, you have a wide range of experience because you play many roles: consumer, student, parent, child, husband or wife, parent, driver, pet owner, athlete. These and many other roles may fit you. In each of your roles, you may have noticed or experienced something that can lead to a topic.

2. Be sure to take a stand in your thesis. That is, don't merely state a problem, but make a point about how to solve or eliminate it.

> **not this:** The potholes on Johnson Road are terrible.
> **but this:** The Department of Public Works must fix the potholes on Johnson Road immediately.

> **not this:** Skateboarders have nowhere to go in Mason Heights.
> **but this:** Mason Heights needs a skateboard park.

3. Use the reasons in your argument as a way to focus your body paragraphs. If you have three reasons, for instance, you can write three body paragraphs.

4. Consider your audience's objections. Always ask yourself who the audience is for your argument. If you are arguing that your office needs a new copier, you will probably be writing to your supervisor. If you are arguing for an after-school program at your child's elementary school, you will probably be writing to the school board. Consider why your audience should support your points and how they might object.

There are several ways to handle objections and apply your critical thinking skills. If you can *refute* an objection (that is, you can prove that it isn't valid), you have removed a major obstacle. Sometimes you may have to admit the other side has a valid objection by *conceding* it. Even by conceding, however, you win confidence by showing that you know both sides of the argument and are fair enough to consider another point of view.

Another way to handle an objection is to *turn an objection into an advantage*. Adopting this ploy, you admit the objection is valid but use it to reinforce your own point. If you are arguing for a new copier and your supervisor says it is too expensive, you can agree that it is expensive but that the office is losing time and money by constantly repairing the old copier. Turning an obstacle into an advantage shows that you are informed, open-minded, resourceful, and a *critical thinker*.

Even if you do not openly refer to objections in your argument essay, being aware of possible objections helps you to frame your points effectively, with your audience in mind.

WRITING THE ARGUMENT ESSAY IN STEPS

PREWRITING **ARGUMENT ESSAY**

Imagine that your instructor has given you this assignment:

> Write a letter to the editor of your local newspaper. Argue for something in your town that needs to be changed.

One way to begin is to brainstorm for some specific issue that you can write about. You can ask questions such as these: Is there a part of town that needs to be cleaned up? Should something be changed at a school? What do I notice on my way to work or school that needs improvement? What could be improved in my neighborhood?

By answering these questions, you may come up with one topic, and then you can list ideas on it.

topic

Cleaning Up Roberts Park

ideas

dirty and overgrown
benches are all cracked and broken
full of trash
could be fixed up
people work nearby
they would use it

You can consider your audience and possible objections:

audience

local people of all ages who read the local paper

possible objections from this audience

would cost money
more important things to spend money on

answering objections

Money would be well spent to beautify the downtown.
City children could play there in the fresh air and in nature; workers could eat lunch there.

Once you have a list, you can start grouping the ideas on your list. Some of the objections you wrote down may actually lead you to reasons that support your argument. That is, by answering objections, you may come up with reasons that support your point. Following is a list with a point to argue, three supporting reasons, and some details about cleaning up Roberts Park.

List for an Argument Essay

Topic: Cleaning Up a Park

point:	We should fix up Roberts Park
reason:	Improving the park would make the downtown area more attractive to shoppers.
details:	Shoppers could stroll in the park or rest from their shopping.
	Friends could meet in the park for a day of shopping and lunch.
reason:	City children could play in the park.
details:	They could get fresh air.
	They could play in a natural setting.
reason:	Workers could eat lunch outdoors.
details:	Several office complexes are nearby.
	Workers would take a break outdoors.

With your reasons and details, you can draft a thesis sentence:

Roberts Park should be cleaned up and improved.

With a thesis sentence, three reasons, and details, you are ready to move on to the planning stage of preparing an argument essay.

PLANNING **ARGUMENT ESSAY**

Following is an outline for an argument essay on cleaning up a park. Study the outline carefully and be prepared to respond to the exercise that follows it.

Outline for an Argument Essay

paragraph 1

I. Thesis: Roberts Park should be cleaned up and improved.

paragraph 2
topic sentence and details

II. Improving the park would make the downtown area more attractive to shoppers.
  A. If the city could clean, landscape, and refurnish the park, it would be a natural refuge for shoppers.
  B. It is located in the middle of the shopping district.

reason 1
a place for shoppers

  C. Those who already shop in the city could stroll through the park or rest there after shopping.
  D. Soon, shoppers would tell their friends about the attractive, new-looking park.
  E. Eventually, friends could agree to meet at the park for a day of shopping and lunch.
  F. City shops and department stores would see business improve.
  G. Business would be good for restaurants, too.

paragraph 3
topic sentence and details

III. Workers from nearby offices and stores could eat lunch outdoors.
  A. Several office buildings are nearby.
  B. During the lunch break, many people, even those who bring their lunch, want to get out of the office or store.

reason 2
a place for workers

  C. Everyone wants to get up and forget the job for a little while.
  D. Some want fresh air.
  E. Others want to read a book or magazine while they eat.
  F. Others want to get some exercise by walking a little.
  G. Others just want to observe nature and people.
  H. An improved park could meet all these needs.

paragraph 4
topic sentence and details

IV. City children could play there.
  A. City children live in apartments.
  B. They don't have backyards to enjoy.
  C. They are reduced to playing in dangerous streets or on narrow sidewalks.

reason 3
a place for children

  D. Many aren't allowed outside at all.

reason 3 (details continued)	E. They go from sitting all day at school to sitting at home.
	F. In the park, children could interact rather than sit alone inside, watching television and playing video games.
	G. They could play on grass, not asphalt.
	H. They would not have to play near traffic.
paragraph 5 conclusion	V. Roberts Park used to be the city's landmark, and it could be once again.

The outline combined some of the details from the list with new details gathered during the planning process. It focused each body paragraph on one reason to clean up the park. As you write and revise your draft, you can continue to add details to each reason. You can also combine sentences, add transitions, and work on word choice.

Exercise 13   **Practice: Recognizing Added Details in the Outline of an Argument Essay**

Many new details help to develop the body paragraphs of the outline. Paragraph 3, for example, contains four new items to support the topic sentence. Underline these items.

DRAFTING AND REVISING   **ARGUMENT ESSAY**

Following is a revised draft of the essay on cleaning up a park. As you read it, you'll notice many changes from the outline on pages 340–341.

- An introduction has been added.
- Transitions have been added within and between paragraphs.
- Details have been added.
- A concluding paragraph has been added.

Study the draft carefully and be prepared to respond to the exercises that follow it.

Draft of an Argument Essay

(Thesis and topic sentences are underlined.)

    Roberts Park was once a pretty little park with a fountain, dark wood benches, carefully landscaped paths, and lush trees and flowers. Today, however, the fountain is cracked and dry, the benches are faded and splintered, and the paths are overgrown. Trash fills the flowerbeds. <u>Roberts Park should be cleaned up and improved.</u>

    There are several reasons why a better park would make a better city. First, <u>improving the park would make the downtown area more attractive to shoppers.</u> If the city could clean, landscape, and refurnish the park, it would be a natural refuge for shoppers. It is right in the middle of the shopping district, making it convenient for those who already shop in the city to stroll through the park or rest there. <u>Soon,</u>

continued

shoppers might tell their friends about the attractive, new-looking park. Eventually, friends could agree to meet at the park for a day of shopping and lunch. City shops and department stores would see an increase in business, and restaurants would benefit, too.

Those who do business in the city would appreciate a renovated park as well. <u>Workers from nearby offices and stores could eat lunch outdoors.</u> Several high-rise office buildings are nearby, full of office workers. During their lunch break, many people, even those who bring their lunch, want to get out of the office or store. Everyone wants to get up and forget the job for a little while. Some want fresh air, and others want to read a book or magazine while they eat. The more ambitious want to get some exercise by walking a little; however, many people just want to observe nature and people. An improved park could meet all these needs.

The most important reason to clean up the park is to help children. <u>City children could play in Roberts Park.</u> City children, who live in apartments, don't have backyards to enjoy. If they go outside, they are reduced to playing in dangerous streets or on narrow sidewalks. Many aren't allowed outside at all. They go from sitting all day at school to sitting at home. In a restored park, children could interact rather than sit alone inside, watching television and playing video games. They could play on grass, not asphalt. Best of all, they would not have to play near traffic.

Today, the words "Roberts Park" describe a run-down, ragged plot of broken benches, weeds, and trash. But the place could be a haven for children, shoppers, and workers. Once the park was green, the fountain shimmered, and the benches shone. <u>Roberts Park </u>used to be<u> the city's landmark, and it </u>could be once<u> again.</u>

Exercise 14 **Practice: Identifying Time Contrasts in the Draft of an Argument Essay**

The introduction to the essay talks about the <u>past</u> of the park (what it "once" was), and its <u>present</u> ("Today" it is in bad shape). The conclusion also refers to time: <u>past</u>, <u>present</u>, and <u>future</u>. Underline the words or phrases in the conclusion that refer to each time.

_____

_____

Exercise 15 **Practice: Recognizing the Importance of Time Sequence Transitions**

Paragraph 2 also organizes its details with time transitions. Underline four time transitions in this paragraph, and consider why time is such an important part of this essay.

_____

_____

PROOFREADING **ARGUMENT ESSAY**

Following is the final version of the essay on cleaning up a park. When you compare it to the draft on pages 341–342, you will notice some changes:

- The introduction needed a transition from the description of the park to the thesis.
- A transition sentence has been added.

- One sentence in paragraph 2 has been revised to eliminate extra words.
- Also in paragraph 2, the words "shop," "shoppers," and "shopping" became repetitive, so one phrase, "these people," replaced one use of "shoppers."
- Some details have been added and word choices improved.
- A new sentence of details has been added to paragraph 4.
- A transition has been added to paragraph 4.
- A title has been added.

Study the final version carefully and be prepared to respond to the exercise that follows it.

Final Version of an Argument Essay

The Case for Renovating Roberts Park

Roberts Park was once a pretty little park, with a bubbling fountain, dark wood benches, carefully landscaped paths, and lush trees and flowers. Today, however, the fountain is cracked and dry, the benches are faded and splintered, and the paths are overgrown. Trash fills the flowerbeds. It is time to make this place park-like again. Roberts Park should be cleaned up and improved.

There are several reasons why a better park would make a better city. First, improving the park would make the downtown area more attractive to shoppers. If the city could clean, landscape, and refurnish the park, it would be a natural refuge for shoppers. Because it is right in the middle of the shopping district, those who already shop in the city would be likely to stroll through the park or rest there. Soon, these people might tell their friends about the attractive, new-looking park. Eventually, friends could agree to meet at the park for a day of shopping and lunch. City shops and department stores would see an increase in business, and restaurants would benefit, too.

Those who do business in the city would appreciate a renovated park as well. Workers from nearby offices and stores could eat lunch outdoors. Several high-rise office buildings are nearby, full of office workers. During their lunch break, many people, even those who bring their lunch, want to get out of the office or store. Everyone wants to get up and forget the job for a little while. Some want fresh air, and others want to read a book or magazine while they eat. The more ambitious want to get some exercise by walking a little; however, many people just want to observe nature and people. An improved park could meet all these needs.

The most important reason to clean up the park is to help children. City children could play in Roberts Park. City children, who live in apartments, don't have backyards to enjoy. If they go outside, they are reduced to playing in dangerous streets or on narrow sidewalks. Many aren't allowed outside at all. They go from sitting all day at school to sitting at home. In a restored park, children could interact rather than sit alone inside, watching television and playing video games. They would get some much-needed exercise. In addition, they could play on grass, not asphalt. Best of all, they would not have to play near traffic.

Today, the words "Roberts Park" describe a run-down, ragged site full of broken benches, weeds, and trash. But the place could be a haven for children, shoppers, and workers. Once the park was green, the fountain shimmered, and the benches shone. Roberts Park used to be the city's landmark, and it could be, once again.

Exercise 16   **Practice: Spotting Changes in the Final Version of an Argument Essay**

Underline the transition sentence added to the introduction; then underline the sentence of details added to paragraph 4.

Topics for Writing an Argument Essay

When you write on any of these topics, work through the stages of the writing process in preparing your essay.

1. Write an essay for readers of your local newspaper, arguing for or against one of the following:
   a. a city-wide curfew for every person under age 18
   b. video surveillance cameras that record all activity in high-crime areas
   c. a ban on using a cell phone (or texting) while driving
   d. an online traffic school for violators of traffic laws
   e. a leash law for dog owners

2. As a consumer, you purchase a number of products and services. Think of one product (like toothpaste, a calculator, or a pair of athletic shoes) or a service (like a flight on a plane, a car repair, or a meal in a restaurant) that you feel needs improvement. Write an essay in the form of a letter to the president of the company that produces the product or offers the service. Argue for the improvement you want. Be specific. For example, if you are dissatisfied with a brand of cereal, you might want less deceptive packaging, a lower price, or less sugar in the cereal.

3. Write to the president of a company whose advertising offends you. The advertising can be television, print, or online advertising. In an essay in the form of a letter, argue for removing that advertising.

4. Argue for one of the following college issues. Your audience will be the president, vice presidents, and deans at your college. Topics to argue:
   a. open parking (with the exception of handicapped spaces) at your college
   b. a laptop (at a minimal rental fee and with a security deposit) for each registered student
   c. a twenty-four-hour study area with computers available
   d. security escorts for all evening students who ask to be accompanied to their cars

5. If you are a parent, a husband or wife, a partner, an employee, an employer, a student, a pet lover, a driver, or a traveler, you have most likely noticed something (in one of your roles) that has irritated or upset you. Write an argument essay about how to change that place, rule, policy, procedure, situation, and so forth.

Topics for Critical Thinking and Writing: Argument Essay

1. Argue for some change in your neighborhood, at your workplace, or on your campus. It must be a change that would not cost any money but would improve the quality of life.

2. Assume an anonymous donor has just given your local government a grant of $200,000 with the stipulation that the money should be used to pay some of the operating costs of city-sponsored programs that help teenagers. After you have researched the needs, operating expenses, and effectiveness of these programs, make your case for allocating most of the money to your choice of the most deserving program.

THE MULTIPATTERN ESSAY

Many essays rely on more than one essay pattern to make their point. For example, if you want to *describe* a city landmark, you might want to include a history (*narration*) of the place. If your goal is to convince a reader to take some action such as to get regular dental check-ups, your essay might include sections on the health risks of avoiding the dentist and the relatively painless process of regularly scheduled appointments. In that case, your essay could use the patterns of *argument* (convincing a reader), *effects* (discussing what can happen to those who avoid the dentist), and *process* (tracing the steps of a typical check-up).

Hints for Writing a Multipattern Essay

1. Start with a topic, not with a concern about the patterns you use. Most conversation and writing begin with a subject. You may tell your best friend about a party, for instance. When you start the conversation, you may be thinking about the story (*narrative*) of the party. However, you may soon find yourself *describing* an attractive stranger at the gathering. Soon, you may be explaining why (*causes*) you had to leave the party early, without getting to meet the stranger. In writing, as in conversation, the patterns you choose depend on what you want to say.

2. When you write a multipattern essay, do not shift patterns within a paragraph. Telling the story of a party and shifting to a description of a stranger in the same paragraph will be (1) confusing and (2) skimpy on development of either pattern.

If you begin with a developed *story*, you tell the reader who held the party, why it was held, where it took place, when it began, what people said and did at the party, and so forth.

If you intend to make the stranger a key part of the essay, he or she deserves a detailed *description* in another paragraph. So does an explanation of your *reasons* for leaving without meeting the good-looking stranger.

3. Your thesis does not have to include a reference to each pattern you are using. Your thesis is about the point of all your body paragraphs, but it can be short and focused.

> **not this:** After spending several hours dancing, eating, gossiping, and flirting at Kim and Mario's housewarming party, I noticed a guest that made my heart beat faster, but we were destined not to meet.
> **but this:** Love and celebration did not come together at a recent party.

4. Be especially careful about transitions between paragraphs. Transitions are always important in clear, smooth writing, but they are particularly important here. Because you are moving from one pattern to another, you need clear transitions that signal these moves.

WRITING THE MULTIPATTERN ESSAY IN STEPS

PREWRITING **MULTIPATTERN ESSAY ON PINE RIVER**

Imagine that you are asked to write about a financial problem that affects you or people you know. You might begin by listing your first thoughts:

> Money is tight
> Unemployment in our area
> Our town relying on summer tourists
> Someone who left town after a foreclosure

You decide that the subject you know best is how much your town relies on summer tourism. To develop and focus the idea, you start listing questions:

> What are summer tourists?
> How do they bring money to our town?
> Why do they visit here?
> Do residents like tourists?
> What do tourists do when they visit?
> What are the attractions in this town?
> Why is it only summer tourism?
> How can the town survive or even grow?
> What does the town need?

Organizing Your Ideas for a Multipattern Essay

By scanning the questions and answering as many as you can, you may realize that your writing is falling into three essay patterns. Following is a list of three patterns and details (formed by answering the questions). The list could be developed into a multipattern essay.

Grouped Details for a Multipattern Essay

Topic: Pine River

description: summer tourists love to visit

the weather is cool and sunny
area has much to do
town has camping, boating, fishing
small bed and breakfasts, a motel
friendly local restaurants, souvenir and crafts shops

effects: tourist economy is part time

after Labor Day, the town is empty
cold weather and storms discourage camping and boating
the bed and breakfasts struggle
the motel closes until spring
local stores suffer

argument: year-round businesses can save the town
a big-box store to employ people all year
store will bring customers from nearby towns all year
a local factory or plant is important
steady jobs mean better income

Grouping the details can help you design a thesis. As you study your list, you realize that the town thrives in the summer but suffers in the winter. Tourists help to support the town, but since they are the main source of income, money dries up after Labor Day. You devise a thesis that makes this point and recommends a solution:

Pine River must grow beyond its reliance on tourist money.

Notice that the thesis includes the name of the town. This thesis can be supported three ways: by *describing* the summer prosperity, by writing about the *effects* on the community when tourist season ends, and by *arguing* for a solution to this problem.

PLANNING   MULTIPATTERN ESSAY ON PINE RIVER

Following is an outline for a multipattern essay on helping Pine River to grow. Study the outline carefully and be prepared to respond to the exercise that follows it.

Outline for a Multipattern Essay

Topic: Pine River

paragraph 1	I. Thesis: Pine River must grow beyond its reliance on tourist money.
paragraph 2 **topic sentence and details**	II. Pine River is a beautiful New England town that thrives when summer tourists visit.
	A. People who visit in the summer love the cool, sunny weather.
description of the town in summer	B. There is much to do in Pine River.
	C. Boating and fishing attract many visitors to the river.
	D. Many people camp in the nearby hills.
	E. There are small bed-and-breakfast establishments.
	F. The one motel is always full in the summer.
	G. Downtown, friendly local restaurants, crafts shops, and souvenir stores charm people.
paragraph 3 **topic sentence and details**	III. When summer ends and the tourists leave, Pine River's economy falls apart.
	A. Cold weather, rain, and storms mean the end of boating, fishing, and camping.
effects of the end of tourist season	B. Bed and breakfasts lose guests.

continued

C. The motel owners close their business until summer.

D. The small downtown area becomes nearly empty.

E. Without a supply of tourists as customers, some restaurants close until late spring.

F. Local people are not likely to buy souvenirs or craftwork.

paragraph 4
topic sentence and details

IV. Pine River must save itself from this dangerous cycle by attracting year-round businesses.

A. A big-box national store would create jobs.

B. Constructing such a store would require local workers of all types.

what should be done
to save Pine River

C. More permanent jobs would be available when the store opened.

D. A large store would attract customers from nearby towns all year.

E. Big-box stores tend to be followed by smaller commercial businesses such as pizza restaurants.

F. Another great addition to Pine River would be a factory or plant.

G. Even a small manufacturing facility would mean more year-round jobs.

H. Local people could have them.

I. Workers at a superstore or factory earn money that can be spent in Pine River year round.

paragraph 5
conclusion

V. Tourist towns suffer ups and downs, but a tourist town with other resources can enjoy steady prosperity.

The outline added many new details gathered during the outlining process. The topic sentences indicate the pattern of each body paragraph: Paragraph 2 uses the descriptive words "beautiful little" town; paragraph 3 begins by discussing effects ("When the summer ends . . . Pine River's economy falls apart"), and Paragraph 4 opens by saying that the town "must save itself" (argument).

Exercise 17   **Practice: Noting the Development of Paragraph 4**

Compare the grouped details in the prewriting stage for paragraph 4 to the same paragraph and details in outline form. Underline what is new in the outline.

DRAFTING AND REVISING   **MULTIPATTERN ESSAY ON PINE RIVER**

Following is a revised draft of a multipattern essay on Pine River, its summer tourists, and the town's needs. As you read it, you will notice many changes from the outline on pages 347–348.

- An introduction has been added.
- Details have been added.
- A conclusion has been written.
- Sentences have been combined.
- One sentence that was in the passive voice in part IV of the outline has been revised so that it is now in the active voice (a better and less wordy choice).

Study the draft carefully and be prepared to respond to the exercises that follow it.

Draft of a Multipattern Essay

(Thesis and topic sentences are underlined.)

Many people like to visit a place that is known for its attractions in one special season. For example, Northerners love to visit Florida in the winter because Florida weather is sunny and warm. At the same time, other people head to Colorado for the snow-covered slopes of the skiing season. In the summer, many tourists go to New England for relaxation and natural beauty. <u>However, if Pine River is to find stability, it must go beyond its reliance on tourist money.</u>

<u>Pine River is a beautiful little New England town that thrives when summer tourists visit.</u> People who visit during the summer months love the cool but sunny weather. There is much to do in Pine River. Boating and fishing attract many to the river. Many people camp in the nearby hills. There are small bed-and-breakfast establishments. The one motel in town is always full in the summer. In the small downtown area, friendly local restaurants, crafts shops, and souvenir stores charm people.

<u>When the summer ends and the tourists leave, Pine River changes.</u> The town falls apart. Cold weather, rain, and storms mean the end of boating, fishing, and camping. Bed and breakfasts lose guests. The motel owners close their business until next summer. The small downtown area becomes nearly empty. Without a supply of tourists as customers, some restaurants close until late spring. Since local people are not likely to buy souvenirs or crafts, many small shops suffer.

<u>Pine River must save itself from this dangerous financial cycle by attracting year-round businesses.</u> For example, bringing a national superstore such as Target or Walmart would create jobs. Constructing such a store would require local workers of all kinds. Staffing the store would mean more year-round jobs, and a large store would attract customers from nearby towns all year. In addition, big-box stores tend to be followed by smaller businesses such as pizza restaurants, home improvement centers, and electronics stores. They, too, employ people year-round. Another great addition to Pine River would be a factory or plant. Even a small manufacturing facility would most likely hire local people. Best of all, workers employed at the new large or small stores could spend money in Pine River all year round.

Pine River in the summer is a beautiful place for residents and tourists. However, when summer ends, life in Pine River changes. <u>Tourist towns suffer ups and downs, but a tourist town with other resources can enjoy economic prosperity.</u>

> Exercise 18   **Practice: Evaluating the Role of Contrasts
> in the Introduction**

The introduction contains a number of contrasts (for example, winter and summer). Underline as many of these contrasts as you can and consider why they are important to the subject of the essay.

_____

_____

> Exercise 19   **Practice: Recognizing the Changes from Outline to Draft**

Compare paragraph 4 of the essay in outline and paragraph form. Underline the added specific details such as brand names and types of businesses.

PROOFREADING   MULTIPATTERN ESSAY ON PINE RIVER

Following is a final version of the essay on Pine River's summer tourists and the town's needs. As you read it, you will notice some changes:

- A title has been added.

- A sentence has been added to the introduction so that the link between the New England towns and one specific town, Pine River, is clear.

- Sentences have been combined in paragraph 2.

- The word choices have been improved; for example, the reference to shops and restaurants that "charm people" has been revised to "appeal to visitors" because "visitors" is more specific and refers to the town's dependence on tourists.

- A transition to emphasize a point has been added to paragraph 4.

- Also in paragraph 4, what became one long sentence loaded with too much information has been divided in two.

- The conclusion has been revised and developed so that it is more specific in describing how the year-round residents of Pine River can begin the work of transformation.

- A final sentence in the conclusion also links the title to the essay's point.

Study the final version carefully and be prepared to respond to Exercise 20 that follows it.

Final Version of a Multipattern Essay

The Two Pine Rivers

Many people like to visit a place that is known for its attractions in one special season. For example, Northerners love to visit Florida in the winter because Florida weather is sunny and warm. At the same time, other people head to Colorado for the snow-covered slopes of the skiing season. In the summer, many tourists go to New England for relaxation and natural beauty. Many of these tourists come to Pine River. However, if Pine River is to find stability, it must go beyond its reliance on tourist money.

Pine River is a beautiful little New England town that thrives when summer tourists visit. People who visit during the summer months love the cool but sunny weather. There is much to do in Pine River. Boating and fishing attract many to the river. Many people camp in the nearby hills. There are small bed-and-breakfast establishments, and the one motel in town is always full in the summer. In the small downtown area, friendly local restaurants, crafts shops, and souvenir stores appeal to visitors.

When the summer ends and the tourists leave, Pine River changes. The town falls apart. Cold weather, rain, and storms mean the end of boating, fishing, and camping. Bed and breakfasts lose guests. The motel owners close their business until next summer. The small downtown area becomes nearly empty. Without a supply of tourists as customers, some restaurants close until late spring. Since local people are not likely to buy souvenirs or crafts, many small shops suffer.

Year-round residents of Pine River have seen this pattern develop each year. Pine River must save itself from this dangerous financial cycle by attracting year-round businesses. For example, bringing a national superstore such as Target or Walmart would create jobs. Constructing such a store would require local workers of all kinds. More important, staffing the store would mean additional permanent, year-round jobs. Such a large store would attract customers from nearby towns all year. In addition, big-box stores tend to be followed by smaller businesses such as pizza restaurants, home improvement centers, and electronics stores. They, too, employ people year-round. Another great addition to Pine River would be a factory or plant. Even a small manufacturing facility would most likely hire local people. Best of all, workers employed at the new large or small stores could spend money in Pine River all year round.

Pine River in the summer is a beautiful place for residents and tourists. However, when summer ends, life in Pine River changes. The leaders of the community such as the mayor and the members of the Chamber of Commerce must work with every citizen to find the ways and means to attract year-round businesses to Pine River. Tourist towns suffer ups and downs, but a tourist town with other resources can enjoy economic prosperity. Then Pine River could have two images: one as an attractive summer place and the other as a thriving year-round community.

<table>
<tr><td>Exercise 20</td><td>**Practice: Analyzing the Significance of an Essay's Title**</td></tr>
</table>

Explain the meaning of the essay's title. To understand its meaning, reread the essay's conclusion and also consider how the "two Pine Rivers" that currently exist could change if the town's economy is transformed.

_____

_____

_____

ANOTHER EXAMPLE OF A MULTIPATTERN ESSAY

The essay on Pine River is just one example of an essay that relies on more than one pattern. There is no rule about how many patterns to choose or how to organize them. You can decide what kind of paragraphs will work best to support your thesis and what order works best for your topic.

Below is another multipattern essay. It relies on narrative and on an analysis of effects to support a thesis.

PREWRITING **MULTIPATTERN ESSAY ON ONE FAMILY'S FIGHT AGAINST AGORAPHOBIA**

Imagine that you are asked to write about a common psychological problem. You decide to write about *agoraphobia*, a fear of open spaces or of being alone in crowded spaces. Because the illness has affected a member of your family, you know something about its effects. You could begin by freewriting.

Freewriting for a Multipattern Essay on One Family's Fight Against Agoraphobia

I only know it from dealing with my sister. She wouldn't leave the house. Started with not going to crowded places like sports arenas or concerts. Later, Sarah didn't want to visit friends. Even family. We didn't know what to do. She lived in fear of everything. Family members get frustrated. Impatient. Insist on trying to drag her out. Then she's a prisoner. We worried about her. Finally, therapy starts. Kinds of therapy. Therapy and the family.

As you consider the freewriting, you decide that you will use two patterns to develop this essay: narrative and effects. You brainstorm and consider what details will help you to develop the essay. With both the details from freewriting and additional details from brainstorming, you devise a possible grouping of the three body paragraphs.

Sarah's fall into fear (narration)

She wouldn't leave the house.
Started with not going to crowded places like sports arenas or concerts.
Later, Sarah didn't want to visit friends, even family.
She lived in fear of everything.
She's a prisoner.

Family panic (effects)

We didn't know what to do.
Family members get frustrated, impatient.
Insist on trying to drag her out.
We worried about her.

Therapy helps (effects)

Finally, therapy starts.
Sarah seeks help.
Kinds of therapy
Therapy and the family.

With a topic for three body paragraphs and some details for each, you can think about a thesis for this multipattern essay. Your thesis does not have to refer to the patterns you will use, but it needs to make some point about Sarah's illness and the family's reaction.

A possible thesis can be the following:

My sister's battles with agoraphobia required the strength of an entire family.

This thesis will work well with the topics of your three body paragraphs because they will cover *the story* of Sarah's illness, its *effects* on the family, and the *effects* of therapy. With a thesis sentence, three topic sentences for the body paragraphs, and a list of details, you are ready to write an outline for your essay.

PLANNING **MULTIPATTERN ESSAY ON ONE FAMILY'S FIGHT AGAINST AGORAPHOBIA**

Following is an outline for a multipattern essay on one family and its fight against agoraphobia. Study the outline carefully and be prepared to respond to the exercise that follows it.

Outline for a Multipattern Essay

Topic: A Family's Fight against Agoraphobia

paragraph 1
I. Thesis: My sister's battle with agoraphobia required the strength of an entire family.

paragraph 2
topic sentence and details
II. Agoraphobia slowly suffocated my sister.
   A. The symptoms started a few months after Sarah's husband left her.

a narrative about agoraphobia
   B. First, she would not go to crowded places such as sports arenas or concerts.
   C. Then she didn't want to join me or her friends on our regular trips to the mall or other places.
   D. She said the trips made her nervous.
   E. Soon she was asking me to pick up items from the supermarket.
   F. I realized that she was no longer leaving her house, even to buy food.
   G. Later, she began to tremble when the doorbell or phone rang.

paragraph 3
topic sentence and details
III. Sarah's loved ones suffered as well.
   A. Neither I nor my parents could persuade her to leave the house.

the effects of Sarah's illness on her family
   B. Our constant visits did not seem to help her.
   C. My parents and I became fearful.
   D. We could not help Sarah.
   E. Our fear became frustration, impatience, and anger.
   F. Sarah sensed these emotions.
   G. We realized that she was dreading our visits.

paragraph 4
topic sentence and details
IV. Therapy brought hope to all of us.
   A. A compassionate therapist convinced Sarah to seek help.
   B. With the support of her family, Sarah was brave enough to begin regular visits to her therapist.

continued

the effects of
therapy on
Sarah and her family

   C. These visits and appropriate medication eased her fears.

   D. Additional group therapy convinced Sarah that she was not alone in her illness.

   E. My parents and I joined a support group for family members.

   F. The group taught us how to help Sarah.

   G. It also taught us how to take care of ourselves.

paragraph 5
conclusion

V. For a long time, everyone in my family was afraid, but courage, love, and the right kinds of support brought us out of a world of terror.

Exercise 21   **Practice: Adding Details to an Outline**

How is part IV of the outline different from the "therapy helps" grouping in the earlier list of effects? Does it add more description of the same points or does it add new information? Give examples.

_____

_____

DRAFTING AND REVISING   **MULTIPATTERN ESSAY ON ONE FAMILY'S FIGHT AGAINST AGORAPHOBIA**

Following is a revised draft of a multipattern essay on one family and its fight against agoraphobia. As you read it, you will notice many changes from the outline on pages 353–354.

- An introduction has been added.
- A conclusion has been written.
- Details have been added, including one sentence in paragraph 2.
- One additional detail in paragraph 4 explains how Sarah managed to leave her home to visit a therapist.
- Transitions have been added, especially in paragraph 4.

Study the draft carefully and be prepared to respond to the exercises that follow it.

Draft of a Multipattern Essay

(Thesis and topic sentences are underlined.)

    In his acclaimed inaugural address at the depth of the Great Depression, President Franklin Delano Roosevelt advised Americans not to let fear consume them, for "the only thing we have to fear is fear itself." This famous quote might well have been describing agoraphobia. It is a fear that grows and grows. I know about this disease because <u>my sister's battles with agoraphobia required the strength of an entire family.</u>

    <u>Agoraphobia slowly suffocated my sister.</u> The symptoms started a few months after her husband left her. First, she would not go to crowded places such as sports

arenas or concerts. Then she didn't want to join me or her friends on our regular trips to the mall and other places. She said the trips made her nervous. Soon she was asking me to pick up items from the supermarket. I realized she was no longer leaving her house, even to buy food. Later, she began to tremble when the doorbell or phone rang. Her fear of the outside world had made her a prisoner in her own home.

Sarah's loved ones suffered when she did. Even if we coaxed her, neither I nor my parents could persuade her to leave the house. Our constant visits did not seem to help her. Soon my parents and I became fearful. We could not do anything for Sarah. Our fear revealed itself as anger, frustration, and impatience. Sarah sensed these emotions. She began to dread our visits.

Therapy brought help to all of us. A compassionate therapist convinced Sarah to seek help. Accompanied by a family member, Sarah became brave enough to begin regular visits to her therapist. These visits and appropriate medication eased her fears. Later, additional group therapy convinced Sarah she was not alone. Meanwhile, my parents and I joined a support group for family members of agoraphobics. The group taught us how to encourage and support Sarah. It also taught us how to take care of ourselves.

Agoraphobia caused our whole family to fight a battle against fear. The war is not over, but Sarah and the rest of us are winning. Courage, love, and the right kinds of support brought us out of a world of terror.

Exercise 22   **Practice: Identifying the Type of Introduction Used in the Essay**

Circle the type of introduction used in this essay: (1) using one or more questions, (2) opening with a contradiction of your main point, or (3) opening with a quotation.

Exercise 23   **Practice: Recognizing the Frame in the Essay**

To understand how the essay opens and closes with words that refer to being afraid or enduring conflict, underline the synonyms for these words in the introduction and conclusion of the draft.

PROOFREADING   MULTIPATTERN ESSAY ON ONE FAMILY'S FIGHT AGAINST AGORAPHOBIA

Following is the final version of a multipattern essay on one family's fight against agoraphobia. As you read it, you will notice some changes.

- A title has been added.
- More specific details have been added.
- A transition has been added to the beginning of one paragraph.
- Sentences have been combined.
- An additional sentence has been added to one paragraph.

Study the final version carefully and be prepared to respond to the exercise that follows it.

Final Version of a Multipattern Essay

One Family's Fight Against an Enemy Within

In his acclaimed inaugural address at the depth of the Great Depression, President Franklin Delano Roosevelt advised Americans not to let fear consume them, for "the only thing we have to fear is fear itself." This famous quote might well have been describing agoraphobia. It is a fear that grows and grows. I know about this disease because my sister's battles with agoraphobia required the strength of an entire family.

Agoraphobia slowly suffocated my sister. The symptoms started a few months after her husband left her. First, she would not go to crowded places such as sports arenas or concerts. Then she didn't want to join me or her friends on our regular trips to the mall and coffee shop. She said the trips made her nervous. Soon she was asking me to pick up items from the supermarket. At that time, I realized she was no longer leaving her house, even to buy food. Later, she began to tremble when the doorbell or phone rang. Her fear of the outside world had made her a prisoner in her own home.

Sarah's loved ones suffered when she did. Even if we coaxed her, neither I nor my parents could persuade her to leave the house. Our constant visits did not seem to help her. Soon my parents and I became fearful because we could not do anything for Sarah. Our fear revealed itself as anger, frustration, and impatience. Sarah sensed these emotions. She began to dread our visits. When Sarah reacted to our visits with fear, we felt guilty.

Everyone seemed to be falling into despair, but therapy brought help to all of us. A compassionate therapist convinced Sarah to seek help. Accompanied by a family member, Sarah became brave enough to begin regular visits to her therapist. These visits and appropriate medication eased her fears. Later, additional group therapy convinced Sarah she was not alone. Meanwhile, my parents and I joined a support group for family members of agoraphobics. The group taught us how to encourage and support Sarah. It also taught us how to take care of ourselves.

Agoraphobia caused our whole family to fight a battle against fear. The war is not over, but Sarah and the rest of us are winning. Courage, love, and the right kinds of support brought us out of a world of terror.

Exercise 24   **Practice: Recognizing the Revisions in the Final Version**

Underline these revisions in the final version: (1) an additional sentence and (2) a paragraph that begins with an added transition.

Topics for Writing a Multipattern Essay

> **Note:** When you choose your own topic for writing an essay, you may decide which pattern (or patterns) are most appropriate to express your ideas. The topics below suggest patterns for a *specific* topic and are meant to give you some possibilities for writing a multipattern essay.

1. This topic requires you to write an essay that will be structured around two patterns. First, tell the story (narration) of a time when you had to make a tough choice. The choice could involve jobs, romantic partners, places to live, or another difficult decision.

After you have told that story, write about the effects of that choice. (Note: You can write two paragraphs of narration and one of effects or vice versa.)

2. Write an essay that is structured around three patterns: process, contrast, and causes. First, write about the wrong way to perform a task (process); second, contrast the wrong way with the correct way; and third, discuss the reasons (causes) why many people choose the wrong way to perform the activity.

3. Write an essay that tells the story of an event that changed your life (narration) and also explains why this event affected you strongly (cause).

4. Write an essay that describes a place in your community where the crime rate is high. Then write about the effects of this environment on the residents of that place. They can be emotional, economic, political, physical, health-related, personal, long-range, or short-range.

Topics for Critical Thinking and Writing: Multipattern Essay

1. Think of three common psychological problems that people in your age group may face. Define each problem and classify it according to its severity, cause, or any other basis that works for you. Once you have completed the classification part of your essay, argue what could be done in your community to help those who suffer from these afflictions.

2. Write an essay about a time you observed or experienced unfair treatment by someone in authority. Relate what happened (narration), why you feel the person in authority acted inappropriately (causes), what resulted from his or her actions (effects), and what should be done to prevent or discourage someone in a similar position from acting so inappropriately (argument).

CHAPTER 14

Using Research to Strengthen Essays

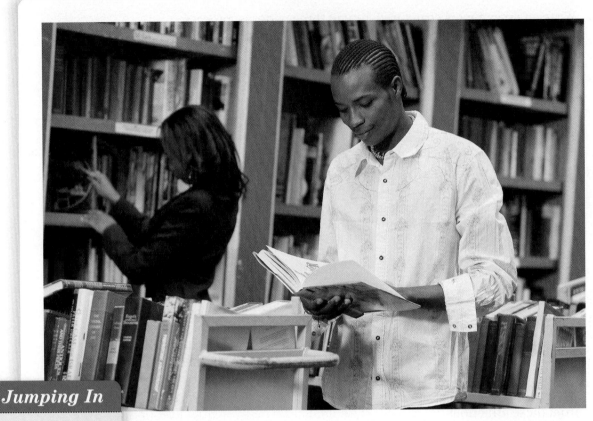

Chapter Objectives

Students will be able to strengthen their essays by (1) incorporating supporting details from valid sources, (2) using proper MLA documentation for internal citation and Works Cited entries, and (3) blending direct quotations and effective paraphrasing.

THE ROLES OF RESEARCH

During your college experience, you will no doubt use research techniques in your coursework as well as in your daily life. Even if you have not yet written a formal paper involving research, you probably have already employed various research techniques to solve problems or make crucial decisions. Asking key questions and organizing your findings are research skills that can serve you well in college and in life.

Most of the writing assignments you have completed thus far have probably been based on your own experiences, observations, or opinions. By writing regularly, you now know the importance of purpose, audience, organization, supporting details, and revision in producing a polished, final version of an essay. By appreciating the basics of effective writing, you can also recognize how essays can be strengthened through research. This chapter shows how a student writer can strengthen his or her original essay by smoothly incorporating supporting material from outside sources.

Starting with a Basic Outline and Essay

The following outline and short essay about dog-rescue groups are based solely on the writer's own experience and knowledge about dog-rescue operations. You may notice that the outline is in the same format as the outlines you reviewed in Chapter 11, "Writing an Essay." The writer's thesis is that such groups perform a humane service by rescuing homeless dogs and by carefully matching potential adopters with suitable pets. (Later in this chapter, you will see how the writer smoothly incorporated information from five sources into an outline, draft, and final version of the essay.)

Outline for an Essay Without Research

I. Dog-rescue organizations perform a humane service by saving homeless dogs and matching responsible adopters with a devoted new family member.

II. Dog-rescue volunteers play several roles.
   A. Some volunteers are "spotters" who look for specific breeds at local shelters.
   B. Experienced rescue volunteers may become coordinators and arrange assistance from various sources.
   C. Volunteers work with national organizations such as Adopt-a-Pet and Petfinder.com, which maintain databases of adoptable dogs from rescue groups throughout the United States and Canada.
   D. Volunteers assist at rescue-dog "Adoption Days" hosted by pet supply chains such as Petco and PetSmart.

III. Rescue groups provide important information and benefits for prospective adopters.
   A. By viewing a rescue group's Web site, potential adopters can read about a dog's age, temperament, adoption fee, and any special medical conditions.
   B. If a potential adopter does not find a suitable dog, he or she can still complete an online application.
   C. On an application, a potential adopter can list his or her preferences for the age, gender, and size of the dog.
   D. Although some dogs are puppies rescued from abusive situations, most are adult dogs already socialized and housebroken.

IV. Careful screening often results in a successful adoption.
   A. Rescue groups routinely conduct home visits to check the living conditions and the neighborhood.
   B. The applicant must have access to veterinary care.
   C. The applicant must agree to return the dog to the rescue organization if he or she can no longer care for the animal.
   D. A foster parent can fully inform the adoptive parent about potential adjustment problems.
   E. Careful attention to such details leads to a winning adoption process.

V. Rescue groups not only provide care for homeless dogs; they also remind us of the joy made possible by compassionate adoption.

An Essay Without Research

The following essay, written from the outline you have just reviewed, contains no research from outside sources; *it is based solely on the writer's own knowledge and experience.* As you read it, you will notice how the points in the outline have been developed through the use of specific details, effective sentence combining, and key transitions. You may also notice that some of the original words and phrases in the outline have been changed for better style.

Draft of an Essay Without Research

The Humane Work of Dog-Rescue Groups

Although the United States is generally regarded as a country that loves and pampers its pets, animal shelters are often filled to capacity with dogs that have been abandoned, abused, or surrendered by their owners. Sadly, some shelters routinely euthanize healthy dogs if no one claims or adopts them after a grace period ranging from just days to a few weeks. Fortunately, however, many shelters work closely with dog-rescue organizations that find loving, temporary homes where foster parents can provide care and, if necessary, rehabilitation. Staffed by dedicated volunteers, rescue groups perform a humane service by saving homeless dogs and enabling responsible adopters to gain a devoted new family member.

From rescuing retired greyhounds to saving mini "mutts," dog-rescue volunteers play several roles. For example, they often serve as "spotters" at local shelters, looking for specific dogs that can be fostered by individuals who specialize in specific breeds such as boxers and golden retrievers. Experienced volunteers may become coordinators who arrange for assistance from a variety of sources, including local veterinarians, groomers, transporters, and Web site designers. Many rescue groups work closely with national organizations such as Adopt-a-Pet and Petfinder.com, whose Web sites publish comprehensive lists of adoptable rescue dogs throughout the United States and Canada. On weekends, rescue volunteers can be seen helping out during "Adoption Days" sponsored by national chains, including Petco and PetSmart.

Rescue groups provide both crucial information and welcome benefits for potential adopters. When one becomes interested in a specific dog on a rescue group's Web site, he or she can read about the animal's medical needs, age, temperament, and adoption fee. Even if he or she does not spot a suitable dog but remains interested in adopting one from rescue, he or she can fill out an application and list preferences regarding a dog's age, gender, and size. Although rescue groups occasionally receive puppies and young dogs that have been picked up during police raids of abusive puppy mills and backyard breeders, the majority of dogs available for adoption are older ones. Any pet owner who has experienced the aggravation of sleepless nights and numerous housetraining "accidents" can appreciate the benefits of adopting an older, socialized, and housebroken dog.

Although the adoption process may take several weeks or even months to find the best match, careful screening improves the chances for a successful adoption. Rescue groups routinely conduct home visits of prospective dog owners to see if both the living conditions and the neighborhood will be suitable for the dog's size, temperament, and exercise needs. In addition, the applicant must have access to veterinary care and agree to return the dog to the rescue organization if he or she can no longer properly care for it. A foster parent can fully inform the adoptive parent about a dog's potential adjustment problems because the animal's behavior has been observed over a period of weeks—if not months—in a home setting. Careful attention to such details leads to a winning adoption process.

Whichever way a dog comes to a rescue group—by an owner surrender, a good Samaritan, or even by a police raid of an illegal breeding operation—it will have an opportunity to live out the rest of its life free from harm and neglect. Rescue groups not only provide care for homeless dogs; they also remind us of the joy made possible by compassion, commitment, and unconditional love.

> **Note:** Later in this chapter, you will see how the outline for this essay and the essay itself are strengthened by research.

FINDING RESEARCH TO STRENGTHEN ESSAYS

Locating Material in Your College Library

The Online Catalog If you decide to use research to strengthen an essay, you can take advantage of a number of options. Your college library probably has an online catalog system that lists all of the library's books and major holdings. You can search the online catalog by a key word related to your subject, or, if you already have information about authors who deal with your subject, you can search by the author's last name or the title of an author's book. An online catalog can provide you with a list of sources, the call number of each source (the number that will help you find the book on the library shelves), and information regarding the availability of the source. If your college has more than one campus, the online catalog can tell you which campus has a copy of the book you want. Be sure to take advantage of any "Help" menu the system provides as well as any library orientation offered on your campus.

Popular Periodical Indexes College libraries commonly subscribe to several index services that provide access to complete articles (called "full-text" articles) from periodicals (magazines, journals, and newspapers). Some of the most widely used periodical indexes include the following: *EBSCOhost*, *InfoTrac*, *LexisNexis*, *NewsBank*, *Reader's Guide to Periodical Literature*, and *WilsonWeb*.

Always preview articles carefully to see if they contain useful information for your research essay. Scan articles online and print copies of the pages that will be useful for highlighting and note taking later. Also, copy the first and last page of the article, which include information you will need for giving credit to the author and the source of the article. Be sure to ask your instructor if he or she will require copies of any of the pages you consulted for your essay.

Internet Search Engines The World Wide Web is the largest component of the Internet, and every Web site has an address, or **URL (uniform resource locator).** Many students now use search engines that help users locate specific Web sites and potential sources if they do not know URL addresses. Here are some of the more popular search engines, along with their URLs:

Google	www.google.com
Bing	www.bing.com
AltaVista	www.altavista.com
Yahoo!	www.yahoo.com

Unfortunately, some links posted on Web sites may be unavailable, and students will have to conduct searches carefully. Also, outdated information may remain posted on a Web site indefinitely, so students need to be cautious about using statistics or expert opinions that are several years old.

Checking for Validity of Sources

The writer of the dog-rescue essay decided to strengthen his paper by adding material from outside sources. The instructor required students to incorporate information from at least one print publication (magazine, newspaper, or book) and two valid electronic (online) sources. While a traditional research paper involves a more comprehensive use of outside sources and a lengthier planning and research process, a short essay can often be enhanced by adding relevant material from experts. Regardless of the scope of any research assignment, *the sources used must be valid.*

The student began his Internet search by typing the key phrase "dog rescue organizations" into the Google search function. This initial search resulted in a list of several hundred potential sources. After consulting with his instructor about the validity of his sources, the student was able to narrow his list to several dozen suitable sources.

Although the Internet and popular search engines are valuable tools for research, students are often tempted to use information from a Web site without checking for accuracy or validity. Students should check the author's credentials, such as educational background, professional experience, and other significant connections. In addition, students should locate any information about the background of the company or individuals responsible for a Web site. For example, if a student is investigating dog-rescue groups, the words of a veterinarian or background information from a nonprofit organization such as the Humane Society of the United States can generally be considered reliable. Since the veterinarian and the nonprofit group are experienced and have no financial ties to the selling of dogs, their information is more valid than opinions from a pet shop owner, who makes money selling pets, or from a chat room popular with pet owners, who may know very little about dog-rescue groups.

Similarly, print sources need to be evaluated just as carefully. For example, a brochure advertising quick or foolproof dog training programs would not be as reliable as an article from a magazine endorsed by the American Society for the Prevention of Cruelty to Animals (ASPCA). Many colleges offer library orientations that include suggestions for determining the validity of a Web site's information and of a print source's reliability.

If you have any doubt about a source's validity, check with your instructor or seek advice from a campus librarian. At the very least, see if an article lists the title or credentials of the author. If you have found an unsigned article, see if the organization responsible for the material lists its history and/or purpose. Also, check for the publication date of the article, the original place of publication, the tone of the article (i.e., Does it avoid slang? Does it appear serious?), and the proper use of statistics and expert opinion. Using valid sources will lend credibility to your work.

INCORPORATING AND ACKNOWLEDGING YOUR SOURCES

Gathering and Organizing Sources

Once you have previewed your potential sources and have selected the ones best suited for your topic, you will need printouts of any online article (or at least the necessary pages) for highlighting and note taking. If you are using a book or a magazine in its original form, you will need to photocopy the relevant pages. To keep track of all the sources you are using, you should staple or paper-clip the pages of each source and label each one clearly.

If you have narrowed your search to eight sources (for example, three magazine articles, two newspaper articles, and one book), you could organize your sources alphabetically by the authors' last names. If an article does not list its author, you can use the first major word of the title in place of the author's last name. Then you can label your sources as Source #1, Source #2, and so forth. This type of labeling will be useful for you later as you develop an outline that includes references to your sources.

Your instructor may want to see a preliminary list of your potential sources and he or she may also require that your notes from sources be written on lined 4" × 6" note cards. *Be sure you follow your instructor's specific guidelines and directions.*

Taking Notes and Acknowledging Your Sources

When you take notes from one of your sources and use the information in your paper, you must acknowledge the source. This acknowledgment is called **documentation** because you are documenting, or giving credit, to the author and the work that provided the information. When you provide documentation within a research essay, you are using what is called **internal citation.** "Citation" means "giving credit," and "internal" means "inside," or "within," the paper. At the end of your essay, you list all the sources you cited within the paper. This list is called **Works Cited.** The list of works cited is on a separate page from the rest of the essay, and it is the last numbered page of the essay.

Avoiding Plagiarism

Plagiarism occurs when you use a source's words or ideas and fail to give proper credit to the author and/or source of the work. Even if you paraphrase (state someone else's ideas in your own wording), you must give credit to the original source.

Whether you summarize material from an outside source, quote directly from it, or even paraphrase from it, you must acknowledge the source. Failure to do so is a form of academic theft. Depending on departmental or college policy, the penalties for plagiarism can be severe, ranging from receiving a failing grade on the plagiarized paper or failing a course, to expulsion. Some departments now use special software programs to check all student papers for plagiarism, and it is simply not worth the risk to submit research assignments without proper documentation.

Options for Acknowledging Your Sources

The **Modern Language Association (MLA) system of documentation** is preferred by English instructors, and you may find that humanities instructors on your campus also want you to follow MLA guidelines. In other departments, such as psychology and social sciences, instructors may ask you to follow the American Psychological Association (APA) system of documentation. Be sure to follow your instructor's directions regarding documentation requirements for your research assignments. There are many handbooks available that contain both MLA and APA styles of documentation, and most freshman composition courses require that students purchase a handbook. You may want to check with your instructor to find out which handbook, manual, or style guide is used for freshman composition on your campus.

Over the next several pages, you will see how MLA documentation is used for summarizing, paraphrasing, and directly quoting information from sources. *You will also see how books, periodicals, and electronic sources should be listed on a Works Cited page that conforms to the latest MLA style and guideline changes.*

MLA Internal ("In-text") Citation   When using internal citations, you have several options for incorporating and giving credit to the source of your information. If you use a combination of techniques, your paper will read more smoothly. The following examples of summarizing, directly quoting, paraphrasing, and combining direct quotation and paraphrase will provide you with sufficient documentation options as you draft your essay. Notice that authors and/or page numbers appear in parentheses, and this form is called **parenthetical documentation.**

A Summary of an Entire Book

One at a Time: A Week in an American Animal Shelter describes the fate of seventy-five animals who passed through a local shelter in Northern California over a seven-day period (Leigh and Geyer).

> **Note:** No page numbers are included in this brief summary because the entire work is summarized. MLA style now requires the use of italics rather than underlining for all titles of published works and names of in-text Web site domains (e.g., *petfinder.com*).

A Direct Quotation

According to Leigh and Geyer, "The safest and most reliable identification is provided by a combination of an ID tag, which is easily visible, and a microchip, which is permanent" (2).

> **Note:** If you do not introduce the author before you quote from his or her work, you must put the author's name in parentheses at the end of the quoted material. In this case, there are two authors. Both of their names could be placed in parentheses, as follows: (Leigh and Geyer 2). Notice that the period goes *after* the parentheses.

A Paraphrase

A clearly marked ID tag, along with a permanent microchip, provides an animal with the best and safest means of identification (Leigh and Geyer 2).

A Combination of a Direct Quote and a Paraphrase

Leigh and Geyer emphasize that the best means of identification for an animal is "provided by a combination of an ID tag, which is easily visible, and a microchip, which is permanent" (2).

A Source Quoted in Another Author's Work

Kathy Nicklas-Varraso, author of *What to Expect from Breed Rescue*, notes that adopters will "most often get an adult whose chewing phase, housebreaking phase, and general puppy wildness are gone" (qtd. in Mohr).

Note: Nicklas-Varraso is the author being quoted; her comment was found in an online magazine by Mohr. Mohr is the source that the student writer found. Therefore, Mohr is the source cited in parentheses. No page numbers are cited when the article comes from an online magazine.

Signal Phrases

In two of the above examples, **signal phrases** have been used to introduce quoted or paraphrased material. Signal phrases such as "Leigh and Geyer emphasize" and "According to Leigh and Geyer" are phrases that enable you to lead smoothly into documented information. Here are some of the more commonly used signal phrases, using Smith as the author:

According to Smith,	Smith reports that
As Smith notes,	Smith claims that
Smith suggests that	Smith points out that
Smith emphasizes that	Smith contends that

Documenting Information from a Source with an Unknown Author

If there is no author listed for a source, you can introduce the full title of the work after a signal phrase or place an abbreviation of the title in parentheses at the end of the information cited. For example, you can choose either of the following forms:

As the article "The Rules of Local Zoning Boards" notes, many counties prohibit businesses from operating out of garages in residential communities (C1).

or

Many counties prohibit businesses from operating out of garages in residential communities ("Rules" C1).

Note: When your source is a newspaper article, as in the examples above, give the section of the newspaper and the page number, as in C1, which stands for section C, page 1. Article titles are placed within quotation marks; book titles are placed in italics according to new MLA rules.

Exercise 1   **Practice: Paraphrasing from Sources**

Paraphrase each of the short excerpts below and include the appropriate parenthetical documentation. Use a signal phrase in at least one of the excerpts you paraphrase. The first excerpt is done for you and shows two options.

1. "A dog's sense of smell is not only exquisitely sensitive, but it communicates with a brain that can make fine discriminations among scents and learn new ones when they become important." (from *How Dogs Think* by Stanley Coren, page 63)

   Paraphrase (no signal phrase): Dogs have a keen sense of smell that enables the brain to distinguish between scents and remember new ones (Coren 63).

   or

   Paraphrase (with a signal phrase): Coren notes that dogs have a very sensitive sense of smell that enables the brain to recognize and remember important scents (63).

2. "The world is full of damaged dogs who desperately need homes. Lots of wonderful people rescue them, and those people deserve our heartfelt appreciation. Patience and hard work can go a long way to rehabilitate dogs damaged in their youth by unstable environments." (from *For the Love of a Dog* by Patricia O'Connelly, page 87)

   Paraphrase: _____

   _____

   _____

   _____

3. "The sniffing ritual is designed in part to help dogs establish who has the more forceful personality and deserves extra respect. This is an essential component of all of their introductions as well as the interactions that follow." (from *The Secret Lives of Dogs* by Jane Murphy, page 64)

   Paraphrase (Use a combination of paraphrasing and direct quoting in your version.): _____

   _____

   _____

   _____

4. "Grieving dogs experience symptoms similar to those experienced by a grieving pet owner. They may show signs of stress or restlessness. They may stop eating and lose weight or become listless and depressed. They may also have trouble sleeping or howl pitifully over the loss of their companion." (from *What's Your Dog's IQ?* by Sue Owens Wright, page 155)

   Paraphrase: _____

   _____

   _____

   _____

WORKS CITED ENTRIES: MLA FORMAT

The Works Cited list of sources contains only the works you cited in your paper. This alphabetized list starts on a separately numbered page after the essay itself. **On the Works Cited page, entries should be double spaced, and the second and subsequent lines of each entry should be indented five spaces. Double spacing should also be used between each entry. MLA now requires that the medium of publication (print, Web, CD, performance, etc.) be listed for all Works Cited entries.**

WORKS CITED ENTRIES: A COMPREHENSIVE LIST (MLA)

Books

Book by One Author

Stevens, Paul Drew. *Real Animal Heroes*. New York: Signet, 1997. Print.

Note: New York is the place of publication, Signet is the publisher, and 1997 is the year of publication. Short forms of the publisher's name should be used, so "Inc.," "Co.," and "Press" can be omitted.

Book by Two Authors

Leigh, Diane, and Marilee Geyer. *One at a Time: A Week in an American Animal*

    Shelter. Santa Cruz: No Voice Unheard, 2003. Print.

Note: When two or three authors are listed, the name of the first author is listed last name first, and the other author(s) are listed in regular order. If there are more than three authors, the name of the first author is listed last name first and followed by the Latin phrase *et al.*, which means *and others*.

A Short Work in an Anthology

Wong, Edward. "A Long Overdue Apology." *Tales from the Times*. Ed. Lisa Belkin.

    New York: St. Martin's Griffin, 2004. 29–34. Print.

Note: An anthology is a book-length collection of short works such as articles, essays, poems, or short stories. It usually has at least one editor who compiles and organizes all of the short works, which are by different authors. When you are citing from an anthology, begin with the author of the short work and its title; then list the name of the anthology and its editor. At the end of the entry, list the page numbers of the short work.

Introduction from a Book

Curtis, Jamie Lee. Foreword. *Second Chances: More Tales of Found Dogs.*

By Elise Lufkin. Guilford: Lyons, 2003. ix–x. Print.

Note: Sometimes a book will contain either an introduction, preface, or foreword written by someone other than the author of the book. When citing from such introductory material, begin with the author of this material, followed by the word "Introduction" (or "Preface" or "Foreword"), the name of the book, the author of the book, place of publication, publisher, date of publication, and the page numbers of the introduction, which will be in small Roman numerals.

Dictionary or Encyclopedia

"Luxate." *The American Heritage College Dictionary.* Third Edition. New York:

Houghton Mifflin, 1993. Print.

Note: *Luxate* is the word you defined by using this dictionary.

Periodicals

Periodicals are newspapers, magazines, and scholarly journals. In Works Cited listings, all months except May, June, and July are abbreviated.

Newspaper Article

Caldwell, Tanya. "Boca Names Its New Dog Park." *South Florida Sun-Sentinel*

10 Aug. 2005: B1+. Print.

Note: B1 refers to the section (B) and page number (1) of the article. The plus sign (+) means that the article was continued on another page.

Newspaper Editorial

"Disaster Aid." Editorial. *South Florida Sun-Sentinel* 9 Aug. 2005: A10. Print.

Note: Newspaper editorials do not list an author.

Magazine Article (From a Monthly or Bimonthly Publication)

Richard, Julie. "The Lost Tigers of China." *Best Friends* Mar. 2005: 27–29. Print.

Magazine Article (From a Weekly Publication)

Boks, Ed. "The Dirty Little Secret in Your Community." *Newsweek* 27 June 2005:

15. Print.

Journal Article

Newkirk, Thomas. "The Dogma of Transformation." *College Composition and*

Communication 56.2 (2004): 251–71. Print.

Note: The number 56 is the volume number, 2 is the issue number, and 2004 is the year of publication.

Electronic Sources

Electronic sources can include professional Web sites, online periodicals, works from subscription services (such as NewsBank), e-mails, and even CD-ROMs.

When you list a Web site as one of your sources, you should include as many of the following items as you can find on the site:

1. Author or group author's name
2. Title of the site
3. Date of publication or date of latest update
4. The company or organization that sponsors the Web site (if it is different from the group author)
5. Date you accessed the Web site
6. Include the URL (list with angle brackets) if your instructor or department requires it.

Entire Web Site

Humane Society of the United States. 2007. Web. 20 June 2007.

Note: In this example, the sponsoring organization, the Humane Society of the United States, is also the group author of the site. 2007 is the date of the Web site's most recent update. The second date is the date of access by the user.

Article or Short Work

Mohr, Lori. "Adopting from a Breed Rescue Group." *Animal Forum*. Web.

23 June 2005.

> **Note:** In this example, no date of publication was available, so the only date given in this listing is the date the online article was accessed by the student.

Article from an Online Magazine

Woolf, Norma Bennett. "Getting Involved in Purebred Rescue." *Dog Owner's Guide*

18 May 2005. Web. 20 June 2005.

Article from an Online Subscription Service

Foss, Brad. "No Braking for Higher Prices." *South Florida Sun-Sentinel* 11 Aug. 2005:

D1. *NewsBank*. Broward County Lib., Fort Lauderdale, Fl. 16 Aug. 2005.

> **Note:** If you use one of your library's online subscription services, you can first follow the same format as a print periodical, but you will need to add the name of the subscription service, the library you used, and the date you accessed the article.

E-mail

Brown, Vernon. "Re: Answers to Your Questions." Message to Jason Roberts.

15 July 2005. E-mail.

Other Sources: Non-Print

Personal Interview

Carter, Michael. Personal Interview. 17 Mar. 2005.

Radio or Television Program

"Babies Having Babies." *Live on Five Series*. Narr. Harry Anderson.

NBC. WPTV, West Palm Beach. 6 Aug. 2004. Television.

Exercise 2   Listing Works Cited Entries in MLA Format

Arrange the items from the basic sources below in correct MLA format. Consult either the "Works Cited Entries" starting on page 367 or the "At a Glance" feature on the next page for proper form and punctuation.

1. **Book**
   City where published: New York
   Publisher: Free Press
   Author: Stanley Coren
   Title: How Dogs Think
   Year published: 2002

   _____

   _____

2. **Newspaper Article**
   Newspaper: Gainesville Sun
   Article title: A Message That Lives On
   Section of newspaper: A
   Date: January 16, 2008
   Author: Alice Wallace
   Pages: 1 and 4

   _____

   _____

3. **Magazine Article** (from a monthly publication)
   Article: The Pug Who Came to Dinner
   Author: Gail MacMillan
   Magazine: Bark
   Pages: 67–69
   Month: March
   Year: 2007

   _____

   _____

4. **Journal Article**
   Journal: Journal of Communication
   Article: Dialogue about the American Family on Television
   Volume: 50
   Issue number: 4
   Year published: 2000
   Pages: 79–110
   Author: Kelly F. Albada

   _____

   _____

AT A GLANCE: SEVEN COMMON TYPES OF WORKS CITED ENTRIES

Book

author · title · city where published · publisher · date

Stevens, Paul Drew. *Real Animal Heroes*. New York: Signet, 1997. Print.

Magazine Article

author · article title · name of magazine

Boks, Ed. "The Dirty Little Secret in Your Community." *Newsweek*

date · page

27 June 2005: 15. Print.

Newspaper Article

author · article title · name of newpaper

Caldwell, Tanya. "Boca Names Its New Dog Park." *South Florida*

name of newspaper · date · year · section and page number

Sun Sentinel 10 Aug. 2005: B1. Print.

Journal Article

author · article title · name of journal

Newkirk, Thomas. "The Dogma of Transformation." *College Compo-*

name of journal · volume and issue number · year · pages

sition and Communication 56.2 (2004): 251–71. Print.

Article from an Online Magazine

author · article title

Woolf, Norma Bennett. "Getting Involved in Purebred Rescue."

name of magazine · date published · date of access

Dog Owner's Guide 18 May 2005. Web. 20 June 2005.

URL address

<http://www.canismajor.com/dog/rescinv.html>.

> **Note:** The medium, "Web," is placed before the date of access. Include the URL address only if requested by your instructor or your department. Page numbers are not listed for online articles because different printers will affect the page numbering of the printed article. *Exception*: If an article is contained within a PDF file, page numbers can be listed because numbers will be consistent regardless of the program used.

Article from an Online Database Subscription Service

author | article title | publication

Foss, Brad.　"No Braking for Higher Prices."　*South Florida*

section, page | subscription service | date published | library used

Sun-Sentinel　11 Aug.　2005:　D1. *NewsBank*.　Broward County

location | date of access

Lib., Lauderdale, FL.　Web.　16 Aug.　2005.

An Entire Web Site (No Named Author)

most recent update | name of sponsoring organization | date of access

Humane Society of the United States.　2007.　Web.　20 June 2007.

> **Note:** The first date is the year listed for the Web site's most recent update.　The second date is the date of access by the user.　The name of the Web site here is also the sponsoring organization and group author.

INCORPORATING RESEARCH INTO YOUR OUTLINE

After you have compiled all of your notes from your sources, you need to determine what information you will use and where it best fits into your essay. The best way to do this is to work with your original outline before you draft a research version of your essay. Here again is the outline for the dog-rescue essay, but it is a bit different from the outline on page 359. This version now includes references to sources; *key information from these sources will be the research that strengthens the essay.*

Notice that the headings "Introduction" and "Conclusion" have been added to the outline. In this version, the writer wanted to include some relevant research in both the introductory and concluding paragraphs as well as in the body paragraphs, so he expanded his outline. By placing research references in the outline, the student writer will know where the new information will be included when he prepares the drafts and final version of his research essay.

> **Note:** The references to the added research appear in bold print below so that you can compare this outline to the previous one without research on page 359.

Outline for an Essay with Research

I. Introduction
    A. Six to eight million dogs and cats are placed in shelters each year; three to four million are euthanized. **See Humane Society, source #2.**
    B. Some shelters euthanize animals routinely. **See Leigh and Geyer, source #3.**
    C. Some shelters work with rescue groups.

    Thesis Statement: Dog-rescue organizations perform a humane service by saving homeless dogs and matching responsible adopters with a devoted new family member.

II. Dog-rescue volunteers play several roles.
    A. Some volunteers are "spotters" who look for specific breeds at local shelters.
    B. Experienced rescue volunteers may become coordinators and arrange assistance from various sources. **See Woolfe, source #5.**
    C. Volunteers work with national organizations such as Adopt-a-Pet and Petfinder.com, which maintain databases of adoptable dogs from rescue groups throughout the United States and Canada.
    D. Volunteers assist at rescue-dog "Adoption Days" hosted by pet supply chains such as Petco and PetSmart.

III. Rescue groups provide important information and benefits for prospective adopters.
    A. By viewing a rescue group's Web site, potential adopters can read about a dog's age, temperament, adoption fee, and any special medical conditions.
    B. If a potential adopter does not find a suitable dog, he or she can still complete an online application.
    C. On an application, a potential adopter can list his or her preferences for the age, gender, and size of the dog.

    D. Although some dogs are puppies rescued from abusive situations, most are adult dogs already socialized and housebroken. **See Nicklas-Varraso in Mohr, source #4.**

  IV. Careful screening often results in a successful adoption.
    A. Rescue groups routinely conduct home visits to check the living conditions and the neighborhood.
    B. The applicant must have access to veterinary care.
    C. The applicant must agree to return the dog to the rescue organization if he or she can no longer care for the animal.
    D. A foster parent can fully inform the adoptive parent about potential adjustment problems.
    E. Careful attention to such details leads to a winning adoption process.

  V. Conclusion
    A. Rescue groups provide an opportunity for a dog to live out the rest of its life free from harm and neglect.
    B. We should "embrace non-lethal strategies" to show we are a humane society. **See Bok, source #1.**

Concluding Statement: Rescue groups not only provide care for homeless dogs; they also remind us of the joy made possible by compassionate adoption.

A Draft of an Essay with Research

The following is a rough version of the original essay on dog-rescue groups; it has been strengthened with some material from outside sources. (The material is underlined so that you can spot it easily.) The marginal annotations will alert you to (1) places where the information is directly quoted or paraphrased, and (2) places where revisions are necessary to achieve a better style.

Draft of an Essay with Research

The Humane Work of Dog-Rescue Groups

statistic and paraphrased statement from online source as part of introduction

    Although the United States is generally regarded as a country that loves and pampers its pets, animal shelters are often filled to capacity with dogs that have been abandoned, abused, or surrendered by their owners. <u>Each year, six to eight million dogs and cats are placed in shelters, and three to four million of them are euthanized (Humane Society).</u> Sadly, some shelters routinely euthanize healthy dogs if no one claims or adopts them after a grace period ranging from just days to a few weeks.

direct quotation from the preface of a book with two authors

These dogs have only <u>"about a fifty percent chance of getting out alive" (Leigh and Geyer viii).</u> Fortunately, however, many shelters work closely with dog-rescue organizations that find loving, temporary homes where foster parents can provide care and, if necessary, rehabilitation. Staffed by dedicated volunteers, rescue groups perform a humane service by saving homeless dogs and enabling responsible adopters to gain a devoted new family member.

continued

From rescuing retired greyhounds to saving mini "mutts," dog-rescue volunteers play several roles. For example, they often serve as "spotters" at local shelters, looking for specific dogs that can be fostered by individuals who specialize in specific breeds such as boxers and golden retrievers. Experienced volunteers may become coordinators who arrange for assistance from a variety of sources, including local veterinarians, groomers, transporters, and Web site designers. <u>Norma Bennett Woolf writes for the online magazine *Dog Owner's Guide*. Woolf states, "There's always room for more foster homes, fund-raisers, dog spotters, kennels, public relations workers, and trainers."</u> Many rescue groups work closely with national organizations such as Adopt-a-Pet and Petfinder.com, whose Web sites publish comprehensive lists of adoptable rescue dogs throughout the United States and Canada. On weekends, rescue volunteers can be seen helping out during "Adoption Days" sponsored by national chains, including Petco and PetSmart.

Rescue groups provide both crucial information and welcome benefits for potential adopters. When one becomes interested in a specific dog on a rescue group's Web site, he or she can read about the animal's medical needs, age, temperament, and adoption fee. Even if he or she does not spot a suitable dog but remains interested in adopting one from rescue, he or she can fill out an application and list preferences regarding a dog's age, gender, and size. Although rescue groups occasionally receive puppies and young dogs that have been picked up during police raids of abusive puppy mills and backyard breeders, the majority of dogs available for adoption are older ones. <u>Kathy Nicklas-Varraso wrote *What to Expect from Breed Rescue*. This writer says, "You'll most often get an adult whose chewing phase, housebreaking phase, and general puppy wildness are gone" (qtd. in Mohr).</u> Any pet owner who has experienced the aggravation of sleepless nights and numerous housetraining "accidents" can appreciate the benefits of adopting an older, socialized, and housebroken dog.

Although the adoption process may take several weeks or even months to find the best match, careful screening improves the chances for a successful adoption. Rescue groups routinely conduct home visits of prospective dog owners to see if both the living conditions and the neighborhood will be suitable for the dog's size, temperament, and exercise needs. In addition, the applicant must have access to veterinary care and agree to return the dog to the rescue organization if he or she can no longer properly care for it. A foster parent can fully inform the adoptive parent about a dog's potential adjustment problems because the animal's behavior has been observed over a period of weeks—if not months—in a home setting. Nicklas-Varraso states, <u>"Borderline pets are offered for adoption within strict guidelines, such as no other pets or fenced yards only"</u> (qtd. in Mohr). Careful attention to such details leads to a winning adoption process.

direct quotation from an online magazine, sentence combining needed

a source quoted in another author's work; needs to be more smoothly blended

direct quote; needs a transition

<table>
<tr>
<td>

print source
is a maga-
zine; sentence
combining
needed; put
Bok's name
in a signal
phrase

</td>
<td>

However a dog finds its way to a rescue group—by an owner sur-
render, a good Samaritan, or even by a police raid of an illegal
breeding operation—it will have an opportunity to live out the
rest of its life free from harm and neglect. <u>Ed Bok is director of
Animal Care and Control for New York City. He believes that we
should embrace preventive, non-lethal strategies that reveal that
at our core we truly are a humane society" (15).</u> Rescue groups
not only follow Bok's advice by providing care for homeless dogs;
they also remind us of the joy made possible by compassion, com-
mitment, and unconditional love.

</td>
</tr>
</table>

Note: A Works Cited page will be included in the final version of this essay.

PREPARING THE FINAL VERSION OF AN ESSAY WITH RESEARCH

Making Final Changes and Refinements

The final version of the research essay includes the refinements suggested in the margins of the previous draft. You will notice that the final essay reflects proper MLA documentation and page numbering format. Other improvements relate to the style of the essay. Changes from the previous draft include the following:

- The title has been changed to be more descriptive and appealing.

- Information from sources has been more smoothly blended by sentence combining and the use of signal phrases.

- An awkward repetition of "he or she" has been changed to the more specific term "a potential adopter" in the third paragraph.

- The word "humane" has been added in the last paragraph to reinforce the idea of compassionate care for animals.

- To conform to MLA format, the writer has placed his name, his instructor's name, the course title, and the date in the upper left-hand corner of the first page.

- Again following MLA style, the writer has placed his last name and page number in the upper right-hand corner of each page of the essay.

- A Works Cited page, in proper MLA format, is included and appears as the last page of the essay.

Note: Pages in the sample paper are not 8 ½ × 11 standard size. MLA format requires margins of at least one inch but no more than an inch and a half on all sides of the page.

Roberts 1

Jason Roberts

Professor Alvarez

English 100

7 December 2012

Crusading for Canines:

Dog-Rescue Groups and Winning Adoptions

Although the United States is generally regarded as a country that loves and pampers its pets, animal shelters are often filled to capacity with dogs that have been abandoned, abused, or surrendered by their owners. Each year, six to eight million dogs are placed in shelters, and three to four million of them are euthanized (Humane Society). Sadly, some shelters routinely euthanize healthy dogs if no one claims or adopts them after a grace period ranging from just days to a few weeks. These dogs have only "about a fifty percent chance of getting out alive" (Leigh and Geyer viii). Fortunately, however, many shelters work closely with dog-rescue organizations that find loving, temporary homes where foster parents can provide care and, if necessary, rehabilitation. Staffed by dedicated volunteers, rescue groups perform a humane service by saving homeless dogs and enabling responsible adopters to gain a devoted new family member.

From rescuing retired greyhounds to saving mini "mutts," dog-rescue volunteers play several roles. For example, they often serve as "spotters" at local shelters, looking for specific dogs that can be fostered by individuals who specialize in specific breeds such as boxers and golden retrievers. Experienced volunteers may become coordinators who arrange for assistance from a variety of sources, including local veterinarians,

Roberts 2

groomers, transporters, and Web site designers. As Norma Bennett Woolf suggests in the online magazine *Dog Owner's Guide*, "There's always room for more foster homes, fund-raisers, dog-spotters, kennels, public relations workers, and trainers." Many rescue groups work closely with national organizations such as Adopt-a-Pet and Petfinder, whose Web sites publish comprehensive lists of adoptable rescue dogs throughout the United States and Canada. On weekends, rescue volunteers can be seen helping out during "Adoption Days" sponsored by national chains, including Petco and PetSmart.

Rescue groups provide both crucial information and welcome benefits for potential adopters. When one becomes interested in a specific dog on a rescue group's Web site, he or she can read about the animal's medical needs, age, temperament, and adoption fee. Even if a potential adopter does not spot a suitable dog but remains interested in adopting one from rescue, he or she can fill out an application and list preferences regarding a dog's age, gender, and size. Although rescue groups occasionally receive puppies and young dogs that have been picked up during police raids of abusive puppy mills and backyard breeders, the majority of dogs available for adoption are older ones. Kathy Nicklas-Varraso, author of *What to Expect from Breed Rescue,* notes that adopters will "most often get an adult whose chewing phase, housebreaking phase, and general puppy wildness are gone" (qtd. in Mohr). Any pet owner who has experienced the aggravation of sleepless nights and numerous housetraining "accidents" can appreciate the benefits of adopting an older, socialized, and housebroken dog.

Although the adoption process may take several weeks or even months to find the best match, careful screening improves the chances for a successful adoption. Rescue groups routinely conduct home visits of prospective dog owners to see if both the living conditions and the neighborhood will be suitable for the dog's size, temperament,

Roberts 3

and exercise needs. In addition, the applicant must have access to veterinary care and agree to return the dog to the rescue organization if he or she can no longer properly care for it. A foster parent can fully inform the adoptive parent about a dog's potential adjustment problems because the animal's behavior has been observed over a period of weeks—if not months—in a home setting. Nicklas-Varraso stresses that the "borderline pets are offered for adoption within strict guidelines, such as no other pets or fenced yards only" (qtd. in Mohr). Careful attention to such details leads to a winning adoption process.

However a dog finds its way to a rescue group—by an owner surrender, a good Samaritan, or even by a police raid of an illegal breeding operation—it will have an opportunity to live out the rest of its life free from harm and neglect. Ed Boks, director of Animal Care and Control for New York City, urges us to "embrace preventive, non-lethal strategies that reveal that at our core, we truly are a humane society" (15). Rescue groups not only provide humane care for homeless dogs; they also remind us of the joy made possible by compassion, commitment, and unconditional love.

Roberts 4

Works Cited

Boks, Ed. "The Dirty Little Secret in Your Community." *Newsweek* 27 June 2005:

15. Print.

Humane Society of the United States. 2007. Web. 20 June 2007.

Leigh, Diane, and Marilee Geyer. Preface. *One at a Time: A Week in an American*

Animal Shelter. Santa Cruz: No Voice Unheard, 2003. vii–viii. Print.

Mohr, Lori. "Adopting from a Breed Rescue Group." *Animal Forum.* Web. 23 June

2005.

Woolf, Norma Bennett. "Getting Involved in Purebred Rescue." *Dog Owner's*

Guide 18 May 2005. Web. 20 June 2005.

Grammar for Writers

INTRODUCTION

Overview

In this section, you'll be working with the basics of grammar that you need to master to be a clear writer. If you are willing to memorize certain rules and work through the activities here, you will be able to apply grammatical rules automatically as you write.

Using "Grammar for Writers"

Since this section of the textbook is divided into self-contained segments, it does not have to be studied in sequence. Your instructor may suggest you review specific rules and examples, or you may be assigned various segments as either a class or group assignment. Various approaches are possible, and thus you can regard this section as a "user-friendly" grammar handbook for quick reference. Mastering the practical parts of grammar will improve your writing, helping you become more sure of yourself and better prepared for future composition courses.

Contents

The Simple Sentence

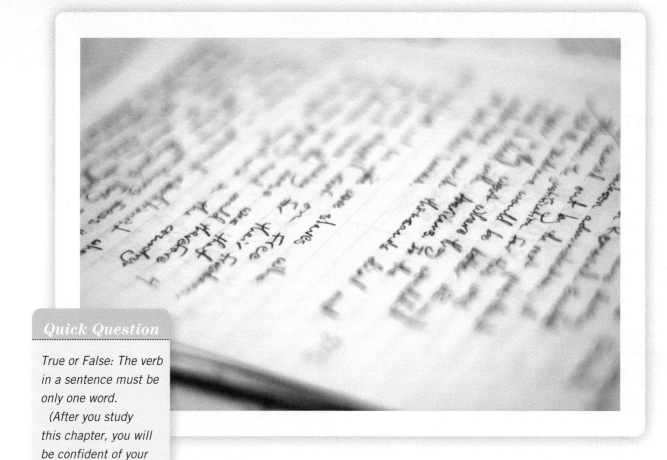

Chapter Objectives

Students will be able to (1) identify subjects and verbs in both simple sentences and in ones with complicated word order, (2) recognize helping verbs, prepositional phrases, and infinitives, and (3) correct errors in faulty sentence construction.

Identifying the crucial parts of a sentence is the first step in many writing decisions: how to punctuate, how to avoid sentence fragments, how to be sure that subjects and verbs "agree" (match). To move forward to these decisions requires a few steps back—to basics.

RECOGNIZING A SENTENCE

Let's start with a few basic definitions. A basic unit of language is a **word.**

examples: *car, dog, sun*

A group of related words can be a **phrase.**

examples: *shiny new car; snarling, angry dog; in the bright sun*

When the group of words contains a subject and a verb, it is called a **clause.** When the word group has a subject and a verb and makes sense by itself, it is called a **sentence** or an **independent clause.** When the word group has a subject and a verb but does not make sense by itself, it is called a **dependent clause.**

If you want to check to see whether you have written a sentence, and not just a group of related words, you first have to check for a subject and a verb. Locating the verbs first can be easier.

RECOGNIZING VERBS

Verbs are words that express some kind of action or being. Verbs about the five senses—sight, touch, smell, taste, sound—are part of the group called **being verbs.** Look at some examples of verbs as they work in sentences:

action verbs:
We *walk* to the store every day.
The children *ran* to the playground.

being verbs:
My mother *is* a good cook.
The family *seems* unhappy.
The soup *smells* delicious.

Exercise 1   Practice: Recognizing Verbs

Underline the verbs in each of the following sentences.

1. A loud cry woke me out of a sound sleep.

2. This game appears simple.

3. You are the hardest worker at the restaurant.

4. Two brave joggers run in the coldest weather.

5. The soldier saluted his mother.

6. Distrust keeps the brothers apart.

7. Vanessa and Chris were my neighbors in Providence.

8. Emilio sounds thrilled about the new baby.

9. On warm days, the cat dozed in the sun.

10. My boss starts each day with a joke.

More on Verbs

The verb in a sentence can be more than one word. First of all, there can be **helping verbs** in front of the main verb, the action or being verb. Here is a list of some frequently used helping verbs: *is, am, are, was, were, do, must, might, have, has, shall, will, can, could, may, should, would.*

I *was watching* the Super Bowl. (The helping verb is *was.*)
You *should have called* me. (The helping verbs are *should* and *have.*)
The president *can select* his assistants. (The helping verb is *can.*)
Leroy *will graduate* in May. (The helping verb is *will.*)

Helping verbs can make the verb in a sentence more than one word long. But there can also be more than one main verb:

Andrew *planned* and *practiced* his speech.
I *stumbled* over the rug, *grabbed* a chair, and *fell* on my face.

Collaborate

Exercise 2   **Collaborate: Writing Sentences with Helping Verbs**

Complete this exercise with a partner or a group. First, ask one person to add at least one helping verb to the verb given. Then work together to write two sentences using the main verb and the helping verb(s). As a final step, appoint one spokesperson for your group to read all your sentences to the class. Notice how many combinations of main verbs and helping verbs you hear.

The first one is done for you.

1. **verb:** named

    verb with helping verb(s): was named _____

    sentence 1: I was named after my father. _____

    sentence 2: Washington, D.C., was named after the first president. ___

2. **verb:** staring

    verb with helping verb(s): _____

    sentence 1: _____

    sentence 2: _____

3. **verb:** forget

    verb with helping verb(s): _____

    sentence 1: _____

    sentence 2: _____

4. **verb:** hurt

    verb with helping verb(s): _____

    sentence 1: _____

    sentence 2: _____

5. **verb:** included

    verb with helping verb(s): _____

    sentence 1: _____

    sentence 2: _____

RECOGNIZING SUBJECTS

After you can recognize verbs, finding the subjects of sentences is easy because subjects and verbs are linked. If the verb is an action verb, for example, the subject will be the word or words that answer the question, "Who or what is doing that action?"

The truck stalled on the highway.

Step 1: Identify the verb: *stalled*

Step 2: Ask, "Who or what stalled?"

Step 3: The answer is the subject: The *truck* stalled on the highway. *Truck* is the subject.

If your verb expresses being, the same steps apply to finding the subject.

Spike was my best friend.

Step 1: Identify the verb: *was*

Step 2: Ask, "Who or what was my best friend?"

Step 3: The answer is the subject: *Spike* was my best friend. *Spike* is the subject.

Just as there can be more than one word to make up a verb, there can be more than one subject.

examples:
David and *Leslie* planned the surprise party.
My *father* and *I* worked in the yard yesterday.

Exercise 3   **Practice: Recognizing the Subjects in Sentences**

Underline the subjects in the following sentences.

1. Nobody has been taking out the trash lately.

2. Something is happening at our neighbor's house.

3. After my last exam, worry and hope battled in my brain.

4. Sometimes shopping offers an escape from my troubles.

5. Airports are becoming more crowded with holiday travelers.

6. Confidence can be an asset for a job seeker.

7. On Mondays, Chris, Bill, and I meet for coffee before class.

8. With great joy, the lost dog greeted its owner.

9. We can finish our conversation in a few minutes.

10. Aunt Teresa could have misunderstood my directions to the house.

More About Recognizing Subjects and Verbs

When you look for the subject of a sentence, look for the core word or words; don't include descriptive words around the subject. The idea is to look for the subject, not for the words that describe it.

The dark blue *dress* looked lovely on Anita.
Dirty *streets* and grimy *houses* destroy a neighborhood.

The subjects are the core words *dress*, *streets*, and *houses*, not the descriptive words *dark blue*, *dirty*, and *grimy*.

PREPOSITIONS AND PREPOSITIONAL PHRASES

Prepositions are usually small words that often signal a kind of position or possession, as shown in the following list:

INFO BOX: Some Common Prepositions

about	before	beyond	inside	on	under
above	behind	during	into	onto	up
across	below	except	like	over	upon
after	beneath	for	near	through	with
among	beside	from	of	to	within
around	between	in	off	toward	without
at					

A prepositional phrase is made up of a preposition and its object. Here are some prepositional phrases. In each one, the first word is the preposition; the other words are the object of the preposition.

Prepositional Phrases

about the movie	of mice and men
around the corner	off the record
between two lanes	on the mark
during recess	up the wall
near my house	with my sister and brother

There is an old memory trick to help you remember prepositions. Think of a chair. Now, think of a series of words you can put *in front of* the chair:

around the chair	*with* the chair
behind the chair	*to* the chair
between the chairs	*near* the chair
by the chair	*under* the chair
of the chair	*on* the chair
off the chair	*from* the chair

Those words are prepositions.

You need to know about prepositions because they can help you identify the subject of a sentence. There is an important grammar rule about prepositions:

Nothing in a prepositional phrase can ever be the subject of the sentence.

Prepositional phrases describe people, places, or things. They may describe the subject of a sentence, but they never include the subject. Whenever you are looking for the subject of a sentence, begin by putting parentheses around all the prepositional phrases.

The restaurant (around the corner) makes the best fried chicken (in town).

The prepositional phrases are in parentheses. Since *nothing* in them can be the subject, once you have eliminated the prepositional phrases, you can follow the steps to find the subject of the sentence:

What is the verb? *makes*
Who or what makes the best fried chicken? The *restaurant.*
Restaurant is the subject of the sentence.

By marking off the prepositional phrases, you are left with the *core* of the sentence. There is less to look at.

(Behind the park), a *carousel* (with gilded horses) delighted children (from all the neighborhoods).
subject: *carousel*

The *dog* (with the ugliest face) was the winner (of the contest).
subject: *dog*

| Exercise 4 | **Practice: Recognizing Prepositional Phrases, Subjects, and Verbs** |

Put parentheses around all the prepositional phrases in the following sentences. Then underline the subject and verb and put an *S* above each subject and a *V* above each verb.

1. Alicia has been wondering about her chances for a job in nursing at a hospital near the military base.

2. An argument (between my mother and father) affected all the children (in the family.)

3. Elderly people (in our neighborhood) are becoming substitute grandparents (to many children without older relatives in the area.)

4. At the top of his lungs, the toddler screamed for his mother and stretched his arms toward her.

5. Nothing in the refrigerator except an apple looks edible to me.

6. Before dinner, I can run to the bakery and get some cookies for dessert.

7. The girl with the long dark hair sat near me during the pep rally inside the gym.

8. A couple of raindrops fell on Cody's newly waxed car and left tiny water marks.

9. Over the weekend, a silly argument caused a serious feud between two families in the neighborhood.

10. From the first day of the term, Charlie has been worrying about his grade in this class.

| Exercise 5 | **Collaborate: Writing Sentences with Prepositional Phrases** |

Collaborate

Complete this exercise with a partner. First, add one prepositional phrase to the core sentence. Then ask your partner to add a second prepositional phrase to the same sentence. For the next sentence, switch places. Let your partner add the first phrase; you add the second. Keep reversing the process throughout the exercise. When you have completed the exercise, be ready to read the sentences with two prepositional phrases to the class. The first one has been done for you as a sample.

1. **core sentence:** Rain fell.

   Add one prepositional phrase: Rain fell on the mountains.

   Add another prepositional phrase: From a dark sky, rain fell on the mountains.

   _____

2. **core sentence:** Eddie shouted.

   Add one prepositional phrase: _____

   Add another prepositional phrase: _____

   _____

3. **core sentence:** A helicopter hovered.

   Add one prepositional phrase: _____

   Add another prepositional phrase: _____

   _____

4. **core sentence:** A cat can be amused.

   Add one prepositional phrase: _____

   Add another prepositional phrase: _____

   _____

5. **core sentence:** The woman yawned.

   Add one prepositional phrase: _____

   Add another prepositional phrase: _____

   _____

WORD ORDER

When we speak, we often use a very simple word order: first comes the subject; then comes the verb. For example, someone would say, "I am going to the store." *I* is the subject that begins the sentence; *am going* is the verb that comes after the subject.

But not all sentences are in such a simple word order. Prepositional phrases, for example, can change the word order.

sample sentence: Among the contestants was an older man.

Step 1: Mark off the prepositional phrase(s) with parentheses: *(Among the contestants) was an older man.* Remember that nothing in a prepositional phrase can be the subject of a sentence.

Step 2: Find the verb: *was*

Step 3: Who or what was? An older *man* was. The subject of the sentence is *man.*

After you change the word order of this sentence, you can see the subject (S) and verb (V) more easily.

          S   V

An older *man was* among the contestants.

`Exercise 6` **Practice: Finding Prepositional Phrases, Subjects, and Verbs in Complicated Word Order**

Prepositional Phrases
↓
Being verb
↓
Subject

Start by putting parentheses around the prepositional phrases in the following sentences. Then underline the subjects and verbs and put an *S* above each subject and a *V* above each verb.

1. Among my favorite pieces of clothing was an old baseball cap from my high school days.

2. Under my grandmother's bed is a box with old photographs of her and my grandfather in their wild teenage years.

3. Beneath the floorboards lurks a family of the craftiest mice on this continent.

4. Between my house on Daley Road and the corner was a huge old house behind a rusted iron fence.

5. From the back of the classroom came the soft snoring sound of a student in dreamland.

6. Beyond the layers of deception and intrigue was a simple answer to the mystery of the hero's death.

7. Among the most irritating programs on television are a talent show for deluded contestants and a comedy without any jokes.

8. Inside my mother's purse are expired coupons from the supermarket and tattered half-price offers from local restaurants.

9. Behind the school cafeteria lie six huge dumpsters in a row.

10. Through all my struggles runs a small hope for a better life.

More on Word Order

The expected word order of subject first, then verb, changes when a sentence starts with *There is/are, There was/were, Here is/are, Here was/were.* In such cases, look for the subject after the verb.

$$\overset{V}{\text{There }} \overset{S}{are \ a \ bakery} \text{ and a } \overset{S}{pharmacy} \text{ down the street.}$$

$$\overset{V}{\text{Here}} \; is \; \text{the} \; \overset{S}{man} \; \text{with the answers.}$$

Here *is* the *man* with the answers.

To understand this pattern, try changing the word order:

A *bakery* and a *pharmacy are* there, down the street.

The *man* with the answers *is* here.

You should also note that even if the subject comes after the verb, the verb has to "match" the subject. For instance, if the subject refers to more than one thing, the verb must also refer to more than one thing.

> There *are* a *bakery* and a *pharmacy* down the road. (Two things, a bakery and a pharmacy, *are* down the road.)

Word Order in Questions

Questions may have a different word order. The main verb and the helping verb may not be next to each other.

question:	Do you like pizza?
subject:	*you*
verbs:	*do, like*

To understand this concept, think of answering the question. If someone accused you of not liking pizza, you might say, "I *do like* it." You would use two words as verbs.

question:	Will he think about it?
subject:	*he*
verbs:	*will, think*
question:	Is Maria telling the truth?
subject:	*Maria*
verbs:	*is, telling*

Exercise 7 **Practice: Recognizing Subjects and Verbs in Complicated Word Order: A Comprehensive Exercise**

Underline the subjects and verbs, putting an *S* above the subjects and a *V* above the verbs.

1. There were a gray cat and a striped kitten in the garden.

2. Will you drive to Biloxi on Saturday?

3. From the end of the long hall came the sound of laughter.

4. Was there anything in your coat pocket?

5. Have Jimmy and Chris spoken about the boat trip on the Hudson River?

6. Here are the most recent photographs of my nephew.

7. Among the stores in the strip mall was a tire store with a section for wheel alignment and balancing.

8. Can we think about a reasonable solution to the problem?

9. Near the end of the movie came a terrifying scene inside a dark cave.

10. Between the yellowed pages of the book was a thin film of dust.

Words That Cannot Be Verbs

Sometimes there are words that look like verbs in a sentence, but they are not verbs. Such words include adverbs (words like *always*, *often*, *nearly*, *rarely*, *never*, *ever*) that are placed close to the verb but are not verbs. Another word that is placed between a helping verb and a main verb is *not*. *Not* is not a verb.

When you are looking for verbs in a sentence, be careful to eliminate words like *often* and *not*.

> Not
> too
> very

> He *will* not *listen* to me. (The verbs are *will listen.*)
> Althea *can* always *find* a bargain. (The verbs are *can find.*)

Be careful with contractions.

> They *haven*'t *raced* in years. (The verbs are *have raced. Not* is not a part of the verb, even in contractions.)
> *Do*n't you *come* from Arizona? (The verbs are *do come.*)
> *Won't* he ever *learn?* (The verbs are *will learn. Won't* is a contraction for *will not.*)

Recognizing Main Verbs

If you are checking to see if a word is a main verb, try the *pronoun test.* Combine your word with this simple list of pronouns: *I, you, he, she, it, we, they.* A main verb is a word such as *drive* or *noticed* that can be combined with the words on this list. Now try the pronoun test.

> For the word *drive:* I drive, you drive, he drives, she drives, it drives, we drive, they drive
> For the word *noticed:* I noticed, you noticed, he noticed, she noticed, it noticed, we noticed, they noticed

But words such as *never* cannot be used alone with the pronouns:

> ~~I never, you never, he never, she never, it never, we never, they never~~
> (Never did what?)

Never is not a verb. *Not* is not a verb either, as the pronoun test indicates:

> ~~I not, you not, he not, she not, it not, we not, they not~~
> (These combinations do not make sense because *not* is not a verb.)

Verb Forms That Cannot Be Main Verbs

There are forms of verbs that cannot be main verbs by themselves either. **An -*ing* verb, by itself, cannot be the main verb,** as the pronoun test shows.

For the word *voting:* ~~I voting, you voting, he voting, she voting, we voting, they voting~~

If you see an *-ing* verb by itself, correct the sentence by adding a helping verb.

> Scott ~~riding~~ his motorcycle. (*Riding*, by itself, cannot be a main verb.)
>
> **correction:** Scott *was riding* his motorcycle.

Another verb form, called an infinitive, also cannot be a main verb. An infinitive is the form of the verb that has *to* placed in front of it.

INFO BOX: Some Common Infinitives

to care	to vote	to repeat
to feel	to play	to stumble
to need	to reject	to view

Try the pronoun test, and you'll see that infinitives cannot be main verbs:

> For the infinitive *to vote:* ~~I to vote, you to vote, he to vote, she to vote, we to vote, they to vote~~

So if you see an infinitive being used as a verb, correct the sentence by adding a main verb.

> We ~~to vote~~ in the election tomorrow. (There is no verb, just an infinitive.)
>
> **correction:** We *are going* to vote in the election tomorrow. (Now there is a verb.)

The infinitives and the *-ing* verbs just do not work as main verbs. You must put a verb with them to make a correct sentence.

Exercise 8 **Practice: Correcting Problems with *-ing* or Infinitive Verb Forms**

Most—but not all—of the sentences below are faulty; an *-ing* verb or an infinitive may be taking the place of a main verb. Rewrite the sentences with errors.

1. Behind the heavy purple curtains, a little girl in a nightgown hiding from the noise of the thunderstorm.

   rewritten: _____

   _____

2. After dinner, Mr. Stein wants to sit in front of his big-screen television until bedtime.

   rewritten: _____

   _____

3. The weeds around the stepping-stones creeping between the cracks and over the broken stones.

   rewritten: _____

   _____

4. After hours of negotiation, an escaped convict from Utah to surrender to police in New Mexico.

   rewritten: _____

   _____

5. At a high point in his career, the internationally known tennis star quitting for personal reasons.

   rewritten: _____

   _____

6. On weekends, my sisters to ride their bicycles to the park near our house.

   rewritten: _____

   _____

7. After the midterm exam, a few of the students in my science class were complaining about the grading scale.

   rewritten: _____

   _____

8. Without a second look, I turned my back on my former friend and walked calmly to my car.

   rewritten: _____

   _____

9. Lindsay and Vince ridiculing the newcomers to the exclusive club.

   rewritten: _____

   _____

10. A famous military leader to present the awards at the banquet for the outstanding members of the graduating class.

    rewritten: _____

    _____

Exercise 9 **Practice: Finding Subjects and Verbs: A Comprehensive Exercise**

Underline the subjects and verbs in these sentences and put an *S* above each subject and a *V* above each verb.

1. There were a pen, a pencil, and a crumpled piece of paper in

   Sophie's book bag.

2. Melanie could have been waiting for you at the coffee shop.

3. At the front of the classroom is a large box with a stack of papers in it.

4. My computer does not offer quick access to the Internet.

5. You have suddenly developed an interest in our handsome neighbor on the third floor.

will

6. Won't you think about a career in mechanical engineering?

7. Alec is dreaming of making a return visit to Cancun.

8. At the top of my list of worries are the fear of missing an opportunity and the fear of failure.

DO

9. Don't you ever take time for fun and relaxation?

Subject is buried in the middle →

10. In November, they are closing their shop and starting a new business in Iowa.

Here and there are not subjects...

| Exercise 10 | Practice: Finding Subjects and Verbs: Another Comprehensive Exercise |

Underline the subjects and verbs in these sentences and put an *S* above each subject and a *V* above each verb.

1. Before my speech to the scholarship committee, I thought about my dream of higher education, looked into each person's eyes, and hoped for the best.

wrong

2. In any marriage, there will be a period of adjustment for both partners.

3. Here is the old scrapbook with the pictures of you in your Little League uniform.

4. Alicia would never ask for help from her brother.

5. Haven't you always wanted a house near the ocean?

6. With his giant television on the living room wall and his huge collection of films, Todd rarely goes to a movie theater for entertainment.

7. Can't the two of you ever think about anyone except yourselves?

8. In the bright light, the large dog seemed weird and dangerous.

9. Inside the old and yellowed envelope were a letter and a key.

10. My uncle kissed me on the cheek and led me on a tour of his new store.

Exercise 11   **Collaborate: Create Your Own Text**

Collaborate

Complete this activity with two partners. Below is a list of rules you've just studied. Each member of the group should write one example of each rule. When your group has completed three examples for each rule, trade your completed exercise with another group, and check their examples while they check yours.

The first rule has been done for you.

Rule 1: The verb in a sentence can express some kind of action.
examples:

a. Wanda sleeps late on the weekends.

b. On Monday I found a wallet in the street.

c. Melted snow covered the sidewalks and steps.

Rule 2: The verb in a sentence can express some state of being or one
of the five senses.
examples:

a. _____

b. _____

c. _____

Rule 3: The verb in a sentence can consist of more than one word.
examples:

a. _____

b. _____

c. _____

Rule 4: There can be more than one subject of a sentence.
examples:

a. _____

b. _____

c. _____

Rule 5: If you take out the prepositional phrases, it is easier to identify the subject of a sentence, since nothing in a prepositional
phrase can be the subject of a sentence. (Write sentences with
at least one prepositional phrase and put parentheses around
the prepositional phrases.)
examples:

a. _____

b. _____

c. _____

Rule 6: Not all sentences have the simple word order of subject first, then verb. (Give examples of more complicated word order.)

examples:

a. _____

b. _____

c. _____

Rule 7: Words like *not, never, often, always,* and *ever* are not verbs. (Write sentences using those words, but write *V* above the correct verb or verbs.)

examples:

a. _____

b. _____

c. _____

Rule 8: An *-ing* verb form by itself or an infinitive (*to* preceding the verb) cannot be a main verb. (Write sentences with *-ing* verb forms or infinitives, but write *V* above the main verb.)

examples:

a. _____

b. _____

c. _____

Exercise 12 **Connect: Recognizing Subjects and Verbs in a Paragraph**

Underline the subjects and verbs in this paragraph and put an *S* above each subject and a *V* above each verb.

verb

subject

My father could never have fit into his old U.S. Army uniform without a

rigorous program of exercise and diet. In January, he received an invitation to

the twenty-fifth reunion of his army buddies. He was eager to attend. However,

he wanted to look like the fit, trim soldier of long ago. He had six months for get-

ting fit before the reunion. During those six months, my father joined a local gym

and arrived faithfully at 6:00 A.M. on every day of the week. In the evening,

he jogged through the neighborhood for two miles. On Saturdays, my

father pushed me into walking long distances in the mountains near our house. In

addition, he rarely drank beer or ate junk food in front of the television. Salads, broiled chicken, and grilled fish became frequent dinner choices. He stuck to his

program for fitness and transformed himself from a typical middle-aged man with

too little energy and too much flab into a perfect model of a former fighting man.

Exercise 13   **Connect: Recognizing Subjects and Verbs in a Paragraph**

Connect

Underline the subjects and verbs in this paragraph and put an *S* above each
subject and a *V* above each verb.

At the age of fifteen, my sister fell in love with vampires and werewolves.

Books about romance between handsome creatures from another world and beau-

tiful young women from this world started her infatuation. In a year or two, the

books became popular films. At that time, my sister and her friends stood in long

lines at the local movie theater. They adored these movies about danger, mystery,

and secret love. Women of all ages turned these films into blockbusters. Beyond

her teenage years, my sister didn't retain her fascination with the otherworldly

books and movies. Today she focuses on the attraction between real men and

women.

Chapter Test **The Simple Sentence**

Underline the subjects and verbs in these sentences and put an *S* above each subject and a *V* above each verb.

1. The smell of freshly baked bread at the bakery near my apartment is making me hungry.

2. After a dental check-up, Dr. Talbott usually gives me a small bag with a new toothbrush and a small tube of toothpaste.

3. Inside the pancake restaurant are bright yellow booths and posters with photos of every kind of pancake and topping in the world.

4. Didn't you ever dream about living in a big city?

5. The warm wind in my hair and the sun in my eyes were a pleasant change from the sleet and snow at home.

6. Kyla never asked about my background or questioned my motives for leaving town suddenly.

7. Manny's nasty tantrum at dinner could have resulted in hurt feelings among the family members at the table.

8. Behind her carefree attitude and silly behavior is a woman with anxieties about her future.

9. My dogs hate to go outside on a cold and rainy day.

10. During the week before final exams, there is no good reason for skipping a class.

PEARSON
mywritinglab   For support in meeting this chapter's objectives, log in to
www.mywritinglab.com and select **Verbs, Subjects and**
Verbs, and Prepositions.

Beyond the Simple Sentence: Coordination

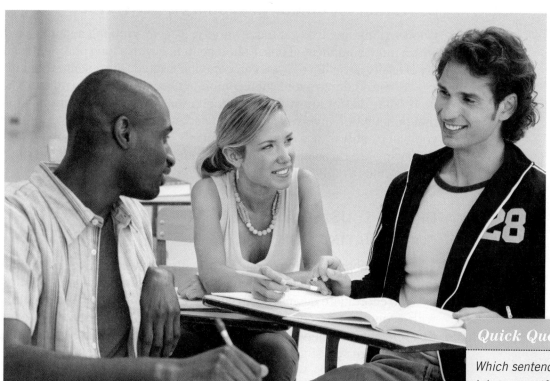

CHAPTER 16

Quick Question

Which sentence(s) is/are correct?

A. Edward owns a motorcycle, but he wants a car.

B. Edward owns a motorcycle but he wants a car.

(After you study this chapter, you will be confident of your answer.)

Chapter Objectives

Students will be able to identify and apply sentence-combining techniques that rely on coordinating conjunctions and conjunctive adverbs.

AVOIDING SIMPLE SENTENCES

A group of words containing a subject and verb is called a **clause.** When that group makes sense by itself, it is called a sentence or an independent clause.

The kind of sentence that is one independent clause is called a **simple sentence.** If you rely too heavily on a sentence pattern of simple sentences, you risk writing paragraphs like this:

> I am a college student. I am also a salesperson in a mall. I am always busy. School is time-consuming. Studying is time-consuming. Working makes me tired. Balancing these activities is hard. I work too many hours. Work is important. It pays for school.

Here is a better version:

> I am a college student and a salesperson at a mall, so I am always busy. School and study are time-consuming, and working makes me tired.

Balancing these activities is hard. I work too many hours, but that work is important. It pays for school.

OPTIONS FOR COMBINING SIMPLE SENTENCES

Good writing involves sentence variety; it means mixing a simple sentence with a more complicated one, a short sentence with a long one. Sentence variety is easier to achieve if you can combine related, short sentences into one.

Some students avoid such combining because they are not sure how to do it. They do not know how to punctuate the new combinations. It is true that punctuation involves memorizing a few rules, but once you know them, you will be able to use them automatically and write with more confidence. Following are three options for combining simple sentences and the punctuation rules to follow in each case.

OPTION 1: USING A COMMA WITH A COORDINATING CONJUNCTION

You can combine two simple sentences with a comma and a coordinating conjunction. The coordinating conjunctions are *for, and, nor, but, or, yet,* and *so.*

To coordinate means to join equals. When you join two simple sentences with a comma and a coordinating conjunction (CC), each half of the combination remains an independent clause, with its own subject (S) and verb (V).

Here are two simple sentences:

   S   V   S   V
He cooked the dinner.   *She worked* late.

Here are the two simple sentences combined with a comma, and with the word *for,* a coordinating conjunction (CC):

   S   V   , CC S   V
He cooked the dinner, *for she worked* late.

The combined sentences keep the form they had as separate sentences; that is, they are still both independent clauses, with a subject and verb and with the ability to stand alone.

The word that joins them is the **coordinating conjunction.** It is used to join equals. Look at some more examples. These examples use a variety of coordinating conjunctions to join two simple sentences.

sentences combined with *and*:

      S   V   , CC   S   V
Jennifer likes Italian food, *and Mark prefers* Korean dishes.

sentences combined with *nor*:

   S V   V   , CC   V S V
I didn't like the book, *nor did I like* the movie made from the book. (Notice what happens to the word order when you use *nor.*)

sentences combined with *but*:

   S   V   , CC S V
I rushed to the bank, *but I was* too late.

   S   V   , CC S   V
She can write a letter to Jim, *or she can call* him.

sentences combined with *yet*:

    S   V   , CC S   V

Leo tried to please his sister, *yet she* never *seemed* appreciative
     of his efforts.

sentences combined with *so*:

    S V   , CC S V

I was the first in line for the concert tickets, *so I got* the best seats in
     the stadium.

> **Note:** One easy way to remember the coordinating conjunctions is to call them, as a group, **fanboys** (**f**or, **a**nd, **n**or, **b**ut, **o**r, **y**et, **s**o).

Where Does the Comma Go?

Notice that the comma comes before the coordinating conjunction (*for, and, nor, but, or, yet, so*). It comes before the new idea, the second independent clause. It goes where the first independent clause ends. Try this punctuation check. After you've placed the comma, look at the combined sentences. For example:

    She joined the army, and she traveled overseas.

Then split it into two sentences at the comma:

    She joined the army. And she traveled overseas. (The split makes sense.)

If you put the comma in the wrong place, after the coordinating conjunction, your split sentences would be:

    She joined the army and. She traveled overseas. (The split doesn't
     make sense.)

This test helps you see whether the comma has been placed correctly—*where the first independent clause ends*. (Notice that you can begin a sentence with *and*. You can also begin a sentence with *but, or, nor, for, yet,* or *so*—as long as you're writing a complete sentence.)

> **Caution:** Do *not* put a comma every time you use the words *and, but, or, nor, for, yet,* or *so;* put it only when the coordinating conjunction joins independent clauses. Do not put the comma when the coordinating conjunction joins words:
>
>   blue and gold   tired but happy   hot or cold
>
> Do not put the comma when the coordinating conjunction joins phrases:
>
>   on the chair or under the table
>   in the water and by the shore
>   with a smile but without an apology

The comma is used when the coordinating conjunction joins two independent clauses. Another way to say the same rule is to say, the comma is used when the coordinating conjunction joins two simple sentences.

Placing the Comma by Using Subject–Verb (S–V) Patterns

An independent clause, or simple sentence, follows one of these basic patterns:

    S   V

    He ran.

or

    S   S V

He and I ran.

or

    S   V   V

He ran and swam.

or

    S   S V   V

He and I ran and swam.

Study all four patterns for the simple sentence, and you will notice that you can draw a line separating the subjects on one side and the verbs on the other:

S	V
SS	V
S	VV
SS	VV

So whether the sentence has one subject (or more than one) and one verb (or more than one), in the simple sentence the pattern is subject(s) followed by verb(s)—one simple sentence.

When you combine two simple sentences, the pattern changes:

two simple sentences:

    S   V   S V

He swam. I ran.

two simple sentences combined:

    S   V   S V

He swam, but I ran.

In the new pattern, *SVSV*, you cannot draw a line separating all the subjects on one side, and all the verbs on the other. This new pattern, with two simple sentences (or independent clauses) joined into one, is called a **compound sentence**.

Recognizing the *SVSV* pattern will help you place the comma for compound sentences.

Here is another way to remember this rule. If you have this pattern:

SV | SV

use a comma in front of the coordinating conjunction. Do not use a comma in front of the coordinating conjunction with these patterns:

S	V
SS	V
S	VV
SS	VV

For example, use a comma for this pattern:

    S   V   ,   S   V

Jane followed directions, *but I rushed* ahead.

Do not use a comma for this pattern:

    S   V   V

Carol cleans her kitchen every week *but* never *wipes* the top of the refrigerator.

You have just studied one way to combine simple sentences. If you are going to take advantage of this method, you have to memorize the coordinating conjunctions—*for, and, nor, but, or, yet,* and *so*—so that your use of them, with the correct punctuation, will become automatic.

Exercise 1   Practice: Recognizing Compound Sentences and Adding Commas

Add commas only where they are needed in the following sentences. Do not add any words.

1. Cruiser Auto Parts offers a wide range of accessories for Toyota Tundras, so Edward spends half his paycheck on gadgets for his truck.

2. Claudia is looking for a two-bedroom apartment in a good neighborhood, or a small house with a porch.

3. My mother won't tell me about her trip to the emergency room, nor will she explain her decision to take a class in self-defense.

4. Antonio seems worried about something but never confides in me or his sister.

5. My best friend can eat every item in the refrigerator yet he has maintained the same healthy weight for years.

6. The kitchen table is covered in scratches and dents for the family cuts and carves food on it every day.

7. Michelle rides her bicycle to class every day so she saves money on gas for her car.

8. Between the rumpled sheets on my bed I found my lost gold earring and I immediately put the earring in a safe place.

9. The cat under the porch meowed at me but it refused to come out from its hideout.

10. A heavy rain crushed the spring flowers into a multicolored mess and turned the grass into streaks of green mud.

[handwritten margin notes: subject, verb, cc; has to be SV, SV for a common]

Exercise 2   Practice: Recognizing Compound Sentences and Adding Commas

Add commas only where they are needed in the following sentences. Do not add any words.

1. The detective at the scene of the crime was neither thorough nor efficient in investigating the site.

2. My van is great transportation for a student with a habit of saving every kind of junk in the world.

3. Next week we can go to the mall, or I can come to your house for coffee.

4. Sam is always complaining about his job yet never has the initiative to look for a better position.

5. Mike saved money, and Melanie worked overtime to buy a new home.

6. Mark and Melanie saved money and worked overtime to buy a new home.

7. Most horror movies rely on the same plots yet the films always attract big crowds.

8. You should drink eight glasses of water a day or you will get dehydrated in the summer heat.

9. One of the instructors at the college is sponsoring a trip to Spain in the summer and told my art class about earning college credit on the trip.

10. Last night someone sprayed paint on my car, and this morning I called the police.

Exercise 3 **Practice: Combining Sentences Using Coordinating Conjunctions**

Combine each pair of sentences using a coordinating conjunction and the appropriate punctuation.

1. Jordan was a wonderful father to his three boys.
   He was not a great husband.

   combined: _____

   _____

2. Kevin made a reservation at the most popular restaurant in town.
   He wanted to please his new girlfriend.

   combined: _____

   _____

3. Many of my friends are sick of the congestion of city life.
   They are looking for jobs in the country.

   combined: _____

   _____

4. He can buy a new car with great style and huge monthly payments.
   He can settle for a used car with less style and much smaller payments.

   combined: _____

   _____

5. Alicia has suffered through several bad relationships.
   Alicia keeps choosing the same, abusive kind of partner.

   combined: _____

   _____

6. Ramon Ramirez played football in high school.
   Hector Ramirez went to college on a baseball scholarship.

   combined: _____

   _____

7. My grandfather always wanted to visit his family in Barbados. He never saved enough money for the trip.

combined: _____

_____

8. I caught a bad cold at the hockey game last weekend. I couldn't go to work yesterday.

combined: _____

_____

9. My current apartment does not have laundry facilities in the building. My current apartment does not have an outlet for cable television.

combined: _____

_____

10. I might send my child to a day care center. I might drop him off at my mother's house.

combined: _____

_____

OPTION 2: USING A SEMICOLON BETWEEN TWO SIMPLE SENTENCES

Sometimes you may want to combine two simple sentences (independent clauses) without using a coordinating conjunction. If you want to join two simple sentences that are related in their ideas and you do not use a coordinating conjunction, you can combine them with a semicolon.

two simple sentences:

S   V   S   V
I cooked the turkey. *She made* the stuffing.

two simple sentences combined with a semicolon:

S   V   ; S   V
I cooked the turkey; *she made* the stuffing.

Here's another example of this option in use:

S   V   V   ; S   V
Rain can be dangerous; *it makes* the roads slippery.

Notice that when you join two simple sentences with a semicolon, the second sentence begins with a lowercase letter, not a capital letter.

You need to memorize the seven coordinating conjunctions so that you can make a decision about punctuating your combined sentences. Remember these rules:

- If a coordinating conjunction joins the combined sentences, put a comma in front of the coordinating conjunction.

  S   V   ,   S   V
  Tom had a barbecue in his back yard, and the *food was* delicious.

- If there is no coordinating conjunction, put a semicolon in front of the second independent clause.

      S   V   ;   S   V
      Tom had a barbecue in his back yard; the *food was* delicious.

OPTION 3: USING A SEMICOLON AND A CONJUNCTIVE ADVERB

Sometimes you may want to join two simple sentences (independent clauses) with a connecting word called a **conjunctive adverb.**

Here is a list of some conjunctive adverbs:

INFO BOX: **Some Common Conjunctive Adverbs**

also	furthermore	likewise	otherwise
anyway	however	meanwhile	similarly
as a result	in addition	moreover	still
besides	in fact	nevertheless	then
certainly	incidentally	next	therefore
consequently	indeed	now	thus
finally	instead	on the other hand	undoubtedly

You can use a conjunctive adverb (CA) to join simple sentences, but when you do, you still need a semicolon in front of the adverb.

two simple sentences:

      S   V   S   V
      My *parents checked* my homework every night. *I did* well in math.

two simple sentences joined by a conjunctive adverb and a semicolon:

      S   V   ; CA S   V
      My *parents checked* my homework every night; *thus I did* well in math.
      S   V   ;   CA   S   V
      She gave me good advice; *moreover, she helped* me follow it.

Punctuating After a Conjunctive Adverb

Notice the comma after the conjunctive adverb in the preceding sentence. Here is the generally accepted rule:

> **Put a comma after the conjunctive adverb if the conjunctive adverb is more than one syllable long.**

For example, if the conjunctive adverb is a word like *consequently, furthermore,* or *moreover,* you use a comma. If the conjunctive adverb is one syllable, you do not have to put a comma after the conjunctive adverb. One-syllable conjunctive adverbs are words like *then* or *thus.*

I saw her cruelty to her staff; *then* I lost respect for her.
We worked on the project all weekend; *consequently,* we finished a week ahead of the deadline.

If 2 or more sylabuls, we put a comma after

ex: ; moreover,

Exercise 4 **Practice: Combining Simple Sentences with Semicolons and Conjunctive Adverbs**

Some of the following sentences need a semicolon; others need a semicolon and a comma. Do not add, change, or delete any words; just add the correct punctuation.

1. Desmond likes insects; in fact, he has a pet spider at home.

2. At the end of dinner came an unpleasant surprise; it was the bill for our fancy meal.

3. My first year in college is almost over; then I'll be a sophomore with a fairly respectable academic record.

4. Professor Mackenzie talks too fast I can't keep up with his explanations of the math problems.

5. Shane never paid me back for the loan of twenty dollars instead he took me to the movies yesterday.

6. You always leave the kitchen a mess furthermore you forget to take out the garbage.

7. My hectic work schedule prevents me from having any fun; on the other hand, the extra hours at my job are paying my bills.

8. I saw a flash of lightning outside my bedroom window last night next I lost electrical power for hours.

9. My mother dislikes her older brother nevertheless she tolerates his constant visits to her home.

10. My room is beginning to look like a storage unit in a row of sleazy warehouses; I must get rid of the clutter.

Exercise 5 **Practice: Combining Simple Sentences with Semicolons and Conjunctive Adverbs**

Below are pairs of simple sentences. Combine each pair into one sentence. You have two options: (1) use a semicolon or (2) use a semicolon and a conjunctive adverb (with a comma if it is needed). Pick the option that makes the most sense for each sentence.

1. Green fuzz covered the leftover chicken and rice.
   The casserole had been in the refrigerator for two weeks.

   combined: _____

   _____

2. The band on the stage started throwing trinkets to the audience.
   A huge crowd pushed toward the first row of seats.

   combined: _____

   _____

3. Amanda bolted the apartment door.
   Connor frantically called an emergency number.

   combined: _____

   _____

4. I wasted three hours on patching and taping a broken lawn chair.
I bought a new chair at a discount store.

combined: _____

_____

5. Tyler refused to speak to me yesterday at school.
He even avoided eye contact.

combined: _____

_____

6. The first snow of the year began to fall.
The white coating transformed the hills and trees into a strange scene.

combined: _____

_____

7. Molly has to do well on her next two Introduction to Sociology tests.
She could fail the course.

combined: _____

_____

8. Skip is turning into a fine dog.
He has learned all the essential skills of obeying commands and
walking on a leash.

combined: _____

_____

9. You don't have to get me a fancy gift for my birthday.
You can take me to the latest Quentin Tarantino movie.

combined: _____

_____

10. I passed my driving test yesterday.
I have to look for a low-priced car.

combined: _____

_____

Exercise 6 **Practice: Combining Simple Sentences Three Ways**

Add a comma, a semicolon, or a semicolon and a comma to the following sentences. Do not add, change, or delete any words; just add the correct punctuation.

1. No one moved; the huge snake remained coiled in the corner.

2. You should apologize to Sean, moreover you should apologize sincerely and soon.

3. We will get to the electronics store early; thus we will be the first ones at the grand opening sale.

4. Kelly buys a lottery ticket every week, yet she has never won a penny.

5. Andrew regretted his angry words to his wife; similarly, his wife felt guilty about the cruelty of her responses.

6. I ran into your old girlfriend at the mall yesterday, incidentally, she is going to be in your biology class next semester.

7. My five-year-old son spent three hours at the beach, now he is a tired but happy child with sand in his hair, toes, and ears.

8. My roommate hasn't paid his share of the rent in two months nor has he paid any part of the other household expenses.

9. Stephen doesn't like coffee in fact he's never been inside a Starbucks coffee shop.

10. Last night my dog barked at the front door for about twenty minutes but I couldn't see anyone in the yard.

Exercise 7 **Collaborate: Using Three Options to Combine Simple Sentences** Collaborate

Below are pairs of simple sentences. Working with a partner or partners, combine each pair into one sentence in two different ways. Remember, you have three options: (1) use a comma and a coordinating conjunction, (2) use a semicolon, or (3) use a semicolon and a conjunctive adverb (with a comma if it is needed). Pick the options that make the most sense for these sentences. The first one has been done for you.

1. Crystal ran out of money for her electric bill.
   I lent her enough to pay it.

   combinations:

   a. <u>Crystal ran out of money for her electric bill, so I lent her enough to pay it.</u>

   _____

   b. <u>Crystal ran out of money for her electric bill; therefore, I lent her enough</u>

   <u>to pay it.</u>

2. All of my shoes are worn out.
   My clothes are falling apart.

   combinations:

   a. _____

   _____

   b. _____

   _____

3. Luis can be an irritating person.
   He deserves a little sympathy at this sad time.

   combinations:

   a. _____

   _____

   b. _____

   _____

4. Uncle Scott could have gotten stuck in traffic.
   Uncle Scott could have taken a wrong turn off the highway.

combinations:

a. _____

_____

b. _____

_____

5. My father never paid me a compliment.
   My father never spent much time with me.
   combinations:

a. _____

_____

b. _____

_____

6. We expected a delicious meal at the stylish and expensive restaurant.
   We got food poisoning.
   combinations:

a. _____

_____

b. _____

_____

7. Allison will take me to school tomorrow.
   She owes me a favor.
   combinations:

a. _____

_____

b. _____

_____

8. Nelson Pinder was offered a great job in Boston.
   He decided to move there.
   combinations:

a. _____

_____

b. _____

_____

9. Summer never seems to last long enough.
   Winter always seems to last forever.
   combinations:

a. _____

_____

b. _____

_____

10. Someone stole my wallet.
I am worried about identity theft.

combinations:

a. _____

_____

b. _____

_____

Exercise 8 Connect: Editing a Paragraph for Errors in Coordination

Connect

Edit the following paragraph for errors in coordination. You do not need to add or change words. Just add, delete, or change punctuation. There are seven errors in the paragraph.

Maintaining a healthy weight is a challenge for Demetrius. He struggles with the temptations of junk food and his mother's ideas about nutrition. Demetrius has a busy schedule at school and at work consequently, he eats most of his meals on the run. He tries to focus on choosing healthy items but the choices are difficult. A salad at a salad bar can be loaded with fat in the choice of toppings such as croutons, meat, cheese, and thick, creamy, or even oily salad dressings. The special sauces on fatty burgers are a double temptation; even a serving of frozen yogurt, can be filled with sugar and fat. Demetrius' goal of eating healthy foods is challenged at home for his mother believes in large helpings of comfort food. Fried chicken, vegetables in creamy sauces, and homemade biscuits tempt him, moreover, his mother has strong feelings about food. To her, feeding people is part of her mission in life; so she pushes huge helpings of food on everyone at her table. In the fight against flab, Demetrius is trying hard but his battle is a tough one.

Exercise 9 Connect: Editing a Paragraph for Errors in Coordination

Connect

Edit the following paragraph for errors in coordination. You do not need to add or change words. Just add, delete, or change punctuation. There are six errors in the paragraph.

One sport dominates in our area. The university in our town has an outstanding basketball team, and thousands of fans from near and far. Home games are especially exciting, as a result, the area fills with visitors at those times. Tickets to the home games become scarce and hotel rooms become scarcer.

Half of the people in our town wear the home team's colors; in fact pets wear the colors, too. Local television news stations report every movement of the players and the coaches. The star players are treated like international celebrities; they appear at charitable functions, promotional events, and press interviews. Children adore them and adults want to be photographed with them. After each game, the local media analyze every second of play, then the speculation about the next game begins. Basketball fever is an epidemic here, and people don't want a cure.

Chapter Test Beyond the Simple Sentence: Coordination

Add a comma, a semicolon, or a semicolon and a comma to the following sentences. Do not add, change, or delete any words; just add the correct punctuation.

1. At the end of the meeting, the president of the club stormed out of the room then the club members looked at each other and smiled.

2. LaShonda has never seen snow nor has she experienced the beauty of spring in a northern climate.

3. Archie is a good-natured person still he won't listen to his cousin's constant criticism.

4. I should have taken a class in yoga years ago now I am enjoying my Yoga for Beginners sessions.

5. The stray cat would not leave our yard for my sister had been feeding it for several days.

6. Rain began to pound the roof next the palm trees bent against the fierce winds.

7. I don't like wearing a heavy coat instead I wear layers of sweaters.

8. Anthony's screen door has been making a creaking sound for years yet he has ignored my hints about repairing it.

9. Carlotta was working on her biology assignment meanwhile her husband gave the baby a bath.

10. Eric may look for work at the local hospital or he may leave the area for more job opportunities.

Avoiding Run-on Sentences and Comma Splices

Chapter Objectives

Students will be able to recognize and correct run-on sentences and comma splices.

RUN-ON SENTENCES

Run-on sentences are independent clauses that have not been joined correctly. This error is also called a *fused sentence.*

> **run-on sentence error:**
> Carol cleans her kitchen every week she shines every pot and pan.
> **run-on sentence error corrected:**
> Carol cleans her kitchen every week; she shines every pot and pan.

> **run-on sentence error:**
> I studied for the test all weekend I am well prepared for it.
> **run-on sentence error corrected:**
> I studied for the test all weekend, so I am well prepared for it.

> **run-on sentence error:**
> People crowded into the stadium they scrambled for seats.
> **run-on sentence error corrected:**
> People crowded into the stadium. They scrambled for seats.

STEPS FOR CORRECTING RUN-ON SENTENCES

When you edit your writing, you can correct run-on sentences by following these steps:

> **Step 1:** Check for two independent clauses.
>
> **Step 2:** Check that the clauses are separated by either a coordinating conjunction and a comma or by a semicolon.

Follow the steps in checking this sentence:

> The meeting was a waste of time the club members argued about silly issues.
>
> **Step 1:** Check for two independent clauses. You can do this by checking for the subject-verb, subject-verb pattern that indicates two independent clauses:
>
> S   V   S   V
> The *meeting was* a waste of time the club *members argued* about silly issues.

The pattern indicates that you have two independent clauses.

> **Step 2:** Check that the clauses are separated by either a coordinating conjunction (*for, and, nor, but, or, yet, so*) and a comma or by a semicolon.

There is no punctuation between the independent clauses, so you have a run-on sentence. You can correct it three ways:

> **run-on sentence corrected with a coordinating conjunction and a comma:**
> The meeting was a waste of time, *for* the club members argued about silly issues.
>
> **run-on sentence corrected with a semicolon:**
> The meeting was a waste of time; the club members argued about silly issues.
>
> **run-on sentence corrected with a period and a capital letter:**
> The meeting was a waste of time. The club members argued about silly issues.

Follow the steps once more as you check this sentence:

> I had the flu I missed class last week.
>
> **Step 1:** Check for two independent clauses. Do this by checking the subject-verb, subject-verb pattern:
>
> S V   S V
> *I had* the flu *I missed* class last week.
>
> **Step 2:** Check that the clauses are separated by either a coordinating conjunction (*for, and, nor, but, or, yet, so*) and a comma or by a semicolon.

There is no punctuation between the independent clauses, so you have a run-on sentence. You can correct the run-on sentence three ways:

> **run-on sentence corrected with a period and a capital letter:**
> I had the flu. I missed class last week.

**run-on sentence corrected with a coordinating conjunction and
a comma:**

I had the flu, *so* I missed class last week.

run-on sentence corrected with a semicolon:

I had the flu; I missed class last week.

Using the steps to check for run-on sentences can also help you avoid unnecessary punctuation. Consider this sentence:

> The manager gave me my schedule for next week and told me about a
> special sales promotion.

Step 1: Check for two independent clauses. Do this by checking the
subject-verb, subject-verb pattern.

>   S   V   V
> The *manager gave* me my schedule for next week and *told* me about
> a special sales promotion.

The pattern is SVV, not SVSV. The sentence is not a run-on sentence. It does
not need any additional punctuation.

Following the steps in correcting run-on sentences can help you avoid
a major grammar error.

| Exercise 1 | **Practice: Correcting Run-on (Fused) Sentences** |

Some of the sentences below are correctly punctuated. Some are run-on
(fused) sentences; that is, they are two simple sentences run together without any punctuation. If the sentence is correctly punctuated, write *OK* in the
space provided. If it is a run-on sentence, put an *X* in the space provided and
correct the sentence above the lines.

1. _____ I can drive you to the clinic now or on Friday after my last
   class.

2. _____ Tamara won't like the movie, she isn't interested in martial
   arts action films.

3. _____ A heavy rain came after lunch *,so* everyone raced for cover.

4. _____ I had two cups of coffee after dinner now I can't get to
   sleep.

5. _____ A smile on your face encourages strangers to let go of their
   natural defensiveness and relax.

6. _____ Mosquitoes first appear as a minor nuisance; then they
   become a constant, hateful threat.

7. _____ The kitten grabs my hand with her front paws she puts her
   tiny teeth into my fingers.

8. _____ Driving on the highway and maneuvering in city traffic
   require different skills.

9. _____ I live next to a police station thus I feel protected at all
   times.

10. _____ Andrew doesn't want to make a speech at the wedding he's
    afraid of making a fool of himself.

COMMA SPLICES

A comma splice is an error that occurs when you punctuate with a comma but should use a semicolon instead. If you are joining two independent clauses without a coordinating conjunction (*for, an, nor, but, or, yet, so*) you must use a semicolon. A comma is not enough.

comma splice error:
The crowd pushed forward, people began to panic.

comma splice error corrected:
The crowd pushed forward; people began to panic.

comma splice error:
I forgot my glasses, thus I couldn't read the small print in the contract.

comma splice error corrected:
I forgot my glasses; thus I couldn't read the small print in the contract.

CORRECTING COMMA SPLICES

When you edit your writing, you can correct comma splices by following these steps:

Step 1: Check for two independent clauses.

Step 2: Check that the clauses are separated by a coordinating conjunction (*for, and, nor, but, or, yet, so*). If they are, then a comma in front of the coordinating conjunction is sufficient. If they are not separated by a coordinating conjunction, you have a comma splice. Correct it by changing the comma to a semicolon.

Follow the steps to check for a comma splice in this sentence:

I dropped the glass, it shattered on the tile floor.

Step 1: Check for two independent clauses. You can do this by checking for the subject-verb, subject-verb pattern that indicates two independent clauses.

S   V   S   V
I dropped the glass, *it shattered* on the tile floor.

The pattern indicates that you have two independent clauses.

Step 2: Check that the clauses are separated by a coordinating conjunction.

There is no coordinating conjunction. To correct the comma splice error, you must use a semicolon instead of a comma.

comma splice error corrected:
I dropped the glass; it shattered on the tile floor.

Be careful not to mistake a short word like *then* or *thus* for a coordinating conjunction. Only the seven coordinating conjunctions (*for, and, nor, but, or, yet, so*) with a comma in front of them can join independent clauses.

comma splice error:
Susie watched television, then she went to bed.

comma splice error corrected:
Susie watched television; then she went to bed.

Then is not a coordinating conjunction; it is a conjunctive adverb. When it joins two independent clauses, it needs a semicolon in front of it.

Also remember that conjunctive adverbs that are two or more syllables long (like *consequently, however, therefore*) need a comma after them as well as a semicolon in front of them when they join independent clauses:

> Harry has been researching plane fares to New York; consequently,
>   he knows how to spot a cheap flight.

(For a list of some common conjunctive adverbs, see Chapter 16, p. 408.)

Sometimes writers see commas before and after a conjunctive adverb and think the commas are sufficient. Check this sentence for a comma splice by following the steps:

> Jonathan loves his job, however, it pays very little.

Step 1: Check for two independent clauses by checking for the
   subject-verb, subject-verb pattern.

> $\quad$ S $\qquad$ V $\qquad\qquad\qquad$ S $\quad$ V
> *Jonathan loves* his job, however, *it pays* very little.

The pattern indicates that you have two independent clauses.

Step 2: Check for a coordinating conjunction.

There is no coordinating conjunction. *However* is a conjunctive adverb, not a coordinating conjunction. Because there is no coordinating conjunction, you need a semicolon between the two independent clauses.

comma splice error corrected:
Jonathan loves his job; however, it pays very little.

Exercise 2 **Practice: Correcting Comma Splices**

Some of the sentences below are correctly punctuated. Some contain comma splices. If the sentence is correctly punctuated, write *OK* in the space provided. If it contains a comma splice, put an *X* in the space provided and correct the sentence above the lines. To correct a sentence, do not add any words, just correct the punctuation.

1. _____ Eric changed the channel, he couldn't watch any more
   celebrity gossip.

2. _____ Melinda and Tony were born in Taiwan and came to
   America as children; therefore, they speak two languages
   fluently.

3. _____ My six-year-old son spent eight months in a hospital, so he
   started first grade late

4. _____ Our math instructor should have reviewed the new material
   before the test; anyway, he should have hinted about the
   kinds of questions on the test.

5. _____ My dog loves to run in an open field, and I often take her to a huge dog park near the university.

6. _____ Most of my friends dress casually for work; a few wear uniforms.

7. _____ A pencil is an inexpensive writing instrument, but I hate the faded look of penciled words on paper.

8. _____ The auditorium was packed, we couldn't find a seat anywhere.

9. _____ My roommates and I are lazy and disorganized, so we often eat nothing but take-out pizza for two or three days.

10. _____ I tried to talk on the phone, meanwhile, the television was blaring across the room.

Collaborate

Exercise 3 **Collaborate: Completing Sentences**

With a partner or group, write the first part of each of the following incomplete sentences. Make your addition an independent clause. Be sure to punctuate your completed sentences correctly. The first one is done for you.

1. The driver ignored the railroad warning signals, ____ and his car was hit by the train.

2. _____ then I ran out of money.

3. _____ incidentally, you also told several lies about me to my friends.

4. _____ he was arrested for driving under the influence of alcohol.

5. _____ otherwise, I won't be able to get a good job.

6. _____ but the caller hung up.

7. _____ or someone will get hurt.

8. _____ now my friend has to testify in court.

9. _____ and lightning struck the control tower.

10. _____ besides, you can always change your mind.

Connect

Exercise 4 **Connect: Editing a Paragraph for Run-on Sentences and Comma Splices**

Edit the following paragraph for run-on sentences and comma splices. There are six errors.

My girlfriend's car was stolen outside of her apartment we were both shocked. The apartment is in a safe neighborhood and many young people live in the area. Most of the residents are college students or people at the beginning of their careers. My girlfriend is usually careful about safety, however, one evening she was careless and left her car doors unlocked. On the next morning, she could not find her car in the parking lot. For half an hour she searched every section of the parking lot and the nearby parking areas. After her desperate search, she called the police and reported the crime. Two days later, the officers called with some news. Her car had been found in a wooded area near the local airport the auto had dented fenders and two smashed windows. First, my girlfriend was horrified by the damage, then she realized her good luck in getting her car back. In the future, she will be more vigilant about securing her car and keeping it safe from car thieves. One careless mistake had cost her money and misery so she doesn't want to make the same error again.

Exercise 5   **Connect: Editing a Paragraph for Run-on Sentences and Comma Splices**

Connect

Edit the following paragraph for run-on sentences and comma splices. There are six errors.

I cannot afford to get sick. I have a full-time job, and I go to college at night. I pay for my own rent, food, clothes, transportation, and tuition. Health insurance is too expensive for me. Sometimes I get a cold or the flu, and I fight it with aspirin and cough drops. I spread germs, but I have no choice. I cannot miss classes; I would be wasting my tuition fees. My job does not pay me for sick days, so I cannot afford any absences. Illness has no place on my calendar or in my budget; however, illness finds a place in my life.

Chapter Test Avoiding Run-on Sentences and Comma Splices

Some of the sentences below are correctly punctuated. Some are run-on sentences, and some contain comma splices. If a sentence is correctly punctuated, write *OK* in the space provided. If it is a run-on sentence or contains a comma splice, put an *X* in the space provided and correct the sentence above the lines. To correct a sentence, add the necessary punctuation. Do not add any words.

1. _____ Kristen has a hot temper thus she has been involved in several feuds with our nosy neighbors.

2. _____ Leon is nearsighted as a result, he likes a seat near the front of the movie theater.

3. _____ The first quarter of the game was full of action but did not please the fans of the visiting team.

4. _____ Eddie was nosy he bombarded me with personal questions.

5. _____ You're a good athlete, so you will enjoy the challenges of this game.

6. _____ I am spending the night at my sister's apartment otherwise, I would go out with you tonight.

7. _____ Our new puppy raced around the back yard for hours today; now he's sleeping.

8. _____ My cell phone was stolen thus I am in a panic about keeping up with the news from my family and friends.

9. _____ Sean will find a shorter route to work in the early morning, or he will set his alarm for an earlier wake-up time.

10. _____ I was constantly in trouble during my years in middle school incidentally my older brother was a discipline problem at the same school.

PEARSON
mywriting**lab** For support in meeting this chapter's objectives, log in to
www.mywritinglab.com and select **Run-ons**.

Beyond the Simple Sentence: Subordination

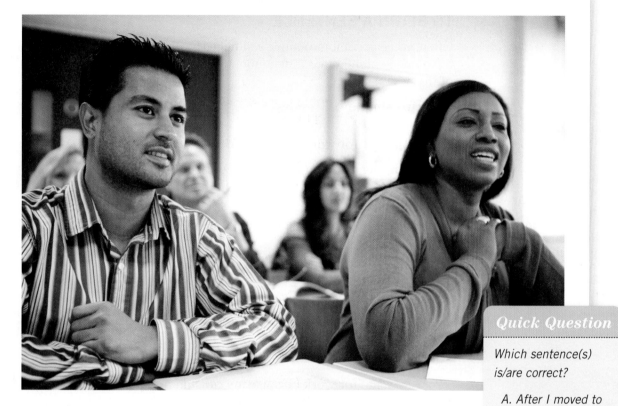

Chapter Objectives

Students will be able to (1) identify sentence-combining techniques that rely on subordinating conjunctions, (2) distinguish between dependent and independent clauses, and (3) generate and punctuate sentences.

MORE ON COMBINING SIMPLE SENTENCES

Before you go any further, look back. Review the following:

- A clause has a subject and a verb.
- An independent clause is a simple sentence; it is a group of words, with a subject and verb, that makes sense by itself.

There is another kind of clause called a **dependent clause**. It has a subject and a verb, but it does not make sense by itself. It cannot stand alone. It is not complete by itself. That is, it *depends* on the rest of the sentence to give it meaning. You can use a dependent clause in another option for combining simple sentences.

> **Note:** Options 1–3 for sentence combining are explained in Chapter 16 on coordination.

OPTION 4: USING A DEPENDENT CLAUSE TO BEGIN A SENTENCE

Often, you can combine simple sentences by changing an independent clause from one sentence into a dependent clause and placing it at the beginning of the new sentence.

two simple sentences:

S V   S V
I was late for work. My *car had* a flat tire.

changing one simple sentence into a beginning dependent clause:

             S   V   S V
Because my *car had* a flat tire, *I was* late for work.

OPTION 5: USING A DEPENDENT CLAUSE TO END A SENTENCE

You can also combine simple sentences by changing an independent clause from one sentence into a dependent clause and placing it at the end of the new sentence:

S V   S   V
I was late for work because my *car had* a flat tire.

Notice how one simple sentence can be changed into a dependent clause in two ways:

two simple sentences:

 S   S   V   S V
Mother and *Dad wrapped* my presents. *I slept.*

changing one simple sentence into a dependent clause:

 S   S   V   S V
Mother and *Dad wrapped* my presents while *I slept.*

or

 S V   S   S   V
While *I slept*, *Mother* and *Dad wrapped* my presents.

Using Subordinating Conjunctions

Changing an independent clause to a dependent one is called **subordinating**. How do you do it? You add a subordinating word, called a **subordinating conjunction**, to an independent clause, making it dependent—less "important," or subordinate—in the new sentence.

Keep in mind that the subordinate clause is still a clause; it has a subject and a verb, but it does not make sense by itself. For example, let's start with an independent clause:

      S   V
Caroline studies.

Somebody (Caroline) does something (studies). The statement makes sense by itself. But if you add a subordinating conjunction to the independent clause, the clause becomes dependent, incomplete, unfinished, like this:

> *When* Caroline studies. (When she studies, what happens?)
> *Unless* Caroline studies. (Unless she studies, what will happen?)
> *If* Caroline studies. (If Caroline studies, what will happen?)

Now, each dependent clause needs an independent clause to finish the idea:

dependent clause   **independent clause**
When Caroline studies, she gets good grades.

dependent clause   **independent clause**
Unless Caroline studies, she forgets key ideas.

dependent clause   **independent clause**
If Caroline studies, she will pass the course.

There are many subordinating conjunctions. When you put any of these words in front of an independent clause, you make that clause dependent. Here is a list of some subordinating conjunctions:

INFO BOX: Subordinating Conjunctions			
after	before	so that	whenever
although	even though	though	where
as	if	unless	whereas
as if	in order that	until	whether
because	since	when	while

[handwritten margin notes: SC / if SC is in front (,) / if SC is in the middle ✗]

If you pick the right subordinating conjunction, you can effectively combine simple sentences (independent clauses) into a more sophisticated sentence pattern. Such combining helps you add sentence variety to your writing and helps to explain relationships between ideas.

simple sentences:

  S   V   V   S   V
Leo could not *read* music. His *performance was* exciting.

new combination:

dependent clause   **independent clause**
Although Leo could not read music, his performance was exciting.

simple sentences:

  S   V   S   V
I caught a bad cold last night. *I forgot* to bring a sweater to the
    baseball game.

new combination:

independent clause   **dependent clause**
I caught a bad cold last night because I forgot to bring a sweater to
    the baseball game.

Punctuating Complex Sentences

A sentence that has one independent clause and one (or more) dependent clause(s) is called a **complex sentence**. Complex sentences are very easy to punctuate. See if you can figure out the rule for punctuating by yourself. Look at the following examples. All are punctuated correctly.

dependent clause   independent clause
Whenever the baby smiles, his mother is delighted.

independent clause   dependent clause
His mother is delighted whenever the baby smiles.

dependent clause   independent clause
While you were away, I saved your mail for you.

independent clause   dependent clause
I saved your mail for you while you were away.

In the examples above, look at the sentences that have a comma. Look at the ones that do not have a comma. Both kinds of sentences are punctuated correctly. Do you see the rule?

> **If the dependent clause comes at the beginning of the sentence, put a comma after the dependent clause. If the dependent clause comes at the end of the sentence, do not put a comma in front of the dependent clause.**

Although we played well, we lost the game.
We lost the game although we played well.

Until he called, I had no date for the dance.
I had no date for the dance until he called.

Exercise 1   Practice: Punctuating Complex Sentences

All the sentences below are complex sentences; that is, they have one independent and one (or more) dependent clause(s). Add a comma to each sentence that needs one.

1. Until I can afford a new car, I have to keep paying for repairs on my old one.

2. Give me a call if you want me to drive you to school tomorrow.

3. After my parents stopped arguing about my bad behavior, I fell into a restless and troubled sleep.

4. I fell into a restless and troubled sleep after my parents stopped arguing about my bad behavior.

5. Kristin never buys much when she and I spend time at the mall on the weekends.

6. Because my supervisor insists on punctuality I come to work early every morning.

7. My brother won't come to dinner unless I make his favorite banana cake.

8. The babysitter became absorbed in her telephone conversation while the children discovered the pleasures of their mother's makeup bag.

9. If I go out with Rebecca on Saturday I will skip the weekend camping trip with my brothers.

10. Before I started college I was secretly afraid of meeting new people and finding my way around the campus.

Exercise 2   **Practice: Punctuating Complex Sentences**

All the sentences below are complex sentences; that is, they have one independent clause and one or more dependent clauses. Add a comma to each sentence that needs one.

1. Gina struggled to hold on to her purse as the crowd around her began pushing forward.

2. The dining room was the biggest room in the house so that the large family could sit comfortably for weekly dinners, birthdays, and holiday celebrations.

3. Whether Al joins the U.S. Army or goes to flight school he will need the support of his old friends.

4. Alicia wouldn't accept a gift from her father because he hasn't been a part of her life for years.

5. While you were wasting your time playing video games I finished my book report for sociology class.

6. Since we had missed the first part of the movie we couldn't understand the plot.

7. When an aggressive driver follows my car too closely I want to scream.

8. I will own my own house even if I have to work and save for ten or twenty years.

9. Although hot pink is not my favorite color it looks good on the kitchen walls.

10. As the forest fire moved closer to the houses the residents prepared for evacuation.

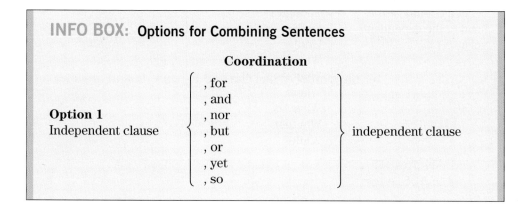

INFO BOX: Options for Combining Sentences

Coordination

| Option 1
Independent clause | { , for
, and
, nor
, but
, or
, yet
, so } | independent clause |

Option 2

Independent clause   ;   independent clause

Option 3
Independent clause

- ; also,
- ; anyway,
- ; as a result,
- ; besides,
- ; certainly,
- ; consequently,
- ; finally,
- ; furthermore,
- ; however,
- ; incidentally,
- ; in addition,
- ; in fact,
- ; indeed,
- ; instead,   independent clause
- ; likewise,
- ; meanwhile,
- ; moreover,
- ; nevertheless,
- ; next
- ; now
- ; on the other hand,
- ; otherwise,
- ; similarly,
- ; still
- ; then
- ; therefore,
- ; thus
- ; undoubtedly,

Subordination

Option 4
Dependent clause
(Put a comma at the
end of the dependent
clause.)

- After
- Although
- As
- As if
- Because
- Before
- Even though
- If
- In order that
- Since   independent clause
- So that
- Though
- Unless
- Until
- When
- Whenever
- Where
- Whereas
- Whether
- While

Option 5 Independent clause	after although as as if because before even though if in order that since so that though unless until when whenever where whereas whether while	dependent clause

SC @ middle

leave it alone!

Note: In Option 4, words are capitalized because the dependent clause will *begin* your complete sentence.

Exercise 3 **Practice: Using the Five Options for Combining Sentences**

Add the necessary commas and/or semicolons to the following sentences. Some are correct as they are.

1. After the rain stopped, the plants in the garden looked fresh and new.

2. One of the puppies in the exercise pen began to bark at the visitor ; then all the puppies joined in the barking.

3. The cardboard box absorbed the constant drip from the ceiling and gradually turned into a soggy mess.

4. Caleb has a hot temper even though he seems easygoing and calm.

5. Whenever the phone rings in the middle of the night, I expect bad news.

6. Unless Samantha gets a good night's sleep she is irritable the next day.

7. Give me your answer I need to know it now.

8. My wild curly hair grows fast; consequently, I spend a significant part of my paycheck on haircuts.

9. Jose spends most of his spare time playing soccer or watching soccer matches on television, so he would love tickets to the World Cup.

10. I can go to the movies with you on Saturday if you meet me for an afternoon show.

SV , SV

, FB

; CA ,

SC

SC ,

Exercise 4   **Practice: Using the Five Options for Combining Sentences**

Add the necessary commas and/or semicolons to the following sentences. Some are correct as they are.

1. My brother turned my parents' wedding anniversary into something special; he made a video out of their old, forgotten home movies.

2. Because I can't stand the smell of smoke on a person's clothing, I rarely socialize with smokers.

3. My house is not the cleanest house in town, but it is warm and comfortable.

4. My sister doesn't spend money on the latest toys for her children instead she takes them to the park, to the zoo, or to the library for new adventures.

5. Some parking lots were designed many years ago and the parking spaces in them are too small for many of today's large cars.

6. I always feel guilty when I gossip about a friend.

7. Although Raymond drives a tow truck at work his own car is a tiny Volkswagen.

8. The pot of spaghetti boiled over while I was distracted by my phone conversation with Eli.

9. Expensive chocolates are an acceptable birthday or Valentine's Day gift; however, they're not a very original one.

10. A couple of my friends from high school are going on a cruise next week they got a great price on a five-day trip to Mexico.

Collaborate

Exercise 5   **Collaborate: Combining Sentences**

Do this exercise with a partner or a group. Below are pairs of sentences. Combine each pair of sentences into one clear, smooth sentence in two different ways. You can add words as well as punctuation. The first pair of sentences is done for you.

1. We always go to Country Ice Cream for a treat.
   The store has the best hot fudge sundaes in the world.

   combination 1: We always go to Country Ice Cream for a treat because the store has the best hot fudge sundaes in the world.

   combination 2: We always go to Country Ice Cream for a treat; the store has the best hot fudge sundaes in the world.

2. My cousin wouldn't drive me to the gym.
   I had to take the bus.

   combination 1: _____

   _____

   combination 2: _____

   _____

3. Oil continued to ooze from the overturned tanker truck.
Motorists struggled to avoid the slick and dangerous part of the highway.

combination 1: _____

_____

combination 2: _____

_____

4. A sleazy towing company removed my car from a no-parking zone.
The company demanded a large cash payment.

combination 1: _____

_____

combination 2: _____

_____

5. Charlie wouldn't listen to Tommy's explanation for the delay.
He wouldn't accept Tommy's apology.

combination 1: _____

_____

combination 2: _____

_____

6. I always wake Mark up in the morning.
He sleeps through the sound of the alarm clock.

combination 1: _____

_____

combination 2: _____

_____

7. My dog has never caught a squirrel.
She begins each day with the dream of catching one.

combination 1: _____

_____

combination 2: _____

_____

8. Bill wanted a career in music.
He became a physician's assistant.

combination 1: _____

_____

combination 2: _____

_____

9. My father lost his wallet.
He became anxious about the possibility of identity theft.

combination 1: _____

_____

combination 2: _____

_____

10. The apartment for rent could be a good deal.
It could be a dump.

combination 1: _____

_____

combination 2: _____

_____

Collaborate

Exercise 6 **Collaborate: Create Your Own Text on Combining Sentences**

Below is a list of rules for coordinating and subordinating sentences. Working with a group, write two examples for each rule.

Option 1: You can join two simple sentences (two independent clauses) into a compound sentence with a coordinating conjunction and a comma in front of it. (The coordinating conjunctions are *for, and, nor, but, or, yet, so.*)

example 1: _____

_____

example 2: _____

_____

Option 2: You can combine two simple sentences (two independent clauses) into a compound sentence with a semicolon between independent clauses.

example 1: _____

_____

example 2: _____

_____

Option 3: You can combine two simple sentences (two independent clauses) into a compound sentence with a semicolon and a conjunctive adverb between independent clauses. (Some conjunctive adverbs are *also, anyway, as a result, besides, certainly, consequently, finally, furthermore, however, in addition, in fact, incidentally, instead, likewise, meanwhile, moreover, nevertheless, next, now, on the other hand, otherwise, similarly, still, then, therefore, thus,* and *undoubtedly.*)

example 1: _____

_____

example 2: _____

_____

Option 4: You can combine two simple sentences (two independent clauses) into a complex sentence by making one clause dependent. The dependent clause starts with a subordinating conjunction. Then, if the dependent clause begins the sentence, the clause ends with a comma. (Some common subordinating conjunctions are _after, although, as, as if, because, before, even though, if, in order that, since, so that, though, unless, until, when, whenever, where, whereas, whether_, and _while_.)

example 1: _____

_____

example 2: _____

_____

Option 5: You can combine two simple sentences (two independent clauses) into a complex sentence by making one clause dependent. Then, if the dependent clause comes after the independent clause, no comma is needed.

example 1: _____

_____

example 2: _____

_____

| Exercise 7 | Connect: Editing a Paragraph for Errors in Coordination and Subordination |

Connect

Edit the following paragraph for errors in coordination and subordination. You do not have to add words to the paragraph; just add, delete, or change punctuation. There are ten errors.

My mother always dreamed about being a nurse finally, her dream will come true. When she was a young woman she wanted an education, so that she could enter the medical field. Poverty and other family struggles prevented her from finishing high school and she went to work at sixteen. My mother married at twenty, and had three children before she was twenty-four. She raised them, while she continued working at various low-paying jobs. After my father died she worked for fifty hours a week and put every penny into a college fund. The college fund began to grow but all of the money in it was spent on her children's education.

When her children were grown up and educated my mother remembered her lost dream of an education. A guidance counselor told my mother about earning a G.E.D. My mother studied hard, moreover, she often studied with the help of her college-educated children. She was proud of earning her high-school diploma then she tackled college. Years of part-time enrollment and constant study passed, and today she is close to her longtime dream. At sixty-two, my mother will graduate from the nursing program at Roosevelt College.

Connect

Exercise 8 Connect: Editing a Paragraph for Errors in Coordination and Subordination

Edit the following paragraph for errors in coordination and subordination. You do not have to add words to the paragraph; just add, delete, or change punctuation. There are eight errors.

Everyone in my family enjoys some type of reality show on the other hand, we do not agree on the best kind of reality program. My mother and older sister like to watch shows about house-hunting and interior decorating. My mother loves them because, she enjoys peering into other peoples' houses. My sister is different she dreams of redoing her bedroom or bathroom. My younger brother will not turn off the television, when a show about restoring, building, or repairing motor-cycles is on. He is fascinated by speed and power but he is too young to drive. Whenever I get a few free minutes I watch the gruesome kind of reality show. A group of people in desolate territory can entertain me when they eat disgusting creatures. Watching those people bond with or betray their teammates keeps me interested because it reveals two sides of human nature. My father ridicules his family's fascination with reality shows yet I have caught him with Animal Planet on the screen late at night. We are a family with a love of real life, even though the the reality is not our own.

Chapter Test   Coordination and Subordination

Some of the following sentences need commas and/or semicolons. Write *X* next to the incorrect sentences and correct them above the lines.

1. ____✓____ I began to feel ill after I ate a seafood dinner at the Oyster House restaurant and had a piece of homemade key lime pie for dessert.

2. ___X___ On the plane, his complaining started at take-off and continued until landing;finally, the other passengers got some relief from the loud and constant whining.

3. ___✓___ I packed my boxes of shoes and clothes in the trunk of my car and then stuffed every space inside the old Kia with pillows, blankets, and sporting goods.

4. ___X___ Trevor was always helpful and polite to the customers at the garden store, for he was afraid of offending someone and losing his job in a time of high unemployment.

5. ___X___ My grandparents have lived in the same house for thirty years;thus they haven't dealt with the ups and downs of the current real estate market.

6. ___✓___ We can save enough money for a summer trip to Yellowstone,if you will sacrifice your annual fishing trip with your cousin.

7. ___✓___ Kira loves dance music yet rarely goes to any of the dance clubs in either of the nearby cities.

8. ___X___ As the water level in the basement began to rise and threaten the first floor of the house, my brother frantically called the number of an emergency plumbing service.

9. ___X___ Once you told me a terrible lie;consequently, I lost all my trust in you.

10. ___X___ You should bring a bottle of water to the beach, or you will become dehydrated in the hot sun.

fanboy

6 are wrong

Avoiding Sentence Fragments

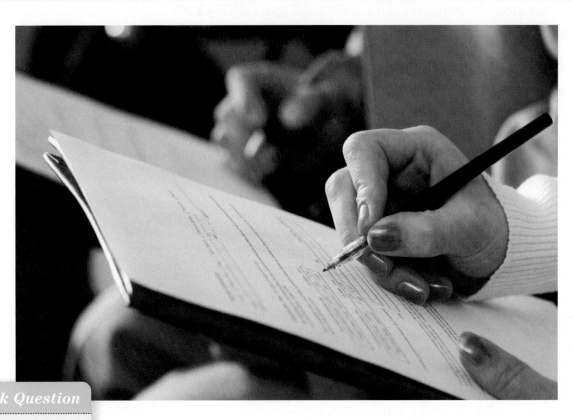

Chapter Objectives

Students will be able to recognize and correct sentence fragments.

AVOIDING SENTENCE FRAGMENTS

A **sentence fragment** is a group of words that looks like a sentence, is punctuated like a sentence, but is not a sentence. Writing a sentence fragment is a major error in grammar because it reveals that the writer is not sure what a sentence is.

The following groups of words are all fragments:

Because customers are often in a hurry and have little time to look
for bargains.
My job being very stressful and fast-paced.
For example, the introduction of salads into fast-food restaurants.

There are two easy steps that can help you check your writing for sentence fragments.

INFO BOX: Two Steps in Recognizing Sentence Fragments

Step 1: Check each group of words punctuated like a sentence, looking for a subject and a verb.

Step 2: If you find a subject and a verb, check that the group of words makes a complete statement.

RECOGNIZING FRAGMENTS: STEP 1

Check for a subject and a verb. Some groups of words that look like sentences may actually have a subject but no verb, or they may have a verb but no subject, or they may have no subject *or* verb.

> The puppy in the pet store window. (*Puppy* could be the subject of a sentence, but there is no verb.)
> Doesn't matter to me one way or the other. (There is a verb, *Does matter*, but there is no subject.)
> In the back of my mind. (There are two prepositional phrases, *In the back* and *of my mind*, but there are no subject and verb.)

Remember that an *-ing* verb by itself cannot be the main verb in a sentence. Therefore groups of words like the ones below may look like sentences, but they lack a verb and are really fragments:

> Your sister having all the skills required of a good salesperson.
> The two top tennis players struggling with exhaustion and the stress of a highly competitive tournament.
> Jack being the only one in the room with a piece of paper.

An infinitive (*to* plus a verb) cannot be a main verb in a sentence, either. The following groups of words are also fragments:

> The manager of the store to attend the meeting of regional managers next month in Philadelphia.
> The purpose to explain the fine points of the game to new players.

Groups of words beginning with words like *also, especially, except, for example, in addition*, and *such as* need subjects and verbs, too. Without subjects and verbs, these groups can be fragments, like the ones below:

> Also a good place to grow up.
> Especially the youngest member of the family.
> For example, a person without a high school diploma.

Exercise 1   **Practice: Checking Groups of Words for Subjects and Verbs**

Some of the following groups of words have subjects and verbs; these are sentences. Some are missing subjects, verbs, or both; these are fragments. Put an *S* by each sentence and an *F* by each fragment.

1. ___F___   Would consider changing the admission fee for the boxing match to be held on Friday night.

2. ___S___   No one at the house is answering the phone.

3. ___F___   My brother Jerome driving me to the Denver airport and my best friend meeting me at O'Hare Airport in Chicago.

No verb

4. ___F___ Two dogs with their noses sticking out of the car window and their ears flapping in the wind.

5. ___S___ Thai food may be too spicy for my mother.

6. _____ Should have asked me about spending our savings on an entertainment unit.

no verb → 7. ___F___ Except one required course in sociology or psychology.

8. _____ My only option being a part-time job at a supermarket warehouse.

9. ___S___ At my back was a sad-looking little boy.

10. _____ Might think about moving to Tennessee in the summer.

RECOGNIZING FRAGMENTS: STEP 2

If a group of words has both a subject and a verb, check that it makes a complete statement. Many groups of words that have both a subject and a verb do not make sense by themselves. They are **dependent clauses.** How can you tell if a clause is dependent? After you have checked each group of words for a subject and verb, check to see if it begins with one of the subordinating conjunctions that start dependent clauses. (Some common subordinating words are _after, although, as, as if, because, before, even though, if, in order that, since, so that, though, unless, until, when, whenever, where, whereas, whether, while._)

A clause that begins with a subordinating conjunction is a dependent clause. When you punctuate a dependent clause as if it were a sentence, you have a kind of fragment called a **dependent clause fragment.**

> After I woke up this morning.
> Because he liked football better than soccer.
> Unless it stops raining by lunchtime.

It is important to remember both steps in checking for fragments:

Step 1: Check for a subject and a verb.

Step 2: If you find a subject and a verb, check that the group of words makes a complete statement.

Exercise 2   **Practice: Checking for Dependent-Clause Fragments**

Some of the following groups of words are sentences. Some are dependent clauses punctuated like sentences, which are sentence fragments. Put an _S_ by each sentence and an _F_ by each fragment.

1. ___F___ After the interview at the bank was over.

2. ___S___ Without a word, Ben took the check.

3. ___F___ Even though the drive to Baton Rouge takes six hours.

4. ___S___ Near the administration building is a patio with stone tables and benches.

5. ___S___ Then my computer shut down.

6. ___F___ Because no one told me about the nosy neighbors next door.

7. _____ Until Carl and Eddie can get some free time to work on restoring the car.

8. _____ Before Francois can choose his classes for the fall term.

9. _S_ With a smile on his face, he handed me the check.

10. _____ When my parents sell their house and move to Arizona.

Exercise 3   **Practice: Using Two Steps to Recognize Sentence Fragments**

Some of the following are complete sentences; some are fragments. To recognize the fragments, check each group of words by using the two-step process:

   Step 1: Check for a subject and a verb.

   Step 2: If you find a subject and verb, check that the group of words makes a complete statement.

Then put an *S* by each sentence and an *F* by each fragment.

1. _F_ If my little boy can take swimming lessons at the community center.

2. _____ Regret was obvious in his tone of voice.

3. _F_ One of my neighbors starting a project to send packages of goodies to American troops in foreign countries.

4. _S_ Without my help, my five-year-old tied her own shoes.

5. _S_ Around the front door was a string of holiday lights.

6. _____ Without a sign of regret for his actions.

7. _F_ Whenever I hear a certain song on the radio.

8. _____ As Gloria and Brian studied the brochure on travel in India.

9. _____ This simple chore is taking me a long time.

10. _____ The reason being a lack of calcium in my grandmother's diet.

[handwritten margin note: 15 SC questions / 15 SF questions]

CORRECTING FRAGMENTS

You can correct fragments easily if you follow the two steps for identifying them.

Step 1: Check for a subject and a verb. If a group of words is a fragment because it lacks a subject or a verb, or both, *add what is missing.*

   fragment: My father being a very strong person. (This fragment lacks a main verb.)

   corrected: My father *is* a very strong person. (The verb *is* replaces *being*, which is not a main verb.)

   fragment: Doesn't care about the party. (This fragment lacks a subject.)

   corrected: *Alicia* doesn't care about the party. (A subject, *Alicia*, is added.)

> **fragment:** Especially on dark winter days. (This fragment has neither a subject nor a verb.)
>
> **corrected:** *I love* a bonfire, especially on dark winter days. (A subject, *I*, and a verb, *love*, are added.)

Step 2: If you find a subject and a verb, check that the group of words makes a complete statement. To correct the fragment, you can turn a dependent clause into an independent one by removing the subordinating conjunction, *or* you can add an independent clause to the dependent one to create a sentence.

> **fragment:** When the rain beat against the windows. (The statement does not make sense by itself. The subordinating conjunction *when* leads the reader to ask, "What happened when the rain beat against the windows?" The subordinating conjunction makes this a dependent clause, not a sentence.)
>
> **corrected:** The rain beat against the windows. (Removing the subordinating conjunction makes this an independent clause, a sentence.)
>
> **corrected:** When the rain beat against the windows, *I reconsidered my plans for the picnic.* (Adding an independent clause turns this into a sentence.)

Sometimes you can correct a fragment by linking it to the sentence before it or after it.

> **fragment (underlined):** I have always enjoyed outdoor concerts. <u>Like the ones at Pioneer Park.</u>
>
> **corrected:** I have always enjoyed outdoor concerts *like the ones at Pioneer Park.*

> **fragment (underlined):** <u>Even if she apologizes for that nasty remark.</u> I will never trust her again.
>
> **corrected:** *Even if she apologizes for that nasty remark*, I will never trust her again.

You have several choices for correcting fragments: you can add words, phrases, or clauses; you can take words out or combine independent and dependent clauses. You can transform fragments into simple sentences or create compound or complex sentences. To punctuate your new sentences, remember the rules for combining sentences.

Exercise 4 **Practice: Correcting Fragments**

Correct each sentence fragment below in the most appropriate way.

1. I spent two hours waiting at the airport. Until Jessica's flight finally arrived.

   corrected: <u>I spent two hours waiting at the airport</u> <u>until Jessica's flight finally arrived.</u>

2. To earn the money for my little brother's series of operations. My father took a second job.

   corrected: <u>To earn the money for my little brother's</u> <u>series of operations, my father took a second job.</u>

3. Colin searched for candles and matches. After the electricity went off.

   corrected: <u>Colin searched for candles and matches</u>
   <u>after the electricity went off.</u>

4. Because a severe drought has struck our area. We are not allowed to water our lawns.

   corrected: _____

   _____

5. Then took a sharp left turn across oncoming traffic and nearly caused a serious accident.

   corrected: _____

   _____

6. One reason for the sharp downturn in the economy being the sharp increase in the price of gasoline.

   corrected: _____

   _____

7. Mosquitoes had bitten every exposed area of David's skin. Especially his neck and feet.

   corrected: _____

   _____

8. Choosing a difficult topic for her speech. Shawna researched her subject for hours.

   corrected: _____

   _____

9. When you eat a substantial meal late in the evening. You may have trouble falling asleep.

   corrected: _____

   _____

10. If a heavy rain falls, the old house has a tendency to leak in several places. Such as the attic and the kitchen.

    corrected: _____

    _____

Collaborate

Exercise 5   **Collaborate: Correcting Fragments Two Ways**

Working with a partner or group, correct each fragment below in two ways. The first one is done for you.

1. Whenever I am waiting for an important phone call.

   corrected: <u>I am waiting for an important phone call.</u>

   _____

corrected: Whenever I am waiting for an important phone call, I am extremely impatient and nervous.

2. Except for three days of blizzard conditions.

corrected: _____

_____

corrected: _____

_____

3. While the hostage negotiators waited.

corrected: _____

_____

corrected: _____

_____

4. You will damage your suede jacket. If you wear it in wet weather.

corrected: _____

_____

corrected: _____

_____

5. On the other side of town, where Tyler lives.

corrected: _____

_____

corrected: _____

_____

6. Although no one at the college knew him well.

corrected: _____

_____

corrected: _____

_____

7. After the returning soldier had hugged his mother and kissed his girlfriend. He noticed the television cameras pointed at him.

corrected: _____

_____

corrected: _____

_____

8. The defense attorney delivering a strong case for acquittal.

corrected: _____

_____

corrected: _____

_____

9. Until I get my check. I can't buy any gifts for the holidays.

corrected: _____

_____

corrected: _____

_____

10. Matt considering his chances for promotion at the company.

corrected: _____

_____

corrected: _____

_____

Connect

Exercise 6 Connect: Editing a Paragraph for Sentence Fragments

Correct the sentence fragments in the following paragraph. There are seven fragments.

There is nothing in the world. Like sleeping under a soft, warm quilt. My grandmother had an old quilt on her guest room bed. I was always thrilled to sleep under that puffy covering. When I was a child. In fact, I always hoped for cold weather during my visits to her house. Then I could enjoy the nighttime comfort of the quilt. In addition, adult enjoyment of a good night's sleep under a quilt. My first purchase for my apartment was a big, warm quilt. To be used not only for my bed but also for napping on the sofa. With my own quilt covering me, a soothing, warm cocoon. I can reenter my childhood place. Everyone needing a quilt. Days of racing to work, sitting on hard plastic chairs, standing behind a counter, staring at a screen, or performing back-breaking labor difficult to endure. Sleeping under a quilt is a little reward for such days.

Connect

Exercise 7 Connect: Editing a Paragraph for Sentence Fragments

Correct the sentence fragments in the following paragraph. There are five fragments.

Most people are forgetful at times, but they could spare themselves the consequences of these memory lapses. It doesn't take much to fight absent-mindedness.

A pencil and some paper. Some people cannot remember class assignments and should write them down. Immediately. Others arrive at the supermarket, do their shopping, but return home without half of the essentials such as milk or bread. A shopping list could save these people time and shopping trips. Many younger people thinking of lists as guides for old people. As a result, the young resist the idea of carrying a list. Others afraid to make a note in front of other people. They fear that others might judge them as too picky or neurotic. However, lists represent freedom. Freedom from frustration, misunderstanding, confusion, missed assignments, and missed appointments. Much of the aggravation of forgetting could be eliminated if people remembered to rely on a pencil and paper.

Chapter Test Avoiding Sentence Fragments

Some of the following are complete sentences; some are sentence fragments. Put an *S* by each sentence and an *F* by each fragment.

1. _F_ A total stranger to assume the job now vacant as a result of the resignation of my supervisor.

2. _F_ Unless someone can drive my mother to her doctor's appointment on Tuesday afternoon.

3. _F_ The fumes in the basement giving Dylan a terrible headache during his two hours of work on the heating system.

4. _S_ On the top shelf of the bookcase sits an old leather catcher's mitt from my father's high school days.

5. _F_ While a group of happy children threw snowballs at each other.

6. _F_ The reason for my lack of enthusiasm about the wedding being my distrust of the groom's intentions.

7. _S_ Unlike the birthday celebrations in my family, Jordan's birthday party was an elaborate and highly planned gathering.

8. _S_ Then a man in a cat mask appeared at the window of the fraternity house.

9. _F_ When I begin a conversation with my girlfriend and see her lack of interest.

10. _F_ For example, several of the summer school classes filling up in the first two days of the registration period.

 For support in meeting this chapter's objectives, log in to www.mywritinglab.com and select **Fragments**.

Using Parallelism in Sentences

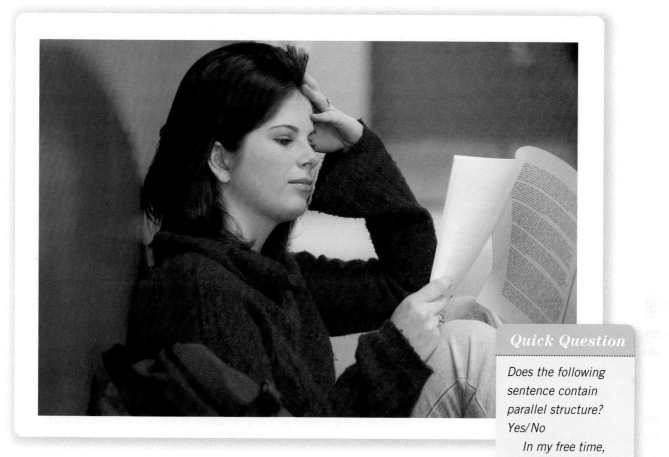

Quick Question

Does the following sentence contain parallel structure? Yes/No

In my free time, I enjoy listening to music, walking on the beach, and socializing with my friends.

(After you study this chapter, you will be confident of your answer.)

Chapter Objectives

Students will be able to recognize parallel structure and use it to revise awkwardly worded sentences.

WHAT IS PARALLELISM?

Parallelism means balance in a sentence. To create sentences with parallelism, remember this rule:

> **Similar points should get a similar structure.**

Often, you will include two or three (or more) related ideas, examples, or details in one sentence. If you express these ideas in a parallel structure, they will be clearer, smoother, and more convincing.

Here are some pairs of sentences with and without parallelism:

not parallel: Of all the sports I've played, I prefer tennis, handball, and playing golf.

parallel: Of all the sports I've played, I prefer *tennis, handball, and golf.* (Three words are parallel.)

// = you have a problem with Perallelism

445

> **not parallel:** If you're looking for the car keys, you should look under the table, the kitchen counter, and behind the refrigerator.
>
> **parallel:** If you're looking for the car keys, you should look *under the table, on the kitchen counter, and behind the refrigerator.* (Three prepositional phrases are parallel.)

> **not parallel:** He is a good choice for manager because he works hard, he keeps calm, and well liked.
>
> **parallel:** He is a good choice for manager because *he works hard, he keeps calm, and he is well liked.* (Three clauses are parallel.)

From these examples you can see that parallelism involves matching the structures of parts of your sentence. There are two steps that can help you check your writing for parallelism.

INFO BOX: **Two Steps in Checking a Sentence for Parallel Structure**

Step 1: Look for the list in the sentence.

Step 2: Put the parts of the list into a similar structure. (You may have to change or add something to get a parallel structure.)

ACHIEVING PARALLELISM

Let's correct the parallelism of the following sentence:

> **sample sentence:** The committee for neighborhood safety met to set up a schedule for patrols, coordinating teams of volunteers, and also for the purpose of creating new rules.

To correct this sentence, we'll follow the steps.

Step 1: Look for the list. The committee met to do three things. Here's the list:
1. to set up a schedule for patrols
2. coordinating teams of volunteers
3. for the purpose of creating new rules

Step 2: Put the parts of the list into a similar structure:
1. *to set up* a schedule for patrols
2. *to coordinate* teams of volunteers
3. *to create* new rules

Now revise to get a parallel sentence.

> **parallel:** The committee for neighborhood safety met *to set up* a schedule for patrols, *to coordinate* teams of volunteers, and *to create* new rules.

If you follow Steps 1 and 2, you can also write the sentence like this:

> **parallel:** The committee for neighborhood safety met to *set up* a schedule for patrols, *coordinate* teams of volunteers, and *create* new rules.

But you cannot write a sentence like this:

> **not parallel:** The committee for neighborhood safety met *to set up* a schedule for patrols, *coordinate* teams, and *to create* new rules.

Think of the list again. You can have:
The committee met

1. to set up
2. to coordinate   } parallel
3. to create

Or you can have:
The committee met to

1. set up
2. coordinate   } parallel
3. create

But your list cannot be:
The committee met to

1. set up
2. coordinate   } not parallel
3. to create

In other words, use the *to* once (if it fits every part of the list), or use it with every part of the list.

Caution: Sometimes making ideas parallel means adding something to a sentence because all the parts of the list cannot match exactly.

---

sample sentence: In his pocket the little boy had a ruler, rubber band, baseball card, and apple.

Step 1: Look for the list. In his pocket the little boy had a
1. ruler
2. rubber band
3. baseball card
4. apple

As the sentence is written, the *a* goes with *a ruler, a rubber band, a baseball card,* and *a apple.* But *a* isn't the right word to put in front of *apple.* Words beginning with vowels (*a, e, i, o, u*) need *an* in front of them: *an apple.* So to make the sentence parallel, you have to change something in the sentence.

Step 2: Put the parts of the list into a parallel structure.

parallel: In his pocket the little boy had *a ruler, a rubber band, a baseball card,* and *an apple.*

Here's another example:

sample sentence: She was amused and interested in the silly plot of the movie.

Step 1: Look for the list. She was
1. amused
2. interested the silly plot of the movie.

Check the sense of that sentence by looking at each part of the list and how it works in the sentence: "She was *interested in* the silly plot of the movie." That part of the list seems clear. But "She was *amused* the silly plot of the movie"? Or "She was *amused in* the silly plot of the movie"? Neither sentence is right. People are not *amused in.*

Step 2: The sentence needs a word added to make the structure parallel.

parallel: She was *amused by* and *interested in* the silly plot of the movie.

When you follow the two steps to check for parallelism, you can write clear sentences and improve your style.

Exercise 1   Practice: Revising Sentences for Parallelism

Some of the following sentences need to be revised so that they have parallel structures. Revise the ones that need parallelism.

1. Billy would rather help people in need than staring at a computer screen all day.

   revised: _____

   _____

2. The wedding reception was the fanciest I have ever attended, also the most expensive, and the biggest of all.

   revised: _____

   _____

3. At my old school, <u>wearing last year's</u> styles was like when you <u>wear a sign that says "loser."</u>

   revised: *At my old school, wearing last years styles was like wearing a sign that says "loser"*

4. The car's price, size, and the condition it was in made it a good buy for a college student.

   revised: *the car's price, size, and condition made a good buy for a college student*

5. After my father bailed me out of jail, he spent the rest of the evening shouting at me, blaming himself for my behavior, and also he worried about my future.

   revised: *After my father bailed me out of jail, he spent the rest of the evening shouting, blaming himself and worring about my future.*

6. Cleaning out closets, having to throw away junk, and packing endless boxes are all part of moving out of your home.

   revised: *Cleaning out closets, throwing away junk, and packing endless boxes are all part of moving out of your home*

7. Put the money in the kitchen drawer or on the dresser.

   revised: _____

   _____

8. Every time I run into Katie, she talks so long that I wind up looking at my watch, making restless motions, and interrupt her before I can get away.

revised: _Everytime I run into catie, she talks so long that I wind up looking at my watch, making restless motions, and interupting her before I can get away_

9. Andrew has good sense, talent that is natural, and intense motivation.

revised: _____

_____

10. The store opens at 7:30 A.M.; 10:00 P.M. is when it closes.

revised: _The store opens at 7:30 am and closes at 10:00 pm_

Exercise 2 **Collaborate: Writing Sentences with Parallelism**

Collaborate

Complete this exercise with a partner or a group. First, brainstorm a draft list; then revise the list for parallelism. Finally, complete the sentence in parallel structure. You may want to assign one step (brainstorming a draft list, revising it, etc.) to each group member, then switch steps on the next sentence. The first one is done for you.

1. Three habits I'd like to break are

draft list

a. worry too much

b. talking on the phone for hours

c. lose my temper

revised list

a. worrying too much

b. talking on the phone for hours

c. losing my temper

sentence: Three habits I'd like to break are worrying too much, talking on the phone for hours, and losing my temper.

2. Three ways to stay healthy are

draft list

a. _____

b. _____

c. _____

revised list

a. _____

b. _____

c. _____

sentence: _____

_____

3. Two reasons why people choose not to marry are

draft list

a. _don't want to commit_

b. _don't want to share_

revised list

a. _____

b. _____

sentence: _Two reasons why people choose not to marry are they dont want to commit and they dont want to share._

4. Three gifts that money cannot buy are

draft list   revised list

a. _____   a. _____

b. _____   b. _____

c. _____   c. _____

sentence: _____

_____

5. Saving money is important because (add three reasons)

draft list   revised list

a. _buy new phone_   a. _you can buy ~~a new~~ phone_

b. _buy a new car_   b. _~~you can~~ buy ~~a new~~ car_

c. _buy a new house_   c. _~~you can~~ buy ~~a new~~ house_

sentence: _Saving money is important because you can buy a phone, a car, and a house_

6. Starting a new job can be stressful because (add three reasons)

draft list   revised list

a. _____   a. _____

b. _____   b. _____

c. _____   c. _____

sentence: _Starting a new job can be stressful because of meeting new people, learning new tasks, and getting use to a working_

7. When I finish college, I want to (add two goals)

draft list   revised list

a. _____   a. _a new car_

b. _____   b. _a new job_

sentence: _When I finish college, I want to get a new job and a new car_

8. People seem to get angry when (add two times or occasions)

draft list   revised list

a. _____   a. _____

b. _____   b. _____

sentence: _____

_____

9. Three characteristics of a good friend are

draft list   revised list

a. _____   a. _____

b. _____   b. _____

c. _____   c. _____

sentence: _____

_____

10. Two household chores most people dislike are

draft list   revised list

a. _____   a. _____

b. _____   b. _____

sentence: _____

_____

Exercise 3   **Practice: Combining Sentences and Creating a Parallel Structure**

Combine each cluster of sentences below into one clear, smooth sentence that includes some parallel structure. The first one is done for you.

1. Before you buy a used car, you should research what similar models are selling for.
It would be a good idea to have a mechanic examine the car.
Also, how much mileage it has racked up is a consideration.

combination: _Before you buy a used car, you should compare prices of_

similar models, get a mechanic to examine the car, and think carefully about

the mileage.

2. The qualifications for the job include some sales experience.
Applicants also have to have good telephone skills.
Another requirement is being trained in computers.

combination: _____

_____

_____

3. Jake was the funniest friend I ever had.
He was more generous than any other friend I ever had.
His loyalty was the best, too.

combination: _____

_____

_____

4. Hundreds of students waited in line to register for their classes.
They also were paying their tuition fees.
Their other goal was to see an advisor.

combination: _____

_____

_____

5. My aunt started as a night security guard at Crescent Rehabilitation Center.
Then she was promoted to head of the night security shift.
Eventually she worked her way up to Director of Security for the Center.

combination: _Starting as a night security gaurd @CRC_
my aunt became head of night security shift
and eventually moved to Director of Security.

6. Shopping malls sell goods.
Contests are often held at shopping malls.
Santa Claus and the Easter Bunny are presented at the malls.
Early morning exercise for mall-walkers is offered.
Special events such as celebrity appearances are another sponsored feature at malls.

combination: _____

_____

_____

7. He was tall.
His skin was dark.
He looked muscular.
He dressed fashionably.
He was the new dean of students.

combination: _____

_____

_____

8. When I need advice, I go to Sean, who is a sensible person.
Sean has insight.
Perceptiveness is another one of his strengths.

combination: _____

_____

_____

9. If you drive me to New York City, we'll go to Times Square.
Eating Korean food is something else we'll do.
In addition, we can walk in Central Park.

combination: _If you drive me to new York City, we can_
go to time square, Eat Korean food and walk through
Central Park.

10. Look in my wallet when you want some spare change.
You can also check the zippered compartment in my handbag.
The pile of coins on the hall table is another place to investigate.

combination: _____

_____

_____

| Exercise 4 | **Connect: Editing a Paragraph for Errors in Parallelism** |

Connect

Correct any errors in parallelism in the following paragraph. There are five errors.

Most people get angry when they lose an argument or losing a game. For instance, my mother is usually a calm and polite individual. However, when she has a difference of opinion with me about my social life, she becomes a wild woman. Her eyes give off a fiery glint, her mouth stiffening into a pout, and her jaw juts out with rage if I make an intelligent observation. She does not like a challenge to her beliefs and opinions even if the challenge is polite. Similarly, my best friend becomes very upset when he loses one of our neighborhood soccer games. These games are supposed to be informal get-togethers where everyone can get a little exercise, release some stress, and to enjoy each other's company. However, to my friend, these competitions are tests. Whenever he plays in a silly little soccer game, he reacts as if he were in the World Cup and becoming an aggressive fool. To him, losing means slinking away in disgrace, misery, and with fury. I would love to advise my mother and my friend that their anger does not win an argument nor change the outcome of a game.

| Exercise 5 | **Connect: Editing a Paragraph for Errors in Parallelism** |

Connect

Correct any errors in parallelism in the following paragraph. There are five errors.

The job of my dreams would offer me a decent salary, opportunity for adventure, and a chance to work outdoors. Although I have held part-time jobs in malls and offices, I would love to work at a wildlife refuge, a boat, or in a helicopter. I prefer being in motion and physical labor to sitting behind a desk. I don't care what kind of climate my job would involve. Rescuing people stranded in blizzards or to patrol the seacoasts would be equally attractive. When I watch dramatic scenes of firefighters saving children from burning buildings, I am fascinated. On the other hand, I would be happy in a less stressful job. Fishing boats, nature preserves, national parks, and great lakes all interest me. As long as the work offers me a fair salary, a chance to enjoy nature, and being challenged by different things every day, I am ready for it.

Chapter Test Using Parallelism in Sentences

Some of the following sentences have errors in parallelism; some are correct. Put an *X* by the sentences with errors in parallelism.

1. __X__ The honors ceremony will celebrate the academic achievements of many scholars, the success of various sports teams, the ability of individual athletes, and award recognition of the many student clubs.

2. __X__ Alonzo is a dear friend, a neighbor who is kind, a hardworking police officer, and a committed volunteer.

3. __✓__ The specialist in tropical diseases was puzzled by and afraid of the new form of malaria.

4. __X__ I packed a pair of socks, a change of underwear, an extra shirt, new toothbrush, an old sweatshirt, and a bottle of deodorant in my overnight bag.

5. __X__ Visiting my grandmother makes me nervous because she asks me personal questions, offers me strange food, and bores with long and pointless stories.

6. __X__ If you get to the movie theater and I am not there yet, you can stand in the ticket line, buy the tickets, and waiting for me at the entrance.

7. __X__ A whining worker can irritate the other employees, the boss, create a negative atmosphere, and take all the energy out of the room.

8. __✓__ I tried the front door, checked every window, and explored the entrance to the basement, but I could not find a way into the house.

9. __✓__ When you have hope, optimism, persistence, and conviction, you can make a difference in your community.

10. __X__ After we arrived at the airport, we were eager to board the plane, fasten our seatbelts, and to begin our adventure.

3 Correct 7 wrong

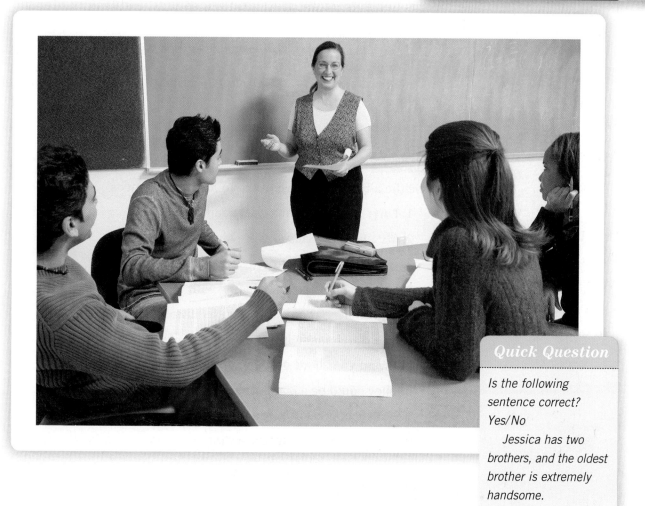

Quick Question

Is the following sentence correct? Yes/No

   Jessica has two brothers, and the oldest brother is extremely handsome.

   (After you study this chapter, you will be confident of your answer.)

Chapter Objectives

Students will be able to identify adjectives and adverbs and incorporate them correctly in their writing.

WHAT ARE ADJECTIVES?

Adjectives describe nouns (persons, places, or things) or pronouns (words that substitute for nouns).

adjectives:
She stood in a *dark* corner. (*Dark* describes the noun *corner.*)
I need a *little* help. (*Little* describes the noun *help.*)
She looked *happy.* (*Happy* describes the pronoun *she.*)

An adjective usually comes before the word it describes.

He gave me a *beautiful* ring. (*Beautiful* describes *ring.*)
A *small* horse pulled the cart. (*Small* describes *horse.*)

Sometimes an adjective comes after a *being* verb, a verb that tells what something is. Being verbs are words like *is, are, was, am,* and *has been.*

[handwritten margin note: what does an adjective do for a living?]

[handwritten margin note: • Describes or limits noun or pronouns]

Words like *feels*, *looks*, *seems*, *smells*, *sounds*, and *tastes* are part of the group called being verbs.

> He seems *unhappy*. (*Unhappy* describes *he* and follows the being verb *seems*.)
> Alan was *confident*. (*Confident* describes *Alan* and follows the being verb *was*.)

[handwritten margin note: adj → n LV adj]

Exercise 1 **Practice: Recognizing Adjectives**

Circle the adjective in each of the following sentences.

[handwritten margin note: what Kind? which ones? how many / much?]

1. Larry got caught in a heavy rainstorm.
2. Mr. and Mrs. Salazar were kind neighbors.
3. A small mouse skittered across the floor.
4. The prisoner seems unhappy with the judge's decision.
5. The enormous snake was curled inside a box.
6. The cough medicine smelled horrible.
7. I want your honest opinion of my performance.
8. Lucy could be a superior singer.
9. A dirty blanket covered the bed.
10. That movie had a weird ending.

ADJECTIVES: COMPARATIVE AND SUPERLATIVE FORMS

[handwritten margin note: we tend to not use the comparative form when needed...]

The **comparative** form of an adjective compares two persons or things. The **superlative** form compares three or more persons or things.

> **comparative:** Your car is *cleaner* than mine.
> **superlative:** Your car is the *cleanest* one in the parking lot.
> **comparative:** Hamburger is *cheaper* than steak.
> **superlative:** Hamburger is the *cheapest* meat on the menu.
> **comparative:** Lisa is *friendlier* than her sister.
> **superlative:** Lisa is the *friendliest* of the three sisters.

For most adjectives of one syllable, add *-er* to form the comparative, and add *-est* to form the superlative:

> The weather is *colder* than it was yesterday, but Friday was the *coldest* day of the year.
> Orange juice is *sweeter* than grapefruit juice, but the *sweetest* juice is grape juice.

For longer adjectives, use *more* to form the comparative, and *most* to form the superlative:

> I thought algebra was *more difficult* than composition; however, physics was the *most difficult* course I ever took.
> My brother is *more outgoing* than my sister, but my father is the *most outgoing* member of the family.

The three forms of adjectives usually look like this:

Adjective	Comparative	Superlative
	(two)	(three or more)
sweet	sweeter	sweetest
fast	faster	fastest
short	shorter	shortest
quick	quicker	quickest
old	older	oldest

They may look like this instead:

Adjective	Comparative	Superlative
	(two)	(three or more)
confused	more confused	most confused
specific	more specific	most specific
dangerous	more dangerous	most dangerous
confident	more confident	most confident
beautiful	more beautiful	most beautiful

However, there are some irregular forms of adjectives:

Adjective	Comparative	Superlative
	(two)	(three or more)
good	better	best
bad	worse	worst
little	less	least
many, much	more	most

Exercise 2   Practice: Selecting the Correct Adjective Form

Write the correct form of the adjective in each of the following sentences.

1. Milk chocolate tastes _Better_ (good) than dark chocolate.

2. After my surgery, I had to make _more_ (many) calls to my insurance company; in fact, I called the insurance company _more_ (many) often than I called my boyfriend.

3. Nick's communications class requires _____ (little) public speaking than my communications class does.

4. Which of the four games would be the _most_ (many) suitable for a four-year-old boy?

5. My brother did a _____ (good) job painting my bathroom, but he would have done a _____ (good) job if he had been painting his own bathroom.

6. My sister is learning to cook and has been trying out her creations on me; of the three dishes I've eaten, the broiled swordfish was the _Worst_ (bad).

7. I love both my brothers, but Oscar is _more_ (much) loveable than Malcolm.

8. *Pirates of the Caribbean, Spiderman,* and *Shrek* all produced sequels; I think *Spiderman* offers the _____ (good) of the sequels.

9. Sticking with a diet is _____ (hard) than starting one; but the _____ (tough) part of dieting is reaching a plateau when the pounds won't come off any longer.

10. You look _____ (good) in short and long hair; however, I think you look much _____ (good) in short hair.

Collaborate

Exercise 3   **Collaborate: Writing Sentences with Adjectives**

Working with a partner or group, write a sentence that correctly uses each of the following adjectives. Be prepared to share your answers with another group or with the class.

1. oldest _____

2. more useful _____

3. richest _____

4. least _____

5. most foolish _____

6. stronger _____

7. longer _____

8. more alert _____

9. worse _____

10. much _____

WHAT ARE ADVERBS?

Adverbs describe verbs, adjectives, or other adverbs.

adverbs:
As she spoke, Steve listened *thoughtfully*. (*Thoughtfully* describes the verb *listened*.)
I said I was *really* sorry for my error. (*Really* describes the adjective *sorry*.)
The cook worked *very* quickly. (*Very* describes the adverb *quickly*.)

Adverbs answer questions like "How?" "How much?" "How often?" "When?" "Why?" and "Where?"

Exercise 4   **Practice: Recognizing Adverbs**

Circle the adverbs in the following sentences.

1. The dog across the street is usually quiet, but he barks uncontrollably at cats.

2. Sometimes, Sarah Sanchez can be very irritable.

3. The burglar moved swiftly and silently through the house.

4. Ethan was extremely proud of his lovingly rebuilt motorcycle.

5. You can hardly expect me to forgive Doug for his dishonesty.

6. Mr. Li regularly complains about the noise from the construction crew.

7. My English professor is <u>genuinely</u> interested in my stories about my childhood in Nigeria.   *How?*
   Adj

8. David Dowd's beautifully <u>designed</u> furniture won first prize at a decorator's showcase.

9. When Brad showed up <u>late</u> for practice, the coach was really upset with him.   *when?*

10. As he reached the finish line, the winning driver smiled <u>triumphantly</u>.

Exercise 5   **Collaborate: Writing Sentences with Adverbs**

Collaborate

Working with a partner or group, write a sentence that correctly uses each of the following adverbs. Be prepared to share your answers with another group or with the class.

1. rarely   _____

2. completely   _____

3. never   _____

4. sadly   _____

5. slowly   _____

6. often   _____

7. viciously   _____

8. truly   _____

9. always   _____

10. really   _____

HINTS ABOUT ADJECTIVES AND ADVERBS

Do not use an adjective when you need an adverb. Some writers make the mistake of using an adjective when they need an adverb.

not this: Talk to me ~~honest~~.
but this: Talk to me *honestly*.

not this: You can say it ~~simple~~.
but this: You can say it *simply*.

not this: He was breathing ~~deep~~.
but this: He was breathing *deeply*.

Exercise 6   **Practice: Changing Adjectives to Adverbs**

In each pair of sentences, change the underlined adjective in the first sentence to an adverb in the second sentence. The first one is done for you.

1. **a.** She is a <u>graceful</u> dancer.

   b. She dances _____*gracefully*_____.

2. **a.** Gloria gave an <u>impatient</u> response.

   b. Gloria responded _____.

3. **a.** Mrs. Goldstein was a <u>recent</u> visitor to Concord.

   b. Mrs. Goldstein _____ visited Concord.

bad≠ good is an adj
badly≠ well is an adv

danced: well / badly
dog = good / bad

linking verbs = be

After a LV we us an adjective

Pie is good
Smells
∧·Pie doesn't have a nose,
taste
·Pie doesn't have a mouth

Dog smells _____
· Both because either
its talking about
us or the dogs
Sense.

Feel is an adj
·Emotion _____
good/bad
↳finger tips · well/badly
↳ You feel bad

4. **a.** As she drove to the emergency room, Abigail was <u>nervous</u>.

   b. Abigail _____ drove to the emergency room.

5. **a.** After the contestant conquered his stage fright, his singing was <u>magnificent.</u>

   b. After the contestant conquered his stage fright, he sang
   _____.

6. **a.** The team's second try for the title had <u>significant</u> differences from its first attempt.

   b. The team's second try for the title was _____ different from its first attempt.

7. **a.** Governor Millburn's defense of his decision was <u>calm.</u>

   b. Governor Millburn _____ defended his decision.

8. **a.** Cristina made a <u>steady</u> advance to the finish line.

   b. Cristina _____ advanced to the finish line.

9. **a.** The store manager's apology seemed <u>sincere.</u>

   b. The store manager apologized _____.

10. **a.** Ali was a <u>regular</u> contributor to the Children's Home Fund.

    b. Ali _____ contributed to the Children's Home Fund.

so it can't preform the action

Don't Confuse *Good* and *Well,* or *Bad* and *Badly*

Remember that *good* is an adjective; it describes nouns. *Well* is an adverb; it describes verbs. (The only time *well* can be used as an adjective is when it means "healthy": *I feel well today.*

not this: You ran that race ~~good~~.
but this: You ran that race *well.*

not this: I cook eggs ~~good~~.
but this: I cook eggs *well.*

not this: How ~~good~~ do you understand grammar?
but this: How *well* do you understand grammar?

Bad is an adjective; it describes nouns. It also follows being verbs like *is, are, was, am, has been.* Words like *feels, looks, seems, smells, sounds,* and *tastes* are part of the group called being verbs. *Badly* is an adverb; it describes action verbs.

not this: He feels ~~badly~~ about his mistake.
but this: He feels *bad* about his mistake. (*Feels* is a being verb; it is described by the adjective *bad.*)

not this: That soup smells ~~badly~~.
but this: That soup smells *bad.* (*Smells* is a being verb; it is described by the adjective *bad.*)

not this: He dances ~~bad~~.
but this: He dances *badly.* (*Dances* is an action verb; it is described by the adverb *badly.*)

Exercise 7   **Practice: Using *Good* and *Well*, *Bad* and *Badly***

health = well ≠ ill

Write the appropriate word in the following sentences.

1. Arthur sold his car to his sister Kathleen, who wanted it _badly_ (bad, badly).

2. Teresa skipped her math class yesterday because she didn't feel _well_ (good, well).

3. A day after I had my computer repaired, it worked _well_ (good, well), but a week later, it started working _badly_ (bad, badly) again.

4. The first firefighter on the scene could have been _badly_ (bad, badly) <u>hurt</u> by smoke inhalation.

5. When Pete concentrates on his game, he does _well_ (good, well) at regional golf tournaments.

6. My sister has never been a _good_ (good, well) liar, but my brother has a gift for <u>lying</u> _well_ (good, well).

7. No one wanted to buy the house because it was _badly_ (bad, badly) decorated.

8. How _good_ (good, well) do you think the movie will be?

9. I shouldn't have bought the new shaving gel; it smells _bad_ (bad, badly) on my skin.

10. I feel _bad_ (bad, badly) about forgetting Charlene's birthday.

Not More + -*er* or Most + -*est*

Be careful. Never write both an -*er* ending and *more*, or an -*est* ending and *most*.

not this: I want to work with someone ~~more smarter~~.
but this: I want to work with someone *smarter*.

not this: Alan is the ~~most richest~~ man in town.
but this: Alan is the *richest* man in town.

Use *Than*, not *Then*, in Comparisons

When you compare things, use *than*. *Then* means "at a later time."

not this: You are taller ~~then~~ I am.
but this: You are taller *than* I am.

a = comparison
e = when

not this: I'd like a car that is faster ~~then~~ my old one.
but this: I'd like a car that is faster *than* my old one.

When Do I Need a Comma Between Adjectives?

Sometimes you use more than one adjective to describe a noun.

I visited a cold, dark cave.
The cat had pale blue eyes.

If you look at the preceding examples, one uses a comma between the adjectives *cold* and *dark*, but the other does not have a comma between the adjectives *pale* and *blue*. Both sentences are correctly punctuated. To decide whether you need a comma, try one of these tests:

Test 1:   Try to put *and* between the adjectives. If the sentence still makes sense, put a comma between the adjectives.

check for comma: I visited a cold, dark cave. (Do you need the comma? Add *and* between the adjectives.)
add *and*: I visited a cold *and* dark cave. (Does the sentence still make sense? Yes. You need the comma.)
correct sentence: I visited a cold, dark cave.

check for comma: The cat had pale, blue eyes. (Do you need the comma? Add *and* between the adjectives.)
add *and*: The cat had pale *and* blue eyes. (Does the sentence still make sense? No. You do not need the comma.)
correct sentence: The cat had pale blue eyes.

Test 2:   Try to reverse the order of the adjectives. If the sentence still makes sense, put a comma between the adjectives.

check for comma: I visited a cold, dark cave. (Do you need the comma? Reverse the order of the adjectives.)
reverse order: I visited a dark, cold cave. (Does the sentence still make sense? Yes. You need the comma.)
correct sentence: I visited a cold, dark cave.

check for comma: The cat had pale, blue eyes. (Do you need the comma? Reverse the order of the adjectives.)
reverse order: The cat had blue pale eyes. (Does the sentence still make sense? No. You don't need a comma.)
correct sentence: The cat had pale blue eyes.

You can use Test 1 or Test 2 to determine whether you need a comma between adjectives.

Connect

| Exercise 8 | Connect: Editing for Errors in Adjectives and Adverbs |

Edit the following paragraph, correcting all the errors in the use of adjectives and adverbs. Write your corrections above the errors. There are six errors.

   When you see my new haircut, I want you to be honestly with me. Don't try

to cover up the truth with tactful remarks or badly disguised lies. The haircut

cost me more money then a week's groceries, so it should be more better

than any other haircut I've ever had. In addition, I don't want to fool myself

about my appearance. I need to know very quick whether I should cover my

head with a cap for a few weeks. Of all the good friends in my life, you are

my better friend, so I am relying on your judgment. Go ahead; breathe deep,

and give me your opinion.

Connect

| Exercise 9 | Connect: Editing for Errors in Adjectives and Adverbs |

Edit the following paragraph, correcting all the errors in the use of adjectives and adverbs. Write your corrections above the errors. There are eight errors.

I always look forward to winter weather, but sometimes a certain kind of winter day depresses me. I feel exhilarated on cold sunny winter days when the sky is a crisp, clear blue. On such days, I don't mind wearing three layers of clothing and feeling the wind sting my face. That kind of winter day is the best kind of day for walking. It is better than a hot sweaty summer day or a dark, rainy winter's day. Those gray winter days depress me. On the wet, cold days, the last leaves on the trees fall silent to the sidewalks and stick to the pavement. Walking becomes treacherously. The wet cold stings my face. The dreary sky offers no hope because it promises only most misery and rain. Such days are a naturally part of winter, but I want them to go away quick. However, a gray day does offer me one opportunity. The miserable weather gives me an excuse to spend a well part of my time indoors.

Chapter Test Using Adjectives and Adverbs

Some of the following sentences have errors in the use of adjectives and adverbs. Some are correct. Put an *X* by each sentence with an error.

1. √ I have had <u>three different phone</u> plans; the first one looked like a bargain, but it turned out to be the <u>worst deal.</u>

2. X The tutor from the student learning center was <u>more kinder</u> to me than any of my math instructors in high school.

3. X I didn't want to tell Brian the truth, but his new shirt looks <u>badly</u> on him.   *Shirt doesn't have eyes to look*
    ↳ Bad

4. ✓ When Maya left the hospital, she looked healthy, but she wasn't feeling <u>well.</u>

5. X On his trip to Savannah, Trevor saw three old friends; one had become a <u>real</u> successful cartoonist.

6. ✓ My sister wants to meet a young, dark, and handsome man   *really*
    with a good job.   *comma's are good*

7. ✓ After I gave her the giant teddy bear, my daughter gave me a great big kiss.   *don't want a ,*

8. X Driving to Providence seems to be a <u>more better</u> idea than spending a great deal of money on plane tickets.

9. √ Brandon presented an <u>extremely good argument</u> for shutting down the contaminated factory.

10. X My cousin became <u>serious</u> involved in protecting marine life   *↱ Seriously*
    after he saw a movie about dying species in the Pacific Ocean.

PEARSON
mywritinglab   For support in meeting this chapter's objectives, log in to
www.mywritinglab.com and select **Adjectives** and **Adverbs**.

CHAPTER 22

Correcting Problems with Modifiers

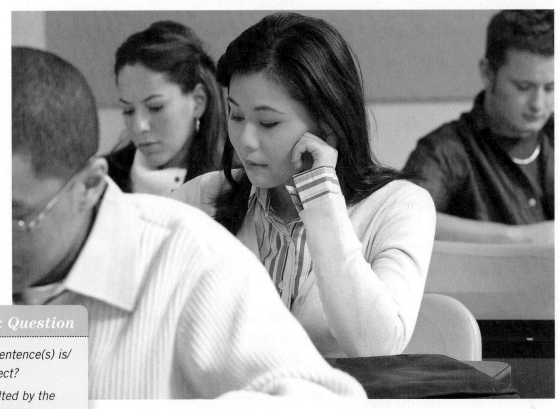

Chapter Objectives

Students will be able to identify modifiers within sentences and correct misplaced or dangling modifiers.

WHAT ARE MODIFIERS?

Modifiers are words, phrases, or clauses that describe (modify) something in a sentence. All the italicized words, phrases, and clauses below are modifiers.

the *blue* van (word)
the van *in the garage* (phrase)
the van *that she bought* (clause)

foreign tourists (word)
tourists *coming to Florida* (phrase)
tourists *who visit the state* (clause)

Sometimes modifiers limit another word. They make another word (or words) more specific.

the girl *in the corner* (tells exactly which girl)
fifty acres (tells exactly how many acres)

the movie *that I liked best* (tells which movie)

He *never* calls. (tells how often)

Exercise 1 Practice: Recognizing Modifiers

In each sentence below, underline the modifiers (words, phrases, or clauses) that describe the italicized word or phrase.

1. *A* chocolate *sundae* with sprinkles on top makes my nephew smile with pleasure.

2. Walking confidently down the red carpet, *the celebrity* waved to his fans.

3. Ava searched through the debris for family *photographs* lost in the flood.

4. Smiling at me from the back row of the classroom, *my sister* applauded my speech.

5. Mark and Aaron have adopted *a friendly stray cat.*

6. *The passengers* waiting at the terminal for hours began to complain loudly.

7. *The woman* selected for the top job once worked at a local bank.

8. My boyfriend was amused by *a little boy* playing with a large beach ball.

9. *The truck* with a dent in its rear bumper belongs to Silvio.

10. Danny couldn't help laughing at *the bully* covered in mud.

[handwritten note: Comma tells us whats being described]

CORRECTING MODIFIER PROBLEMS

Modifiers can make your writing more specific and more concrete. Used effectively and correctly, modifiers give the reader a clear, exact picture of what you want to say, and they help you to say it precisely. But modifiers have to be used correctly. You can check for errors with modifiers as you revise your sentences.

INFO BOX: **Three Steps in Checking for Sentence Errors with Modifiers**

Step 1: Find the modifier.

Step 2: Ask, "Does the modifier have something to modify?"

Step 3: Ask, "Is the modifier in the right place, as close as possible to the word, phrase, or clause it modifies?"

If you answer no in either Step 2 or Step 3, you need to revise your sentence. Let's use the steps in the following example.

[handwritten note: Misplaced]

sample sentence: I saw a girl driving a Mazda wearing a bikini.

Step 1: Find the modifier. The modifiers are *driving a Mazda, wearing a bikini.*

Step 2: Ask, "Does the modifier have something to modify?" The answer is yes. The girl is driving a Mazda. The girl is wearing a bikini. Both modifiers go with *a girl*.

Step 3: Ask, "Is the modifier in the right place?" The answer is yes and no. One modifier is in the right place:

I saw a *girl driving a Mazda*

The other modifier is *not* in the right place

a *Mazda wearing a bikini*

The Mazda is not wearing a bikini.

> **revised:** I saw a girl *wearing a bikini* and *driving a Mazda*.

Let's work through the steps once more:

sample sentence: Scampering through the forest, the hunters saw two rabbits.

Step 1: Find the modifier. The modifiers are *scampering through the forest*, and *two*.

Step 2: Ask, "Does the modifier have something to modify?" The answer is yes. There are *two rabbits*. The *rabbits* are *scampering through the forest*.

Step 3: Ask, "Is the modifier in the right place?" The answer is yes and no. The word *two* is in the right place:

two rabbits

But *scampering through the forest* is in the wrong place:

Scampering through the forest, the hunters

The hunters are not scampering through the forest—the rabbits are.

> **revised:** The hunters saw two rabbits *scampering through the forest*.

Caution: Be sure to put words like *almost, even, exactly, hardly, just, merely, nearly, only, scarcely*, and *simply* as close as possible to what they modify. If you put them in the wrong place, you may write a confusing sentence.

---

sample sentence: Etienne only wants to grow carrots and zucchini. (The modifier that creates confusion here is *only*. Does Etienne have only one goal in life—to grow carrots and zucchini? Or are these the only vegetables he wants to grow? To create a clearer sentence, move the modifier.)

revised: Etienne wants to grow *only* carrots and zucchini.

The examples you have just worked with show one common error in using modifiers. This error involves **misplaced modifiers**, words that describe something but are not where they should be in the sentence. Here is the rule to remember:

> **Put a modifier as close as possible to the word, phrase, or clause it modifies.**

Exercise 2 **Practice: Correcting Sentences with Misplaced Modifiers**

Some of the following sentences contain misplaced modifiers. Revise any sentence that has a misplaced modifier by putting the modifier as close as possible to whatever it modifies.

1. Hanging from the ceiling, I noticed a giant spider.

    revised: _I noticed a gaint spider hanging from the_
    ceiling

2. The village is well known for its giant garbage dump where I was born.

    revised: _The village where I was born is well know_
    for its gaint garbage dump

3. Ray lent the tools to a friendly neighbor that he bought at a garage sale.

    revised: _Ray lent the tools that he bought at a_
    garage sale to a friendly neighbor

4. Callie and Jeremy were surprised by the sudden appearance of two deer driving in the national forest.

    revised: _Driving in the national forest, Callie &_
    Jermy were suprised by the sudden appearance of
    two deer.

5. Painted a pale green, the old house looked new again.

    revised: _____

    _____

6. Dipped in chocolate, my aunt enjoyed the large, plump strawberries.

    revised: _My Aunt enjoyed the large, plump strawberries_
    dipped in chocolate

7. Standing in line at the ticket counter, the children grew restless and bored.

    revised: _____

    _____

8. Right from the oven, Annie served the cinnamon cookies.

    revised: _____

    _____

9. Tommy was so hungry that he almost ate everything on the table.

    revised: _____

    _____

10. The twins nearly waited for an hour before an emergency vehicle came to help them.

    revised: _the twins waited_ for _nearly an hour before an_
    emergency vehicle came to help them

CORRECTING DANGLING MODIFIERS

The three steps for correcting modifier problems can help you recognize another kind of error. Let's use the steps to check the following sentence.

> **sample sentence:** Strolling through the tropical paradise, many colorful birds could be seen.

> **Step 1:** Find the modifier. The modifiers are *Strolling through the tropical paradise,* and *many colorful.*

> **Step 2:** Ask, "Does the modifier have something to modify?" The answer is yes and no. The words *many* and *colorful* modify birds. But who or what is *strolling through the tropical paradise*? There is no person mentioned in this sentence. The birds are not strolling.

This kind of error is called a **dangling modifier**. It is a modifier that does not have anything to modify; it just dangles in the sentence. To correct this kind of error, you cannot just move the modifier:

> **still incorrect:** Many colorful birds could be seen strolling through the tropical paradise. (There is still no person strolling.)

The way to correct this kind of error is to add something to the sentence. If you gave the modifier something to modify, you might come up with several different revised sentences:

> **revised sentences:** *As I strolled through the tropical paradise, I saw* many colorful birds.

> or

> Many colorful birds could be seen *when we were strolling through the tropical paradise.*

> or

> *While the tourists strolled through the tropical paradise, they saw* many colorful birds.

Try the process for correcting dangling modifiers once more:

> **sample sentence:** Ascending in the glass elevator, the hotel lobby glittered in the light.

> **Step 1:** Find the modifier. The modifiers are *Ascending in the glass elevator,* and *hotel.*

> **Step 2:** Ask, "Does the modifier have anything to modify?" The answer is yes and no. The word *hotel* modifies lobby, but *ascending in the glass elevator* doesn't modify anything. Who is ascending in the elevator? There is nobody mentioned in the sentence.

To revise this sentence, put somebody or something in it for the modifier to describe:

> *As the guests ascended in the glass elevator,* the hotel lobby glittered in the light.

> or

> *Ascending in the glass elevator, she* saw the hotel lobby glitter in the light.

Remember that you cannot correct a dangling modifier just by moving the modifier. You have to give the modifier something to modify; you have to add something to the sentence.

Exercise 3 **Practice: Correcting Sentences with Dangling Modifiers**

Some of the following sentences use modifiers correctly. Some sentences have dangling modifiers. Revise the sentences with dangling modifiers. To revise, you will have to add words and change words.

1. When accelerating to make a green light, an accident can occur.

   revised: *when accelerating to make a green light, the driver can cause an accident.*

2. While volunteering at an animal shelter on the weekends, Christopher met a beautiful woman.

   revised: _____

   _____

3. To find a house in a lower price range, looking farther from the city is necessary.

   revised: *To find a house in a lower price range, the buy must look farther from the city*

4. Having trained as a paramedic in the army, Jose's skills would help him to find a job in civilian life.

   revised: *Having trained as a paramedic in the army, Jose hoped his skills would help him find a job.*

5. Unprepared for a hot day, people began shedding their coats and sweaters.

   revised: _____

   _____

6. Listening to another of his father's rants, anger began to fill David's head.

   revised: *listening to another of his father's rants, David began to be angry.*

7. With hard work and a positive attitude, many of the setbacks and disappointments of a new job can be handled.

   revised: *with hard work & positive attitude, the new worker can handle the set backs & dissappointments*

8. At the age of five, my brother was born, and I had some difficulty being the older brother.

   revised: *When I was 5, my*

   _____

9. After much discussion and some argument, an agreement was reached.

revised: _____

_____

10. Reading the letter for the second time, the terrible reality of the situation hit Ashley.

revised: _____

_____

REVIEWING THE STEPS AND THE SOLUTIONS

It is important to recognize problems with modifiers and to correct these problems. Modifier problems can result in confusing or even silly sentences. And when you confuse or unintentionally amuse your reader, you are not making your point.

Remember to check for modifier problems in three steps and to correct each kind of problem in the appropriate way.

INFO BOX: **A Summary of Modifier Problems**

Checking for Modifier Problems

Step 1: Find the modifier.

Step 2: Ask, "Does the modifier have something to modify?"

Step 3: Ask, "Is the modifier in the right place?"

Correcting Modifier Problems

If the modifier is in the wrong place (a misplaced modifier), put it as close as possible to the word, phrase, or clause it modifies.

If the modifier has nothing to modify (a dangling modifier), add or change words so that it has something to modify.

Collaborate

Exercise 4 **Collaborate: Revising Sentences with Modifier Problems**

All of the following sentences have modifier problems. Working with a partner or group, write a new, correct sentence for each incorrect one. You may move words, add words, change words, or remove words. The first one is done for you.

1. Written in stone, the archaeologist could not understand the ancient message.

revised: The archaeologist could not understand the ancient message written in stone.

2. Looking for a compatible mate, friends and family members may know several potential partners.

revised: _____

_____

3. Without time to study and do homework, surviving in college becomes impossible.

   revised: _____

   _____

4. Daniel is so absentminded that he nearly loses a pen every time he goes to class.

   revised: _____

   _____

5. Proudly carrying a shoe in his mouth, Tommy saw his dog Rocco emerge from the closet.

   revised: _____

   _____

6. Exhausted after a long day at work, Tina only watched half an hour of television before she fell asleep.

   revised: _____

   _____

7. An angry man stormed into the police station covered in mud.

   revised: _____

   _____

8. Before buying a new home, the needs of all the family members should be considered.

   revised: _____

   _____

9. To restore the downtown plaza to its place as the center of the community, the support of all the citizens is necessary.

   revised: _____

   _____

10. Covered in fudge icing, I couldn't stop eating the brownies.

    revised: _____

    _____

Exercise 5 **Connect: Editing a Paragraph for Modifier Problems**

Connect

Correct any errors in the use of modifiers in the following paragraph. There are six errors. Write your corrections in the space above the line.

I have been hearing about more restrictions on driving lately, and I have

mixed reactions. Of course, every state has laws against drunk driving, and such

laws save lives. However, after briefly studying old and proposed driving rules, the need for real enforcement is clear. For example, some states are focusing on the seat belt rules and making it easier for an officer to check for a seat belt violation. Other states want to pass a law that will prohibit the use of a GPS system while in a moving car. Another proposed law would forbid the use of a hand-held phone while driving. Concerned about other driving hazards, banning drivers from texting is being considered in some states. I understand the good intentions behind all the current and proposed driving laws, but not how they will be enforced. Police officers have already too many responsibilities and too few hours for additional work.

Connect

Exercise 6　Connect: Editing a Paragraph for Modifier Problems

Correct any errors in the use of modifiers in the following paragraph. There are seven errors. Write your corrections above the line.

When two roommates and I moved into our first home, we were lucky to have my uncle checking the premises for safety hazards. First, my roommates and I would nearly have missed all the problems in the electrical system. My uncle found fire hazards in the wiring. I brought another danger into the house. Wanting to save on heating costs, an old space heater from a garage sale was brought into our new home. On its first use, the condition of the heater would have been a fire hazard. Heat became an issue in the kitchen, too. Without a fire extinguisher, there was danger in the kitchen. A pantry near the kitchen filled with stacks of old newspapers could ignite, and we would not see the fire until it spread past the pantry. My uncle also noticed cracked many windows that created security problems. Finally, my uncle explored our yard and installed bright lights at the front door. We were grateful for his careful inspection, although we had only wanted a quick survey of our home.

Chapter Test Correcting Problems with Modifiers

Some of the sentences below have problems with modifiers; some are correct. Put an *X* by each sentence with a modifier problem.

1. ____✓____ Stuck in an endless line of traffic and late for work, nothing seemed to be going well for me on Wednesday morning.

2. ____✓____ At the age of nineteen, a beautiful baby entered my mother's life.

3. __wrong__ In order to make money in a small business, patience and a realistic attitude about profit and loss are necessary.

4. ____✓____ Racing through the airport, I nearly made the last flight to Puerto Rico but arrived at the gate as the doors of the plane closed.

5. __wrong__ When cleaning the interior of a car, a portable vacuum cleaner, a brush, and a few soft cloths can be helpful.

6. ____✓____ Caught in a lie, Sean and Mason tried talking fast as a way to cover their dishonesty.

7. ____✓____ Whipped by strong winds, the beach cabana did not seem a safe place for us to to take shelter in a tropical storm.

8. __wrong__ Martin became acquainted with several kind and friendly drivers while hitchhiking to school.

9. __wrong__ The flat-screen television on sale at the discount store is not what I <u>exactly</u> wanted.

10. __wrong__ Discouraged by a long and difficult job search, hope is essential but often hard to find.

3 wrong

PEARSON
mywritinglab For support in meeting this chapter's objectives, log in to
www.mywritinglab.com and select **Adjectives** and **Misplaced**
or Dangling Modifiers.

Using Verbs Correctly: Standard Verb Forms, Irregular Verbs, Consistency, and Voice

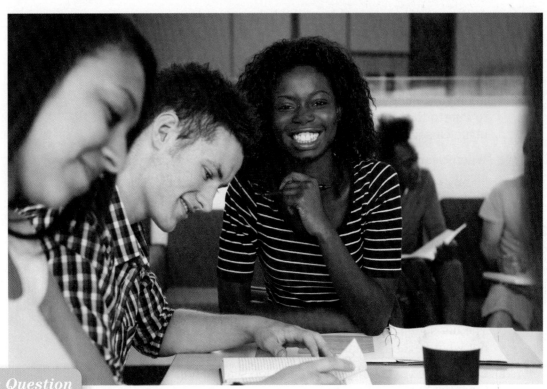

Quick Question

Which sentence(s) is/
are correct?

A. Last weekend,
   I catched a bad
   cold.
B. Last weekend, I
   caught a bad cold.

(After you study
this chapter, you will
be confident of your
answer.)

Chapter Objectives

Students will be able to (1) identify standard and irregular verb forms, (2) recognize errors in verb tense or consistency, and (3) distinguish between passive and active voice.

THE ROLE OF VERBS

Verbs are words that show some kind of action or being. The following verbs show action or being:

> He *runs* to the park.
> Melanie *is* my best friend.
> The pizza *tastes* delicious.

Verbs also tell about time.

> He *will run* to the park. (The time is future.)
> Melanie *was* my best friend. (The time is past.)
> The pizza *tastes* delicious. (The time is present.)

The time of a verb is called its *tense.* You can say a verb is in the *present tense, future tense,* or many other tenses.

Using verbs correctly involves knowing which form of the verb to use, choosing the right verb tense, and being consistent in verb tense.

USING STANDARD VERB FORMS

Many people use nonstandard verb forms in everyday conversation. But everyone who wants to write and speak effectively should know different levels of language, from the slang and dialect of everyday conversation to the **standard English** of college, business, and professional environments.

In everyday conversation, you may use **nonstandard forms** like these:

I goes	he don't	we was
you was	it don't	she smile
you be	I be	they walks

But these are not correct forms in standard English.

THE PRESENT TENSE

Look at the standard verb forms for the present tense of the word *listen:*

verb: listen

I listen	we listen
you listen	you listen
he, she, it listens	they listen

Take a closer look at the standard verb forms. Only one form is different:

> he, she, it *listens*

This is the only form that ends in *s* in the present tense.

> **INFO BOX:** In the present tense, use an *-s* or *-es* ending on the verb only when the subject is *he, she,* or *it,* or the equivalent, such as a proper name or a singular noun.

> *He calls* his mother every day.
> *She chases* the cat away from the bird cage.
> *It runs* like a new car.

> *Jim calls* his mother every day.
> *Samantha chases* the cat away from the bird cage.
> *The jalopy runs* like a new car.

Take another look at the present tense. If the verb is a standard verb, it will follow this form in the present tense.

> *I attend* every lecture.
> *You care* about the truth.
> *He visits* his grandfather regularly.
> *She drives* a new car.
> The new *album sounds* great.
> *We follow* that team.

You work well when you both compromise.
They buy the store brand of cereal.

Practice: Picking the Correct Verb in the Present Tense

Underline the subject and circle the correct verb form in parentheses in each sentence below.

1. In the spring, my allergies (make, makes) me miserable.

2. The frog in the garden (get, gets) fatter every day.

3. My cousins in Puerto Rico (turn, turns) my visits into special occasions.

4. With a smile, my daughter's kindergarten teacher (welcome, welcomes) each child to class.

5. The construction workers across the street never (arrive, arrives) before 8:00 A.M.

6. Around the corner (stand, stands) an old house and a new apartment building.

7. Arriving quickly and without warning, thunderstorms (strike, strikes) the area on summer afternoons.

8. A cat (require, requires) less attention than a dog.

9. Trying to please his boss, Caleb (take, takes) weekend classes in accounting and business law.

10. Here (come, comes) Jerome and Denise.

THE PAST TENSE

The past tense of most verbs is formed by adding *-d* or *-ed* to the verb.

verb: listen
I listened	we listened
you listened	you listened
he, she, it listened	they listened

Add *-ed* to *listen* to form the past tense. For some other verbs, you may add *-d*.

sun *faded* from the sky.
He *quaked* with fear.
She *crumpled* the paper into a ball.

Practice: Writing the Correct Verb Forms in the Past Tense

Write the correct past tense form of each verb in parentheses in each sentence below.

1. You _____ (ignore) the slow leak in the basement for months.

2. Last night, Ira _____ (play) cards for two hours.

3. In sixth grade, I _____ (earn) an award for perfect attendance.

4. For many years, my father _____ (talk) about coming to America.

5. A truck driver _____ (cross) the center line on the highway.

6. On Friday, someone _____ (call) me in the middle of the night.

7. After the movie, my friends _____ (invite) me to a Chinese restaurant.

8. After getting lost on the highway, we finally _____ (discover) the correct exit to the Miami airport.

9. My husband _____ (blame) me for our recent argument.

10. Like many young men, Michael _____ (want) instant success.

THE FOUR MAIN FORMS OF A VERB: PRESENT, PAST, PRESENT PARTICIPLE, AND PAST PARTICIPLE

When you are deciding which form of a verb to use, you will probably rely on one of four forms: the present tense, the past tense, the present participle, and the past participle. Most of the time, you will use one of these forms or add a helping verb to it. As an example, look at the four main forms of the verb *listen*.

Present	**Past**	**Present Participle**	**Past Participle**
listen	listened	listening	listened

You use the four verb forms—present, past, present participle, past participle—alone or with helping verbs, to express time (tense). Forms of regular verbs like *listen* are very easy to remember. Use the present form for the present tense:

We *listen* to the news on the radio.

The past form expresses past tense:

I *listened* to language tapes for three hours yesterday.

The present participle, or *-ing* form, is used with helping verbs:

He *was listening* to me.
I *am listening* to you.
You *should have been listening* more carefully.

The past participle is the form used with the helping verbs *have, has,* or *had:*

I *have listened* for hours.
She *has listened* to the tape.
We *had listened* to the tape before we bought it.

Of course, you can add many helping verbs to the present tense:

present tense:
We *listen* to the news on the car radio.

add helping verbs:
We *will* listen to the news on the car radio.
We *should* listen to the news on the car radio.
We *can* listen to the news on the car radio.

When a verb is regular, the past form is created by adding *-d* or *-ed* to the present form. The present participle is formed by adding *-ing* to the present form, and the past participle form is the same as the past form.

IRREGULAR VERBS

Irregular verbs do not follow the same rules for creating verb forms that regular verbs do. Three verbs that we use all the time—*be, have, do*—are irregular verbs. You need to study them closely. Look at the present tense forms for all three, and compare the standard, present tense forms to the nonstandard ones. *Remember to use the standard forms for college or professional writing.*

verb: be

Nonstandard	Standard
~~I be~~ or ~~I is~~	I am
~~you be~~	you are
~~he, she, it be~~	he, she, it is
~~we be~~	we are
~~you be~~	you are
~~they be~~	they are

verb: have

Nonstandard	Standard
~~I has~~	I have
~~you has~~	you have
~~he, she, it have~~	he, she, it has
~~we has~~	we have
~~you has~~	you have
~~they has~~	they have

verb: do

Nonstandard	Standard
~~I does~~	I do
~~you does~~	you do
~~he, she, it do~~	he, she, it does
~~we does~~	we do
~~you does~~	you do
~~they does~~	they do

Caution: Be careful when you add *not* to *does*. If you are writing a contraction of *does not*, be sure you write *doesn't*, not *don't*.

not this: ~~The light don't work.~~
but this: The light doesn't work.

Exercise 3   **Practice: Choosing the Correct Form of *be, have,* or *do* in the Present Tense**

Circle the correct form of the verb in parentheses in each sentence below.

1. If you (has, have) a free afternoon, you can spend some time with Karen and her children.

2. My feet (be, are) sore; these shoes pinch my toes.

3. The blue paint (has, have) the right tint of green to match your turquoise chairs.

4. Alicia won't come to the party because she (doesn't, don't) care about her old friends.

5. Dogs can be wonderful pets, but they (has, have) to be treated humanely.

6. Before I socialize with a stranger, I (do, does) a little investigating into his or her background.

7. Rick can be critical of his parents, but he (do, does) care about them.

8. Caroline (has, have) dreams of moving to Massachusetts.

9. At this moment, I (be, am) the luckiest man in the world.

10. A cup of hot tea (do, does) not soothe my sore throat much.

The Past Tense of *be, have, do*

The past forms of these irregular verbs can be confusing. Again, compare the nonstandard forms to the standard forms. *Remember to use the standard forms for college or professional writing.*

verb: be

Nonstandard	Standard
I were	I was
you was	you were
he, she, it were	he, she, it was
we was	we were
you was	you were
they was	they were

verb: have

Nonstandard	Standard
I has	I had
you has	you had
he, she, it have	he, she, it had
we has	we had
you has	you had
they has	they had

verb: do

Nonstandard	Standard
~~I done~~	I did
~~you done~~	you did
~~he, she, it done~~	he, she, it did
~~we done~~	we did
~~you done~~	you did
~~they done~~	they did

> **Exercise 4**   **Practice: Choosing the Correct Form of *be, have,* or *do* in the Past Tense**

Circle the correct verb form in parentheses in each sentence below.

1. Years ago, my family (have, had) pizza for dinner once a week.

2. I do not feel guilty about ignoring Todd's calls because he (done, did) nothing but argue with me for two days.

3. Yesterday Shakira (had, have) to pay for a new cell phone.

4. After our senior year, Jamie Perez and I (was, were) best friends for a while.

5. Last Wednesday, several members of the local crime watch group (had, have) a meeting with residents in the Birch Glen area.

6. When we won the raffle, we (were, was) too surprised to say anything.

7. My sister bought the plants for a garden, but my brother-in-law (done, did) the planting, watering, clipping, and fertilizing.

8. Ben drove me to the clinic when I (was, were) sick.

9. Before Brian moved to New York, he (have, had) never been on a subway.

10. The North Road area and Soldier Plaza (was, were) once the busiest sections of town.

More Irregular Verb Forms

Be, have, and *do* are not the only verbs with irregular forms. There are many such verbs, and everybody who writes uses some form of an irregular verb. When you write and you are not certain if you are using the correct form of a verb, check the list of irregular verbs on pages 480–482.

For each irregular verb listed below, the *present,* the *past,* and the *past participle* forms are given. The present participle isn't included because it is always formed by adding *-ing* to the present form.

Irregular Verb Forms

Present	Past	Past Participle
(Today I *arise.*)	(Yesterday I *arose.*)	(I have/had *arisen.*)
arise	arose	arisen
awake	awoke, awaked	awoken, awaked

Present	**Past**	**Past Participle**
bear	bore	born, borne
beat	beat	beaten
become	became	become
begin	began	begun
bend	bent	bent
bite	bit	bitten
bleed	bled	bled
blow	blew	blown
break	broke	broken
bring	brought	brought
build	built	built
burst	burst	burst
buy	bought	bought
catch	caught	caught
choose	chose	chosen
cling	clung	clung
come	came	come
cost	cost	cost
creep	crept	crept
cut	cut	cut
deal	dealt	dealt
draw	drew	drawn
dream	dreamed, dreamt	dreamed, dreamt
drink	drank	drunk
drive	drove	driven
eat	ate	eaten
fall	fell	fallen
feed	fed	fed
feel	felt	felt
fight	fought	fought
find	found	found
fling	flung	flung
fly	flew	flown
freeze	froze	frozen
get	got	got, gotten
give	gave	given
go	went	gone
grow	grew	grown
hear	heard	heard
hide	hid	hidden
hit	hit	hit
hold	held	held
hurt	hurt	hurt
keep	kept	kept
know	knew	known
lay (means to put)	laid	laid
lead	led	led

continued

Present	Past	Past Participle
leave	left	left
lend	lent	lent
let	let	let
lie (<u>means to recline</u>)	lay	lain
light	lit, lighted	lit, lighted
lose	lost	lost
make	made	made
mean	meant	meant
meet	met	met
pay	paid	paid
ride	rode	ridden
ring	rang	rung
rise	rose	risen
run	ran	run
say	said	said
see	saw	seen
sell	sold	sold
send	sent	sent
sew	sewed	sewn, sewed
shake	shook	shaken
shine	shone, shined	shone, shined
shrink	shrank	shrunk
shut	shut	shut
sing	sang	sung
sit	sat	sat
sleep	slept	slept
slide	slid	slid
sling	slung	slung
speak	spoke	spoken
spend	spent	spent
stand	stood	stood
steal	stole	stolen
stick	stuck	stuck
sting	stung	stung
stink	stank, stunk	stunk
string	strung	strung
swear	swore	sworn
swim	swam	swum
teach	taught	taught
tear	tore	torn
tell	told	told
think	thought	thought
throw	threw	thrown
wake	woke, waked	woken, waked
wear	wore	worn
win	won	won
write	wrote	written

Exercise 5 **Practice: Choosing the Correct Form of Irregular Verbs**

Write the correct form of the verb in parentheses in each sentence below. Be sure to check the list of irregular verbs.

1. You have never _swung_ (swim) in a pool like this one.

2. Yesterday someone _told_ (tell) me about a place to buy vitamins and herbs.

3. She wore a necklace of glass beads _strung_ (string) on a silver chain. (Describing word)

4. Once Leila picked a major, she _felt_ (feel) more focused and motivated in college.

5. Marie Elena has _sworn_ (swear) to lose weight so that she can fit into her favorite jeans.

6. I wish I had never _lent_ (lend) my car to Calvin.

7. My mother _wore_ (wear) the same old coat for years.

8. The police found a warehouse full of electronic goods that the thieves had _stole_ (steal).

9. My neighbor's burglar alarm has _rung_ (ring) every morning for a week.

10. Until yesterday, Stephen's parents _thought_ (think) he was attending school regularly.

Exercise 6 **Collaborate: Writing Sentences with Correct Verb Forms**

Collaborate

With a partner or a group, write two sentences that correctly use each of the verb forms below. In writing these sentences, you may add helping verbs to the verb forms, but do not change the verb form itself. The first one is done for you.

1. sent

   a. He sent her a dozen roses on Valentine's Day.

   b. I have sent him all the information he needs.

2. lie (means to recline)

   a. _____

   b. _____

      _____

3. shrank

   a. _____

   b. _____

4. meant

   a. _____

   b. _____

5. paid

a. _____

b. _____

6. lain

a. _____

b. _____

7. shined

a. _____

b. _____

8. seen

a. _____

b. _____

9. wore

a. _____

b. _____

10. born

a. _____

b. _____

Connect

Exercise 7 **Connect: Editing a Paragraph for Correct Verb Forms**

Correct the errors in verb forms in the following paragraph. There are six errors.

My father should stop nagging me about my future. I has been in college

for only a few weeks, and since my first day of class, he has been a nuisance.

Last spring, he were thrilled when I received a grant and some other financial

aid, and he burst with pride when I registered for my first semester. However,

lately he has chose to lay a million questions on me whenever he sees me. For

instance, he constantly asks me about my choice of a college major. Since I have

not yet decided, I try to explain to him that at this time I do not need to select

a major. He never lets me gets to the second part of my explanation when I

patiently tell him that my current courses are useful and required for any major.

Instead, he interrupts me and recites a list of possible careers for me. The list

include everything from brain surgeon to accountant. I have grown to ignore his lists and simply remain silent. However, his constant quizzing has begun to wear me down. I know he means well, but his pressure don't help me to succeed in college.

Connect

Exercise 8   Connect: Editing a Paragraph for Correct Verb Forms

Correct the errors in verb forms in the following paragraph. There are eleven errors.

After years of shyness, Alicia has came to be a confident and attractive person. I have knowed Alicia since we was both in our early teens, but I never understood her. She was too shy to talk much and rarely mixed with more than one or two friends. Because she is my cousin, I sometimes seen her at family gatherings where she usually hided in a quiet part of the room and avoided conversation. Something must have happen to her in the past few years. I had not run into her for a long time, but recently I noticed an attractive woman in my uncle's home. She was talking to my aunt in the kitchen. As I moved toward kitchen, the two women breaked into laughter. Suddenly I realize that the person with my aunt was Alicia. Her eyes was bright, and her smile came from her heart. This was a new Alicia. She revealed the real person that had lay behind the years of fear and shyness. Alicia had finded her true self.

Section Test   Using Verbs Correctly

Some of the sentences below use verbs correctly; others do not. Put an *X* by each sentence with an error in using verbs correctly.

1. __X__   We swum in the pool until sunset, when the water became too cold. *swam*

2. __X__   My mother sewed like a professional but never teached me how to do anything as simple as threading a needle. *taught*

3. __✓__   For three nights, the moon has risen in a cloudless sky, and the moonlight covered my summer garden.

4. __✓__   Yesterday morning I lay on the couch so I could rest my eyes until my headache medicine began to work.

5. __X__   Chelsea will do well in her new position at the bank as long as she don't become impatient with rude customers.

6. __X__   A social worker visited my uncle when he was in the hospital, but she done nothing about arranging home healthcare for him. *doesn't* *did*

7. ✓ If I <u>had known</u> the cake was loaded with fat, I <u>wouldn't</u> ✓
have eaten an extra piece.

8. ✗ Daniel and Lucy <u>have chose</u> to have a small wedding and *chosen*
<u>have found</u> a perfect place for the ceremony.

9. ✓ Before the rare plants <u>froze</u> overnight, my father <u>flung</u> a big
sheet over them and <u>held</u> it in place with stones.

10. ✓ Richard <u>told</u> me to get gas at the cheapest service station in
town, but I <u>went to</u> the nearest place instead.

Remember that your choice of verb form indicates the time (tense) of
your statements. Be careful not to shift from one tense to another unless you
have a reason to change the time.

CONSISTENT VERB TENSES

Staying in one tense (unless you have a reason to change tenses) is called
consistency of verb tense.

incorrect shifts in tense:
The waitress *ran* to the kitchen with the order in her hand, *raced*
back with glasses of water for her customers, and *smiles* calmly.
He *grins* at me from the ticket booth and *closed* the ticket window.

You can correct these errors by putting all the verbs in the same tense.

consistent present tense:
The waitress *runs* to the kitchen with the order in her hand, *races*
back with glasses of water for her customers, and *smiles* calmly.
He *grins* at me from the ticket booth and *closes* the ticket window.

consistent past tense:
The waitress *ran* to the kitchen with the order in her hand, *raced*
back with glasses of water for her customers, and *smiled* calmly.
He *grinned* at me from the ticket booth and *closed* the ticket window.

Whether you correct the errors by changing all the verbs to the present tense,
or by changing them to the past tense, you are making the tenses consistent.
Consistency of tense is important in the events you are describing because it
helps the reader understand what happened and when it happened.

Exercise 9 **Practice: Correcting Sentences That Are Inconsistent
in Tense**

In each sentence following, one verb is inconsistent in tense. Cross it out and
write the verb in the correct tense above the space.

1. My brother asked me to dinner, picked a fancy restaurant, and then
leaves me with the entire bill.
left

2. Tanisha takes evening classes because they don't interfere with

her work schedule, require attendance only once a week, attracted serious students, and offer a highly concentrated version of the course content.

3. As soon as Rick saved enough money, he packed up his car, drove across the country, and gets a job near a ski resort.
   got

4. Because a new version of a popular phone was about to be introduced, people line up outside the local phone store and camped out overnight.

5. Charlyce slammed the front door on her angry neighbor; then the neighbor shouts insults at the closed door until Marvin called the police.

6. Yesterday, my boss didn't show up at the office; at the same time, major problems occur in the phone system, and no one knew how to handle the emergency.

7. Sometimes Matthew is good-natured and open, but occasionally he worries about minor problems, lost his temper, and hurts his closest friends.

8. At the courthouse, the police department made plans for the highly publicized trial; it increased the number of security guards, made room for members of the media to file reports, and blocks many entrances to the building.
   blocked

9. Every Tuesday and Thursday, I get up at 6:30 A.M., grab a Diet Pepsi, pulled on some clothes, stagger outside, and ride my bike to my 7:30 A.M. English class.

10. Whenever my dog wants to go for a walk, she jumps on the sofa, stares right into my eyes, and began licking me until I give in and pick up her leash.

Connect

| Exercise 10 | **Connect: Editing a Paragraph for Consistency of Tenses** |

Read the following paragraph. Then cross out any verbs that are inconsistent in tense and write the corrections above. There are six errors.

My best friend Ryan tried college years ago but gave up after one wasted semester. He had no real purpose in going to college. He was a recent high school graduate and starts college because all his friends were going. Ryan has no idea of the demands of higher education. He took advantage of the freedom of college, skipped classes, avoids completing assignments, and relied on taking makeup tests instead of keeping up with the class. Ryan never thinks about the outcome. He just floated through the semester until he starts drowning. Unfortunately, he fails all his courses and dropped out of college. He swore that college was not right for him, but he was sad and a little defensive.

Connect

| Exercise 11 | **Connect: Editing a Paragraph for Consistency of Tenses** |

Read the following paragraph. Then cross out any verbs that are inconsistent in tense and write the corrections above. There are five errors.

At least once a year, Luke's bad behavior causes trouble for him and me. This trouble always begins at a party where Luke drinks too much and got too loud. Soon Luke manages to insult at least one stranger. Then the stranger and his friends become aggressive. I pulled my friend out of the fight, take him to the emergency room, and wait. Hours later, Luke returns. He had stitches on his face or a body part in a cast. I accuse him of behaving like a fool. I swore never to go to a party with him again. Unfortunately, we both have bad habits. His are drinking and fighting. Mine is enabling him to continue his self-destructive behavior. We were both getting hurt because we can't break these habits.

Exercise 12 Collaborate: Writing a Paragraph with Consistent Verb Tenses

The following paragraph has many inconsistencies in verb tenses; it shifts between past and present tenses. Working with a group, write two versions of the paragraph: *write it once in the present tense, then a second time in the past tense.* Divide your activity; half the group can write it in one tense while the other half can write it in the other tense.

After both rewrites are complete, read the new paragraphs aloud to both parts of the team as a final check.

My best friend took me for a ride in the country and tells me some bad news. He says that in two weeks he was moving to another state. This news is very sudden and shocks me to my core. My friend is more than a friend; he was a brother, a partner in pranks, a teammate in games, and a keeper of secrets. After he told me, we walk in the woods together. We find it hard to say much because we each knew what the other is feeling. After what seems like hours, he stops walking and faces me. He says the move wasn't what he wanted, but he added that his family needs him. I see sadness in his eyes, and I knew he saw the sorrow in mine.

Paragraph Revised for Consistent Tenses:

_____

_____

_____

_____

_____

_____

_____

_____

_____

_____

_____

_____

_____

_____

_____

_____

THE PRESENT PERFECT TENSE

When you are choosing the right verb tense, you should know about two verb tenses, the present perfect and the past perfect, that can make your meaning clear.

The **present perfect tense** is made up of the past participle form of the verb plus *have* or *has* as a helping verb. Use this tense to show an action that started in the past but is still going on in the present.

past tense: My father *drove* a truck for five months. (He doesn't drive a truck anymore, but he did drive one in the past.)
present perfect tense: My father *has driven* a truck for five months. (He started driving a truck five months ago; he is still driving a truck.)

past tense: For years, I *studied* ballet. (I don't study ballet now; I used to.)
present perfect tense: For years, I *have studied* ballet. (I still study ballet.)

Remember, use the present perfect tense to show that an action started in the past and is still going on.

> **Exercise 13** Practice: Distinguishing Between the Past Tense and the Present Perfect Tense

Circle the correct verb in parentheses in each sentence below. Be sure to look carefully at the meaning of the sentences.

1. Janet (sent, *has sent*) me a text message every morning for months now.

2. After heavy rain hit the area, the brakes on my car (*felt*, have felt) less efficient.

3. A burglar (*cut*, has cut) a hole in the roof of a jewelry store and managed to steal the safe.

4. The Addison Steak House (won, *has won*) Kansas City's best restaurant award for several years now.

5. One of the instructors in the business department at the college (was, has been) a well-known banker but now teaches classes in finance.

6. My four-year-old son (was, has been) clinging to my leg for five minutes and is still begging me for ice cream.

7. Yesterday I finally confronted my roommate and (demanded, have demanded) an explanation for the unpaid light bill.

8. Chris and Ben (were, have been) working in an unsafe building, but they won't complain to their supervisor.

9. My mother (volunteered, has volunteered) at the local food bank since it opened last year.

10. In August, Charles (signed, has signed) a contract with a professional hockey team.

THE PAST PERFECT TENSE

The **past perfect tense** is made up of the past participle form of the verb and *had* as a helping verb. You can use the past perfect tense to show more than one event in the past—that is, when two or more things happened in the past but at different times.

past tense: He *washed* the dishes.
past perfect tense: He *had washed* the dishes by the time I came home. (He washed the dishes *before* I came home. Both actions happened in the past, but one happened earlier than the other.)

past tense: Susan *waited* for an hour.

past perfect tense: Susan *had waited* for an hour when she gave up on him. (Waiting came first; giving up came second. Both actions are in the past.)

The past perfect tense is especially useful because you write most of your essays in the past tense, and you often need to get further back into the past. Remember, to form the past perfect tense, use *had* with the past participle of the verb.

Exercise 14   **Practice: Distinguishing Between the Past Tense and the Past Perfect Tense**

Circle the correct verb in parentheses in each sentence below. Be sure to look carefully at the meaning of the sentences.

1. Most of the audience (guessed, had guessed) the ending to the mystery before the movie was half finished.

2. Melissa was not sure whether Jerry (tried, had tried) to call her earlier that morning.

3. On Mother's Day, my daughter (surprised, had surprised) me with a necklace she had made at her preschool arts and crafts class.

4. By the time Nelson remembered the soup, it (boiled, had boiled) over on the stove.

5. As Brianna brushed her hair, she (studied, had studied) her face in the mirror.

6. Jacob looked at the exam questions and wondered if he (read, had read) the right chapters in his textbook.

7. The defense attorney examined the transcripts of the trial that (took, had taken) place two years earlier.

8. On Sunday morning, I took part in a charity walk-a-thon because my sister (was, had been) nagging me about it for weeks.

9. While my boyfriend devoured a breakfast of bacon, eggs, and pancakes, I (limited, had limited) myself to fruit and yogurt.

10. By the time Amber and I got to the movies, a huge crowd (took, had taken) all the good seats for the new Harry Potter film.

PASSIVE AND ACTIVE VOICE

Verbs not only have tenses, but they also have voices. When the subject in the sentence is doing something, the verb is in the **active voice.** When something is done to the subject—when it receives the action of the verb—the verb is in the **passive voice.**

active voice:
I painted the house. (*I,* the subject, did it.)
The people on the corner made a donation to the emergency fund.
    (The *people,* the subject, did it.)

passive voice:
The house was painted by me. (The *house,* the subject, didn't do anything. It received the action—it was painted.)

A donation to the emergency fund was made by the people on the corner. (The *donation*, the subject, didn't do anything. It received the action—it was given.)

Notice what happens when you use the passive voice instead of the active:

active voice:
I painted the house.

passive voice:
The house was painted by me.

The sentence in the passive voice is two words longer than the one in the active voice. Yet the sentence that uses the passive voice does not say anything different, and it does not say it more clearly than the one in the active voice.

Using the passive voice can make your sentences wordy, it can slow them down, and it can make them boring. The passive voice can also confuse readers. When the subject of the sentence is not doing anything, readers may have to look carefully to see who or what *is* doing something. Look at this sentence, for example:

A decision to fire you was reached.

Who decided to fire you? In this sentence, it is hard to find the answer to that question.

Of course, there will be times when you have to use the passive voice. For example, you may have to use it when you do not know who did something, as in these sentences:

Our house was broken into last night.
A leather jacket was left behind in the classroom.

But in general, you should avoid using the passive voice and rewrite sentences so they are in the active voice.

Exercise 15 **Practice: Rewriting Sentences, Changing the Passive Voice to the Active Voice**

In the following sentences, change the passive voice to the active voice. If the original sentence does not tell you who or what performed the action, add words that tell who or what did it. An example is done for you.

example: Sandy Adams was appointed chief negotiator last night.

rewritten: The union leaders appointed Sandy Adams chief negotiator last night.

1. A twenty-two-year-old man from Idaho has been arrested and charged with the kidnapping of Kelly Romano.

rewritten: _____

_____

2. Questions are being asked about the missing funds at the health center.

rewritten: _____

_____

3. The true story of his mother's death was never told to Arthur.

   rewritten: His family never told Arther the true story of his mothers death.

4. Several paintings were donated to the museum by a wealthy woman.

   rewritten: _____

   _____

5. Once a month, the kindergarten class is entertained by a professional storyteller.

   rewritten: Once a month, a professional story teller entertained the kindergarden class.

6. Just before takeoff, an airline safety demonstration was conducted by a flight attendant.

   rewritten: _____

   _____

7. Due to the rising costs of energy, a slight increase in your cable bill has been instituted.

   rewritten: _____

   _____

8. Finally, the ringing phone was answered by the man behind the counter.

   rewritten: _____

   _____

9. Later today, a contract with an international music company will be signed by the popular performer.

   rewritten: _____

   _____

10. A search for the missing weapon was conducted last night.

    rewritten: _____

    _____

Avoiding Unnecessary Shifts in Voice

Just as you should be consistent in the tense of verbs, you should be consistent in the voice of verbs. Do not shift from active voice to passive voice, or vice versa, without some good reason to do so.

          active   passive

shift: *I designed* the decorations for the dance; *they were put up* by Chuck.

          active   active

rewritten: *I designed* the decorations for the dance; *Chuck put* them *up.*

passive active

shift: Many *problems were discussed* by the council members, but *they found* no easy answers.

active active

rewritten: The council *members discussed* many problems, but *they found* no easy answers.

Being consistent in voice can help you to write clearly and smoothly.

| Exercise 16 | **Practice: Rewriting Sentences to Correct Shifts in Voice**

Rewrite the sentences below so that all the verbs are in the active voice. You may change the wording to make the sentences clear, smooth, and consistent in voice.

1. I enjoyed the party until red wine was spilled all over my silk shirt.

   rewritten: _____

   _____

2. If a window was broken by my son, I never knew about the incident.

   rewritten: _____

   _____

3. Esther screamed with rage when she was called a liar.

   rewritten: _____

   _____

4. My uncle used to be a pilot; airplanes and airports are loved by him.

   rewritten: _____

   _____

5. Today a shy fisherman was honored by the city council; the fisherman had risked his life to save a drowning woman.

   rewritten: _____

   _____

6. The local roads were packed by frustrated drivers when flash floods closed two major highways.

   rewritten: _____

   _____

7. Because Paul is my old friend, he can be trusted by me.

   rewritten: _____

   _____

8. The county commissioners decided that every section of the budget will be cut next year.

   rewritten: _____

   _____

9. The schedule of summer classes is being posted online today; the college will also distribute paper copies of the schedule throughout the campus.

   rewritten: _____

   _____

10. The cousins wanted to surprise their grandfather with a fancy party, but specific plans for a party were never discussed.

   rewritten: _____

   _____

A Few Tips About Verbs

There are a few errors that people tend to make with verbs. If you are aware of these errors, you'll be on the lookout for them as you edit your writing.

Used to: Be careful when you write that someone *used to* do, say, or feel something. It is incorrect to write *use to.*

   not this: Janine ~~use to~~ visit her mother every week.
   They ~~use to~~ like Thai food.
   but this: Janine *used to* visit her mother every week.
   They *used to* like Thai food.

Could Have, Should Have, Would Have: Using *of* instead of *have* is another error with verbs.

   not this: I ~~could of~~ done better on the test.
   but this: I *could have* done better on the test.

   not this: He ~~should of~~ been paying attention.
   but this: He *should have* been paying attention.

   not this: The girls ~~would of~~ liked to visit Washington.
   but this: The girls *would have* liked to visit Washington.

Would Have/Had: If you are writing about something that might have been possible, but that did not happen, use *had* as the helping verb.

   not this: If I ~~would have~~ taken a foreign language in high school, I wouldn't have to take one now.
   but this: If I *had* taken a foreign language in high school, I wouldn't have to take one now.

   not this: I wish they ~~would have~~ won the game.
   but this: I wish they *had* won the game.

   not this: If she ~~would have~~ been smart, she would have called a plumber.
   but this: If she *had* been smart, she would have called a plumber.

Collaborate

Exercise 17 **Collaborate: Writing Sentences with the Correct Verb Forms**

Do this exercise with a partner or a group. Follow the directions to write or complete each sentence below.

1. Complete this sentence and add a verb in the correct tense: My dog had chewed my best pair of shoes before

   _____

   _____

2. Write a sentence that is more than eight words long and that uses the words *would have been happier* in the middle of the sentence.

   _____

   _____

3. Write a sentence that uses the past tense form of these words: *act* and *lose.*

   _____

   _____

4. Write a sentence in the passive voice.

   _____

   _____

5. Write a sentence in the active voice.

   _____

   _____

6. Write a sentence that uses *would have* and *had.*

   _____

   _____

7. Write a sentence that is more than six words long and that uses the words *had decided* and *before.*

   _____

   _____

8. Write a sentence of more than six words that uses the words *used to.*

   _____

   _____

9. Write a sentence that contains two verbs in the same tense.

   _____

   _____

10. Write a sentence that uses the words *should have.*

   _____

   _____

Exercise 18   **Connect: Editing a Paragraph for Errors in Verbs:**
Consistency, Tense, and Voice

Connect

Edit the following paragraph for errors in verb consistency, tense, or voice. There are six errors.

Noticing an attractive person in school can be an opportunity for making a new friend; on the other hand, it can lead to embarrassment. Whether you notice the interesting stranger in class, in the library, in the student center, or in the gym, certain rules must be observed. First, you must find a casual, carefree way to initiate a conversation. Cool dialogue or a cute line should not be attempted by you. A simple "How are you doing?" worked better. Second, don't assume that the stranger is open to meeting you. Many people are too shy to accept a smile and some friendly words from a stranger. However, if the interesting person does respond to your opening lines, you must go slowly. It was never wise to expect more than friendship. All these rules may seem discouraging to you, but one additional rule was more important than any of the others. The golden rule for meeting people is "If a chance isn't taken, you will never gain anything."

Exercise 19   **Connect: Editing a Paragraph for Errors in Verbs:**
Consistency, Tense, and Voice

Connect

Edit the following paragraph for errors in verb consistency, tense, or voice. There are six errors.

My great aunt Emma Paluska has a pretty glass bowl that is a piece of family history. The bowl comes from Poland. Only one factory near Warsaw made this type of bowl, and during World War II, the Nazis bombed the factory. The bowl has been in the family for years. If my Aunt Emma's mother would not have brought the bowl to America in 1937, it could of been destroyed by the bombing near the Paluska home. Generations of Paluskas have cherished this bowl. I remember the bowl from the big Saturday night dinners of years ago. We use to eat the contents of the bowl, fruits and nuts, for dessert. Today the bowl is displayed by my great aunt on special occasions. She fills it with glittery pine cones in the winter; in spring, flowers are put in the bowl. I hope that one day, the bowl will be passed on to me by my great aunt.

Section Test Verbs: Consistency and Voice

Some of the sentences below are correct; others have errors in verb consistency, correct tense, and voice. Put an *X* next to the sentences with errors.

1. _____ If I had checked the oil in my car, I would have been spared hundreds of dollars in car repairs and the misery of begging rides from family members.

2. _____ Hope for a better life came to the peasants of France and Spain when a treaty between the warring nations was signed.

3. _____ After the noise of the trucks at the dump site stopped, the workers can hear the the thunder approaching from the western part of the woods.

4. _____ Amanda worked at the preschool for two years; then she left for a position at Memorial Hospital where she has enjoyed her interactions with the physical therapy patients.

5. _____ My sister had been nagging me about my hair until I finally agreed to get it cut before her wedding.

6. _____ Two of my cats ate a special treat of leftover turkey but had refused a small portion of sweet potatoes.

7. _____ I had finished my homework after I had spent two hours procrastinating and playing games on my computer.

8. _____ My vacation in South Carolina was terrible; for three days, I have done nothing but sweat and swat buzzing mosquitoes away from every part of my body.

9. _____ Every year on Independence Day, my mother and father bring out all the lawn chairs, set the outdoor table with plastic dishes, filled the grill with chicken and ribs, and invite the neighbors to a celebration.

10. _____ You could have been more tactful when you thought of bringing your new girlfriend to your former girlfriend's birthday party.

Chapter Test Using Verbs Correctly: Standard Verb Forms, Irregular Verbs, Consistency, and Voice

Some of the sentences below use verbs correctly; other have errors in standard verb forms, irregular verbs, consistency, and voice. Put an *X* by each sentence with an error.

1. _____ My grandparents are wonderful; every weekend, they takes me out to dinner at my favorite diner.

2. _____ The air conditioner in my bedroom is working, but it do make a strange noise every time I turn it on.

3. _____ Nathan is my oldest friend; therefore, he should be introduced by me at the sports banquet.

4. _____ If I had known about the surprise party, I would have dressed better and washed my hair.

5. _____ For five months, Marcy has worked as a receptionist at a dentist's office; unfortunately, the dentist plans to close his office next month.

6. _____ Olivia stared at her reflection in the mirror and wondered whether she had chosen the right haircut.

7. _____ By the time Caleb was in his early twenties, his tendency to borrow money and never repay it had caused his brother and sister to avoid Caleb's desperate calls and woeful stories.

8. _____ I will ask my sister-in-law to take care of my dog over the weekend; she have done this chore for me before.

9. _____ Yesterday Bill took his daughter to the mall, helps her find a birthday gift for her cousin, and dropped her off at the birthday girl's sleepover party.

10. _____ The heavy rain had flooded the streets near the river by the time Jacob tried to drive home.

Making Subjects and Verbs Agree

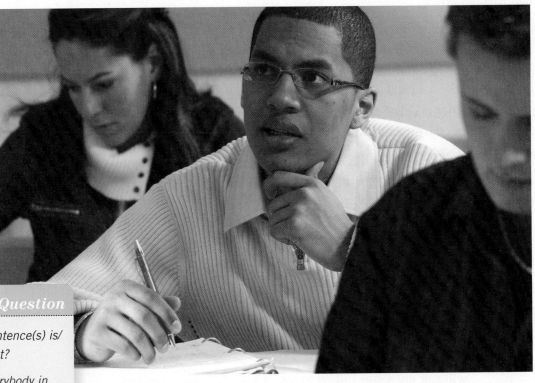

Quick Question

Which sentence(s) is/
are correct?

A. Everybody in
   the office needs
   a raise.
B. Either the
   manager or the
   owners need to
   find the money.

(After you study
this chapter, you will
feel confident of your
answer.)

Chapter Objectives

Students will be able to (1) identify correct subject–verb agreement and (2) recognize prepositional phrases, compound subjects, indefinite pronouns, and collective nouns.

SUBJECTS AND VERBS: SINGULAR VS. PLURAL

Subjects and verbs have to agree in number. That means a singular subject must be matched to a singular verb form; a plural subject must be matched to a plural verb form.

> **singular subject, singular verb:**
> My *sister walks* to work every morning.

> **plural subject, plural verb:**
> *Mary, David,* and *Sam believe* in ghosts.

> **singular subject, singular verb:**
> That *movie is* too violent for me.

> **plural subject, plural verb:**
> Bulky *packages are* difficult to carry.

Caution: Remember that a regular verb has an -*s* ending in only one singular form in the present tense—the form that goes with *he, she, it,* or their equivalents:

He *makes* me feel confident.
She *appreciates* intelligent conversation.
It *seems* like a good buy.
Bo *runs* every day.
That girl *swims* well.
The machine *breaks* down too often.

Exercise 1 **Practice: Subject–Verb Agreement: Selecting the Correct Verb Form**

Circle the correct form of the verb in each sentence.

1. My nephew (is, are) a natural athlete with a great future.

2. The camera sometimes (give, gives) a false impression of the size of a room.

3. My five-year-old son and my three-year-old daughter rarely (go, goes) out to eat.

4. That watch (cost, costs) more than you can afford.

5. By 10:00 P.M., the bar (smell, smells) like spilled beer.

6. People in the middle of a crisis may become startled when a phone (ring, rings).

7. Driving a hundred miles for a picnic (seem, seems) silly.

8. Constantly blaming others (appear, appears) to be John's way of avoiding responsibility.

9. If the television is on, Anna (complain, complains) that she can't concentrate on her homework.

10. After a bad day at work, you (need, needs) a quiet place to relax.

Exercise 2 **Connect: Correcting Errors in Subject–Verb Agreement in a Paragraph**

Connect

There are errors in subject–verb agreement in the paragraph below. If a verb does not agree with its subject, change the verb form. Cross out the incorrect verb form and write the correct one above. There are seven errors in agreement in the paragraph.

Malcolm always bring a present when he visits his mother. He does not have much money but manage to find an appropriate gift every time. Sometimes he arrives with a bunch of flowers or some fresh fruit from a nearby fruit stand. His mother love his thoughtfulness; it make her feel valued. Occasionally, she scolds him for spending money on her. In addition, when he arrives with a small box of chocolates, she say, "Malcolm, you are tempting me to get fat." However, he know

his mother too well to believe her complaints. She actually looks forward to his

small surprises. Besides, he, too, like to eat a little of the fruit or chocolate.

PRONOUNS AS SUBJECTS

Pronouns can be used as subjects. Pronouns are words that take the place of nouns. When pronouns are used as subjects, they must agree in number with verbs.

Here is a list of the subject pronouns and the regular verb forms that agree with them, in the present tense:

INFO BOX: Subjective Pronouns and a Present Tense Verb

pronoun	verb	
I	listen	
you	listen	all singular forms
he, she, it	listens	
we	listen	
you	listen	all plural forms
they	listen	

In all the sentences below, the pronoun used as the subject of the sentence agrees in number with the verb:

> **singular pronoun, singular verb:**
> *I make* the best omelet in town.

> **singular pronoun, singular verb:**
> *You dance* very well.

> **singular pronoun, singular verb:**
> *She performs* like a trained athlete.

> **plural pronoun, plural verb:**
> *We need* a new refrigerator.

> **plural pronoun, plural verb:**
> *They understand* the situation.

SPECIAL PROBLEMS WITH AGREEMENT

Agreement seems fairly simple: if a subject is singular, you use a singular verb form, and if a subject is plural, you use a plural verb form. However, there are special problems with agreement that will come up in your writing. Sometimes, it is hard to find the subject of a sentence; at other times, it is hard to determine if a subject is singular or plural.

Finding the Subject

When you are checking for subject–verb agreement, you can find the real subject of the sentence by first eliminating the prepositional phrases. To find the real subject, put parentheses around the prepositional phrases. Then it is easy to find the subject because nothing in a prepositional phrase is the subject of a sentence.

prepositional phrases in parentheses:

S   V
One (of my oldest friends) *is* a social worker.

     S   V
A *student* (from one)(of the nearby school districts) *is* the winner.

      S   V
The *store* (across the street) (from my house) *is* open all night.

   S   V
Jim, (with all his silly jokes), *is* a nice person.

Note: Words and phrases such as *along with, as well as, except, in addition to, including, plus,* and *together with* introduce prepositional phrases. The words that follow them are part of the prepositional phrase and cannot be part of the subject.

      S   V   V
My *sister*, (along with her husband), *is planning* a trip to Bolivia.

      S   V
Tom's *house*, (as well as his apartment), *is* part of a family
   inheritance.

Exercise 3 | **Practice: Finding the Real Subject by Recognizing Prepositional Phrases**

Put parentheses around all the prepositional phrases in the sentences below. Put an *S* above each subject and a *V* above each verb.

    S   ✓
1. Jealousy, in addition to lack of trust, threatens the stability

of a marriage.

2. Cristina, plus her mother-in-law, is visiting Venezuela over the

summer.

3. Without much thought, a loud customer made a cruel comment

on the server's appearance.

4. In the early morning, a tall man with a Great Dane jogs through

the park.

5. The truth behind the actors' brawl at the nightclub is a simple story of too much alcohol.

6. Yogurt, as well as low-fat cheese, is a good source of calcium in any diet.

7. My best friend from high school arrived a day early for the reunion.

8. A guest speaker from Children in Distress is coming to my psychology class on Tuesday.

9. Two of the men in the car are friends of Alicia's cousin.

10. The old house, including the yard and driveway, is in good condition.

Exercise 4 **Practice: Selecting the Correct Verb Form by Identifying Prepositional Phrases**

Put parentheses around all the prepositional phrases in the sentences below. Then circle the verb that agrees with the subject.

1. A motel with clean rooms, a small pool, and free breakfast (is, are) at the exit to Masonville.

2. Mr. Kelly's patience, in addition to his years of experience, (explain, explains) his popularity with students.

3. Gossiping about friends (is, are) a clear sign of a deficiency in loyalty.

4. One of the most handsome men in town (is, are) my best friend, Tyler.

5. Under suspicion of murder, the young man, together with his fiancée, (was, were) the subject of a police search.

6. The house with the blue shutters (has, have) been sold to a family from Missouri.

7. Tennis players at summer tournaments often (compete, competes) in dangerously hot weather.

8. One of the judges on the daytime television shows (go, goes) into a

   fit of anger during every episode.

9. Many of the tests, plus the regular quizzes, (seem, seems) designed

   for a higher-level mathematics class.

10. The dirty dishes on the kitchen table (need, needs) to be washed

    and dried before dinner time.

Changed Word Order

You are probably used to looking for the subject of a sentence in front of the verb, but not all sentences follow this pattern. Questions, sentences beginning with words like *here* or *there*, and other sentences change the word order. So you have to look carefully to check for subject–verb agreement.

>   **V**   **S**
> Where *are* my *friends?*
>   **V** **S** **V**
> When *is he going* to work?
>   **V**   **S**
> Behind the elm trees *stands* a huge *statue.*
>   **V**   **S**
> There *are potholes* in the road.
>   **V**   **S**
> There *is* a *reason* for his impatience.

| Exercise 5 | **Practice: Making Subjects and Verbs Agree in Sentences with Changed Word Order** |

In each of the sentences below, underline the subject; then circle the correct verb in parentheses.

1. Besides Scott's bad temper, there (is, **are**) his cruel and violent tendencies.

2. Across the courtyard in the Student Center (**is**, are) an area with concrete benches and tables.

3. Beneath the layers of dirt and grime (**was**, were) a beautiful marble bathtub in pale beige stone.

4. About an hour after dark, there (was, **were**) an ambulance with flashing lights and a police car in front of the house across the street.

5. Stuck in the small space between the refrigerator and the cabinet (was, **were**) the lost Super Bowl tickets.

6. On the walls of the waiting room at the dentist's office (**was**, were) a large collection of posters about dental hygiene.

7. Inside the flea market (is, are) an endless row of stalls with all kinds of merchandise from tee-shirts to ten-foot artificial plants.

8. After a few awkward moments, there (was, were) smiles and laughter among the guests at the singles-only party.

9. Where on Earth (is, are) your pack of emergency supplies?

10. Near the huge multiplex movie theater (is, are) an amusement park with rides and games for children.

COMPOUND SUBJECTS

A **compound subject** is two or more subjects joined by *and, or,* or *nor*.

When subjects are joined by *and,* they are usually plural.

    S   S   V
Jermaine and *Lisa are* bargain hunters.

      S   S   V
The *house* and the *garden need* attention.

   S   S   V
A *bakery* and a *pharmacy are* down the street.

> **Caution:** Be careful to check for a compound subject when the word order changes.

     V   S   S
There *are* a *bakery* and a *pharmacy* down the street. (Two things, a *bakery* and a *pharmacy, are* down the street.)

     V   S   S
Here *are* a *picture* of your father and a *copy* of his birth certificate. (A *picture* and a *copy,* two things, *are* here.)

When subjects are joined by *or, either . . . or, neither . . . nor, not only . . . but also,* the verb form agrees with the subject closer to the verb.

           singular S   plural S, plural V
Not only the restaurant *manager* but also the *waiters were* pleased with the new policy.

         plural S   singular S, singular V
Not only the *waiters* but also the restaurant *manager was* pleased with the new policy.

      plural S   singular S, singular V
Either the *parents* or the *boy walks* the dog every morning.

     singular S   plural S, plural V
Either the *boy* or the *parents walk* the dog every morning.

     plural S   singular S, singular V
Neither the *tenants* nor the *landlord cares* about the parking situation.

    singular S   plural S, plural V
Neither the *landlord* nor the *tenants care* about the parking situation.

Exercise 6   **Practice: Making Subjects and Verbs Agree: Compound Subjects**

Circle the correct form of the verb in parentheses in each sentence below.

1. Either the woman in the upstairs apartment or the men across the street (is, **are**) leaving garbage in the street.

2. Not only the fried chicken but also the vegetables (taste, **tastes**) homemade.

3. Neither the slipcovers on the sofa nor the huge pillow on the chair (hide, **hides**) the decrepit condition of the furniture.

4. Here (is, **are**) the baby's formula and his blanket.

5. There (**was**, were) a problem with the oil in my car and with a strange grinding sound in the engine.

6. After dinner, either my mother or my brother (clear, **clears**) the table while I do the dishes.

7. Anger and bitterness never (**solve**, solves) a problem.

8. Neither hot tea nor chicken soup (has, **have**) much effect when I get a bad cold.

9. In the middle of the night, there (come, **comes**) a time when my child wakes up crying.

10. When I have a stressful day, either a call to my girlfriend or an hour at the gym (help, helps) me relax.

INDEFINITE PRONOUNS

Certain pronouns that come from a group called **indefinite pronouns** always take a singular verb.

INFO BOX: Indefinite Pronouns

one	nobody	nothing	each
anyone	anybody	anything	either
someone	somebody	something	neither
everyone	everybody	everything	

If you want to write clearly and correctly, you must memorize these words and remember that they always take a singular verb. Using your common sense is not enough because some of these words seem plural: for example, *everybody* seems to mean more than one person, but in grammatically correct English, it takes a singular verb. Here are some examples of the pronouns used with singular verbs:

singular S   singular V

Everyone in town *is talking* about the scandal.

singular S   singular V

Each of the boys *is* talented.

singular S singular V
One of their biggest concerns *is* crime in the streets.

singular S singular V
Neither of the cats *is* mine.

> **Hint:** You can memorize the indefinite pronouns as the -*one*, -*thing*, and -*body* words (every*one*, every*thing*, every*body*, and so forth) plus *each*, *either*, and *neither*.

Exercise 7   Practice: Making Subjects and Verbs Agree: Using Indefinite Pronouns

Circle the correct verb in parentheses in each sentence below.

1. (Was/Were) anybody from school at the club on Friday night?

2. Either of the cell phones (cost, costs) too much for my budget.

3. (Is/Are) someone taking photographs during the ceremony?

4. Each of Mrs. Todd's painted bowls (has, have) a personal value.

5. Neither of the boys (has, have) ever given me any trouble.

6. In the coldest weather of the year, everyone in the Polar Bear Club (gather, gathers) at the icy lake for one quick swim.

7. Something about most romantic movies (bore, bores) me.

8. Beyond the chain-link fence there (was, were) nothing except some stunted trees and dusty weeds.

9. After the party, (was, were) anyone talking to Michelle?

10. Everyone in my night classes (seem, seems) much smarter than I am.

COLLECTIVE NOUNS

Collective nouns refer to more than one person or thing:

team	company	council
class	corporation	government
committee	family	group
audience	jury	crowd

Most of the time, collective nouns take a singular verb.

singular S   singular V
The *committee is sponsoring* a fundraiser.

singular S   singular V
The *audience was* impatient.

singular S, singular V
The *jury has reached* a verdict.

The singular verb is used because the group is sponsoring, or getting impatient, or reaching a verdict, *as one unit*.

Collective nouns take a plural verb only when the members of the group are acting individually, not as a unit.

> The sophomore *class are fighting* among themselves. (The phrase *among themselves* shows that the class is not acting as one unit.)

Exercise 8   Practice: Making Subjects and Verbs Agree: Using Collective Nouns

Circle the correct verb in parentheses in each sentence below.

1. The Green Corporation (give, gives) all its full-time employees ten vacation days.

2. The family from Nevada (is, are) looking for a house to rent for at least one year.

3. Some members of the jury (was, were) falling asleep in the late afternoon sessions.

4. My son's kindergarten class (sing, sings) songs at the start of each day.

5. The Merrill College Student Council (was, were) determined to raise the issue of student fees.

6. The most popular team in baseball history (is, are) deeply divided on the issue of steroid use.

7. Although rain delayed the outdoor concert, the crowd at the park (was, were) patient and cheerful.

8. When a movie is boring or slow, the audience (begin, begins) to talk among themselves.

9. Once a year, the motorcycle club (donate, donates) toys to children in hospitals and orphanages.

10. For years, the board of directors at the computer company (has, have) discussed the problem of overseas competition.

MAKING SUBJECTS AND VERBS AGREE: THE BOTTOM LINE

As you have probably realized, making subjects and verbs agree is not as simple as it first appears. But if you can remember the basic ideas in this section, you will be able to apply them automatically as you edit your own writing. Below is a quick summary of subject–verb agreement.

> **INFO BOX: Making Subjects and Verbs Agree: A Summary**
>
> 1. Subjects and verbs should agree in number: singular subjects get singular verb forms; plural subjects get plural verb forms.
>
> 2. When pronouns are used as subjects, they must agree in number with verbs.
>
> 3. Nothing in a prepositional phrase can be the subject of the sentence.
>
> 4. Questions, sentences beginning with *here* or *there,* and other sentences can change word order, making subjects harder to find.
>
> 5. Compound subjects joined by *and* are usually plural.
>
> 6. When subjects are joined by *or, either . . . or, neither . . . nor,* or *not only . . . but also,* the verb form agrees with the subject closest to the verb.
>
> 7. Indefinite pronouns always take singular verbs.
>
> 8. Collective nouns usually take singular verbs.

Exercise 9 **Practice: A Comprehensive Exercise on Subject–Verb Agreement**

Circle the correct verb form in parentheses in each sentence below.

1. Yesterday, there (was, were) a dining room table and four chairs on sale at Furniture Warehouse.

2. Around the back of the restaurant (is, are) a huge dumpster and a recycling bin.

3. Neither the child nor his parents (use, uses) the front porch very often because the house is on a busy street.

4. Before the wedding begins, someone (has, have) to direct the guests to the parking area.

5. When (was, were) your brothers planning to visit?

6. Everything in Jackie's room (seem, seems) dusty and grimy.

7. Every time I get home after 9:00 P.M., someone (has, have) taken my parking space.

8. Either of my sisters (is, are) capable of handling a family emergency.

9. Aaron Manelli, as well as Josh Hines, (bowl, bowls) in a league for hospital employees.

10. Neither my dogs nor my cat (like, likes) the sound of thunder very much.

Collaborate

Exercise 10 **Collaborate: Writing Sentences with Subject–Verb Agreement**

With a partner or a group, turn each of the following phrases into a sentence—twice. That is, write two sentences for each phrase. Use a verb that fits, and put the verb in the present tense. Be sure that the verb agrees with the subject.

1. A large bag of rocks _____

_____

A large bag of rocks _____

_____

2. Either cake or ice cream _____

_____

Either cake or ice cream _____

_____

3. The company _____

_____

The company _____

_____

4. Mickey and Minnie _____

_____

Mickey and Minnie _____

_____

5. Everything on the menu _____

_____

Everything on the menu _____

_____

6. Someone on the Safe City Council _____

_____

Someone on the Safe City Council _____

_____

7. Not only my friends but also my brother _____

_____

Not only my friends but also my brother _____

_____

8. Anybody from this state _____

_____

Anybody from this state _____

_____

9. One of children's greatest fears _____

_____

One of children's greatest fears _____

_____

10. Neither broccoli nor other green vegetables _____

_____

Neither broccoli nor other green vegetables _____

_____

| **Exercise 11** | **Collaborate: Create Your Own Text on Subject-Verb Agreement** |

Collaborate

Working with a partner or a group, create your own grammar handbook. Below is a list of rules on subject–verb agreement. Write one sentence that is an example of each rule. The first one is done for you.

Rule 1: Subjects and verbs should agree in number: singular subjects get singular verb forms; plural subjects get plural verb forms.

example: _____

_____

Rule 2: When pronouns are used as subjects, they must agree in number with verbs.

example: _____

_____

Rule 3: Nothing in a prepositional phrase can be the subject of the sentence.

example: _____

_____

Rule 4: Questions, sentences beginning with _here_ or _there_, and other sentences can change word order, making subjects harder to find.

example: _____

_____

Rule 5: When subjects are joined by _and_, they are usually plural.

example: _____

_____

Rule 6: When subjects are joined by _or, either . . . or, neither . . . nor,_ or _not only . . . but also,_ the verb form agrees with the subject closest to the verb.

example: _____

_____

Rule 7: Indefinite pronouns always take singular verbs.

example: _____

_____

Rule 8: Collective nouns usually take singular verbs.

example: _____

_____

Connect

Exercise 12 **Connect: Editing a Paragraph for Errors in Subject–Verb Agreement**

Edit the following paragraph by correcting any verbs that do not agree with their subjects. Write your corrections above the lines. There are seven errors.

There is either thoughtlessness or cruelty in hurting someone's feelings. Spite, jealousy, and anger often prompt a person to lash out at another. Such behavior is deliberate and open. Children, who are less skilled in handling their emotions than adults are, can be cruel to another child. There is times when one four-year-old may call another "stupid" or "disgusting" while both children plays a game on the street. The speaker is simply venting his or her rage and soon forgets, but the victim shamed in front of other children may not forget. Adult cruelty are more sophisticated. This cruelty can be the critical remark a boss make to an employee or the constant sarcasm of a wife speaking to her husband. Habitual cruelty often turns into thoughtless cruelty. When one person constantly belittles another, the victim suffer with every repetition of the meanness, but the attacker feels very little. Another kind of thoughtless cruelty is the assignment of a nickname. A man often cringes for years because some childhood "buddies" was too eager to call him "Moose" or "Skinny," and the nickname stuck. Although adults may try to laugh about their nicknames, neither the intentionally cruel names or a thoughtlessly assigned name is a person's choice. In all stages of life, people need to show a little kindness and restraint. Not only the child on the playground but also adults in all their interactions deserves some of that kindness.

Connect

Exercise 13   **Connect: Editing a Paragraph for Errors in Subject–Verb Agreement**

Edit the following paragraph by correcting any verbs that do not agree with their subjects. Write your corrections above the lines. There are seven errors.

Marlene, my friend from the Bahamas, have a strange but charming accent. She has a type of rhythm in her speech. Neither the music of the Caribbean nor the rhythm of Latin music sound like her voice. When she talk, I can understand almost every word, but some words and phrases is pronounced strangely. For example, she say "man," but it sounds like "mon." Her voice travels up and down more than mine do. In every part of the world, people speak a variety of languages, but she and I speaks the same language in different ways. I can think of only one way to describe her accent. It sounds like the voice on an old television commercial asking viewers to visit the Bahamas Islands. When the television speaker says, "It's better in the Bahamas," she has Marlene's voice.

Chapter Test Making Subjects and Verbs Agree

Some of the sentences below are correct; others have errors in making subjects and verbs agree. Put an *X* next to the sentences with errors.

1. _____ After the Safety Committee approves the new street signs, the signs will be placed in the school zones at the two elementary schools and the middle school.

2. _____ Everybody on the three highest floors of the skyscraper gets a wonderful view of Central Park.

3. _____ There is a certain taste and a special texture in the cornbread from Ed's Barbecue Hut in Asheville, North Carolina.

4. _____ Neither a long day at work nor a long ride to our home in the suburbs keeps my father from maintaining a positive attitude.

5. _____ Something about seeing my son in a school play make me want to smile and cry at the same time.

6. _____ We need a television stand for our new television, and the stand on sale at Electric Bargains seem like a good deal.

7. _____ At the end of the dirt road in the dilapidated part of town was an old barn and a broken-down gate to the nearby pasture.

8. _____ Your concern about the price of car insurance make me worry about your ability to handle the costs of driving and maintaining your own car.

9. _____ Not only my two brothers but also my father has severe allergies to pollen and dust.

10. _____ What is the real causes of this massive forest fire?

Using Pronouns Correctly: Agreement and Reference

CHAPTER 25

Quick Question

Is the following sentence correct?
Yes No

No one eats at the Homewood Grill anymore because they stopped serving bargain dinners.

(After you study this chapter, you will be confident of your answer.)

Chapter Objectives

Students will be able to (1) recognize proper pronoun case, (2) identify pronoun antecedents, indefinite pronouns, and collective nouns, and (3) correct errors in pronoun and agreement and reference.

NOUNS AND PRONOUNS

Nouns are the names of persons, places, or things.

Jack is a good friend. (*Jack* is the name of a person.)
The band is from *Orlando*. (*Orlando* is the name of a place.)
I hated the *movie*. (*Movie* is the name of a thing.)

Pronouns are words that substitute for nouns. A pronoun's **antecedent** is the word or word it replaces.

antecedent   pronoun
Jack is a good friend; *he* is very loyal.

antecedent   pronoun
I hated *the movie* because *it* was too violent.

antecedent   pronoun

Playing tennis was fun, but *it* started to take up too much of my time.

antecedent   pronoun

Mike and Michelle are sure *they* are in love.

antecedent   pronoun

Sharon gave away *her* old clothes.

antecedent   pronoun

The dog rattled *its* dish, begging for dinner.

Exercise 1   **Practice: Identifying the Antecedents of Pronouns**

Underline the word or words that are the antecedent of the italicized pronoun in each sentence below.

1. A short walk is healthy for workers because *it* takes them away from the workplace and relieves stress.

2. Your brother called me yesterday; *he* seemed a little depressed.

3. Camille looked at two used cars this afternoon; *they* were overpriced and unattractive.

4. My husband loves sushi, but I refuse to eat *it*.

5. The baby can't go outside without *his* down jacket.

6. The television show lost *its* special charm a few episodes ago.

7. Luis, do *you* need a ride to work?

8. The parrots have finally ended *their* conversation.

9. Meeting new people is difficult for me; *it* seems like a scary job interview.

10. Your father and I will talk about moving to Maryland after *we* visit Baltimore.

AGREEMENT OF A PRONOUN AND ITS ANTECEDENT

A pronoun must agree in number with its antecedent. If the antecedent is singular; the pronoun must be singular. If the antecedent is plural, then the pronoun must be plural.

singular antecedent   singular pronoun

Susan tried to arrive on time, but *she* got caught in traffic.

plural antecedent   plural pronoun

Susan and Ray tried to arrive on time, but *they* got caught in traffic.

plural antecedent   plural pronoun

The visitors tried to arrive on time, but *they* got caught in traffic.

Agreement of pronoun and antecedent seems fairly simple. If an antecedent is singular, use a singular pronoun. If an antecedent is plural, use a plural pronoun. There are, however, some special problems with agreement of pronouns, and these problems will come up in your writing. If you become familiar with the explanations, examples, and exercises that follow, you will be ready to handle the special problems.

INDEFINITE PRONOUNS

Certain words called **indefinite pronouns** always take a singular verb. Therefore, if one of these indefinite pronouns is the antecedent, the pronoun that replaces it must be singular. Here are the indefinite pronouns:

INFO BOX: Indefinite Pronouns

one	nobody	nothing	each
anyone	anybody	anything	either
someone	somebody	something	neither
everyone	everybody	everything	

You may think that *everybody* is plural, but in grammatically correct English, it is a singular word. Therefore, if you want to write clearly and correctly, memorize these words as the *-one*, *-thing*, and *-body* words: every*one*, every*thing*, every*body*, and so on, plus *each*, *either*, and *neither*. If any of these words is an antecedent, the pronoun that refers to it is singular.

singular antecedent   **singular pronoun**
Each of the Boy Scouts received *his* merit badge.
singular antecedent   **singular pronoun**
Everyone in the sorority donated *her* time to the project.

Avoiding Gender Bias

Consider this sentence:

Everybody in the math class brought _____ own calculator.

How do you choose the correct pronoun to fill in the blank? If everybody in the class is male, you can write:

Everybody in the math class brought *his* own calculator.

Or if everybody in the class is female, you can write:

Everybody in the math class brought *her* own calculator.

Or if the class has students of both genders, you can write:

Everybody in the math class brought *his or her* own calculator.

In the past, most writers used the pronoun *his* to refer to both men and women. Today, many writers try to use *his or her* to avoid gender bias. If you find using *his or her* is getting awkward or repetitive, you can rewrite the sentence and make the antecedent plural:

correct: *The students* in the math class brought *their* own calculators.

But you cannot shift from singular to plural:

incorrect: ~~Everybody in the math class brought their own calculators.~~

Exercise 2 **Practice: Making Pronouns and Antecedents Agree**

Write the appropriate pronoun in the blank in each sentence below. Look carefully for the antecedent before you choose the pronoun.

1. During the men's semifinals, one of the tennis players seemed to lose _his_ confidence as the match went into its final minutes.

2. Everyone in the Women's Sculptors Association hopes to exhibit _her_ best work at the Richardson Museum.

3. When the first snow falls, Chet and Nelson strap _their_ skis on the car and head for the mountains.

4. One of the windows was so filthy that _it_ was mistaken for a wall.

5. All the dogs learned to beg for _their_ after-dinner treats.

6. Once I visited the tiny set of a popular television comedy, everything about the show lost _its_ glamour.

7. Yesterday, somebody on the girls' gymnastics team left _her_ gym bag in the practice area.

8. Nothing in Andrea's closet looked as if _it_ had ever been worn.

9. When Stephen is hungry, you can feed him anything, and he will eat _it_.

10. Either of the singer's former husbands could have sold _his_ personal stories about her to the media.

Singular

COLLECTIVE NOUNS

Collective nouns refer to more than one person or thing:

team	company	council
class	corporation	government
committee	family	group
audience	jury	crowd

Most of the time, collective nouns take a singular pronoun.

    collective noun   **singular pronoun**
The *team* that was ahead in the playoffs lost *its* home game.

    collective noun   **singular pronoun**
The *corporation* changed *its* policy on parental leave.

Collective nouns are usually singular because the group is losing a game or changing a policy as one, as a unit. Collective nouns take a plural pronoun only when the members of the group are acting individually, not as a unit.

    The *class* picked up *their* class rings this morning. (The members of the class pick up their rings individually.)

Exercise 3 **Practice: Making Pronouns and Antecedents Agree: Collective Nouns**

Circle the correct pronoun in each sentence below.

1. The commissioners at the Sprucedale City Council gave (its, their) approval to the construction of a new teen center.

2. A gang of my brother's army buddies met for (its, their) annual picnic at Still Waters Park.

3. Before the court adjourned for the day, the judge gave the jury (its, their) directions.

4. A family from China opened (its, their) second furniture company in Baton Rouge.

5. After the club meets, one of (its, their) members always suggests adjourning to a nearby restaurant.

6. Marilyn no longer orders movies from the Film Net company because of (its, their) poor delivery record.

7. Several of the drawing and design classes held (its, their) last class meeting outdoors because of the beautiful spring weather.

8. The retreating army disintegrated when the difficult journey caused the leaders to fight among (itself, themselves).

9. After waiting ninety minutes for the star of the show to appear, the audience lost (its, their) patience.

10. Because of the recent scandals about contaminated food, the global corporation has changed (its, their) inspection procedures.

Exercise 4 **Collaborate: Writing Sentences with Pronoun–Antecedent Agreement**

Collaborate

With a partner or a group, write a sentence for each pair of words below, using each pair as a pronoun and its antecedent. The first pair is done for you.

1. women . . . their

   sentence: Women who work outside the home have to plan their time

   carefully.

2. family . . . its

   sentence: _____

   _____

3. anybody . . . his or her

   sentence: _____

   _____

4. drivers . . . they

   sentence: _____

   _____

5. security . . . it

sentence: _____

_____

6. either . . . her

sentence: _____

_____

7. everybody . . . his or her

sentence: _____

_____

8. America . . . it

sentence: _____

_____

9. music videos . . . they

sentence: _____

_____

10. Identity theft . . . it

sentence: _____

_____

Connect

Exercise 5 **Connect: Editing a Paragraph for Errors in Pronoun–Antecedent Agreement**

Read the following paragraph carefully, looking for errors in agreement of pronouns and their antecedents. Cross out each pronoun that does not agree with its antecedent and write the correct pronoun above it. Six pronouns need correcting.

My job at the reception desk at Millennium General Hospital can be challenging. My work is stressful when the hospital is busy. During visiting hours, I have to be helpful, cheerful, and alert because many people are in the hospital for the first time and don't know the layout of the place. They get anxious when they are faced with too many signs and hallways. In addition, each visitor is worrying about their loved one, sick and alone in a hospital bed. When the hospital is busy, time goes quickly for me. When visiting hours are over and nobody is with their family, time drags on. For example, in the quiet hours of the holidays, when patients want to be back in his or her homes, the staff works extra hard to cheer up patients and visitors. Fortunately, special events brighten up the atmosphere.

Sometimes everyone in a local club visits the wards and does their best to entertain the staff, patients, and visitors in the hospital. At other times, the Steely Corporation, which owns Millennium General, brings a little brightness to their patients and staff. It lights up the corridors with bright lights, plays holiday music, and even brings clowns to the lounges. On Independence Day, the corporation has been known to celebrate by offering a small fireworks display on their front lawn.

Connect

| **Exercise 6** | **Connect: Editing a Paragraph for Errors in Pronoun–
Antecedent Agreement** |

Read the following paragraph carefully, looking for errors in agreement of pronouns and their antecedents. Cross out each pronoun that does not agree with its antecedent and write the correct pronoun above it. There are five pronouns that need correcting.

My two close friends, Bradley and Briana, are funny and supportive. In middle school, Bradley used to make faces at me. At other times, when the teacher had her back turned to the class, Bradley would make strange noises, and everybody in the room had to stifle their laughter. The class enjoyed their moment of fun, and Bradley liked playing the class clown. Briana is funny, but most of the time she doesn't intend to be funny. She makes people laugh because she is so trusting. She is always ready to believe someone when he or she tells her the most obvious fibs. For example, anyone can tell her a ridiculous story about their encounter with the Abominable Snowman, and she will accept the story as real. Then she is astonished to hear the truth: nobody can prove their so-called encounters are real, I say. Instead of becoming angry at being tricked, she just laughs at herself. Briana finds humor in her own foolishness, and Bradley makes others laugh when he deliberately acts silly. We have laughed together, but we have also shared some tough times. Both of my friends gave me their true loyalty in those times. I think of Bradley as my brother and Briana as my little sister. Neither of them would ever break their bond with me.

PRONOUNS AND THEIR ANTECEDENTS: BEING CLEAR

Remember that pronouns are words that replace or refer to other words, and the words that are replaced or referred to are antecedents.

Make sure that a pronoun has one clear antecedent. Your writing will be vague and confusing if a pronoun appears to refer to more than one antecedent or if it doesn't have any specific antecedent to refer to. In grammar, such confusing language is called a problem with *reference of pronouns*.

When a pronoun refers to more than one thing, the sentence becomes confusing or silly. The following are examples of unclear reference:

> Jim told Leonard his bike had been stolen. (Whose bike was stolen? Jim's? Leonard's?)

> She put the cake on the table, took off her apron, pulled up a chair, and began to eat it. (What did she eat? The cake? The table? Her apron? The chair?)

If there is no one clear antecedent, you must rewrite the sentence to make the reference clear. Sometimes the rewritten sentence may seem repetitive, but a little repetition is better than a lot of confusion.

> **unclear:** Jim told Leonard his bike had been stolen.
> **clear:** Jim told Leonard Jim's bike had been stolen.
> **clear:** Jim told Leonard, "My bike has been stolen."
> **clear:** Jim told Leonard that Leonard's bike had been stolen.
> **clear:** Jim told Leonard, "Your bike has been stolen."

> **unclear:** She put the cake on the table, took off her apron, pulled up a chair, and began to eat it.
> **clear:** She put the cake on the table, took off her apron, pulled up a chair, and began to eat the cake.

Sometimes the problem is a little more tricky. Can you spot what's wrong with this sentence?

> **unclear:** Bill decided to take a part-time job, which worried his parents. (What worried Bill's parents? His decision to work part time? Or the job itself?)

Be very careful with the pronoun *which*. If there is any chance that using *which* will confuse the reader, rewrite the sentence and get rid of *which*.

> **clear:** Bill's parents were worried about the kind of part-time job he chose.
> **clear:** Bill's decision to work part time worried his parents.

Sometimes, a pronoun has nothing to refer to; it has no antecedent.

> **no antecedent:** When Bill got to the train station, they said the train was going to be late. (Who said the train was going to be late? The ticket agents? Strangers Bill met on the tracks?)
> **no antecedent:** Maria has always loved medicine and has decided that's what she wants to be. (What does "that" refer to? The only word it could refer to is "medicine," but Maria certainly doesn't want to be a medicine. She doesn't want to be an aspirin or a cough drop.)

If a pronoun lacks an antecedent, add an antecedent or get rid of the pronoun.

add an antecedent: When Bill got to the train station and asked the ticket agents about the schedule, they said the train was going to be late. ("They" refers to the ticket agents.)

drop the pronoun: Maria has always loved medicine and has decided she wants to be a physician.

> **Note:** To check for clear reference of pronouns, underline any pronoun that may not be clear. Then try to draw a line from that pronoun to its antecedent. Are there two or more possible antecedents? Is there no antecedent? In either case, you need to rewrite.

Exercise 7 Practice: Rewriting Sentences for Clear Reference of Pronouns

Rewrite the following sentences so that the pronouns have clear references. You may add, take out, or change words.

1. Leonard took his mother to a violent movie, which was stupid.

2. Years ago, they believed that black cats were a sign of bad luck.

3. The heavy bowl fell on the tile floor, and it cracked.

4. Laura told her best friend Celia that she worried too much.

5. I'm glad I didn't go to Emerson High School because they're all snobs and phonies.

6. My brother has always been fascinated by space flight, and that's what he dreams of being.

7. Most of the conflicts between teenagers and their parents occur because they always think age makes people wiser.

8. Searching in his grandparents' attic, Tyler found some old love letters which shocked him.

9. When we go to lunch at Sun Ray, they always offer a daily special.

10. Brian discussed his bad temper with Marco.

Exercise 8 Connect: Editing a Paragraph for Errors in Pronoun Agreement and Reference

Connect

Correct any errors in pronoun agreement or reference in the following paragraph. There are six errors. Write your corrections above the line.

My family doesn't fly often, and after fifteen years of traveling solely by car,

my sister, her children, and I found many changes when we decided to fly again.

The rules for passenger security are dramatically different. They have designed a new and long process for keeping passengers safe. Although I had heard about some of the new precautions, nobody in my family was ready for their long wait in the check-in area. The process of removing our shoes, offering our carry-on luggage for inspection, and enduring the other parts of the inspection was a little intimidating for us. When we finally boarded a plane packed with passengers, we struggled to find their seats. I soon wondered whether the space in the aircraft had shrunk or I had gained weight. I tried to shove one of my legs under the seat in front of me but ended up bumping it. Looking around at the other passengers, I realized I was not alone in my misery. Nobody in any of the seats had enough room to stretch their legs. By the time the plane had arrived at our destination, I had reached a conclusion. All of today's passengers must realize that nothing about his or her flights, from check-in to arrival, will ever again be easy or quick.

Connect

Exercise 9 Connect: Editing a Paragraph for Errors in Pronoun Agreement and Reference

Correct any errors in pronoun agreement or reference in the following paragraph. There are six errors. Write your corrections above the line.

Anyone with a strong will and enough motivation can change their attitude from negative to positive. I am living proof of this statement. Each day I used to focus on what could go wrong, which made me constantly anxious. I was also terribly self-conscious. Every time I entered a room or spoke in public, I was extremely nervous. I imagined everyone looking at me with their attention focused on my flaw. Each member of my family tried their best to brighten my moods and boost my confidence, but their efforts couldn't help. Fortunately, I signed up for a class in psychology and it led me to an important discovery. About halfway through the term, the assigned readings and class lectures helped me to realize that I was suffering from depression. I decided to do something about it. I began to see a counselor, and I am now learning to think of myself and my future in a new way. I am ready to focus on hope, not fear.

Chapter Test **Using Pronouns Correctly: Agreement and Reference**

Some of the sentences below are correct; others have errors in pronoun agreement or reference. Put an *X* next to the sentences with errors.

1. _____ When Brendan came home, Colton announced that his dog had chewed up a leather sandal.

2. _____ I want to go to the University of Springfield because their business school has an excellent reputation for placing recent graduates in good jobs.

3. _____ Everyone in my old neighborhood wanted to sell their home before major road construction started nearby.

4. _____ Graham had always had a dream of musical stardom, which made him special.

5. _____ We desperately wanted the local football team to win, but it was no match for the opponents from out of town.

6. _____ After the argument, either of my sisters could have offered their apologies, but the feud continued for months.

7. _____ I have bright red hair, and I get angry when they call me "Carrot Top" or "Crazy Redhead."

8. _____ After dinner, somebody took the leftover cookies from the kitchen counter and put them in his or her pocket.

9. _____ A few people in the audience began to complain because their seats were extremely far from the stage.

10. _____ Dave grabbed a large hoagie roll, several slices of cheese, a chunk of leftover ham, a jar of mustard and one of mayonnaise, put the food on the counter, and began to make an enormous sandwich.

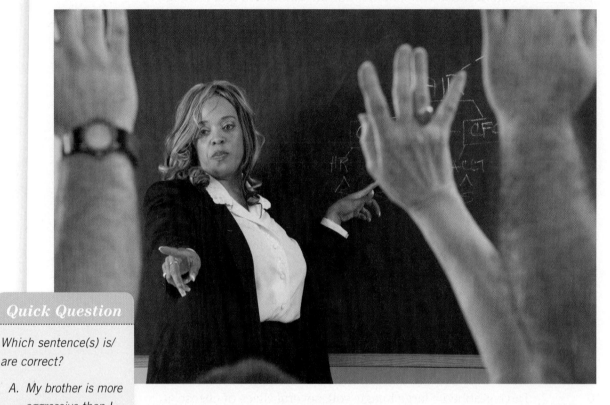

CHAPTER 26 Using Pronouns Correctly: Consistency and Case

Quick Question

Which sentence(s) is/ are correct?

A. My brother is more aggressive than I.

B. You have to keep this story a secret between you and me.

(After you study this chapter, you will be confident of your answer.)

Chapter Objectives

Students will be able to (1) recognize first-, second-, and third-person points of view, (2) correct errors in pronoun inconsistency, and (3) use appropriate pronoun cases in their writing.

POINTS OF VIEW AND PRONOUN CONSISTENCY

When you write, you write from a point of view, and each point of view gets its own form. If you write from the first-person point of view, your pronouns are in the *I* (singular) or *we* (plural) forms. If you write from the second-person point of view, your pronouns are in the *you* form, whether they are singular or plural. If you write from the third-person point of view, your pronouns are in the *he*, *she*, or *it* (singular) or *they* (plural) forms.

Different kinds of writing may require different points of view. When you are writing a set of directions, for example, you may use the second-person (*you*) point of view. An essay about your childhood may use the first-person (*I*) point of view.

Whatever point of view you use, be consistent in using pronouns. That is, do not shift the form of your pronouns without some good reason.

not consistent: Every time *I* go to that mall, the parking lot is so crowded *you* have to drive around for hours, looking for a parking space.

consistent: Every time *I* go to that mall, the parking lot is so crowded *I* have to drive around for hours, looking for a parking space.

Exercise 1 **Practice: Consistency in Pronouns**

Correct any inconsistency in point of view in the sentences below. Cross out the incorrect pronoun and write the correct one above it.

1. Taking a long nap doesn't work well for me; you can wake up feeling more tired than ever.

2. After the arriving airline passengers stare at the empty revolving luggage carousel for ten or twenty minutes, a long stream of luggage rolls slowly before you.

3. My favorite aunt is the kind of relative who praises the smallest success you achieve.

4. Drivers on the interstate highways need to be careful about entering the road; you have to be sure to gather enough speed to merge into traffic.

5. Hallie and I like to shop at the Dollar Bargain Bin because you can always find cheap cosmetics or jewelry there.

6. Sometimes I don't return Joe's calls, for once I start talking to him, he keeps you on the phone for hours.

7. My boyfriend and I like camping near Lake Lion, but you have to be prepared for hordes of mosquitoes in the summer.

8. Whenever I take the time to eat breakfast, I realize how a decent breakfast can give you the energy to face a long day.

9. When I learned English at night school, the instructor was always patient with you and gave me confidence in my abilities.

10. After one meeting with Tom, I believed he was a man who would always be honest with you and would invest my money carefully.

Exercise 2 **Practice: Correcting Sentences with Consistency Problems**

Rewrite the following sentences, correcting any errors with consistency of pronouns. To make the corrections, you may have to change, add, or take out words.

1. Unless a teenager is strong enough to resist peer pressure and smart enough to recognize true friends, you will not have an easy trip to adulthood.

   rewrite: _____

   _____

2. Pierre becomes aware of his mother's sadness whenever she tells you about her childhood in Haiti.

   rewrite: _____

   _____

3. Children attending Middlebrook Elementary School this fall must bring your certificate of vaccination before they are admitted to class.

   rewrite: _____

   _____

4. Laura and I cannot trust her cousin Miranda; if you tell her a secret, she reveals it to the whole neighborhood.

   rewrite: _____

   _____

5. Students who have never used the college library should not be nervous because, after their library tour, you will discover that everything is easy to find.

   rewrite: _____

   _____

6. My seven-year-old likes the first day of school; he likes seeing his old school friends, wearing your new school clothes, and showing off his superiority to the scared kindergartners.

   rewrite: _____

   _____

   _____

7. Some people can make friends easily because you know how to listen and are genuinely interested in others.

   rewrite: _____

   _____

8. To me, Mrs. Carmichael is a strict teacher; you can give her a million excuses, but she will never let me out of class early.

   rewrite: _____

   _____

9. I can't let Cade go outside by himself anymore; since he learned to open the gate, you can't trust him to stay in the yard.

   rewrite: _____

   _____

10. If a man wants a woman to admire him, you shouldn't brag about his money, status, or popularity with the ladies.

    rewrite: _____

    _____

CHOOSING THE CASE OF PRONOUNS

Pronouns have forms that show number and person, and they also have forms that show **case.**

Singular Pronouns	Subjective Case	Objective Case	Possessive Case
1st person	I	me	my
2nd person	you	you	your
3rd person	he, she, it	him, her, it	his, her, its
	who, whoever	whom, whomever	whose

(handwritten left margin: speaker / spoken2 / spoken about)

Plural Pronouns			
1st person	we	us	our
2nd person	you	you	your
3rd person	they	them	their
	who, whoever	whom, whomever	whose

The rules for choosing the case of pronouns are simple:

1. When a pronoun is used as a subject, use the subjective case.
2. When a pronoun is used as the object of a verb or the object of a preposition, use the objective case.
3. When a pronoun is used to show ownership, use the possessive case.

   pronouns used as subjects:
   He practices his pitching every day.
   Bill painted the walls, and *we* polished the floors.
   Who is making that noise?

   pronouns used as objects:
   Sarah called *him* yesterday.
   He gave all his money to *me.*
   With *whom* did you argue?

   pronouns used to show possession:
   I am worried about *my* grade in Spanish.
   The nightclub has lost *its* popularity.
   I wonder *whose* dog this is.

Pronoun Case in a Related Group of Words

You need to be careful in choosing case when the pronoun is part of a related group of words. If the pronoun is part of a related group of words, isolate the pronoun. Next, try out the pronoun choices. Then decide which pronoun is correct and write the correct sentence. For example, which of these sentences is correct?

Aunt Sophie planned a big dinner for Tom and *I*.

or

Aunt Sophie planned a big dinner for Tom and *me*.

Step 1: Isolate the pronoun. Eliminate the related words *Tom and*.

Step 2: Try each case:

Aunt Sophie planned a big dinner for *I*.

or

Aunt Sophie planned a big dinner for *me*.

Step 3: The correct sentence is

Aunt Sophie planned a big dinner for Tom and me.

The pronoun acts as an object, so it takes the objective case.

Try working through the steps once more to be sure that you understand this principle. Which of the following sentences is correct?

Last week, *me* and my friend took a ride on the new commuter train.

or

Last week, *I* and my friend took a ride on the new commuter train.

Step 1: Isolate the pronoun. Eliminate the related words *and my friend*.

Step 2: Try each case:

Last week, *me* took a ride on the new commuter train.

or

Last week, *I* took a ride on the new commuter train.

Step 3: The correct sentence is

Last week, I and my friend took a ride on the new commuter train.

The pronoun acts as a subject, so it takes the subjective case.

> **Note:** You can also write it this way:
> Last week my friend and I took a ride on the new commuter train.

COMMON ERRORS WITH CASE OF PRONOUNS

Be careful to avoid these common errors:

1. *Between* is a preposition, so the pronouns that follow it are objects of the preposition: between *us*, between *them*, between *you and me*. It is never correct to write *between you and I*.

   not this: ~~The plans for the surprise party must be kept a secret between you and I.~~
   but this: The plans for the surprise party must be kept a secret between you and me.

2. Never use *myself* as a replacement for *I* or *me*.

   not this: ~~My father and myself want to thank you for this honor.~~
   but this: My father and I want to thank you for this honor.

   not this: ~~She thought the prize should be awarded to Arthur and myself.~~
   but this: She thought the prize should be awarded to Arthur and me.

3. The possessive pronoun *its* has no apostrophe.

   not this: ~~The car held it's value.~~
   but this: The car held its value.

   not this: ~~The baby bird had fallen from it's nest.~~
   but this: The baby bird had fallen from its nest.

4. Pronouns that complete comparisons can be in the subjective, objective, or possessive case.

   subjective: Christa speaks better than *I*.
   objective: The storm hurt Manny more than *her*.
   possessive: My car is as fast as *his*.

   > **Note:** To decide on the correct pronoun, add the words that complete the comparison and say them aloud:

   Christa speaks better than I *speak*.
   The storm hurt Manny more than *the storm hurt* her.
   My car is as fast as his *car*.

5. *Who* and *whoever* are in the subjective case. *Whom* and *whomever* are in the objective case.

   subjective: *Who* came to the house?
   subjective: *Whoever* wants the books can take them.
   objective: *Whom* did Larry bring to the house?
   objective: You can bring *whomever* you like to the house.

   > **Note:** If you have trouble choosing between *who* and *whom*, or *whoever* and *whomever*, substitute *he* for *who* and *whoever*, and *him* for *whom* and *whomever* to check the correctness of your choice.

Check this sentence:

> *Who* made the cake?

Is it correct? Change the sentence, substituting *he* in one version, and *him* in another version.

> *He* made the cake.
> *Him* made the cake.

If *he* is correct, then *who* is correct.
Check another sentence:

> With *whom* are you arguing?

Is it correct? Change the sentence, substituting *he* in one version, and *him* in another version. To make your choice simpler, write the sentence as a statement, not a question:

> You are arguing with *he*.
> You are arguing with *him*.

If *him* is correct, then *whom* is correct.

Exercise 3 Practice: Choosing the Right Case of Pronoun

Circle the correct pronoun in parentheses in each of the following sentences.

1. (She, Her) and Mr. Bergman were married in Austin many years ago.

2. My parents' messy divorce caused a series of disagreements between my sister and (me, myself).

3. Moving to Montana was the right decision for Josh and (I, me) because it offered a new beginning in a new place.

4. Captain Stacy Matella is a highly admired leader, but Captain Harry Hutchins has just as many good qualities as (she, her).

5. Our long-awaited trip to the big city ended in disappointment for my parents and (I, me).

6. You and Tony both majored in business, but your skills in closing a deal are different from (him, his).

7. The water company is taking (its, it's) time in sending me a refund for a billing error.

8. Sometimes I become impatient with Joe and (she, her); they procrastinate about making even the smallest choices.

9. (Who, Whom) were you arguing with when I saw you in the hallway?

10. (I, Me) and my best friend have known each other for ten years.

Exercise 4 **Collaborate: Write Your Own Text on Pronoun Case**

With a partner or with a group, write two sentences that could be used as examples for each of the following rules. The first one is done for you.

Rule 1: When a pronoun is used as a subject, use the subjective case.

examples: _He complained about the noise in the street._

Tired and hungry, they stopped for lunch.

Rule 2: When a pronoun is used as the object of a verb or the object of a preposition, use the objective case.

examples: _____

_____

Rule 3: When a pronoun is used to show ownership, use the possessive case.

examples: _____

_____

Rule 4: When a pronoun is part of a related group of words, isolate the pronoun to choose the case. (For examples, write two sentences in which the pronoun is part of a related group of words.)

examples: _____

_____

Exercise 5 **Connect: Editing a Paragraph for Errors in Pronoun Consistency and Case**

In the following paragraph, correct any errors in pronoun consistency and case. There are seven errors. Write your corrections above the line.

I am very grateful for this award from the Community Cares Club. Many people encouraged, supported, and even changed me in my work with local homeless children. One is my mother, whom introduced me to the organization several years ago. At that time, I thought of my mother's work in the club as worthy but depressing. I never realized how mistaken I was until you actually met the children. Because of my mother's involvement in the club, I had a chance to learn about the spirit, courage, and strength of disadvantaged boys and girls. Interacting with these children created a bond between them and I. I gave them the stability of regular attention, academic support, and physical activity. Around them, I became a more positive person. They were a good influence on I. Them and me were a good combination. Therefore I have to thank the Community Cares Club. They brought me and the children together.

Exercise 6   **Connect: Editing a Paragraph for Errors in Pronoun Consistency and Case**

In the following paragraph, correct any errors in pronoun consistency and case. There are five errors. Write your corrections above the line.

My fiancée and myself recently witnessed a strange scene in a jewelry store. We were looking at engagement rings when another couple approached a sales clerk. The couple wanted to see several rings in the display case. The man and woman were well dressed. He was wearing an expensive leather jacket, and she had on designer jeans and a cashmere sweater. Me and my girlfriend could not afford the clothes this couple wore. First, the two examined some expensive rings. The woman didn't like any of them; neither did the man. As we continued eavesdropping on the conversation, we heard the man ask the clerk about several lower-priced rings. When the clerk produced the rings, the woman became unhappy. She pushed two of the rings aside; then she jammed the third ring into it's velvet box. "Who is this ring for?" she shouted at her boyfriend. "Certainly not *me*. I would never wear such junk." She scowled and added, "You'd better find yourself another girlfriend. You can marry whoever you want. Find somebody as cheap as you are." She pushed her way to the door as my fiancée and I stared in horror. We didn't think she'd be marrying the man in the leather jacket anytime soon. In addition, we felt sorry for the man she would find to replace him.

Chapter Test   Using Pronouns Correctly: Consistency and Case

Some of the sentences below are correct; others have errors in pronoun consistency or case. Put an *X* next to the sentences with errors.

1. _____   Who did you gossip about after I left the party?

2. _____   Sometimes I get angry at Claudia and he; they take advantage of my generosity.

3. _____   It was difficult for my parents and I to leave our house in the suburbs and move to a small apartment in a decrepit part of the city.

4. _____   Whoever gets to the restaurant first needs to find a table for six.

5. _____   I am a little upset with my brother; he always gets better grades in English than me.

6. _____   The events of that dark November night remain a mystery to everyone except me and Alex.

7. _____   After the blizzard, Kate and myself were grateful for the emergency vehicles that rescued us from the huge drifts of snow around the cabin.

8. _____   Whom do you expect at the farewell party for your supervisor?

9. _____   After I and the head of campus security ran out of the building, a flame appeared at one of the open windows.

10. _____   Casey and I will never again try to sneak into a movie; after you have dealt with the theater manager and the threats of arrest, the lure of criminal adventure soon disappears.

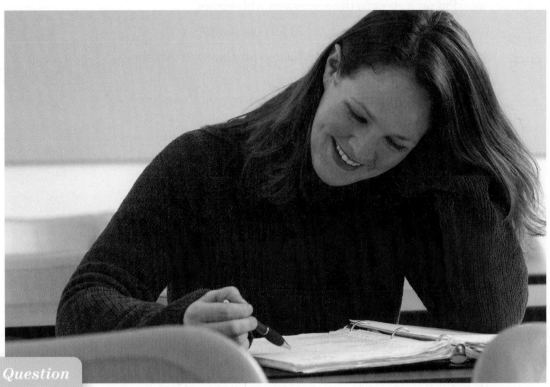

Quick Question

Which sentence(s) is/
are correct?

A. Will Lisa ever
trust her instincts
again?

B. I wonder if Lisa
will ever trust her
instincts again?

(After you study
this chapter, you will
feel confident of your
answer.)

Chapter Objectives

Students will be able to demonstrate proficiency in basic punctuation skills, including (but not limited to) the proper use of commas, semicolons, colons, apostrophes, parentheses, numbers, capital letters, and abbreviations.

THE PERIOD

Periods are used two ways:

1. Use a period to mark the end of a sentence that makes a statement.

> We invited him to dinner at our house.
> When Richard spoke, no one paid attention.

2. Use a period after abbreviations.

> Mr. Ryan
> James Wing, Sr.
> 10:00 P.M.

> **Note:** If a sentence ends with a period marking an abbreviation, do not add a second period.

Exercise 1   Practice: Using Periods

Add periods where they are needed in each of the following sentences.

1. Oscar bought about fifteen lbs of special food for his sick terrier

2. When the elementary school children went on field trips, they were nervous around people like Mr Carlson, the principal

3. Isaac wants to get a B S degree in Biology, and his friend, Dr Hamilton, told him to prepare by taking many science classes in high school

4. Tell Ms Marko or Mr Scanlon about the parking problems in the gymnasium parking lot.

5. Last night I studied for my social sciences test until nearly 2:00 A M and didn't sleep well.

6. Nicholas Anderson, Sr, is a better businessman than his son

7. Someday, I want to be known as Cecilia Knowles, R N, so I am going to college to study nursing.

8. We had a traditional Thanksgiving dinner with turkey, stuffing, cranberry sauce, pumpkin pie, etc at my mother's house

9. After Sgt Albury left the scene, people crowded around the yellow tape to see what was left of the burned car.

10. You could have asked Aunt Maya to visit us next September

THE QUESTION MARK

Use a question mark after a direct question.

> Isn't she adorable?
> Do you have car insurance?

If a question is not a direct question, it does not get a question mark.

> They asked if I thought their grandchild was adorable.
> She questioned whether I had car insurance.

Exercise 2   Practice: Punctuating with Periods and Question Marks

Add any missing periods and question marks to each sentence below.

1. Are the people upstairs moving out of their apartment

2. Have you ever thought about getting a B A in graphic design

3. Two of my friends have been asking me about my plans for semester break

4. Were there any good-looking men sitting in the food court

5. I'm not certain that the meeting will take place as scheduled

6. How has the old school changed since you graduated ten years ago

7. Don't you think 6:00 A M is a little early to start driving to Tallahassee

8. Is it possible that Mrs Mikulski forgot to lock the front door

9. I wonder why you never call me on Saturdays

10. The supervisors questioned whether Miss Chen would want to leave a secure, high-level position for a potentially better but risky one

Connect

Exercise 3 Connect: Editing a Paragraph for Errors in Periods and Question Marks

In the following paragraph, correct errors in punctuating with periods and question marks. The errors may involved missing or incorrect punctuation. There are eight errors.

Last Tuesday, a simple errand started me wondering if I had lost my mind? First, I visited my allergy doctor for a routine check of my sinuses and bronchial tubes. Then I went to my local pharmacy to refill a prescription for an antihistamine. This is a regular prescription for me; I have been taking the medicine since I developed seasonal allergies several years ago. After I received the bag with the vial of pills in it, I ran several more errands. I returned to my house at about 6:30 PM. for dinner and a good night's sleep. The next morning, I opened the plastic container with my allergy pills inside. Suddenly I noticed a problem with the pills. The pills were large and blue. My allergy pills are always small and pink. I didn't know what to do. First, I asked myself whether I had paid enough attention to Dr Kasabian during my visit a day earlier? Had he changed my medication. Or had the pharmacist given me the wrong pills? What would happen if I took one of the new pills? I needed my allergy medicine, and I was slipping into a state of panic. After obsessing for a few more minutes, I decided not to take an allergy pill until I called the pharmacist. My heart beat wildly as I waited to be connected to the pharmacy department at the drug store. The woman who answered the phone was Ms Patel, and she seemed very calm. I wondered how she could be so calm when my life might be at stake? Soon, I learned the real story. My prescription medicine was now being manufactured by a new company. The company was producing the same pill in the same dose, but the

pill was now large and blue. I began to feel calm, and my voice lost its hysterical

tone I swallowed my pill, smiled, and vowed never again to create a crisis out of

nothing.

Section Test **Punctuation: The Period and the Question Mark**

Some of the sentences below are correct; others have errors in the use of periods and question marks. Put an *X* next to the sentences with errors.

1. _____ After I got to know Dr Stefanovic, I trusted her with my medical care.

2. _____ Carl was not sure whether the restaurant was open for breakfast.

3. _____ The officer could have asked Kate Gomez about the time of the break-in.

4. _____ Now that Eddie has finished medical school, he has become Edward Obara, M D

5. _____ At the Crosstown Market, Mr O'Neill was selling two lbs of organic sweet potatoes for two dollars.

6. _____ Will Abraham ever finish restoring his old Ford Mustang?

7. _____ My roommate woke me up at 6:00 AM yesterday so that we could study for our botany test.

8. _____ Uncle Colin has been calling and questioning me about my plans for St. Patrick's Day.

9. _____ Do you think about Nate very often?

10. _____ Since my father and I share the same first, middle, and last names, he is Calvin B Kiyosaki, Sr.

THE COMMA

There are four main ways to use a comma, as well as other, less important ways. *Memorize the four main ways.* If you can learn and understand these four rules, you will be more confident and correct in your punctuation. That is, you will use a comma only when you have a reason to do so; you will not be scattering commas in your sentences simply because you think a comma might fit, as many writers do.

The four main ways to use a comma are as a lister, a linker, an introducer, or an inserter (use two commas).

Use a Comma as a Lister

Commas support items in a series. These items can be words, phrases, or clauses.

> **comma between words in a list:** Her bedroom was decorated in shades of blue, green, and gold.

> **comma between phrases in a list:** I looked for my ring under the coffee table, between the sofa cushions, and behind the chairs.
>
> **comma between clauses in a list:** Last week he graduated from college, he found the woman of his dreams, and he won the lottery.

Note: In a list, the comma before *and* is optional, but many writers use it.

Exercise 4 Practice: Using a Comma as a Lister

Add commas only where they are needed in the following sentences. Do not add any other punctuation or change existing punctuation.

1. Meat fish cheese beans and dairy products are sources of protein.

2. Nicole can do the laundry Mike can vacuum the house and I can clean the kitchen.

3. The thief caught with the money was silent snarling and slippery.

4. Bargain prices for DVD players satellite radios and flat-screen televisions drew shoppers to the electronics store.

5. I will wash dry and fold your dirty clothes when you take them off the floor and put them in the laundry basket.

6. My aunt knew she was spending too much time and money on television shopping channels when boxes of glittering jewelry expensive makeup and household gadgets started piling up in her house.

7. Eric is self-centered he lacks any sense of responsibility and he lies to his friends.

8. Sweaters pajamas and scarves are the only gifts my aunt ever gave me.

9. I misplaced my backpack with my chemistry workbook cell phone and student ID card in it.

10. There are certain creatures I hope never to see in my house; these include rats mice snakes and lizards.

Use a Comma as a Linker

A comma and a coordinating conjunction link two independent clauses. The coordinating conjunctions are *for, and, nor, but, or, yet, so.* The comma goes in front of the coordinating conjunction:

> I have to get to work on time, or I'll get into trouble with my boss.
> My mother gave me a beautiful card, and she wrote a note on it.

Exercise 5 Practice: Using a Comma as a Linker

Add commas only where they are needed in the following sentences. Some sentences do not need commas. Do not change words or add any other punctuation.

1. Dr. Pinsky used to clean my teeth and he would give me a new toothbrush afterward.

2. My daughter can spend the weekend with her father or she can stay at her grandmother's house.

3. A day with my best friend lets me escape from my worries and act like a child again.

4. Todd wouldn't talk to his wife nor would he listen to his friend's advice.

5. Sophie must be sick for she has missed every class this week.

6. George had planned a perfect holiday party but something went wrong.

7. Jerry has tried several diets and exercise plans yet can't seem to lose weight.

8. Lisa's cousin Lev is quiet and rarely goes out to the movies or sports events.

9. My dog missed me so he went to sleep with an old sock of mine in his mouth.

10. Tim does all his assignments at the last minute yet he always manages to turn them in on time.

Use a Comma as an Introducer

Put a comma after introductory words, phrases, or clauses in a sentence.

a comma after an introductory word:
Yes, I agree with you on that issue.
Dad, give me some help with the dishes.

a comma after an introductory phrase:
In the long run, you'll be better off without him.
Before the anniversary party, my father bought my mother a necklace.

a comma after an introductory clause:
If you call home, your parents will be pleased.
When the phone rings, I am always in the shower.

Exercise 6   Practice: Using a Comma as an Introducer

Add commas only where they are needed in the following sentences. Some sentences do not need commas. Do not change words or add any other punctuation.

1. In the back of the dark room stood a man from my past.

2. Unless the weather improves we won't be able to hunt tomorrow.

3. Sure I can take care of your cat while you are away.

4. Courtney do you have an extra pencil or pen?

5. On my little brother's birthday I took him to a water park.

6. While Bernard grills the fish you can make the rice and beans.

7. Behind the curtains are two children playing hide-and-seek.

8. After a few days Luisa got used to the noisy city streets.

9. If he calls tell him I went away for the weekend.

10. Under the circumstances you should be the one to apologize for the misunderstanding.

Use a Comma as an Inserter

When words or phrases that are *not* necessary are inserted into a sentence, put a comma on *both* sides of the inserted material:

The game, unfortunately, was rained out.
My test score, believe it or not, was the highest in the class.
Potato chips, my favorite snack food, are better-tasting when they're fresh.
James, caught in the middle of the argument, tried to keep the peace.

Using commas as inserters requires that you decide what is essential to the meaning of the sentence and what is nonessential. Here is a good rule to remember:

If you do not need material in a sentence, put commas around the material. If you need material in a sentence, do not put commas around the material.

For example, consider this sentence:

The girl who called me was selling magazine subscriptions.

Do you need the words "who called me" to understand the meaning of the sentence? To answer that question, write the sentence without those words:

The girl was selling magazine subscriptions.

Reading the shorter sentence, you might ask, "Which girl?" The words *who called me* are essential to the sentence. Therefore you do not put commas around them.

correct: The girl who called me was selling magazine subscriptions.

Remember that the proper name of a person, place, or thing is always sufficient to identify it. Therefore any information that follows a proper name is inserted material; it gets commas on both sides.

Carlton Furniture, which is nearby, has the best prices on futons and sofa beds.
Sam Harris, the man who won the marathon, lives on my block.

> **Note:** Sometimes the material that is needed in a sentence is called *essential* (or *restrictive*), and the material that is not needed is called *nonessential* (or *nonrestrictive*).

Exercise 7 Practice: Using Commas as Inserters

Add commas only where they are needed in the following sentences. Some sentences do not need commas.

1. A house full of toys will not always make a troubled child happy.

2. My best friend his eyes red and swollen mourned the loss of his cousin.

3. Mr. Murdock could of course decide to raise the rent.

4. Drivers who take the shortcut to the airport can save at least ten minutes and avoid the congestion at the toll plaza.

5. Our neighbor an enthusiastic gardener has transformed his yard into a small park.

6. *The Polar Express* which both children and adults enjoy was created with an experimental animation process.

7. The little girl at the end of the line has dropped the ice cream out of her cone.

8. Ultimate Books the bookstore in the Midland Mall has the biggest collection of fantasy books and magazines.

9. The woman in the gray suit introduced the guest of honor at the luncheon.

10. Baltimore where I was born has changed a great deal since I was a child.

> Remember the four main ways to use a comma—as a lister, a linker, an introducer, and an inserter—and you'll solve many of your problems with punctuation.

Exercise 8 Practice: Punctuating with Commas: The Four Main Ways

Add commas only where they are needed in the following sentences. Do not add any other punctuation, and do not change any existing punctuation. Some sentences do not need commas.

1. As Philip turned the key in the front door he heard a strange noise coming from the second floor.

2. The giant shrimp the best item on the buffet table disappeared in about five minutes.

3. Anyone who loves a bargain will want to visit the new outlet mall on Gibbons Road.

4. I had to work overtime at the hospital of course and couldn't go to the lake with Martin.

5. A house with a fireplace seems more appealing to me than a house with a pool.

6. Well you can do whatever you want and I'll just stay home and watch television.

7. Because we bought an old house we spent a year painting the exterior refinishing the wooden floors repairing the plumbing and remodeling the kitchen.

8. Shelley would you like a mango cake from the Cuban bakery for your birthday?

9. Dealing with frazzled travelers and enforcing airline rules was too much for me so I quit my job at Dynamic Airlines.

10. It will take me hours but I'll fix your computer.

Other Ways to Use a Comma

There are other places to use a comma. Reviewing these uses will help you feel more confident as a writer.

1. Use commas with quotations. Use a comma to set off a direct quotation from the rest of the sentence.

My father told me, "Money doesn't grow on trees."

"Let's split the bill," Raymond said.

Note that the comma that introduces the quotation goes before the quotation marks. But once the quotation has begun, commas or periods go inside the quotation marks.

2. Use commas with dates and addresses. Use commas between the items in dates and addresses.

August 5, 1980, is Chip's date of birth.

We lived at 133 Emerson Road, Lake Park, Pennsylvania, before we moved to Florida.

Notice the comma after the year in the date, and the comma after the state in the address. These commas are needed when you write a date or address within a sentence.

3. Use commas in numbers. Use commas in numbers of one thousand or larger.

The price of equipment was $1,293.

4. Use commas for clarity. Put a comma when you need it to make something clear.

Whoever it is, is about to be punished.

While hunting, the eagle is swift and strong.

I don't like to dress up, but in this job I have to, to get ahead.

Exercise 9   **Practice: Punctuation: Other Ways to Use a Comma**

Add commas wherever they are needed in the following sentences. Do not add any other punctuation, and do not change any existing punctuation.

1. "There isn't any milk in the refrigerator" my little boy complained.

2. On January 1 2002 Suzanne and Colin moved into a small house in Clifton New Jersey.

3. Be sure that anything you do you do for the right reasons.

4. The electric bill at my father's restaurant can run as high as $1500 a month.

5. "I have lived at 535 Orchid Place Denver Colorado for more than six years" Alex told me.

6. Kevin graduated from high school on June 15 2007 and soon started work as a landscaper in Mobile Alabama.

7. Melissa stood in front of the clothes in her closet and muttered "I have got to clean out this mess."

8. "Let's talk this over like adults" my cousin pleaded.

9. "It's going to be twins" my wife said on March 22 2009.

10. The car salesman said "The sticker price for that car is only $26299."

Exercise 10   Practice: Punctuating with Commas: A Comprehensive Exercise

Add commas only where they are needed in the following sentences. Do not add any other punctuation, and do not change any existing punctuation. Some of the sentences do not need commas.

1. The spoiled little boy refused to eat any of his chicken nuggets nor would he touch his French fries.

2. Whenever I start to worry about the future my boyfriend shrugs his shoulders and says "Whatever happens happens and there is nothing you can do about it."

3. My old sneakers are in bad shape yet they are more comfortable than any other shoes I own.

4. Cough syrup in tasty flavors should be kept out of children's reach because the children might drink the syrup for its taste.

5. Island Treats the most popular restaurant in town is opening another restaurant in Maybrook Georgia.

6. People who enter the theater after a movie has started should stay in one place until their eyes adjust to the darkness.

7. Tim can meet me at the coffee shop or call me when he gets home.

8. Running as fast as he could the officer shouted "Get out of the building!"

9. Dr. Levin the famous psychiatrist has written a book about depression and teenagers.

10. My mother cautioned me threatened me and even begged me but I would not give up the woman that my family disliked.

Exercise 11   Connect: Editing a Paragraph for Errors in Commas

Connect

In the following paragraph, correct any errors related to punctuating with commas. The errors may involve missing or incorrect use of commas. There are nineteen errors.

My grandparents live in an old but very sturdy home. Whoever built it built

it well. They bought it in 1970 for $35450 and it was a bargain even in those days.

The house has survived several blizzards and my grandfather has never had to

make major repairs for heating problems or burst pipes. When a huge hurricane

hit the area the house suffered only minor roof damage. The home a two-story wooden house is strong solid, and stable. Part of the story of the house is of course a story of luck. Cable Road where the house sits on several acres of land is full of old houses. Many, have survived bad times and bad weather but most have been hit by a falling tree or flooded by melting snow. My grandparents have watched their neighbors pump the water out of basements cut tree limbs away from the roof or tape broken windows on the storm side of a house. My grandfather and grandmother have helped the other residents of Cable Road deal with the effects of time and weather. On the other hand the neighbors have never had to come to my grandparents' rescue. "We're just grateful for our home" my grandfather says and I envy his good luck.

Section Test **Punctuation: The Comma**

Some of the sentences below are correct; others have errors in punctuating with commas. Put an *X* next to the sentences with errors.

1. _____ Christina Roberts, my best friend since high school was born in Fort Lauderdale, during a powerful hurricane.

2. _____ The damage to the empty house was senseless, and whoever did it, did it out of pure meanness.

3. _____ No I don't want your old computer, printer, or digital camera.

4. _____ Sam had an enjoyable evening with Cassie last weekend but never bothered to to call her again.

5. _____ Super Foods, which is open twenty-four hours a day, is the best place for last-minute grocery shopping.

6. _____ A little girl from the children's hospital led the group in singing a popular song.

7. _____ Angry and frightened, the woman whose purse had been stolen screamed loudly, picked herself up off the pavement, and ran after the thief.

8. _____ "No one will criticize you for telling the truth," my brother told me.

9. _____ Ella, her face shining with happiness, graduated from college on May 22, 2007 with a degree in physical therapy.

10. _____ Getting my truck repaired cost me $1214, but it was cheaper than making enormous car payments on a new truck.

THE SEMICOLON

There are two ways to use semicolons:

1. Use a semicolon to join two independent clauses:

> Michael loved his old Camaro; he worked on it every weekend.
> The situation was hopeless; I couldn't do anything.

> **Note:** If the independent clauses are joined by a conjunctive adverb, you will still need a semicolon. You will also need a comma after any conjunctive adverb that is more than one syllable long.

conjunctive adverb

> He was fluent in Spanish; *consequently,* he was the perfect companion for our trip to Venezuela.

conjunctive adverb

> I called the hotline for twenty minutes; *then* I called another number.

> **For your information:** A list of common conjunctive adverbs is on page 408.

Independent clauses joined by coordinating conjunctions (the words *for, and, nor, but, or, yet, so*) do not need semicolons. Use a comma in front of the coordinating conjunction:

coordinating conjunction

> Michael loved his old Camaro, *and* he worked on it every weekend.

coordinating conjunction

> He was fluent in Spanish, *so* he was the perfect companion for our trip to Venezuela.

2. Use semicolons to separate the items on a list that contains commas. Adding semicolons will make the list easier to read:

> The contestants came from Rochester, New York; Pittsburgh, Pennsylvania; Trenton, New Jersey; and Boston, Massachusetts. (The semicolons show that Rochester is a city in the state of New York, Pittsburgh is a city in the state of Pennsylvania, and so forth.)

> The new officers of the club will be Althea Bethell, president; Francois Riviere, vice-president; Ricardo Perez, secretary; and Lou Phillips, treasurer. (The semicolons link the person, Althea Bethell, with the office, president, and so forth.)

Exercise 12 **Practice: Punctuating with Semicolons**

Add any missing semicolons to the following sentences. In some sentences, you may have to change commas to semicolons.

1. The noise of construction workers outside the building grew louder meanwhile, I was trying to conduct a serious conversation on the telephone.

2. Two years ago, I was terrified of water now I love to jump into the deep end of the pool.

3. My aunt took me to a fancy restaurant for dinner in addition, she bought me two new CDs at a music store.

4. Stacey is smart, attractive, and outgoing, yet she longs to be more like her younger sister.

5. Mario, my father, Mark, my older brother, Michael, my younger brother, and Michelle, my sister, all have first names that begin with *M*.

6. Gene is upset about something you need to talk to him.

7. Arthur was wearing a new jacket and had just gotten a haircut in fact, he looked quite handsome.

8. I studied hard for my grammar test thus I didn't think it was too difficult.

9. Sarah will call the cable company or stop by its office for an explanation of the latest bill.

10. I have to pack my suitcase tonight otherwise, I might forget something in the morning rush to the airport.

THE COLON

A colon is used at the end of a complete statement. It introduces a list or an explanation:

colon introduces a list: When I went grocery shopping, I picked up a few things: milk, eggs, and coffee.

colon introduces an explanation: The room was a mess: dirty clothes were piled on the chairs, wet towels were thrown on the floor, and an empty pizza box was tossed in the closet.

Remember that the colon comes after a complete statement. What comes after the colon explains or describes what came before the colon. Look once more at the two examples, and you'll see the point.

When I went grocery shopping, I picked up a few things: milk, eggs, and coffee. (The words after the colon—*milk, eggs, and coffee*—explain what few things I picked up.)

The room was a mess: dirty clothes were piled on the chairs, wet towels were thrown on the floor, and an empty pizza box was tossed in the closet. (In this sentence, all the words after the colon describe what the mess was like.)

Some people use a colon every time they put a list in a sentence, but this is not a good rule to follow. Instead, remember that a colon, even one that introduces a list, must come after a complete statement.

not this: ~~When I go to the beach, I always bring: suntan lotion, a big towel, and a cooler with iced tea.~~

but this: When I go to the beach, I always bring my supplies: suntan lotion, a big towel, and a cooler with iced tea.

A colon may also introduce long quotations.

On December 8, 1941, the day after the Japanese attacked Pearl Harbor, President Franklin Delano Roosevelt summed up the situation:

"Hostilities exist. There is no blinking at the fact that our people, our territory, and our interests are in grave danger." *(Note that what comes after the colon explains what came before it.)*

Exercise 13   **Practice: Punctuating with Colons**

Add colons where they are needed in the following sentences. Some sentences do not need a colon.

1. When you go to the cabin for the weekend, be sure to fill your car with groceries, extra blankets, insect repellent, books, binoculars, and fishing gear.

2. My brother did a superb job of cleaning the bathroom a shining bathtub, a spotless sink, a gleaming toilet, and even a floor free of footprints.

3. Since I had twenty dollars left over at the end of the week, I bought some small surprises for my husband a can of cashews, a bottle of wine, and his favorite magazine.

4. Until we cleaned out the garage, we had a collection of tools, ladders, empty boxes, lawn chairs, broken appliances, and rags crowded into the space.

5. My cat brings me what he thinks are trophies a dead lizard, a mouse, even a small snake.

6. Our neighborhood has several Fourth of July traditions flags flying in people's yards, a parade of small children on their bikes or in strollers, and a community barbecue on a dead-end street.

7. If you want to contribute to the food drive for victims of the storm, you can bring canned food, bread and rolls, bottled water, and paper plates and towels.

8. My grandmother believes that there are two kinds of children the ones who behave and the ones who don't.

9. The bridesmaids had their choice of three colors for their dresses pink, yellow, or lavender.

10. The men looked like rap celebrities lots of jewelry, designer clothes, and shoes that cost more than my monthly salary.

Exercise 14   **Practice: Using Semicolons and Colons**

Add semicolons and colons where they are needed in the following sentences. You might have to change a comma to a semicolon.

1. I will never go to a sushi restaurant the idea of eating raw fish makes me sick.

2. You need floor mats for your car, and be sure to look for the usual auto supplies motor oil, car wax, and windshield wiper fluid.

3. Leroy sent me a get-well card he's always thoughtful.

4. If you go to the drug store, get me some toothpaste, hair gel, and aspirin.

5. Arthur seems like a trustworthy employee, on the other hand, I don't know that much about him.

6. There has been a shake-up in the managerial staff of Tompkins Motors, so the new leaders are Karen Killian, manager, Pierre LaValle, assistant manager, Ron Jessup, service manager, and Lorena Robles, business manager.

7. After my father got a job with a hotel, he took classes in accounting, customer relations, restaurant management, and business law.

8. Your parents love Luisa, also, she is fond of them.

9. Every time I take my father to a good restaurant, he orders the same thing a salad with thousand island dressing, a steak, and a baked potato.

10. Marianne skipped dinner last night then she left the house at 10:00 A.M.

Connect

> ### Exercise 15   Connect: Editing a Paragraph for Errors in Semicolons and Colons

In the following paragraph, correct any errors related to punctuating with semicolons or colons. The errors may involve missing or incorrect use of semicolons or colons. There are nine errors.

On one subzero day in Minnesota, my friend and I dreamed of a tropical vacation, but we did not exactly find our dream. We started by listing all the warm places we craved Miami; Florida; Cancun; Mexico; Honolulu; Hawaii; and Kingston; Jamaica. Of course, we soon discovered that the price of traveling to and staying at any of these four places was well beyond our means. We were ready to give up our dreams, then we thought of another way to enjoy fun in the sun without spending thousands of dollars. My sister and her husband had recently returned from a bargain cruise in the Bahamas. The reasonable price included the following round-trip airfare to the port of departure, accommodations in a double cabin, all meals, and all entertainment. Our ship would stop at two ports and also spend a day at a private island where we could swim, snorkel, and soak up the sun. This trip sounded like a perfect way for us to spend our spring break. Of course, nothing is perfect, and we soon experienced many small and large snags. Just as we flew into the city where we would board the ship, a rare winter rain storm hit the tropics. As we left the port of departure, we stood on deck and held giant umbrellas over our heads. The storm followed us to the ports we visited it also hit the private island. Dancing the limbo on a rain-swept patio is not exciting even when the steel drums play. Snorkeling in the rain is not much fun even when the setting is a private island. By the time we returned to Minnesota, we had learned one hard lesson; pack more than sunscreen and swimsuits when you prepare for any cruise.

Section Test **Punctuation: The Semicolon and the Colon**

Some of the following sentences are correct; others have errors in the use of semicolons and colons. Put an *X* next to the sentences with errors.

1. _____ Drawn by the famous country singer's last concert, people came from all over the southern states: Gainesville, Florida; Savannah, Georgia; Huntsville, Alabama; and Jackson, Mississippi.

2. _____ Don't try to convince me; I'm not going anywhere with you.

3. _____ Amanda forgot to pack her medication; so we had to turn around and drive fifty miles back to her house.

4. _____ Chris will eat just about any cookie in the world: stale cookies, cookie crumbs, half-eaten cookies, even cookies that have fallen on the floor.

5. _____ My cousin got stuck in traffic: then his car overheated.

6. _____ If you go to the islands, be sure to enjoy the natural beauty: the turquoise water, the powdery white beaches, and the amazing undersea creatures.

7. _____ Three of my former teachers have won teaching awards: Mrs. Anthony, my first-grade teacher, Mrs. Evans, my fifth-grade teacher; and Mr. Goldfarb, my tenth-grade history teacher.

8. _____ Charlie won't talk to me about his worries; nor will he share them with his mother.

9. _____ When Danny shops for clothes, he buys sneakers, tee-shirts, jeans, and hooded jackets; he never buys a dress shirt or slacks.

10. _____ In my first term in college, I took Fundamentals of Mathematics, Introduction to Sociology, and Art Appreciation.

THE APOSTROPHE

Use the apostrophe in the following ways:

1. Use an apostrophe in contractions to show that letters have been omitted.

do not   = don't
I will   = I'll
is not   = isn't
she would = she'd
will not   = won't

Also use the apostrophe to show that numbers have been omitted:

the summer of 1998 = the summer of '98

> ### Exercise 16   Practice: Using Apostrophes in Contractions
>
> Add apostrophes where they are necessary in each sentence below.
>
> 1. Dr. Fanelli is a great veterinarian; shell tell you whats wrong with your potbellied pig.
>
> 2. My grandfather never stops talking about the blizzard of 84 and how he didnt think hed live through it.
>
> 3. The trip wasnt what Id expected, but Ill never forget it.
>
> 4. Hows your new baby doing?
>
> 5. Terry wont tell you that theres a problem with the financing for the car.
>
> 6. Henry and Lori couldnt make the trip this week; theyll come next month when theyve got more time.
>
> 7. I havent seen Monica lately; I hear shes got a new job.
>
> 8. If youre sick, youd better stay home from work today.
>
> 9. Its wonderful to see dolphins in their natural habitat.
>
> 10. Parents shouldnt argue in front of their small children; the children dont know how to cope with family conflict.

2. Use an apostrophe to show possession. If a word does not end in *s*, show ownership by adding an apostrophe and *s*.

the ring belongs to Jill   = Jill's ring
the wallet belongs to somebody   = somebody's wallet
the books are owned by my father   = my father's books

If two people jointly own something, put the *'s* on the name of the second person listed.

Ann and Mike own a house = Ann and Mike's house

If a word already ends in *s* and you want to show ownership, just add an apostrophe.

the ring belongs to Frances   = Frances' ring
two boys own a dog   = the boys' dog
the house belongs to Ms. Jones = Ms. Jones' house

Caution: Be careful with apostrophes. These words, the possessive pronouns, do not take apostrophes: *his, hers, theirs, ours, yours, its.*

---

not this: ~~The pencils were their's.~~
but this: The pencils were theirs.

not this: ~~The steak lost it's flavor.~~
but this: The steak lost its flavor.

Exercise 17 **Practice: Using Apostrophes to Show Possession**

Add apostrophes where they are needed in the following sentences. Some sentences do not need apostrophes.

1. Mrs. Noriko promised to improve the companys marketing division and expand its overseas office.

2. I went to Charles and Agnes wedding yesterday, and I thought their wedding cake tasted better than yours.

3. I tried to put the dinner dishes, pots, and pans away quietly, but I dropped one pots lid against the stoves hood, creating a horrible, clanking sound.

4. Catherine and Anthony are creative people, and the credit for renovating the pediatric wing of the hospital is all theirs.

5. I hope that, when I mentioned the changes at the womens club, I did not hurt anyones feelings.

6. Be careful when you pack my aunts photograph albums; her whole life is contained in them.

7. I miss San Diegos weather, but I love Bostons college life and its sense of history.

8. My sister Allisons musical ability is all hers; no one else in the family can sing, play an instrument, or read music.

9. I had to describe the lost suitcase to the airport cargo manager so that he could be sure the bag was ours.

10. In a week or two, the beautiful tree will have lost all its gold and scarlet leaves.

3. Use the apostrophe for special uses of time, and to create a plural of numbers mentioned as numbers, letters mentioned as letters, and words that normally do not have plurals.

special uses of time: It will take a week's work.
numbers mentioned as numbers: Take out the 5's.
letters mentioned as letters: Cross your *t*'s.
words that normally do not have plurals: I want no more *maybe*'s.

> **Caution:** Do not add an apostrophe to a simple plural.

not this: ~~He lost three suitcase's.~~
but this: He lost three suitcases.

Exercise 18 **Practice: Special Uses of Apostrophes**

Add apostrophes where they are needed in the following sentences. Some sentences do not need apostrophes. Do not change or add any words.

1. I have *B*s on all my science quizzes, so I feel confident about the test.

2. Alice is going to New Zealand for three weeks; she will stay with relatives who live there.

3. Jennifer deserves a days pay for all the time she spent on cleaning up your office.

4. There are two *es* in the word *coffee.*

5. The winner of the lottery won an amount of money with six *0*s at the end, so it has to be at least one million dollars.

6. It will be several months before I can save up enough vacation days for a trip to Wyoming.

7. My mother writes very fancy capital *A*s because she used to study calligraphy.

8. The down payment on my new house is less than a years worth of rent on my old one.

9. Don wants to spend hundreds of dollars on an anniversary party for our parents, but I think we can give them a memorable day for less money.

10. Dont forget your "*excuse me*s" and "*please*s" when you visit Aunt Claudia.

Exercise 19   **Practice: Using Apostrophes: A Comprehensive Exercise**

Circle the correct form in parentheses in each sentence below.

1. I think the notebook belongs to (Carlos, Carlo's).

2. Could the white rabbit in our yard be (someones, someone's) pet?

3. (Theres, There's) nothing wrong with your computer.

4. A new (mens, men's) store just opened in the Palms Plaza.

5. The mail carrier delivered the package to our neighbors, but it was (ours, our's).

6. I fell in love for the first time in the spring of (99, '99).

7. My brother was in Korea for two (years, year's).

8. Tell me if you like (Laura's and Kim's, Laura and Kim's) new roommate.

9. Lamont's answers to my requests are too full of (*no*s, *no*'s).

10. Staying out late began to lose (its, it's) appeal for me when I became a father.

Exercise 20   **Connect: Editing a Paragraph for Errors in Apostrophes**

Connect

In the following paragraph, correct any errors related to punctuating with apostrophes. The errors may involve missing or incorrect use of apostrophes. There are eleven errors.

Watching the Super Bowl in Aunt Kathleen's and Uncle Manny's basement

lounge is almost as good as being in the stadium. First of all, the room is huge,

and its filled with sports memorabilia, comfortable chairs, and a giant television

screen. A big refrigerator is packed with food and beverages that are all our's.
This basement is soundproof, so the crowd in front of the screen can cheer or cry
loudly. Everyone can look at this years most outrageous commercials and wait
for the surprise's of the halftime show. Enjoying the Super Bowl while we sit in
my aunt and uncles basement has become a tradition for me, my cousin Anthony,
my parent's, and my fathers' best friend, Patrick. Also, new faces appear at the
party each year. After some games, it takes me a weeks worth of family calls to
identify newcomers such as the woman sitting with my cousin or the old man who
kissed my aunt. I know that I would love to sit in the seat's at the Super Bowl, but
I also love game day with my aunt and uncle. That special Sunday has it's own
pleasures.

Section Test Punctuation: The Apostrophe

Some of the sentences below are correct; others have errors in using punctuation. Put an *X* by each sentence with an error.

1. _____ Morris is sure to say his "*thank you*s" when he visits his grandfather's house.

2. _____ I'm not sure if Mark and Maria left behind the serving bowls, but I know the platters are theirs.

3. _____ The stray kitten has to be somebodys pet, so we'll post the kitten's photo throughout the neighborhood and keep the little cat safe until it's owner shows up.

4. _____ Although Adam and Jackson look like twins, the brother's personalities are different.

5. _____ We'll go to Rita's and Carlos' party after we've had dinner.

6. _____ Tammy got a months salary as a bonus after she'd broken the company's record for sales.

7. _____ I'd like to see a few more *0*'s at the end of my income tax refund check.

8. _____ There's no one under the bed; the monster is a product of Charles imagination.

9. _____ My father's southern relatives always drop the "*g*'s" when they say words like "fishing" and "running."

10. _____ Years from now, when we've saved enough money, a house in a good neighborhood will be ours.

THE EXCLAMATION MARK

The exclamation mark is used at the end of sentences that express strong emotion:

> **appropriate:** You've won the lottery!
> **inappropriate:** We had a great time! (*Great* already implies excitement.)

Be careful not to overuse the exclamation mark. If your choice of words is descriptive, you should not have to rely on the exclamation point for emphasis. Use it sparingly, for it is easy to rely on exclamations instead of using better vocabulary.

THE DASH

Use a dash to interrupt a sentence. It usually indicates a dramatic shift in tone or thought.

> I picked up the crystal bowl carefully, cradled it in my arms, walked softly—and tripped, sending the bowl flying.

Two dashes set off dramatic words that interrupt a sentence.

> Ramon took the life preserver—our only one—and tossed it far out to sea.

Because dashes are somewhat dramatic, use them sparingly.

PARENTHESES

Use parentheses to enclose extra material and afterthoughts.

> I was sure that Ridgefield (the town I'd just visited) was not the place for me.
> Her name (which I have just remembered) was Celestine.

> **Note:** Commas in pairs, dashes in pairs, and parentheses are all used as inserters. They set off material that interrupts the flow of the sentence. The least dramatic and smoothest way to insert material is to use commas.

THE HYPHEN

A hyphen joins two or more descriptive words that act as a single word.

> The old car had a souped-up engine.
> Bill was a smooth-talking charmer.

Use a hyphen in the written form of compound numbers from twenty-one to ninety-nine.

Exercise 21   **Practice: Punctuating with Exclamation Marks, Dashes, Parentheses, and Hyphens**

Add any exclamation marks, dashes, parentheses, and hyphens that are needed in the sentences below.

1. Larry took the airline ticket my last chance at freedom and threw it into the incinerator.

2. There's someone hiding in the closet

3. Lenny Montalbano the boy who used to live next door grew up to start his own medical research company.

4. Mr. Okada is a caring, competent, and good natured supervisor.

5. Mr. Thompson is known for his eccentric ways; one day he came to work in a handsome blue blazer, striped silk tie, gray flannel slacks and bright orange sneakers.

6. Get off the train tracks

7. The salesperson said the radio was a top of the line product.

8. The Aces Club where my cousin said all the single people meet turned out to be a loud, dirty bar and grill.

9. The killer drew a breath his last one and fell to the ground.

10. Amanda married a battle weary veteran of the war in Iraq.

QUOTATION MARKS

Use quotation marks for direct quotes, for the titles of short works, and for other special uses.

1. Put quotation marks around direct quotes, a speaker or writer's exact words:

> My mother told me, "There are plenty of fish in the sea."
> "I'm never going there again," said Irene.
> "I'd like to buy you dinner," Peter said, "but I'm out of cash."
> My best friend warned me, "Stay away from that guy. He will break your heart."

Look carefully at the preceding examples. Notice that a comma is used to introduce a direct quotation, and that at the end of the quotation, the comma or period goes inside the quotation marks:

> My mother told me, "There are plenty of fish in the sea."

Notice how direct quotes of more than one sentence are punctuated. If the quote is written in one unit, quotation marks go before the first quoted word and after the last quoted word:

> My best friend warned me, "Stay away from that guy. He will break your heart."

But if the quote is not written as one unit, the punctuation changes:

> "Stay away from that guy," my best friend warned me. "He will break your heart."

> **Caution:** Do *not* put quotation marks around indirect quotations.

> **indirect quotation:** He asked if he could come with us.
> **direct quotation:** He asked, "Can I come with you?"
>
> **indirect quotation:** She said that she wanted more time.
> **direct quotation:** "I want more time," she said.

2. Put quotation marks around the titles of short works. If you are writing the title of a short work like a short story, an essay, a newspaper or magazine article, a poem, or a song, put quotation marks around the title:

> In middle school, we read Robert Frost's poem "The Road Not Taken."
> My little sister has learned to sing "Itsby Bitsy Spider."

If you are **handwriting** the title of a longer work like a book, movie, magazine, play, television show, or CD, underline the title:

> Last night I saw an old movie, <u>The Godfather.</u>
> I read an article called "Campus Changes" in <u>Newsweek.</u>

In typed papers and printed publications such as books or magazines, titles of long works are italicized:

> Last night I saw an old movie, *The Godfather*.
> I read an article called "Campus Changes" in *Newsweek*.

3. There are other, special uses of quotation marks. You use quotation marks around words mentioned as words in a sentence.

> When you said "never," did you mean it?
> People from the Midwest pronounce "water" differently than I do.

If you are using a quotation within a quotation, use single quotation marks.

> My brother complained, "Every time we get in trouble, Mom has to say 'I told you so.'"
> Kyle said, "Linda has a way of saying 'Excuse me' that is really very rude."

CAPITAL LETTERS

There are ten main situations in which you capitalize:

1. Capitalize the first word of every sentence:

> Yesterday we saw our first soccer game.

2. Capitalize the first word in a direct quotation if the word begins a sentence:

> My aunt said, "This is a gift for your birthday."
> "Have some birthday cake," my aunt said, "and have some more ice cream." (Notice that the second section of this quote does not begin with a capital letter because it does not begin a sentence.)

3. Capitalize the names of persons:

> Nancy Perez and Frank Murray came to see me at the store.
> I asked Mother to feed my cat.

Do not capitalize words like *mother, father,* or *aunt* if you put a possessive in front of them.

> I asked my mother to feed my cat.

4. Capitalize the titles of persons:

> I spoke with Dr. Wilson.
> He has to see Dean Johnston.

Do not capitalize when the title is not connected to a name:

> I spoke with that doctor.
> He has to see the dean.

5. Always capitalize countries, cities, languages, nationalities, religions, races, months, days of the week, documents, organizations, holidays, and historical events or periods:

> In high school, we never studied the Vietnam War.
> The Polish-American Club will hold a picnic on Labor Day.

Use small letters for the seasons:

> I love fall because I love to watch the leaves change color.

6. Capitalize the names of particular places:

> We used to hold our annual meetings at Northside Auditorium in
>   Springfield, Iowa, but this year we are meeting at Riverview
>   Theater in Langton, Missouri.

Use small letters if a particular place is not given:

> We are looking for an auditorium we can rent for our meeting.

7. Use capital letters for geographic locations:

> Jim was determined to find a good job in the West.

But use small letters for geographic directions:

> To get to my house, you have to drive west on the turnpike.

8. Capitalize the names of specific products:

> I always drink Diet Pepsi for breakfast.

But use small letters for a kind of product:

> I always drink a diet cola for breakfast.

9. Capitalize the names of specific school courses:

> I have to take Child Psychology next term.

But use small letters for a general academic subject:

> My advisor told me to take a psychology course.

10. Capitalize the first and last words in the titles of long or short works, and capitalize all other significant words in the titles:

> I've always wanted to read *The Old Man and the Sea.*
> Whenever we go to see the team play, my uncle sings "Take Me Out to
>   the Ballgame."

> **Note:** Remember that the titles of long works, like books, are italicized (unless these titles are handwritten; then they are underlined). The titles of short works, like songs, are placed within quotation marks.

Exercise 22   Practice: Using Quotation Marks, Underlining, and Capital Letters

Add any missing quotation marks, underlining, and capital letters to the sentences below. You can assume that all these sentences are in printed form.

1. When I was growing up, uncle Richard was my favorite relative, but I later discovered my uncle had a dangerous temper.

2. When Melanie signed up for her winter term at college, she registered for classes in social science, writing, and music.

3. I can't stand it, my girlfriend said, when you say maybe instead of giving me a definite answer.

4. I finally found a good preschool for my son; it's the Madison school for early childhood education, and dr. Howard of Miller university is the director.

5. One night, my brother Jason was watching a television show called Dirty Jobs; I watched it for a minute and said, Ugh! Turn off that disgusting program. "

6. David is looking for a job in the midwest because he wants to be near his parents, who live north of Chicago.

7. Whenever Mimi says the word love, she means the word infatuation.

8. Gerry, stop complaining, his father said. It doesn't do any good to complain.

9. Last night my boyfriend and I watched an old Clint Eastwood movie called The Good, The Bad, And The Ugly.

10. There is nothing funnier than listening to my grandfather sing Marvin Gaye's old song, I heard It Through the Grapevine.

NUMBERS

Spell out numbers that take one or two words:

> Alice mailed two hundred brochures.
> I spent ninety dollars on car repairs.

Use the numbers themselves if it takes more than two words to spell them out.

> We looked through 243 old photographs.
> The sticker price was $10,397.99.

Also use numbers to write dates, times, addresses, and parts of a book.

> We live at 24 Cambridge Street.
> They were married on April 3, 1993.
> Chapter 3 had difficult maps to read, especially the one on page 181.

ABBREVIATIONS

Although you should spell out most words rather than abbreviate them, you may abbreviate *Mr.*, *Mrs.*, *Ms.*, *Jr.*, *Sr.*, and *Dr.* when they are used with a proper name. You should abbreviate references to time and to organizations widely known by initials.

> The moderator asked Ms. Steinem to comment.
> The bus left at 5:00 P.M., and the trip took two hours.
> He works for the FBI.

You should spell out the names of places, months, days of the week, courses of study, and words referring to parts of a book:

> **not this:** ~~I missed the last class, so I never got the notes for Chap. 3.~~
> **but this:** I missed the last class, so I never got the notes for Chapter 3.

> **not this:** ~~He lives on Chestnut Street in Boston, Mass.~~
> **but this:** He lives on Chestnut Street in Boston, Massachusetts.

> **not this:** ~~Pete missed his psych. test.~~
> **but this:** Pete missed his psychology test.

Exercise 23   **Practice: Using Numbers and Abbreviations**

Correct any errors in the use of numbers or abbreviations in the following sentences. Some sentences may not need corrections.

1. Ellen came into our soc. class last Mon., carrying her research

   paper, which looked about three in. thick.

2. Mr. and Mrs. Chang sent one hundred fifty five invitations to their

   daughter's wedding in Minneapolis, Minn.

3. My parents' apartment on Sunset Ave. had 4 rooms.

4. Matthew left Fla. on Mar. third, 2004, to begin a job with the Abraham and Braun Co. in N. Dakota.

5. My phys. ed. teacher starts class promptly at 8:30 A.M. every Fri.

6. It took me two hrs. to finish Chap. 3 of my sociology textbook.

7. Gregory charges twenty-five dollars an hour to help people with their computer problems.

8. Charles Woods, Jr., was an executive with the NFL for ten years before he took a job with ABC Sports.

9. My father and his 3 brothers arrived in New York on a cold Feb. day in 1975.

10. Dr. Hoffman used to live on 5723 Elm Street, Boston, Mass., until he took a job at the Univ. of Wisconsin in Madison.

> **Note:** Exercises incorporating concepts from all punctuation sections follow the section test.

Section Test **Other Punctuation**

Some of the sentences below are correct; others have errors in using quotation marks, capital letters, numbers, and abbreviations. Put an *X* next to the sentences with errors.

1. _____ My mother warned, "Before you do anything impulsive, think about your future".

2. _____ Carlotta spent one thousand and eighty dollars on new curtains for her house even though she owes her brother hundreds of dollars for fixing her roof.

3. _____ At my aunt's wedding reception, my sister sang "I Will Always love You" as the bride and groom danced.

4. _____ Dr. Gillespie is teaching an online course in Intro. to Psychology in the summer term.

5. _____ In our elementary school library, there was a framed copy of the Declaration of Independence on the wall.

6. _____ You always say "eventually" when I ask you whether you will ever get married.

7. _____ "Give me a few minutes," Father said, "and I'll take you to the park."

8. _____ I used to walk down the fashionable streets in Chicago, Ill., and stare at the the expensive cars and luxury stores.

9. _____ The spoiled heiress picked up the heavy china plate—a hand-painted antique—and smashed it against the wall.

10. _____ Nathan was so eager to leave Springfield (the town where he was born) that he took a job at a broken-down gas station five hundred miles away.

Exercise 24   **Practice: A Comprehensive Exercise on Punctuation**

Add any missing punctuation to the following sentences. Also, correct any errors in capitalization and in the use of numbers or abbreviations. Assume that all the sentences are in printed or typed form.

1. We had a second rate meal at Frank and Maries house of Ribs last Sat. night we can't recommend the place to you.

2. I'm looking for a book called the rule of four my friend recommended it.

3. The five year old boy began to pour chocolate syrup on the kitchen floor meanwhile the babysitter dozed on the living room couch.

4. Lance took 2 spanish courses at National H.S. so he does not have to take a foreign language class at Centenary college.

5. The star athlete wanted to know if she could miss a days practice.

6. The star athlete asked Can I miss a days practice

7. I love Its a whole new world, the song from the movie Aladdin.

8. Now that we live in Buffalo N.Y. I need some warm clothes sweaters, gloves, hats, and a coat with a heavy lining.

9. lll keep your secret Bill as long as your secret doesnt hurt anyone elses chance at happiness.

10. An old man with a cane walked slowly down the sidewalk for the ice made the pavement treacherous.

Exercise 25   **Practice: A Comprehensive Exercise on Punctuation**

Add any missing punctuation to the following sentences. Also, correct any errors in capitalization and in the use of numbers or abbreviations.

1. Tonya Brillstein my best friend told me she is sick of Lance and Marcus teasing.

2. The oral surgery will cost me $2321 nevertheless I intend to have it as soon as possible.

3. All I can say, dad is that youve hurt Nicoles feelings.

4. Let me see your license, the officer said and give me your registration too.

5. A man with bright red hair was seen leaving the scene of the crime but witnesses could not identify him.

6. The teenagers wonder whether their favorite teacher will ever return to the classroom at Penn. State University.

7. The movie Friday Night Lights was based on a book about a real High school football team in Texas.

8. When Vincent takes a trip with his Great Danes, he packs his van full of the animals possessions two large dog beds giant bags of dog food special spill proof water bowls and at least a dozen dog toys.

9. Theres a red Mustang in the parking lot with its lights on maybe the car is yours.

10. No don't buy me that book called The 7 Habits of Highly Effective People I have to break my bad habits before I can start developing good ones.

Connect

Exercise 26 Connect: Editing a Paragraph for Errors in Punctuation

In the following paragraph, correct any errors related to punctuation or mechanics. The errors may involve missing or incorrect punctuation, capitalization, use of numbers, or abbreviations. There are twenty-one errors.

When I agreed to do some work at a dirty old house I was not prepared, for the consequences. The house had belonged to my Mothers second cousin. When he died, he left it to my mother. She persuaded me and my brother to clean the house for her. After it was cleaned, she planned to sell the property. As my brother Sam and I approached the decrepit house we noticed that a dark, blue sky covered us. Beneath the brooding sky, the roof of the house had lost many of it's shingles. The rickety gate creaked ominously when we entered the yard. I reached the front entrance, and grabbed the rusty doorknob. Almost immediately, a hairy spider crawled across my hand. The atmosphere did not improve when we entered the house. Spider webs, and dust covered each room, then a horrible smell repelled us as we moved toward the basement stairs. The stairs to the basement were creaky. Some were missing. My brother stumbled and had to grab my hand, after he put his foot into an open space where a stair should have been. Soon we saw more horror. At least 100 rats were crawling around the dark basement spaces. Racing back to the smelly safety of the upper floor's, I wondered, "What else was waiting for us in this miserable place?" We decided not to explore any more of this crazy place. Our short time in the house had made us feel like ready made victims in a movie like *Dawn Of The Dead.*

Exercise 27 **Connect: Editing a Paragraph for Errors in Punctuation**

Connect

In the following paragraph, correct any punctuation errors. Errors may involve missing or incorrect punctuation, capitalization, use of numbers, or abbreviations. There are sixteen errors.

    My boyfriend loves shoe's. He has a closet full of sneakers, athletic shoes, running shoes, dress shoes, and boots. He has pair's and pairs of each kind. He must spend more than, two hundred dollars a month on shoes. Shoes are his addiction. Some of the shoes are brands that I recognize, such as nike and New balance. Other shoes come from foreign countries like Italy and I have never heard of the brand names. My boyfriend will travel from his home in Teaneck, NJ to Long Island, NY for a great sale on shoes. My boyfriend is also unusual because he wont get rid of his old shoes. "I love the look of a new pair of shoes, he says, but I also love the comfort of an old pair. Like my boyfriend, I love shoes. However, I don't love them as much as my boyfriend does. When womens shoes are on sale, I am always ready to buy a new pair but I will toss out an old pair at the same time.

Chapter Test **Punctuation**

Some of the sentences below are punctuated correctly; others have errors. Put an *X* next to the sentences with errors.

1. _____ I wonder if you would like me to bake a cake for your birthday.

2. _____ Andrew tried to fit in with his brother's friends, but never felt at ease around them.

3. _____ At the back of the house was a large patio surrounded by palm trees.

4. _____ Burgers and More, the most popular restaurant near campus, is closing its doors.

5. _____ Lisa warned her sister, "Stay away from people who love to gossip."

6. _____ Lightning struck the old school; fortunately no one was hurt.

7. _____ I would never drive a long distance without: my phone, water, and snacks.

8. _____ The credit for Jan and Jimmy's success in business is all theirs.

9. _____ My father warned me that "I'd better start saving some money."

10. _____ I look forward to Independence Day when Hanover Park hosts a big celebration.

Quick Question

Does the following sentence contain a spelling error? Yes/No

A week in the mountains appealled to me because I could find relief from the city's heat.

(After you study this chapter, you will be confident of your answer.)

Chapter Objectives

Students will be able to (1) distinguish between vowels and consonants, (2) apply basic spelling rules to determine proper word endings and variations, and (3) recognize when a one- or two-word spelling applies to certain terms.

No one is a perfect speller, but there are ways to become a better speller. If you can learn a few spelling rules, you can answer many of your spelling questions.

VOWELS AND CONSONANTS

To understand the spelling rules, you need to know the difference between vowels and consonants. **Vowels** are the letters a, e, i, o, u, and sometimes y. **Consonants** are all the other letters.

The letter y is a vowel when it has a vowel sound.

silly (The y sounds like ee, a vowel sound.)

cry (The y sounds like i, a vowel sound.)

The letter y is a consonant when it has a consonant sound.

yellow (The y has a consonant sound.)

yesterday (The y has a consonant sound.)

SPELLING RULE 1: DOUBLING A FINAL CONSONANT

When you add an ending, double the final consonant of a word if all three of the following are true:

1. The word is one syllable, or the accent is on the last syllable.
2. The word ends in a single consonant preceded by a single vowel.
3. The ending you are adding starts with a vowel.

begin	+	ing	=	beginning
shop	+	er	=	shopper
stir	+	ed	=	stirred
occur	+	ed	=	occurred
fat	+	est	=	fattest
pin	+	ing	=	pinning

Exercise 1   **Practice: Doubling a Final Consonant**

Add -ed to the following words by applying the rules for double consonants.

1. stammer _____   6. repel _____

2. swat _____   7. uncoil _____

3. trick _____   8. stop _____

4. order _____   9. excel _____

5. admit _____   10. defer _____

SPELLING RULE 2: DROPPING THE FINAL e

Drop the final e before you add an ending that starts with a vowel.

observe	+	ing	=	observing
excite	+	able	=	excitable
fame	+	ous	=	famous
create	+	ive	=	creative

Keep the final e before an ending that starts with a consonant.

love	+	ly	=	lovely
hope	+	ful	=	hopeful
excite	+	ment	=	excitement
life	+	less	=	lifeless

Exercise 2   **Practice: Dropping the Final e**

Combine the following words and endings by following the rule for dropping the final e.

1. imagine + able _____

2. care + less _____

3. arrange + ment _____

4. resource + ful _____

5. behave + ing _____

6. home   +   less   _____

7. expense   +   ive   _____

8. intense   +   ly   _____

9. adore   +   able   _____

10. refuse   +   ing   _____

SPELLING RULE 3: CHANGING THE FINAL *y* TO *i*

When a word ends in a consonant plus *y*, change the *y* to *i* when you add an ending:

try	+	es	=	tries
silly	+	er	=	sillier
rely	+	ance	=	reliance
tardy	+	ness	=	tardiness

> **Note:** When you add *-ing* to words ending in *y*, always keep the *y*.

cry	+	ing	=	crying
rely	+	ing	=	relying

Exercise 3   **Practice: Changing the Final *y* to *i***

Combine the following words and endings by applying the rule for changing the final *y* to *i*.

1. happy   +   er   _____

2. apply   +   ing   _____

3. convey   +   er   _____

4. penny   +   less   _____

5. marry   +   ed   _____

6. deny   +   es   _____

7. ally   +   ance   _____

8. comply   +   ant   _____

9. ready   +   ness   _____

10. imply   +   ing   _____

SPELLING RULE 4: ADDING *-s* OR *-es*

Add *-es* instead of *-s* to a word if the word ends in *ch*, *sh*, *ss*, *x*, or *z*. The *-es* adds an extra syllable to the word.

box	+	es	=	boxes
witch	+	es	=	witches
class	+	es	=	classes
clash	+	es	=	clashes

Exercise 4 **Practice: Adding** *-s* **or** *–es*

Apply the rule for adding *-s* or *-es* to the following words.

1. polish _____

2. defeat _____

3. march _____

4. stock _____

5. distress _____

6. fix _____

7. pass _____

8. smash _____

9. back _____

10. tax _____

SPELLING RULE 5: USING *ie* OR *ei*

Use *i* before *e*, except after *c*, or when the sound is like *a*, as in *neighbor* and *weigh*.

i before *e*:
relief   convenience   friend   piece

e before *i*:
conceive   sleigh   weight   receive

Exercise 5 **Practice: Using** *ie* **or** *ei*

Add *ie* or *ei* to the following words by applying the rule for using *ie* or *ei*.

1. dec _ _ t

2. fr _ _ ght

3. conc _ _ t

4. bel _ _ f

5. perc _ _ ve

6. ch _ _ f

7. n _ _ ce

8. f _ _ ld

9. ingred _ _ nt

10. sh _ _ ld

Exercise 6 **Practice: Spelling Rules: A Comprehensive Exercise**

Combine the following words and endings by applying the spelling rules.

1. blur   +   ed   _____

2. carry   +   ed   _____

3. fizz   +   s or es   _____

4. tidy   +   er   _____

5. perch   +   s or es   _____

6. harass   +   s or es   _____

7. plan   +   ed   _____

8. ready   +   ness   _____

9. ply   +   able   _____

10. concur +   ed   _____

11. unhappy +   est   _____

12. devote + ion   _____

13. spite + ful   _____

14. impulse + ive   _____

15. confine + ment   _____

16. rely + es   _____

17. apply + ance   _____

18. catch + s or es   _____

19. offer + ed   _____

20. suffer + ing   _____

Exercise 7   **Connect: Editing a Paragraph for Spelling**

Connect

Correct the spelling errors in the following paragraph. Write your corrections above each error. There are ten errors.

Buying store-brand products, which are usually cheaper than national-brand products, is a good way to save money. I used to think that buying national brands of items such as cereal or peanut butter meant getting food of better quality. However, I have stoped beleiving in that distinction. For example, how much difference can there be in two boxs of raisin bran from different companys? In addition, I have learned that many of the store brands are produced in the same mills or factorys as the national brands. It is quite possible that Kellogg's raisin bran and Publix raisin bran were made with the same bran, sugar, raisins, and other ingredients and were made in the same place. The only difference between a can of peachs sold by a national brand and one sold by a store brand may be the price. The national brand usually costs more because nationally known companies have to pay more for their expensive national advertising campaigns. Recently, I have tryed to be a smarter shoper, and I have concentrated on buying store brands of such items as bottled water, English muffinns, ice cream, and peanuts. In most cases, I cannot tell the difference between the national and the store brands. Now, when I visit my nieghborhood supermarket, I am a little smarter than I used to be.

DO YOU SPELL IT AS ONE WORD OR TWO?

Sometimes you can be confused about certain words. You are not sure whether to combine them to make one word or to spell them as two words. The lists below show some commonly confused words.

Words That Should Not Be Combined

a lot	each other	high school	every time
even though	good night	all right	no one
living room	dining room	in front	

Words That Should Be Combined

another	newspapers	bathroom
bedroom	playroom	good-bye, goodbye, or good-by
bookkeeper	roommate	cannot
schoolteacher	downstairs	southeast, northwest, etc.
grandmother	throughout	nearby
worthwhile	nevertheless	yourself, himself, myself, etc.

Words Whose Spelling Depends on Their Meaning

one word: *Already* means "before."
He offered to do the dishes, but I had *already* done them.
two words: *All ready* means "ready."
My dog was *all ready* to play Frisbee.

one word: *Altogether* means "entirely."
That movie was *altogether* too confusing.
two words: *All together* means "in a group."
My sisters were *all together* in the kitchen.

one word: *Always* means "every time."
My grandfather is *always* right about baseball statistics.
two words: *All ways* means "every path" or "every aspect."
We tried *all ways* to get to the beach house.
He is a gentleman in *all ways*.

one word: *Anymore* means "any longer."
I do not want to exercise *anymore*.
two words: *Any more* means "additional."
Are there *any more* pickles?

one word: *Anyone* means "any person at all."
Is *anyone* home?
two words: *Any one* means "one person or thing in a special group."
I'll take *any one* of the chairs on sale.

one word: *Apart* means "separate."
Liam stood *apart* from his friends.
two words: *A part* is "a piece or section."
I read *a part* of the chapter.

one word: *Everyday* means "ordinary."
Tim was wearing his *everyday* clothes.
two words: *Every day* means "each day."
Sam jogs *every day*.

one word: *Everyone* means "all the people."
Everyone has bad days.
two words: *Every one* means "all the people or things in a specific
    group."
My father asked *every one* of the neighbors for a donation to the Red
    Cross.

Exercise 8   **Practice: Do You Spell It as One Word or Two?**

Circle the correct word in parentheses in each sentence below.

1. Jason apologized to me yesterday; he said he wanted to make everything (all right, allright) between us.

2. Terry would be happy to own (any one, anyone) of the beautiful houses being built on Pinewood Avenue.

3. If you have (all ready, already) seen the new Jamie Foxx movie, let's go see the one with Jennifer Lopez and Matt Damon.

4. Robin is thinking of moving back to the (North East, Northeast); she misses her friends in Vermont.

5. Being snowed in at the airport was an (all together, altogether) horrible experience.

6. My father sold insurance, and my mother was a (school teacher, schoolteacher) in an elementary school.

7. (Every time, Everytime) I hear that song, I think of Luis.

8. My math professor says he doesn't want to hear (any more, anymore) complaints about the homework.

9. Lynn told me to return (every one, everyone) of the CDs I borrowed from her.

10. Tom will have to get a new (room mate, roommate) if Bernard leaves town.

Exercise 9   **Connect: Do You Spell It as One Word or Two? Correcting Errors in a Paragraph**

Connect

The following paragraph contains errors in word combinations. Correct the errors in the space above each line. There are ten errors.

My friends all ways want to go to a club on Saturday nights, but I am not will-

ing to go with them any more. Like many women, I want to meet people, but I

don't think I want to meet men in a bar. Everytime I go to a bar, I meet two kinds

of men: drunk men or arrogant men. Of course, most of my girlfriends and I drink

too much at a bar or a club, too. Perhaps we also appear to be arrogant. I have

begun to think that, a part from putting men and women under the same roof,

bars don't do much to help people get to know eachother. Loud music, crowded

spaces, and role-playing don't help anyone make a new friend. Worth while rela-

tionships are likely to begin in a more natural environment such as a classroom,

snack bar, gym, workplace, or place of worship. I can not put myself in the same

situation of dressing up, trying to look cool, and scanning the crowd for any one who might become a friend. The night all ways ends in a headache, a disappoint-

ment, or a mistake. I am saying goodby to my Saturday night routine and looking

for something healthier.

A LIST OF COMMONLY MISSPELLED WORDS

Following is a list of words you use often in your writing. Study this list and use it as a reference.

1. absence	43. believe	85. copy
2. absent	44. benefit	86. cough
3. accept	45. bicycle	87. cousin
4. achieve	46. bought	88. criticism
5. ache	47. breakfast	89. criticize
6. acquire	48. breathe	90. crowded
7. across	49. brilliant	91. daily
8. actually	50. brother	92. daughter
9. advertise	51. brought	93. deceive
10. again	52. bruise	94. decide
11. a lot	53. build	95. definite
12. all right	54. bulletin	96. dentist
13. almost	55. bureau	97. dependent
14. always	56. buried	98. deposit
15. amateur	57. business	99. describe
16. American	58. busy	100. desperate
17. answer	59. calendar	101. development
18. anxious	60. cannot	102. different
19. apparent	61. career	103. dilemma
20. appetite	62. careful	104. dining
21. apology	63. catch	105. direction
22. appreciate	64. category	106. disappearance
23. argue	65. caught	107. disappoint
24. argument	66. cemetery	108. discipline
25. asked	67. cereal	109. disease
26. athlete	68. certain	110. divide
27. attempt	69. chair	111. doctor
28. August	70. cheat	112. doesn't
29. aunt	71. chief	113. don't
30. author	72. chicken	114. doubt
31. automobile	73. children	115. during
32. autumn	74. cigarette	116. dying
33. avenue	75. citizen	117. early
34. awful	76. city	118. earth
35. awkward	77. college	119. eighth
36. balance	78. color	120. eligible
37. basically	79. comfortable	121. embarrass
38. because	80. committee	122. encouragement
39. becoming	81. competition	123. enough
40. beginning	82. conscience	124. environment
41. behavior	83. convenient	125. especially
42. belief	84. conversation	126. etc.

127. every
128. exact
129. exaggeration
130. excellent
131. except
132. exercise
133. excite
134. existence
135. expect
136. experience
137. explanation
138. factory
139. familiar
140. family
141. fascinating
142. February
143. finally
144. forehead
145. foreign
146. forty
147. fourteen
148. friend
149. fundamental
150. general
151. generally
152. goes
153. going
154. government
155. grammar
156. grateful
157. grocery
158. guarantee
159. guard
160. guess
161. guidance
162. guide
163. half
164. happiness
165. handkerchief
166. heavy
167. height
168. heroes
169. holiday
170. hospital
171. humorous
172. identity
173. illegal
174. imaginary
175. immediately
176. important
177. independent
178. integration
179. intelligent
180. interest
181. interfere
182. interpretation
183. interrupt
184. irrelevant
185. irritable
186. iron
187. island
188. January
189. jewelry
190. judgment
191. kindergarten
192. kitchen
193. knowledge
194. laboratory
195. language
196. laugh
197. leisure
198. length
199. library
200. loneliness
201. listen
202. lying
203. maintain
204. maintenance
205. marriage
206. mathematics
207. meant
208. measure
209. medicine
210. million
211. miniature
212. minute
213. muscle
214. mysterious
215. naturally
216. necessary
217. neighbor
218. nervous
219. nickel
220. niece
221. ninety
222. ninth
223. occasion
224. o'clock
225. often
226. omission
227. once
228. operate
229. opinion
230. optimist
231. original
232. parallel
233. particular
234. peculiar
235. perform
236. perhaps
237. permanent
238. persevere
239. personnel
240. persuade
241. physically
242. pleasant
243. possess
244. possible
245. potato
246. practical
247. prefer
248. prejudice
249. prescription
250. presence
251. president
252. privilege
253. probably
254. professor
255. psychology
256. punctuation
257. pursue
258. quart
259. really
260. receipt
261. receive
262. recognize
263. recommend
264. reference
265. religious
266. reluctantly
267. remember
268. resource
269. restaurant
270. ridiculous
271. right
272. rhythm
273. sandwich
274. Saturday
275. scene
276. schedule
277. scissors
278. secretary
279. seize
280. several
281. severely
282. significant
283. similar
284. since
285. sincerely

continued

286. soldier
287. sophomore
288. strength
289. studying
290. success
291. surely
292. surprise
293. taught
294. temperature
295. theater
296. thorough

297. thousand
298. tied
299. tomorrow
300. tongue
301. tragedy
302. trouble
303. truly
304. twelfth
305. unfortunately
306. unknown
307. until

308. unusual
309. using
310. variety
311. vegetable
312. Wednesday
313. weird
314. which
315. writing
316. written
317. yesterday

Words That Sound Alike/Look Alike

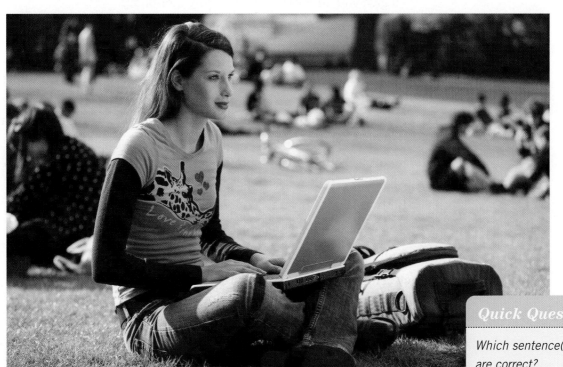

CHAPTER 29

Chapter Objectives

Students will be able to distinguish between common sound-alike and look-alike words and incorporate such distinctions in their writing.

WORDS THAT SOUND ALIKE/LOOK ALIKE

Words that sound alike or look alike (often called *homonyms*) can be confusing. Here is a list of some of the confusing words. Study this list, and make a note of any words that give you trouble.

a/an/and *A* is used before a word beginning with a consonant or consonant sound:

> Jason bought *a* car.

An is used before a word beginning with a vowel or vowel sound:

> Nancy took *an* apple to work.

And joins words or ideas:

> Pudding *and* cake are my favorite desserts.
> Fresh vegetables taste delicious, *and* they are nutritious.

accept/except *Accept* means "to receive":

I *accept* your apology.

Except means "excluding":

I'll give you all my books *except* my dictionary.

addition/edition An *addition* is something that is added:

My father built an *addition* to our house in the form of a porch.

An *edition* is an issue of a newspaper or one of a series of printings of a book:

I checked the latest *edition* of the *Daily News* to see if my advertisement is in it.

advice/advise *Advice* is an opinion offered as a guide; it is what you give someone:

Betty asked for my *advice* about finding a job.

Advise is what you do when you give an opinion offered as a guide:

I couldn't *advise* Betty about finding a job.

affect/effect *Affect* means "to influence something":

Getting a bad grade will *affect* my chances for a scholarship.

Effect means "a result" or "to cause something to happen":

Your kindness had a great *effect* on me.
The committee struggled to *effect* a compromise.

allowed/aloud *Allowed* means "permitted":

I'm not *allowed* to skateboard on those steps.

Aloud means "out loud":

The teacher read the story *aloud*.

all ready/already *All ready* means "ready":

The dog was *all ready* to go for a walk.

Already means "before":

David had *already* made the salad.

altar/alter An *altar* is a table or place in a church:

They were married in front of the *altar*.

Alter means "to change":

My plane was delayed, so I had to *alter* my plans for the evening.

angel/angle An *angel* is a heavenly being:

That night, I felt an *angel* guiding me.

An *angle* is the space within two lines:

The road turned at a sharp *angle*.

are/our *Are* is a verb, the plural of *is*:

We *are* friends of the mayor.

Our means "belonging to us":

We have *our* family quarrels.

beside/besides *Beside* means "next to":

He sat *beside* me at the concert.

Besides means "in addition":

I would never lie to you; *besides*, I have no reason to lie.

brake/break *Brake* means "to stop" or "a device for stopping":

That truck *brakes* at railroad crossings.
When he saw the animal on the road, he hit the *brakes*.

Break means "to come apart," or "to make something come apart":

The eggs are likely to *break*.
I can *break* the seal on that package.

breath/breathe *Breath* is the air you take in, and it rhymes with *death:*

I was running so fast, I lost my *breath*.

Breathe means "to take in air":

He found it hard to *breathe* in high altitudes.

buy/by *Buy* means "to purchase something":

Sylvia wants to *buy* a shovel.

By means "near," "by means of," or "before":

He sat *by* his sister.

I learn *by* taking good notes in class.

By ten o'clock, Nick was tired.

capital/capitol *Capital* means "city" or "wealth":

Albany is the *capital* of New York.
Jack invested his *capital* in real estate.

A *capitol* is a building where a legislature meets:

The city has a famous *capitol* building.

cereal/serial *Cereal* is a breakfast food or type of grain:

My favorite *cereal* is Cheerios.

Serial means "in a series":

Look for the *serial* number on the appliance.

choose/chose *Choose* means "to select." It rhymes with *snooze:*

Today I am going to *choose* a new sofa.

Chose is the past tense of *choose:*

Yesterday I *chose* a new rug.

close/clothes/cloths *Close* means "near" or "intimate." It can also mean "to end or shut something":

We live *close* to the train station.
James and Margie are *close* friends.
Noreen wants to *close* her eyes for ten minutes.

Clothes are wearing apparel:

> Eduardo has new *clothes*.

Cloths are pieces of fabric:

> I clean the silver with damp *cloths* and a special polish.

coarse/course *Coarse* means "rough" or "crude":

> The top of the table had a *coarse* texture.
> His language was *coarse*.

A *course* is a direction or path. It is also a subject in school:

> The hurricane took a northern *course*.
> In my freshman year, I took a *course* in drama.

complement/compliment Complement means "complete" or "make better":

> The colors in that room *complement* the style of the furniture.

A *compliment* is praise:

> Trevor gave me a *compliment* about my cooking.

conscience/conscious Your *conscience* is your inner, moral guide:

> His *conscience* bothered him when he told a lie.

Conscious means "aware" or "awake":

> The accident victim was not fully conscious.

council/counsel A *council* is a group of people:

> The city *council* meets tonight.

Counsel means "advice" or "to give advice":

> I need your *counsel* about my investments.
> My father always *counsels* me about my career.

decent/descent *Decent* means "suitable" or "proper":

> I hope Mike gets a *decent* job.

Descent means "going down, falling, or sinking":

> The plane began its *descent* to the airport.

desert/dessert A *desert* is dry land. To *desert* means "to abandon":

> To survive a trip across the *desert*, people need water.
> He will never *desert* a friend.

Dessert is the sweet food we eat at the end of a meal.

> I want ice cream for *dessert*.

do/due *Do* means "perform":

> I have to stop complaining; I *do* it constantly.

Due means "owing" or "because of":

> The rent is *due* tomorrow.
> The game was canceled *due* to rain.

does/dose *Does* is a form of *do:*

> My father *does* the laundry.

A *dose* is a quantity of medicine.

> Whenever I had a cold, my mother gave me a *dose* of cough syrup.

fair/fare *Fair* means "unbiased." It can also mean "promising" or "good":

> The judge's decision was *fair*.
> Jose has a *fair* chance of winning the title.

A *fare* is the amount of money a passenger must pay.

> I couldn't afford the plane *fare* to Miami.

farther/further *Farther* means "a greater physical distance":

> His house is a few blocks *farther* down the street.

Further means "greater" or "additional." Use it when you are not describing a physical distance:

> My second French class gave me *further* training in French conversation.

flour/flower *Flour* is ground-up grain, an ingredient used in cooking:

> I use whole-wheat *flour* in my muffins.

A *flower* is a blossom:

> She wore a *flower* in her hair.

forth/fourth *Forth* means "forward":

> The pendulum on the clock swung back and *forth*.

Fourth means "number four in a sequence":

> I was *fourth* in line for tickets.

hear/here *Hear* means "to receive sounds in the ear":

> I can *hear* the music.

Here is a place:

> We can have the meeting *here*.

heard/herd *Heard* is the past tense of *hear:*

> I *heard* you talk in your sleep last night.

A *herd* is a group of animals:

> The farmer has a fine *herd* of cows.

hole/whole A *hole* is an empty place or opening:

> I see a *hole* in the wall.

Whole means "complete" or "entire":

> Silvio gave me the *whole* steak.

isle/aisle An *isle* is an island:

> We visited the *isle* of Capri.

An *aisle* is a passageway between sections of seats:

> The flight attendant came down the *aisle* and offered us coffee.

its/it's *Its* means "belonging to it":

> The car lost *its* rear bumper.

It's is a shortened form of *it is* or *it has*:

> *It's* a beautiful day.
> *It's* been a pleasure to meet you.

knew/new *Knew* is the past tense of *know:*

> I *knew* Teresa in high school.

New means "fresh, recent, not old":

> I want some *new* shoes.

know/no Know means "to understand":

> They *know* how to play soccer.

No is a negative:

> Carla has *no* fear of heights.

Exercise 1 **Practice: Words That Sound Alike/Look Alike**

Circle the correct words in parentheses in each sentence below.

1. I need to look (farther, further) into the circumstances of the crime before I can (advice, advise) you about possible suspects.

2. The rich investment banker collects first (additions, editions) of famous books; he has an expert tell him which ones to (buy, by).

3. Edward must have no (conscience, conscious), for he was willing to (desert, dessert) his children in order to satisfy his own desires.

4. Whenever Kim (complements, compliments) me, I (hear, here) a hint of insincerity in her voice.

5. Eric needs a (does, dose) of reality before he makes plans to walk to the (altar, alter) with Sabrina.

6. I spent a (hole, whole) lot of money on dresses and other (close, clothes, cloths) last month, and now payment is (do, due).

7. When I had to speak in front of the town (council, counsel), I was so nervous I could hardly (breath, breathe).

8. One of (are, our) trees was struck by lightning; a huge branch fell at a crazy (angel, angle).

9. A large man crowded in (beside, besides) me on the bus right before I tried to reach the (isle, aisle).

10. I'm lazy, and I don't know how to cook, so I live on (cereal, serial) and Pop Tarts unless someone cooks me a (decent, descent) meal.

Collaborate

Exercise 2 **Collaborate: Words That Sound Alike/Look Alike**

Working with a partner or group, write one sentence for each word below.

1. a. its _____

   b. it's _____

2. a. coarse _____

   b. course _____

3. a. fair   _____

   b. fare   _____

4. a. forth   _____

   b. fourth   _____

5. a. capital   _____

   b. capitol   _____

6. a. accept   _____

   b. except   _____

7. a. brake   _____

   b. break   _____

8. a. affect   _____

   b. effect   _____

9. a. know   _____

   b. no   _____

10. a. flour   _____

   b. flower   _____

Exercise 3   **Connect: Editing a Paragraph for Words That Sound Alike/ Look Alike**

Connect

The following paragraph has errors in words that sound alike/look alike. Correct each error in the space above it. There are ten errors.

Driving an old truck presented several challenges for me recently. I usually ride my bike to school and sometimes drive my girlfriend's car. However, one afternoon she called me and asked for help. She was stranded on a country road about ten miles from home. Her car had broken down, and she needed me to pick her up. I couldn't leave her desperate and desserted, waiting alone for a tow truck. Since I had no car, I borrowed my friend's old truck. I had never driven a truck before; beside, I was nervous about driving on strange roads. Nevertheless, I set fourth bravely. As soon as I started the engine, I was conscience of weird sounds. They seemed to be coming from the engine. A few minutes later, I hit a whole in the road. I imagined the worst consequences. Maybe I had broken something important under the truck. Perhaps I had lost the ability to steer. Nervously, I drove further down the rough road. My next challenge was a steep decent down a hill. At that moment, I feared a loss of break power, but fortunately, I made it safely down the hill. Several miles later, I saw my girlfriend and her car at the side of a wooded area. After a long wait, we managed to get her car towed and to return safely to town. The series of mishaps involved in driving that truck led me to make a promise to myself: I will never drive that truck again. I would rather pay bus or even taxi fair, hitchhike, or even stay home. I will do anything accept get behind the wheel of that decrepit vehicle.

MORE WORDS THAT SOUND ALIKE/LOOK ALIKE

lead/led When *lead* rhymes with *need*, it means "to give directions, to take charge." If *lead* rhymes with *bed*, it is a metal:

> The marching band will *lead* the parade.
> Your bookbag is as heavy as *lead*.

Led is the past form of *lead* when it means "to give directions, to take charge":

> The cheerleaders *led* the parade last year.

lessen/lesson *Lessen* means make less or reduce:

> I took an aspirin to *lessen* the pain of my headache.

A *lesson* is something to be learned or studied:

> I had my first guitar *lesson* yesterday.

loan/lone A *loan* is something you give on the condition that it be returned:

> When I was broke, I got a *loan* of fifty dollars from my aunt.

Lone means "solitary, alone":

> A *lone* shopper stood in the checkout line.

loose/lose *Loose* means "not tight":

> In the summer, *loose* clothing keeps me cool.

To *lose* something means "to be unable to keep it":

> I'm afraid I will *lose* my car keys.

medal/meddle/metal A *medal* is a badge of honor or a coinlike piece of bronze, silver, or similar substance used to commemorate an event.

> Mandy won a *medal* for swimming at the regional competition.
> At the Revolutionary War museum, visitors could buy souvenir *medals* depicting famous battles.

To *meddle* means to interfere when the interference is not justified.

> Ben didn't think his mother should *meddle* in his romantic attachments.

Metal is an element such as gold or silver that often has a particular luster.

> Her bracelet was a thick cuff of a beaten *metal*.

moral/morale *Moral* means "upright, honorable, connected to ethical standards":

> I have a *moral* obligation to care for my children.

Morale is confidence or spirit:

> After the game, the team's *morale* was low.

pain/pane *Pain* means "suffering":

> I had very little *pain* after the surgery.

A *pane* is a piece of glass:

> The girl's wild throw broke a window *pane*.

pair/pear A *pair* is a set of two:

> Mark has a *pair* of antique swords.

A *pear* is a fruit:

> In the autumn, I like a *pear* for a snack.

passed/past *Passed* means "went by." It can also mean "handed to":

> The happy days *passed* too quickly.
> Janice *passed* me the mustard.

Past means "the time that has gone by":

> Let's leave the *past* behind us.

patience/patients *Patience* is calm endurance:

> When I am caught in a traffic jam, I should have more *patience*.

Patients are people under medical care:

> There are too many *patients* in the doctor's waiting room.

peace/piece *Peace* is calmness:

> Looking at the ocean brings me a sense of *peace*.

A *piece* is a part of something:

> Norman took a *piece* of coconut cake.

personal/personnel *Personal* means "connected to a person." It can also mean "intimate":

> Whether to lease or own a car is a *personal* choice.
> That information is too *personal* to share.

Personnel are the staff in an office:

> The Digby Electronics Company is developing a new health plan for its *personnel*.

plain/ plane *Plain* means "simple, clear, or ordinary." It can also mean "flat land":

> The restaurant serves *plain* but tasty food.
> Her house was in the center of a windy *plain*.

A *plane* is an aircraft:

> We took a small *plane* to the island.

pray/prey A person who *prays* is speaking to a spiritual being:

> Every night, my mother *prayed* for my safe return from the war.

Prey is a victim, whether it is an animal killed for food or a person. It can also mean to make another person into a victim:

> Small animals such as rabbits are often the *prey* of larger ones.
> The robber *preyed* on those who walked alone at night.

presence/presents Your *presence* is your attendance, your being somewhere:

> We request your *presence* at our wedding.

Presents are gifts:

> My daughter got too many birthday *presents*.

principal/principle *Principal* means "most important." It also means "the head of a school":

> My *principal* reason for quitting is the low salary.
> The *principal* of Crestview Elementary School is popular with students.

A *principle* is a guiding rule:

> Betraying a friend is against my *principles*.

quiet/quit/quite *Quiet* means "without noise":

> The library has many *quiet* corners.

Quit means "stop":

> Will you *quit* complaining?

Quite means "truly" or "exactly":

> Victor's speech was *quite* convincing.

rain/reign/rein *Rain* is wet weather:

> We have had a week of *rain*.

To *reign* is to rule; *reign* is royal rule:

> King Arthur's *reign* in Camelot is the subject of many poems.

A *rein* is a leather strap in an animal's harness:

> When Charlie got on the horse, he held the *reins* very tight.

residence/residents A *residence* is a place to live.

> For years, my *residence* was a garage apartment with no kitchen.

Residents are the people who live in a certain place.

> *Residents* of the Florida Keys are used to the uncertainty of hurricane season.

right/rite/write *Right* is a direction (the opposite of left). It can also mean "correct":

> To get to the gas station, turn *right* at the corner.
> On my sociology test, I got nineteen out of twenty questions *right*.

A *rite* is a ceremony:

> I am interested in the funeral *rites* of other cultures.

To *write* is to set down in words:

> Brian has to *write* a book report.

sight/site/cite A *sight* is something you can see:

> The truck stop was a welcome *sight*.

A *site* is a location:

> The city is building a courthouse on the *site* of my old school.

Cite means "to quote an authority." It can also mean "to give an example":

> In her term paper, Christina wanted to *cite* several computer experts.
> When my father lectured me on speeding, he *cited* the story of my best
> friend's car accident.

soar/sore To *soar* is to fly upward. It can also mean to rise higher.

> We watched the eagle *soar* from its perch in the tree.
> Sam sang at the audition and *soared* above the competition.

Sore means "painful."

> After I spent the afternoon raking leaves, I had a *sore* back.

sole/soul A *sole* is the bottom of a foot or shoe:

> My left boot needs a new *sole*.

A *soul* is the spiritual part of a person:

> Some people say meditation is good for the *soul*.

stair/stare A *stair* is a step:

> The toddler carefully climbed each *stair*.

A *stare* is a long, fixed look:

> I wish that woman wouldn't *stare* at me.

stake/steak A *stake* is a stick driven into the ground:

> The gardener put *stakes* around the tomato plants.

A *steak* is a piece of meat or fish:

> I like my *steak* cooked medium rare.

stationary/stationery *Stationary* means "standing still":

> As the speaker presented his speech, he remained *stationary*.

Stationery is writing paper:

> For my birthday, my uncle gave me some *stationery* with my name
> printed on it.

steal/steel To *steal* means "to take someone else's property without permission or right":

> Last night, someone tried to *steal* my car.

Steel is a form of iron:

> The door is made of *steel*.

than/then *Than* is used to compare things:

> My dog is more intelligent *than* many people.

Then means "at that time":

> I lived in Buffalo for two years; *then* I moved to Albany.

their/there/they're *Their* means "belonging to them":

My grandparents donated *their* old television to a women's shelter.

There means "at that place." It can also be used as an introductory word:

Sit *there*, next to Simone.
There is a reason for his happiness.

They're is a contraction of *they are*:

Jaime and Sandra are visiting; *they're* my cousins.

thorough/through/threw *Thorough* means "complete":

I did a *thorough* cleaning of my closet.

Through means "from one side to the other." It can also mean "finished":

We drove *through* Greenview on our way to Lake Western.
I'm *through* with my studies.

Threw is the past tense of *throw*:

I *threw* the ball to him.

to/too/two *To* means "in a direction toward." It is also a word that can go in front of a verb:

I am driving *to* Miami.
Selena loves *to* write poems.

Too means "also." It also means "very":

Anita played great golf; Adam did well, *too*.
It is *too* kind of you to visit.

Two is the number:

Mr. Almeida owns *two* clothing stores.

vain/vane/vein *Vain* means "conceited." It also means "unsuccessful":

Victor is *vain* about his dark, curly hair.
The doctor made a *vain* attempt to revive the patient.

A *vane* is a device that moves to indicate the direction of the wind:

There was an old weather *vane* on the barn roof.

A *vein* is a blood vessel:

I could see the *veins* in his hands.

waist/waste The *waist* is the middle part of the body:

He had a leather belt around his *waist*.

Waste means "to use carelessly." It also means "thrown away because it is useless":

I can't *waste* my time watching trashy television shows.
That manufacturing plant has many *waste* products.

wait/weight *Wait* means "to hold yourself ready for something":

I can't *wait* until my check arrives.

Weight means "heaviness":

> He tested the *weight* of the bat.

weather/whether *Weather* refers to conditions outside.

> If the *weather* is warm, I'll go swimming.

Whether means "if":

> *Whether* you help me or not, I'll paint the hallway.

were/we're/where *Were* is the past form of *are:*

> Only last year, we *were* scared freshmen.

We're is the contraction of *we are:*

> Today *we're* confident sophomores.

Where refers to a place:

> Show me *where* you used to play basketball.

whined/wind/wined *Whined* means "complained":

> Polly *whined* about the weather because the rain kept her indoors.

Wind (if it rhymes with *find*) means "to coil or wrap something" or "to turn a key":

> *Wind* that extension cord, or you'll trip on it.

Wind (if it rhymes with *sinned*) is air in motion:

> The *wind* blew my cap off.

If someone *wined* you, he or she treated you to some wine:

> My brother *wined* and dined his boss.

who's/whose *Who's* is a contraction of *who is* or *who has:*

> *Who's* driving?
> *Who's* been leaving the door unlocked?

Whose means "belonging to whom":

> I wonder *whose* dog this is.

woman/women *Woman* means "one adult female person":

> A *woman* in the supermarket gave me her extra coupons.

Women means "more than one woman":

> Three *women* from Missouri joined the management team.

wood/would *Wood* is a hard substance made from trees:

> I have a table made of a polished *wood.*

Would is the past form of *will:*

> Albert said he *would* think about the offer.

your/you're *Your* means "belonging to you":

> I think you dropped *your* wallet.

You're is the short form of *you are:*

> *You're* not telling the truth.

Exercise 4 **Practice: More Words That Sound Alike/Look Alike**

Circle the correct words in each sentence below.

1. During the (rain, reign) of King George III of England, the American colonies lost (patience, patients) with the king's restrictive laws and fought for (their, there, they're) freedom.

2. (Moral, Morale) at the fraternity has declined since the group was criticized for its reckless initiation (rights, rites, writes).

3. The poor and trusting are often the (pray/prey) of con artists who offer get-rich-quick schemes such as fake overseas lotteries and worthless (medal/meddle/metal) disguised as gold.

4. It was (quiet, quit, quite) noisy in the library today until the librarian asked the three elderly men to (quiet, quit, quite) laughing and chatting at the computers.

5. We thought we were lost at first, but eventually Diane's directions (lead, led) us to a large red barn with a (weather, whether)(vain, vane, vein).

6. The (whined, wind, wined) swept the rain against the car with such force that we hardly knew (were, we're, where) we (were, we're, where) going.

7. I want to know (who's, whose) responsible for making that (woman, women) wait for an hour and (than, then) giving her the wrong prescription.

8. If (your, you're) looking for a (loan, lone) to start your business, you will have to (site, cite) other, similar projects that have been successful.

9. Edward knew he (wood, would) be (to, too, two) busy to stop for a meal, so he put a (pair, pear), a bottle of water, and a granola bar in his briefcase.

10. It will take time to (lessen, lesson) the heartache of Rick's loss, but eventually he will find (peace, piece).

Collaborate

Exercise 5 **Collaborate: More Words That Sound Alike/Look Alike**

Working with a partner or group, write one sentence for each of the words below.

1. **a.** loose _____

   b. lose _____

2. **a.** stationary _____

   b. stationery _____

3. **a.** residence _____

   b. residents _____

4. a. passed _____

   b. past _____

5. a. plain _____

   b. plane _____

6. a. thorough _____

   b. through _____

   c. threw _____

7. a. sole _____

   b. soul _____

8. a. stake _____

   b. steak _____

9. a. wait _____

   b. weight _____

10. a. stair _____

   b. stare _____

| Exercise 6 | Connect: Editing a Paragraph for Errors in More Words That Sound Alike/Look Alike |

Connect

The following paragraph has errors in words that sound alike or look alike. Correct each error in the space above it. There are sixteen errors.

Silvio hated his job. He didn't know how he would make it threw another day

at work. Yet he was afraid to loose his job because times were tough. Moral at the

party and costume store was low. Months of misery had past. Silvio didn't know if

he could endure many more days of dissatisfaction. The principle problem was the

assistant manager. He had no idea how to deal with personal and had no patients.

Most of the staff worked in quite despair, but Silvio's days past in a silent, growing

anger. Then the horrible rain of the assistant manager ended. He resigned when

the owner of the store discovered a discrepancy between the sales records and the

bank deposits. Soon the assistant manager was identified as the one who had been

steeling money. Rumors spread. Supposedly, the assistant manager had pleaded in

vane for another chance. As the news of the assistant manager's departure spread,

Silvio and the other employees we're relieved. Surely a new boss wood have to be

better then there old one, they felt. At last, Silvio was able to let go of his anger.

Exercise 7 **Practice: Words That Sound Alike/Look Alike:**
A Comprehensive Exercise

Circle the correct words in parentheses in each sentence below.

1. As the officer began to (advice, advise) Lucy of her (rights, rites, writes), Lucy remained (stationary, stationery).

2. Mrs. Kowalski is such a good (sole, soul) that I sometimes feel she is an (angel, angle) (hear, here) on earth.

3. (Its, It's) a sad day when a science fiction movie loses (its, it's) power to entertain me, but this movie is a (waist, waste) of my time.

4. Todd's shirt (complements, compliments) the color of his eyes, and that color (wood, would) look good on you, (to, too, two).

5. I was not (conscience, conscious) of Anita's bad temper until she jerked hard on her horse's (rains, reigns, reins) and (than, then) kicked the poor animal.

6. It was so cold that I could see my (breath, breathe) on the window (pane, pain) and (knew, new) that winter had arrived.

7. Sam was not willing to (accept, except) his brother's (council, counsel) about applying for financial aid.

8. (Your, You're) behavior in court can (affect, effect) the outcome of the trial, no matter how (fair, fare) the jury tries to be.

9. As I walked down the (isle, aisle) with my bride, I suddenly realized that we were about to go (forth, fourth) into a (knew, new) life.

10. My doctor is encouraging his (patience, patients) to try a (does, dose) of an over-the-counter cold medicine instead of overusing antibiotics.

11. My brother's class is taking a trip to Tallahassee, the (capital, capitol) of Florida, as part of a (coarse, course) in political science.

12. I hope that the loss of his home will have no (farther, further) (affect, effect) on the (all ready, already) unhappy child.

13. Larry doesn't follow fashion trends; when he needs (close, clothes, cloths), he buys (plain, plane) old jeans and flannel shirts from discount stores.

14. My first goal is to find a (decent, descent) apartment; (then, than) I want to meet someone (who's, whose) (principals, principles) are the same as mine.

15. I (wander, wonder) if I should go to the (personal, personnel) department of Satellite Services and apply for a job; I've (heard, herd) that (moral, morale) is high among the staff.

16. The actress is so (vain, vane, vein) that she expects fresh (flours, flowers) in her dressing room every night.

17. I want to take my toddler to Felipe's wedding, but I don't (know, no) (weather, whether) children are (aloud, allowed) at the ceremony.

18. Residents of the area are nervous about the rumors of a (cereal, serial) killer; (their, there, they're) locking (their, there, they're) doors at night.

19. It was difficult for the employees at the plant to (wait, weight) for a decision from the company president when so many jobs (were, we're, where) at (stake, steak).

20. The famous athlete's (presence, presents) at the local basketball game caused many people to (stair, stare).

| Exercise 8 | Connect: Editing a Paragraph for Errors in Words That Sound Alike/Look Alike: A Comprehensive Exercise |

Connect

The following paragraph has errors in words that sound alike or look alike. Correct each error in the space above it. There are eleven errors.

A family tradition in are house was celebrated every Sunday when we

enjoyed homemade pancakes. Although many advertisements show woman

cooking, a man made our Sunday breakfast. I wood stand beside my father as he

stirred the batter and carefully poured spoonfuls into a buttered pan. I learned to

weight for him to flip each pancake at the rite time. A pancake cannot be too soft

or too solid when it is flipped, he said. My father new the right way to make them:

he showed patients. Whether he made plane or blueberry pancakes, he made

delicious ones. My memories of this ritual came to me recently when I was far

from home. I was in the U. S. Army, and I woke to the sight of the sun rising in the

dessert. Suddenly I thought of my father's pancakes. I wanted to be in the family

kitchen, watching my father make breakfast. Someday I will enjoy the quite plea-

sure and piece of such a day.

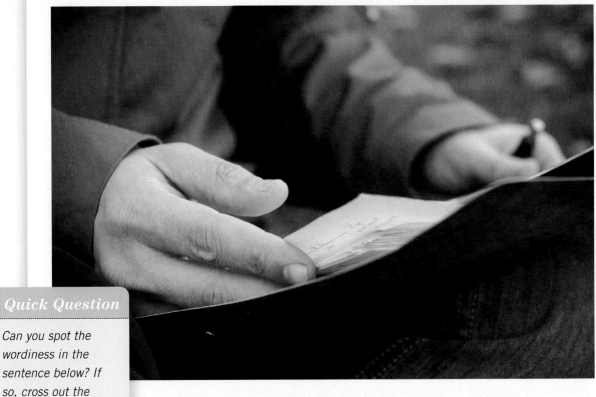

Quick Question

Can you spot the wordiness in the sentence below? If so, cross out the wordiness.

We should meet as soon as we can in order to share in common each and every one of our concerns about a tuition hike.

(After you study this chapter, you will be confident of your answer.)

Chapter Objectives

Students will be able to (1) identify examples of wordiness, slang, and clichés and (2) gain an appreciation for precise word choice (diction) in their writing.

PRECISE LANGUAGE

One way to improve your writing is to pay close attention to your choice of words. As you revise and edit, be careful to use precise language and avoid wordiness, clichés, and slang.

Try to be as specific as you can in explaining or describing. Replace vague, general words or phrases with more precise language.

> **not this:** Last night, I made a lot of money in tips.
> **but this:** Last night, I made *fifty dollars* in tips.

> **not this:** He gave me a nice smile.
> **but this:** He gave me a *friendly* smile.
> **or this:** He gave me a *reassuring* smile.
> **or this:** He gave me a *welcoming* smile.

not this: Maggie is a ~~good~~ friend.
but this: Maggie is a *loyal* friend.
or this: Maggie is a *devoted* friend.

Exercise 1   **Practice: Using Precise Language**

In the following sentences, replace each italicized word or phrase with a more precise word or phrase. Write your revisions above the lines.

1. I had a *nice* weekend with my folks.

2. You need to buy *a lot* of potato chips for the party.

3. I think about you *often*.

4. Take Mr. Benson for English; he's *nice*.

5. Mitchell had another *bad* day at work.

6. This time, let's go to an *interesting* movie.

7. I am going to need *a lot* of help with this course.

8. I tried to practice my speech, but it sounds *stupid*.

9. What's wrong? You sound *funny* today.

10. You will make a *great* father someday.

WORDINESS

As you revise and edit your work, check for *wordiness:* the use of extra words. If you can convey the same idea in fewer words, do so. You can be precise *and* direct.

not this: After the accident, I thought ~~in my mind that~~ I was to blame.
but this: After the accident, *I thought* I was to blame.

not this: ~~In my opinion,~~ I think children should exercise daily.
but this: *I think* children should exercise daily.

not this: Jorge bought a CD for ~~the price of~~ $10.95.
but this: Jorge bought a CD *for* $10.95.

Here is a list of some wordy expressions and possible substitutes:

Wordy Expressions	Possible Substitutes
alternative choices	alternatives, choices
asset group	assets
attach together	attach
at a later date and time	later
at a future date	later
at that time	then
at the present moment	now, presently

Wordy Expressions	Possible Substitutes
at the present time	now, presently
at this point in time	now, today
basic essentials	essentials
blend together	blend
bring together	unite
by means of	by
by the fact that	because
change out	replace
combine together	combine
consider the fact that	consider
continue on	continue
day in and day out	daily
deep down inside he believed	he believed
due to the fact that	because
each and every one	each one
end result	result
for all intents and purposes	realistically
for the reason that	because
gather together	gather
have a need for	need
have a realization of	realize
I felt inside	I felt
I personally feel	I feel
I thought in my head	I thought
in the field of art (music, etc.)	in art (music, etc.)
in the near future	soon
in this day and age	today
in this modern world	today
in my mind, I think	I think
in my opinion, I think	I think
in order to	to
in today's society	today
join together	join
maximum amount	maximum
mix together	mix
of a remarkable kind	remarkable
on a daily basis	daily
on and on	endlessly
on a regular basis	regularly
past experience	experience
point in time	time
reached a decision	decided
really and truly	really
reason why	reason
refer back	refer
reflect back	reflect
repeat again	repeat
separate out	separate
shadow of a doubt	doubt
share in common	share
short in stature	short
small in size	small

Wordy Expressions	Possible Substitutes
skills set	skills
start off	start
switch out	replace
the reason being	because
things of that nature	similar traits/objects
top priority	priority
true facts	facts
two different kinds	two kinds
unite together	unite
until and unless	until, unless
very unique	unique

Exercise 2 Practice: Revising for Wordiness

Revise the following sentences, eliminating the wordiness. Write your revisions in the space above the lines.

1. At this point in time, I personally feel that better office technology should be the company's top priority.

2. I cannot approve a promotion for Walter Ford because in my opinion I think that his skills set would not be adequate in the new position.

3. By means of researching the alternatives, our committee has reached a decision to continue the office's contract with the Info-Fix computer maintenance company due to the fact that Info-Fix offers us the maximum amount of service at a reasonable price.

4. In this day and age, consumers are willing to spend their money on some computer products of a remarkable kind.

5. I thought to myself that I had better start studying on a regular basis if I really and truly wanted to finish college.

6. Todd asked me to repeat my refusal again because deep down inside he believed that I would never say "no" to him.

7. Christina is small in size and short in stature, yet she has a powerful personality and a very unique ability to motivate others.

8. Past experience has taught me that in today's society we can blend together two different kinds of music and create a popular and profitable sound.

9. By the fact that I plan to be an artist, I would rather not take a

course in the field of mathematics, but I have to learn the basic

essentials as a college requirement.

10. I want to know the true facts of the store's bankruptcy, but you just

refer back to gossip and rumors.

CLICHÉS

Clichés are worn-out expressions. Once they were a new way of making a point, but now they are old and tired. You should avoid them in your writing.

not this: I know that Monica will always ~~be there for me~~.
but this: I know that Monica will always support me.

not this: Alan experienced the ~~trials and tribulations~~ of late
  registration.
but this: Alan experienced the difficulties of late registration.

Following are some common clichés. If you spot clichés in your writing, replace them with more direct or thoughtful statements of your own.

Some Common Clichés

acting like there's no tomorrow	in the blink of an eye
all in all	in the final analysis
all the time in the world	information superhighway
at the end of the day	I wouldn't be where I am today
avoid like the plague	It is what it is
beat around the bush	kick the bucket
between a rock and a hard place	let bygones be bygones
break the ice	light as a feather
break new ground	live and let live
breathtaking	live life to the fullest
by the same token	make ends meet
can't hold a candle to	on the same page
climb the ladder of success	on top of the world
cold as ice	one day at a time
cry my eyes out	over the hill
cutting edge	pure as the driven snow
dead as a doornail	quick as a wink
dead tired	ready on day one
down in the dumps	rock solid
down on his luck	shoulder to cry on
a drop in the bucket	sick as a dog
few and far between	smooth as silk
first and foremost	state of the art
free as a bird	the ball's in your court
give it your best shot	the sky's the limit
go the distance	through thick and thin
go the extra mile	trials and tribulations
good as gold	tried and true
grass is always greener	up at the crack of dawn

hard as a rock   when all is said and done
he (she) is always there for me   worked and slaved
hit the ground running   worked like a dog
hit the nail on the head
hot under the collar
hustle and bustle

Exercise 3   **Collaborate: Revising Clichés**

Collaborate

The following sentences contain clichés (italicized). Working with a partner or a group, rewrite the sentences, replacing the clichés with more direct or thoughtful words or phrases. Write in the space above the lines.

1. When I lost my best friend, I was ready to *cry my eyes out.*

2. An accident can change a person's life *in the blink of an eye.*

3. *I wouldn't be where I am today* without Professor Miyori's inspiring classes.

4. Since I lost my weekend job at the hospital, I am struggling to *make ends meet.*

5. Hank has a *tried and true* method of repairing leaky windows.

6. When I take my dog for a walk, she acts like she is *on top of the world.*

7. Once my dog smelled the turkey roasting, she ran to the kitchen *as quick as a wink.*

8. Tanika has been *down in the dumps* ever since she had an argument with her sister.

9. If I am not qualified for the job, *don't beat around the bush* about the situation.

10. Some people might have envied my family, but that's only because they believed *the grass is always greener* in somebody else's home.

Exercise 4   **Practice: Identifying Clichés**

Underline all the clichés in the following paragraph. There are nine clichés.

Since first grade, you and I have been best friends. Our disagreements have been few and far between. Thinking about our shared history, our talents, and our goals, I have come to an important conclusion. If we can maintain our friendship through thick and thin, then the sky's the limit if we want to start a small business together. However, we have to be on the same page about our goals and financial arrangements. Once we have learned to go the distance in the early days of building our business, we will break new ground in our cutting-edge technology lab. It may be a challenge to climb the ladder of success as quickly as we would like. However, in the final analysis, our achievements will be great if we can become just as loyal business partners as we are friends.

Connect

Exercise 5 Connect: Editing for Imprecise Language, Wordiness, and Clichés

Edit the following paragraph for imprecise language, clichés. Cross out wordiness and write your revisions above the lines. There are nine places that need editing.

A few years ago, my boyfriend Jimmy had a hard time finding work by the fact that he never finished high school and had no clear goals. At this point in time, he is studying for his GED and at a future date wants to study law enforcement at a community college. Without a shadow of a doubt he has changed dramatically from the teenager with no direction and no self-esteem. After a long struggle with dead-end jobs and family conflicts, Jimmy has reached a decision to look forward with determination and things. Now he needs to work on his skills set and stay patient and focused through the trials and tribulations of testing, training, and preparing for a career. When I look at the hardships he has already survived, I really and truly believe in Jimmy's future.

SLANG

Slang is an informal vocabulary frequently used during conversations among friends. It is also used by fiction writers when they try to create realistic dialogue. Slang expressions and their meanings can change frequently. "Cool" and "hot" can both mean "popular," while "bad" as a slang term can mean "good." Today, "guys" as slang refers to males and females. Slang expressions change often, and because they can easily be misunderstood, you should avoid them in formal writing assignments that require precise word choice.

The following list may contain slang that you use in everyday conversation, but you may also notice several expressions that are now considered outdated. See how many you recognize from your own daily conversations.

Slang	**Standard English**
a slam dunk	a certainty
All bets are off.	The future is uncertain.
awesome	terrific
back in the day	in the past (or when I was younger)
been there for me	supported me
bent out of shape	upset
big time	major
blowback	harsh reaction
bounce (verb)	leave
Bring it on.	Challenge me.
bummed	disappointed
call him/her out	criticize (or shame him/her)
chill (or chill out)	relax (or calm down)
creeps me out	makes me uneasy
Don't do me like that.	Don't treat me that way.
don't have a clue	have no idea
Don't mess with me.	Don't bother me.
Dial it back.	Be less intense.
ditch (verb)	throw away
Do you know what I'm saying?	Do you understand?
Don't go there.	Don't talk about it.
Feel me?	Do you understand?
For real?	Really?
for sure	certainly
from the get go	from the beginning
get his/her act together	become more organized or focused
get his/her groove on	regain momentum or confidence
get (or wrap) my head around	understand (or imagine)
Get real.	Be realistic.
gets me down	upsets me, saddens me
give it up for; give a shout out	applaud for; recognize
Give me a break.	Be more lenient with me.
got game	has excellent skills
he/she goes	he/she says
he's all about	he's very interested in
here's the thing (or here's the deal)	here's what's important
Hold up.	Wait.
I freaked.	I became upset.
I got your back.	I'll protect you.
I'm down with that	I agree with that; I accept that.
I'm into	I'm interested in
I'm not buying it.	I don't believe it.
I'm with you.	I agree with you.
It's all good.	Everything is fine.
It's on you.	It's your fault.
jazzed	excited
keeping it real	being realistic
Lighten up.	Be less serious.
mess up	make a mistake
mix it up	fight (or use a variety of tactics)

continued

Slang	**Standard English**
my bad	my mistake
my ride	my car
No problem. (after "Thank you.")	You're welcome.
not feelin' it	don't like it
party (verb)	socialize (or celebrate)
pushback	resistance
seal (or close) the deal	reach an agreement (or win)
set of wheels	automobile
Show me some love.	Be considerate (or kind) to me.
That's how we roll.	That's what we do.
That's on you.	That's your fault.
That's sick.	That's the best. (or That's terrific.)
That's what I'm talkin' about.	That's what I like.
They got served.	They were soundly defeated/insulted.
They're tight.	They are close friends.
This is huge.	This is very important
totaled	destroyed
tripping	acting strangely (or irrationally)
True story?	Is it true?
true that	definitely
wasted	inebriated
What's the deal?	Why (or How) did that happen?
What's up with that?	What does that mean?

Collaborate

Exercise 6   **Collaborate: Identifying Slang**

Working with a partner or group, write your own examples of slang that you and your friends use today. After each example of slang, write its meaning in standard English.

1. slang: _____

   standard English: _____

2. slang: _____

   standard English: _____

3. slang: _____

   standard English: _____

4. slang: _____

   standard English: _____

5. slang: _____

   standard English: _____

Collaborate

Exercise 7   **Collaborate: Revising Slang**

Working with a partner or group, revise each sentence to eliminate slang. For smoother style, you can change the word order as well as wording that is not slang.

1. My brother was really bummed about losing his job, so I told him he should just chill for a few days until he could get his act together and be ready to look for another job.

   _____

   _____

   _____

2. Driving down a dark, deserted road creeps me out at times, but my sister can't even lighten up enough to drive anywhere.

   _____

   _____

   _____

3. Kesha hopes to win a lead role in our civic center's production of *Rent*, but she knows that all bets are off if professional actors are allowed to audition.

   _____

   _____

   _____

4. Back in the day, my father was all about being the starting quarterback for his high school, and he often brags that he's still got game.

   _____

   _____

   _____

5. In my speech at the academic awards ceremony, I gave a shout out to my parents because they had always been there for me. Their support was huge for me.

   _____

   _____

   _____

6. Whenever Jenna drinks too much, she starts tripping and shouting at strangers, "Bring it on!"

   _____

   _____

   _____

7. I really messed up when I lied to my manager about my accounting skills; unfortunately, any spreadsheet mistakes will now be all on me.

   _____

   _____

   _____

8. When I saw the architect's plans for our new office, I wasn't feeling any of it at all.

_____

_____

_____

9. My little brother and I are tight, so I told him that he should get real about living on his own since he works only part time and barely has enough money for the security deposit on a small apartment.

_____

_____

_____

10. Sometimes it gets me down when my parents argue, but I know that's just how they roll and they'll always have each other's back.

_____

_____

_____

Connect

Exercise 8 **Connect: Editing for Imprecise Language, Wordiness, Clichés, and Slang**

Edit the following paragraph for imprecise language, wordiness, clichés, and slang. Cross out problem areas and write any necessary revisions above the lines. There are thirteen places that need editing.

Nina and I stopped seeing each other because she didn't know how to dial it back, and I couldn't find a way to get her to chill. We never seemed to be on the same page in our emotional responses. She expressed a lot of anger and anxiety if I did things with other people. I began to feel funny about having a girlfriend who acted as if we were married. At the present moment she is not speaking to me, and I feel relieved of stress and guilt. Nina and I are two different kinds of people, and I am not crying my eyes out about the situation. I only hope that Nina can learn to lighten up. I personally feel that she is a nice person who needs to change out her emotional dramas with a little self-confidence.

Sentence Variety

Chapter Objectives

Students will be able to recognize a variety of sentence patterns and incorporate an effective balance of long and short sentences in their writing.

BALANCING LONG AND SHORT SENTENCES

One way to improve your writing is to work on *sentence variety*, the use of different lengths and kinds of sentences. You can become skilled in sentence variety by (1) revising your writing for a balance of short and long sentences and for a mix of sentence types, and (2) being aware of the kinds of sentences you can use.

There are no grammar errors in the following paragraph, but it needs revision for sentence variety.

> I have a routine for waking up. First, I grab a can of Diet Pepsi. I gulp it down. I turn on the TV at the same time. I watch cartoons. I sit for about half an hour. Then the caffeine in the Pepsi starts working. I move to the shower. I make the water temperature very hot. Steam fills the bathroom. My muscles come alive. I begin to feel fully awake.

The paragraph is filled with short sentences. Read it aloud, and you will notice the choppy, boring style of the writing. Compare it to the following revised paragraph, which contains a variety of short and long sentences:

> I have a routine for waking up. First, I grab a can of Diet Pepsi and gulp it down while I turn on the TV. Then I watch cartoons for about half an hour. When the caffeine in the Pepsi starts working, I move to the shower. I make the water temperature so hot that steam fills the bathroom. My muscles come alive as I begin to feel fully awake.

The revised paragraph balances short and long sentences. Read it aloud, and you will notice the way the varied lengths create a more flowing, interesting style.

Some writers rely too heavily on short sentences; others use too many long sentences. The following paragraph contains too many long sentences.

> Randall wanted to make new friends because his old friends had become a bad influence. Randall loved his old friends, especially Michael, but they had begun to be involved in some dangerous activities, and Randall didn't want to be part of these crimes because Randall wanted to apply to the police academy, and he knew that having a record would destroy his chances of admission. Consequently, Randall was honest with Michael, and Randall told him that Randall couldn't risk his future by mixing with people who liked to joyride in stolen cars or steal from neighborhood stores. Soon Randall's friends stopped asking him out, and for a while Randall felt lonely and isolated, but eventually, Randall formed some new friendships, and he was happy to be part of a new group and happy it was one that didn't break the law.

Read the previous paragraph aloud, and you will notice that the sentences are so long and complicated that part of their meaning is lost. Piling on one long sentence after another can make a paragraph boring and difficult to follow. Compare the previous paragraph to the following revised version.

> Randall wanted to make new friends because his old friends had become a bad influence. Randall loved his old friends, especially Michael. However, they had begun to be involved in some dangerous activities, and Randall didn't want to be a part of these crimes. He wanted to apply to the Police Academy and knew that having a record would destroy his chances of admission. Consequently, Randall spoke honestly to Michael. Randall explained that he couldn't risk his future by mixing with people who liked to joyride in stolen cars or steal from neighborhood stores. Soon Randall's friends stopped asking him out, and for a while, Randall felt lonely and isolated. Eventually, Randall formed some new friendships and was happy to be part of a new, law-abiding group.

Read the revised paragraph aloud, and you will notice the combination of long and short sentences makes the paragraph clearer and smoother. Careful revision helps you achieve such a mix.

Connect

Exercise 1   **Connect: Revising Short Sentences**

The following paragraph is composed entirely of short sentences. Rewrite it so that it contains a mix of short and long sentences. Write your revisions above the lines.

My great aunt leads an active life for a woman of seventy-five. She works at a drug store. She has worked there for thirty years. She works five days a week. Every Friday night she meets her friends. They drink coffee and play cards. They also gossip about their neighbors. Each weekend, she sings in a choir. Afterwards, the members of the choir go out for brunch. My great aunt also keeps up with the latest fashions. She is well known for her style. It is clearly expressed in her elaborate hats. She is a young woman of seventy five. I'd like to be like her someday.

Exercise 2 **Connect: Revising Long Sentences**

Connect

The following paragraph is composed entirely of long sentences. Rewrite it so that it contains a mix of short and long sentences. Write your revisions above the lines.

Yesterday I heard a conversation that hurt me deeply. I am still upset about it because I cannot figure out why people would be so unkind about me when they hardly know me or have any right to assess me so negatively. It all began at work as I was about to enter the break room and I heard two people I considered to be my friends talking. All I heard was my name, and then someone laughed as if I were a joke of some kind, and by this point I decided to stay outside the door and listen. Soon I heard one of my so-called friends say, "Jerome? He's not invited." I decided to walk away from the room so the two wouldn't notice me outside and since I couldn't walk in without them wondering what I might have heard. I have spent hours trying to understand why they laughed at me and, even worse, why I'm being left out of some party or other event. I know I'm being silly, and I tell myself I heard only part of a conversation that could be interpreted in a different way, but I still feel that hearing others discuss me was a terrible experience.

USING DIFFERENT WAYS TO BEGIN SENTENCES

Most of the time, writers begin sentences with the subject. However, if you change the word order, you can break the monotony of using the same pattern over and over.

Begin with an Adverb

One way to change the word order is to begin with an adverb, a word that describes verbs, adjectives, or other adverbs. (For more on adverbs, see Chapter 21.) You can move adverbs from the middle to the beginning of the sentence as long as the meaning is clear.

> **adverb in middle:** Ricky opened the package *carefully* and checked the contents.
> **adverb at beginning:** *Carefully*, Ricky opened the package and checked the contents.

> **adverb in middle:** The policewoman *calmly* issued a ticket to the aggressive driver.
> **adverb at beginning:** *Calmly*, the policewoman issued a ticket to the aggressive driver.

Exercise 3 **Practice: Writing Sentences That Begin with an Adverb**

In the following sentences, move the adverb to the beginning of the sentence.

1. Isabel smiled slyly at the unsuspecting new team member.

2. Emilio searched frantically for his lost concert tickets.

3. The big dog barked angrily at the strange man in the yard.

4. Ernie stroked the horse rhythmically to calm it.

5. My mother frequently spends her Saturdays at garage sales.

6. Amber walked carefully between the shelves filled with antiques.

7. The evil scientist in the film laughed cruelly at his victim.

8. Andrew thoughtlessly revealed his sister's infatuation with his new friend.

9. Charlie silently accepted the blame for the incident.

10. The little boy slept blissfully in his father's arms.

Begin with a Prepositional Phrase

A prepositional phrase contains a preposition and its object. (For more on prepositions, see Chapter 15.) You can change the usual word order of a sentence by moving a prepositional phrase from the end of a sentence to the beginning. You can do this as long as the meaning of the sentence remains clear.

> **prepositional phrase at the end:** A gleaming silver convertible suddenly passed me *in the left lane.*
> **prepositional phrase at the beginning:** *In the left lane*, a gleaming silver convertible suddenly passed me.

> **prepositional phrase at the end:** The bulldog growled and snarled *with fierce intensity.*
> **prepositional phrase at the beginning:** *With fierce intensity*, the bulldog growled and snarled.

Note: Usually, you should put a comma after a prepositional phrase that begins a sentence. However, you do not need a comma if the prepositional phrase is short.

Exercise 4 Practice: Writing Sentences That Begin with a Prepositional Phrase

Rewrite the following sentences, moving a prepositional phrase to the beginning of the sentence. Write your revisions above the lines.

1. Oscar was in bed with the flu during most of spring break.

2. The white van with a dented rear panel remained abandoned in the alley.

3. Daniel felt most lonely on the weekends.

4. You can get homemade lemon cake at the Superior Bakery.

5. Ardeese can't write a letter or an essay without her dictionary.

6. I'll do the laundry before I go to work.

7. The heroic soldier received letters and gifts from hundreds of strangers.

8. An old letter was concealed inside a dusty leather book.

9. There is a kind person underneath Vinnie's rough exterior.

10. We swam in the ice-cold lake after the rain stopped.

Exercise 5 Collaborate: Creating Sentences That Begin with Prepositional Phrases

Collaborate

Working with a partner or group, write sentences that begin with the following prepositional phrases.

1. In a year _____

2. On long weekends _____

3. After the accident _____

4. For amusement _____

5. Under too much pressure _____

6. Between us _____

7. Near my house _____

8. With no regret _____

9. Before you go _____

10. At the end of class _____

USING DIFFERENT WAYS TO JOIN IDEAS

Another way to create sentence variety is to try different methods of combining ideas. Among these methods are (1) using an *-ing* modifier, (2) using an *-ed* modifier, (3) using an appositive, and (4) using a *who*, *which*, or *that* clause.

Use an *-ing* Modifier

You can avoid short, choppy sentences by using an *-ing* modifier. This way, one of the short sentences becomes a phrase. (For more on modifiers, see Chapter 22.)

> **two short sentences:** Sarah was talking on her cell phone. She drove into a tree.
>
> **combined with an *-ing* modifier:** Talking on her cell phone, Sarah drove into a tree.

Note: If the modifier begins the sentence, be sure that the next word is the one the modifier describes.

> **two short sentences:** Mr. Martinez loves to read travel books. He plans his next vacation.
>
> **combined with an *-ing* modifier:** Mr. Martinez loves to read travel books, *planning his next vacation.*

Exercise 6 **Practice: Using *-ing* Modifiers**

Following are pairs of sentences. Combine each pair by using an *-ing* modifier.

1. A fat black cat sat by the window. It was licking its paws.
   combined: _____

   _____

2. The earrings gleamed in the velvet box. They invited me to try them on.
   combined: _____

   _____

3. Tonya wiped her little boy's tears. She struggled to comfort the child.
   combined: _____

   _____

4. The sound of my neighbor's television blasted through my apartment walls.
   It irritated me all weekend.
   combined: _____

   _____

5. One of my friends hoped to get good tips. She took a job at a popular restaurant.
   combined: _____

   _____

6. Aggressive drivers tailgate at high speeds. They risk their own and others' lives.
   combined: _____

   _____

7. My mother worried about my first job away from home. She called me three times a day.
   combined: _____

   _____

8. Philip Delgado needed a favor. He showed up at my house last night.
   combined: _____

   _____

9. Carrie Swenson dreamed of a career as a dancer. She enrolled in a high school dedicated to the arts.
   combined: _____

   _____

10. The bride wore a black dress. She shocked all the wedding guests.
    combined: _____

    _____

Use an *-ed* Modifier

You can also avoid short, choppy sentences by using an *-ed* modifier. This way, one of the short sentences becomes a phrase. (For more on modifiers, see Chapter 22.)

> **two short sentences:** The fish was broiled with lemon and butter. The fish was delicious.
> **combined with an *-ed* modifier:** *Broiled with lemon and butter,* the fish was delicious.

Note: If the modifier begins the sentence, be sure that the next word is the one the modifier describes.

> **two short sentences:** Sam gave me a jewelry box. It was painted with silver and blue flowers.
> **combined with an *-ed* modifier:** Sam gave me a jewelry box *painted with silver and blue flowers.*

Exercise 7 **Practice: Using *-ed* Modifiers**

Following are pairs of sentences. Combine each pair, using an *-ed* modifier.

1. The chicken was stuffed with herb dressing. The chicken was delicious.
   combined: _____

   _____

2. Armand's boat was a total loss. Armand's boat was wrecked in a fierce storm.
   combined: _____

   _____

3. Alan followed every rule. Alan was motivated by fear of his supervisor.
   combined: _____

   _____

4. I lost a beautiful bracelet. The bracelet was studded with coral beads.

combined: _____

_____

5. My new belt had a large silver buckle. The buckle was engraved with an elaborate design.

combined: _____

_____

6. Sergeant Thomas Levy was named Officer of the Year. He risked his life to save a woman drowning in a canal.

combined: _____

_____

7. The old house was designed for a large family. It was converted into three spacious apartments.

combined: _____

_____

8. Patrick is inspired by his famous mother. He is studying to become a child psychologist.

combined: _____

_____

9. Samantha was married at eighteen. She has never experienced living on her own.

combined: _____

_____

10. Now that I have my own place, I miss my mother's kitchen. It was stocked with snacks and treats.

combined: _____

_____

Collaborate

Exercise 8 **Collaborate: Completing Sentences with *-ing* or *-ed* Modifiers**

Working with a partner or group, complete each sentence below.

1. Stranded in the airport _____

_____

2. Looking for trouble _____

_____

3. Taking the wrong turn _____

_____

4. Suspected of murder _____

_____

5. Deprived of sleep _____

_____

6. Smiling at me _____

_____

7. Trapped in the cave _____

_____

8. Dropping the ball _____

_____

9. Excited by the news _____

_____

10. Trusting his friend _____

_____

Use an Appositive

Another way to combine short, choppy sentences is to use an appositive. An **appositive** is a phrase that renames or describes a noun. Appositives can go in the beginning, middle, or end of a sentence. Use commas to set off the appositive.

> **two short sentences:** Chocolate milk contains calcium and vitamins. It is a favorite of children.
> **combined with an appositive:** Chocolate milk, *a favorite of children*, contains calcium and vitamins.

> **two short sentences:** Richard is my best friend. He has been a wrestler for several years.
> **combined with an appositive:** Richard, *my best friend*, has been a wrestler for several years.

> **two short sentences:** I am looking forward to Thanksgiving. It is my favorite holiday.
> **combined with an appositive:** I am looking forward to Thanksgiving, *my favorite holiday*.

Exercise 9   Practice: Using Appositives

Following are pairs of sentences. Combine each pair by using an appositive.

1. Inez is an accountant. She is helping me with my taxes.
combined: _____

_____

2. Island Theaters is an old movie house. It is being sold to a restaurant chain.
combined: _____

_____

3. I want to take you to Electronics Unlimited. It is the cheapest computer store in the area.
combined: _____

_____

4. My new boyfriend took me to dinner at Sunflower. It is the fanciest restaurant in the city.
   combined: _____

   _____

5. Kima is a warm-hearted person. She adopted a shelter cat last week.
   combined: _____

   _____

6. Arrogance and impatience are my brother's worst qualities. They show up whenever he is under stress.
   combined: _____

   _____

7. Yesterday, I heard the buzz of a mosquito. It is a sure sign of summer.
   combined: _____

   _____

8. Dr. Harjo dresses like a college student. He is a world-renowned scientist.
   combined: _____

   _____

9. Chicken nuggets and French fries are full of fat. They are my son's favorite foods.
   combined: _____

   _____

10. Lucille Okara is a respected negotiator. She is heading an international peace conference in Guatemala.
    combined: _____

    _____

Use a *Who*, *Which*, or *That* Clause

Clauses beginning with *who*, *which*, or *that* can combine short sentences.

two short sentences: Jacob is my favorite cousin. He won the golf tournament.
combined with a *who* clause: Jacob, *who is my favorite cousin*, won the golf tournament.

two short sentences: Good running shoes can be expensive. They make running easier.
combined with a *which* clause: Good running shoes, *which can be expensive*, make running easier.

two short sentences: The cinnamon buns were delicious. I tasted them.
combined with a *that* clause: The cinnamon buns *that I tasted* were delicious.

Punctuating *who, which,* or *that* clauses requires some thought. Decide whether the information in the clause is *essential* or *nonessential.* If the information is essential, do not put commas around it:

essential clause: Students *who like history* will love the movie. (Without the clause *who like history,* the sentence would not have the same meaning. Therefore the clause is essential and is not set off by commas.)

nonessential clause: Mel, *who has been singing for years,* deserves to win. (The clause *who has been singing for years* is not essential to the meaning of the sentence. Therefore, it is set off by commas.)

If you have to choose between *which* and *that, which* usually begins a nonessential clause, and *that* usually begins an essential clause.

essential clause: The car *that he was driving* is expensive.

nonessential clause: The car, *which I've had for years,* needs a new muffler.

> **Note:** Essential and nonessential clauses are also referred to as *restrictive* and *nonrestrictive* clauses.

Exercise 10   Practice: Using *Who, Which,* or *That* Clauses

Following are pairs of sentences. Combine each pair by using a *who, which,* or *that* clause.

1. Sharon told me a secret. The secret shocked me.
   combined: _____

   _____

2. Belgian chocolate is available in the United States. Some consider it the best chocolate in the world.
   combined: _____

   _____

3. Clara works with a young man. The young man teaches yoga in the evenings.
   combined: _____

   _____

4. Tyler Nelson is married to my sister. He used to play baseball on a minor league team.
   combined: _____

   _____

5. People love their pets. They will spend a great deal of money to keep their animals healthy and happy.
   combined: _____

   _____

6. Pocket scooters are popular with children. The scooters can be dangerous on public roads.
   combined: _____

   _____

7. Joanna bought a new coffeemaker. The coffeemaker brews one cup of coffee at a time.

   combined: _____

   _____

8. Selena wants to go back to Albuquerque. Albuquerque is her favorite vacation spot.

   combined: _____

   _____

9. I need to thank my father. He worked at two jobs to help me finish college.

   combined: _____

   _____

10. Talking to strangers once made me nervous. Talking to strangers is now an important part of my job.

    combined: _____

    _____

Connect

Exercise 11 **Connect: Revising for Sentence Variety: A Comprehensive Exercise**

Rewrite the following paragraph, combining each pair of underlined sentences using one of the following: an *-ing* modifier, an *-ed* modifier, an appositive, or a *who, which,* or *that* clause. Write your revisions in the spaces above the lines.

Jealousy is like a poison. <u>My last girlfriend was a beautiful woman. She swore she had not a drop of jealous blood.</u> At first, she was understanding and tolerant of the time I spent without her. Then I noticed a slight change. <u>She would check my eyes carefully. She tried to detect any lies about my social activities.</u> This subtle surveillance made me somewhat uneasy. <u>Antonio was my best friend. He advised me to break off the relationship.</u> Antonio said I would soon see my girlfriend become more possessive. <u>I was blinded by my infatuation. I hoped that my girlfriend would change.</u> She did, but the change made me jealous. She left me when she found someone she liked better.

Appendix: Readings for Writers

WRITING FROM READING

One way to find topics for writing is to draw on your ideas, memories, and observations. Another way is to write from reading you have done. You can *react* to it; you can *agree* or *disagree* with something you have read. In fact, many college assignments or tests ask you to write about an assigned reading: an essay, a chapter in a textbook, an article in a journal. This kind of reading is done in steps:

1. Preread
2. Read
3. Reread with a pen or pencil

After you have completed these steps, you can write from your reading. You can write about what you have read, or you can react to what you have read.

PREREADING

Prereading takes very little time, but it helps you immensely. Some students believe it is a waste of time to scan an assignment; they think they should jump right in and get the reading over with. However, spending just a few minutes on preliminaries can save hours later. Most importantly, prereading helps you to become a *focused reader*.

If you scan the length of an assignment, you can pace yourself. And if you know how long a reading is, you can alert yourself to its plan. A short reading, for example, has to come to its point fairly soon. A longer essay may take time to develop its point and may use more details and examples. Any highlighted material, including subheadings, charts, graphs, boxes, or illustrations, is important enough that the author wants to emphasize it. A list of vocabulary words and their definitions that accompanies a reading selection is worth scanning, too. Looking over that material *before* you read gives you an overview of the important points the reading will contain.

Introductory material or introductory questions will also help you know what to look for as you read. Background on the author or on the subject may hint at ideas that will come up in the reading. Sometimes even the title of the reading will give you the main idea.

You should preread so that you can start reading with as much knowledge about the writer and the subject as you can get. Then, when you read the entire assignment, you will be reading *actively* for more knowledge.

If you want to read with a focus, it helps to ask questions before you read. Form questions by using the information you gained from prereading. For example, if the title of the article is "Manners Matter Online," you may turn the title into a question: "What basic etiquette is required online?" You can jot write down such questions, but it's not necessary. Just forming questions and keeping them in the back of your mind helps you read actively and stay focused.

READING

The first time you read, try to get a sense of the whole piece you are reading. Reading with questions in mind can help you do this. If you find that you are confused by a certain part of the reading selection, go back and reread that part. If you do not know the meaning of a certain word, check the list of vocabulary words if the article includes one. If there is no list or the word is not defined, try to figure out the meaning from the way the word is used in the sentence.

If you find that you have to read more slowly than you usually do, don't worry. People vary their reading speed according to what they read and why they are reading it. If you are reading for entertainment, for example, you can read quickly; if you are reading a chapter in a textbook, you must read more slowly. The more complicated the reading selection is, the more slowly you will read it.

REREADING WITH A PEN OR PENCIL

The second reading is the crucial one. At this point, you begin to *think on paper* as you read. In this step, you can make notes or write about what you read. Some students are reluctant to do this, for they are not sure what to note or write. Think of these notes as a way of learning, thinking, reviewing, and reading. Reading with a pen or pencil in your hand keeps you alert. With that pen or pencil, you can do the following:

> Mark the main point of the reading.
> Mark other points.
> Define words you don't know.
> Question parts of the reading you're not sure of.
> Evaluate the writer's ideas.
> React to the writer's opinions or examples.
> Add ideas, opinions, and examples of your own.

There is no single system for marking or writing as you read. Some readers like to underline the main idea with two lines and to underline other important ideas with one line. Some students like to put an asterisk (a star) next to important ideas, while others like to circle key words.

Some people like to use the margins to write comments like, "I agree!" or "Not true!" or "That's happened to me!" Sometimes readers put questions in the margins; sometimes they summarize a point in the margin next to its location in the essay. Some people make notes on the white space above the reading and list important points, and others use the space at the end of the reading. Every reader who writes while he or she reads has a personal system; what these systems share is an attitude. If you write as you read, you concentrate on the reading selection, get to know the writer's ideas, and develop ideas of you own.

AN EXAMPLE OF REREADING WITH A PEN OR PENCIL

Following is the article, "Manners Matter Online: Basic Etiquette Applies Even for E-Mail." It has been marked as if a student reader were rereading it after prereading and reading the selection.

Manners Matter Online: Basic Etiquette Applies Even for E-mail

Amritha Alladi

Alladi wrote this article for the <u>Gainesville Sun</u> (Fla.), and she focuses on why students and other young people seeking employment need to sharpen their e-mail communication skills.

Words You May Need to Know (Corresponding paragraph numbers are in parentheses.)

jargon (3): language used by a specific group or profession
indecipherable (3): impossible to understand
protocol (5): a formal procedure
hierarchical (5): organized by a person's rank or status
sublimated the role of the gatekeeper (6): eliminated the traditional, more rigid channels of communication
incoherent (6): not logically consistent
psychosocial implications (7): psychological and social effects
demeanor (9): behavior

1   Before you click "Send," reread the last line of that e-mail, will you?

2   After all, you wouldn't appreciate a message from your boss that read, "Dude, what's up with ur presentation? CU in my office ASAP," so it's best to extend him or her the same courtesy. When it comes to professional e-mails, business etiquette is no Laughing Out Loud matter.

3   Eric Hall, assistant director for employer relations at the University of Florida's Career Resource Center, says he has heard from job recruiters that <u>students are too casual when corresponding with prospective employers and professors.</u> *thesis* <u>Many young professionals have become accustomed to sending quick messages to friends and peers, and they sometimes forget that abbreviations and jargon may be inappropriate, or at times, even indecipherable.</u> *example* "In this day and age of text messaging, there are occasionally the LOLs," Hall says.

4   Meanwhile, communications professors feel the issue goes beyond e-mail etiquette. Professors at UF's Warrington College of Business say the problem is rooted more in the generation's behavioral trends rather than in technological ones.

5   <u>Jane Douglas,</u> associate professor of management communication, <u>says young people entering the work force are generally unaware of protocol with</u> *example* <u>regard to addressing people in higher positions.</u> "There is this illusion that communication is horizontal. They don't understand that it's hierarchical." Douglas says that during her twenty-five years of teaching, she has noticed a huge difference in the way students interact with faculty.

6   E-mail communication and the Internet have sublimated the role of the gatekeeper entirely, said Douglas. Last year, her college faced some "very problematic undergrads" <u>who took it upon themselves to address their</u> *Why is this so awful?*

complaints directly to the dean and provost. "It's just one keystroke from the dean, and usually it's incoherent," she says. "Students seldom proofread or think of the entire impression."

improper actions

7   Basic etiquette teaches that you avoid the obvious (improprieties) — abbreviations, slang, poor grammar, and informal greetings—no matter who you're sending an e-mail to. Formality is necessary anytime you are communicating with someone for the first time. However, Douglas, who has done extensive research in the psychosocial implications of communication, says she has noted some other major pitfalls that land this budding generation of professionals in hot water with future employers.

example

8   "You see a lot of unprofessional e-mail addresses like tequilagirl@aol.com," Douglas says. "They don't understand that when you're communicating with someone you don't know, you need to be somewhat formal."

no one has time

9   Hall says UF's Career Resource Center tries to teach students appropriate business demeanor through outreach programs that focus on etiquette workshops, business attire, and interviewing tips. Experts at the center also review resumes and cover letters and give the students feedback for employment. Communication at all stages is important because managers are not just assessing your professional communication within the office. "They're also examining how you might work with potential clients," Hall says. "It's in a person's best interest to use formal language at all times. "

10   Of course, if you don't know whether your e-mail is appropriate, seek advice. "If you have any professional contacts, especially in the way of networking," Hall says, "they can be a good guiding force."

What the Notes Mean

In the sample above, the underlining indicates sentences or phrases that seem important. The words in the margin, such as "thesis" or "example," can refer to important sections of the reading. Sometimes a word is circled in the selection itself and defined in the margin; for instance, "improprieties" is circled in paragraph 7 and defined in the margin as "improper actions."

Sometimes words in the margin are personal reactions. When a university administrator, Eric Hall, notes that his university offers outreach programs for teaching students about business demeanor and interviewing, the reader notes "no one has time" for such programs. The marked-up article is a flexible tool. If you are asked to write a summary of the article, you can use the thesis and the examples you noted as important components of the summary. A comment about students' lack of time for workshops or outreach programs may lead a reader to develop his or her own writing that agrees or disagrees with a point made in the article. Another underlined part, about some undergraduate students who went directly to high-level administrators instead of talking to their professors, could be the basis for writing on a related topic about student–faculty interaction.

The marked-up article is a flexible tool. You can go back and mark it further. Writing as you read involves you in the reading process. It can help you to write about or react to important points in the article. In addition, if you are to be tested on the reading selection or asked to discuss it, you can scan your markings and notations later for a quick review.

A SAMPLE SUMMARY

A summary of a reading tells the important ideas in brief form. It includes (1) the writer's main idea, (2) the ideas used to explain the main idea, and (3) some examples used to explain the ideas. It also refers to the author and the title of the article you are summarizing. Following is a sample summary of "Manners Matter Online: Basic Etiquette Applies Even for E-Mail."

A Summary

   "Manners Matter Online: Basic Etiquette Applies Even for E-Mail" by Amritha Alladi warns that college students tend to be "too casual when corresponding with prospective employers and professors." The article refers to concerned professors who believe that technology, which has made e-mail and texting so popular, is partly to blame. When younger people rely on such quick communication, they may forget that abbreviations and jargon can be out of place or confusing. Other professors believe that the cause of this violation of business etiquette is linked to this generation's belief that employee and employer, student and professor are equals. Alladi's research into business etiquette stresses that if today's students can learn correct communications skills, they can improve their relationships with faculty and employers.

> **Note:** When you refer to an author in something that you write, use the author's first and last name the first time you make a reference. For example, you write "Amritha Alladi" the first time you refer to this author. Later in the paragraph, if you want to refer to the same author, use only his or her last name. Thus, a second reference would be to "Alladi," as in the summary, which refers to "Alladi's research."

WRITING A REACTION TO A READING

A summary is one kind of writing you can do after reading, but there are other kinds. You can react to a reading by agreeing or disagreeing with some idea within the reading or by writing on a topic related to the reading. The effectiveness of your reaction will depend on your careful evaluation of the reading selection.

THE ROLE OF CRITICAL THINKING

When you start forming opinions based on what you observe, hear, read, or discuss, you are applying **critical thinking skills.** Thinking critically as you read involves examining an issue from different sides as well as evaluating the validity, or truthfulness, of the information presented.

Applying the critical thinking process to evaluate what you are reading requires that you ask yourself the following questions:

- What is the writer's main idea or proposal?

- Is the main idea supported by facts? Personal experience? Expert opinion(s)?

- Does the writer reach logical conclusions based on his or her evidence?

Sharpening your critical thinking skills by using this type of questioning as you read can enable you to form reasonable opinions and express them confidently. Reading critically can help you succeed in all of your college classes, and it will be especially beneficial in your future composition courses.

DEVELOPING POINTS OF AGREEMENT OR DISAGREEMENT

One way to use a reading selection to lead you to a topic is to review the reading selection and jot down any statements that provoke a strong reaction in you. You will be looking for statements with which you agree or disagree. If you already marked "Manners Matter Online: Basic Etiquette Applies Even for E-Mail," you might focus your own writing on your disagreement with the point that outreach programs can change students' modes of communication with potential employers. The sample writing that follows acknowledges that students need help in learning how to communicate with potential employers, but *disagrees* that outreach programs will reach everyone who needs them.

Developing Points of Agreement or Disagreement

One part of "Manners Matter Online: Basic Etiquette Applies Even for E-mail" by Amritha Alladi discusses college students' lack of the skills they need to communicate with employers. It also refers to one university that offers outreach programs that can teach students proper business etiquette, business attire, interviewing tips, and resume writing. Outreach programs are valuable, but I do not agree that they are an effective way to train many students who want to find jobs. Most students will not find time for these sessions because participating in any "outreach" means spending extra time and doing extra work. The realistic way to motivate students is to include lessons on interviewing, conducting job searches, and professional communications in a for-credit course. It could be a one-credit course tailored for different fields of study, or it could be part of an already required course in such fields as business, education, science, and so forth. Students would get the information they need, and prospective employers would get the type of employees they need.

WRITING ON A RELATED IDEA

Another type of writing requires critical thinking and writing. Your instructor might ask you to react by writing about some idea connected to your reading. For example, your instructor might ask you to react to "Manners Matter Online: Basic Etiquette Applies Even for E-mail" by writing about whether all the descriptions of college students in the article are accurate.

Writing on a Related Idea

In Amritha Alladi's article, "Manners Matter Online: Basic Etiquette Applies Even for E-Mail," she refers to one university professor who was concerned when some undergraduate students "took it upon themselves to address their complaints directly to the dean and provost." This action seemed to create a problem because the students did not go first to their professors and other teaching staff. I understand why students should not skip steps in dealing with their problems. But I don't agree that all students who bring their problems directly to a dean or provost are being impatient or unreasonable. Sometimes student concerns have been ignored so often that undergraduates become frustrated. Unfortunately, some professors do not respond to students' e-mail. When students try to talk to their instructors after class, most faculty are on their way to another class or an appointment. A few faculty do not always keep their office hours. Some part-time faculty do not have offices or are busy teaching at more than one campus. While people in high positions should not have to deal with everyday student concerns, students need to have their voices heard.

Writing from reading can develop your abilities to challenge others' ideas, widen your perspective, and build confidence in your critical-thinking skills.

READINGS FOR WRITERS: THE WRITING PROCESS

Getting Carded

David Migoya

"Getting carded" usually means getting checked for identification at bars, restaurants, or clubs, but Denver Post writer David Migoya uses it to mean getting one's first credit card, a milestone for many college students. He warns that the card, a symbol of maturity, has its dangers.

Words You May Need to Know (Corresponding paragraph numbers are in parentheses.)

bombard (1): attack
entice (1): draw on by exciting hope or desire
"maxed out" (3): slang for "used to the maximum amount allowed"
rescinded (4): taken back
droves (5): herds
savvy (6): knowledgeable
jalopy (6): an old car that is falling apart

travesty (6): grotesque imitation (in this case, of graduating with a bright future)
cavalier (7): free and easy
pitfalls (8): hidden dangers
vulnerable (8): liable to be hurt
ultimately (9): eventually
perks (10): slang for "perquisites" (extra payments)

1 They remember their first love, their first car, and, if financial institutions have it right, their first credit card. Because the result could be a commitment that outlasts the first two, banks bombard college students with credit offers designed to entice them to sign up and start

charging. And the unsuspecting will be lured by methods ranging from free tee shirts and university-logo coffee mugs to inconceivably low interest rates and high spending limits. "Every year, there's a fresh pack of prospects called freshmen," said Kim McGrigg of Consumer Credit Counseling Services in Denver. "College students are the largest identifiable segment of new customers."

2   It didn't take long for the credit-card offers to land at Jeffrey Kaczmarek's feet. "It seemed like they showed up the moment I moved into the dorm," said Kaczmarek, an Iowa State University graduate. "Most of the problems I created have been behind me for only two years." The thirty-three-year-old computer programmer recalls a freshman year filled with important purchases—"pizza, beer, cigarettes, and other really useful things for college," he said with sarcastic tone—all of them on a $500-limit credit card, his first.

3   With one card "maxed out," Kaczmarek said, getting a second card was easy. "It was a chain reaction," the Denver resident said. "And when all was said and done, I was into it for $4,500." Not only did the debt follow him, but the creditors did, too. "When you're in school and the creditors are calling all the time, it's stress you don't need," he said. "I turned off my phone; I screened calls; it was a terrible way to live."

4   The time after college wasn't any better because a poor credit history affected interest rates Kaczmarek was offered on car loans. He said he even suspects a job offer was rescinded because of it. "As a freshman, I had no way to pay the $500 card," he said, "but it looked soooo good."

5   As colleges and universities begin the new school year, the credit offers come in droves. More than fifty-eight percent of college students said they saw credit-card marketers on campus for two or more days at the beginning of a semester, and seventy-eight percent of all students say they have a card, according to the U.S. Public Interest Research Group. "There's significant data supporting the theory that if you can be the first card in their wallet, they'll remain loyal, " said John Ulzheimer, president of education services at Credit.com. "Some issuers mail over a billion pieces a year."

6   The savvy student will use the new card to build credit responsibly so that it later comes in handy to rent an apartment, get a car loan, obtain a mortgage, or even land a job. Used improperly, though, a credit card can cause more heartache to a student than a breakup and cost a lot more than a tune-up. In the end, some students learn it's easier to part ways with a jalopy than with the bad credit they got from buying it. "That low credit score is the grade they never thought about or wanted to earn," Ulzheimer said. "The students spend their time working on an impressive GPA, and they get a degree in one hand and a bad credit score in the other. It's a sad travesty."

7   The worst problems occur not from overspending or maxing out credit limits—which typically are kept low to start—but from fees associated with late payments or interest rates. Put simply, a student who consistently pays only the monthly minimum is likely to hit financial ruin quickly. In fact, the number of eighteen-to-twenty-four-year-olds who filed for bankruptcy has ballooned by ninety-six percent in the past decade, according to the Richmond Credit Abuse Resistance Education Program. "The biggest issue is in the attitude toward using the card, and it's usually very cavalier," McGrigg of Consumer Credit Counseling said. "It's a tool of convenience, not an extension of your income."

8   Problems come from a lack of understanding about how credit cards work and the everlasting pitfalls of abuse. Some students just aren't ready for them, said Judy McKenna, a Fort Collins–based financial planner. "It's a particularly vulnerable population that may not come from much money, or it's a group of the temporarily poor," McKenna said. "The pulls to use the cards can be very strong." The average college student has a credit-card balance of $552, according to the Credit Research center at Georgetown University. Yet forty-five percent of students say they're in serious debt with balances averaging $3,000, Jumpstart Coalition reports.

9   Despite the possible long-term association, why do credit card issuers pursue students if they pose such a financial risk? The answer, according to experts, is Mom and Dad. "Ultimately, the cards get paid by parents who swoop in and save them," said Susan Black, director of financial planning at eMoney Advisor. Said Ulzheimer, "It's actually a safer bet to sign up a student than what common sense tells you."

10   The experts offer several approaches to avoiding problems. The easiest, McKenna said, is simply to avoid problems, at least until a student gets a full-time job. "Living on a checkbook or cash is smarter," she said. If a student must have a card, he or she should shop around for the best offer, including a competitive interest rate, low or no annual fee, a payment grace period, and user perks such as bonus points or cash back. Sometimes, the perks can pay for a student's trip home or a spring break destination. "Credit isn't for you if you're not serious enough about your financial future to take the time and research which card is best," McGrigg said.

11   Alternatives to credit cards and good ways to build a student's credit history include secured cards—those that require a deposit equaling the credit limit—and charge cards, which require full payment for all purchases each month. Prepaid cards, known as "stored-value cards," are popular because they limit spending. They are accepted like a credit card but are more like a gift certificate. The owner buys an amount on the card and spends it down, either by purchases or cash advances. "They're easy to control and can't be abused," Ulzheimer said.

Discussion Prompts/Writing Options

If you write on any of the following topics, work through the stages of the writing process in preparing your assignment.

1. "Getting Carded" discusses the dangers that shadow a student getting his or her first credit card. Write a summary of the article. Describe the short-term and long-term dangers, and explain how a student bombarded with credit card offers can avoid "maxing out" or can find a better alternative to a credit card.

2. If you have one or more credit cards, write about how well (or badly) you cope with the temptations to spend beyond your limit.

3. Write about three items (small or large) that many people pay for with a credit card, but that should be bought only with cash or a check. Explain why these items should not be purchased on credit.

4. Write about a purchase that you regret making. Did you buy the item on impulse? Did you buy it to cheer yourself up? To impress someone? To reward yourself? To fit in? How did you feel at the time you made the purchase? How did you feel later?

Collaborate

5. Although college students must cope with the dangers and temptations of credit cards, students also enjoy the advantages of owning at least one credit card. Working with a partner or group, brainstorm some examples of these advantages. When you have at least five examples, work individually on writing about these advantages.

Topics for Critical Thinking and Writing

If you write on any of the following topics, work through the stages of the writing process in preparing your assignment.

1. If you were the parent of a college student, would you advise him or her to get a credit card? Why or why not?

2. Why do so many college students fall into debt? What financial pressures make the college years a difficult time?

3. As you read "Getting Carded," did you notice some of the phrases that revealed the attitudes of some financial experts? For example, Judy McKenna, a Fort Collins–based financial planner, called first-year college students "a particularly vulnerable population that may not come from much money," or "a group of the temporarily poor." Do you believe these are valid descriptions? Another expert, Susan Black, director of financial planning at eMoney Advisor, said that credit card issuers pursue student business even when the companies expect many students to fall into debt because "the cards get paid by parents who swoop in and save them." In your experience, do parents save their college freshmen from credit card debt? Are these experts creating an accurate picture of the freshman student population?

READINGS FOR WRITERS: ILLUSTRATION

A Life Full of Riches

Karl R. Green

Karl R. Green lives in Cedar Rapids, Iowa. In this essay, originally published in <u>Newsweek</u> in 2007, Green gives many examples of the "riches" he enjoys. He notes, "This material world constantly reminds me of what I don't have. But somehow I still feel wealthy."

Words You May Need to Know (Corresponding paragraph numbers are in parentheses.)

whim (4): a sudden but short desire
fabricate (6): put together
efficiency (8): a one-room apartment

dated (8): no longer stylish
went south (8): ended, fell apart
affluent (11): wealthy
tangible (13): capable of being touched

1   It was early December, 2003, my first season as a Salvation Army bell ringer, when I was confronted with the question. I was standing just outside the door of a Walmart, offering a "thank you" and a smile to each person who dropped a donation into my red kettle. A neatly dressed woman and her young son walked up to the kettle stand. While she searched her purse for some cash, the boy looked up at me. I can still see the confusion and curiosity in his eyes as he asked, "Are you poor?"

2   "Well," I stammered, trying to think, "I have more than some people, but not as much as others." His mother scolded him for the social no-no, and they hurried off to do their shopping. His question, however, did not leave me.

3   I've never thought of myself as "poor," but I can't deny certain facts. Every time I fill out my 1040 form, I fall into one of the lowest income brackets. In the past 35 years, I've taken just one vacation trip. My TV is a black-and-white set that someone gave me eight years ago.

4   Yet I feel nothing more than a passing whim to attain the material things that so many other people have. My 1999 car shows the wear and tear of 105,000 miles. But it is still dependable. My apartment is modest, but quiet and relaxing. My clothes are well suited to my work, which is primarily outdoors. My minimal computer needs can be met at the library.

5   In spite of what I don't have, I don't feel poor. Why? I've enjoyed good health for 53 years. It's not just that I've been illness free, it's that I feel vigorous and spirited. Exercising is actually fun for me. I look forward to long, energizing walks. And I love the "can-do" attitude that follows.

6   I also cherish the gift of creativity. When I write a beautiful line of poetry or fabricate a joke that tickles someone, I feel rich inside. I'm continually surprised at the insights that come through my writing process, and talking with some of my interesting writer friends is one of my main sources of enjoyment.

7   But there is one vital area of my life where I am not so well off. In a society that spends so much emotional energy on the pursuit of possessions, I feel out of place.

8   When I was younger, there was an exceptionally interesting person I dated. What was most important to her, she told me, was what's on the inside. I thought I had found someone special to share my life with. Then I took her to see my apartment. At the time, I lived in a basement efficiency with a few pieces of dated furniture. Shortly after her visit, our relationship went straight south.

9   The seemingly abrupt change in her priorities was jolting. It remains a most memorable turning point in my personal journey.

10   In contrast to relationships, stuff just doesn't mean that much to me. I think most people feel the same way—except when there are social consequences to having particular items. There is a commercial on the radio that begins, "Everybody wants a high-end TV." The pressure to purchase is real. It may be true that everybody wants a high-end TV. After all, nobody wants to be a nobody.

11   But I'm happy to live without one. In fact, not being focused on material goods feels quite natural to me. There are many people throughout the world who would consider my lifestyle to be affluent.

12   Near the end of the year, when I put on the Salvation Army's red apron, something changes inside me. Instead of feeling out of place economically, I begin to feel a genuine sense of belonging. As I ring my bell, people stop to share their personal stories of how much it meant to be helped when they were going through a rough time. People helping people is something I feel deeply connected to. When I'm ringing the bell, complete strangers have brought me hot chocolate, leaving me with a lingering smile. Countless individuals have helped to keep me warm with the sentiments of the season: "Thank you for ringing on such a cold day." "Can I get you a cup of coffee?" "Bless you for your good work." December is the time of year I feel wealthiest.

13   Over the past four years, I've grown to understand more about myself because of a single question from a curious child. As I've examined what it means to be poor, it has become clear to me what I am most thankful for: both my tangible and my intangible good fortune.

Discussion Prompts/Writing Options

If you write on any of the following topics, work through the stages of the writing process in preparing your assignment.

1. In your own life, what makes you feel rich? Give examples, either tangible or intangible.

2. Can you think of examples of items that "everybody" wanted? How long did the craving for each item last? Is this item still

valued, taken for granted, or considered out of date or out of style?

3. Are there "riches" in your own life that you take for granted? What would happen if you lost them?

4. Karl R. Green writes, "People helping people is something I feel deeply connected to." He gives three examples of this connection: (1) he collected money for the Salvation Army, (2) people who donated shared their stories of struggle, and (3) some offered coffee or hot chocolate. Write about the times when you felt most connected to others. To support your main idea, be sure to use as many specific examples as you can.

Topics for Critical Thinking and Writing

If you write on one of the following topics, work through the stages of the writing process in preparing your assignment.

1. Do you think that peer pressure causes children or teens to want certain items in order to fit into a certain group? Give examples of such items and illustrate how the list of desired objects changes quickly.

2. Is there a social division on your campus? That is, are students identified by their clothing, means of transportation, or other signs of style, affluence, or status? if so, give examples of the style or possessions that make some students appear more respected or admired than others.

READINGS FOR WRITERS: DESCRIPTION

The Colors

Gary Soto

In this essay, Gary Soto describes his childhood world of Fresno, California. The Mexican-American poet, essayist, and short story writer relies heavily on the senses of sight, smell, sound, and touch as he writes of the summer days at his grandparents' house.

Words You May Need to Know (Corresponding paragraph numbers are in parentheses.)

slug (2): an obviously fake coin
frijoles (8): beans
Danish (8): a large pastry with a fruit or cheese filling

viejo (9): old man
m'ijo (10): a shortened form of *"mi hijo,"* which means "my boy" or "my son"

1   Grandfather's favorite color was the green of dollar bills. On summer evenings he watered his lawn, the jet of water cooling his thumb from eight hours of stapling crates at Sun Maid raisin. He knew that his house, pink as it was, was worth money. He knew that if he kept the rose bushes throwing out buds of sweet flowers, the value of the house would increase. The fruit trees would grow and thicken with branches to feed his family and neighbor.

2   Grandmother was also fond of green but preferred the silver shine of coins that made her eyebrows jump up and down. She showed me a nickel slug from the county fair stamped: MILK IS GOOD. She could not read or write in Spanish or English and thought the coin was worth more than a brown child realized. I wanted to say that it was nothing. It could sparkle in the sun or make a nice necklace, but it was no rare coin. I drank my purple Kool-Aid, crunched spines of air trapped in the ice cubes, and made my eyebrows jump up and down like hers.

3   Yellow was her favorite color. Yellow roses floated in a bowl on the windowsill. The yellow sunshine clock hummed on the wall, and her yellow refrigerator, the first on the block, blended well with the floor, a speckled affair with some yellow but mostly black. From a top shelf of the hallway closet, she took down a shoe box of papers, including a single stock certificate from a sewing machine company. I looked closely at the yellowed paper and noted "one share" and the date "1939." It was now 1961, and even though I was young, nine at the time, I guessed that the stock was worth the memory of hope but little else.

4   "When you marry, honey, I will give this to you," she said, shaking the paper at me. "You'll be a rich man."

5   My eyebrows jumped up and down, and I went outside to the back yard to play with my favorite color, mud. At my grandparents' house there were no toys, no pets, no TV in English, so when I stayed there I had to come up with things to do. I tried rolling summer-warmed oranges around the yard in a sort of bowling game in which I tried to knock over sparrows that had come in search of worms. But after twenty minutes of this, I was bored. I did chin-ups on the clothesline pole, but that was sweaty work that bored me even more.

6   So I fashioned mud into two forts and a great wall on which I stuck flags of straw-like weeds. When the mud dried hard as a turtle, I pounded the hell out of the forts and wall, imagining that a Chinese war had come. I made bomb sounds and moaned for the dying. My thumb pressed a red ant, and I said, "Too bad."

7   Mud was a good color, and the purple of plums made my mouth water. Peaches did the same, and the arbor of greenish grapes that I spied in the neighbor's yard. Their German Shepherd, ears erect, spied me too, so I couldn't climb the fence and help myself. But looking was almost like eating, and noon was near.

8   The brown of frijoles was our favorite color as steam wavered in our faces. Grandfather, who came home for lunch, left his shoes near the door, smothered his beans with a river of chile and scooped them with big rips of tortilla. I ate with a fork and a tortilla, savoring little mouthfuls of beans with a trickle of chile. The clear color of water washed it all down, and the striped candy cane left over from Christmas sweetened the day.

Grandfather, patting his stomach, smiled at me and turned on the radio to the Spanish station. For dessert, there was dark coffee and a powdered donut on a white plate. Grandmother sipped coffee and tore jelly-red sweetness from a footprint-sized Danish.

9   While Grandfather played a game of solitaire, I fooled with the toothpicks in the wooden, pig-shaped holder, the only thing that resembled a toy in the house or yard. I swept the crumbs from the table and pinched the donut crumbs from Grandfather's plate. Grandmother did the dishes, ever mindful of the sweep of the sunshine clock. "Viejo," she said, "it's time."

10   I walked Grandfather to the front yard, where he stopped and said to me, "A pink house is worth lot of money, m'ijo." We both stood admiring the house, trimmed with flowers and a wrought-iron gate, a plastic flamingo standing one-legged in front of a geranium. This was home, the color of his life. We started up the block, me taking two steps for every one of his, and he said no one's lawn was as green as his. When we looked back, when Grandfather said I should go because it was time to work, Grandmother was at the front door beating the dusty windowsills with a dish towel, waving goodbye until later.

Discussion Prompts/Writing Options

If you write on any of the following topics, work through the stages of the writing process in preparing your assignment.

1. Describe a place where, as a child, you had to spend some time. The place could be a family member's yard, a waiting room at a doctor's or dentist's office, a car on a long road trip, or some other place. Include details about what you did to amuse yourself.

2. What is your favorite color? Describe the objects or scenes that you associate with that color.

3. Gary Soto associates a certain color or colors with different people. For example, the young boy notices his grandfather's fondness for green. He also connects that color to his grandfather's desire to prosper; he notes that his grandfather's favorite color was "the green of dollar bills." Write a description of someone you connect to a specific color. Describe the connections that link the person to that color. For instance, Grandmother's favorite color was yellow, and she valued yellow flowers, sunshine, and a yellowed stock certificate that she thought would make her grandson rich.

4. Describe someone you know who has become too fond of one color. Include descriptions of the color's role in the person's clothes, home, book bag, and so forth.

5. A meal can be a good indicator of a family's background, economic status, or level of contentment. Describe a meal with family, friends, or strangers and consider how the meal and the way the people shared it reflected the background, status, or level of contentment of the diners.

Topics for Critical Thinking and Writing

If you write on one of the following topics, work through the stages of the writing process in preparing your assignment.

1. Soto's essay is about generational change. The grandparents speak Spanish, but their grandson wants to watch television in English. His grandmother cannot read, but her grandson can understand that the stock certificate she holds is worthless. He is bored at his grandparents' house, but they enjoy the pleasure of their simple routine and care for their house as a treasure. In spite of these differences, the boy respects and loves his grandparents. Write about a generational divide that you have experienced in your own family. Be sure to write specific descriptions of how this divide reveals itself.

2. Write about some part of your heritage that you love or that gives you pride. For example, some people are proud to be the children of men or women who died for their country; others love to hear stories of the first generation of their family to come to America. Sometimes the pride or love comes from past achievements; sometimes it comes from past sacrifices. Describe what part of your family's past has become part of your identity.

READINGS FOR WRITERS: NARRATION

The Good Father

Alisa Valdes-Rodriguez

In this essay, best-selling author Alisa Valdes-Rodriguez writes about her father. He was orphaned, shipped to one foster home after another, and later abandoned by his wife to raise their children alone. Yet, despite it all, this Latino father maintained an open heart and became his only daughter's hero and best friend.

Words You May Need to Know (Corresponding paragraph numbers are in parentheses.)

elitist (2): people who believe they belong to a superior group and deserve special treatment
tantamount (2): equal to
scarlet letter (2): a sign of shame; the term comes from Nathaniel Hawthorne's novel about a woman forced to wear a scarlet letter as punishment for committing adultery
transplanted (4): moved or relocated from one place to another
confronted (4): stood in front of, faced
***arroz con pollo* (6):** chicken with rice

1 For years I have sent my father a Mother's Day card. I'm not trying to insult him, and I'm not trying to make a joke. Rather, I am acknowledging the fact that from the time I was eleven, when my parents divorced and my mother left us, my father served as both a mother and a father to me. A single father raising a daughter through her adolescence

is unusual. But that my Cuban dad raised me to be strong, confident, and brave is all the more remarkable considering the details of his early life.

2   The story begins in Santa Clara, Cuba, in the 1940s. My grandmother Eugenia Leyba was a beautiful teenager, the maid in the home of a wealthy family. The family had two sons. The sons made a bet, each thinking that he would be the first to sleep with the maid. My grandfather Ricardo Hernandez "won" that bet (no one knows whether by force or through charm). What we do know is that my father, Nelson, was the product of this unhappy union, and Ricardo, now living in Miami, never claimed him. When Ricardo's parents discovered that the maid was pregnant by their son, they did what most class- and color-conscious elitists would have done at the time: they fired Eugenia and spread rumors about her around town, rumors that made it impossible for her to find work. Being a single mother—and a single teen mother from the working class—is difficult anywhere in Latin America, even today; in the 1940s it was tantamount to wearing a scarlet letter.

3   The young Eugenia gave birth to my father on the kitchen table in her mother's house. She then moved to Havana, shamed, and took jobs as a domestic servant. When my father was seven, his mother married. The man's name was Elpidio Valdes. In those days it was scandalous for a man to marry a woman who had a child, so Eugenia and Elpidio pretended that he was my dad's father, even changing my dad's last name to Valdes. When my dad was nine, Eugenia died of leukemia. No one told him she was dead until the funeral. Elpidio stood at the grave with my father as the casket was lowered and said simply, "That's your mother. Men don't cry."

4   When my dad was fifteen, Elpidio heard about Operation Pedro Pan, a U.S.-based program that arranged for children to be taken out of the newly communist Cuba, and thought it was a marvelous idea. He sent my father, alone, to the United States. (Ultimately the program transplanted 14,000 children.) Unlike many of the other kids, however, my father never saw his family again. Elpidio did not come after him or even try to reach him. At fifteen my father was on his own in a new country, placed in the fourth grade because he knew no English, and shuffled from one foster home to another until he was eighteen. Then he fell in love with a tall American woman, married her, and had a son. He took a job as a janitor at the University of New Mexico at Albuquerque and started reading student papers he found on teachers' desks. He thought the papers in the sociology department were particularly interesting and confronted the head of the department, saying that he, the lowly janitor, could do a better job than the students.

5   The department head took my father under his wing, and within six years, during which time I was born, my dad had a Ph.D. in sociology. He eventually became a professor at the same university where he had once cleaned toilets. My mother, a woman with a history of picking low-life men to scandalize her parents and to match her terrible self-esteem, did not have

as much interest in a successful academic as she'd had in an immigrant janitor with limited English. She moved out of the state with scarcely a second thought—leaving behind my brother, Ricardo, and me.

6   My father, despite his own troubled history, embraced the opportunity to raise me. He taught himself to cook, and some of my fondest memories are of him whipping up *arroz con pollo* in the kitchen of our house near the university. And when I was twelve and got my period, my dad—an orphan boy from the mean streets of Havana—celebrated by buying me flowers and having a female friend of his take me out for ice cream.

7   When I wanted to be a jazz saxophonist, my father bought me the most expensive tenor sax he could find. He listened as I practiced and came to my room with tears in his eyes to tell me how talented I was. When I decided that I wanted to be a journalist, my dad told me to apply to Columbia University, which had the best graduate school for journalism in the nation. I was afraid I wouldn't get in, but Dad told me I would. He was right. When I decided to leave newspapers—and my steady salary—to write novels, my dad opened his home to me and told me to stay as long as I needed to. I was thirty-two years old, married, with a baby. My dad did not care; he knew I could do it. He read pages of what I'd written and told me it was great. As always, my father believed in me before I believed in myself, and helped guide me toward publication of my first novel and a whole new career as an author.

8   I hear so many Latinas bashing our men as if somehow this will help move us to equality. And I know that many men are rotten to women. But many are not. Many are like my father: wonderful, sensitive human beings who stand behind their daughters. Papi, I love you. Happy Father's Day.

Discussion Prompts/Writing Options

If you write on any of the following topics, work through the stages of the writing process in preparing your assignment.

1. One of the author's fondest memories is of her father "whipping up *arroz con pollo*," a chicken and rice dish. What is one of your fondest memories of a family ritual? If you write a narrative of this memory, be sure to arrange the details in a clear, logical order.

2. When he was a janitor at a university, Nelson Valdes was brave enough to confront the head of the sociology department. Write a narrative about the first time you tried to conquer a particular fear, such as speaking in front of an audience, flying for the first time, asking someone out on a first date, and so forth.

3. When Nelson Valdes was only fifteen years old, he was sent to the United States all alone and was placed in the fourth grade because he could not speak English. Write about an experience that seemed negative for you at the time but that proved to be a positive turning point in your life. Although you will be writing your narrative in time order, try to use a variety of transitional words and phrases. (Avoid repetitive use of "then" and "next.")

4. Nelson Valdes supported his daughter's changing career goals even when she had to give up a steady salary and move back home with a husband and baby. Recall the first time you realized that a friend or family member would accept you, no matter how risky your choices may have seemed.

Topics for Critical Thinking and Writing

If you write on any of the following topics, work through the stages of the writing process in preparing your assignment.

1. Valdes-Rodriguez doesn't write much about her mother (saying only that she "had a history of picking low-life men to scandalize her parents" and suffered from "terrible self-esteem"). Imagine this story from her mother's point of view, Do you think the mother felt the loss of her children and guilt about her choices?

2. Why was Nelson Valdes able to suffer such abandonment and pain yet still have the strength to become a loving, caring parent? Are there any clues in his daughter's descriptions of his childhood, early struggles, and ultimate success? What qualities emerge as he finds his way to a good life?

3. In many ways, "The Good Father" is about people trapped in roles: the servant girl who has no power, the single teen mother, the janitor who is invisible to most people on a university campus, and so forth. Consider how roles—being a victim of or breaking out of such roles—create the conflicts in this essay.

READINGS FOR WRITERS: PROCESS

Breath of Life

Judith Sachs

Judith Sachs, an expert on stress management, has taught the subject in places from universities and corporate settings to holistic health centers. She is also the author or coauthor of more than twenty books on preventive health and stress management. In this excerpt from her book, Twenty-Minute Vacations, Sachs explains how a simple process—breathing correctly—can give us a vacation from stress.

Words You May Need to Know (Corresponding paragraph numbers are in parentheses.)

ledge (2): rim
slack (2): loose
pubic bone (3): the front bone of the pelvis

sternum (3): the breastbone
stray (10): wander
acknowledge (10): recognize

1   nhaling and exhaling—you probably aren't even conscious of those precious breaths that occur over and over during the course of each day and night. You can turn this involuntary physical activity into a meaningful twenty-minute vacation that will get you in touch with the deeper sense of yourself that you probably ignore most of the time.

2   Find a place you like: it may be a corner of your living room, or out in the sun on a warm rock or on a ledge of a pool near an office building. Get as comfortable as possible and lie down. Loosen your belt and take off your shoes. You want your head in line with your neck, the chin slightly tucked in. Let your shoulders go slack, draining into the floor or ground under you.

3   In order to breathe—really let go and breathe!—you have to allow the stomach muscles to release. Just for a minute, hold your breath, and tighten everything, from your pubic bone to your xiphoid process (the small bone beneath the sternum). Now let it out with a huge sigh. Roll your head from side to side, yawning as you do so. Okay, you're ready to begin.

4   It's important to become aware of the way you breathe normally, something of which you probably never were conscious. So start your vacation as an observer of the process. Watch what happens as you take breath in and let it out. Do you breathe quickly or slowly? Are your inhalations and exhalations even, or does one take more time than the other? Do you stop and catch your breath, then inhale some more? Do you draw your nostrils closed in an attempt to take in more air? Does your chest rise as you do this? Do you pause after you've exhaled, getting ready to breathe again? Do you hold your breath? Do you sigh a lot?

5   Don't judge yourself or decide that your breathing is "wrong" or "right." You're on vacation and should be enjoying yourself. As you get deeper into the process, you'll find that it becomes easier and easier to fill and empty all the various cavities of your body—not just your lungs, nose, and mouth, but also, if you can imagine them clearly enough, your heart, your liver, and your bones.

6   Breathing should come right from your belly. Don't worry about your lungs; they'll get oxygen no matter what you do. Put your hand on your lower abdomen and push against it with your stomach muscles as though you were pushing the air out. See your belly as a balloon, expanding and growing as you inhale, deflating as you exhale. Be sure you inhale and exhale at the same pace, in the same rhythm. Loosen all your limbs and allow them to be stirred by your breath. Breathe in and out through your nose, keeping your mouth lightly closed.

7   For the next part of this vacation, breathe normally, which probably will give you rather shallow breaths (this is the way most people breathe most of the time). Then, as your belly opens up and you are able to take in more air, let the breaths deepen and intensify. If at any point in this vacation you feel lightheaded or dizzy, just go back to your regular breathing.

8   Now you are going to get creative with your breathing by dividing it into three parts. In the first part, inhale into your belly just a little; then bring the air up into your chest, and finally all the way into your throat. When you have as much air as you can possibly take, begin the three-part exhale: first, let the air out from the throat, then from the chest, then from the stomach. Continue this pattern as long as it feels comfortable. You can

always switch back to your normal breathing at any point if the three-part breathing is too intense.

9   While you are on vacation, you are going to think of nothing but the breath: how cool the inhalation feels as it rushes in through your nostrils, how warm the exhalation feels on your upper lip as you let the air escape. The gentle in and out of breathing is like a wave, never really ending and never really beginning. There is always just a little left in your lungs, even when you've exhaled completely, and always a small gap at the top when you think you can't take in any more.

10   Your thoughts doubtless will stray in the midst of this journey; if you find yourself thinking about anything else at all, simply acknowledge the thought, let it go, and return to your focus on the breath. You want to feel like a passenger in a car, watching the scenery go by, acknowledging each view but attaching to none. A twenty-minute session of breathing will leave you refreshed and relaxed, ready for the rest of your day.

Discussion Prompts/Writing Options

If you write on any of the following topics, work through the stages of the writing process in preparing your assignment.

1. Almost everyone engages regularly in a stressful process. Write about one process that adds to your daily stress. For instance, you may write about the stress of opening your email at work each morning or about cleaning up your children's mess at the end of the day. As you write about the steps of the process, be sure to include details about your stress level building or decreasing.

2. Exercise is considered an effective stress-buster. Do you regularly engage in some physical activity (anything from walking to boxing) that helps you to relax? If so, describe the process involved in relieving your stress while you are engaged in this exercise.

3. Do you allow yourself a brief "vacation" during a busy day? That is, do you take a ten- or twenty-minute break to clear your head and catch your breath? What do you do during that break? Describe the steps of your "vacation" process.

4. Reducing stress is an important part of healing in a number of illnesses. You can learn more about the role of stress reduction in healing and wellness by researching online. You can begin by researching one or more of the following terms:

   meditation and strokes
   meditation and heart attacks
   alternative medicine
   stress and cancer
   guided imagery and pain management
   mind–body connection
   mind–body medicine

   After you have explored the role of stress reduction in healing and wellness, write about one process that minimizes pain or helps heal illness by reducing stress.

Topics for Critical Thinking and Writing

If you write on any of the following topics, work through the stages of the writing process in preparing your assignment.

1. Do you believe that a breathing exercise can help a person relieve stress? Would you feel silly trying the "Breath of Life" activity? Explain why or why not.

2. For five minutes, focus only on your breathing. If, after five minutes, you realize that you found yourself being distracted often, ask yourself why it is difficult to focus only on your breathing. Does it take discipline to maintain that focus? Is it possible that modern life, with its constant multitasking and ever-present electronic stimulation, makes focusing on one thing more difficult for most people than it used to be? If you agree, write about one typical process (such as studying, planning, or decision making) that can be made more difficult by distractions.

3. How much of our daily stress would disappear if we changed our lifestyles? For example, would life be less stressful if we spent less, bought less, cut back on unnecessary driving, chose a smaller living space, and found meaningful work that might pay less? What stands in the way of most people who would like to make such changes? Could it be financial demands, career ambitions, or family pressures?

READINGS FOR WRITERS: COMPARISON AND CONTRAST

Honesty and Dishonesty

Jo-Ellan Dimitrius and Mark Mazzarella

Although Jo-Ellan Dimitrius is not a lawyer, she has been closely connected to some of the most famous trials of the past twenty-five years. Dimitrius' gift for decoding the hidden messages in the appearance, facial expression, tone of voice, and personal habits of jurors, witnesses, lawyers, and judges has enabled her to predict their behavior. Her book, Reading People, which contains the section "Honesty and Dishonesty," applies the skills she uses in the courtroom to everyday life so that readers can learn how to "read people" and learn how others "read" us.

Words You May Need to Know (Corresponding paragraph numbers are in parentheses.)

furrowed (4): wrinkled
brow (4): forehead
deviations (6): departures from customary behavior

subtle (8): delicate, difficult to notice or understand
disbelief (8): refusal to believe

1 ┃magine a young boy insisting to his mother that he wasn't the one who took the cookies out of the cookie jar. He can't bring himself to look her in the eye for more than an instant. He's shifting from foot to foot and stuttering to beat the band. Honest people are generally relaxed and open. Dishonest people aren't.

2   Any trait that shows tension, nervousness, or secretiveness indicates possible dishonesty. There are four different types of liars: occasional, frequent, habitual, and professional. Two of those types, habitual and professional, are difficult to spot by their body language alone. The habitual liar is so accustomed to lying that he may not care or fully realize he's lying, so he usually won't show it. The professional liar has rehearsed his lies so well that his behavior will give little away.

3   Like drug and alcohol abusers, people who lie won't usually admit it. But lying is often easy to detect when you know what to look for. The symptoms listed here are reliable tip-offs to the occasional and frequent liar. These physical clues generally appear only when someone knows he's lying and is at least somewhat troubled when he does. Luckily, most people are at worst occasional liars and reveal their discomfort in many ways.

4   Symptoms of dishonesty include shifty or wandering eyes, any type of fidgeting, rapid speech, change in voice, shifting back and forth on one's feet or in a chair, any signs of nervousness, an exaggerated version of the "sincere," furrowed-brow look, sweating, and shaking. Other symptoms include any activity that obscures the eyes, face, or mouth, such as putting the hand over the mouth while talking, rubbing the nose, or blinking the eyes. Symptoms may also be licking the lips, running the tongue over the teeth, leaning forward, and inappropriate familiarity, such as backslapping, other touching, and getting too close (invading personal space).

5   The signs of honesty are just the opposite of those listed above. Honest people are relaxed and calm. They usually meet your gaze. A sincere smile and the warm, kind eyes that most of us know when we see them also indicate honesty.

6   When things get stressful, it can be difficult to tell the difference between honest nervousness or defensiveness and dishonesty. If your employee has made a horrible mistake and you've asked him to explain it, chances are he'll look nervous and defensive no matter how truthful he is. I've watched hundreds of nervous witnesses, and I've found the surest way to detect a lie in a stressful situation is to watch for their patterns of behavior, looking for consistencies and deviations.

7   Several years ago, I worked on a case in which the owner of a real estate development company was being sued by his partner for fraud. One of the key witnesses was an employer who had worked closely with both men. A very nervous woman under the best of circumstances, she shook like a leaf from the moment she was sworn in until the moment she left the witness stand. She showed all the classic signs of dishonesty: failing to maintain eye contact, shaking, fidgeting in her chair, and fussing with small paper cups on the witness stand. But I couldn't conclude from this that she was lying because had she simply been dishonest, she probably would have been more comfortable during at least some portion of her

testimony—when describing her personal background, for instance. The fact that this woman's discomfort was constant revealed that she was nervous, not necessarily dishonest.

8   You have to pay close attention to someone's normal pattern in order to notice a deviation from it when he or she lies. Sometimes the variation is as subtle as a pause. Other times it's obvious and abrupt. I recently saw a news interview with an acquaintance who I was certain was going to lie about a few sensitive issues, and lie she did. During most of her interview she was calm and direct, but when she started lying, her manner changed dramatically: she threw her head back, laughed in "disbelief," and shook her head back and forth. It's true the questions dealt with very personal issues, but I've found that *in general, if a person is telling the truth, his or her manner will not change significantly or abruptly.* But you won't see those changes if you're not watching carefully.

Discussion Prompts/Writing Options

If you write on any of the following topics, work through the stages of the writing process in preparing your assignment.

1. According to Dimitrius, what body language is a sign of an honest person, and what body language may signal a liar? Write a summary of her article, and include her warnings about confusing nervousness with dishonesty and about the need to know a person's normal behavior patterns before judging his or her honesty.

2. Contrast the body language of two celebrities who have recently been in trouble with the law. Which celebrity appeared to be more honest, and why?

3. Have you ever "misread" a person's body language? Contrast how you interpreted the person's signals with the reality of the person's intentions.

4. Write about the different body languages of the attentive student and the inattentive student in a college classroom.

5. Reread the signs or symptoms of dishonesty in paragraph 4 of Dimitrius' essay. Pick any five of them, and show how these signs may indicate a trait or emotion different from dishonesty.

Topics for Critical Thinking and Writing

If you write on any of the following topics, work through the stages of the writing process in preparing your assignment.

1. Why do some people lie more than others? Consider whether fear, insecurity, greed, a desire to feel powerful, or other traits can prompt a person to lie.

2. Dimitrius stresses that knowing the background and setting of an action is essential to judging it. That is, a person may appear dishonest because he or she is nervous, but, Dimitrius warns, "nervousness can be an honest response to a difficult situation." Can

you think of times in which a person might be misjudged because the background or setting of his or her behavior was misunderstood? For example, a person who runs at the sight of a police officer may have grown up in a country where terror squads in uniform administered justice, or a person might laugh inappropriately in a serious setting because he or she is nervous.

3. Are there situations in everyday life in which people *expect* to hear lies? Buying or trading a car is one such situation. Can you think of others? Think about business, legal, or personal interactions in which most people are accustomed to dishonesty.

READINGS FOR WRITERS: CLASSIFICATION

The Dog Ate My Disk, and Other Tales of Woe

Carolyn Foster Segal

Carolyn Foster Segal originally wrote this article for <u>The Chronicle of Higher Education</u>, *a magazine for college teachers. An English professor, Segal classifies student excuses according to the kind of misfortune they describe. Note that this essay was written for college teachers and see if you, as a student, find it amusing.*

Words You May Need to Know (Corresponding paragraph numbers are in parentheses.)

feline (1): an animal in the cat family

veracity (2): truthfulness

revered (2): highly respected

conjures up (3): brings about as if by magic

Louisa May Alcott (3): author of *Little Women*, a beloved nineteenth-century novel about four sisters

Pilgrim's Progress (3): a classic account of a spiritual journey

adjunct (5): at a college or university, an instructor who is hired from term to term

motifs (5): themes

bizarre (8): strange

harp on (9): speak repetitiously

trauma (9): bodily injury or mental shock

bedraggled (9): untidy or dirty

whirlwind (10): rushing and forceful

rendezvous (10): meet at an arranged time

papal (10): connected to the Roman Catholic pope

1   Taped to the door of my office is a cartoon that features a cat explaining to his feline teacher, "The dog ate my homework." It is intended as a gently humorous reminder to my students that I will not accept excuses for late work, and it, like the lengthy warning on my syllabus, has had absolutely no effect. With a show of energy and creativity that would be admirable if applied to the (missing) assignments in question, my students persist, week after week, semester after semester, year after year, in offering excuses about why their work is not ready. Those reasons fall into several broad categories: the family, the best friend, the evils of dorm life, the evils of technology, and the totally bizarre.

2   **The Family** The death of the grandfather/grandmother is, of course, the grandmother of all excuses. What heartless teacher would dare to question a student's grief or veracity? What heartless student would lie, wishing death on a revered family member, just to avoid a deadline? Creative students may win extra extensions (and days off) with a little careful planning and plot development, as in the sequence of "My grandfather/grandmother is sick"; "Now my grandfather/grandmother is in the hospital"; and finally, "We could all see it coming—my grandfather/grandmother is dead."

3   Another favorite excuse is "the family emergency," which (always) goes like this: "There was an emergency at home, and I had to help my family." It's a lovely sentiment, one that conjures up images of Louisa May Alcott's little women rushing off with baskets of food and copies of *Pilgrim's Progress*, but I do not understand why anyone would turn to my most irresponsible students in times of trouble.

4   **The Best Friend** This heartwarming concern for others extends beyond the family to friends, as in "My best friend was up all night, and I had to (a) stay up with her in the dorm, (b) drive her to the hospital, or (c) drive to her college because (1) her boyfriend broke up with her, (2) she was throwing up blood [no one catches a cold anymore; everyone throws up blood], or (3) her grandfather/grandmother died."

5   At one private university where I worked as an adjunct, I heard an interesting spin that incorporated the motifs of both best friend and dead relative: "My best friend's mother killed herself." One has to admire the cleverness here: A mysterious woman in the prime of her life has allegedly committed suicide, and no professor can prove otherwise! And I admit I was moved, until finally I had to point out to my students that it was amazing how the simple act of my assigning a topic for a paper seemed to drive large numbers of otherwise happy and healthy middle-aged women to their deaths. I was careful to make that point during an off week, during which no deaths were reported.

6   **The Evils of Dorm Life** These stories are usually fairly predictable; almost always feature the evil roommate or hallmate, with my student in the role of innocent victim; and can be summed up as follows: My roommate, who is a horrible person, likes to party, and I, who am a good person, cannot concentrate on my work when he or she is partying. Variations include stories about the two people next door who were running around and crying last night because (a) one of them had boyfriend/girlfriend problems; (b) one of them was throwing up blood; or (c) someone, somewhere, died. A friend of mine in graduate school had a student who claimed that his roommate attacked him with a hammer. That, in fact, was a true story; it came out in court when the bad roommate was tried for killing his grandfather.

7   **The Evils of Technology** The computer age has revolutionized the student story, inspiring almost as many new excuses as it has Internet businesses. Here are just a few electronically enhanced explanations:

- The computer wouldn't let me save my work.
- The printer wouldn't print.
- The printer wouldn't print this disk.
- The printer wouldn't give me time to proofread.
- The printer made a black line through all my words, and I know you can't read this, but do you still want it, or wait, here, take my disk. File name? I don't know what you mean.
- I swear I attached it.
- It's my roommate's computer, and she usually helps me, but she had to go to the hospital because she was throwing up blood.
- I did write to the news group, but all my messages came back to me.
- I just found out that all my newsgroup messages came up under a different name. I just want you to know that it's really me who wrote all those messages, you can tel which ones our mine because I didn't use the spelcheck! But it was yours truly :) Anyway, just in case you missed those messages or don't belief its my writing. I'll repeat what I sad: I thought the last movie we watched in clas was borring.

8   **The Totally Bizarre** I call the first story "The Pennsylvania Chain Saw Episode." A commuter student called to explain why she had missed my morning class. She had gotten up extra early so that she would be wide awake for class. Having a bit of extra time, she walked outside to see her neighbor, who was cutting some wood. She called out to him, and he waved back to her with the saw. Wouldn't you know it, the safety catch wasn't on or was broken, and the blade flew right out of the saw and across his lawn and over her fence and across her yard and severed a tendon in her right hand. So she was calling me from the hospital, where she was waiting for her surgery. Luckily, she reassured me, she had remembered to bring her paper and a stamped envelope (in a plastic bag, to avoid bloodstains) along with her in the ambulance, and a nurse was mailing everything even as we spoke.

9   This wasn't her first absence. In fact, this student had missed most of the class meetings, and I had already recommended that she withdraw from the course. Now I suggested again that it might be best if she dropped the class. I didn't harp on the absences (what if even some of this story were true?). I did mention that she would need time to recuperate and that making up so much missed work might be difficult. "Oh no," she said, "I can't drop this course. I had been planning to go on to medical school and become a surgeon, but since I won't be able to operate because of my accident, I'll have to major in English, and this course is more important than ever to me." She did come to the next class wearing—as evidence of her recent trauma—a bedraggled Ace bandage on her left hand.

10   You may be thinking that nothing could top that excuse, but in fact I have one more story, provided by the same student, who sent me a letter to explain

why her final assignment would be late. While recuperating from her surgery, she had begun corresponding on the Internet with a man who lived in Germany. After a one-week, whirlwind Web romance, they had agreed to meet in Rome, to rendezvous (her phrase) at the papal Easter Mass. Regrettably, the time of her flight made it impossible for her to attend class, but she trusted that I—just this once—would accept late work if the pope wrote a note.

Discussion Prompts/Writing Options

If you write on any of the topics below, work through the stages of the writing process in preparing your assignment.

1. Have you ever listened to a string of excuses from a person? Do they fall into categories? For example, your brother might have several kinds of excuses for borrowing, damaging, or not returning your possessions. Write a paragraph that classifies these excuses. You can decide what basis you will use to place these excuses into three or more categories.

2. As a college student, you might have a different point of view about assignment deadlines than Carolyn Foster Segal does. In fact, you may want to classify your professors according to their policies about late assignments or makeup tests.

3. Classify three kinds of college students that attend classes with you. You may choose a basis (such as friendliness, behavior in class, age, etc.) for the classification.

Topics for Critical Thinking and Writing

If you write on one of the following topics, work through the stages of the writing process in preparing your assignment.

1. Consider the distance between each student and teacher. That is, how much can an instructor really know about a student's motivations or circumstances? How much can a student know about what motivates or concerns the person at the head of the classroom? Classify students (or instructors) according to the image they present in class, but also consider how limited the image is.

2. Classifications can, unfortunately, be linked to stereotyping. That is, they can be quick assessments of others based on little evidence. Write about three stereotypes (such as snob, shallow person, or jock) that people might mistakenly use to classify you. Include reasons why others might label you with these terms and why you do not fit the stereotypes.

READINGS FOR WRITERS: DEFINITION

Terrorism

Ron Cunningham

Ron Cunningham is the editorial page editor of the <u>Gainesville Sun</u> (Fla.). In this 2010 editorial, he defines terrorism two ways: (1) as the national fear of flying, bombing, and other attacks by enemies abroad, *and (2) as a fear that we ignore each time we drive. As he notes, "In a typical month, more of us are killed in traffic than perished in the attacks of 9–11." Consider whether his definitions make too little of global terrorism or make the reader think about highway safety.*

Words You May Need to Know (Corresponding paragraph numbers are in parentheses.)

bumbled Christmas Day bombing attempt (2): a reference to an airline passenger who carried the makings of a bomb in his underwear

fanatics (3): people earnestly devoted to a cause

warped (3): distorted

curtail (5): reduce, limit

e.g. (5): for example

bureaucracy (6): a group of government administrators

devolution (7): becoming, changing into

retard (9): slow down

nah (10): slang for "no"

Big Brother (10): In George Orwell's famous novel *1984*, the evil and all-powerful ruler is called Big Brother.

gut (10): destroy the insides of

amorphous (10): without a definite shape

1   Periodically, I get e-mails from an outfit called HCD Research that are essentially public opinion snapshots. In a survey of 300 Americans, HCD Research recently found that an overwhelming number, seventy four percent, think the government should spend more money on airport security. In addition, after watching an interview with a former federal inspector about security issues, twenty five percent said they would feel "not at all safe" about flying, while only eight percent said they feel "very safe" on a plane.

2   None of this is especially surprising given the news of the bunbled Christmas day bombing attempt and subsequent disclosures about holes in our Homeland Security system. We're at war with terrorism, you know. Everybody says so. Dick Cheney. Even President Barack Obama. Why would anybody want to fly when terrorists with explosive underwear are slipping past the screeners? Better to drive, instead. Or maybe not.

3   Most of us don't think twice about driving. It's what we auto-Americans do. It's not as scary to most of us as flying, and we almost never see fanatics trying to set fire to their underwear while sitting in a traffic jam (although some of us have seen far stranger things in traffic). But our perception of what's safe and what isn't can be a bit warped.

4   Last year, I read Tom Vanderbilt's terrific book *Traffic: Why We Drive the Way We Do (and What It Says About Us)*. One of the things Vanderbilt's book says about us is that we are pretty lousy when it comes to the whole business of risk assessment. For instance, Vanderbilt points out that since the 1960s, fewer than 5000 people have died in the United States as a result of terrorism. On the other hand, something like 40,000 Americans are killed every year, year in and year out, in auto accidents.

In a typical month, more of us are killed in traffic than perished in the attacks of 9–11.

5   "In the wake of those attacks, polls found that many citizens thought it was acceptable to curtail civil liberties to help counter the threat of terrorism, to help preserve our 'way of life,' " Vanderbilt wrote. "Those same citizens, meanwhile, in polls and in personal behavior, have routinely resisted traffic measures designed to reduce the annual death toll (e.g., lowering speed limits, introducing more red light cameras, stiffer blood alcohol limits, stricter cell phone laws)."

6   Sure enough, this week came yet another poll, this from McClatchy-Ipsos, in which a majority agreed that "it is necessary to give up some civil liberties in order to make the world safe from terrorism." To wage a "war" that has claimed fewer than 5,000 American lives in half a century, we have put occupying armies into two countries on the other side of the world, created a Homeland Security bureaucracy on steroids and turned our airports into miniature police states.

7   In addition, we've done it all on enough borrowed money to practically guarantee our eventual devolution into an economic colony of the People's Republic of China. Everybody feel safer now? But what about that other form of terrorism? You know, the one that claims 40,000 American lives, year in and year out? Well, we know how to fight terrorism on the highway. It's not rocket science, and it's not nearly as expensive as rooting out bin Laden's disciples.

8   We could post cameras to catch red-light runners. We could ban texting while driving and cell phone use in cars. We could reinstate the helmet law for motorcyclists. We could narrow urban streets, lower the speed limit, and adopt other "traffic calming" measures that would force motorists to slow down and behave themselves.

9   Speed is the auto-terrorist's weapon of choice. Slowing down traffic would not only save lives at home but retard the threat of terrorism abroad. Driving slower means using less gas, which means fewer oil profits for the petroleum states that finance terrorism. Hey, here's a radical idea: We could stop manufacturing automobiles that are capable of driving twice as fast as our highest speed limits.

10   Nah. That would be Big Brother style meddling into our personal lives. So Americans are willing to gut the Bill of Rights in order to feel a little safer against the rather amorphous threat of international terrorism. But when it comes to defending that most sacred of all American rights—the right to drive as much and as fast as we care to—we are resolute.

11   Even if that means sacrificing tens of thousands of lives every year right at home. "Driving, with its exhilarating speed and the boundless personal mobility it grants us, is strangely life-affirming," Vanderbilt writes, "but also, for most of us, the most deadly presence in our lives." Go figure.

Discussion Prompts/Writing Options

If you write on any of these topics, be sure to work through the stages of the writing process in preparing your assignment.

1. How would you define "terror" in a personal definition? That is, what circumstances or events are you most afraid of? Why?

2. Write your personal definition of "safety." You can use examples from your experience or the experience of others.

Collaborate

3. Can you define yourself as a driver? For example, are you a nervous, confident, impatient, or aggressive driver? Feel free to come up with your own term. Support your definition with personal examples.

4. Have you ever lost a friend or loved one in a traffic accident? Pick a word or phrase that best expresses your reaction and explain that choice of word(s).

Topics for Critical Thinking and Writing

If you write on any of the following topics, work through the stages of the writing process in preparing your assignment.

1. Cunningham took the current meaning of "terrorism" and applied it to another form of "terrorism," the widely unrecognized terrorism of speed and recklessness on the road. Using Cunningham's method, write a personal definition (with examples) of some other widely used term such as *unemployment, crime victim, good neighborhood, star athlete, role model*, and so forth.

2. You may find Cunningham's comparison of international terrorism and terrorism on the road unconvincing or even foolish. You may be annoyed by his use of irony or sarcasm. However, those writing techniques are employed to make a point about America's love of driving fast. Do you think his point is valid? Explain.

READINGS FOR WRITERS: CAUSE AND EFFECT

Say Something

Lucie Prinz

Lucie Prinz writes about some adults' fear of teenagers and explains the effects of that fear. She uses two incidents, both of which take place on a subway, to ask why these adults are reluctant to interact with "the ordinary, harmless children we all come in contact with every day."

Words You May Need to Know (Corresponding paragraph numbers are in parentheses.)

engrossed (2): giving all their attention to
disdain (2): scorn
imperative (3): obligation
distended (4): swollen
testosterone (5): a male hormone

ebullient (7): very excited
collective (7): combined
rambunctious (9): noisy and unrestrained
recoil (10): spring back
flourish (10): thrive

1   I was sitting on a subway a few weeks ago when I looked up and saw a baby, just a little less than a year old, swinging from the overhead bar. She was flanked by two young teenage girls who thought this was a great way to entertain their little sister. As the train began to move, I could visualize the baby flying across the car. Without really thinking, I said to the girls, "Hey, that's not a good idea. That baby is going to get hurt. You better sit down with her on the seat." The kids gave me one of those "Who do you think you are?" looks they reserve for meddling adults, but they took the baby off the bar and sat down.

2   I was suddenly struck by the silence in the subway car. The normal hum of conversation had vanished. My fellow passengers, who had witnessed my encounter with the kids, were now engrossed in their newspapers and books or staring at something fascinating on the subway-tunnel wall. The car was not very crowded, and everyone had seen that endangered baby just as I had, but they had chosen not to get involved. Although most of them now avoided eye contact with me, a few treated me to the kind of disdain reserved for troublemakers. Could it be that my fellow passengers didn't care about that baby? Or were they just afraid to interfere?

3   We've all heard the old African saying, "It takes a whole village to raise a child." Americans have adopted it, and I understand why. It expresses some things that we can all easily accept: family values, shared responsibility, community spirit. But do we really believe in it as a guiding principle? When we repeat it, are we pledging ourselves to carry out its imperative? I don't think so.

4   Americans are known for generosity. We're ready to rescue the suffering children of the world. We send food to Ethiopia after our television screens show us little kids with huge eyes and distended bellies. We help the victims of floods, and we fund agencies to take care of refugees and abandoned children. We are the nation that invented the poster child and the telethon. These nameless suffering children touch our hearts—but they do not touch our lives.

5   The same adults who are profoundly moved by the plight of children they will never know seem to be willing to ignore the children they encounter every day, even if it is obvious that these children are in trouble or that they need a little guidance. I've watched adults actually move away from children they see approaching. I'm not talking about hostile, swaggering gangs of teenage boys—although even some of them are just exhibiting the high that comes with that first surge of testosterone. I'm talking about the ordinary, harmless children we all come in contact with every day on the streets of our cities, towns, and yes, villages.

6   I'm keeping score, counting the number of times I find myself the only person in a crowd who dares to interact with a child she doesn't know.

7   A few days after the swinging-baby incident, I was waiting on a crowded subway platform when someone pushed me from behind. I turned to see three teenage girls, giggling, ebullient, and so eager to get on the train just pulling into the station that they were shoving. Again I reacted without thinking. "Stop pushing – we'll all get on," I said. After a few murmured remarks along the lines of "Get lost, lady," they stopped. So did the conversation around me. Eyes swiveled away. I felt a collective intake of breath. Disapproval hung in the air, but mainly I sensed fear.

8   Seconds later the train doors opened, and we all stepped in. The woman who dropped into the seat next to me said, "Wow, that was a brave thing to do." When I suggested that it was no such thing, she said, "Well, you can't be too careful these days." That's just it, I thought. You *can* be too careful.

9   In both these encounters I treated harmless children as if they were indeed harmless. They may have been foolish, thoughtless, rambunctious, rude, or annoying. But the only one in any danger was that baby swinging on the bar.

10   I live in a big city. I know that there are violent armed children, hopeless and desperate kids out there. There is no way that I can attack the serious urban problems we all hear about on the evening news. But I am convinced that I can contribute to the larger solutions by refusing to recoil from kids just because they are acting like kids. A lost child who encounters fear instead of concern is twice lost. By responding to these children, we may begin to build a village where they will flourish and adults can live without fear.

Discussion Prompts/Writing Options

If you write on any of the following topics, work through the stages of the writing process in preparing your assignment.

1. Prinz wrote this article in 1996. What do you think might happen today if adults in public places followed her advice about dealing with "kids acting like kids" in public places? Are there appropriate times for adults to intervene and other times when adult guidance can be misinterpreted?

2. If an adult in your neighborhood cautioned or scolded two or more teens at a bus stop, in a store, or on the street, what could be the result? Would the reaction be different if only one teen was present?

3. Consider some of the reasons that teens tend to "act out" in public.

4. If a stranger on a bus, in line, or on the street cautioned you about your bad behavior (for instance, cutting in line, deliberately littering on the sidewalk), how would you react? Why?

5. What public behavior would make you intervene? Careless or cruel behavior involving a pet? A child? How would you become involved? Would you call a police officer or take action yourself?

Topics for Critical Thinking and Writing

If you write on any of the following topics, work through the stages of the writing process in preparing your assignment.

1. Some people believe that bad behavior in public places has increased among all age groups. For example, brawls in sports arenas (on the court, field, or among the crowd) have multiplied, people have been crushed in the stampede to enter stores at after-holiday sales, some airline passengers have refused to remain seated until the plane has come to a complete stop even though the safety of others is jeopardized. Do you believe that we have lost our sense of civility? If so, what has caused the change? If you believe that public behavior is better than it used to be, give examples of the improvement and explain what has caused the change.

2. What does Prinz mean when she says that "A lost child who encounters fear is twice lost"? Who is afraid? Who is lost, and how is the child lost twice?

3. Consider people you know who are your age but who do not attend college. Are their lives as stressful as yours? Why or why not?

READINGS FOR WRITERS: ARGUMENT

The Case for a Tax on Sodas

Jo Ivey Boufford

Boufford, president of the New York Academy of Medicine, writes about a growing concern in this country: the role of sugary drinks in the obesity epidemic. The statistics and studies in her article, published in 2010, are used to argue that a tax on sodas (combined with other programs and policies) could save lives.

Words You May Need to Know (Corresponding paragraph numbers are in parentheses.)

afoot (1): under way   **prominent (4):** easily seen
- laden (4): loaded   **surcharges (5):** extra charges

1   There is a movement afoot across the nation encouraging consumers to think twice before popping open a can of soda. The reason is clear, and the medical evidence is in: sugar-sweetened beverages, or SSBs, have been linked to the obesity explosion taking place throughout America.

2   Unlike other foods, SSBs—which include soda, sports drinks, energy drinks, sweetened bottled coffee or tea, and sweetened fruit or vegetable drinks—have no nutritional value. They are empty calories that simply deliver sugar rather than replacement calories for other foods a person might eat. SSBs are the only foods that researchers have consistently linked to the obesity epidemic.

3   According to the Centers for Disease Control and Prevention, two-thirds of American adults are overweight or obese, and obesity is now the

second-largest contributor to premature death in the United States. According to a report issued last July, U.S. health care costs due to obesity have reached $147 billion, double what they were ten years ago. Worse yet, children who consume more soft drinks consume more calories (about 55 to 190 per day) than kids who drink fewer soft drinks, and are more likely to become overweight.

4   The public health risks associated with the consumption of SSBs top the list of critical medical issues facing millions of children and adults each year. Sugar-sweetened beverages play an especially prominent role in our sugar-laden diets. The beverage industry spends billions of dollars each year marketing its products, with a special focus on children and adolescents. The result is that the average American is consuming 46 gallons of SSBs a year—the equivalent of 40 pounds of sugar.

5   Our only hope for reducing rates of obesity is to prevent people, especially children, from consuming excess calories in the first place. The Institute of Medicine has recommended surcharges as a strategy for reducing consumption of sugar-sweetened beverages. Multiple studies show that when the prices of unhealthy food or products are raised, people switch to healthier foods.

6   Combined with educational programming in schools and communities and with policies that increase the options available to families who want and need better access to fresh, healthy foods, SSB taxes could be part of a successful approach to combating obesity.

Discussion Prompts/Writing Options

If you write on any of the following topics, work through the stages of the writing process in preparing your assignment.

1. Among the SSBs (sugar-sweetened beverages) may be one that you drink often. Argue for excluding this drink from the list of SSBs that Bouffard says deserve a surcharge to discourage consumption. Your reasons will be personal.

2. Do you approve of the intense and widespread marketing of "junk food" (such as sugary drinks) to children? Or do you believe that, in a free market economy, parents (and not the government) should be responsible for choosing what their children eat and drink?

3. Bouffard refers to a need for "policies that increase the options available to families who want and need better access to fresh, healthy foods." Write an argument to convince readers that one of the following groups needs better access to fresh, healthy, and affordable foods: residents of poor, urban neighborhoods (which often do not have supermarkets); college students (who live in places such as dorm rooms with no refrigerators); those who depend on food banks for much of their food; or young working adults who eat all their meals at cheap, fast-food outlets.

Topics for Critical Thinking and Writing

If you write on any of the following topics, work through the stages of the writing process in preparing your assignment.

1. Do you consume an excessive amount of sugar? If so, what is your weakness? Sugary snacks? Candy? Soda? Explain why the sweet food or drink appeals to you. Does the sweet food serve as a reward, an energy booster, or a comforter on a tough day? How are emotions connected to overindulgence in sweet foods or drinks?

2. Argue that another major cause of obesity, such as the trans-fat found in cookies, cakes, chips, and other popular foods, should become the focus of a campaign for healthy eating. You may need to research trans-fat to familiarize yourself with this subject.

READINGS FOR WRITERS: THE ESSAY

How to Twitter

Julia Angwin

Writing widely on issues of media and technology, Julia Angwin has published the book Stealing MySpace about the rise and power of the social networking site MySpace and, as a columnist for the Wall Street Journal, writes about technology. In this 2009 article from the Wall Street Journal, she writes about joining Twitter, finding followers, and distinguishing them from friends.

Words You May Need to Know (Corresponding paragraph numbers are in parentheses.)

decode (1): translate a message from code
medium (1): a means of mass communication
character (2): a mark, such as a letter or number, made in printing
narcissism (3): an abnormal tendency to admire one's own perfections

prodding (3): urging
reciprocal (5): mutual
devotee (5): a dedicated member
cobbled (7): patched together
obscure (8): used as a verb, it means *hide*
gaggle (9): a flock (usually used as "a gaggle of geese")
musings (9): thoughts
eliciting (9): drawing out

1   When I first joined Twitter, I felt like I was in a noisy bar where everyone was shouting and nobody was listening. Soon, I began to decode its many mysteries: how to find a flock of followers, how to talk to them in a medium that blasts to lots of people at once and how to be witty in very tiny doses.

2   Twitter is a mass text-messaging service that allows you to send short 140-character updates—or "tweets"—to a bunch of people at once. They are your "followers." It was designed to be read on a cell phone, though many people read it online, too.

3   Suddenly a lot of non-tweeters are starting to feel left out. On "The Daily Show" this week, host John Stewart reported on Twitter with a wink (or was it a twink?) at the narcissism of the personal broadcasting system. It has a world-wide audience of six million unique visitors a month, up from 1.2 million a year ago, according to ComScore Media Metrix. But I have to admit I didn't understand the appeal of Twitter when I joined, at the prodding of friends, in November. One answer that explains its popularity: It's not about chatting with your friends—it's about promoting yourself.

4   My name was available, so I set up a profile at twitter.com/JuliaAngwin. On Twitter, however, you do not exist without followers, who subscribe to receive your messages. So I set out to follow some people in the hope that they would follow me.

5   I had to learn the crucial distinction between a "follower" and a "friend." On Facebook, if I'm your friend, you're my friend, and we can read all about each other. Relationships on Twitter are not reciprocal: People you follow do not have to follow you or give you permission to start following them. You just sign up and start following them. It's a bit like stalking. Heather Gold, a comedian and Twitter devotee, points out that for all its flaws, the term follower is more honest than "friend."

6   At first, I was the loneliest of social creatures—a leader without followers. I tried searching for my actual real-world friends using Twitter's "Find People" function, but it was down the day I joined. (Twitter is growing so fast that short outages are not unusual.) So I asked a few colleagues for their Twitter addresses and started following them. I also searched their public list of followers and who they followed.

7   Eventually, I cobbled together a mix of people I could follow: media colleagues, friends, bloggers and various people who are known as great "tweeters," such as the chief executive of online retailer Zappos.com, Tony Hsieh, who has written quite movingly on his blog about how Twitter changed his life. He says that being forced to bear witness to his life in 140-character bursts of prose has made him more grateful for the good moments and more amused by the bad moments.

8   I discovered that a better way to get followers was to tweet. Every time I tweeted, I got a surge of followers. Where were they coming from? The likely answer illuminates Twitter's greatest strength: It's easily searchable. During the terrorist attacks in Mumbai in November 2009, people scoured Twitter for postings from eye witnesses. When US Airways Flight 1559 landed in the Hudson River, one of the first pictures was posted as a link on Twitter. Similar items may have appeared on other social networks, but they were not as easy to discover. On Facebook, most people's information is viewable only by their approved friends. MySpace profile pages are searchable, but not its blogs or status updates, and it is hard to find anyone you know because most people obscure their real names.

9   Now, a gaggle of unknown followers were finding something in my tweets—and following me! I quickly found that my general musings about life such as "Thank God they have wifi on jury duty" fell like a dead weight, eliciting no response. A larger problem was that it was hard to tweet when I didn't know whom I was tweeting to. Unlike Facebook, where I know each and every one of my 287 friends, I have never met or heard of the 221 people following me on Twitter.

10   To understand the medium, I studied others' Tweets. I spent a surprising amount of time trying out tweets in my head before tweeting. I aimed to tweet once a day but often came up short. I found it difficult to fit in both news and opinion. Without a point of view, though, my updates were pretty boring. So, for instance, I changed "eating strawberries during a snowstorm" into "eating strawberries during a snowstorm. not carbon efficient but lovely." Another trick, including a short link to a Web site or to my own stories (using link-shrinking services like TinyURL), let me use most of the 140 characters to compose a thought.

11   I found a good way to get followers was to get "retweeted," meaning that someone would pick up my tweet and send it to their followers preceded by the code "RT@juliaangwin." When I tweeted about being interviewed by Wired.com recently, two colleagues retweeted my tweet. Seven of their followers then retweeted it. As a result, I gained 22 new followers.

12   People also seem eager to answer questions on Twitter. I came across twenty-five-year-old Justin Rockwell, who was spending so much time answering people's tweets about how to build better Web pages that he says he decided to try it as a business. He now makes about $350 a week scouring Twitter for people tweeting about their problems building Web pages. Using the Twitter ID ThatCSSGuy (which refers to a Web program called CSS), he offers to help solve their problems and asks for a tip in return.

13   But I found it difficult to acknowledge answers I received on Twitter. Twitter's reply features felt clumsy. The easiest way to reply to a tweet is to hit the @reply icon which broadcasts your answer to all your followers, essentially Twitter's equivalent of the "reply all" email function. As a result, I often didn't reply because I didn't want to spam everyone with a bunch of "thanks for your feedback" messages. So I was silent, which made me feel even more antisocial.

14   Twitter wasn't designed for these kinds of social interactions or conversations. As Twitter cofounder Biz Stone told me, "Twitter is fundamentally a broadcasting system." The messaging features were ad-ons.

15   Twitter is useful precisely because so many people are talking about different things at once. When he was president of Sling Media, for instance, Jason Hirschhorn constantly monitored the word "sling" on Twitter. "It's an up-to-the-minute temperature of what people are saying about your brand," he said. He left the consumer electronics company last month.

16   There are more than 2000 Twitter applications made by other people to help you sort through all the tweets. One of my favorites is Twitturly.com, which tracks the most popular URLs (or Web links) being shared across Twitter. Others, such as Tweetdeck and Whirl, help you manage and organize your tweets.

17   Still, the beauty of Twitter is that you don't have to commit to it; no one expects you to read all the tweets rolling in. As a result, Twitter makes for very good people watching—even if you don't go home with anyone there.

Discussion Prompts/Writing Options

If you write on any of the following topics, work through the stages of the writing process in preparing your assignment.

1. Have you ever joined Twitter? If so, are you still a member? Why or why not?

2. Compare two social networking sites such as Facebook and the less-popular MySpace, or any others you know well. You might compare them on a basis such as their appeal to a specific age group or groups, uses, general popularity today, special features, privacy protections, and so forth.

3. Describe the steps of your first daily check of the Web. What do you look at first? Second? How long do you spend at each site? Which are most important to you? Which are most irritating or time-consuming?

4. If you had to give up one item of technology such as a cell phone, tablet device, laptop, or digital camera, what would it be? Why?

5. Angwin explains that "on Twitter you do not exist without followers." She is referring to those who choose to read your tweets. Angwin struggled to attract followers until she found several methods that worked. Followers are more like an audience for a person's tweets than they are friends, the term used on Facebook. However, the sites on the social network all offer connections between people who may never meet in person. Do you believe that some people find a great deal of comfort or even identity through these Web connections? If so, explain.

Topics for Critical Thinking and Writing

If you write on any of the following topics, work through the stages of the writing process in preparing your assignment.

1. Julia Angwin says that Twitter is "not about chatting with friends—it's about promoting yourself." If you are familiar with Twitter, do you agree with Angwin's assessment? Why or why not? If you are not familiar with Twitter, consider another social networking Web site that you know better. What are its purposes and how can you recognize them?

2. Do the social networking sites stretch or break the bounds of privacy? Give examples to support your answer.

READINGS FOR WRITERS: THE ESSAY

A Brother's Murder

Brent Staples

In 1984, writer Brent Staples received news of his younger brother's murder. In this essay, he explores how two black men growing up in poverty and pain can take such different paths. As he traces his escape from anger and desperation, he grieves the loss of the brother he could not rescue.

Words You May Need to Know (Corresponding paragraph numbers are in parentheses.)

emerged (1): came out of
massive (1): large
inseparable (1): very close
escalated (1): increased
posturing (1): trying to look tough
assailant (1): attacker
wrenched (2): suddenly pulled
light-years (2): a long way
mortality (2): death
brash (2): fast-moving, impulsive
donned (2): put on
noncommissioned officer (3): an enlisted member of the armed forces appointed to lead other enlisted men and women
affluent (3): prosperous
machismo (3): a strong sense of manhood that includes aggressiveness, domination of women, and physical courage

paranoia (3): extreme irrational distrust of others
incursions (3): attacks, violations
upwardly mobile (4): likely to move up in wealth and status
ensconced (4): securely settled
grim (4): gloomy
umbilical (4): a connection between family members
desolate (5): deserted, lifeless
idle (5): unemployed, inactive
embittered (5): made bitter
forays (5): trips, ventures
terrain (5): ground
dive (6): a rundown bar or nightclub
affected (6): imitated, put on
alarm (7): sudden fear
earnestly (8): seriously
recurrent (8): occurring repeatedly

1 It has been more than two years since my telephone rang with the news that my younger brother Blake—just twenty-two years old—had been murdered. The young man who killed him was only twenty-four. Wearing a ski mask, he emerged from a car, fired six times at close range with a massive .44 Magnum, then fled. The two had once been inseparable friends. A senseless rivalry—beginning, I think, with an argument over a girlfriend—escalated from posturing to threats, to violence, to murder. The way the two were living, death could have come to either of them from anywhere. In fact, the assailant had already survived multiple gunshot wounds from an incident much like the one in which my brother lost his life.

2 As I wept for Blake, I felt wrenched backwards into events and circumstances that had seemed light-years gone. Though a decade apart, we both were raised in Chester, Pennsylvania, an angry, heavily black, heavily poor, industrial city southwest of Philadelphia. There, in the 1960s, I was introduced to mortality, not by the old and failing, but by beautiful young men who lay wrecked after sudden explosions of violence. The first, I remembered from my fourteenth year—Johnny, brash lover of fast cars, stabbed to death two

doors from my house in a fight over a pool game. The next year, my teenage cousin, Wesley, whom I loved very much, was shot dead. The summers blur. Milton, an angry neighbor, shot a crosstown rival, wounding him badly. William, another teenage neighbor, took a shotgun blast to the shoulder in some urban drama and displayed his bandages proudly. His brother, Leonard, severely beaten, lost an eye and donned a black patch. It went on.

3   I recall not long before I left for college, two local Vietnam veterans—one from the Marines, one from the Army—arguing fiercely, nearly at blows about which outfit had done the most in the war. The most killing, they meant. Not much later, I read a magazine article that set that dispute in a context. In the story, a noncommissioned officer—a sergeant, I believe—said he would pass up any number of affluent, suburban-born recruits to get hard-core soldiers from the inner city. They jumped into rice paddies with "their manhood on their sleeves," I believe he said. These two items—the veterans arguing and the sergeant's words—still characterize for me the circumstances under which black men in their teens and twenties kill one another with such frequency. With a touchy paranoia born of living battered lives, they are desperate to be *real* men. Killing is only machismo taken to the extreme. Incursions to be punished by death were many and minor, and they remain so: they include stepping on the wrong toe, literally; cheating in a drug deal; simply saying "I dare you" to someone holding a gun; crossing territorial lines in a gang dispute. My brother grew up to wear his manhood on his sleeve. And when he died he was in that group—black, male, and in its teens and early twenties—that is far and away the most likely to murder or be murdered.

4   I left the East Coast after college, spent the mid- and late 1970s in Chicago as a graduate student, taught for a time, then became a journalist. Within ten years of leaving my hometown, I was overeducated and "upwardly mobile," ensconced on a quiet, tree-lined street where voices raised in anger were scarcely ever heard. The telephone, like some grim umbilical, kept me connected to the old world with news of deaths, imprisonings, and misfortune. I felt emotionally beaten up. Perhaps to protect myself, I added a psychological dimension to the physical distance I had already achieved. I rarely visited my hometown. I shut it out.

5   As I fled the past, so Blake embraced it. On Christmas of 1983, I traveled from Chicago to a black section of Roanoke, Virginia, where he then lived. The desolate public housing projects, the hopeless, idle young men crashing against one another—these reminded me of the embittered town we'd grown up in. It was a place where once I would have been comfortable, or at least sure of myself. Now, hearing of my brother's forays into crime, his scrapes with police and street thugs, I was scared, unsteady on foreign terrain.

6   I saw that Blake's romance with the street life and the hustler image had flowered dangerously. One evening that late December, standing in some Roanoke dive among drug dealers and grim, hair-trigger losers, I told him I feared for his life. He had affected the image of the tough he wanted to be.

But behind the dark glasses and the swagger, I glimpsed the baby-faced toddler I'd once watched over. I nearly wept. I wanted desperately for him to live. The young think themselves immortal, and a dangerous light shone in his eyes as he spoke laughingly of making fools of the policemen who had raided his apartment looking for drugs. He cried out as I took his right hand. A line of stitches lay between the thumb and index finger. Kickback from a shotgun, he explained, nothing serious. Gunplay had become part of his life.

7   I lacked the language simply to say: Thousands have lived this for you and died. I fought the urge to lift him bodily and shake him. This place and the way you are living smells of death to me, I said. Take some time away, I said. Let's go downtown tomorrow and buy a plane ticket anywhere, take a bus trip, anything to get away and cool things off. He took my alarm casually. We arranged to meet the following night—an appointment he would not keep. We embraced as though through glass. I drove away.

8   As I stood in my apartment in Chicago holding the receiver that evening in February 1984, I felt as though part of my soul had been cut away. I questioned myself then, and I still do. Did I not reach back soon enough or earnestly enough, for him? For weeks I awoke crying from a recurrent dream in which I chased him, urgently trying to get him to read a document I had, as though reading it would protect him from what had happened in waking life. His eyes shining like black diamonds, he smiled and danced just beyond my grasp. When I reached for him, I caught only the space where he had been.

Discussion Prompts/Writing Options

If you write on any of the following topics, work through the stages of the writing process in preparing your assignment.

1. Brent Staples tried to connect emotionally with his brother. He warned Blake about the dangers of staying on a violent path. Do you think Staples did everything he could to save his brother? Use specific details from the article to support your point of view.

2. If you have witnessed or experienced a particularly disturbing or violent event in your neighborhood, describe the event and its consequences. You can include its immediate impact on you and your neighbors as well as its lasting effects.

3. Although "A Brother's Murder" was first published in 1986, some of Staples' descriptions, such as "idle young men crashing against one another," can apply to some violent and angry young males today. Select three or four descriptions or statements from the article that are still relevant and accurate. Be sure to include specific connections to senseless violence today.

4. Imagine all that could have happened in Staples' recurrent dream. What was the chase like, why is he "urgently" trying to get his

brother to read a document, what did the document say, how did his brother react, and so forth. Focus on creating a clear picture of what each man sees and feels.

Topics for Critical Thinking and Writing

If you choose to write on any of the following topics, work through the stages of the writing process in preparing your assignment.

1. Put yourself in Blake Staples' shoes. Why do you think his life took such a different turn than his brother's?

2. How would you define a "real" man? How do you think Brent Staples defined it? How did Blake Staples define it?

3. Do you think that people who live in relatively safe areas can become numb to daily reports of violence locally or nationally? What kinds or instances of violence can shock people who are accustomed to tuning out the daily crime news?

READING FOR WRITERS: THE ESSAY

Navajo Code Talkers: The Century's Best Kept Secret

Jack Hitt

In this essay, Jack Hitt talks of the secret heroism of a group of Native Americans during World War II. By using the language of their tribe, the Navajo code talkers made an "incredible contribution" to "winning history's biggest war."

Words You May Need to Know (Corresponding paragraph numbers are in parentheses.)

decisive (1): unmistakable
Iwo Jima (1): a Japanese island in the Pacific
momentous (1): important
guttural (1): harsh, grating
intonations (1): tones
baffled (1): confused
infuriated (1): made angry
conformed (1): followed the rules of
linguistic (1): language
cryptographers (1): people who study secret codes
decipher (1): solve or decode
clandestine (1): secret
cryptographic (2): secret code
intercepted (2): stopped, interrupted, or turned aside

proficient (2): expert
sabotage (2): destroy
the Pentagon (2): the United States military establishment
gambits (2): maneuvers
virtually (3): practically
artillery (3): weapons
coined (3): created
neologisms (3): new words
pyrotechnic (4): resembling fireworks
elite (5): high status
solemnly (5): gravely
messaging apparatus (6): means for sending messages

1   During World War II, on the dramatic day when Marines raised the American flag to signal a key and decisive victory at Iwo Jima, the first word of this momentous news crackled over the radio in odd guttural noises and complex intonations. Throughout the war, the Japanese were repeatedly

baffled and infuriated by these seemingly inhuman sounds. They conformed to no linguistic system known to the Japanese. The curious sounds were the military's one form of conveying tactics and strategy that the master cryptographers in Tokyo were unable to decipher. This perfect code was the language of the Navajo tribe. Its application in World War II as a clandestine system of communications was one of the twentieth century's best-kept secrets.

2   After a string of cryptographic failures, the military in 1942 was desperate for a way to open clear lines of communication that would not be intercepted by the enemy. In the 1940s, there was no such thing as a "secure line." All talk had to go out onto the public airwaves. Standard codes were an option, but the cryptographers in Japan could quickly crack them. And there was another problem: the Japanese were proficient at intercepting short-distance communications, on walkie-talkies for example, and then having well-trained English-speaking soldiers either sabotage the message or send out false commands to set up an ambush. That was the situation in 1942 when the Pentagon authorized one of the boldest gambits of the war.

3   The solution was conceived by the son of missionaries to the Navajos, a former Marine named Philip Johnston. His idea: station a native Navajo speaker at every radio station. Since Navajo had never been written down or translated into any other language, it was an entirely self-contained human communication system restricted to Navajos alone; it was virtually indecipherable without Navajo help. Without some key or way into a language, translation is virtually impossible. Not long after the bombing of Pearl Harbor, the military dispatched twenty-nine Navajos to Camp Elliott and Camp Pendleton in California to begin a test program. These first recruits had to develop a Navajo alphabet since none existed. And because Navajo lacked technical terms of military artillery, the men coined a number of neologisms specific to their task and war.

4   According to Chester Nez, one of the original code talkers, "Everything we used in the code was what we lived with on the reservation every day, like the ants, the birds, bears." Thus, the term for a tank was "turtle," a tank destroyer was "tortoise killer." A battleship was "whale." A hand grenade was "potato," and plain old bombs were "eggs." A fighter plane was "hummingbird," and a torpedo plane "swallow." A sniper was "pick 'em off." Pyrotechnic was "fancy fire."

5   It didn't take long for the original twenty-nine recruits to expand to an elite corps of Marines, numbering at its height 425 Navajo Code Talkers, all from the American Southwest. Each Talker was so valuable, he traveled everywhere with a personal bodyguard. In the event of capture, the Talkers had solemnly agreed to commit suicide rather than allow America's most valuable war code to fall into the hands of the enemy. If a captured Navajo did not follow that grim instruction, the bodyguard's instructions were understood: shoot and kill the Code Talker.

6   The language of the Code Talkers, their mission, and every detail of their messaging apparatus were secrets they were all ordered to keep, even

from their own families. They did. It wasn't until 1968, when the military felt convinced that the Code Talkers would not be needed for any future wars, that America learned of the incredible contribution a handful of Native Americans made to winning history's biggest war. The Navajo Code Talkers, sending and receiving as many as 800 errorless messages at fast speed during "the fog of battle," are widely credited with giving U.S. troops the decisive edge at Guadalcanal, Tarawa, Saipan, Iwo Jima, and Okinawa.

Discussion Prompts/Writing Options

If you write on any of the following topics, work through the stages of the writing process in preparing your assignment.

1. The language of the Navajo tribe was the perfect language to use for secret code. Are you familiar with any regional language or slang that would be hard to decipher by anyone unfamiliar with this form of communication? If so, describe where this language developed, how often it is used, and why it would be so difficult to decipher or translate.

2. The Navajo Code Talkers could be considered unsung heroes because their heroic contributions during World War II went unrecognized for so many years. Write a short essay about someone whom you regard as an unsung hero in your school, community, city, or state.

3. Jack Hitt, author of "Navajo Code Talkers," states that the Talkers "are widely credited with giving U.S. troops the decisive edge at Guadalcanal, Tarawa, Saipan, Iwo Jima, and Okinawa." Conduct an online search for information about one or more of these battles, and see if the contributions of the Navajo Code Talkers are mentioned. If so, summarize the specific contributions of the Talkers. If not, summarize the main points of the article(s); you may want to include details about the purpose of the battle, the length of the battle, the number of casualties, and the degree of success.

Topics for Critical Thinking and Writing

If you choose to write on any of the following topics, work through the stages of the writing process in preparing your assignment.

1. As the creators of a secret code, the "elite corps of Marines" known for many years as the Navajo Code Talkers were secret heroes. Consider what benefits and rewards (from family, society, and the government) this group of Native Americans were denied because of this secrecy.

2. The members of the Navajo Code Talkers had to promise to commit suicide if they were ever captured by the enemy. Would you want a loved one to join a similar secret group and make a similar promise?

3. The Navajo Code Talkers' most valuable skill came from their brains, not from their physical abilities. How much does winning a war depend on physical strength, troop numbers, and weapons, and how much does it depend on mental abilities? In considering these questions, give examples of the power of all these components of battle.

Text Credits

Page 619: Amritha Alladi, "Manners Matter Online: Basic Etiquette Applies Even for E-Mail" in *The Gainesville Sun*, June 2, 2008, © 2008. Reprinted with permission.

Page 623: David Migoya, "Getting Carded." *The Denver Post* (August 23, 2007) C-01, Business Section. Reprinted by permission of The Denver Post.

Page 627: Karl R. Green, "A Life Full of Riches" from *Newsweek*, December 24, 2007, © 2007 *The Newsweek/Daily Beast Company LLC*. All rights reserved. Used by permission and protected by the Copyright Laws of the United States. The printing, copying, redistribution, or retransmission of this Content without express written permission is prohibited. www.newsweek.com.

Page 629: Gary Soto, "The Colors" in *A Summer Life*, copyright © University Press of New England, Lebanon, NH. Reprinted with permission.

Page 632: Alisa Valdes-Rodriguez, "The Good Father." *Latina*, June 2004, pp. 79-80. Reprinted with permission.

Page 635: Judith Sachs, "Breath of Life." Reprinted from *Twenty Minute Vacations* © 2001 by The Stonesong Press and Judith Sachs and used with permission of The Stonesong Press, LLC.

Page 638: From *Reading People* by Jo-Ellan Dimitrius, Ph.D. and Mark Mazzarella. Copyright © 1998, 1999 by Jo-Ellan Dimitrius,Ph.D. and Mark Mazzarella. Used by permission of Random House, Inc.

Page 641: Carolyn Foster Segal, "The Dog Ate My Disk, and Other Tales of Woe," Originally published in *The Chronicle of Higher Education*, August 11, 2000. Copyright Carolyn Foster Segal. Reprinted with permission of the author.

Page 644: Ron Cunningham, "Terrorism," in *The Gainesville Sun*, January 17, 2010, © 2010. Reprinted with permission.

Page 647: Lucie Prinz, "Say Something" from *The Atlantic Online*, October 1996. Copyright © 2010, The Atlantic Media Co. as published in The Atlantic Online. Distributed by Tribune Media Services. Reprinted with permission.

Page 650: Jo Ivey Boufford, "The Case for a Tax on Sodas," as appeared in *The Gainesville Sun*, May 2, 2010, page 3F. © McClatchy-Tribune Information Services. All Rights Reserved. Reprinted with permission.

Page 652: Reprinted by permission of *The Wall Street Journal*, Copyright © 2009 Dow Jones and Company, Inc. All Rights Reserved Worldwide. License number 2703800427595.

Page 656: Brent Staples, "A Brother's Murder" from *The New York Times Magazine*, March 30, 1986, © 1986 The New York Times. All rights reserved. Used by permission and protected by the Copyright Laws of the United States. The printing, copying, redistribution, or retransmission of this Content without express written permission is prohibited. www.nytimes.com.

Page 659: Jack Hitt, "Navajo Code Talkers" from *American Greats*. Copyright © 1999 Robert Wilson. Reprinted by permission of Public Affairs, a member of the Perseus Books Group.

Photo Credits

Page 2: Hemera Technologies/Thinkstock; **Page 36 (top):** Francisco Romero/iStockphoto.com; **(bottom):** RonTech2000/iStockphoto.com; **Page 37:** Meredith Parmelee/Stone; **Page 39:** George Clerk/iStockphoto.com; **Page 57:** Peter Arnold, Inc./Alamy; **Page 58:** Ann Boyajian/Photodisc/Getty Images; **Page 60:** Photos.com; **Page 82 (top):** Photos.com; **(bottom):** Photodisc/Getty Images; **Page 85:** Ned White/iStockphoto.com; **Page 109:** David Young-Wolff/PhotoEdit; **Page 110:** AP Photo/Dave Martin; **Page 112:** George Doyle/Stockbyte/Getty Images; **Page 130:** Todd Bigelow/Aurora Photos; **Page 131:** Jeff Gross/Getty Images; **Page 133:** Ron Chapple/Photodisc/Getty Images; **Page 160:** Peter Wilson/Dorling Kindersley; **Page 161:** Joseph Sohm; ChromoSohm Inc./CORBIS; **Page 163 (left):** Jupiterimages/Thinkstock; **(middle):** Jupiterimagest/Thinkstock; **(right):** Stockbyte/Thinkstock; **Page 179:** Gary Conner/PhotoEdit; **Page 181:** iofoto/Shutterstock.com; **Page 201:** AFP/Getty Images; **Page 203:** A. Ramey/PhotoEdit; **Page 222:** China Tourism Press/The Image Bank/Getty Images; **Page 223:** Jose Luis Pelaez, Inc./CORBIS; **Page 225:** TommL/iStockphoto.com; **Page 245 (top):** Bill Bachmann/Photo Researchers, Inc.; **(bottom):** Alex L. Fradkin/Photodisc/Getty Images; **Page 248:** Photos.com; **Page 282:** Michael Newman/PhotoEdit; **Page 283:** Getty Images, Inc.- Photodisc/Royalty Free; **Page 285:** Photos.com; **Page 317:** iStockphoto/Thinkstock; **Page 358:** Photos.com; **Page 384:** Matty Symons/iStockphoto; **Page 401:** Stockbyte/Thinkstock; **Page 415:** Doug Menuez/Photodisc/Getty Images; **Page 423:** Chris Schmidt/iStockphoto.com; **Page 436:** iStockphoto/Thinkstock; **Page 445:** Photos.com; **Page 455:** Photos.com; **Page 464:** Photos.com; **Page 474:** iStockphoto.com/Thinkstock; **Page 500:** Photos.com/Thinkstock; **Page 515:** Hemera Technologies/Thinkstock; **Page 526:** Jupiterimagest/Thinkstock; **Page 536:** Photos.com/Thinkstock; **Page 567:** iStockphoto/Thinkstock; **Page 577:** iStockphoto/Thinkstock; **Page 594:** iStockphoto/Thinkstock; **Page 605:** Joshua Hodge Photography/iStockphoto.com.

INDEX

> **Note:** Reading Selections are listed under, "readings." Each selection contains vocabulary definitions, discussion prompts, writing options, and topics for critical-thinking and writing.